MindTap™ — QUICK START GUIDE

1. To get started, navigate to: **www.cengagebrain.com** and select "Register a Product".

A new screen will appear prompting you to add a Course Key. A Course Key is a code given to you by your instructor - this is the first of two codes you will need to access MindTap. Every student in your course section should have the same Course Key.

2. Enter the Course Key and click "Register".

If you are accessing MindTap through your school's Learning Management System such as BlackBoard or Desire2Learn, you may be redirected to use your Course Key/Access Code there. Follow the prompts you are given and feel free to contact support if you need assistance.

3. Confirm your course information above, and proceed to the log in portion below.

If you have a CengageBrain username and password, enter it under "Returning Students" and click "Login". If you are new to the site, register under "New Students" and click "Create a New Account".

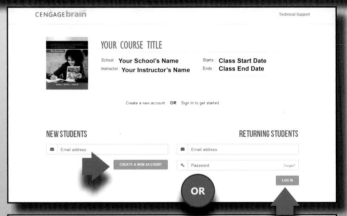

4. Now that you are logged in, you can access the course for free by selecting "Start Free Trial" for 20 days, or enter in your Access Code.

Your Access Code is unique to you and acts as payment for MindTap. You may have received it with your book or purchased it separately in the bookstore or at **CengageBrain.com**. Enter it and click "Register".

NEED HELP?

For CengageBrain Support: Login to **Support.Cengage.com**. Call **866-994-2427** or access our **24/7 Student Chat!** Or access the **First Day of School PowerPoint Presentation** found at cengagebrain.com.

Archetypes of Wisdom

An Introduction to Philosophy

Ninth Edition

Archetypes of Wisdom

An Introduction to Philosophy

Ninth Edition

Douglas J. Soccio

CENGAGE
Learning

Australia • Brazil • Mexico • Singapore • United Kingdom • United States

Archetypes of Wisdom, Ninth Edition
Douglas J. Soccio

Product Manager: Debra Matteson

Managing Content Developer: Joanne Dauksewicz

Content Developer: Florence Kilgo

Product Assistant: Abby Hess

Media Developer: Anais Wheeler

Marketing Manager: Christine Sosa

Senior Content Project Manager: Catherine G. DiMassa

Art Director: Kristina Mose-Libon

Manufacturing Planner: Sandee Milewski

IP Analyst: Alexandra Ricciardi

IP Project Manager: Farah Fard

Production Service/Compositor: Cenveo® Publisher Services

Text Designer: Lumina Datamatics, Inc.

Cover Designer: Lumina Datamatics, Inc.

Cover Image: Sistine Chapel Ceiling: Delphic Sibyl (fresco, 1508-1512), by Michelangelo Buonarroti, (1475-1564)/Vatican Museums and Galleries, Vatican City/The Bridgeman Art Library

Library of Congress Control Number: 2014951251

ISBN: 978-1-285-87431-9

Cengage Learning
20 Channel Center Street
Boston, MA 02210
USA

Cengage Learning is a leading provider of customized learning solutions with office locations around the globe, including Singapore, the United Kingdom, Australia, Mexico, Brazil and Japan. Locate your local office at **international.cengage.com/global.**

Cengage Learning products are represented in Canada by Nelson Education, Ltd.

To learn more about Cengage Learning Solutions, visit **www.cengage.com.**

Purchase any of our products at your local college store or at our preferred online store **www.cengagebrain.com.**

Printed in Canada
Print Number: 01   Print Year: 2015

For Minerva

How can I not smile when I see her?

©iStock.com/seanjolly

Brief Contents

©iStock.com/seanjolly

Contents

©iStock.com/efilippou

ix

© FineShine/Shutterstock.com

©iStock.com/m-1975

©iStock.com/Thomas Lammeyer

©iStock.com/seanjolly

Preface

The ninth edition modifications to *Archetypes of Wisdom* refine the qualities that make it unique among introductory philosophy textbooks. Chief among these is the respect it pays to the common notion that philosophy ought to have something to do with living issues—with the search for wisdom.

All changes in this book, big and small, have been made with an eye to balance academic rigor with student engagement. Throughout the text, references to contemporary concerns have been refreshed to reflect the everyday experiences of student readers without pandering to them or to anyone else. In these ways *Archetypes of Wisdom* allows students to discover for themselves that (1) philosophy, considered broadly, is already part of their lives and (2) that they are up to the task of engaging with important thinkers about important matters on increasingly sophisticated levels. As in prior editions, all elements of the text and its ancillary material are fully integrated to introduce students of diverse backgrounds and reading levels to first-rate philosophy that is interesting and worthwhile for its own sake.

New to This Edition

Beginning with the second edition, each revision of *Archetypes of Wisdom* has benefited from an ongoing collaboration with readers ranging from highly specialized philosophers and philosophy teachers to students and individuals who read philosophy for pleasure and out of personal curiosity. In this light, the ninth edition of *Archetypes of Wisdom* sports a number of changes that will be obvious to readers familiar with earlier incarnations:

Chapter 2: The Presocratic Sophos This edition's most obvious change is this chapter-length treatment of the Presocratics. Users of earlier editions recognize this as a reinstatement of material that was reduced in an effort to expand coverage of contemporary philosophy without making the text prohibitively long. This change left many instructors dissatisfied enough with that deletion to ask for a return of the deleted chapter—a desire I shared. In addition to offering instructors who wish it included a fuller look at these intriguing and important proto-scientists, this change provides more flexibility for all instructors.

Chapter 9: The Rationalist: René Descartes An updated look at Susan Bordo's critique of what she describes as the fantasy of Cartesian dualism challenges students to reflect on the ways Enlightenment optimism affects our efforts to defy aging and death. Bordo's questions about the possibility and desirability of a "view from nowhere" can be used to help students bring philosophically technical questions down to earth and see how deeply ingrained Cartesian dualism is in their lives. This capstone to Chapter 9 offers students and instructors fertile opportunities for discussion and reflection.

Chapter 10: The Skeptic: David Hume A new modestly expanded look at Alison Jaggar's assessment of the role emotions play in our lives raises questions that occur to many, if not most, beginning philosophy students: Can knowledge be divorced from social conditions? Can suffering give us a clearer understanding of life than objectivity? Is emotional acumen a "women's issue," and, if not, why have so many philosophers overlooked emotions as sources of knowledge? Jaggar's questions are natural occasions for encouraging students to search for signs of emotional—as well as intellectual—interests in some of the philosophers they've already studied.

Chapter 12: The Utilitarian: John Stuart Mill A new section based on the work of Sarah Conly's controversial book *Against Autonomy: Justifying Coercive Paternalism* is engaging, controversial stuff that should get students fired up—one way or another. Calling for radical restrictions on our liberties to "protect us from ourselves," Conly takes on Mill's high regard for personal liberty. This new material promises to be pedagogically effective because Conly challenges an icon of liberty and encourages increasing efforts to legislate whether restaurants can put salt shakers on their tables and how big our Big Gulps can get. This is sure to get students' attention.

Chapter 14: The Existentialist: Søren Kierkegaard The touching story of Regine Olsen's last encounter with Søren Kierkegaard and the consequences his death had for her underscores the existential price paid by the philosopher and his beloved for Kierkegaard's anguished struggle to reconcile conflicting desires.

Chapter 18: Philosophy as a Way of Life New material concerning the underrepresentation of women and other groups in philosophy includes data from Sally Haslanger's article "Women in Philosophy? Do the Math" and Laurie Calhoun's essay "Feminism Is a Humanism." Demographic data, only recently collected after much difficulty by Haslanger and other feminist philosophers, makes the issue of representation less abstract and thereby more engaging to students, who may well find themselves surprised, disturbed, and intrigued by actual percentages and the questions they raise.

Strengths, Improved and Refined

Every effort has been made to enhance and refresh *Archetypes of Wisdom*'s original search-for-wisdom motif without impairing the presentation of core philosophical issues. This classroom-proven approach respects the age-old association of philosophy with the "search for meaning" that some professional philosophers see as philosophically naive. I prefer to see it as an indicator of common ground that unites most of us in a shared desire to live meaningful lives. To that end, *Archetypes of Wisdom* employs an integrated mix of academic and personal elements to draw student-readers into those core issues. Chief among these features are the following:

Learning Objectives This edition contains Learning Objectives that can serve multiple pedagogical purposes. They are helpful previews of the material to be covered in the chapter that alert readers to key concepts, figures, and terms. There are also pre-written quiz and discussion questions and can, with some modification, serve as a basis for essay topics. All Learning Objectives have been thoroughly revised and vetted to conform to Bloom's Taxonomy, a pedagogical grammar that many of today's students have been exposed to as K–12 students.

For Deeper Consideration questions Many of these boxed questions have been updated to link current events to philosophical arguments and issues. New considerations concern socialism and the Affordable Care Act and class consciousness and labor union bosses' salaries (Chapter 13, "The Materialist: Karl Marx"); what the tender-/tough-minded distinction might tell us about the hostility between staunch political partisans (Chapter 15, "The Pragmatist: William James"); and what role one's behavior over time can tell us about authentic political, moral, or religious belief (Chapter 18, "Philosophy as a Way of Life"). As always, For Deeper Consideration prompts are placed where they will make the most sense to students and encourage them to look for more than information as they read. Without intruding on the joy of discovering new ideas for themselves, these broad, deep questions nurture students' critical thinking habits by giving them some important and interesting things to think about in the context of each chapter's philosophical focus.

Philosophical Queries Narrower in scope than For Deeper Consideration questions, Philosophical Queries directly address readers, prompting them to react critically to specific passages of text. They range from the theoretical to the personal and can be readily modified for use as essay questions or as a topic of in-class discussion. Some of these queries are integrated into the MindTap for this book as Discussing Philosophy forum topics, to promote interactive online discussion.

Compelling visual pedagogy Through carefully selected and integrated images keyed to important philosophical questions and individuals, *Archetypes of Wisdom*'s overall aesthetic takes advantage of students' exposure to visual variety and mixed-media presentations of information. Images are integrated with the text through engaging, focused captions. They are not add-ons or pictures-for-pictures'-sake, but an evolution of one of the founding assumptions of *Archetypes of Wisdom*: The wise teacher begins where the student is, and today's students expect, appreciate, and learn from aesthetically inviting sources. With that in mind, I have selected illustrations that catch the reader's eye and capture even the most casual reader's mind with thought-provoking captions. This judicious use of illustrations enriches the narrative and nurtures any reader's encounter with philosophical ideas, their origins, and contexts.

Special Pedagogical Features

As in previous revisions, the entire text has been edited and modified with an emphasis on precision, compelling biographical narratives, historical flow, and useful cross-references. Here are some of the features that students, instructors, and general readers have consistently identified as enhancing *Archetypes of Wisdom*'s effectiveness and readability:

Multiple levels of sophistication The philosophical material presented here varies in degree of difficulty. Sophisticated philosophical arguments are always presented as part of a cultural context. Philosophical passages are explained in an unobtrusive way that shows students how to read critically and carefully by asking them pointed questions and by connecting philosophical issues to students' current interests in a natural, unforced, and nontrivializing way.

Open, visually appealing format encourages readers of many levels *Archetypes of Wisdom*'s spacious format makes possible the illustrations, margin quotes, margin glossary, and boxed passages that entice readers of various levels to "just look around." Responses from students and instructors consistently report that many readers begin looking at pictures and reading margin quotes and boxed material out of curiosity and for pleasure, only to find that they are also learning something about philosophy. Without a doubt, the most rewarding and touching comments I receive about *Archetypes of Wisdom* refer to the combined effects of these inviting features and take the form of "I never thought I would be able to understand philosophy, but this book has helped me to see that I can."

Integrated margin quotes and boxed passages From its inception, the carefully chosen and positioned margin quotes have been a particularly popular feature of *Archetypes of Wisdom*, cited by students and general readers alike as "fun" and "intriguing." Many readers indicate that they learn a great deal just by reading margin quotes. Margin quotes come from the central figures in each chapter, other philosophers, and a variety of other sources. Margin quotes and boxed passages enrich the content of the main text and make excellent discussion material.

The pull of stories Even the most uninterested and resistant students respond to personal anecdotes about philosophers. With the exception of the first chapter, every chapter contains a brief but engaging philosophical biography of one or two main figures. These biographies provide cultural and historical context for the philosophical ideas covered in the chapter by showing students how philosophers respond to important concerns of their times.

Accessible depth *Archetypes of Wisdom* solves the problem of choosing between accessibility and depth by covering selected philosophers and philosophical ideas on a fundamental level. Careful juxtaposition of secondary commentary with primary source material of varying length and difficulty helps students learn how to read philosophical literature.

Cultural breadth *Archetypes of Wisdom* blends traditional Western philosophy, non-Western and nontraditional philosophy, and contemporary issues. Whenever appropriate, the figure of the sophos (sage) is used to link traditional and academic philosophical concerns with "everyday meaning needs." Nontraditional and non-Western selections include Asian humanism (philosophical Taoism, Confucianism, and Buddhism), existential iconoclasm (Søren Kierkegaard and Friedrich Nietzsche), public philosophy (Martha Nussbaum and Peter Singer), prophetic philosophy (Martin Luther King, Jr.), philosophical feminism (Alison Jaggar, Susan Bordo, Susan Moller Okin, Sarah Conly, Laurie Calhoun, Sally Haslanger, Carol Swaim, and Carol Gilligan), philosophy of religion (Augustine, Abu Hamid Muhammad al-Ghazali, Thomas Aquinas, David Hume, Søren Kierkegaard, William James, and Friedrich Nietzsche), and postmodern philosophy (Friedrich Nietzsche, Ludwig Wittgenstein, Martin Heidegger, and Jean-Paul Sartre).

A wide range of contemporary sources *Archetypes of Wisdom* includes a variety of contemporary sources that address philosophical issues from beyond academic philosophy. These show—rather than merely tell—students that philosophy occurs outside philosophy class and in other guises.

Flexible structure Each chapter is a self-contained unit. It is not necessary to cover sections in chronological order, nor is it necessary to cover every chapter to have an effective class. Material not covered by the instructor can be used for independent writing assignments, group presentations, and the like.

Overviews of philosophical themes Two strongly visual summaries of classical and modern philosophical themes give students a story-like preview of key philosophical issues and a sense of historical context and continuity.

Chapter commentaries Chapters conclude with clearly identified brief commentaries that include general evaluations or personal reflections concerning the philosophical ideas covered in the chapter; often they connect chapter ideas to contemporary issues.

Summaries of Main Points Highlights of key ideas can be used as a handy preview, review, and discussion aid for each chapter.

Post-Reading Reflections and pedagogical framing Each chapter opens with Learning Objectives and concludes with post-reading questions keyed to the text. These range from specific to general and can be used as review questions and as test or essay questions. Individual questions can be taken as they are or easily modified for use as reading quizzes, essay assignments, or paper topics. Together, Learning Objectives and Post-Reading Reflections frame each chapter's core content in a way that is especially helpful to students who are unfamiliar with sophisticated writing or who *believe* that philosophy has nothing to offer them.

Sources A Notes section documents all sources for primary source extracts.

Two Glossaries In addition to a handy margin glossary, which defines key terms in the margins, highlighting their importance and facilitating text reviews, an alphabetical glossary with chapter and page references makes it easy to locate key terms in the text.

Bibliography of Philosophical Delights Arranged by chapter, this little collection of books contains brief descriptions of some overlooked gems. Unlike standard academic bibliographies, the focus here is on the joy of reading and discovering just how far philosophy reaches. It is encouraging to students who want to go beyond the textbook for academic or personal reasons.

Index of Margin Quote Authors This popular feature helps students locate authors of margin quotes featured throughout the text.

Student-oriented Index Geared toward novice philosophers, the Index is extensively cross-referenced to help budding researchers and readers unfamiliar with philosophy find what they are looking for—and what they did not know they were looking for until they found it (serendipity).

Digital Solutions for Students and Instructors

MindTap for *Archetypes of Wisdom* is a highly personalized, customizable teaching and learning experience that improves learning outcomes. Through a carefully designed chapter-based learning path, MindTap allows students to easily identify the chapter's learning objectives, complete readings and activities organized into short, manageable blocks, and test their content knowledge through a variety of tools and "MindApps." Analytics and reports provide a snapshot of class progress, time in course, engagement and completion rates. Instructors can customize the MindTap platform to design a pedagogically meaningful path by using any of the following:

- **MindTap Reader.** Cengage Learning's re-imagination of the traditional eBook, is specifically designed for how students assimilate content and media assets—in a mobile reading environment. The MindTap Reader provides the entire text of *Archetypes of Wisdom*, 9e, and allows students to make notes, highlight text, and find definitions right from the page. It also includes chapter-specific resources such as quizzes, flashcards, and more.

- **Aplia MindApp.** The Aplia™ learning solution significantly improves outcomes and elevates thinking by increasing student effort and engagement. Developed by teachers and used by more than 1,000,000 students, Aplia assignments provide automatically graded assignments with detailed, immediate explanations on every question.

- **Questia MindApp.** Access to the premier trusted online research library Questia provides the resources needed to complete college-level, core-curriculum course assignments. Featuring 24/7 online access to a collection of full-text books and academic journals along with a complete suite of organizational and productivity tools.

- **Questia Writing Center.** Questia can also help students throughout the entire research process, from finding good topics and appropriate scholarly sources to organizing notes, drafting paper outlines, and properly citing references. Questia helps students write better papers by providing an extensive array of scholarly sources, and enabling them to organize what they've learned into a better thought-out paper.

- **Supplemental Primary Source Readings.** Access to the Questia library also brings the ability to assign a wide range of philosophy primary source readings with cleared digital permissions. Instructors can pick and choose from suggested readings integrated into the MindTap chapter learning path or use the database to add their own selections.

- **Philosophy videos.** A thoughtfully curated selection of video clips provides in-depth analyses of key philosophical topics using writings of past philosophers and expert interviews from pre-eminent scholars and philosophers. These videos do more than reiterate the reading, jump-starting student learning with thought-provoking perspectives on philosophical issues.

- *How to Get the Most Out of Philosophy, seventh edition.* Written by textbook author, Douglas J. Soccio, this companion student success manual equips students with the skills necessary to succeed in an introductory Philosophy course. Beginning with how to study philosophical texts, continuing through test-taking and writing strategies, and ending with tips for ongoing college achievement, this handy guide prepares students for long-term accomplishment.

- **Additional Activities.** A discussion board with "Discussing Philosophy" forum topics from the textbook and ability to add additional topics, interactive "Philosophy Timelines," and chapter-based multiple choice and essay questions complete the selection of activities that can be assigned for each chapter learning path.

MindTap for *Archetypes of Wisdom* goes well beyond an eBook, a homework solution, a resource center website, or a Learning Management System. To learn more, ask your Cengage Learning sales representative to demo it for you —or go to www. Cengage.com/MindTap.

Online instructor's manual with tests In addition to the sections containing over 1,300 true/false, multiple-choice, and essay questions, this unique manual includes a section on the philosophy of testing (how to prepare tests), lecture and discussion tips for all chapters, tips for new philosophy teachers (which are useful for all teachers), a discussion of the special pedagogical features of *Archetypes of Wisdom*, and a list of more than 100 "philosophical films." Few, if any, instructor aids are as practical or complete. This is not a cursory job, but a substantial and truly useful compendium of tips, time-saving classroom-tested test questions, and flexible lecture guides. These instructor resources are available on the **Instructor Companion Website**. This website is an all-in-one resource for class preparation, presentation, and testing for instructors and is accessible through www.Cengage.com/login with your faculty account.

Cengage Learning Testing, powered by Cognero® is a flexible, online system that allows you to: import, edit, and manipulate content from the text's test bank or elsewhere, including your own favorite test questions; create multiple test versions in an instant; and deliver tests from your LMS, your classroom, or wherever you want.

How to Get the Most Out of Philosophy, seventh edition This companion student success manual equips students with the skills necessary to succeed in an introductory Philosophy course. Beginning with how to study philosophical texts, continuing through test-taking and writing strategies, and ending with tips for ongoing college achievement, this handy guide prepares students for long-term accomplishment. *How to Get the Most Out of Philosophy* is available as a bundled supplement at a significantly reduced cost for adopters of *Archetypes of Wisdom*, as an independent text, or as a free eBook with MindTap.

CengageCompose This text is available in CengageCompose, our custom book building site. Instructors can preview content, and work with a Custom Project Manager to build a custom text by selecting chapters from multiple texts, collections, or adding their own original material.

Acknowledgments

I am grateful to these busy philosophy professors and teachers for time, care, and detailed advice they provided to help us improve *Archetypes of Wisdom*—both as a textbook and an invitation to readers to join "the great conversation."

For their advice and insight regarding this revision, I convey my gratitude to the following reviewers:

Ken Adams, University of Arkansas Community College Hope; Owen Anderson, Arizona State University; Mark Arandia, North Lake College; Jennifer Caseldine-Bracht, Indiana University-Purdue University Fort Wayne; Chung Chang, Montclair State University; Matthew Clark, Coastal Carolina University; Alan Clark, Del Mar College; Brad Cohen, Jamestown Community College; Vincent Dever, Marymount College; Jonathan Gainor, Harrisburg Area Community College; Russ Jacobs, Washburn University; Aleksandr Kragh, Averett University; Klaus Ladstaetter, Washburn University; Sandor Marai, Sinclair Community College; Barbara McIntyre, Cayuga Community College; Alexandra Perry, Bergen Community College; and Christopher Rodkey, Penn State York

For their feedback on Aplia, I am thankful to the following reviewers:

Jeremy Byrd, Tarrant County College; Nathan Draluck, University of South Florida; Melissa Ebbers, University of Memphis; Roel Feys, University of South Carolina; Cheryl McKinley, Northern Kentucky University; Alexander Miller, Piedmont Technical College; Herminia V. Reyes, San Diego State University; Dennis L. Slivinski, Cal State Channel Islands; Tim Sundell, University of Kentucky; Dan Taylor, Arizona Western College; and David Vessey, Grand Valley State University

Finally, for their ongoing committed participation in our introduction to philosophy digital advisory board, I wish to thank the following board members:

Kent Anderson, Clarke University; Tara Blaser, Lake Land College; David Burris, Arizona Western College; Dan Dutkofski, Valencia College; Bryan Hilliard, Mississippi University for Women; Sharon Kaye, John Carroll University; Terry Sader, Butler Community College; Julio Torres, Los Angeles City College; Jere Vincent, Great Bay Community College; Tim Weldon, University of Saint Francis.

Alas, I have had to make some difficult decisions. Had I been able to take all of your great suggestions, *Archetypes of Wisdom* would look like the hardback, multi-volume edition of the Oxford English Dictionary!

Archetypes of Wisdom has always been a very complicated book to put together. And although, more often than not, I have been the beneficiary of some excellent teams over the course of its lifespan, each new revision prompts some initial anxiety. A project with so many features and players is a lot like an extended trip with new in-laws and distant relatives. Will we get along? Are we all going in the same direction? From the beginning of this project, my anxieties about the unknown were quickly assuaged, beginning with Debra Matteson, Cengage Learning Product Manager for Philosophy & Religion. A philosopher herself, Debra has shown a personal interest in my book *as a book* and not merely a project. I am especially grateful to her for going to bat for me regarding modifications to the original revision schedule when I had other pressing concerns. Debra has been encouraging from the get-go and set the tone for what has turned out to be a truly generous revision team.

The frustrating early stages of a revision always demand extra concentration and energy as unused skills have to be refreshed and limbered up. Much to my delight, this stage of the task was often enjoyable thanks to Content Developer Florence Kilgo. Florence's attention to detail, wit, warmth, patience, and kindness quickly transformed a professional relationship into a long-distance friendship, without sacrificing the attention to detail so important to this kind of complicated work. At the risk of sounding like a broken record—a risk my readers know I indulge routinely—I want to thank Jeanine Furino of Cenveo Publisher Services for watching over this book that I think of as one of my children as if it were one her own. Jeanine managed to coordinate a disparate team of folks on this and other projects without ever once approaching this revision in a detached or cursory manner. Thanks also to Senior Content Project Manager Cathie DiMassa. By itself the term "manager" conveys images of herding cats or directing folks from a distance. My experience with Cathie was the opposite of this stereotype. Cathie protected this revision with grace, concern, and sincere interest in our progress, playing a vital role in helping all of us produce the book I envisioned. As Lao-tzu might have said, Cathie managed without managing. Lastly, Kitty Wilson has been a gem of a copy editor, saving me embarrassment by catching errors before they got into print, smoothing away awkward constructions, even finding the tiniest of spacing errors, and (gulp) picking up a few stealth spelling errors that managed to survive multiple professional readers and revisions. Kitty has accomplished the difficult task of making substantive improvements without being heavy-handed or intrusive.

I've been around long enough to know and cherish the delicate balance between the personal and the professional that marks those who bring integrity and grace to their work. This has been a team of just such individuals.

A Personal Note

I thank my friends and family for supporting me through this revision by putting into practice so many of the qualities that make a good philosopher: Relentless questioning. Willingness to listen and reconsider. Tolerance without sentimentalism. Courage, forbearance, and integrity. Good humor. Acceptance of loss. And, best of all, openness to new ideas, new ways of being, and new people.

Most importantly, I thank my wife, Margaret, the heart of my philosophy and lodestone of my life, without whom this book and I would be so much the poorer. She it is who has shown me that just as philosophy is a way of life, our way of life is our true philosophy. When I am ready to clip the coin a trifle and settle for "not too bad," she reminds me that every reader pays for every book with more than money. Readers pay with trust and irrecoverable time. And so she asks, sometimes outright, more often with a glance, "Good enough?" And we both know the answer. But more than being my editorial conscience, Margaret is a ferocious student advocate and a lover of philosophy. It matters to her that every reader, and especially every student reader, gets true, fair value from *Archetypes of Wisdom*. So she reads and rereads and re-rereads every jot and tittle, patiently, carefully, lovingly. Margaret was *Archetypes of Wisdom*'s first reader. She will always be its best reader. And she will always be my favorite reader.

Life's meaning—however we conceive it—does not depend on who the president is or on how many people agree with us about politics or religion or about anything else. As interesting or important as such things may be, they are not primary matters. Why, then, do we devote so much energy to them and to things like them? Perhaps because we are prone to forgetting what matters most to us, were we to stop and think about it—maybe not in Plato's sense of forgetting but forgetting nonetheless. We routinely experience bouts of philosophical amnesia, the cure for which is not navel-gazing or logic-chopping but philosophical conversation and reflection.

I offer *Archetypes of Wisdom* as one small antidote against forgetting philosophy and hope that in some small way I have done right by the philosophers I have been able to include in it. They are superb company, and it is a privilege to share them with you.

Yiorgos Karahalis/Reuters/Landov

Introduction

Philosophy and the Search for Wisdom

Grey-eyed Athena sent them a favorable breeze, a fresh wind, singing over the wine-dark sea.

— *Homer*

Learning Objectives

 MindTap™

After you complete this chapter, you should be able to:

- Define the term *philosophy*.

- Outline the four primary areas of philosophy.

- Identify five philosophical archetypes.

- Differentiate between archetypes and stereotypes.

- Based on your own educational experience, analyze James Q. Wilson's claim that radical relativism is rampant on college campuses.

- Explain why wisdom is often associated with age.

- Contrast practical and theoretical knowledge.

- Distinguish belief from knowledge.

- Distinguish belief from mere belief.

- Explain willed ignorance.

Philosophy Timelines

philosophy
From Greek roots meaning "the love of wisdom."

Beggars get handouts before philosophers because people have some idea of what it's like to be blind and lame.

— Diogenes

PHILOSOPHY is already an important part of your life, whether you know it or not. The word **philosophy** comes from Greek roots meaning "the love of wisdom." The earliest philosophers were considered wise men and women, or sages, because they devoted themselves to asking "big questions": What is the meaning of life? Where did everything come from? What is the nature of reality? For a long time, most philosophers were wisdom-seeking amateurs. That is, philosophy was a way of living for them, not a way of making a living. (The original meaning of *amateur* is one who is motivated by love rather than by profit.)

We use the term *philosophy* in a similar sense when we think of a person's basic philosophy as the code of values and beliefs by which someone lives. Sometimes we talk about Abby's philosophy of cooking or Mikey's philosophy of betting on the horses. In such instances, we are thinking of philosophy as involving general principles or guidelines. Technically, that's known as *having a philosophy*; it is not the same thing as *being a philosopher*.

You don't have to be a philosopher to ask philosophical questions; you just have to be a naturally curious and thoughtful person. Here's a sampling of the kinds of questions philosophers study:

- Does God exist?
- What's the meaning of life?
- Why do innocent people suffer?
- Is everything a matter of opinion?
- Are all people really equal, and if so, in what sense?
- What is the best form of government?
- Is it better to try to make the majority happy at the expense of a few or make a few happy at the expense of many?
- How are minds connected to bodies?
- Is there one standard of right and wrong for everyone, or are moral standards relative?
- Is beauty in the eye of the beholder?
- Does might make right?
- Is objectivity possible? Desirable?

For Deeper Consideration

Reflect on your own education up to this point. In what ways has it hindered, and in what ways has it supported, a love of wisdom?

What to Expect from This Book

Although the idea of studying selected highlights of nearly three thousand years of (mostly) Western philosophizing may seem *exhausting*, this is not meant to be an *exhaustive* history of philosophy or survey of philosophical topics. That is,

"Surely, Life Is Not Merely a Job"

Why do we go through the struggle to be educated? Is it merely in order to pass some examinations and get a job? Or is it the function of education to prepare us while we are young to understand the whole process of life? Having a job and earning one's livelihood is necessary—but is that all? Are we being educated only for that? Surely, life is not merely a job, an occupation; life is wide and profound, it is a great mystery, a vast realm in which we function as human beings. If we merely prepare ourselves to earn a livelihood, we shall miss the whole point of life; and to understand life is much more important than merely to prepare for examinations and become very proficient in mathematics, physics, or what you will.

Jiddu Krishnamurti, from "The Function of Education" quoted in Daniel Kolak and Raymond Martin, *The Experience of Philosophy* (Belmont, Calif.: Wadsworth, 1990), pp. 20–21.

Archetypes of Wisdom is not meant to be "complete," covering every significant philosopher or every significant contribution made by the philosophers it does include. Rather, it's meant to be a *representative* and inviting introduction to interesting and important questions of value, meaning, and knowledge and the cultural conditions that gave rise to them.

If you're reading this book as part of an academic course, I recommend treating your introduction to philosophy as an opportunity to distinguish between saying philosophical-sounding things and actually philosophizing. Perhaps the chief difference between just talking about philosophical ideas and actually philosophizing about them involves the degree of rigor and discipline you apply to your reflections.

We can say, then, that philosophy consists of careful reasoning about certain kinds of issues. Philosophical thinking includes careful assessment of terms, evaluation of logical reasoning, willingness to make refined distinctions, and so forth. Philosophers are especially interested in the arguments (reasons) offered to support our ideas.

Philosophical issues concern ultimate values, general principles, the nature of reality, knowledge, justice, happiness, truth, God, beauty, and morality. Philosophy addresses questions that other subjects do not address at all, and it addresses them in a more thorough way.

That's not to say, however, that we can tell whether or not a person is a philosopher just by his or her job description. Physicists, psychologists, physicians, literary critics, artists, poets, novelists, soldiers, housewives—all sorts of folks—engage in philosophical reflection without necessarily being labeled as philosophers. The quality of philosophical reasoning should concern us most, rather than the label "philosopher."

Because of their nature, philosophical questions cannot be answered in the way that a mathematical or factual question can be answered with "4" or "the year 1066." Certain questions must be asked and answered anew by each culture and by any person who awakens to what Plato and Aristotle called the *philosophical sense of wonder*. Indeed, thoughtful individuals wrestle with philosophical questions all their lives.

Of what use is a philosopher who doesn't hurt anybody's feelings?
— Diogenes

Discussing Philosophy

Areas of Philosophy

In practice, philosophy consists of the systematic, comprehensive study of certain questions that center on meaning, interpretation, evaluation, and logical or rational consistency. The primary areas of philosophy are listed here:

- *Metaphysics* encompasses the study of what is sometimes termed "ultimate reality." As such, metaphysics raises questions about reality that go beyond sense experience, beyond ordinary science. Metaphysical questions involve free will, the mind–body relationship, supernatural existence, personal immortality, and the nature of being. Some philosophers (see Chapters 10, 11, 13, and 15–17) question the very possibility of a reality beyond human experience, while others (see Chapters 1, 2, 3, 5, 7, 8, and 9) base their philosophies on metaphysical notions.

- *Epistemology*, from the Greek for "knowledge," is the branch of philosophy that asks questions about knowledge, its nature and origins, and whether it is even possible. Epistemological questions involve standards of evidence, truth, belief, sources of knowledge, gradations of knowledge, memory, and perception. Epistemological issues cut across all other branches of philosophy. (See, in particular, Chapters 1–6, 8–11, and 13–17.)

- *Ethics*, from the Greek word *ethos*, encompasses the study of moral problems, practical reasoning, right and wrong, good and bad, virtues and vices, character, moral duty, and related issues involving the nature, origins, and scope of moral values. Today, it is not uncommon for ethicists to specialize in medical ethics, business ethics, environmental ethics, academic ethics, issues of ethnicity and gender, and the nature of the good life. Ethical issues include benevolence, truth-telling, relativism, and universality. (See Chapters 1–7, 10–13, 16, and 17.)

- *Social and political philosophy* are concerned with the nature and origins of the state (government), sovereignty, the exercise of power, the effects of social institutions on individuals, ethnicity, gender, social status, and the strengths and weaknesses of different types of societies. (See Chapters 1, 4, 5, 7, 12, 13, 16, and 17.)

An unlikely epistemologist, the comedian Stephen Colbert coined the term *truthiness* as a tongue-in-cheek definition of a "truth" that a person claims to know from the gut, without regard for evidence or logic.

Other important areas of philosophy include logic, the study of the rules of correct reasoning; axiology, the study of values; aesthetics, the study of perceptions, feelings, judgments, and ideas associated with the appreciation of beauty, art, and objects in general; and ontology, the study of being and what it means to "Exist."

Philosophers sometimes concentrate on only one of these primary areas. Today some philosophers go so far as to reject whole areas of philosophy as unfit for study.

For example, a logician might view metaphysics as overly abstract and confused; a moral philosopher might see the study of symbolic logic as belonging to mathematics, rather than philosophy. Whenever philosophers concern themselves with the meaning of life or the general search for wisdom, however, all of these primary areas are involved, even if some are not dealt with explicitly.

Contemporary academic philosophers tend to specialize even within these areas, concentrating on historical periods; certain philosophers; the philosophy of music, religion, or law; or particular philosophical issues, such as What is justice? Is objectivity possible? More than two hundred areas of specialization are currently listed by the Philosophical Documentation Center, a professional organization dedicated to compiling and disseminating research data and articles about philosophy.

Philosophical Archetypes

In the ancient world, the wise person was known as the sage; in parts of Asia, a bodhisattva, yogi, or guru; in parts of Africa, a witch doctor; among Native Americans and the nomadic tribes of Asia, a shaman. In the Bible, the prophets were people of wisdom. In many cultures, the "grandmother" or "grandfather" or some other elder represents the basic image of the wise person. In the West, the wise person is often depicted as a male, but not always. In cartoons, the "wise man" is often caricatured as an oddball or a hermit wearing a robe of some sort, maybe carrying a staff, and sporting a long white beard. Why do you suppose that is? Because even cartoonists tap into this nearly universal image—and we recognize it.

This kind of basic image is sometimes referred to as an *archetype*. According to psychologist C. G. Jung (1875–1961), an **archetype** is an image that has been shared by the whole human race from the earliest times. In its more traditional sense, an archetype represents our conception of the essence of a certain kind of person. An archetype is a fundamental, original model of some type: mother, warrior, trickster, cynic, saint, pessimist, optimist, atheist, rationalist, idealist, and so on. A **philosophical archetype** is a philosopher who expresses an original or influential point of view in a way that significantly affects subsequent philosophers and nonphilosophers.

The difference between an archetype and an *ideal* is that the archetype need not be good or perfect. The difference between an archetype and a *stereotype* is in their depth. A stereotype is a simplistic distortion of a type of person. An archetype, by contrast, is a powerful representation of a fundamental response to universal experiences. Archetypes exemplify essential ways of coping with the universal aspects of life (suffering, death, loss, society, wealth, knowledge, love, purpose) in uncommonly pure ways. There are archetypes of evil as well as good and of fools as well as of wise people.

This introduction to philosophy is organized around philosophical archetypes. Even people who have not studied philosophy recognize the basic qualities of many philosophical archetypes. Most likely you have already encountered individuals who resemble some of them. Two brief examples will show you what I mean.

One philosophical archetype is the *skeptic* (Chapter 10). Skeptics believe that any claim to knowledge must be personally verified by their own sensory experience. They want to see, touch, taste, or measure everything. The New Testament contains

archetype
A basic image that represents our conception of the essence of a certain type of person; according to psychologist C. G. Jung, some of the images have been shared by the whole human race from the earliest times.

archetype (philosophical)
A philosopher who represents an original or influential point of view in a way that significantly affects philosophers and nonphilosophers: cynic, saint, pessimist, optimist, atheist, rationalist, idealist, and so on.

Erich Lessing/Art Resource, NY

The Protected Art Archive/Alamy

Archetypes of wisdom appear in many forms, from the rational Greek sophos (left) to this Native American wise woman, or shaman (right).

"It Is a Shameful Question"

The idea that devoting time to philosophy distracts us from "practical" concerns is an old one. And, of course, the very suggestion that philosophy is not as useful or practical as other subjects or activities is itself a philosophical idea that requires justification. In the following passage, the prolific philosophical historian Will Durant challenges the notion that being useful is supremely important:

> The busy reader will ask, is all this philosophy useful? It is a shameful question: We do not ask it of poetry, which is also an imaginative construction of a world incompletely known. If poetry reveals to us the beauty our untaught eyes have missed, and philosophy gives us the wisdom to understand and forgive, it is enough, and more than the world's wealth. Philosophy will not fatten our purses, nor lift us to dizzy dignities in a democratic state; it may even make us a little careless of these things. For

what if we should fatten our purses, or rise to high office, and yet all the while remain ignorantly naive, coarsely unfurnished in the mind, brutal in behavior, unstable in character, chaotic in desire, and blindly miserable?

> . . . Perhaps philosophy will give us, if we are faithful to it, a healing unity of soul. We are so slovenly and self-contradictory in our thinking; it may be that we shall clarify ourselves, and pull ourselves together into consistency, and be ashamed to harbor contradictory desires or beliefs. And through unity of mind may come that unity of purpose and character which makes a personality, and lends some order and dignity to our existence.

Will Durant, *The Mansions of Philosophy* (New York: Simon & Schuster, 1929), p. x.

an excellent example of this archetype in the person of "Doubting" Thomas, the disciple who would not believe that Jesus had risen from the grave until he carefully examined Jesus' wounds for himself.

Another philosophical archetype is the *utilitarian* (Chapter 12). Utilitarians believe that pain is inherently bad, that pleasure is inherently good, and that all creatures strive to be as happy as possible. Thus, utilitarians argue that our private and communal behavior should always maximize pleasure and minimize pain. You might recognize their famous formula: Always act to produce the greatest possible happiness for the greatest number of people. You probably also recognize utilitarian thinking in all sorts of "majority rules" reasoning.

The philosophers we will study include these two archetypes as well as exemplars of other significant philosophical schools and orientations. Philosophical archetypes are often the founders of the schools they represent, but not always. Sometimes the archetypal representatives of a philosophy are individuals who refine and develop others' ideas. In addition to their significance in the history of philosophy, archetypes confront universally important philosophical questions in ways that continue to be interesting and engaging.

Two special virtues of archetypal figures are the intensity and purity of their belief in their philosophies. Philosophical archetypes are strict advocates of a philosophical worldview or philosophical method. The intensity with which they hold to their views, combined with exceptional philosophical depth and rigor, almost always challenges our own, often unclarified, beliefs—whether we want to be challenged or not. Never fear. You alone always remain responsible for what you choose to believe, reject, or modify.

Learning about philosophical archetypes is a good way to get an initial picture of a philosophical orientation and the kinds of philosophers who are drawn to it. Learning about philosophical archetypes may also give you a better sense of your own present philosophy of life, or at least some aspects of it.

Are Philosophers Always Men?

The history of Western philosophy contains mostly male representatives, most of them of European ancestry. This has led to the sarcastic but important charge that Western philosophy is nothing but the study of "dead white males." Even though increasing numbers of women are entering the ranks of professional philosophy today, men still outnumber women among professional philosophers.

Although throughout history individual women were recognized for their insight and brilliance, most of them remained—or were kept—outside of the formal history of philosophy. In our own times, the recognition of women philosophers is improving: Susanne Langer, L. Susan Stebbing, Simone de Beauvoir, Simone Weil, Ayn Rand, Christina Hoff Sommers, Alison Jaggar, Susan Moller Okin, and Martha Nussbaum, among many others, have achieved renown as philosophers. Women philosophers are still generally not as well known, however, as women in fields such as psychology. (The fact that women are still underrepresented in many fields underscores the serious consequences that pervasive cultural prejudices have on the search for truth.)

Erich Lessing/Art Resource, NY

One of the first women philosophers to leave a substantial written record, Hildegard Von Bingen (1098–1179), receives one of her divine visions, as the monk Volmar looks on in amazement.

"The Prejudices of Practical Men"

If we are not to fail in our endeavour to determine the value of philosophy, we must first free our minds from the prejudices of what are wrongly called "practical" men. The "practical" man, as this word is often used, is one who recognizes only material needs, who realizes that men must have food for the body, but is oblivious of the necessity of providing food for the mind. If all men were well off, if poverty and disease had been reduced to their lowest possible point, there would still remain much to be done to produce a valuable society; and even in the existing world the goods of the mind are at least as important as the goods of the body. It is exclusively among the goods of the mind that the value of philosophy is to be found; and only those who are not indifferent to these goods can be persuaded that the study of philosophy is not a waste of time.

...Philosophy is to be studied, not for the sake of any definite answers to its questions, since no definite answers can, as a rule, be known to be true, but rather for the sake of the questions themselves; because these questions enlarge our conception of what is possible, enrich our intellectual imagination and diminish the dogmatic assurance which closes the mind against speculation; but above all because, through the greatness of the universe which philosophy contemplates, the mind also is rendered great, and becomes capable of that union with the universe which constitutes its highest good.

Bertrand Russell, *The Problems of Philosophy* (Oxford: Oxford University Press, 1912), selections from Chapters 1, 14, and 15.

Because, until recently, Western philosophy has been dominated by an emphasis on logical reasoning and written argument, other expressions of philosophical insight have been given less attention. Until the eighteenth century, most Western philosophers represented a small class of highly educated men, able to support themselves independently or associated with the Church or some other source of income. Only with the emergence of great public universities were higher education and philosophy open to people from other backgrounds. And even then, philosophers tended to remain members of an educated male elite.

In the following passage, Mary Ellen Waithe, the head of a team of scholars that has compiled a valuable series called *A History of Women Philosophers*, notes first-hand the difficulty of filling in some of the gaps in the history of philosophy:

> On a sweltering October afternoon in 1980...I sought comfort in the basement library of City University of New York's Graduate Center. I came upon a reference to a work by Aegidius Menagius [on the history of women philosophers] published in 1690 and 1692. I had never heard of any women philosophers prior to the 20th century with the exceptions of Queen Christina of Sweden, known as Descartes' student, and Hildegard von Bingen, who lived in the 12th century....It took sixteen months to obtain a copy of Menagius' book....
>
> As it turns out, many of the women he listed as philosophers were astronomers, astrologers, gynecologists, or simply relatives of male philosophers. Nevertheless, the list of women alleged to have been philosophers was impressive.
>
> ...By the end of 1981 I had concluded that the accomplishments of some one hundred or more women philosophers had been omitted from the standard philosophic reference works and histories of philosophy. Just check sources such as *The Encyclopedia of Philosophy*, Copleston, Zeller, Bury, Grote and others. If the women are mentioned at all, it is in passing, in a footnote.[1]

I do not know how to teach philosophy without becoming a disturber of the peace.
— Baruch Spinoza

There is no escaping the fact that Western philosophy has been predominantly male influenced throughout its history, shaped by a strong preference for rational and objective evidence rather than by more holistic and intuitive approaches to problems. The pervasiveness of this orientation makes it imperative that we acknowledge this problem. Chapters 9, 11, and 13–17 include some intriguing critiques of rationalism and universalism.

For Deeper Consideration

To what extent do you think gender and ethnic background should be considered in evaluating an individual's philosophical beliefs? Do gender, ethnic background, and other personal factors (age, income, and so on) control what we think? Is your response to this question dependent on such factors? How would—or could—you find out without being unduly influenced by the very factors under scrutiny?

Philosophy and the Search for Truth

Even with its cultural limits and biases, philosophy is perhaps the most open of all subjects. Its primary goals are clarity of expression and thought, and its chief components are reason, insight, contemplation, and experience. No question or point of view is off-limits.

The best philosophers—no matter what their personal beliefs—defer to the most compelling arguments regardless of their origins. Such important philosophers as Plato, Augustine, Thomas Aquinas, John Stuart Mill, Søren Kierkegaard, Friedrich Nietzsche, and Martin Heidegger, to name but a few, radically questioned and revised their own thinking over the course of their lives, reacting to what they saw as more compelling evidence.

Today, the philosophical arguments raised by women and other philosophical "outsiders" have expanded the ever-growing philosophical community. The history of philosophy is, in the words of Walter Kaufmann, the history of heresy.

There has always been a powerful philosophical tradition that challenges the status quo and confronts social institutions. In recent times, this tradition has found effective and powerful expression among philosophers concerned with the environment, animal rights, family structure, racism, and sexism.

Because archetypal figures exert such far-reaching influence, it is hard to predict who they will be with any certainty. That's understandable—we cannot merely assign archetypal status to a person, no matter how tempting that seems. In this regard, philosophy is no different from other fields. History teaches us that most of any given era's significant and popular figures don't usually retain their significance much beyond their own lifetimes. So predicting the emergence of archetypal philosophers must be approached with caution. In Chapters 17 and 18, we will look

Reason or a halter.
— Diogenes

at some important twentieth-century philosophers and reflect on the persistence of philosophical questions.

The history of philosophy is a living thing. It is still being written. Perhaps you will contribute to it. Eventually all facets of wisdom may be equally welcome—and future textbooks will not have sections like this one. And as you will quickly see, the ultimate issue is not who said something or who said it first but whether it is true and worthwhile. Wisdom, it seems, transcends color, gender, social class, and ethnicity.

"Isn't All This Just a Matter of Opinion?"

Does it ever occur to you that there's no way to settle the kinds of philosophical issues we have been discussing because they are only about beliefs and opinions? Perhaps you believe that "What's right for someone else might not be right for me. It's best to just let others believe whatever they want, and I'll believe whatever I want." This kind of thinking is a form of "mellow" relativism. **Relativism** is the belief that knowledge is determined by specific qualities of the observer. In other words, absolute (universal) knowledge of the truth is impossible—one opinion is as good as another.

People who see themselves as sophisticated sometimes adopt a relativistic attitude toward such "philosophical" questions as What is the meaning of life? or Is democracy the best form of government? They reason that there are nearly as many answers to such questions as there are lifestyles, religions, cultures, and individuals.

Then, too, relativists can also point to the seemingly endless differences of opinion about abortion, the right to die, capital punishment, the existence and nature of God, affirmative action, immigration policies, the president's moral character, or the greatest rock and roll singer or basketball player in history. We haven't even gotten to evolution versus intelligent design, alien autopsies, whether men are from Mars and women are from Venus, whether one ethnicity or gender is superior to another, or whether homosexuals are fit to raise children. With all this diversity of opinion, the relativist wonders how we can ever agree on who is really wise.

Amateur relativists can be heard saying things like, "Well, there's no way to decide if this particular affirmative action policy is better than that one. African Americans, women, and members of other protected classes favor it because they'll get first crack at all the good jobs, government grants, and scholarships. Middle-aged white males don't like it because now it's their turn to ride in the back of the social bus. It's always a matter of *perspective*." Relativists say things like, "Professor, I think my essay grade is unfair. It's only your *opinion*. I mean, this is not like science or math. Here in philosophy class, there's no real way to determine which opinion about Plato's theory of justice is true. Just because you've got a Ph.D. doesn't mean you're right. You're still just giving your opinion."

Somewhat more sophisticated versions of this sort of relativistic reasoning are made by some social scientists, who argue that there is no way for one culture to judge another. In America, for instance, most of us think it's wrong to treat women

relativism
The belief that knowledge is determined by specific qualities of the observer, including age, ethnicity, gender, and cultural conditioning.

Relativism is tricky. When former President George W. Bush was seen holding hands with another man, Saudi Prince Abdullah, as a sign of mutual respect, Bush's gesture made many Americans uncomfortable, as did President Barack Obama's courteous bow as he shook hands with Japanese Emperor Akhito and Empress Michiko. Why do you suppose so many Americans were as troubled as they were by these gestures? Is there any difference between graciousness and pragmatic calculation?

as second-class citizens who should defer to their fathers, brothers, and husbands. But in some Middle Eastern countries, the notion that women should have social equality is viewed as absolutely wrong. Who are we, the relativist asks, to judge a completely different way of life?

In the following passage, the sociologist James Q. Wilson describes his experiences with relativism in the classroom:

> In my classes, college students asked to judge a distant people, practice, or event will warn one another and me not to be "judgmental" or to "impose your values on other people." These remarks are most often heard when they are discussing individual "lifestyles," the modern, "nonjudgmental" word for what used to be called character. . . . If asked to defend their admonitions against "being judgmental," the students sometimes respond by arguing that moral judgments are arbitrary, but more often they stress the importance of tolerance and fair play, which, in turn, require understanding and even compassion. Do not condemn some practice—say, drug use or unconventional sexuality—that ought to be a matter of personal choice; do not criticize some group—say, ghetto rioters—whom you do not know and whose beliefs and experiences you do not understand. . . .
>
> These students are decent people. In most respects, their lives are exemplary. Thus it was all the more shocking when, during a class in which we were discussing people who at great risk to themselves had helped European Jews during the Holocaust, I found that there was no general agreement that those guilty of the Holocaust itself were guilty of a moral horror. "It all depends on your perspective," one said. "I'd first have to see those events through the eyes of people affected by them," another remarked. No doubt some perpetrators were caught up in that barbaric episode for reasons that we might understand and even excuse. What worried me was not that the students were prepared to accept some excuses, but that they began their moral reasoning on the subject by searching for excuses. They seemed

to assume that one approaches a moral question by taking a relativist position and asking, "How, given the interests and values of another person, might we explain what happened?"...To...many of my students..."What counts as a decent human being is relative to historical circumstance, a matter of transient consensus about what attitudes are normal and what practices are unjust."[2]

Wilson claims that such radical relativism is "rampant" among college students (and many professors) today. That's difficult to say. Regardless of how common relativism is, the issue of relativism remains controversial. Sometimes relativism is advocated as a form of tolerance, as in the example Wilson cites.

Conflicts between relativists and nonrelativists are found throughout the history of philosophy. Indeed, the first major Western philosopher, Socrates, emerged as a public figure partly because of his struggles with early relativists, known as *sophists*. The struggle between relativists and nonrelativists is one of the most exciting in the history of ideas. We'll study it in Chapters 3, 4, and 5 and then again toward the end of our survey of philosophy in Chapters 11 and 14–17.

(By the way, just about every relativist I have met *argues* for his relativism or at least tries to give *reasons* why my nonrelativism is inferior, misguided, mistaken, or intolerant. As if that weren't odd enough, the relativist often gets angry when I simply point out that, according to his own relativistic claims, it is impossible for his views to be "righter" than mine. After all, relativism is "just his opinion.")

Whether or not we're relativists, let's do our best to give philosophers a chance to make their cases before we accept or reject them.

Wisdom, Knowledge, and Belief

wisdom
A fundamental understanding of reality as it relates to living a good life; reasonable and practical, focusing on the true circumstances and character of each individual; good judgment about complex situations involving reflection, insight, and a plausible conception of the human condition.

knowledge
True belief.

knowledge (theoretical)
The accurate compilation and assessment of factual and systematic relationships.

The chief goal of **wisdom** is a fundamental understanding of reality as it relates to living a good life. At its core, wisdom is reasonable and practical, focusing on the true circumstances and character of each individual. We might say then, that wisdom is good judgment about complex situations. Consequently, wisdom involves reflection, insight, a capacity to learn from experience, and some plausible conception of the human condition. Unlike forms of knowledge that require formal education and specialized intelligence, wisdom has been associated with experience in a way that theoretical and intellectual knowledge has not. That may be why wisdom is so often associated with the elders of a tribe or clan. Yet, clearly, age alone cannot guarantee wisdom, nor can intelligence. Wisdom has also been associated with personal virtue far more than knowledge has.

Philosophers generally agree that **knowledge** is some form of true belief. Questions then arise as to how to distinguish true belief from mistaken belief; and, as you might expect, different philosophers give different answers involving the roles of reason, perception, experience, intuition, and social agreement in this process. Some philosophers go so far as to deny the possibility of knowledge entirely. (See Chapters 3, 5, 9, 10, 14–17.)

Philosophers also distinguish between theoretical and practical knowledge. **Theoretical knowledge** involves the accurate compilation and assessment of factual and systematic information and relationships. **Practical knowledge** consists of skills needed to do things like play the piano, use a band saw, remove a tumor, or bake a cake.

Depending on their nature, evaluating knowledge claims involves logical argumentation, scientific experiments and predictions, or the demonstration of some skillful performance. It would seem, then, that to know *X* means, first, that *X* actually is true; second, that I believe *X* to be true; and third, that I can justify or establish my belief in *X* by providing adequate evidence.

Knowledge *claims* raise some interesting and thorny questions. For example, Is a strong personal feeling adequate evidence? How much proof is enough? According to whose criteria? Philosophers demand that we provide reasons to justify our knowledge claims.

In contrast to knowledge, **belief** refers to the *subjective mental acceptance* that a claim is true. Beliefs—unlike knowledge—need not be true. Because beliefs are subjective mental states, it is possible to be firmly convinced that a belief is correct when it is not. On the other hand, sometimes our beliefs are true, but we're unable to offer adequate evidence for them.

Although beliefs can be either true or false, technically speaking, "false knowledge" is impossible. The very idea is self-contradictory. For the most part, our everyday language reflects an understanding of this important distinction. We rarely say "I had false knowledge that peach pits boost intelligence." Instead, we say something like "I had pretty good reasons to think that peach pits boost intelligence, but I've since learned that I was mistaken." Or we say "I used to believe that peach pits boost intelligence, but now I know better." In other words, sometimes what we *thought we knew* turns out to be mistaken.

Some beliefs are more reasonable than others, and there's a big difference between *informed* belief and *mere* belief. **Mere belief** refers to a conviction that something is true for which the only evidence is the conviction itself. If that sounds circular, it's because it is. Mere belief validates itself—or tries to. Most philosophers and scientists believe that truth cannot be reduced to merely believing something. For example, you do not have cancer just because you believe that you do. The best way to distinguish reliable beliefs from problematic ones is to subject important ideas to careful scrutiny. To a certain extent, we can, and must, do this for ourselves.

Ignorance Is Not an Option

Because we are all limited by our experiences, abilities, and preferences, we cannot just rely on our own untested thinking. We need to consider others' ideas, and we need to subject our beliefs to the scrutiny of others. In the realm of philosophy, we would be wise to take advantage of those thinkers and ideas that have stood the test of time and significance. (Of course, we do not want to accept the arguments of philosophers just because they are considered great or important.)

Even though we need to think for ourselves, impulsively or defensively rejecting important philosophical arguments before we have really thought about them is foolish—and arrogant. It is foolish because we cannot really know what value

knowledge (practical)
The skills needed to do things like play the piano, use a band saw, remove a tumor, or bake a cake.

belief
Conviction or trust that a claim is true; an individual's subjective mental state; distinct from knowledge.

belief (mere)
A conviction that something is true for which the only evidence is the sincerity of the believer.

willed ignorance
An attitude of indifference to the possibility of error or enlightenment that holds on to beliefs regardless of the facts.

there is in a position if we do not give it fair hearing. It is arrogant because summarily rejecting (or mocking) ideas that have influenced careful thinkers from the past and present implies that *without any background knowledge* we know more than philosophers, scientists, and theologians who have devoted years of study to these issues.

More subtly, we can shut off challenging questions by prejudging them, by being inattentive and bored when they come up, or by mocking other points of view without investigating them. When we do this, we put ourselves in the position of holding on to a belief regardless of the facts. In such a state, we become indifferent to the possibility of error or enlightenment. Willed ignorance is the name of this closed-minded attitude, and it is as opposite from the love of wisdom as any attitude I can think of.

For most of us, ignorance is not a serious option. As thoughtful people, our choices are not between philosophical indifference and philosophical inquiry but between a life lived consciously and fully or a life that just happens. Because of its fragility and finiteness, life is just too important not to philosophize about—and we know it.

Aplia

Summary of Main Points

- The word *philosophy* comes from Greek roots meaning "the love of wisdom." Philosophy in the archetypal sense is an activity as well as a fixed body of knowledge. A philosopher is a lover of wisdom, someone who has a compelling need to pursue wisdom. Areas of philosophy include metaphysics, epistemology, axiology, ethics, aesthetics, political philosophy, social philosophy, and logic.

- Philosophical archetypes are philosophers who express an original or influential point of view in a way that significantly affects subsequent philosophers and nonphilosophers.

- The history of Western philosophy has been dominated by males of European ancestry, but increasing numbers of women philosophers are expanding the scope and nature of philosophy.

- The chief goal of wisdom is a fundamental understanding of reality as it relates to living a good life. Wisdom is reasonable and practical, focusing on the true circumstances and character of each individual; wisdom is good judgment about complex situations that involves reflection, insight, and some plausible conception of the human condition.

- Philosophers generally agree that knowledge is some form of true belief. This raises questions about distinguishing true belief from mistaken belief; and different philosophers give different weights to the roles reason, perception, experience, intuition, and social agreement play in this process. Some philosophers deny the possibility of knowledge entirely.

- Philosophers distinguish between theoretical and practical knowledge. Theoretical knowledge involves the accurate compilation and assessment of factual and systematic relationships. Practical knowledge consists of skills needed to do things like play the piano, use a band saw, remove a tumor, or bake a cake.

- Relativism is the belief that knowledge is determined by specific qualities of the observer. In other words, absolute (universal) knowledge of the truth is impossible; "one opinion is as good as another."

- Willed ignorance is indifference to the possibility of one's error or one's enlightenment; people with this attitude hold on to beliefs regardless of the facts.

Post-Reading Reflections

Now that you've had a chance to learn about philosophy, use your new knowledge to answer these questions.

1. Is our culture suffering from a kind of philosophical illiteracy? Cite specific examples and identify patterns to support your answer.

2. If you could make only one improvement in the American educational system, what would it be? Why?

3. Are there better reasons for studying philosophy than just meeting some academic requirement? If yes, what are they? If no, why not? Don't be hesitant to give your honest opinion.

4. What is the difference between knowledge and belief? How are they related?

5. Popular and historical conceptions of wise men and women usually present them as elders. Do you think this is accurate? Is the notion of a wise young person somehow flawed? Explain, citing examples.

6. How would you explain what philosophy is to someone who did not already know?

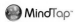 MindTap

Experience MindTap through the activities highlighted in this chapter. Further explore this online, personalized learning tool to deepen your comprehension and improve your grades.

Overview of Classical Themes

Empty is the philosopher's argument by which no human suffering is therapeutically treated. For just as there is no use in a medical art that does not cast out the sicknesses of the bodies, so too there is no use in philosophy, unless it casts out the suffering of the soul.

    — *Epicurus*

There is, I assure you, a medical art for the soul. It is philosophy, whose aid need not be sought, as in bodily diseases, from outside ourselves. We must endeavor with all our strength to become capable of doctoring ourselves.

    — *Cicero*

All humanity is sick.
I come therefore to you as a physician who has diagnosed this universal disease and is prepared to cure it.

    — *Buddha*

The unexamined life is not worth living.

    — *Socrates*

Learning Objectives

- Describe the role of mythology in ancient Greek culture.

- Describe what the transition from the mythological worldview to a more philosophic worldview resulted in.

- Identify the two crucial principles inherent in mythological accounts of life that are still disputed and discussed by contemporary philosophers.

- Give an example of the fallacy of anachronism.

- Give an example of the *ad hominem* fallacy.

- Critique the rationale behind the principle of empathetic understanding, paying special attention to the context in which it is first introduced.

WESTERN PHILOSOPHY BEGAN in ancient Greece about eight hundred years before the time of Christ. At that time, the chief component of Greek culture was a powerful religious mythology. These early myths offered primitive explanations of natural phenomena, human history, and the gods. They provided standards of conduct, morality, social obligations, education, art, religious practices, and so on. The most important mythical view of life was expressed in the *Iliad* and the *Odyssey*, two epic poems attributed to the ancient Greek poet Homer (c. eighth century B.C.E.).

For the Greeks of Homer's era, everything happened through some kind of divine agency. They believed, for example, that the sun was carried around the heavens by Apollo's golden chariot, that thunder and lightning were hurled down from the top of Mount Olympus by Zeus, and that the motion of Poseidon's trident created waves. Other natural phenomena were thought to have similar divine origins. The nature of the community, victory or defeat in war, the course of love, and other human affairs were also directly tied to the gods.

The ancient Greek gods were exaggerated human beings: bigger, stronger, and faster. Like human beings, they were also jealous, sneaky, biased, lazy, promiscuous, and violent. They were not, however, morally or spiritually superior to humans. In fact, the gods were often indifferent to human affairs, including human suffering, because they were involved in complicated soap operas of their own. Occasionally, the gods took an interest in an individual human being or involved themselves in wars or politics, often treating people as pieces in an elaborate chesslike game.

World History Archive/Image Asset Management Ltd./Alamy

Homer's *Iliad* had a major impact on ancient Greek culture. This powerful tale of the Trojan War intertwined the lives of humans with the whims of Olympian gods and provided a mythical ideal of the hero.

Although the ancient Greeks' mythological accounting of events ultimately failed, it implied two crucial principles that are still disputed by philosophers:

1. There is a difference between the way things *appear* and the way they *really* are.

2. There are unseen *causes* of events.

These principles marked a major advance beyond less analytic mythological characterizations of nature and society.

Greek mythology was not sheer fantasy; it was the product of a desire to find explanations. Science grew out of this search for explanations, and philosophy grew out of attempts to provide rational justification for these early prescientific explanations.

As ancient Greece developed, its social structure became less restrictive (though by no means democratic in the modern sense). Colonization of outlying cities and communities contributed to the rise of philosophy, as increased social and political freedom combined with an established culture to permit increasingly free inquiry and exchange of ideas. As Greek civilization grew, colonization led to increasing interaction with sophisticated nearby Eastern cultures and the mythological worldview became less effective. Explaining events with "the gods willed it" became less and less satisfying.

Presocratic Western philosophers challenged the mythological worldview by asking for rational explanations of questions that mythology could not adequately answer: "What causes earthquakes?" "Where do islands come from?" "Why doesn't the earth fall out of the sky like an apple from a tree?" "What holds it up? And what holds that up?" "Why don't the stars fall out of the sky?" Or, more subtly yet, "How come if I eat fish and grain, I don't look like a fish or stalk of wheat? How does 'fish stuff' become fingernail 'stuff'?" "Where does the stone go that is worn away by the waterfall? I cannot see it being chipped away. What is this invisible

Greek mythology was a product of a search for explanations. Ancient storytellers did more than just entertain; they excited curiosity and helped preserve and transmit a shared sense of culture.

In its heyday, the Athenian agora, seen here below the Acropolis (left), would have been abuzz with Greek citizens mingling with merchants, artisans, and philosophers from as far away as what we now know as Italy, Turkey, and Iran. Ancient shoppers would have chosen from much the same colorful variety of goods as those offered in a modern Turkish bazaar (right).

'stuff' that 'goes away'?" And, again: "Where did 'stuff' come from? Where does it go?" (See Chapter 2 for a fuller account of this stage of philosophical development.)

Nature and Convention

In their efforts to provide *unified* rational explanations, these early philosophers first concentrated on the "world order" (*kosmos* in Greek) and "nature" (*phusis* or *physis* in Greek). You may recognize the roots of the English words *cosmos* and *physics* in these ancient Greek terms.

Around the fifth century, an element of specialization emerged throughout the ancient world. Actually, the word *division* is probably more accurate than *specialization* because philosophers began to distinguish between nature (*physis*) and convention (*nomos*) rather than to specialize along narrower lines. The terms *norm, normative,* and *normal* derive from the Greek root *nomos*. In the West, humanistic philosophers known as Sophists (Chapter 3) turned away from the study of nature and toward the study of "man." In China and Southeast Asia, humanistic sages (Chapter 1) turned away from the study of gods and spirits and toward the study of "man" and nature.

Contemporary Lessons from the Past

You're right to wonder about the use of the word *man* here: The ancient world was socially hierarchical and chauvinistic in its divisions of people into social classes of varying status, influence, and power according to nationality, bloodlines (a crude form of "racial" thinking), gender, language and dialect, talent, and beauty.

The Olympian god Poseidon (Neptune), god of the sea, also known as Earth-shaker, was said to cause both calm and chaotic waters, create islands, and, when provoked, cause earthquakes by stabbing the ground with his trident.

For many—but not all—classical philosophers, women were, by nature, not capable of philosophical reasoning. Of course, in this, the philosophers were not alone; they reflected the norms of their times, as did many women. The Asian sage Confucius (Chapter 1), for example, compared women to servants who were easily offended. Plato, arguably the single most influential Western philosopher, thought of women as "lesser men," although he also allows women in the ranks of the philosopher-kings who occupy the highest strata in his ideal state (Chapter 5). Aristotle (Chapter 6), one of the most significant thinkers in the history of Western philosophy, thought of women as "mistakes" of nature—"incomplete" or "misbegotten" men. The hedonist Epicurus, on the other hand, made no philosophical distinctions between men and women (Chapter 7).

Some of the most important and complex questions philosophers ask today concern proper attitudes toward thinkers from the past. Chapters 9, 11, 17, and

In ancient Asia, sages such as Buddha turned toward the study of nature and man (humanity), not separately, but as a harmonious whole.

For classical philosophers, women were by nature incapable of philosophical reasoning. But, as we'll discover, Plato, Epicurus, and Epictetus were among those who thought otherwise.

18 address this issue directly, and reference to it recurs throughout our philosophical journey. But at the beginning of this inquiry, let me encourage you to *seek empathetic understanding before passing judgment on new ideas and those who advocate them*. Practicing this principle helps avoid confusing issues and arguments with the persons who advocate them.

When we uncritically and rigidly apply contemporary values to past practices and ideas, we commit the *fallacy of anachronism*. Even though we can never be sure that our current understanding of the past is accurate, we can make good-faith efforts to understand the conditions that affected people's thinking and acting. Doing so does not commit us to some form of relativism or prevent us from evaluating ideas from other times and cultures. Rather, understanding the historical context that gives rise to a philosophical point of view allows us to cull from the richness and complexity of the entire human condition. Further, we do not need to reject an entire philosophical enterprise just because we find some aspect of it unacceptable—unless what's unacceptable is the heart of the enterprise or is entailed by essential components of it.

Just as we do not want to uncritically impose contemporary values on ancient philosophers, neither do we want to reject a philosopher's arguments because we object to that philosopher's personal habits or beliefs. When we do that, we commit what is known as the *ad hominem* fallacy. *Ad hominem* is Latin for "at the man." In this context it means "against the arguer, against the person making the argument." (Ironically, the term *ad hominem* presents us with an example of the pervasiveness and ambiguity of terms based on the root "man": *mankind, human, chairman, humanistic*, and even *woman*.)

The Search for Excellence

One of the major themes in ancient philosophy is the search for general human excellence, or virtue. The Greek word for virtue (*arete*) means "excellence" and is associated with potency and functionality. The Chinese word for virtue (*jen*) connotes benevolence, humanity, and being a real, authentic person. Thus, something lacking in virtue fails to function in some way. Without virtue, things are dysfunctional, incomplete, not themselves, not what they are meant to be.

In the West, the philosophical search for human excellence links the Sophists (Chapter 3) to Socrates (Chapter 4), Plato (Chapter 5), Aristotle (Chapter 6), and the Stoics (Chapter 7). In Asia, the ancient sages also produced longstanding theories of virtue and well-being (Chapter 1).

The Search for Happiness

As a rule, ancient philosophers did not distinguish between "being good" and "being happy" the way many of us do today. Rather, they thought of living the good life as living well, in the sense of thriving, of being healthy or "fully human."

Today, it is common to equate being happy with almost any form of personal satisfaction. If happiness is a feeling, then I cannot be wrong about being happy: If I *feel* happy, I *am* happy. This particular view of happiness defines "being happy" in purely subjective and individualistic terms.

Classical notions of happiness were more complicated. A helpful analogy here is between *being* healthy and *feeling* healthy and *being* happy and *feeling* happy. It's easy to understand that Margaret may not be well even though Margaret feels well. In other words, Margaret can be unhealthy and feel fine. Conversely, Joe can be convinced that he is dying from cancer even though he is cancer-free. Further, unhealthy individuals can—because they are unhealthy—get used to being sick. Thus the habitual smoker "feels good" when she poisons herself with a puff on a cigarette, but "feels bad" when she acts wisely and refrains from smoking.

If, however, more than subjective conditions are necessary for happiness, then the individual is not the determiner of happiness. In such a view, it is possible to think you are happy and be wrong. If that sounds crazy to you, you are not alone. But before dismissing classical notions of happiness, wait and see what sorts of reasons the ancient philosophers give for their views.

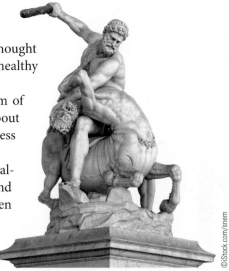

©iStock.com/snem

Although today Heracles is best known for his prodigious physical strength, this son of Zeus and a mortal woman became the greatest of heroes for learning to combine that strength with the "excellence" of perseverance, courage, and intelligence, without which sheer strength is brutish.

1

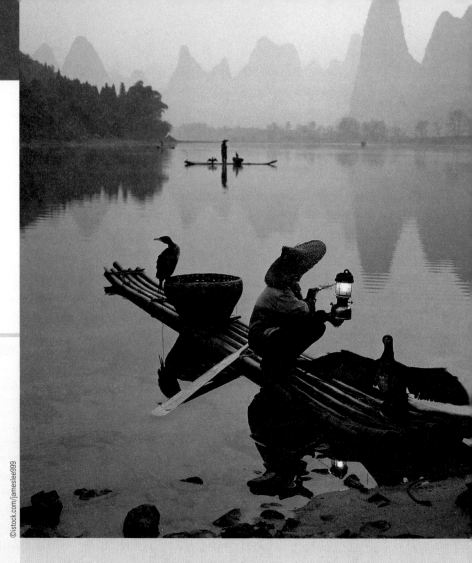

The Asian Sages
Lao-tzu, Confucius, and Buddha

Who knows why Heaven dislikes what it dislikes? Even the sage considers it a difficult question.
— *Lao-tzu*

He who learns but does not think is lost; he who thinks but does not learn is in danger.
— *Confucius*

If you will now and at all times, whether walking, standing, sitting, or lying, only concentrate on eliminating analytic thinking, at long last you will inevitably discover the truth.
— *Buddha*

Learning Objectives

After you complete this chapter, you should be able to:

- Differentiate between an archetype and a sage.
- Characterize Tao.
- Relate *yin* and *yang*.
- Utilize the Golden Mean to distinguish between the inferior man and the superior man according to Confucius.
- Describe humanism.
- Define the term *li*.
- Define the term *jen*.
- Explain asceticism.
- List the Four Noble Truths.
- Describe a bodhisattva.
- Explain the problem posed by talking about nirvana.

OUR SURVEY OF PHILOSOPHICAL ARCHETYPES begins with a look at three of the most influential philosophical archetypes of all time, the sages Lao-tzu, Confucius, and Buddha. A therapeutic figure who combines religious inspiration with extraordinary insight into the human condition, the **sage** is the oldest of the philosophical archetypes. The English word *sage* is derived from the Latin *sapiens*, meaning "wise." The term *sage* has been used to refer to masters associated with religious traditions and to the wise elders of a group or tribe. Philosophers who address how we live and whose lives reflect noteworthy integrity, compassion, and courage are also referred to as sages. As a rule, the ancient sages focused on identifying the root causes of happiness and unhappiness. Today, the title *sage* is associated with individuals who manifest a deep, lifelong commitment to learning and teaching that extends beyond an academic or merely theoretical interest in living wisely.

The Harmony of Heaven and Earth

In ancient Asian cosmologies, all events were said to be interconnected. In ancient Chinese cosmology, everything was influenced by the harmonious working together of Heaven and Earth following the *Tao* of all existence. Literally "way" or "path," **Tao** (or **Dao**) cannot be precisely defined or named. Among contemporary scholars, there is a dispute about whether to refer to the "way" as Tao or Dao in English. So don't be surprised to come across both (or to discover alternate renderings of the names of the sages Lao-tzu and Chuang-tzu as Laozi and Zhuangzi or Lao-zi and Zhuang-zi). The older system of rendering these terms is known as Wade-Giles and the contemporary as Pinyin. For the most part, I use Wade-Giles because there are so many beautiful, inexpensive, and handy editions available that use it. Whether we refer to it as Dao or Tao, the "way" is usually translated as the source of all existence, the principle of all things, the way or path of the universe, or the moral law. Tao "unfolds" and "influences" all of nature while remaining hidden from empirical (sensory) experience.

In this cosmology, Heaven and Earth constitute a single reality, a sort of Heaven–Earth, rather than two diametrically opposed and separate realities; nature consists of the continual interaction of two opposing, but not separable, forces known as *yin* (Earth, passive element) and *yang* (Heaven, active element). **Yin** is weak, negative, dark, and destructive; **yang** is strong, positive, light, and constructive. Heaven (yang) and Earth (yin) exist in a perpetually harmonious balance, actually a perpetual *balancing*, according to Tao. Yin and yang go so far back in Chinese history that we cannot be sure of their original meanings. The classic Confucian text *The Doctrine of the Mean* says, "Equilibrium is the great foundation of the world, and harmony its universal "path."[1]

By the fifth century B.C.E., yin and yang were thought of as inextricably linked together. Each was viewed as an expression of the other, operating together in a never-ending cycle of coming together and falling apart, birth and death, wet and dry, day and night, good and evil, male and female, full and empty. This ceaseless interplay of opposing forces is the natural order of things. "Part" and "whole" cannot be understood—much less exist—without each other. How could they? The very

MindTap
Philosophy Timelines

sage
An archetypal figure who combines religious inspiration and extraordinary insight into the human condition; the English word *sage* is derived from the Latin *sapiens*, meaning "wise."

Tao
Literally "way" or "path," Tao (or Dao) is variously translated as the source of all existence, the principle of all things, the way or path of the universe, or the moral law; key concept in Confucian and Taoist philosophy.

yin
In Ancient Chinese metaphysics, weak, negative, dark, and destructive natural force or principle; Earth; linked with yang.

yang
In Ancient Chinese metaphysics, strong, positive, light, and constructive natural force or principle; Heaven; linked with yin.

essence of being a part requires a whole to be a part of, and there can be no whole without parts.

Thus, there are no firm (permanent and fixed) divisions between the spiritual and the physical or between the natural and the supernatural, nor is there a distinct division between the divine and the human, between reason and intuition.[2] Therefore, Tao, the way of Heaven–Earth, cannot be understood analytically or considered piecemeal, individually.

But if life consists of some fundamental, never-ending, and harmonious exchange, why do we so often experience it as a series of apparently discrete, independent events and either/or options? We experience life, or more properly the illusion of life, as discrete events because we are unenlightened and confused. Unaware that the flow of Tao cannot be trapped, we identify with particularities; we prefer the familiar to the exclusion of all else; we cling to things for fear of losing them; we confuse words (labels) with perception (experience). It falls to the sage to identify and preserve Tao by refining the way we talk about it.[3]

So elusive is this goal that even the sages, with all their wisdom, remain susceptible to the partial view. They disagree over whether human beings are naturally good or naturally evil, over whether Tao is best realized actively through social customs and training (Confucius) or through setting aside all personal striving while spreading compassion to others (Buddha). Lao-tzu recommends passively going with the flow of Tao by abandoning social cultivation and following our natural instincts. Yet for all their apparent differences, the sages insist—if that's the word for it—that suffering, division, and strife need not be our permanent condition, for we share a common human nature from which we can learn. Religion, philosophy, culture, and politics are themselves manifestations of Tao; they interact as complementary parts of a single reality perpetually seeking balance.

Sagehood

When you find something that is bad or that turns out bad, drop it and leave it alone.
— Sitting Bull

The sages' focus on achieving harmony and virtue here and now is a response to the social conditions in which they lived. For Lao-tzu and Confucius, this was a time of such widespread political and social turmoil that it came to be known as the Period of the Warring States. Although traditional Chinese history holds that the Period of the Warring States began in 453 B.C.E. and lasted for nearly 550 years, some historians push the beginning as far back as 771 B.C.E.

The Period of the Warring States was marked by fierce struggles for power waged by a succession of warring princes. The resulting civil wars became increasingly violent as armies ignored the customs and traditional rules of conduct known as *li* that had previously prevented wholesale pillage and destruction. Each atrocity was answered with an equal or greater atrocity. In one notorious incident, soldiers from one army were not paid until they showed the paymaster the severed heads of their enemies.

A. C. Graham, a leading authority on Chinese thought and grammar, describes the teachings of the ancient sages as responses to the "breakdown of the rule of Heaven" and the moral and political chaos that resulted. Instead of asking "What is the truth?" as early Western philosophers did, the Asian sages asked "Where is the Way (Tao)?" Where, they wondered, is the way back to social order and proper conduct?[4] As a result of their practical concerns, the teachings of the sages are marked by what the philosopher Michael Brannigan characterizes as "an intimate rapport between philosophy and its actualization in society."[5]

A "fully human" sensitivity links the three sages we'll look at in this chapter, each of whom speaks from intimate knowledge of suffering and disappointment. Offering anyone who will listen the fruits of their hard-earned "research," sages perform a complex social function: part physician of the soul, part prophet, part preacher, part philosopher, part fellow seeker. In subsequent chapters, we'll look at the Western sages Socrates (Chapter 4), Epicurus, Epictetus, and Marcus Aurelius (all Chapter 7).

Unsurprisingly, the sage has no exact equivalent today, at least not in this culture, a culture that encourages individuation and competition, seemingly perpetual social war—precisely what the sages sought to overcome. In this regard, you might find it interesting to contrast the sage with the more warlike Sophist, a might-makes-right seller of methods for getting whatever one wants, whose philosophy seems surprisingly contemporary. Sophists are discussed in Chapter 3.

If you are unfamiliar with the teachings of the ancient philosophical sages, don't be fooled into thinking that because they talk about harmony and balance sages are preachy "anti-life" figures who don't have anything practical to offer a high-tech, high-energy, individualistic, competitive society. Perhaps the high-tech, specialized (disharmonious) nature of our lives means that just the opposite is true. The lasting appeal and influence of the sages suggests that we're not completely sold on the pursuit of fame, power, riches, and prestige, even though we can't just toss our interest in them aside. In distinct but overlapping ways, these archetypal figures encourage us to achieve sagehood for ourselves.

> *Only the most intelligent and the most stupid do not change.*
> — Confucius

PHILOSOPHICAL QUERY

Based on what you've read so far, can you think of any contemporary examples of sages? If you can, what specific qualities or teachings impress you as sage-like? If you can't, why do you suppose you can't?

The Do-Nothing Sage: Lao-tzu

Legend says that **Lao-tzu** (c. 575 B.C.E.) was a bureaucrat in ancient China, known only by a nickname variously translated as Old Master, Old Man, Old Boy, or Old Philosopher. He may have compiled his book, the *Tao te Ching*, under a pseudonym as a form of self-preservation, since he lived during the instability of the Period of the Warring States. The scholar A. C. Graham suggests that living in a state of "perpetual fear" taught the reclusive Lao-tzu (whoever he really was) to develop a self-preserving "habit of evasive speech."[6] In fact, however, we know very little of Lao-tzu.

According to legend, when he was 160 years old, Lao-tzu grew so disgusted with the hypocrisy and decay of his time that he decided to resign from his position as a bureaucrat to pursue virtue in a more natural environment. Heading west, Lao-tzu

Lao-tzu

© Cengage Learning®

reached the Han-ku Pass, where the keeper of the pass recognized the old sage and said, "You are about to withdraw yourself from sight. I pray you compose a book for me." Lao-tzu honored the man's request by producing a little (5,000-word) book known today as the *Tao te Ching*.[7]

Next to the *Analects* of Confucius, the *Tao te Ching* is the most influential book in Chinese history. Nearly a thousand commentaries on it have been written in China and Japan alone. The *Tao te Ching*, or *The Classic of the Way and the Power (Virtue)*, is second only to the Bible in the number of English translations available. Today interpretations of Taoism are continuously emerging in popular philosophical, spiritual, and psychological literature.

What accounts for the power of this slim volume, usually divided into eighty-one "chapters" of a page or less in length? Some scholars claim that the *Tao te Ching* is so cloudy and obscure, so romantic and poetic, that the reader is free to make it mean anything. To them, the popularity of the *Tao te Ching* derives from its lack of clarity, from its ability to mean all things to all people, and from its brevity.

A more intriguing possibility is that the book credited to the secretive, perhaps fearful Old Philosopher expresses genuine, timeless wisdom. Let's see what Lao-tzu has to say to us in the twenty-first century.

The Way

Rather than presenting a philosophic *system*, Lao-tzu struggled to express a sense of the ultimate, underlying great principle, rule, or cause of "the way all things are."

Lao-tzu refers to Tao in poetic, suggestive terms. He appeals to our "natural instincts" and intuitions. In so doing, he hopes to render as little injustice as possible to the throbbing, rich, ever-flowing stream of the Way. Tao is, he implies, too rich, too big and too small, simply "too much" to be "trapped" by definition, description, or system. Thus, this Taoist sage often speaks in apparent contradictions, in pairs of opposites. He points out "the rest of the story" by calling our attention to overlooked, but essential, aspects of the Way. In *A Source Book in Chinese Philosophy*, Wing-Tsit Chan points out that Tao does not refer to a system or moral truth but to a way of life. Tao is

> the One which is natural, eternal, spontaneous, nameless, and indescribable....
> As a way of life, it denotes simplicity, spontaneity, tranquility, weakness, and most important of all, non-action (*wu wei*). By the latter is not meant literally "inactivity" but rather "taking no action that is contrary to Nature"—in other words, letting Nature take its own course.[8]

In the opening stanza of the *Tao te Ching*, Lao-tzu signals us that this is not an attempt to articulate Tao according to the limiting rules of rational consistency. Ever-flowing, Tao cannot be captured in systems or in words. Consider the subtle differences among the following two translations of the famous opening lines of Chapter 1 of the *Tao te Ching*:

> (1) The Tao that can be told of
>   Is not the absolute Tao;
>   The Names that can be given

Xinhua/Landov

"Since all things are longing for peace, why not let them alone?"
—*Chuang-tzu*

> Are not the Absolute Names.
> The Nameless is the origin of Heaven and Earth;
> The Named is the Mother of All Things.[9]
> (2) As for the Way, the Way that can be spoken of is not the constant Way;
> As for names, the name that can be named is not the constant name.
> The nameless is the beginning of the ten thousand things;
> The named is the mother of the ten thousand things.[10]

Each translation *approximates* a "sense of something"; it circles but cannot explicitly define the Way. In Lao-tzu's phrase, words cannot "trap" Tao. The sage must find a way to "speak without speaking" and "discuss what cannot be discussed." The sage will attempt to communicate the experience of a cosmic or spiritual pattern; this is quite different from expressing a concept, idea, or principle.

People Cannot Stop Talking About It

Why doesn't Lao-tzu just come right out and tell us straightforwardly that the Way cannot be expressed in words, that it is the source of all things, and that it is only discovered by ridding ourselves of desire? Perhaps because that's not precisely what he means. "The trouble with words," Graham says, "is not that they do not fit at all but that they always fit imperfectly."[11] Just because the Way cannot be "reduced" to words or principles does not mean that nothing important and useful can be said about it. Poignantly, Lao-tzu says that although we cannot talk about Tao, "people cannot cease discussing It." And that includes, of course, Lao-tzu.

> *What we cannot speak about we must pass over in silence.*
> — Ludwig Wittgenstein

Next to the *Analects* of Confucius, the *Tao te Ching* (or *Dao de Jing*) is the most influential book in Chinese history, second only to the Bible in the number of English translations currently available.

Lao-tzu's solution to the problem of expressing what cannot be trapped in words is to develop a kind of paradoxical way of communicating in which contradictory assertions and demands keep us from fixing on one "trapped" or "dead" interpretation. The sage's hope is that this kind of giving with one hand and taking with the other will "draw us in the direction which is the Way."[12]

Western philosophers as diverse as Heraclitus (Chapter 3), Søren Kierkegaard (Chapter 14), William James (Chapter 15), Friedrich Nietzsche (Chapter 16), and Martin Heidegger and Ludwig Wittgenstein (Chapter 17) struggle with the "problem of language" and adopt their own indirect strategies for dealing with what cannot be said, usually with more sting than the Old Boy.

In many ways, the history of philosophy is a history of struggling to say what must be said in ways that do justice to human experience. The sages are not alone in confronting the problem of language. Yet the problem of language lingers because, upon reflection, experience always seems to elude us, to defy complete verbalization. No matter what we say about life, *living itself* is always something more. It seems as if our best attempts to define or explain "the Way of life" always fall short. Yet the attempts themselves, Lao-tzu reminds us, the very failures themselves, are Tao, are part of life. It is the mark of a sage to know when to stop talking—and when not to.

When we consider all the philosophical, religious, and scientific talk—chatter—about life, virtue, and ultimate Reality with a capital R, Meaning with a capital M, and Truth with a capital T, Lao-tzu's puzzling opening lines attain the power of insight: Talk in the form of once-and-for-all, absolute, fixed systems, dogmas, objective truths, and universal theories pales beside *living itself*.

"Saying" (talk) can help, but saying can also hurt. Saying helps when it draws us to the Way, when it awakens us to something more, something beyond ordinary understanding. Saying hurts when labels substitute for perception, when abstract ideas and rigid, exclusive notions of good or bad, right or wrong, true or false block feeling and intuition.

Ancient sages and prophets took "saying" or "naming" very seriously. Across cultures, names, incantations, curses, blessings, and classifications have governed our sense of who we are, who the other is, how we should live, feel, think, and even perceive the world or reality. The more "names" there are, the more things there are. Once a thing has been named (right, wrong, true, false, God, man, higher, lower), we tend to cling to its name, to one perspective. We become "dead" in Lao-tzu's scheme of things—because we lose sight of the ever-flowing range of possibilities, perspectives, and conditions that always go beyond the name. Unlike the "myriad things," "The Way is constantly nameless."[13]

And yet...from another point of view, it is convenient to think of the Way in words, to think of it as a thing with a name:

> As for the thing the Way is
> It is vague and dim.
> Dim! Vague!
> Within it is a model.
> Vague! Dim!
> Within it is a thing. . . .
> From the present to the past
> Its name does not depart.[14]

The best of man is like water, Which benefits all things, and does not contend with them, Which flows in places that others disdain, Where it is in harmony with the Way.
—*Tao te Ching*

The Way of Reversal

Lao-tzu often calls the "undivided" the One. Subsequent commentators sometimes refer to it as Being or Reality. Whatever Lao-tzu means, he does not *conceive* of the Way at all. That is, the Way (or the One) is not a concept to grasp cognitively or logically. Lao-tzu is not trying to discover something "more real" than what appears to the senses, but a "constant Way behind the changing and conflicting ways of life and government claimed by competing schools" as the official, one, true, way.[15]

Lao-tzu's nonrational, nonlogical approach presents difficulties for more analytically inclined Western philosophers, some of whom refuse to classify Lao-tzu among the philosophers, suggesting that he belongs with prophetic or religious figures. This is not satisfactory, however, for Asian scholars distinguish between religious Taoism, with its various rituals and beliefs, and philosophical Taoism, exemplified by the *Tao te Ching* and the *Chuang-tzu*.

Where does that leave us? How can we evaluate a "philosophy" that does not attempt to be systematic, rational, or even organized in any ordinary sense? Indeed, what are we to make of a philosophy that suggests that what are often thought of as the basic tools of philosophy—systems, theories, logical reasoning, and linguistic precision—are, in fact, impediments to reality and truth? It is hardly surprising that some philosophers reject Taoism as unphilosophical babbling. Nor is it surprising that other philosophers share Taoism's discomfort with objectivity, dogmatism, rationalism, scientism, and technology. (See Chapters 14–17.)

We must, Lao-tzu suggests, sometimes violate our own carefully crafted rules and systems if we wish to be decent human beings responsive to the ebb and flow of *living itself. Living itself* is not a problem to be solved; consequently, it cannot be contained in any system. We must do more than understand, more than provide rules, more than explain with tightly reasoned precision. We must respond and resonate to the "ultimate something" that throbs with life just beyond the edge of understanding. Lao-tzu says:

> When the people of the world all know beauty as beauty
>   There arises the recognition of ugliness.
> When they all know the good as good,
>   There arises the recognition of evil. Therefore:
>   Being and non-being produce each other;
>   Difficult and easy complete each other;
>   Long and short contrast each other;
>   High and low distinguish each other;
>   Sound and voice harmonize with each other;
>   Front and back follow each other.[16]

But how can we turn off our need to classify, arrange, judge, and label things? How can we stop thinking (analyzing) so much and still remain conscious, alert, and intelligent? Lao-tzu suggests that we adopt an astonishing method of "getting mind out of the way" as it were.

PHILOSOPHICAL QUERY

The tension between "beliefs" and "facts" recurs throughout the history of Western philosophy and explodes in our own time in the form of challenges to the very possibilities of objectivity and universality. Can you spot signs of this division in current affairs? Religion? Politics? Among your friends? Which side of the fence are you on? Do you think this problem has a solution that is fair to both sides?

Prefer Yin to Yang

As we have seen, according to ancient Chinese cosmology, the whole of nature consists of the continual interaction of two opposing forces known as yin (passive, weak, negative, dark, and destructive) and yang (active, strong, positive, light, and constructive), inextricably linked together, each an expression of the other, operating together in a never-ending cycle of coming together and falling apart, part of one seamless cycle. According to Lao-tzu, the true sage, recognizing this, realizes that conditions call up opposite conditions and, thus, nothing is permanent.

What we call the bad "produces" the good (and the good is but the necessary other side of the bad). The reverse is also true: What we call the good "produces" the bad. The bad is but the necessary other side of the good, just as the good is necessary for the bad. Understanding this, the sage is patient, knowing that today's unfortunate circumstance will change into something good. (Nietzsche will say much the same thing in his critique of morality—only without the sage's patience. See Chapter 16.)

Lao-tzu preaches his "doctrine without words" as a strategy for surviving in difficult times (the Period of Warring States) by turning away from common values and reversing common priorities. He repeatedly advises his readers to *prefer* (choose or lean toward) yin rather than yang. The following chains of oppositions are culled from the *Tao te Ching*:

Yang (to be resisted)	*Yin* (to be preferred)
Something	Nothing
Doing something	Doing nothing
Knowledge	Ignorance
Male	Female
Full	Empty
Above	Below
Before	After
Moving	Still
Big	Small
Strong	Weak
Hard	Soft
Straight	Bent[17]

The Union of Relative Opposites

If Lao-tzu is correct, if there is one undivided Way, then neat, fixed, hard distinctions are arbitrary and misleading. Nothing is purely matter or spirit (energy). Nothing is completely male or female, wet or dry, good or bad. As the Western philosopher Heraclitus said, "All things are becoming." (See Chapter 3.)

The good and the bad exist in an everlasting exchange, and the names we give conditions depend on our circumstances and temperaments. For instance, rain is good in a time of drought, bad in a time of flood. Great size might be good on the football field; great size will be bad trying to squeeze through a tiny window opening during a fire. The good and the bad are relative opposites. Things become good or bad according to our reactions. They are not fixed.

According to Lao-tzu, we glimpse Tao in the flux of life. Chaos and disorder are only apparent. They are interpretations and judgments made from a small or fixed perspective. Things seem out of control when we focus on isolated particulars instead of looking for patterns. The sage embraces opposition and flux—yin and yang.

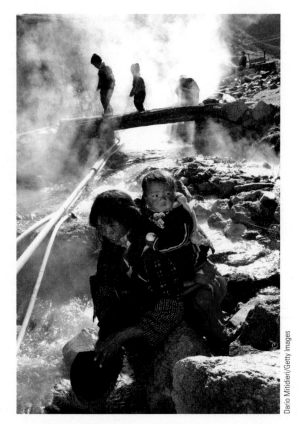

Dario Mitidieri/Getty Images

The sage teaches that the bad is but the necessary other side of the good, just as the good is necessary for the bad. Understanding this, the sage is patient. Do you agree? Would you think the same way if you were this Daocheng mother?

PHILOSOPHICAL QUERY

Stop and reflect on this point. In various forms, it recurs regularly in what is known as wisdom literature. See, for example, how Lao-tzu's position compares with what the Stoics (Chapter 7) say about our attitudes (labels) determining whether things appear to us as good or bad. What is lost if we accept Lao-tzu's teaching? What is gained?

If everything is part of one whole, why bother to resist yang and to prefer yin? To understand what Lao-tzu is doing, it helps to remember two things. First, Lao-tzu was interested in surviving during a period of widespread corruption, intrigue, and violence. The common reaction of people in such conditions, then as now, was to meet force with counterforce. Rulers, their underlings, and even the common people were constantly taking action—doing things, planning, scheming, trying to get what they wanted through force, seduction, any way they could.

The result, then as now, was continuous commotion, busy-ness, frustration, stress, and exhaustion as individuals, groups, and rulers fought to impose their wills on each other. Can you recognize the operant yang principle here? It is *control*. But, as Lao-tzu saw it, no one really has control. There is always Something Beyond, Some Process, Something that seems to have its own purposes (if we can use such a word). And that Something, as you no doubt now know, is Tao (the Way). (Compare what Lao-tzu suggests about being in control and Tao with what the Stoics Epictetus and Marcus Aurelius say about control and *Logos* in Chapter 7.)

If Lao-tzu pushed to *get people to let go of attempts at control*, then he would violate his own insight. Besides, it was (and is) only natural for push to come to shove, for force to produce counterforce. If Lao-tzu actively and forcefully argued for or promoted his doctrine, he would engender its very opposite. What to do?

Lao-tzu's (to us) odd answer is "Do nothing (and great deeds are accomplished)."

The Way of Inaction

wu wei

Literally "not to act"; in the *Tao te Ching*, a warning against unnatural or demanding action.

Often translated as "do nothing," the doctrine of **wu wei** is a most intriguing aspect of Taoism. The literal translation of *wu wei* is "not to act," but it is probably more accurate to think of it as a warning against unnatural or demanding action, demanding as in, "I demand X!" In the following passage, A. C. Graham calls our attention to the paradoxical nature of this crucial Taoist principle:

> The paradox that the way to attain a goal is to cease to aim at it deliberately is most explicit in Lao-tzu's constant appeals to "do nothing" (*wu wei*). This term, which goes back to Confucius, is often translated by such innocuous phrases as "non-action" to avoid giving the impression that Taoists recommend idleness, but it seems better to keep the paradoxical force of the Chinese expression. *Wei* is ordinary human action, deliberated for a purpose, in contrast with the spontaneous processes of nature. … Man takes pride in distinguishing himself from nature by his purposive action; *Lao-tzu* by a classic reversal describes the behavior of the sage as Doing Nothing.[18]

Here, "natural" does not mean common or widespread, but natural in the sense of healthy, spontaneous, and in harmony with Tao. Spontaneity stands in contrast to calculation, deliberation, and the careful (crafty) weighing of advantages and disadvantages, profit and gain, social image, and other priorities and considerations that get us out of touch with the natural order of things: Tao.

Doing Something—planning, pushing, scheming, fixing, saving the world—is exhausting because Doing Something never ends; it never completely accomplishes its goal. Doing Nothing, on the other hand, relaxes the body, calms the mind, loosens the grip of categories [judgments and labels] made habitual by naming, frees the current of thought for more fluid differentiations … and instead of pondering choices lets … problems solve themselves as inclination spontaneously finds its own direction, which is the Way.[19]

When Lao-tzu says that "by doing nothing great deeds are accomplished," he does not mean "by sitting like a lump, no matter what, great deeds are accomplished." He means that by taking no contrived, calculated, "controlling" action, we are most likely to contribute to improving conditions around us. Rather than set out to "save the environment," the sage spontaneously picks up trash while he takes his morning walk. Rather than agitate and argue to put an end to racism, the sage naturally and spontaneously (without calculation or ulterior motive) associates with all sorts of people—and naturally and spontaneously (and unaggressively) walks away when a co-worker tells racist jokes. Thus the sage preaches without preaching and teaches without lecturing.

Concentrating on being a cheerful, helpful, tolerant "friend of Tao," the sage is consistently nonjudgmental. He acts, to be sure, but not through his specific efforts or words, or with concern over precise results:

> I treat those who are good with goodness,
> And I also treat those who are not good with goodness.
> Thus goodness is attained.
> I am honest with those who are honest,
> And I am also honest with those who are not honest.
> Thus honesty is attained.[20]

According Lao-tzu, the best way to deal with social turmoil is "not to do anything about it." If this sounds crazy to you, you are not alone. Just think of how much time and energy we devote to "solving problems," "fixing things," "saving the environment," "winning the war on drugs," "ending racism and poverty." In today's jargon, we are encouraged to be *proactive*, not *reactive*.

Does aggressive social and political action really accomplish its goals—or does it result in contest after contest, with proliferating factions struggling against each other for control? Can social "progress" be linked directly to specific efforts, or does something more mysterious and more complex account for social and technological change? Is there such a thing as progress, pure and simple, or is the very notion of progress itself a judgment—a judgment with which others disagree?

For most readers of this book, I hope, circumstances are not as bad as those Lao-tzu lived through. Yet in many ways, we, too, live without guarantees of physical safety, financial security, or social harmony. Sometimes it seems as if we live in our own Period of Warring Factions, a time during which almost any significant action taken to legislate or enforce one faction's notion of social order and harmony generates a counterforce from opposing factions as generations, nations, ethnic coalitions, political affiliations, and religious groups ceaselessly jump into action with grand plans to proactively fix things.

No matter what is accomplished, struggle and turmoil remain, just in different forms. Lao-tzu says

> The more taboos in the world
> The poorer the people:

When the government is muddled and confused, The people are genuine and sincere. When the government is discriminate and clear, The people are crafty and cunning.
— Lao-tzu

The more sharp tools among the people
The stupider the state.
The more men's arts and skills,
The more oddities arise:
The more laws and edicts are proclaimed
The more thieves and bandits there will be.

Hence the sage says:

If I do nothing, of themselves the people are transformed.
If I love stillness, of themselves the people are correct.
If I meddle in nothing, of themselves the people are rich.
If I desire nothing, of themselves the people are unhewn.[21]

According to Lao-tzu, we would be wise to learn to live in harmony with Tao in the midst of this world, a world of overpopulation, rampant commercialism, aggressive politicians, global terrorism, environmental insult, and our own strong, willful desires to get things done, to get ahead, to hoard wealth—the whole seemingly irresistible, frustrating commotion that we know as life in the high-tech twenty-first century. In harmony with Tao, we can survive, even blossom, in stressful times. Are there any other kinds?

For Deeper Consideration

According to ancient Chinese cosmology, the whole of nature consists of the continual interaction of two opposing forces, yin and yang. Discuss how this belief (or is it an observation?) leads Lao-tzu to the "way of inaction." What kind of action does Lao-tzu warn against? Why? Cite some current real-life examples of "action that rebounds" to support Lao-tzu. On balance, do you think the doctrine of inaction is sound? Feasible? Explain.

The Social Sage: Confucius

Confucius (551–479 B.C.E.) is the Latinized name of K'ung Fu-tzu or Master K'ung, the honorific name of K'ung Ch'iu of Lu, a legendary teacher who vainly sought high political office so that he could initiate a series of governmental reforms. In response to what he saw as widespread social decline, Confucius took a more active approach than Lao-tzu and promoted social order based on humanity (benevolence), custom, and personal moral cultivation.

As a teacher and would-be political reformer, Confucius tried to produce political harmony by cultivating moral harmony within each individual. "Guide the people by governmental measures," he said, "and regulate them by the threat of punishment, and the people will have no sense of honor and shame. Guide the people by virtue and regulate them by *li* (rules of conduct and sense of propriety), and the people will have a sense of honor and respect.[22]

One disciple characterized Confucius as "gentle but dignified, austere, yet not harsh, polite and completely at ease." When another disciple admitted that he had

Confucius

© Cengage Learning®

been unable to describe Confucius to the king, Confucius said, "Why didn't you tell him that I am a man who forgets all worries when he is happy, and who is not aware that old age is coming on?" To a disciple who liked to criticize people, Confucius said, "Ah Sze, you are very clever, aren't you? I have no time for such things." On another occasion, some young people from a village known for its mischief-making came to see Confucius, who welcomed them. This surprised his disciples. "Why be harsh with them?" the sage gently replied. "What concerns me is how they come and not what they do when they go away. When a man approaches me with pure intentions, I respect his pure intentions, although I cannot guarantee what he does afterwards."[23]

Confucius was not always so accepting, however, particularly when it came to "the inferior (or petty) man." He especially disliked hypocrites, whom he called goody-goody thieves of virtue and "rice bags"—that is, people only good for filling their bellies with rice. Confucius took good manners and proper social customs seriously because he was convinced that they are necessary for social order and individual moral cultivation. He is said to have struck an elderly man on the shin with a walking stick for singing disrespectfully at the man's mother's funeral. "As a young boy," Confucius said to the ill-mannered fellow, "you were unruly; when grown up, you have accomplished nothing; and now in your old age you refuse to die. You are a thief!"[24]

Great Man demands it of himself; Petty Man, of others.
— Confucius

The Teacher

Confucius probably began teaching in his twenties or thirties. Legend has it that he was the first man in Chinese history to devote his whole life to teaching, teaching even when he worked as a public official in his home province of Lu. Although today he has a reputation as a conservative wedded to tradition, in his time Confucius was a daring and radical educator who defied traditional practices by making a new form of character education—as opposed to vocational training— available to all social classes. He is said to have had as many as three thousand pupils at once. In spite of his open-door approach to education, Confucius attracted a special class of gentlemen-scholars known as *literati;* the literati dominated Chinese history and culture for thousands of years.[25]

When he was fifty-six years old, Confucius retired from civil service because his superiors were uninterested in his ideas. For the next thirteen years he wandered and taught in what Wing-Tsit Chan calls a "desperate attempt" at social reform, traveling from state to state in search of a ruler who would listen to him. He seems to have had almost no success selling his reforms, although he did manage to win audiences with at least four dukes. At sixty-eight, dejected and disappointed, Confucius returned to Lu, where he continued to teach, write, and edit until his death.

I do not instruct the uninterested. I do not help those who fail to try. If I mention one corner of a subject and the pupil does not deduce therefrom the other three, I drop him.
— Confucius

Despite his failures as a political reformer, Confucius remains one of the great teachers of all time, probably surpassing even Socrates (Chapter 4) in the subsequent influence he has had on his culture. Like Socrates, Confucius was witty, humane, complicated, confident, and modest. Like Socrates, Confucius was unimpressed by wealth and social standing. "The people who live extravagantly," he said, "are apt to be snobbish (or conceited), and the people who live simply are apt to be vulgar. I prefer the vulgar people to the snobs."[26]

Shortly before he died, Confucius wept and said, "For a long time the world has been living in moral chaos, and no ruler has been able to follow me." Leaning on a stick, he walked slowly around his door, singing, "Ah! The Mountain is crumbling down! The pillar is falling down! The Philosopher is passing out!"[27]

A collection of Confucius's conversations known as the *Analects* is the single most influential book of Asian philosophy. Two other important Confucian texts are *The Book of Mencius* and *The Hsun Tzu*, named after their authors, the Confucian philosophers Mencius (c. 372–c. 298 B.C.E.) and Hsun Tzu (c. 313–c. 238 B.C.E.).

Confucian Humanism and the Golden Mean

humanism
The name given to any philosophy that emphasizes human welfare and dignity; the belief that human intelligence and effort are capable of improving conditions in the here and now.

If one word characterizes the overall approach of the ancient sages, it is **humanism**, the name given to any philosophy that emphasizes human welfare and dignity. In general, humanism is based on the belief that human intelligence and effort are capable of improving present conditions.

Confucius's humanistic notion that "man can make the Way (Tao) great" was a radical departure from the traditional Chinese emphasis on nature spirits.[28] In the *Analects* we are told that "The Master did not talk about marvels, feats of strength, irregularities, gods."[29] When he was asked about serving ghosts and gods, Confucius said, "Until you can serve men, how can you serve the ghosts?" When he was asked about death, he said, "Until you know about life, how can you know about death?" In other words, we should not be distracted by nonhuman matters that do not concern us.[30] Asked about wisdom, Confucius said, "To work at doing right for the people, and to be reverent to the ghosts and gods but keep them at a distance, may be called wisdom."[31]

Confucian humanism is rooted in Confucius's vision of himself as a preserver and restorer of a declining culture rather than as an inventor or creator of something new.[32] "It is in transmitting but not originating, trusting in and loving the ancient, that I would venture to compare myself," he said.[33] In contrast to contemporary educational practices, Confucius stressed social preservation over individual creation. Confucius acknowledged the need to think, but focused on the importance of learning. "I used to go without food all day, without sleep all night, to think," he said. "No use, better to learn."[34]

chung-yung
Literally "centrality and universality," the Golden Mean of Confucius, consisting of moderation and normality, universal moral law, also equilibrium or harmony.

Learn what? Learn the way of **chung-yung**, the Golden Mean. Variously translated as the Mean, moderation, normality, and universal moral law, *chung-yung* literally means "centrality and universality." According to Wing-Tsit Chan, the Mean is the same as equilibrium or harmony. By restoring equilibrium to the individual, Confucius thought, order would be restored to the family, to other relationships, to the state, to the world, to the universe. *The Doctrine of the Mean*, a text that some ancient scholars attributed to Confucius's grandson, expresses Confucius's characterization of Tao as a universal moral Mean:

2. Chung-ni (Confucius) said, "The superior man [exemplifies] the Mean (*chung- yung*). The inferior man acts contrary to the Mean. The superior man [exemplifies] the Mean because, as a superior man, he can maintain the Mean at any time. The inferior man [acts contrary to] the Mean because, as an inferior man, he has no caution."

3. Confucius said, "Perfect is the Mean. For a long time few people have been able to follow it."[35]

The pity is that, if Confucius is right, the Way is not far off, yet we fail to find it, choosing instead the little by-paths of imbalance and partiality. We eat and drink too much or too little, thereby savoring less. When we do seek self-improvement for ourselves, we seek it for *ourselves;* we step away from the Mean (centrality and universality) into partiality:

4. Confucius said, "I know why the Way is not pursued. The intelligent go beyond it and the stupid do not come up to it. I know why the Way is not understood. The worthy go beyond it and the unworthy do not come up to it. There is no one who does not eat and drink, but there are few who can really know flavor." …

13. Confucius said, "The Way is not far from man. When a man pursues the Way and yet remains away from man, his course cannot be considered the Way. The *Book of Odes* says, 'In hewing an axe handle, in hewing an axe handle, the pattern is not far off.' If we take an axe handle to hew another axe handle and look askance from the one to the other, we may still think the pattern is far away. Therefore the superior man governs men as men, in accordance with human nature, and as soon as they change [what is wrong], he stops. Conscientiousness (*chung*) and altruism (*shu*) are not far away from the Way. What you do not wish for others, do not do unto them."[36]

> *Great Man reaches complete understanding of the main issues; Petty Man reaches complete understanding of the minute details.*
> — Confucius

PHILOSOPHICAL QUERY

Interestingly, the concept of a mean serves as the basis for Aristotle's *Nicomachean Ethics*, one of the most influential moral philosophies in the Western philosophical tradition. Compare Aristotle's more linear characterization of the mean with Confucius's more holistic or poetic one. Why do you suppose two of the most influential moral philosophers of all time stressed moderation and balance as the basis for human well-being and happiness? Aristotle's mean is discussed in Chapter 6.

Virtue and Ceremony

In contrast to Lao-tzu's let-it-be sense of Tao, Confucius confines the meaning of Tao to the proper course of human conduct and the organization of government. Confucius's focus on the organic relation of Tao and human virtue (*te*) marked the first time those concepts came to philosophical prominence in Chinese philosophy.[37]

Traditionally, **te** (virtue) meant potency, the power to affect others without using physical force. In this sense, *te* is morally neutral in the way that a knife's "virtues"—strength, flexibility, sharpness—are neutral. The same knife can be used to save a life in surgery or to take a life in anger. For both good and bad purposes, strength, flexibility, and sharpness are virtues in a knife. Although Confucius sometimes uses *te* in this functional, morally neutral sense, he also expands it to mean the capacity

te
Traditionally, morally neutral virtue; potency, the power to affect others without using physical force; expanded by Confucius to mean the capacity to act according to Tao and to bring others to Tao.

Zhu Zheng/Xinhua/Landov

By following *li*, we become gracious and well mannered in all aspects of life. Here, descendants of Confucius honor *li* and Confucius by participating in an ancestor worship ceremony.

to act according to Tao and to bring others to Tao. In that use, Tao and *te* cannot be separated.[38]

According to Confucius, producing a harmonious society based on a good government and benevolent (virtuous) human relationships can only be accomplished by mastering and honoring *li*. Literally, "ceremony," li encompasses rites, customs, and conventions ranging from ritual sacrifices honoring one's ancestors to everyday etiquette and good manners. If we don't master *li*, we stray from Tao and *te* and degenerate into disorder (dysfunction) and imbalance (disharmony).

By following *li*, we become gracious and well mannered in all aspects of life, treating all people with dignity and respect. There is more at stake here than mere good manners because there is a sacred quality to *li* that transforms human relations from barbaric, not-truly-human interactions to fully human ones. This quality is independent of the particular ritual or ceremony involved, be it a religious service, a greeting or leave-taking, a shared meal, or observation of participation in a musical performance.[39]

Without mastering good manners and ceremonial forms (*li*), even our good acts will be lacking. We will behave "insincerely," doing the right thing out of obedience rather than "with sincerity" and harmony. Without *li*, even great knowledge lacks virtue, potency, *te*: "Where things are not on course, if you harmonize by knowledge of harmony without regulating it by ceremony, they still cannot be put on course."[40]

Discussing Philosophy

li

Literally, "ceremony"; encompasses rites, customs, and conventions ranging from ritual sacrifices honoring one's ancestors to everyday etiquette and good manners.

PHILOSOPHICAL QUERY

In broad strokes, human history can almost be reduced to an ongoing struggle between two distinct approaches to managing human affairs. One advocates minimal governance—managing by not managing—and the cultivation of healthy (natural) instincts. The other calls for the inculcation of formal manners and habits of repression combined with rules and regulations covering all aspects of our lives. See if you can find examples of each approach in contemporary politics, education, or parenting. Do you think one approach is (generally) superior to the other? Why? Do you agree that these two approaches to life seem to persist throughout history? Discuss.

The Example of the *Chun-tzu*

Whereas his great contemporary Lao-tzu associated Tao and *te* with nature independent of man, and with passivity and psychological withdrawal, Confucius associated them with human conduct and social order. He believed that in addition to rules and regulations (*li*), a harmonious society requires an elaborate bureaucracy of highly cultured and learned men to provide examples of conscientiousness and altruism.

To this end, Confucius, in another move away from tradition, modified the concept of the *chun-tzu*, or superior man. Prior to Confucius, **chun-tzu**, literally the lord's son, could refer to either the sovereign himself or to a "cultivated gentleman." Although Confucius himself occasionally uses the term *chun-tzu* in these traditional ways, for the most part, and most significantly, he uses it to refer to the morally superior man, the great or noble soul. That the morally superior man is also a cultivated gentleman reflects Confucius's emphasis on the importance of *li*. So important are the nature and example of the superior man to Confucius that the term *chun-tzu* occurs 107 times in the *Analects*.[41]

The opposite of the *chun-tzu* is the **hsiao-jen**, the small or vulgar man. The *hsiao-jen* is petty and base.[42] The *chun-tzu* thinks of humanity; the *hsiao-jen* thinks of himself and perhaps those he sees as his "kind." The *chun-tzu* does not seek to put himself above or below others but seeks to help others by becoming noble himself. The *hsiao-jen* looks to others for help and competes with them; he is, in today's vernacular, partial to himself. Consequently, he disrespects *li* and departs from the Mean. When his disciple Yen Yüan asked about this, Confucius said:

> "By conquest of self returning to ceremony one becomes noble. If by conquest of self you return to ceremony for a single day, the whole world will acknowledge you as noble. Becoming noble derives from oneself, not from others!"
>
> "I would ask you to itemize it."
>
> "What isn't according to ceremony don't look at, don't listen to, don't say, don't do."[43]

Confucius's faith in the moral power of the example of the superior man is particularly evident in an anecdote concerning a rapacious, rich official, an obviously inferior man. The greedy *hsiao-jen* told Confucius that he was worried about the high number of robbers in his province. Confucius's reply was blunt: "If you yourself don't love money, you can give the money to thieves and they won't take it."[44]

chun-tzu

Literally, "the lord's son"; originally the sovereign himself or a "cultivated gentleman"; Confucian morally superior man; a great or noble soul.

hsiao-jen

Small or vulgar man; in Confucian philosophy, the opposite of the *chun-tzu*; a petty and base individual.

Would a sick person be helped merely by reading a medical text?

— Shantiveda

PHILOSOPHICAL QUERY

The notion of the noble or great soul has intrigued philosophers from Confucius's time to our own. Does it have any resonance for you? Is the concept of the petty or inferior soul clearer? If it is, why do you suppose that it is easier to come up with examples of pettiness than of nobility? What do you think Confucius was really saying in his reply to the rapacious official? (Hint: Are giving and taking ambiguous?) Discuss.

MindTap

Discussing Philosophy

Note the harmonious blending of aesthetic, moral, social, and personal qualities that constitute Confucius's characterization of the *chun-tzu* in the *Analects*. Note, too, how unappealing the character of the inferior or petty *hsiao-jen* is in contrast—that is, by way of counterexample.

The Thread of Humanity

The nobility that characterizes the Confucian *chun-tzu* is not a matter of bloodline (ethnicity) or political power (social status), but of character, specifically of humanity, or *jen*. **Jen** is a general human virtue, the humane principle rooted in empathy and fellow feeling. The Chinese character for *jen* is composed of "two" and "man," signifying the relationship between men. *Jen* has been translated as human, humane, humanitarian, humanity, and benevolence. According to Chinese American philosopher Lin Yutang, *jen* can have the double meaning of humankind and kindness, as well as referring to a man or woman who is truly himself or herself, a "real person," as it were.[45] *Jen* is expressed by conscientiousness (*chung*) and altruism (*shu*), which in combination constitute the "one thread" of Confucianism.

Realization of *jen* leads to "full humanness," which we only achieve by learning how to balance the needs of self and others, the individual and society. Full humanness (nobility of soul) and harmony are the goals of Confucian moral cultivation, something to which all people are susceptible, at least to some degree. Because *jen* cannot be realized for oneself alone, good manners, proper customs, kindness, and social harmony converge:

> A man of humanity wishing to establish his own character, also establishes the character of others, and wishing to be prominent himself, also helps others to be prominent. To be able to judge others by what is near to ourselves may be called the method of realizing humanity.[46]

Jen
General human virtue; translated as human, humane, humanitarian, humanity, and benevolence; can mean both humankind and kindness; also a man or woman who is truly himself or herself; a "real person."

> *When there is a motive to be virtuous, there is no virtue.*
> — Lie Zi

Candice B. Villarreal/MAI/Landov

Jen is expressed by conscientiousness (*chung*) and altruism (*shu*), the "one thread" of Confucianism. Why do you suppose that, so often, it takes a crisis for us to recognize our shared humanity, so evident in this photo of American servicemen helping a young victim of a Haitian earthquake?

To be a fully human person, a real person, one "merely" has to start out by being a good son or daughter or brother or sister or citizen:

> There are five universal ways [in human relations], and the way by which they are practiced is three. The five are those governing the relationship between the ruler and the minister, between father and son, between husband and wife, between elder and younger brothers, and those in the intercourse between friends. These five are universal paths in the world. Wisdom, humanity, and courage, these three are universal virtues. The way by which they are practiced is one.

> Some are born with the knowledge [of these virtues]. Some learn it through study. Some learn it through hard work. But when the knowledge is acquired, it comes to the same thing. Some practice them naturally and easily. Some practice them for their advantage. Some practice them with effort and difficulty. But when achievement is made, it comes to the same thing.

> Confucius said, "Love of learning is akin to wisdom. To practice with vigor is akin to humanity. To know to be shameful is akin to courage. He who knows these three things knows how to cultivate his personal life. Knowing how to cultivate his personal life, he knows how to govern other men. And knowing how to govern other men, he knows how to govern the empire, its states, and the families."[47]

Great Man is always at ease; Petty Man is always on edge.
— Confucius

Interestingly, Confucius did not teach about *jen* directly, perhaps because *jen* itself is not susceptible to precise formulation, perhaps because humanity is not something that can be taught, or perhaps because Confucius, like so many other sages, was as aware of his own limits as he was of humanity's promise. Confucius said:

> I have never seen one who really loves humanity or one who really hates inhumanity. One who really loves humanity will not place anything above it. One who really hates inhumanity will practice humanity in such a way that inhumanity has no chance to get at him. Is there anyone who has devoted his strength to humanity for as long as a single day? I have not seen any one without sufficient strength to do so. Perhaps there is such a case, but I have never seen it.[48]

Confucius's distinction between the superior individual (*chun-tzu*) and the petty individual (*hsiao-jen*) strikes some philosophers as elitist, as does his advocacy of ceremony (ritual and manners). At first glance, it is easy to see why, given the value we place on egalitarianism and equality and given our distrust of "artificial" values. But are we, perhaps, exalting individuality at the expense of humanity and, thus, ultimately trapping the very selves we are trying to protect from repressive, "uptight" artificiality?

The Buddha

So powerful was the person and vision of **Siddhartha Gautama** (c. 560–480 B.C.E.) that he was recognized during his lifetime as an archetype unto himself. Today, the archetype of the Buddha is a major source of meaning and purpose for over two billion people. The Buddha was a sage, yet more than a sage. Among his many names, perhaps the most enduring are the Awakened or Enlightened One (the original

Siddhartha Gautama

meaning of "the Buddha" in Sanskrit) and the Compassionate Buddha. Yet for all his influence, we have very little factual information about him; most of what we know comes from oral tradition and myth.[49]

Unlike Lao-tzu and Confucius, Siddhartha Gautama was born into wealth and power as the son of a prince (rajah) in what is today Nepal. Siddhartha was intelligent and alert, a talented student and athlete. Legend says that he was a first-rate hunter and archer and enjoyed a rich and active life. An only son, Siddhartha was spoiled and indulged by his family; he became a hedonist and a womanizer. At sixteen he married his cousin, but this does not seem to have slowed his pleasure seeking.

The young prince lived in protected isolation, surrounded by servants who catered to his slightest whim. One version of his life claims that Siddhartha's parents took great pains to shield him from the ugliness of life, even surrounding him with young, attractive servants to spare him the sight of the ravages of age. His parents tried to protect him from knowing about poverty, hunger, sickness, and death by seducing him with every imaginable delight—and by trying to confine him within their palatial grounds. Siddhartha should experience only luxury and pleasure.

But Siddhartha was not content. As with many young people, curiosity and rebelliousness led him away from home. During secret trips outside the palace to a nearby city, he saw three of the now-famous Four Signs that altered his life forever: a destitute and homeless beggar, a dead man being prepared for cremation by weeping mourners, and a diseased and handicapped person. The seeds of the Buddha were planted when Siddhartha encountered his first sight of suffering.

Siddhartha the Seeker

Before his forbidden excursions outside the family compound, Siddhartha had no real idea of what sickness or old age could do to the body and spirit. He had no sense of the depths that poverty could reach. He was unaware of the power of grief. The price he had paid for living in a cocoon of soft pleasures and hidden from the suffering of others was a feeling of bored unease. But ignorance could not protect him forever. Driven by the restless boredom that almost always accompanies an unproductive, self-indulgent life, Siddhartha felt compelled to stray outside. All the pleasures of his wealthy family could not quell his nagging sense of discomfort. He simply had to know more.

The young prince had no one to talk with about his troubling questions except his servant Channa, a hired companion and charioteer, who was also his guardian and bodyguard. To every question Siddhartha raised about life outside the family compound, good Channa could only reply, with great sadness and resignation, "Yes, master, there is no escape. Old age, sickness, death—such is the lot of all men."[50]

In today's language, we might say that Siddhartha "had his eyes opened." His naive unawareness was spoiled forever. No longer were his pleasures as sweet. Try as he might, Siddhartha could not shake the haunting images of old age, sickness, and death. His anxiety grew. How, he asked himself again and again, could anyone be happy if—ultimately—there is absolutely no escape from suffering, disappointment, sadness, and loss? If no one escapes, why be born at all? How could any woman want to give birth knowing what awaited her child? None of his family or servants could answer him.

The sage is neither elated by prosperity nor depressed by adversity. His endeavor always is to rely on himself and to seek his whole satisfaction within himself.

— Seneca

Walking outside the palace grounds one day, deep in despair, Siddhartha saw a wandering monk, an ascetic. **Ascetics** turn away from pleasure and severely limit all sensual appetites in order to achieve salvation or peace of mind. Asceticism involves long hours of prayer and fasting, living on plain food, and wearing simple clothes. Monks in many cultures live ascetic lives. In Western traditions, Old Testament prophets were often ascetics. When John the Baptist and Jesus went into the desert and fasted or lived on locusts, honey, and water, they were going through ascetic trials.

When Siddhartha looked closely into the face of the wandering monk, he was astonished to see serenity, purpose, and detachment. This experience was the last of the Four Signs. Here, finally, was a promise of escape from suffering via self-discipline and a program of resistance to the ego's cravings and fears.

Siddhartha concluded that he must leave the security of his home and live as a monk, homeless, with only a simple robe and beggar's bowl. He would go to the wisest sages, no matter how far and difficult the journey. He would find someone to tell him the answers to life's most basic questions: Why live if suffering is inescapable? Is it possible to be happy in the face of inevitable sickness, old age, and death? What is the real meaning of life?

ascetics
An individual who turns away from pleasure and severely limits all sensual appetites in order to achieve salvation or peace of mind.

The Long Search

Siddhartha wandered for years with his beggar's bowl, seeking one master or guru after another. Even though many of them were wise and deeply interested in helping Siddhartha, he did not find his answer. He found only more teachers, and though he learned many clever philosophical notions, as well as techniques for meditating and disciplining the body, he found no satisfying answers to his basic, timeless questions.

Finally tiring of gurus and ordinary sages, he settled in a grove of trees on the outskirts of the village of Uruvela, India. There he formed a little community with a few other seekers. For six years he meditated, fasted, and concentrated daily on his original questions. During this time, he is said to have conquered most physical appetites and weaknesses and learned how to control "the mad monkey of the mind."[51] But still he found no answers.

In his efforts to subdue his body, Siddhartha nearly destroyed it. He is supposed to have said, "When I touched my stomach I felt my backbone." His extreme asceticism left him a wasted shell. In Buddhist art portraying him during this period, bone and muscle push through his skin. Ultimately, Siddhartha realized that his body was an important instrument in his search, and he realized that he must honor the spirit by honoring the body that houses it. This lesson was clear: The Way cannot be found by either indulgence or denial. We must walk a Middle Path.

Siddhartha's fellow monks were disgusted when he began to take proper nourishment. They had been impressed with his ascetic ways as signs of strength and willpower. From this Siddhartha learned another lesson: We must stop worrying about what others think of us and quit trying to impress people if we are ever to find wisdom. He realized that ascetic self-denial can be of value as a temporary corrective

In his efforts to subdue his body, Siddhartha nearly destroyed it: "When I touched my stomach I felt my backbone."

If a fool is associated with a wise man even all his life, he will perceive the truth as little as a spoon perceives the taste of soup.
— Buddha

I once went a day without food and all night without sleep to enable me to think. I found no advantage in it; it's best to study.
— Confucius

for indulgences or as a momentary cleansing, but it is not an adequate way of life. To subdue the appetites to show strength and willpower is a way of showing off, which prevents one from growing wise.

So Siddhartha returned to his lonely wandering. One day when he was thirty, as he sat in meditation under a fig tree, he was given a special bowl of rice milk by a young woman because he reminded her of a figure she had seen in a vision. In her vision, she had presented rice milk in a golden bowl to a single figure seated under a tree. She took this figure to be a god because of a special glow she saw around him. He was, of course, the Buddha.

Siddhartha accepted the rice milk and, according to one legend, did not eat again for forty-nine days. Another legend says that he divided the milk into numerous portions, and these sustained him during his deepening meditation. After Siddhartha had finished the rice milk, he threw the golden bowl into a nearby river, where it miraculously floated upstream. (This symbolizes the fact that the Buddha's teachings go against the currents of our ordinary, unenlightened thinking, just as Lao-tzu's do.) Siddhartha then ceremoniously bathed in the river, and, taking the lotus position, once more sat under the fig tree and said: "Here I shall remain until I am answered or dead." The tree under which the Buddha sat became known as the Bodhi Tree—the Tree of Wisdom.

Finally, the awakening came. What Buddhist tradition refers to as the "greatest event in human history" occurred during the full moon of May, c. 524 B.C.E. Refusing to be swayed from his goal, heeding some inner call despite all costs, Siddhartha Gautama had transformed himself from a spoiled, pampered young man into "the one who had awakened": the Buddha.

The Bodhisattva

According to Buddhist teachings, it is impossible to explain the awakening. Nonetheless, we can get a rough idea of what the Buddha "saw." Siddhartha saw himself and all life as part of an unending process of change, a great chain of being through which things come into and leave one form of existence for another. Everything is one. The whole universe is a system of interconnected, inseparable parts, rich and complex, composed of all varieties of life forever moving from one form to another.

The Buddha did not arrive at this perception intellectually. He saw it all at once, in what we in the West might call a mystical vision. The now-Buddha realized instantly how difficult it would be to teach a doctrine that could not be grasped by mere reasoning and that could not be realized by blind faith, but only by unswerving personal diligence. Only by the greatest effort could an individual achieve release from suffering. The price of wisdom is love of the whole rather than love of any one part—including, especially, ourselves.[52]

PHILOSOPHICAL QUERY

Compare what Marcus Aurelius says about "the perpetual renewing of the world's youthfulness" (Chapter 7) with Buddha's insight that the whole universe is "forever moving from one form to another." To what philosophical and personal use do Marcus and the Buddha put their notions in this regard?

Siddhartha had reached a state of bliss and utter detachment called *nirvana*. Nirvana is annihilation of the ego, a state of emptiness or "no-thing-ness." It is described as a state of bliss because there is only "pure consciousness" with no sense of individuality, separateness, discrimination, or intellectualizing. It cannot be explained in words because words are limiting and exist to identify similarities and differences. Nirvana is beyond even similarity. It can only be talked around or expressed in contradictions. It transcends all ordinary experience. Nirvana is release from suffering while conscious. (If you do not "understand" what nirvana is, don't feel inadequate. Nirvana must be experienced; it cannot be described or understood.)

Siddhartha now had to make another important choice. He could stay in nirvana, meditating and remaining uninvolved with the commotion and suffering of life. Or he could share his vision. Legend says that "the very earth trembled" while waiting for his decision. At last, the "Great Buddha Heart of Infinite Compassion prevailed."[53] Siddhartha refused ultimate release and, because he chose to stay and help others, became the Buddha, "He Who Awoke," or "He Who Became Aware." This helpful part of him is sometimes referred to as "The Walking Buddha," the man who wandered about once more, only now as a teacher rather than as a seeker.

The Buddha who chose to remain among people giving help to other lost souls is known as the Bodhisattva in some branches of Buddhism. A **bodhisattva** is an enlightened being who voluntarily postpones his own nirvana to help all other conscious life-forms find "supreme release." A bodhisattva is *not* a savior. The Buddha did not *intercede* for others; he showed them a path (a Way). A bodhisattva no longer perceives separateness on any level. A bodhisattva no longer even perceives a separate self, a being, a person.

nirvana
Annihilation of the ego; a state of emptiness or "no-thing-ness"; a state of bliss: "pure consciousness" that leads to release from suffering while remaining conscious.

bodhisattva
An enlightened being who voluntarily postpones his own nirvana in order to help all other conscious life-forms find "supreme release"; not a savior.

PHILOSOPHICAL QUERY

Compare the Buddha's decision to become a bodhisattva with Plato's characterization of the enlightened figure who escapes from the Cave and then returns to help others. See Chapter 5.

His consciousness forever altered, Siddhartha was at last ready to teach personal transformation through compassion. It did not take long for the Buddha to acquire many followers. As with other great sages, who the Buddha was became as significant as what he taught. Siddhartha's once-disappointed ascetic companions even became disciples of the Buddha, as did his wife and son. To share his message with everyone, Siddhartha sent groups of his earliest disciples out as teachers. He did not seek converts, and his monks were not missionaries. Their goal was to spread information that all people could use for themselves to reduce suffering.

The Death of the Buddha

Legend teaches that the Buddha died from either poisonous mushrooms or tainted pork. His last meal was at the humble home of a blacksmith (significantly, a person of low status in ancient Asian culture). Soon after eating, the Buddha took sick. He asked his host to bury the rest of the food so that no one else would eat it. Calling upon the

> *All humanity is sick. I come therefore to you as a physician who has diagnosed this universal disease and is prepared to cure it.*
> — Buddha

discipline learned through years of meditation, he was able to control his pain well enough to travel to a certain river. He bathed in the river and then lay down in a mango grove "on his right side in the attitude of a lion with one foot on the other."[54]

As he lay dying, the Buddha made a special point to tell his closest disciple, Ananda, that the blacksmith was not to blame. The Buddha also sent special word to the blacksmith thanking him for his "alms." By this the Buddha meant that the blacksmith was blessed for having been the vehicle by which the Buddha would escape "the wheel of suffering" and attain nirvana. After sending this message, the Buddha crossed the river and resumed the lion's pose in a different grove.

Just as Socrates reassured his disciples while the hemlock was being prepared for his execution (Chapter 4), Siddhartha reassured his followers that change— including death and decay—is universal, natural, and inescapable. "Do not weep, do not mourn, oh ye monks," the Buddha said.

> *Who knows why Heaven dislikes what it dislikes? Even the sage considers it a difficult question.*
> — Lao-tzu

As a mother, even at the risk of her own life, protects and loves her child, her only child, so let a man cultivate love without measure toward the whole world, above, below, and around, unstinted, unmixed with any feeling of differing or opposing interests. Let a man remain steadfastly in this state of mind, walking, sitting or lying down. This state of mind is the best in the world.[55]

After his death, the teachings of the Buddha were handed down in the form of an oral tradition, and not until the first century B.C.E. did monks begin to transcribe

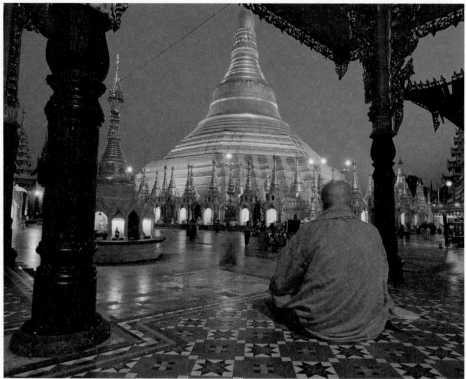

Throughout the ages, Buddhist monks have emulated the "Way of Siddhartha" in their attire and daily meditations.

"Three in the Morning"

Chuang-tzu (c. 399–295 B.C.E.) is the second great Taoist sage. Very little is known about his life, but the book bearing his name contains some of the richest stories in Taoist literature. The stories attributed to him reflect a generous soul, capable of great humor and great sadness. Here's an excellent example:

> On Knowing and Not Knowing the Oneness of Things. Only the truly intelligent understand this principle of the leveling of all things into One.... But to wear out one's intellect in an obstinate adherence to the individuality of things, not recognizing the fact that all things are One—this is called "Three in the Morning." What is "Three in the Morning"? A keeper of monkeys said that with regard to their rations of nuts each monkey was to have three in the morning and four at night. At this the monkeys were very angry. Then the keeper said they might have four in the morning and three at night, with which arrangement they were well pleased. The actual number of nuts remained the same, but there was a difference owing to (subjective evaluations of) likes and dislikes. It also derives from this (principle of subjectivity). Wherefore the true Sage brings all the contraries together and rests in the natural Balance of Heaven. This is called (the principle of following) two courses (at once).

Chuang-tzu, in *The Wisdom of Laotse*, trans. and ed. Lin Yutang (New York: Modern Library, 1976), p. 244.

these discourses onto ola leaves. These teachings remained so until modern times, when the Pali Text Society took up the task of editing and printing them. They are now known collectively as the "three baskets": the *Vinaya Pitaka* (rules for monks), the *Sutta Pitaka* (basic teachings of the Buddha), and an organized later commentary known as the *Abhidhamma Pitaka*. Today, so many people produce books, journal articles, YouTube lectures, podcasts, tweets, and #hashtags commenting on Buddhism that the diligent seeker will have trouble keeping up with a year's worth. Perhaps this is a tribute both to the profundity of the Buddha's pivotal insight and to a common human hunger for enlightenment.

Although our brief look at this great sage can be no more than a glimpse of the rich and profound legacy left by Buddha's great experiment, even reflected wisdom casts valuable light. So let us tread tentatively and respectfully through a tiny corner of one of the world's greatest wisdom traditions.

Karma

Among the insights Buddha gained during his arduous search for enlightenment, three "realities" command our attention: impermanence, suffering, and egolessness. In simplistic, contemporary terms, we can sum up this part of Buddha's teaching like this: "Although nothing lasts, suffering is everywhere, and the 'me' that suffers isn't even real."

At the core of the Buddha's doctrine is the concept of the primal unsatisfactoriness (*dukkha*) generated by the perilousness of the human condition and by the inescapability of physical suffering and sickness, psychological conflict, anxiety, and anguish. As if this is not enough, Buddha reminds us that beneath our dissatisfaction lies a profounder insight: the insubstantiality of existence.[56]

Awareness of insubstantiality is related to the Buddhist doctrines of impermanence (ever-change) and egolessness. According to the Buddha, what we usually

> *"He abused me, he beat me, he defeated me, he robbed me"— in those who harbor such thoughts hatred will never cease. For hatred does not cease by hatred at any time; hatred ceases by love— this is an eternal law.*
>
> — Buddha

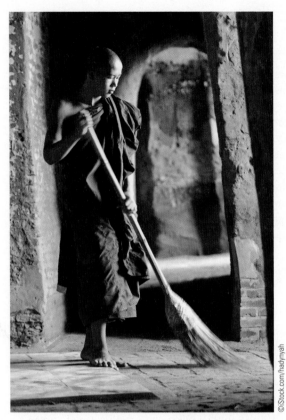
©iStock.com/hadynyah

Buddha promised that through a discipline of meditation, we can learn to control unruly desires.

karma
From the Pali *kamma*; according to Buddhist tradition, the law of moral causation (moral cause and effect); it includes past and present actions and is not to be confused with fate or predestination: good or bad karma results from our own actions.

think of as "I" or "an individual" is a continuously changing combination of physical and psychological elements. Out of ignorance, we project a sense of permanence onto impermanent conditions. Because all is in flux, we are inevitably disappointed by change, destruction, and loss.[57]

Is this vision of the fundamental human condition pessimistic? Perhaps it would be if Buddha had nothing more to teach. But Buddha promised that through a discipline of meditation, we can learn to control unruly desires and realize that happiness is possible given the *facts*—not our *projections*—of the human condition. Central to Buddha's teachings is a notion of free will, a belief that we can control our thoughts, attitudes, and behavior and that thoughts, attitudes, and behavior have consequences. These consequences, their causes, and their control are called *karma*.

The word *karma* comes from the Pali word *kamma*, a term referring to acts of the will that are expressed in thought, word, and deed. The concept of karma combines *kamma* (action–cause) with *vipaka* (reaction–effect). According to Buddhist tradition, karma is the law of moral causation (moral cause and effect); it includes past and present actions and is not to be confused with fate or predestination. Good or bad karma results from our own actions.[58]

Buddha did not teach that everything that happens is due to karma. In the first place, different laws govern natural change, physical phenomena, certain psychological processes, and so forth. In the second place, if karma alone accounted for the human condition, a person with good karma would always be good, and a person with bad karma would always be bad. Yet such is not the case. Indeed, self-reliance and peace of mind come only from understanding karma and living wisely in light of that understanding. "No one," said the Buddha, "can escape the wheel of suffering who does not understand the causes of suffering."

The Four Noble Truths

The Buddha's basic teachings rest on what are called the **Four Noble Truths**:

1. No one can deny that suffering is the condition of all existence.

2. Suffering and general dissatisfaction come to human beings because they are possessive, greedy, and, above all, self-centered.

3. Egocentrism, possessiveness, and greed can, however, be understood, overcome, rooted out.

4. This rooting out, this vanquishing, can be brought about by following a simple, reasonable Eightfold Path of behavior in thought, word, and deed. Change of viewpoint will manifest itself in a new outlook and new patterns of behavior.[59]

The Buddha taught that we suffer because we are partial to ourselves, as anyone who has ever thrown a temper tantrum eventually discovers. Perhaps enlightenment involves outgrowing a sense of entitlement, whether we're two years old or eighty, like this eighty-year-old man who has just been sentenced to prison for killing another man in a road rage incident.

In a nutshell, the Buddha taught that we suffer because we are partial to ourselves. For example, I cannot be bored listening to you complain about your philosophy class for the umpteenth time unless I am judging you or wishing you were talking about something interesting to *me*. It's the *me* that gets bored. I cannot be envious of the attention *my* parents give *my* brother without being greedy for more attention for *me*. If I were not greedy for *my* share, I would be delighted by his delight. The more self-conscious I am, the more me there is to suffer.

Contemporary Buddhist commentators and philosophers use the term *ego* differently from psychologists; they use it to refer to various self-centered, immature, and selfish tendencies. A person with too much ego thinks of himself or herself as unique and special in ways that emphasize differences. The loss or annihilation of this false *ego projection* results in the emergence of the soul or true self, the *Buddha nature*. The awakened or reborn soul/self sees similarities rather than differences, acts from love rather than fear, helps rather than judges. The bliss of nirvana comes from the annihilation of the self-consciousness, judgmentalism, greed, and fear that characterize ego.

The Buddha taught that the way to transcend the ego and see the interconnected whole of life is through loving-kindness. At the moment we feel love for others we cannot be bored or hostile with them. But it is difficult to maintain our compassion even with those we already love. Can we really alter our viewpoint to love every living thing?

Four Noble Truths
The foundation of Buddha's teachings: (1) to exist is to suffer; (2) self-centeredness is the chief cause of human suffering; (3) the cause of suffering can be understood and rooted out; (4) suffering can be alleviated by following the Eightfold Path.

> *Those in the prime of their beauty are proud, those in the prime of their strength are impetuous; you cannot talk to them about Tao.*
> — Lie Zi

PHILOSOPHICAL QUERY

Think back to circumstances in which you were bored or hostile. Did "ego" play a role in your discomfort? Do you believe that all suffering comes from self-partiality? Discuss.

The Eightfold Path

According to Buddha, understanding the Four Noble Truths and following the law of karma are keys to release from suffering, but only if combined as a new way of life that combines three vital components of Buddhist practice into an **Eightfold Path** of wisdom (*panna*), right conduct (*sila*), and right mental training (*samadhi*). The first two steps along the Eightfold Path are the steps of *panna;* steps three, four, and five are the steps of *sila*; and steps six, seven, and eight are the steps of *samadhi:*

1. Right understanding (or views)
2. Right purpose
3. Right speech
4. Right conduct
5. Right livelihood
6. Right effort
7. Right mindfulness (or awareness)
8. Right meditation[60]

Now let's look at a modified version. Gerald Heard, an Anglo-Irish historian and philosopher, phrased the Eightfold Path in an especially contemporary and insightful form:

1. First you must see clearly what is wrong.
2. Next you must decide that you want to be cured.
3. You must act and
4. speak so as to aim at being cured.
5. Your livelihood must not conflict with your therapy.
6. That therapy must go forward at the "staying speed," that is, the critical velocity that can be sustained.
7. You must think about it incessantly and
8. learn how to contemplate with the *deep mind.*[61]

It is probably quite an understatement to note that the wisdom expressed in the Eightfold Path sounds so obvious, almost trivially simple. But simple is not always easy, and we often overlook the obvious. Consider: In many schools of psychology, the most important therapeutic event is the *moment of insight*, in which the client sees for the first time some important factor in his or her unhappiness. Something similar occurs in many religions, either at the moment of "rebirth" or during periods of atonement. The fallen soul sees by the grace of God its fallen nature and the way of salvation. One of the most effective treatment programs for alcoholism is Alcoholics Anonymous (AA), which is based on a list of guidelines for living called the Twelve Steps. The very first step begins, "We admitted we were powerless over alcohol and that our lives were unmanageable." The key to the first step is to see fully our own actual condition, whatever it involves. This "seeing" is, of course, the first step on the Eightfold Path.

It helps to remind ourselves that the Eightfold Path is designed to change us by changing our way of seeing things (consciousness), changing our behavior, and changing our emotions. It is designed to subdue our egocentric sense of identity, replacing the self-centered *me* with a compassionate heart. If I can change the way I view things, I have, in effect, changed the *world*. The difficulty of doing this is underscored by a poignant version of the Buddha's deathbed statement to his monks that ends, "Perhaps someone, somewhere will not misunderstand me."

Discussing Philosophy

PHILOSOPHICAL QUERY

Discuss some of the difficulties you might encounter by trying to follow the Eightfold Path. What, for example, might consist of "wrong livelihoods" (or "wrong college majors")? Are there some jobs that no truly enlightened person could perform? What determines whether an occupation (or college major) is "right"? Explain.

"One Day"

Some of the richest Buddhist literature consists of stories that reveal the process of enlightenment indirectly. Though highly refined, these gemlike little tales leave the heart of the story unspoken. Thus they function like spiritual inkblots, drawing new insights from each listener's response. Here's a sampler of four:

One day a potential suicide was talking to a Buddhist monk, asking whether he had the right to commit suicide if he wanted to. The monk replied, "Anyone has the right to do anything. Everyone else has the right to resist it."

The student said, "Do you see suicide as a moral act?"

The monk answered, "Where there is no victim, every act is morally right, but I personally think suicide is a symptom of taking oneself too seriously."

One day the Buddhist monk Joshu fell down in the snow. He began wailing and crying for help. Seeing his distress, another monk lay down beside him and began thrashing about, crying and wailing as well. Joshu got up and left.

One day Chinso was up in a tower with some important people, and one of them saw a group of monks approaching. "Look," he said, "holy men." "No, they aren't," Chinso said, "and I'll prove it." When the monks were directly below, Chinso leaned out of the tower window and yelled, "Hey! Holy men!" When they all looked up in response to his call, he said to his companions, "See?"

One day a rich man asked Sengai to write something ensuring the continued prosperity of his family. Sengai wrote, "Father dies, son dies, grandson dies." This angered the rich man, who said, "I asked you to write something for the happiness of my family! Why do you make such a joke as this?" "This is no joke," Sengai explained. "If your son dies before you do, you would grieve greatly. If your grandson dies before your son, both of you would be brokenhearted. If your family, generation after generation, passes away in the order I have named, it will be the natural course of life. I call this real prosperity."

The first story is from Camden Benares, *Zen Without Zen Masters* (Berkeley: And/Or Press, 1977), p. 37. The next three are paraphrased from Paul Reps, *Zen Flesh, Zen Bones: A Collection of Zen and Pre-Zen Writings* (Garden City, N.Y.: Anchor, 1973), p. 67.

The Buddha's Legacy

Buddha was a perceptive psychological observer who realized that even though we all must actively work for our own enlightenment, most of us benefit from the support and guidance of regular, intimate association with others working toward a common goal.[62] What he envisioned was the free association of seekers on all levels of the path. What developed was something else. In the twenty-five centuries since the Buddha lived, his basic message has been transformed into "schools of Buddhism," each with its own prescribed rules of dress, diet, habitation, and so on.

Buddha himself, however, did not think it mattered where one lived, what one ate, and so on. Any serious seeker following the Eightfold Path would avoid extremes and remain in the *Middle Way*. Awareness, compassion, and helpfulness are more important than the particular clothes we wear or food we eat or place we live: "Let those who wish to dwell in the forest, dwell in the forest, and let those who wish to live in the village, live in the village."[63] Speaking ironically, Buddha said:

> If the mere wearing of a robe could banish greed, malice and other weaknesses, then as soon as a child was born his friends and kinfolk would make him wear the robe and would press him to wear it saying, "Come thou favored of fortune! Come wear the robe; for by the mere wearing of it the greedy will put from them their greed, the malicious their malice, and so on!"[64]

As happened among the followers of Socrates, Moses, Jesus, and Muhammad, Buddhist sects and divisions arose after Siddhartha's death. "Experts" in theory and ritual emerged, quarreling and competing for the title of true successor. The two main branches of Buddhism are Hinayana (or Theravada), "the Way of the Elders," and Mahayana, after its founder Mahayana, "the Greater Vehicle of Salvation." Other Buddhist sects such as Tibetan Buddhism and Japanese Zen Buddhism are usually seen as branches of the many-sided Mahayana branch.

The quarrels among Buddhists tend to take less hostile and more tolerant tones than do the quarrels among other philosophies and religions. The power

> *Whether you believe in God or not does not matter so much; whether you believe in Buddha or not does not matter so much; as a Buddhist, whether you believe in reincarnation or not does not matter so much. You must lead a good life.*
> — The Dalai Lama

of the Buddha's original vision is perhaps nowhere more clearly felt than in this restraint. Buddhists of one school tend to accept Buddhists of another, for in all cases, "the individual disciple is seen as directly, personally involved in his own salvation, a point of view which allows exceptional latitude in matters of instruction and practice."[65]

What the Buddha Did Not Explain

Some Western philosophers and theologians find it difficult to accept Buddha's refusal to present a theology or system of metaphysics. But Buddha's goal was existential and pragmatic. He was not a scholar or philosopher in a technical sense, but a sage, an insightful teacher who believed that questions of theology and complex philosophy confuse and distract us from our search for wisdom. Buddha believed that we are best served by dealing with the here and now in helpful, uncomplicated ways rather than by fretting and quibbling over unanswerable metaphysical claims and theological doctrines.

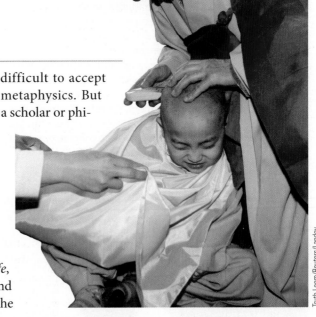

The Buddha said, "If the mere wearing of a robe could banish greed, malice and other weaknesses, then as soon as a child was born his friends and kinfolk would make him wear the robe."

Ultimately, Buddha calls on us to adopt a *way of life*, rather than "a philosophy," as we in the West understand "having a philosophy." Buddha insisted that to discover the truth, we must somehow set aside the kind of "analytic thinking" that leads to establishing schools of Buddhism or to quibbling over the correct interpretation of various texts. (In this, he reminds us of Lao-tzu and other Taoist sages.) Buddha said,

> If you will now and at all times, whether walking, standing, sitting, or lying, only concentrate on eliminating analytic thinking, at long last you will inevitably discover the truth. ... [Relying on analytic thinking is] like using yellow leaves of gold to stop the crying of a child, and [is] decidedly not real. If you take it for something real, you are not one of our sect and, moreover, what relation can it [analytic thinking] have to your real self? ... In reality, everything is pure and glistening, neither square nor round, big nor small, long nor short; it is beyond passion and phenomena, ignorance and Enlightenment.... [66]

> *The greatest eloquence seems to stutter.*
> — Lao-tzu

The function of a sage is to engage us, to challenge us to ask the deepest questions: Who am I? How am I to live? And it is to Buddha the sage that we shall turn as we take our leave of the Compassionate One. Perhaps we can experience a pale reflection of the power of Buddha's transforming vision by considering one of his most famous and intriguing sermons, called "On Questions Not Tending Toward Edification." Another title might be, "What You Don't Need to Know to Live Wisely and Compassionately." This sermon touches on one of the most difficult things for most of us to accept: We need to find a way of living a meaningful life in the absence of absolute answers.

"You Must Attune Your Inner Ear"

You do not like these quirky phrases? Paradoxes put you off? Ah well, no [Asian] sage ever promised you a garden of platitudes....It is not cruelty that makes good gurus demanding. It is unusual kindness. In the spiritual life you become what you do...outer persona and inner self must come closer and closer together.

What doth it profit a person if she can assemble any stereo and never hears the music of the spheres? What doth it profit a person to place all his energies in the stock market? Stereos and the stock market have their place— all the Eastern sages allow them. What the Eastern sages do not allow them is primacy of place....To hear the Tao in the morning or in the evening, to die content, one must

vacate assembling and selling. The business of life is not business. The business of life is being....It does not matter that many of our schools know nothing of such Eastern wisdom. The college catalogue is seldom a great book. Real learning occurs in dark nights and painful passages. Wisdom to live goes far below figures and facts.

...If today you would possess your soul, you must empty it of what is tawdry. If today you would hear the Tao, you must attune your inner ear.

Denise L. Carmody and John T. Carmody, **Eastern Ways to the Center: An Introduction to Religions of the East** (Belmont, Calif.: Wadsworth, 1981), pp. 201–203.

"In reality," said the Buddha, "everything is pure and glistening, neither square nor round, big nor small, long nor short; it is beyond passion and phenomena, ignorance and Enlightenment."

Here's a brief excerpt from one of the richest passages in Buddhist literature (and one my favorite passages in all wisdom literature):

It is as if... man had been wounded by an arrow thickly smeared with poison, and his friends and companions, his relatives and kinsfolk, were to procure for him a physician or surgeon; and the sick man were to say, "I will not have this arrow taken out until I have learnt... the name of the man who wounded me or whether the man who wounded me was... tall, or short, or of the middle height... whether the man who wounded me was black, or dusky, or of a yellow skin... whether the man who wounded me was from this or that village, or town, or city...." That man would die without ever having learnt this....

In exactly the same way ... anyone who should say, "I will not lead the religious life under the Blessed One until the Blessed One shall explain to me that the world is eternal or that the world is not eternal... or that the saint either exists or does not exist after death";—that person would die... before [it was] ever explained to him.

The religious life... does not depend on the dogma....

Accordingly... bear always in mind what it is that I have not explained.... And what... have I explained? Misery... have I explained; the origin of misery have I explained; the cessation of misery have I explained. And why... have I explained this? Because... this does profit, has to do with the fundamentals of religion, and tends to... [tranquillity], knowledge, supreme wisdom, and Nirvana; therefore, I have explained it.[67]

PHILOSOPHICAL QUERY

Aplia

Compare what Buddha "did not say" with what Confucius did not discuss concerning spirits. Do you think indifference to these matters is wise? Is it indifference or something else? Explain.

Commentary

As we will discover in the next chapter, Western philosophy (and science) developed in the direction of objective, rational knowledge rather than the intuitive, holistic wisdom of the sages. One result is a technologically oriented Western culture that provides us with material comforts beyond our ancestors' wildest imaginings. But—as the sages remind us—the price for concentrating on this objective, rational paradigm has been alienation from nature and other rich sources of knowledge and wisdom.

The sage did not separate the human from the divine, or daily life from a sacred Way. The sage saw himself *as a part of* nature and the cosmos, not *apart from it*. In our rediscovery of the importance of nature (the environment), we move a little more in the direction of the sage. In our growing awareness of what Carol Gilligan called the "different voice" of compassion and care expressed by women and non-traditional Western philosophers, we move a little more in the direction of the sage.

In our haste to acquire sophisticated knowledge and its fruits—prestige, gadgets, the satisfaction of being "experts"—we can easily become unbalanced. Aggressive efforts (yang) to manage, analyze, and possess nature overlook the inevitability of flux (yin must follow yang). For example, using complex engineering principles, people build elaborate houses in the floodplains of the Mississippi River or crowd together in California coastal canyons (yang), only to see storms and fires bring them down (yin). To pursue sophisticated pleasures, we crowd into cities, which run short of water; we dirty the air; we pile up on freeways. Perhaps it would be wiser to pursue harmony, a Golden Mean, and live where we work and build simpler homes where nature welcomes us.

In recent years, philosophers, psychologists, ministers, environmentalists, and others have increasingly turned toward Asia to complement—as in "complete"—Western knowledge of technique and mastery. Social criticisms of elitist divisions have reawakened us to the need to see beyond differences to some kind of commonality. Perhaps these trends reflect greater sensitivity to the sacred essence the sages "stammer" about. Perhaps not.

Yet in acknowledging the wisdom of the sages, we must not make the mistake of elevating their teachings above Western science and philosophy—or vice versa. To do either is merely to perpetuate the chief problems the sages address: judgmentalism, partiality, alienation and division, argumentation, and "Doing Something" all the time.

The Asian sage stands between the traditional Western models of a philosopher and a saint or prophet. Saints and prophets of the major Western religious traditions differ from the sage in important ways. The most significant difference is in their relationship to "the one, true God," the Creator who is distinct from His creatures. For the sages, "all is one," and there is no equivalent to the separate God of the Bible.

For the sages, only those who actively work to achieve awareness deserve the title "sage"—and then only if they act on and live

> *To be born when you will be born, that's good fortune. To die when you will die, that's good fortune. To be born and yet not to cherish life, that's opposing heaven. Not to want to die when it's time to die, that's opposing heaven.*
>
> — Lie Zi

"As there was no more to be said, everybody went away."

©iStock.com/hadynyah

by what they have discovered to be true for themselves. No teachings, no scriptures, no theories take the place of experience. When we see clearly, we do not need teachers, scriptures, or theories. When we do not see clearly—for ourselves—nothing else matters.

"All right," you may grant, "but what about when we do see clearly?" Then, too, it seems "nothing else matters," as this delightful story from the teachings of the ninth-century Chan (Zen) master Hsi Yun hints:

> Stepping into the public hall [His Reverence] said: "The knowledge of many things cannot compare to giving up the search. The sage is one who puts himself outside the range of objectivity. There are not different kinds of mind, and there is no doctrine which can be taught."
> As there was no more to be said, everybody went away.[68]

Summary of Main Points

- The sage is an archetypal figure who combines religious inspiration with a love of wisdom. Sages understand and teach the requirements of the good life. Sages tend to be humanists who believe that human intelligence and effort are capable of improving conditions in the here and now.

- In ancient Chinese cosmology, everything was influenced by the harmonious working together of Heaven and Earth following the Tao, literally "way" or "path." Tao, which cannot be precisely defined, is translated as the source or principle of all existence, the way or path of the universe or moral law. Heaven and Earth constitute a single reality perpetually balancing between two opposing, but not separable, forces: yin (Earth, passive element) is weak, negative, dark, and destructive; yang (Heaven, active element) is strong, positive, light, and constructive.

- According to legend, Lao-tzu (c. 575 B.C.E.) was a bureaucrat in ancient China, known only by a nickname, variously translated as the Old Master, the Old Man, the Old Boy, or the Old Philosopher. He is thought to be the author of the *Tao te Ching*, a slim classic that advocates harmony with Tao. Lao-tzu developed a nonlogical and paradoxical manner of communicating his belief that Tao is not a concept that can be grasped cognitively or logically. According to Lao-tzu, error, suffering, and unhappiness accompany all attempts to separate things, to understand the part without the whole.

- The *Tao te Ching* advocates reversing common priorities by preferring yin to yang. According to Lao-tzu's doctrine of inaction (*wu wei*), the best way to deal with social turmoil is "not to do anything about it." Although *wu wei* means "not to act," Lao-tzu uses the phrase as a warning against unnatural or demanding action. Natural action is "natural" in the sense of being spontaneous, healthy, and in harmony with Tao.

- Confucius (551–479 B.C.E.) is the Latinized name of K'ung Ch'iu of Lu, a legendary teacher who vainly sought high political office so that he could initiate a series of governmental reforms. He promoted social order based on personal moral cultivation of *jen* (humanity) and *li* (custom and ceremony). Confucian humanism, the name given to any philosophy that emphasizes human welfare and dignity, focuses on moderation according to the Golden Mean. A collection of Confucius's sayings known as the *Analects* is one of the most influential works in Asian philosophy.

- Confucius placed great emphasis on the moral example of the *chun-tzu*. Conventionally either the sovereign or a "cultivated gentleman," the Confucian *chun-tzu* is the morally superior man, a great and noble soul as well as a cultivated gentleman. His undesirable opposite is the small or vulgar *hsiao-jen*. The *chun-tzu* is a "real person" because he has realized *jen*, general human virtue rooted in empathy and fellow-feeling. Expressed through conscientiousness and altruism, *jen* is the "one thread" of Confucianism.

- Siddhartha Gautama (c. 560–480 B.C.E.) was born into wealth and power as the son of a prince in what today is Nepal. Siddhartha was so disturbed by his first encounters with old age, sickness, and death that he began a search for enlightenment that resulted in his transformation into the Buddha (the One Who Awakened).

- Rejecting the extremes of indulgence or denial, Siddhartha proposed a Middle Path. By choosing to remain among people to help other lost souls, the Buddha became a bodhisattva—an enlightened being who voluntarily postpones his own nirvana to help all other conscious life-forms find "supreme release." A bodhisattva is not a savior.

- The Buddha's basic teachings rest on what are called the Four Noble Truths: (1) Suffering is the condition of all existence. (2) Suffering comes from possessiveness, greed, and self-centeredness. (3) These traits can, however, be understood and overcome. (4) This overcoming can be accomplished by following an Eightfold Path, a practical cure for the suffering caused by being partial to ourselves: (1) right understanding, (2) right purpose, (3) right speech, (4) right conduct, (5) right livelihood, (6) right effort, (7) right mindfulness, (8) right meditation. The resultant state of emptiness or "no-thing-ness" is known as nirvana.

Post-Reading Reflections

Now that you've had a chance to learn about the Asian sages, use your new knowledge to answer these questions.

1. What is the relation between Heaven and Earth in ancient Chinese cosmology?
2. How did living during the Period of Warring States affect Confucius's and Lao-tzu's philosophies?
3. What is Lao-tzu trying to say about language when he claims to "say without saying"?
4. What is *chung-yung*, and how does it figure into Confucius's teaching?
5. What is *te*? What is its relation to Tao?
6. What is *li*? Why was it important to Confucius?
7. How did the Buddha's protected early life contribute to his enlightenment?
8. What role did asceticism play in Buddha's search for wisdom and what did Buddha teach concerning it?
9. Identify key elements in Buddha's long search for enlightenment and explain their significance.
10. What is the relationship between nirvana and becoming a bodhisattva?
11. Did the Buddha establish a religion? Explain.
12. What is the Middle Way? What are the Four Noble Truths? What is their place in Buddha's teaching?
13. What is the Eightfold Path? What is its relationship to the Four Noble Truths?
14. What is significant about "what the Buddha did not explain"?
15. What is the lesson of "Three in the Morning"?

 MindTap

Experience MindTap through the activities highlighted in this chapter. Further explore this online, personalized learning tool to deepen your comprehension and improve your grades.

2

The Presocratic Sophos

Men have talked about the world without paying attention to the world or to their own minds, as if they were asleep or absent-minded.

—*Heraclitus*

Christie's Images/Corbis

Learning Objectives

After you complete this chapter, you should be able to:

- Distinguish between a *sophos* and a philosopher.
- Define the term *apeiron*.
- Define the term *pneuma*.
- Explain what Heraclitus means by *war*.
- Compare the *Logos* and God.
- Define the term *cosmology*.
- Contrast *being* and *not-being*.
- Define the concept of monism.
- Define the concept of pluralism.
- Describe the *plenum*.
- Critique Zeno's paradox of Achilles and the Tortoise.
- Construct a *reductio ad absurdum*.
- Characterize *Nous*.
- Define what an atom is.
- Characterize the void.

AS EARLY GREEK CIVILIZATION became increasingly refined and sophisticated (c. 500 B.C.E.), a new kind of thinker emerged, known as a sophos, from the Greek word for "wise." These "wise men"(and they were almost exclusively men) asked increasingly sophisticated questions about all sorts of things, but especially about natural processes and the origins and essence of life. Although mythology and religion continued to play important roles in the lives of most people for centuries, these first philosophers were noted for their attempts to use reason and observation to "figure out" for themselves how the world works.

In a wonderful book called *Philosophy as a Way of Life*, French philosopher Pierre Hadot describes how, in the ancient world, a true philosopher was usually viewed as someone out of step with daily life. To be a "philosopher" was to be "different." As you learn more about the ancient *sophos*, you can decide for yourself whether this "difference" is good or not.

The sorts of atypical traits Hadot has in mind include a lack of concern with such "normal" things as practicing a trade (having a regular job), pursuing wealth, or desiring fame and power. The *sophos* was someone who devoted himself to asking questions that other people thought had already been answered (by religion and mythology) or were unanswerable (and thus a waste of time). The *sophos* lived and spoke in ways that were interpreted as showing disregard for conventional values and that set him apart from "regular folks" living "normal" lives.[1]

It is hardly surprising, then, that one of the earliest popular images of philosophers is the stereotype of a shabby, unkempt, "absent-minded," starry-eyed dreamer and an asker of silly questions. Socrates (Chapter 4), perhaps the most-recognized example of the ancient Western *sophos*, was even called "unclassifiable" (*atopos*) because he was a "philo-sopher" in the archetypal sense: a person in love with wisdom. In Plato's *Symposium*, Diotima, an ancient woman philosopher whom Socrates referred to as one of his teachers, says that wisdom is not a human state at all, but a "divine" level of perfection and knowledge. If these ancient commentators are correct, the *sophos* is always a "stranger to the world."[2]

From Sophos to Philosopher

In his earliest incarnations, the Western *sophos* was predominantly a sage, or "wise man," in the general or generic sense. He was not a professional thinker. That is, he did not charge people fees (tuition) to study with him or to accompany him. His relationships with his students were personal, complex, and long-lasting. In many cases his pupils were more like disciples than like paying students.

The very first Western thinkers identified as *philosophers* were initially concerned with questions about the nature of nature (*physis*) and of the "world order" (*kosmos*). Today, we would classify many of their concerns as scientific. It would be a mistake, however, to think that ancient philosophers "specialized" in the modern sense. Indeed, Plato and Aristotle (Chapters 5 and 6) were interested in ethics, logic, language, art, human nature, politics, and mental and physical health. Aristotle was also interested in physics, biology, botany, and anatomy.

Whereas the *sophos* (sage, or wise man) was seen as a kind of prophet-priest-therapist, the *philosopher*, who is in love with wisdom but not necessarily wise, was seen as an unusual sort of thinker and truth-seeker. Thus, we notice

🌐 MindTap·

Philosophy Timelines

sophos
Sage or wise man; term applied to the first philosophers; from the Greek word for "wise."

> *I have heard many men talk, but none who realized that understanding is distinct from other knowledge.*
> —Heraclitus

We cannot help but wonder what philosophy may have lost by overlooking the contributions of women philosophers for so long.

Dea/G. Nimatallah/De Agostini Picture Library/Getty Images

"Woman as Sophos"

Aesara of Lucania (c. fourth century B.C.E.–first century C.E.) was a Pythagorean philosopher who has only recently attracted any attention. In the single existing fragment of her book—*On Human Nature*, she says that through the introspection and contemplation of our own souls we can discover the "natural" foundation of all law and the structure of morality. In the following passage, Aesara wisely acknowledges the importance of reason as a guide, without overlooking the importance of emotions. Reading it, we cannot help but wonder what philosophy may have lost by overlooking the contributions of women philosophers for so long:

> By following the tracks within himself whoever seeks will make a discovery: Law is in him and justice, which is the orderly arrangement of the soul. Being threefold, it is organized in accordance with triple functions: That which effects judgment and thoughtfulness is [the mind]...that which effects strength and ability is [high spirit]...and that which effects love and kindness is desire. These are all so disposed relatively to one another that the best part is in command, the most inferior part is governed, and the one in between holds a middle place; it both governs and is governed.
>
> ...And indeed, a certain unanimity and agreement in sentiment accompanies such an arrangement. This sort would justly be called good order,

whichever, due to the better part's ruling and the inferior part's being ruled, should add the strength of virtue to itself. Friendship and love and kindliness, cognate and kindred, will sprout from these parts. For closely-inspecting mind persuades, desire loves, and high spirit is filled with strength; once seething with hatred, it becomes friendly to desire.

Mind having fitted the pleasant together with the painful, mingling also the tense and robust with the slight and relaxed portion of the soul, each part is distributed in accordance with its kindred and suitable concern for each thing: mind closely inspecting and tracking out things, high spirit adding impetuosity and strength to what is closely inspected, and desire, being kin to affection, adapts to the mind, preserving the pleasant as its own and giving up [reasoning] to the thoughtful part of the soul. By virtue of these things the best life for man seems to me to be whenever the pleasant should be mixed with the earnest, and pleasure with virtue. Mind is able to fit these things to itself, becoming lovely through systematic education and virtue.

Holger Thesleff, "Pythagorean Texts of the Hellenistic Period," in Mary Ellen Waithe, ed., **Introduction to the Series, A History of Women Philosophers**, vol. 1, 600 B.C.–A.D. 500. trans. Vicki Lynn Harper (Dordrecht: Martinus Nijhoff, 1987), pp. 20–21.

an ambiguity in the early use of the word "philosopher" that carries over into the present day. Whereas initially the philosopher, like the *sophos*, was expected to live a "philosophical life," today a philosopher is not required to live a wise life but to devote his or her energies to "thinking" about certain things in a rigorous way. In Chapter 18 we will see the very notion of being a philosopher come under scruting as contemporary philosophers challenge the possibility of objectivity and universal truth.

MindTap
Discussing Philosophy

PHILOSOPHICAL QUERY

How do you think it would go over today if we treated philosophers, preachers, and anyone who professes not to value money and wealth as much as integrity, honor, God, or truth as if they mean what they say and hold them personally and legally accountable for *living like they talk*? Is it reasonable—or fair—to judge a person's philosophical claims in terms of behavior? Do we trivialize "being" a philosopher—or "being" a Christian or Muslim or liberal or conservative—when we make a radical distinction between persons and their beliefs?

The Search for a Common Principle

The earliest Western *philosophers* are referred to as the *Presocratics* because they appeared prior to Socrates, the first major figure in the Western philosophical tradition. Some of the Presocratic philosophers are described as *proto-scientists* because they initiated the transformation of mythology into rational inquiry about nature and the cosmos. In the beginning, the difference between a *philosopher* and a *proto-scientist* was one of subject matter; later it became one of method. A general understanding of the development of Presocratic philosophy is helpful for placing subsequent philosophical issues and disagreements in context.

As you study the Presocratics, note how they struggle to offer rational arguments and explanations for their views. Note, too, their efforts to be objective and to uncover universal (general) principles. Also note the role that language plays in the development of philosophy. These emphases are historically significant and mark the beginning of Western philosophical and intellectual history.

As significant and interesting as the Presocratics are, they lived and thought in a radically different world from ours. Consequently, what is obvious to us might have been unthinkable in their world, and what was obvious to them might be obscure or unfathomable to us. Don't be surprised or discouraged if some of their ideas seem alien to you.[3]

> *In Greece wise men speak and fools decide.*
> —Anacharsis

> *Knowledge is not intelligence.*
> —Heraclitus

Rational Discourse

Traditionally, the first Western philosopher is said to have been **Thales** (c. 624–545 B.C.E.). Thales lived in the city of Miletus, part of a Greek colony on the Asian coast in an area known as Ionia. His parents are thought to have been Phoenician. For the most part, it seems that Thales devoted himself to his speculative studies, devoting only the minimum effort necessary to his financial affairs. In one of the earliest "absent-minded professor" stories, Plato records that Thales fell into a well "when he was looking up to study the stars...being so eager to know what was happening in the sky that he could not see what lay at his feet."[4]

Philosophically, Thales is significant for his attempt to find a common source, a single substance underlying all things. For him, this basic "stuff" was water. Aristotle says that Thales "observed" that "the nutriment of everything is moist, and that...the seeds of everything have a moist nature;...and that from which everything is generated is always its first principle."[5]

The real force of Thales' insight was not his specific conclusion that all things are water but, rather, his reduction of all things to one substance. The name for such single-substance philosophies is monism, the belief that reality is essentially one—either one reality, one process, one substance, one structure, or one "ground."

Thales' assertion that everything is composed of water was a major move beyond mythological accounts of nature because it rested on *systematic, rational evidence* and *careful observation*, rather than on mythical stories and poetic images. In other words, Thales tried to "figure out" or reason his way to a theoretical explanation of the changes he saw throughout nature. In presenting arguments for his beliefs, Thales inspired others to refine or reject his ideas with their own carefully *reasoned* counterarguments.

monism
The general name for the belief that everything consists of only one, ultimate, unique substance such as matter or spirit.

rational discourse
The interplay of carefully argued ideas; the use of reason to order, clarify, and identify reality and truth according to agreed-upon standards of verification.

principle of sufficient reason
The principle that nothing happens without a reason; consequently, no adequate theory or explanation can contain any brute, crude, unexplained facts. First specifically encountered in the work of the medieval philosopher Peter Abelard (1079–1142), it is usually associated with the rationalist philosopher Gottfried Wilhelm Leibniz (1646–1716), who used it in his famous "best of all possible worlds" argument.

apeiron
According to Anaximander, the first principle from which all existing things develop, a vast "Indefinite–Infinite"; the *apeiron* is an infinite mass of forces with no specific qualities.

The resulting interplay of carefully argued ideas is known as **rational discourse**, the use of reason to order, clarify, and identify reality and truth according to agreed-upon standards of verification.

As Thales' ideas became known, other philosophers offered rational explanations and modifications of his claims. For example, Thales claimed that the earth floats on water. But what "holds up" the water? A pupil of Thales named Anaximander (611–546 B.C.E.), who was also from Miletus, made another contribution to philosophical reasoning by offering a purely rational explanation for what holds the earth in place. This explanation was "rationalistic" because it did not rely exclusively on experience since Anaximander could not perceive the earth in its entirety or observe whatever held it up.

Anaximander reasoned that the earth stays where it is because it is at the precise center of the cosmos, "not supported by anything but resting where it is because of its equal distance from everything."[6] Aristotle said that Anaximander's reasoning rested on the principle that *nothing happens without a reason*. (Today, this principle is known as the **principle of sufficient reason**.)

According to Aristotle, Anaximander argued that there was "no reason" why the earth should move in one direction rather than in any other direction. And the earth cannot move in all directions because "it cannot move in opposite directions at the same time. So it necessarily rests where it is."[7] Anaximander also claimed that in the beginning, the earth was fluid and that an external source of heat dried some of it. The dried sections became land. Variations in temperature caused winds, and living organisms arose at varying stages of this drying-out process.[8] In theorizing this way, Anaximander underscored the importance of Thales' recognition of the need for some unifying principle to explain natural occurrences by providing a *systematic explanation* of natural phenomena.

Anaximander thought that particular "stuffs" emerged in pairs of opposites (hot–cold, dry–wet, hard–soft, and so on) from a vast "Indefinite–Infinite" called the **apeiron**. He believed that a continuous exchange of opposites can be seen throughout nature, as cold winter becomes warm spring, which becomes hot summer, which becomes cool fall, which becomes cold winter, and on and on. When, for example, hot comes into existence, cold returns to the *apeiron* and vice versa. The single surviving fragment of Anaximander's actual words refers to this continuous, mutual destruction of opposites: "They give justice and reparation to one another for their injustice in accordance with the arrangement of time."[9]

Anaximander's theory of opposites reminds us of Lao-tzu's "relative opposites" (yin–yang), and the *apeiron* is at least superficially reminiscent of Lao-tzu's Tao. But whereas Lao-tzu spoke in deliberately paradoxical language to express "what cannot be said," Anaximander was trying to articulate a systematic rational argument. (Lao-tzu is discussed in Chapter 1.)

The Problem of Change

Thales' direct legacy culminated in Anaximander's pupil, Anaximenes (died c. 500 B.C.E.), the third of the Presocratic Milesian philosophers. Anaximenes' notion that the first, universal, underlying element is *air*, or *pneuma*, was yet a further refinement of philosophical reasoning. **Pneuma** is the ultimate, pervasive spirit that holds the world together.

Just as Anaximander identified problems in Thales' thinking, Anaximenes recognized an important muddle at the heart of Anaximander's doctrine: On one hand, Anaximander characterized the *apeiron* as indefinite or "boundless"; on the other hand, he insisted that the *apeiron* is one thing. How can *one thing* contain *many particular things* and still be only one thing? In what sense is it "one thing" then? If it is indefinite, limitless, how can it be a "single thing"?

Anaximenes advanced the search for a common principle with the introduction of the argument that *qualitative* differences can result from *quantitative* changes. Rather than pairs of opposite stuffs, Anaximenes proposed two opposing *processes of exchange: condensation and rarefaction*. In Anaximenes' cosmology, air (*pneuma*) is invisible in its pure, original state. Pure air becomes progressively denser through the process of condensation, in the following stages: air → fire → wind → cloud → water → earth → stone. Matter becomes progressively lighter during the process of rarefaction: stone → earth → water → cloud → wind → fire → air. Thus, the ongoing cosmic and natural cycle of generation and destruction provides a *single underlying world order* that itself stays the same throughout all change: air ↔ fire ↔ wind ↔ cloud ↔ water ↔ earth ↔ stone.

The Logos

A native of Ephesus, a city on the Ionian coast north of Miletus, **Heraclitus** (c. 500 B.C.E.) took up the question of what holds the real substance of the world together—what makes it an *ordered whole, a cosmos*. Heraclitus is one of the most important and enigmatic of the Presocratics. Although virtually nothing is known of his life, the extant fragments of his writings reveal a powerful intellect, a profound artist, and a withering social critic.[10] Greatly admired by the Cynics and Stoics (Chapter 7), Heraclitus was claimed by Nietzsche (Chapter 16) as a philosophical ancestor. The Sophists, Plato, and Aristotle (Chapters 3, 5, and 6) were also influenced by Heraclitus's ideas.

Because the available fragments of Heraclitus's work are pronouncements rather than arguments, philosophers disagree about their meaning. The summary that follows concentrates on the Heraclitean emphasis on the power of discourse, the underlying "tension" or struggle between opposites that sustains all existing things. Note, too, the disturbing use of "war" as a dominant philosophical motif.

According to Heraclitus, ignorance occurs when people do not comprehend the basic structure of the human **psyche** (soul) and its relationship to the universal principle through which all things come to exist. Heraclitus called this universal principle *logos*.

The complex Greek word *logos* is intriguing. It meant all of the following: "intelligence," "speech," "discourse," "thought," "reason," "word," "meaning," "study of," "the record of," "the science of," "the fundamental principles of," "the basic principles and procedures of a particular discipline," "those features of a thing that make it intelligible to us," and "the rationale for a thing." Although *logos* retains these associated meanings for Heraclitus, in its most important sense the **Logos** was *the rule according to which all things are accomplished and the law which is found in all things*.[11]

pneuma
According to Anaximenes, the ultimate, pervasive spirit that holds the world together; all things are produced by either "rarefaction" of the *pneuma*, which creates fire, or condensation of the *pneuma*, which creates (in order of density) wind, cloud, water, earth, and stone.

psyche
Greek for "soul"; in today's terms, a combination of mind and soul, including the capacity for reflective thinking.

logos
One of the richest and most complex terms in ancient philosophy; associated meanings include "intelligence," "speech," "discourse," "thought," "reason," "word," "meaning"; the root of "log" (record), "logo," "logic," and the "ology" suffix found in terms like sociology and physiology. According to Heraclitus, the rule according to which all things are accomplished and the law which is found in all things.

Heraclitus

"The Cosmic Music of the Spheres"

About 530 B.C.E., Pythagoras of Samos (sixth century B.C.E.) left Greece for the Greek colony of Crotona in southern Italy, where he established a religious community that existed in one form or another for hundreds of years. The Pythagorean community eventually developed important mathematical and philosophical ideas that grew out of efforts to purify the psyche.

Although we know that Pythagoras was a historical figure, it is difficult to determine exactly what Pythagoras himself taught. He wrote nothing, and the ideas of other members of the community were attributed to him as a sign of respect and as a way of lending weight to the ideas. Plato and Aristotle rarely assign ideas to Pythagoras himself, although Pythagorean ideas seem to have influenced Plato's philosophy.

Pythagoreans asserted that number is the first principle of all things. They were the first systematic developers of mathematics in the West and discovered that natural events could be described in mathematical terms, especially as ratios.

To the Pythagoreans, the "principle of number" accounted for everything. Number was a real thing. Somehow, numbers existed in space, not just as mental constructs. *One*, for instance, was a point, *two* a line, *three* a surface, *four* a solid, and so forth. The earth, being a solid, was associated with the cube; fire was associated with the pyramid, air the octahedron, and water the icosahedron. From this perspective, all things "follow rules" and are "ordered."

According to Pythagorean doctrine, the entire universe is an ordered whole consisting of harmonies of contrasting elements. The Greek for "ordered whole" is cosmos. The Pythagoreans were the first philosophers to use the term *cosmos* to refer to the universe in this way. In contrast to the nearly mystical quality of the Heraclitean *Logos*, the Pythagorean cosmos is accessible to arithmetic, geometry, and rationality on a far greater scale. Rationality and truth are both functions of number.

The "celestial music of the spheres" is the hauntingly beautiful phrase the Pythagoreans coined to describe the sound of the heavens as they rotate according to cosmic number and harmony. One point of view held that because we have been exposed to the music of the spheres from birth we do not hear it. Other Pythagoreans thought that the music of the spheres was beyond the range of human hearing.

---

cosmos

Greek term for "ordered whole"; first used by the Pythagoreans to characterize the universe as an ordered whole consisting of harmonies of contrasting elements.

Heraclitus said that there is one *Logos* to which everyone ought to listen, although he thought that most people are unable to comprehend it. Some recent commentators suggest that the Heraclitean *Logos* is both *an account of reality* and *that which is revealed by* the account. This *Logos* is the fundamental reason for things being as they are; it is the fundamental principle of the world.[12]

The Heraclitean capital-L *Logos* is like God, only without the anthropomorphizing (humanizing) by the earlier philosophers and poets who attributed human qualities to the gods. According to Heraclitus's impersonal view of God, the *Logos* is a process, not an entity. As such, the *Logos* is unconcerned with individuals and human affairs, in much the same way that gravity affects us but is unconcerned with us.

Some scholars see the Heraclitean *Logos* as a Western expression of Tao (Chapter 1), but such cross-cultural comparisons are difficult. In this case, comparisons are particularly tricky because Heraclitus's war motif is not only active but also aggressive. Although fuller discussion of this topic is beyond the scope of our inquiries, you might find researching it worthwhile.

Like other ancient philosophers, Heraclitus relied on poetic language to express a transcendent concept. His use of the imagery of fire, thunderbolt (lightning), war, and perpetual change add a mystical quality to fragments about the *Logos*, which may account for some of Heraclitus's persistent appeal. Another possible source of his long-standing appeal may be rooted in a widespread affinity with Heraclitus's conviction that the world order must be intelligent. That is, a nonintelligent world order is impossible.

Appearance and Reality

Heraclitus distinguished "comprehension" and "understanding" from "knowledge," and being "asleep" or "dreaming" (ignorance and foolishness) from being "awake" (seeing beyond ignorance to the wisdom that comes only from recognizing the *Logos*). He also thought that the *Logos* is very close to us. For Heraclitus, the love and pursuit of wisdom is the love and pursuit of the *Logos*. He rejected all other conceptions of wisdom because they were not based on comprehension of the *Logos* as it operates in all things: "There is only one wisdom: to recognize the intelligence who steers all things through all things."[13]

According to Heraclitus, even though many things *appear* to remain the same, "Change alone is unchanging."[14] Traditionally, it has been held that Heraclitus went so far as to claim that *everything is always changing all the time*. But whether he really meant that everything is always changing or that individual things are held together by energy (change) remains unclear.

Heraclitus's concept of change is not what you and I usually mean by change. Our common experience suggests that, on the contrary, many things "stay the same" for very long periods of time. Most things do not change all the time. In order to reconcile the common perception of permanence with his belief that everything is always changing, Heraclitus distinguished between *appearance* and *reality* in a way that contrasted *apparent permanence* with *hidden reality*.[15]

According to Heraclitus, the harmonious quality of the "hidden reality" cannot be grasped by the senses, but only by "seeing" or "hearing" the *Logos:* "The unseen design of things is more harmonious than the seen."[16] The harmony that Heraclitus refers to is not, as you might expect, a pleasant and gentle mixing or commingling of complementary forces. Rather, it is harmony created by tension.

According to Heraclitus, the world (cosmos) exists as a constant struggle between opposing forces. He compared stability (permanence) to the kind of tension that a bent bow or stringed musical instrument is under.[17] A bow appears to be "at rest" only because the bowstring and bow pull "equally" against each other. According to Heraclitus, in both nature and convention (society), stability (permanence) is the result of tension between equal and opposite forces.

For example, social struggle is the maneuvering of various "forces" for domination. Peace and stability exist only when equal opposing forces or pressures hold each other in check. Social stability is roughly analogous to two equally powerful wrestlers pushing in opposite directions. So long as their strength, angle of attack,

"When Homer said he wished war might disappear from the lives of gods and men, he forgot that without opposition all things would cease to exist."–*Heraclitus*

You would not by your going discover the limits of soul though you traveled over every path, so deep has it a Logos.
—Heraclitus

and the like are identical, they will appear to be immobile—even though they are locked in a mighty struggle—a war.

The One

Parmenides of Elea (fl. fifth century B.C.E.) radically transformed the early philosophers' interest in cosmology, the study of the universe as a rationally ordered system (cosmos), into ontology, the study of "being." Parmenides was probably born around 515 B.C.E. in Elea, a Greek colony in southern Italy. His work was a major influence on Plato, who suggests that Parmenides and his pupil Zeno (see the box "Zeno's Paradoxes" in this chapter) came to Athens, where they met young Socrates.[18]

According to Parmenides, none of his predecessors adequately accounted for the process by which the one basic stuff of the cosmos changes into the many individual things we experience every day. In his search for a solution to the problem of "the one and the many," Parmenides turned away from the study of individual things and devoted his attention to an analysis of the process of change itself.

Like Lao-tzu, Parmenides presented his philosophy in the form of a poem. *On Nature* recounts how a goddess revealed "the whole truth" to him. Unlike Lao-tzu's *Tao te Ching, On Nature* is a complex rational and linguistic analysis. In this poem, a goddess identifies three possible "paths" of study and understanding and indicates that only one is true.

Parmenides' reasoning is based on two key premises: "What is, is" and "What is not, is not." "What is not" equals "not being"—nothing, or not anything at all. In other words, the term *nothing* does not name anything. It is impossible to even imagine nothing. According to Parmenides, strictly speaking, "nothing" can never refer to any thing or object. Thus, strictly speaking, the sentence "Nothing exists" is self-contradictory. The Parmenidean nothing paralyzes reason: Lacking any content whatsoever, it cannot be comprehended at all. Since it cannot be comprehended, it cannot be described—there is nothing to refer to.

Parmenides was a *monist* who characterized the one real thing as *being*. "What is" equals *being*. According to Parmenides, *being* is purely positive, simple, and unconditioned. That is, *being* is one, eternal, and indivisible; it is the "unchanging one." *Not-being*, in contrast, is negative, complex, and impure. *Being* ("what is") can be conceived of and expressed. *Not-being* ("what is not") is unintelligible. *Not-being* "paralyzes" thought and is inexpressible.

Being and Change

Parmenides placed all sensations in the realm of appearance. According to Parmenides, *reality* cannot be apprehended by the senses. Change and variety (the many) are only *appearances;* they are not *real*. If this is true, then our most commonly held opinions are "mere opinions," and most of us are unaware of reality, which is one *being*. Consequently, Parmenides associated *being* with correct thinking and *not-being* with illusion. Correct thinking is always about *being* because we can only think about subjects that exist, that *are:* "In fact it is the same thing to think and to be."[19]

cosmology
From the Greek word *kosmos*, meaning "world," "universe," or "orderly structure," the study of the universe as an ordered system or cosmos.

ontology
The study of being.

reductio ad absurdum
From the Latin for "reduce to absurdity"; form of argument that refutes an opponent's position by showing that accepting it leads to absurd, unacceptable, or contradictory conclusions because (1) accepting it leads to a logical contradiction, or (2) it leads to a logical conclusion that is somehow obviously ridiculous because it offends either our reason or common sense.

"Zeno's Paradoxes"

Zeno of Elea (c. 490–430 B.C.E.) forcefully defended the idea that change in the form of motion is impossible. These intriguing paradoxes present one of the earliest examples of a particular method of proof known as a **reductio ad absurdum** (reduce to absurdity). In a *reductio*, an opponent's position is refuted by showing that accepting it leads to absurd, unacceptable, or contradictory conclusions. Zeno is credited with perfecting a way of revealing an idea's absurdity by (1) showing that accepting it leads to a logical contradiction or (2) showing that it leads to a logical conclusion that is somehow obviously ridiculous because it offends either our reason or common sense.

Using a form of the *reductio*, Zeno tried to show that the Heraclitean claim that everything is always changing is absurd because the very idea of change or motion is absurd. The paradoxes also reveal the ultimate inadequacy of the Presocratic notion of the continuum.

Zeno's paradoxes were admired by ancient philosophers and continue to generate lively discussions among contemporary philosophers. See what you make of his three most famous paradoxes.

The Dichotomy

The first argument is this: If movement exists, it is necessary that the mobile [moving thing] traverse an infinite number of points in a finite time; but this is impossible, hence movement does not exist. Zeno demonstrated his position affirming that whatever is moved must traverse a certain distance: but any distance is divisible to infinity, what is moved must first traverse half of the distance and then the whole of it. But first he must traverse the entire half of the distance, and the half of that and the new half of the previous half. But if the halves are infinite in number, since for every whole taken it is possible to take half, then it is impossible to traverse in a finite time an infinite number of points.... Then, given that every magnitude admits of infinite divisions, it is impossible to traverse any magnitude in a finite time.

Simplicius, **In Aristotle's Physics**, 1013.4ff.; quoted in Giovanni Reale, **A History of Ancient Philosophy**, vol. 1, **From the Origins to Socrates**, trans. John R. Catan (Albany: State University of New York Press, 1987), p. 91.

Achilles and the Tortoise

The second [paradox] is the so-called Achilles, and it amounts to this, that in a race the quickest runner can never overtake the slowest, since the pursuer must first reach the point whence the pursued started, so that the slower must always hold a lead. This argument is the same in principle as that which depends on bisection [cutting the distance in half], though it differs from it in that the spaces with which we successively have to deal are not divided into halves. The result of the argument is that the slower is not overtaken: but it proceeds along the same lines as the dichotomy argument (for in both, a division of the space in a certain way leads to the result that the goal is not reached, though the Achilles goes further in that it affirms that even the quickest runner in legendary tradition must fail in his pursuit of the slowest)....

Aristotle, **Physics**, Hardie and Gaye translation, 239B.14ff.

The Flying Arrow

The argument of Zeno, beginning from the premise that everything which occupies a space equal to itself either is in motion or is at rest, that nothing is moved in an instant, and that the mobile always occupies in each instant a space equal to itself, seems to adjust itself in this way: The flying arrow in every instant occupies a place equal to itself, and thus, for the whole time of its motion. But what occupies in an instant a place equal to itself does not move because nothing is moved in an instant. Hence the flying arrow, as long as it is in motion, does not move for the whole time of its flight.

Simplicius, **In Aristotle's Physics**, 1015.19ff.; in Reale, **A History of Ancient Philosophy**, vol. 1, **From the Origins to Socrates**, trans. John R. Catan (Albany: State University of New York Press, 1987), p. 93.

Parmenides reasoned that *being* must be eternal because to come from something other than *being* would be to come from *not-being*—which would be to come from nothing, and nothing can come from nothing. *Being* cannot change into something else because to do so would require *being* to be *not-being*—a clear impossibility.

The classicist John Dillon explains that

> In the context of Greek thought…"being" (often characterized by the additional qualification "real" or "true") denotes some single, permanent, unchanging, fundamental reality, to which is habitually opposed the inconstant flux and variety of visible things…. In short, "being" (*on*, or *orousia*) becomes in Greek philosophy the repository of all the concepts that can be thought up to characterize the idealized opposite of what we see around us—its counterpart, which comprises all aspects of the everyday physical world, being termed "becoming" (*genesis*).[20]

Being is not a "principle" or fundamental "stuff" like the basic principles of the earlier Presocratic philosophers. Parmenides thought that *being* is perfect and complete, or "whole." Thus, it cannot move or change. Philosophical historian Giovanni Reale characterizes Parmenidean *being* as "the *being* of the visible cosmos, immobilized, and to a great extent purified, but still clearly recognizable."[21]

Parmenidean *being* is recognized by *reason* as a perfect whole, as One. Yet our senses only experience *becoming*: living and dying, moving, changing. The senses cannot recognize being, much less discover that *being* is One. In other words, you cannot see, touch, taste, hear, or smell *being*.

In his poem, the goddess advises Parmenides to follow reason rather than the senses because only by reasoning can *being* be recognized as One. The senses can only perceive things as discrete, as many. Parmenides' poem views the world of the senses as corrupted by appearances and by "mere belief" in the reality of *not-being*.

Most startling of all, Parmenides "solved" the problem of the *appearance of change* by concluding that the very concept of change is self-contradictory. What we think of as change is really an illusion. The reasoning runs as follows: "Change" equals transformation into something else. When a thing becomes "something else," it becomes what it is not. But because it is impossible for "nothing" (what is not) to exist, there is no "nothing" into which the old thing can disappear. (There is no "no place" for the thing to go into.) Therefore, change cannot occur.[22] This counterintuitive conclusion triggered Zeno's infamous paradoxes.

Whatever the power of Parmenides' vision of *being* as One, change and motion remain basic facts of experience for most of us. The unpopularity of an opinion is not a measure of its merit, however. And Parmenides' position was the product of careful reasoning in a way that "common sense" rarely is. Further, Parmenides' contemporaries took his arguments seriously, and Parmenides' notion of *being* played an important part in the development of Plato's theory of Forms (Chapter 5).

> *How could being perish? How could it come into being? If it came into being, it is not; and so too if it is about to be at some future time.*
>
> —Parmenides

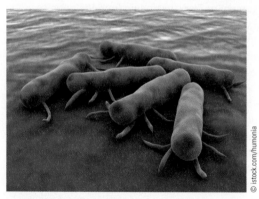

© istock.com/humonia

Absent today's sophisticated tools and technologies, the observations of ancient protoscientists prompted them to provide rational explanations for orderly change, growth, and decay, leading to speculations that the universe is ordered at levels beyond our perception, ordered at its core. Does this microscopic picture of Salmonella bacteria support the sophos's primal "hunches" that there is more order to reality than meets the eye—or any merely human other sense?

PHILOSOPHICAL QUERY

Compare the way Parmenides discusses the One as being with the way Lao-tzu refers to it as Tao and with Heidegger's Concept of Being. (See Chapters 1 and 17.)

The Many

The next major shift in Presocratic philosophy was the emergence of **pluralism**, the belief that there exist many realities or substances. Building on Parmenides' belief that motion is impossible because there is no empty space (no "what is not"), **Empedocles** (c. fifth century B.C.E.) concluded that reality must be "completely full." According to Empedocles, reality is a *plenum* without any gaps.

Because he agreed with Parmenides that nothing comes into existence or goes out of existence, Empedocles decided that all motion and change take place *within* existing reality. Things do not move into empty space but "exchange places" with each other. Rather than an unmoving One (*being*), reality consists of six basic components: four basic "roots" and two basic "motions." The roots are earth, air, fire, and water. Each root is eternal—uncreated, indestructible, and unchanging. The two basic motions are *Love*, which unites different things, and *Strife*, which breaks things up into their basic elements. At the beginning of the "world cycle," the four roots were all mixed together, under the motion of Love. Eventually, Strife took over and the four roots separated into their own individual domains. Once Strife dominates and the four elements are completely separate, Love reemerges, and the process repeats itself.[23]

Empedocles claimed that in the beginning of the separation process, certain "mixtures" of elements could not survive. But in the course of the great random "mixing together" of different combinations, survivable combinations would eventually result. It is chance, in the form of "random combinations," then, that accounts for human beings and all other things that are part of this particular world cycle.

Empedocles was not consistent in his attitude toward the evolutionary cycle he described. Although he sometimes talked about "accidental" combinations, his whole tone shifted when he talked about the world cycle or *process itself*. He used the term *god* for the process—which he worships. The god of Empedocles lacked a body and was "only a sacred and unutterable mind flashing through the whole world with rapid thoughts."[24]

Mind

Anaxagoras (c. 500–428 B.C.E.) realized that Empedocles' four basic roots were no more helpful in explaining change and transformation than water, *apeiron*, or *pneuma* were. "How," he wondered, "could hair come from what is not hair or flesh from what is not flesh?"[25]

Anaxagoras rejected Empedocles' two fundamental motions, Love and Strife. In their place he posited **Nous** (Greek for "mind"). *Nous* is the "all-pervading Mind which imposes (brings about) an intelligible pattern in an otherwise unintelligible

---

pluralism
The belief that there exist many realities or substances.

Nous
From the Greek for "mind"; according to Anaxagoras, "the all-pervading Mind which imposes (brings about) an intelligible pattern in an otherwise unintelligible universe"; a material being that affects all things without being in them.

> *For already have I
> once been a boy and a
> girl, a bush and a bird
> and a dumb sea fish.*
> —Empedocles

universe." *Nous* affects all things without being in them, but it is not a process or force in the contemporary scientific sense. The fragments of Anaxagoras reveal difficulty in clearly articulating the nature of *Nous*. Some passages stress that *Nous* "sets all things in order," but others treat it as purely mechanical.[26] Even so, Anaxagoras's concept of *Nous* provided "one of the most powerful intuitions…in the whole course of Presocratic philosophy…that the [basic] principle is an infinite reality, separate from everything else." Fragment 12 expresses Anaxagoras's insight with haunting poetic power:

> All things which have life, both the greater and the less, are ruled by mind [*Nous*]. Mind took command of the universal revolution, so as to make [things] revolve at the outset. At first things began to revolve from some small point, but now the revolution extends over a greater area, and will spread even further. And the things which were mixed together, and separated off, and divided, were all understood by mind. And whatever they were going to be, and whatever things were then in existence that are not now, and all things that now exist and whatever shall exist— all were arranged by mind, as also the revolution now followed by the stars, the sun and moon, and the air and aither [ether] which were separated off. It was this revolution which caused the separation off. And dense separates from rare, and hot from cold, and bright from dark, and dry from wet. There are many portions of many things. And nothing is absolutely separated off or divided the one from the other except mind. Mind is all alike, both the greater and the less. But nothing else is like anything else….[27]

Anaxagoras believed that "in everything there is a portion of everything."[28] A fingernail, for example, contains bits of whale and plum. Any given sensible stuff contains bits of an infinite variety of ultimate stuffs or "seeds." What we see when we look at a fingernail "or at anything" is the dominant stuff in the mixture. Our eyes and other senses are too gross (unrefined) to see everything: "From the weakness of our sense we are not able to judge the truth. What appears is a vision of the unseen."[29]

> *Mind began to
> revolve first from a
> small beginning; but
> the revolution now
> extends over a larger
> space, and will extend
> over a larger still.…
> And this revolution
> caused the separating
> off, and the rare is
> separated off from the
> dense, the warm from
> the cold, the light
> from the dark, and the
> dry from the moist.*
> —Anaxagoras

If there are seeds of every kind of stuff in every sensible thing, clearly they must be very, very small. Indeed, in order for a very small thing like a speck of dust or diamond chip to contain seeds of *every* other kind of thing, these seeds must be infinitely small. If this is so, then things as we perceive them must be composed of tiny "bits" or seeds that we cannot see individually. We can see things only when seeds are combined in sufficient quantity. The wedge between appearance and reality has been driven in another notch.

Atoms and the Void

Although Anaxagoras and Empedocles did not solve the problem of "the one and the many," they helped further clarify it by drawing more refined attention to the key questions that any adequate explanation must answer: How does the world of things as we ordinarily perceive them "emerge from" some kind of basic stuff that is quite different in its characteristics from the things of our experience? How can the variety of colors, textures, odors, densities, and so on that we see all around us "come from" a single, completely different something else?

The Parmenidean assault on the senses was not adequately "resolved" until the middle of the fifth century B.C.E., when **Leucippus** of Miletus (c. fifth century B.C.E.) and **Democritus** of Abdera (c. 460–370 B.C.E.) argued that there are actually many "ones." Leucippus is credited with being the originator of *atomism*, and Democritus further developed his ideas.

Atomism is the materialistic view that the universe consists entirely of empty space and ultimately simple entities that combine to form objects. The most thorough expression of early atomism occurs in the Roman poet Lucretius's (c. 98–55 B.C.E.) great poem, *De Rerum Natura*. Lucretius's poem helped popularize the ideas of both Democritus and the hedonist Epicurus (Chapter 7).

Rather than reject Parmenidean *being* by denying what is so obvious to our senses—the existence of motion, variety, and change—Leucippus argued that there are many "ones," or beings. Democritus termed these "ones" *atoms*.

The word *atom* comes from the Greek *atomos*, meaning "indivisible," "having no parts," or "uncuttable." **Atoms** are minute material particles, the ultimate material constituents of all things. According to Democritus, atoms have properties such as size, shape, position, arrangement (combination), and motion, but they do not possess sensible qualities like color, taste, temperature, or smell. However, combinations (compounds and composites) of atoms can grow large enough for us to perceive.

Democritus argued that atoms must be so small that they are invisible to the naked eye. Being so small, they are "uncuttable"—thus they cannot be destroyed. In other words, atoms are eternal. Because motion is an inherent property of atoms, they are constantly moving, bumping into each other and bouncing away or quivering in one spot.

Building on Parmenides' fundamental division between *being* and *not-being*, Democritus reasoned that *not-being* cannot even exist since it "is not." Further, he argued, the absence of *not-being* is not the same thing as the absence of empty space. Space is empty when it does not contain "things" or "bodies." Space can be empty of bodies without being empty of *being*.

Democritus further reasoned that it is possible to separate "ones" from each other by empty space, which is devoid of any bodies. The **void** is Democritus's term for no-things (no-bodies), or empty space. *No-thing* is not the same as *nothing*—a crucial distinction that Parmenides failed to make. Empty space is something, an empty something, but something nonetheless.

SuperStock/Getty Images

"Sweet exists by convention, bitter by convention, color by convention; but in reality atoms and the void alone exist."–Democritus

atomism

An early Greek philosophy developed by Leucippus and Democritus and later refined by Epicurus and Lucretius; materialistic view that the universe consists entirely of empty space and ultimately simple entities that combine to form objects.

atoms

From the Greek *atomos*, meaning "indivisible," "having no parts," or "uncuttable"; minute material particles; the ultimate material constituents of all things. Atoms have such properties as size, shape, position, arrangement (combination), and motion, but lack qualities like color, taste, temperature, or smell.

Being and Not-being

PARMENIDES

Being	*Not-being*
(What Is)	(What Is Not)

DEMOCRITUS

Being	*Not-being*
(What Is)	(What Is Not)
Atoms Void	
(Things) (No-Things)	

Reason and Necessity

According to Democritus, things come into existence when atoms combine in certain ways, and they go out of existence when their parts or atoms separate. Stable substances and things are composed of highly compatible atoms, and less stable ones are composed of less compatible atoms. Marble, for instance, contains more stable atoms than nitroglycerin does.

If we ask *why* certain things exist, Democritus's answer is that given the eternal swirling of atoms, some collisions are bound to stick because of the nature of the atoms involved. There is no divine order, no *Nous* or intelligence guiding or combining these atoms. All that exists in this view are atoms and the void—nothing else. There is no intentional order or *purpose* to the universe, though there is *predictability*. That is, "nothing occurs at random." Mechanical laws of motion explain everything; there is no deeper or higher explanation. What appears to be chance is simply a lack of information and knowledge. If we could observe a long sequence of atomistic behavior the way we might observe a game of billiards, we could—in theory—predict the future positions and combinations of various atoms.

Nature and Convention

We never experience atoms directly, according to Democritus. Shape, taste, and other sensible properties are the result of "effluences" and "images" as we sense atoms striking the eye, ear, skin, tongue, and so on. Thus, we are "cut off from the real" because our sensations are products of our own particular condition: our sensory acuity, whether we are sick, and so forth.

Not only do we never experience atoms directly, but even perceptual qualities—like sweet and sour, hot and cold, smooth and rough, hard and soft—are matters of convention, not nature: "Sweet exists by convention, bitter by convention, color by convention; but in reality atoms and the void alone exist," according to Democritus.

Although Democritus rejected the skeptical implications of this insight, subsequent philosophers have elaborated on them with stunning effect. In subsequent chapters we shall look at some of the far-reaching consequences engendered by the issue of what is true by nature and what is true by convention. (See especially Chapters 3–5, which cover some of the most exciting aspects of this struggle, and Chapters 9–11 and 16–17, which concern the modern search for an answer to skepticism.)

void

Democritus's term for no-thing (no-bodies); empty space in Atomist theory.

Aplia

Commentary

When the *sophos* first emerged from the mists of prehistory, knowledge and wisdom were not neatly divided. As early Greek civilization became more refined and sophisticated, mythology and religion developed into philosophy (and later branched off into science).

> *Character is fate.*
> —Heraclitus

Social historian Amaury de Riencourt traces the early history of philosophy as a series of increasingly abstract steps, until a "fanatical concern" with logical consistency and rules of thinking (Parmenides and Zeno, for example) led to theories, which, though logically consistent, did not match observed facts.[30]

The result, de Riencourt says, was "The absolute predominance of the dissociating, analytical...principle in Greek [thought]...its strength and its weakness."[31]

Philosophical speculation became increasingly alienated from common experience, and unemotional, implacable reason (modeled after the *logos*) threatened to dominate other sources of knowledge and wisdom. Seemingly bizarre theories and countertheories struggled for dominance as the first principle of existence: water, *apeiron, pneuma,* fire, *being, Nous,* atoms, and the void. Everyday experiences and the evidence of the senses were rejected as illusory, products of ignorance.

> *The fairest universe is but a heap of rubbish thrown up at random.*
> —Heraclitus

To many people, the philosophers were the ones utterly out of touch with reality. Philosophical speculation was sometimes viewed as an indulgence suitable only for those not fit for "real life"—individuals supported by friends or family and obsessed with pointless "intellectual squabbles." Philosophy became a subject of confusion and ridicule as well as of awe and respect.

A clouded reputation haunts philosophy to this day, as we saw in the Introduction, and will see in Chapter 17. "What," we are asked, "is philosophy good for, if philosophers can hold contradictory and absurd ideas that bear no resemblance to common sense? How can we take seriously charges that we can never experience reality, that our most cherished and widely held beliefs are merely illusions? If careful thinkers end up in such tangles, maybe it's better to think less and live more."

> *Everything flows; nothing remains.*
> —Heraclitus

This suspicious attitude toward philosophy contributed to a kind of philosophical revolution that occurred when the first "professional" thinkers, known as Sophists, turned from the study of the cosmos to the study of human beings. The Sophists' demands for practical philosophy blew through the early history of philosophy like a bracing wind. This is the subject of the next chapter.

Summary of Main Points

- Although the ancient Greeks' mythological accounting of events ultimately failed, it established two crucial principles: (1) There is a difference between the way the things appear and the way they *really* are. (2) There are unseen causes of events; things happen as they do for some reason.

- The first Western philosophers challenged the mythological worldview by asking for *rational* explanations of questions that mythology could not adequately answer. These first philosophers were called *sophos,* or sage, from the Greek word for "wise."

- Traditionally, the first Western philosopher is said to have been Thales, who is significant for his attempt to find a common source, a single substance underlying all things. For him, this basic "stuff" was water. The name for such single-substance philosophies is monism.

- Thales' pupil Anaximander thought that the first principle was a vast "Indefinite–Infinite," which he called the *apeiron*. Anaximander's pupil Anaximenes argued that the first, universal, underlying element is air, or *pneuma*, the ultimate, pervasive spirit that holds the world together.

- Heraclitus used fire imagery to help solve the problem of "the one and the many" because a burning fire is an ongoing process, an "exchange," rather than a static "thing." He also distinguished between *appearance* and *reality* in a way that contrasted apparent permanence with the hidden reality of continuous change. Heraclitus suggested that the world is in a constant struggle between opposing forces. Heraclitus's principle was the *logos*, the law which is found in all things.

- Parmenides of Elea radically transformed the early philosophers' interest in cosmology, the study of the universe as a rationally ordered system (cosmos), into ontology, the study of "being." According to Parmenides, the sentence "nothing exists" is self-contradictory because when we talk about "nothing", we always refer to something—just not the particular thing we are using the word "nothing" to refer to. The Parmenidean "nothing" was thought to paralyze reason. A monist, Parmenides characterized the one real thing as *being*, which is positive, simple, and unconditioned.

- Pluralism is the belief that there exist many realities or substances. Empedocles was a pluralist who concluded that reality must be "completely full," a *plenum* without any gaps. According to Empedocles, reality consists of four basic "roots" (earth, air, fire, and water) and two basic "motions" (Love and Strife). Anaxagoras rejected Empedocles' two fundamental motions Love and Strife. Anaxagoras believed that "in everything there is a portion of everything." He posited *Nous* as the "all-pervading Mind which brings about an intelligible pattern in an otherwise unintelligible universe."

- The atomists Leucippus of Miletus and Democritus of Abdera argued that there are really many Parmenidean "ones." The *void* is Democritus's term for no-things (no-bodies). No-thing is not the same as "nothing." According to Democritus, Parmenides failed to make this important distinction. Democritus termed the Parmenidean "ones" *atoms*, minute material particles. Although atoms have size, shape, position, arrangement (combination), and motion, they do not possess sensible qualities like color, taste, temperature, or smell. Atoms are constantly moving around.

Post-Reading Reflections

1. Distinguish between a *sophos* and a philosopher.

2. What role did the need for explanations play in the development of Presocratic philosophy?

3. Who was Thales? Summarize his fundamental insight. What is the *apeiron*? How is it related to Thales' philosophy?

4. How does Anaximander explain the origin of particular things?

5. What is the *pneuma*? What significant distinction does it involve?

6. What does Heraclitus mean by "fire"? By "war"?

7. What question was "fire" supposed to solve for Heraclitus?

8. What is the *Logos*? How does it differ from God?

9. What is cosmology? What is ontology?

10. What is *being*? What is *not-being*?

11. Reconstruct Parmenides' rejection of *not-being*.

12. What is monism? Pluralism?

13. What is the *plenum*?

14. Name and explain each of Zeno's paradoxes.

15. What is a *reductio ad absurdum*? Construct one.

16. Identify the four roots and two motions of Empedocles.

17. What is *Nous*?

18. How did Democritus deal with Parmenides' problem of reconciling *being* with motion?

19. What are atoms? What is the void?

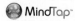 MindTap

Experience MindTap through the activities highlighted in this chapter. Further explore this online, personalized learning tool to deepen your comprehension and improve your grades.

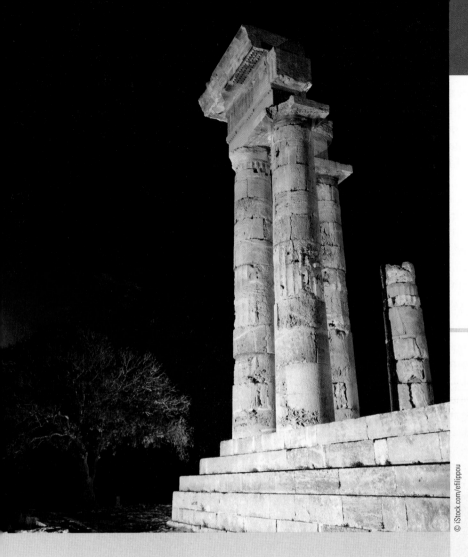

© iStock.com/efilippou

3

The Sophist
Protagoras

Man is the measure of all things, of the things that are, [how] they are, and the things that are not, [how] they are not.

— *Protagoras of Abdera*

Learning Objectives

 MindTap

After you complete this chapter, you should be able to:

- Identify examples of ethnocentrism from your own experience.
- Explain the change from *sophos* to Sophist.
- Identify different kinds of relativism.
- Define the term *pragmatism*.
- Appraise the doctrine of the superior individual.
- Critique the Sophists' claim that conventional morality favors weak and inferior individuals at the expense of superior individuals.
- Critique the idea that might makes right.
- Identify two current examples of political sophistry, one from the liberal side of the political spectrum and the other from the conservative side.
- Assess the claim that the Sophists have been given a bad rap.

Ancients of our culture sought clarity: Plato portrays Socrates tirelessly splitting hairs to extract essential truth from the ambiguities of language and thought. Two thousand years later we are reversing that, for now we pay intellectual talent a high price to amplify ambiguities, distort thought, and bury reality.... One of the discoveries of the twentieth century is the enormous variety of ways of compelling language to lie.

— Jules Henry

THE SCENE. A society showing signs of tension and strain, yet still exciting and important. The privileges of the establishment are being challenged by immigrants and more liberal democratic groups. Wealthy parents pay outrageous tuitions to have their children taught by prestigious educators, only to have these very same children then reject their parents' ideals and beliefs. People complain that atheistic, relativistic trends are permeating the schools and that basic values are breaking down. Traditional religions and beliefs are challenged by intellectuals, by occult practices, and by competing "foreign" religions. Scientific, mathematical, and intellectual advances compete for social control and influence with conservative, fundamentalist religious and moral tenets. Political corruption is pervasive and public. People take one another to court for a variety of real and inflated slights and transgressions. Success, prestige, and power become the overriding goals of many. Consider one commentator's description:

> It seems as if the dominant drive of more and more citizens is the objective of getting as rich as possible.... Meanwhile the money-makers, bent on their business,... continue to inject their poisoned loans wherever they can, and to demand high rates of interest, with the result that drones and beggars multiply.... Yet even when the evil becomes flagrant [the rulers] will do nothing to quench it.... This being so, won't everyone arrange his life as pleases him best? It's a wonderfully pleasant way of carrying on in

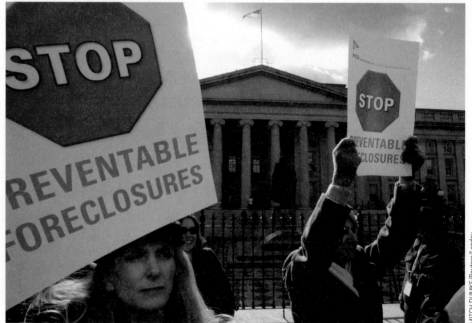

"Meanwhile the moneymakers...continue to inject their poisoned loans...and to demand high rates of interest, with the result that drones and beggars multiply."
–Plato

MITCH DUMKE/Reuters/Landov

the short-run, isn't it? It's an agreeable, anarchic form of society, with plenty of variety, which treats all men as equal, whether they are or not.

It is a picture easy to recognize.[1]

America today? No. You have just read Plato's characterization of the "democratic" state of Athens. Because of their sophisticated, successful civilization, the Athenians had long viewed themselves as unique, special, superior to all others. The Athens of around 500–400 B.C.E. attracted aspiring entrepreneurs from all over Greece and parts of Asia. Those who considered themselves "original, true Athenians" grew uncomfortable and defensive.

> *The Ethiopians say that their gods are snub-nosed and black, the Thracians that theirs have light blue eyes and red hair.*
> — Xenophanes

ethnocentrism
From Greek roots meaning "the race is the center"; belief that the customs and beliefs of one's own culture are inherently superior to all others.

Dogs bark at strangers.
— Heraclitus

barbarian
From a rude "bar-bar" noise used to mock dialects considered crude by the ancient Greeks; originally referred to other cultures considered "less than human" or uncivilized.

The religion of one seems madness unto another.
— Sir Thomas Browne

Social scientists call this attitude **ethnocentrism** (from Greek roots meaning "the race or group is the center"). Ethnocentric individuals see their ways as inherently superior to all others: Their religion is the one true religion. Their science, music, tastes in all areas of life are unsurpassed. The ethnocentric person thinks, "The gods speak *our* language, look like *us*, are *our* color. *Our* family practices are *natural*, others are *deviant*."

Yet things aren't so simple. In some cultures eating the flesh of a cow is forbidden. In other cultures, it is not. Some people get sick at the mere idea of eating a dog or monkey; to others, such culinary practices are normal. Ethnocentrism is what makes us laugh at the way other people dress or talk. We even do this to other citizens of our own country. Some Southerners make fun of people with a "New York accent," while certain New Yorkers mock those with "Southern accents." The ethnocentric person thinks that he or she doesn't even have an accent!

The Greeks of this time were so ethnocentric that they invented the term **barbarian** to mock people who spoke other languages. They mimicked the way foreigners talked by making a sound something like "bar, bar, bar." Today we would probably say, "blah, blah, blah." So the outsiders were bar-bar-ians (or blah-blah-ians)—people whose language sounded like noise or nonsense to the Greeks. To these Greeks, other cultures were simply "uncivilized," "less human." But what happens when a closed-off culture begins to interact with other highly civilized cultures on a regular basis?

PHILOSOPHICAL QUERY

Can you think of any ways you are ethnocentric? What are some close parallels between Athens of the fifth century B.C.E. and America after September 11, 2001? Discuss.

Ultimately—and understandably—for many people philosophy developed a conflicted and confused reputation, something at once noble and somehow ridiculous.

This clouded reputation haunts philosophy to this day, as we saw in the Introduction. "What are you philosophers good for," we are asked, "if you can hold contradictory and absurd ideas that bear no resemblance to common sense? How can the rest of us take seriously your charges that we can never experience reality, that our most cherished and widely held beliefs are merely illusions, that our thinking is muddled, that *we*, the majority, are wrong and that our unwillingness to agree with you is a symptom of our ignorance rather than your own? If even the most careful philosophical thinkers end up in such tangles, maybe it's better to think less and enjoy life more."

This suspicious attitude toward philosophy contributed to a philosophical and cultural revolution that occurred when the first "professional" thinkers, known as Sophists, turned from the study of the cosmos to the study of human beings and brought philosophy back down to Earth. The Sophists' demands for "philosophy that pays" blew through the ancient world like a bracing wind.

The Advent of Professional Educators

Ancient Athens was chauvinistic in many respects. For example, full citizenship was originally confined to males from certain aristocratic families. The ambitious, talented young immigrants from throughout the Mediterranean area who were attracted by Athens' vitality as a trading center had fewer rights and opportunities than did Athenian citizens. Regardless of their abilities, it was difficult, if not impossible, for noncitizens to achieve the same levels of success as those lucky enough to have been born into the right families.

As the number of capable immigrants settling in and around Athens grew, tension and conflict became inevitable. The Athenians' snobbery was challenged. Some Persians and Spartans and Milesians were smarter, quicker, stronger, more attractive; some of their goods were of higher quality; their traders sometimes outfoxed Athenians. Thus, the Athenians' image of themselves as unique and superior people became increasingly difficult to maintain as interaction with people from other cultures increased (as is always ultimately the case). Indeed, great deliberate effort was required to maintain a view of unquestioned superiority.

As the lively trade center flourished, the privileges of birth were challenged by the emergence of a wealthy new business class. Good business sense, personal charm and persuasiveness, the willingness to work hard, and individual ability began to be as important as having been born in the right place to the right kind of family.[2]

In this changing climate, more and more individuals were allowed both to speak before the Athenian Assembly and to sue one another over business and personal matters. The ability to think clearly and speak persuasively was a means for members of the new middle class to enter political life and to improve their social status. These conditions combined to create a demand for something unknown in the Mediterranean world before this time: formal, specialized higher education in such subjects as letters, rhetoric (persuasive speaking), science, statesmanship, and philosophy.[3]

These social changes also affected philosophy. Presocratic philosophers had inconsistently asserted various explanations of "reality" that did not conform to common experience. Each theory was flawed. Each philosopher's position was criticized logically by a newer point of view, which was in turn criticized. Even good logic and sound reasoning seemed ultimately unhelpful in sorting things out. One problem was with the characteristics of arguments themselves. All arguments consist of two aspects: their logical structure and the truth (or falsity) of their content. Sound arguments consist of good reasoning based on true premises. If one or more premises of an argument are false, the conclusion will be unreliable. Thus, if its starting point is flawed, even the most tightly reasoned argument or theory will be flawed.

Overwhelmed by so many conflicting theories, the new *sophos* of the fifth century B.C.E., now called a **Sophist**, concluded that it is impossible to discover "the Truth" because the only difference between a "good" argument and a "bad" argument is custom and individual preference. (See Chapters 14–17 for subsequent challenges to "the Truth.")

Sophists
In the fifth century B.C.E., teachers of rhetoric (who were paid); relativists who taught that might makes right, truth is a matter of appearance and convention, and power is the ultimate value.

Dea Picture Library/De Agostini Picture Library/Getty Images

The original Sophists were wandering teachers and the first philosophers to charge fees for their knowledge.

Power and Education

The original Sophists were wandering teachers who gravitated toward Athens during the fertile fifth century B.C.E. They were also the first professional teachers, charging a fee to teach anyone who wished to study with them. They made Athenian education democratic, at least in the sense that all who could pay were equal. It was no longer necessary to belong to a certain family—as long as you had enough money to pay high tuitions. The *sophos*, in contrast to the Sophist, had followers and disciples rather than paying students.

The Sophists also differed from the *sophos* in that the Sophists turned increasingly from the study of nature to the formal study of human life and conduct. Many of them had traveled rather widely and thus were "sophisticated," or worldly wise. (We get the word *sophisticated* from this period.) The Sophists knew firsthand about various cultures; they had witnessed a variety of religious practices and had experienced a variety of tastes in clothing, food, family patterns, legal values, and morals.

In many ways, the Sophists can be thought of as the first social scientists, combining, as it were, anthropology, psychology, and sociology to produce a particular view of social life and human nature. Their sophistication was a direct threat to the chauvinistic elite that ruled Athens. The idea that anyone with the fee could be educated was offensive to those who saw themselves as inherently superior.

The Sophists looked closely at "what worked" in various cultures and concluded that virtually nothing was good or bad by nature, but that good and bad were matters of custom and preference. Further, they noticed that although different individuals desire different things, *everyone seeks some form of power*. The Sophists argued that every living thing seeks to be happy and to survive as long as possible, so the only "natural" good is power because power increases control over the conditions of happiness and survival. For instance, getting a new car won't make you happy if you cannot keep it. Being right about something at work won't help if you lack the ability (power) to get your boss to recognize it. Based on such observations, the Sophists concluded that so-called truth is subservient to power.[4]

The Sophists remained professionals, in the sense of always demanding payment, eventually becoming infamous for their insistence on being well paid. It was widely believed that the worst of them would teach anything they could get someone to pay for. The Sophists' reputation also suffered because of their emphasis

If a man were really able to instruct mankind, to receive money for giving instruction would, in my opinion, be an honour to him.

— Socrates

"What Would You Do with the Ring of Gyges?"

The technical name for the view that all morality reduces to self-interest is *egoism*. It is usually associated with moral skepticism, since it is the only source of values left for the moral skeptic. One of the earliest and most interesting presentations of the egoist's position occurs in Plato's *Republic:*

> Even those who practise justice do so against their will because they lack the power to do wrong. This we would realize if we clearly imagined ourselves granting to both the just and the unjust the freedom to do whatever they liked. We could then follow both of them and observe where their desires led them, and we would catch the just man redhanded travelling the same road as the unjust. The reason is the desire for undue gain which every organism by nature pursues as good, but the law forcibly sidetracks him to honour equality. The freedom I just mentioned would most easily occur if these men had the power which they say the ancestor of the Lydian Gyges possessed. The story is that he was a shepherd in the service of the ruler of Lydia. There was a violent rainstorm and an earthquake which broke open the ground and created a chasm at the place where he was tending sheep. Seeing this and marvelling, he went down into it. He saw, besides many other wonders of which we are told, a hollow bronze horse. There were window-like openings in it; he climbed through one of them and caught sight of a corpse which seemed of more than human stature, wearing nothing but a ring of gold on its finger. This ring the shepherd put on and came out.

He arrived at the usual monthly meeting which reported to the king on the state of the flocks, wearing the ring. As he was sitting among the others he happened to twist the hoop of the ring towards himself, to the inside of his hand, and as he did this he became invisible to those sitting near him and they went off talking as if he had gone. He marvelled at this and, fingering the ring, turned the hoop outward again and became visible. Perceiving this he tested whether the ring had this power and so it happened: if he turned the hoop inwards he became invisible, but he was visible when he turned it outwards. When he realized this, he at once arranged to become one of the messengers of the king. He went, committed adultery with the king's wife, attacked the king with her help, killed him, and took over the kingdom.

> Now if there were two such rings, one worn by the just man, the other by the unjust, no one, as these people think, would be so incorruptible that he would stay on the path of justice or bring himself to keep away from other people's property and not touch it, when he could with impunity take whatever he wanted from the market, go into houses and have sexual relations with anyone he wanted, kill anyone, free all those he wished from prison, and do other things which would make him like a god among men.

Plato, **Republic**, trans. G. M. A. Grube (Indianapolis: Hackett, 1974), p. 32f.

on winning debates in and out of court at all costs. Since they believed that power was the ultimate value, the key issue became not right or wrong, but getting your own way.

As the Sophists became expert debaters and advertisers, they learned to use emotional appeals, physical appearance, and clever language to sell their particular point of view. These characteristics have led to the modern meaning of a **sophistry** as an example of overly subtle, superficially plausible, but ultimately fallacious reasoning. Plato characterizes the Sophist this way:

> First, I believe he was found to be a paid hunter after the young and wealthy... secondly a kind of merchant in articles of knowledge for the soul...third did he not turn up as a retailer of these same articles of knowledge?...and in the fourth place

sophistry
The teachings and practices of the original Sophists; modern usage refers to subtle, plausible, but fallacious reasoning used to persuade rather than discover truth.

> *The art of the Sophist is the semblance of wisdom without the reality, and the Sophist is one who makes money from an apparent but unreal wisdom.*
> — Aristotle

we found he was a seller of his own products of knowledge...and in the fifth he was an athlete in contests of words, who had taken for his own the art of disputation...the sixth case was doubtful, but nevertheless we agreed to consider him a purger of souls, who removes opinions that obstruct learning.[5]

Socrates (Chapter 4), the first great Western philosopher, lived at the same time as the Sophists and was also a famous educator. He often had what he claimed were *discussions* with Sophists; the Sophists, however, thought they were *contests*. Many Athenians weren't sure whether Socrates was a Sophist or a *sophos*. Socrates himself, though, was clear on one thing: It is wrong to charge money for teaching philosophy. He said:

> [I believe] that it is possible to dispose of beauty or of wisdom alike honorably or dishonorably; for if a person sells his beauty for money to anyone who wishes to purchase it, men call him a male prostitute; but if anyone makes a friend of a person whom he knows to be an honorable and worthy admirer, we regard him as prudent. In like manner those who sell their wisdom for money to any that will buy, men call sophists, or, as it were, prostitutes of wisdom; but whoever makes a friend of a person whom he knows to be deserving, and teaches him all the good that he knows, we consider him to act the part which becomes a good and honorable citizen.[6]

PHILOSOPHICAL QUERY

Discuss some of the pros and cons of personal education versus commercialized education. Try to consider a variety of factors: efficiency; effects of money on pupils, teachers, and institutions; mediocrity; conformity. Do you agree that it is wrong to "sell wisdom"? Is it realistic to expect teachers (or philosophers) to teach for free, for love only? Can't any source of financial support lead to bias? Must it?

Relativism

relativism
The belief that knowledge is determined by specific qualities of the observer, including age, ethnicity, gender, and cultural conditioning.

The Sophists were among the first systematic thinkers to conclude that the truth is relative. **Relativism** is the belief that knowledge is determined by specific qualities of the observer. The Sophists, for example, claimed that place of birth, family habits, personal abilities and preferences, religious training, age, and so forth control an individual's beliefs, values, and even perceptions. (Don't confuse relativism with subjectivism, the belief that we can only know our own sensations.)

Based on this tenet, the Sophists argued that we need only accept what, according to our culture, seems true at the moment. The most extreme Sophists claimed that even within the same culture, individuals have their own truths. The consequences of this position can be unsettling, to say the least. If no ultimate truth exists, no moral code is universally correct or absolutely superior to any other. The Sophists taught that each culture (or individual!) only *believes* that its ways are best, but the person who has studied many cultures *knows* better: One way is as good as another if you believe in it.

There are two basic variants of relativism: cultural and individual. *Cultural relativism* is the belief that all values are culturally determined. Values do not reflect a divine order or a natural pattern, but merely the customs and preferences that develop in a given culture. Thus, what is right in America is not necessarily right in Saudi Arabia or Brazil. Your grandmother's sexual morality was right for a particular person at a particular time and place, but not for all people all the time and in every place. What is right for a twenty-year-old African American woman will be different from what is right for a ninety-year-old Chinese American man, and so on. Consequently, what's right for you may very well be different from what's right for people of different ages and backgrounds.

Individual relativism simply carries the logic of cultural relativism to a more radical conclusion. It goes like this: Even in the same place and time, right and wrong are relative to the unique experiences and preferences of the individual. There is no unbiased way to say that one standard is better than another because the standard used to make that claim is itself the reflection of a preference, ad infinitum. No matter how far back we push "ultimate" reasons, they always reduce to someone's preference. Hence, moral and social values are matters of individual taste and opinion.

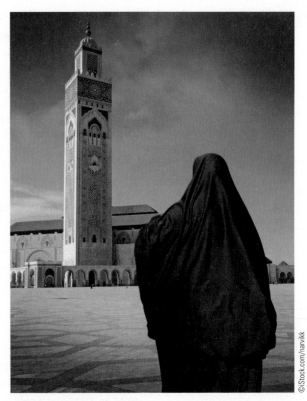

Comparing the lifestyle and beliefs of this contemporary Islamic woman to those of contemporary American women shows how difficult it is to dispute the Sophists' claim that all values are culturally determined.

Discussing Philosophy

PHILOSOPHICAL QUERY

Today, some English teachers hesitate to impose "relative" standards of English grammar. They see all grammar—dialects, that is—as "preferences" Do you agree? Ask your English teacher about the notion of imposing standards.

Protagoras the Pragmatist

Perhaps the greatest of the Sophists was **Protagoras** of Abdera (481–411 B.C.E.). Attracted to Athens around the middle of the fifth century B.C.E., he became a famous teacher there. He was befriended by wealthy and powerful Athenians and, consequently, became rich and powerful himself. Plato even named a dialogue after him.

Protagoras was an archetypal Sophist: an active traveler and first-rate observer of other cultures who noted that although there are a variety of customs and beliefs, each culture believes unquestioningly that its own ways are right—and roundly condemns (or at least criticizes) views that differ from its own. So he asked himself,

Protagoras

"It's All Relative. Period!"

If ethical relativism is correct, it is clearly impossible for the moral beliefs of a society to be mistaken because the certainty of the majority that its beliefs were right would prove that those beliefs were right for that society at that time. The minority view would therefore be mistaken, no matter what it was. Needless to say, most people who state that "in morals everything is relative" and who proceed to call themselves ethical relativists are unaware of these implications of their theory....

"What is right in one group is wrong in another," he says. But what exactly is a group? and which group is one to select? Every person is a member of many different group—his nation, his state, his city, his club, his school, church, fraternity, or athletic association. Suppose that most of the people in his club think that a certain kind of act is wrong and that most of the people in his nation think it is right; what then?

Probably most people who call themselves ethical relativists are not so at all, for they believe in one moral standard which applies in different ways to different societies because of the various conditions in which they live. One might as well talk about gravitational relativism because a stone falls and a balloon rises; yet both events are equally instances of one law of universal gravitation.

John Hospers, **Human Conduct: Problems of Ethics** (Belmont, Ca.: Wadsworth Publishing), 1995, pp. 33–35.

"What really makes something right or wrong? Is anything really right or wrong? What is truth? Can we know it? Can we know that we know it, or are we limited to mere beliefs?" His answers may strike you as surprisingly contemporary. And they are—as the term *Sophist* suggests—quite sophisticated.

Based on his observations and travels, Protagoras concluded that morals are nothing more than the social traditions, or mores, of a society or group. What makes the Athenian way right for someone living in Athens is that following the mores of one's place is the best way to live successfully and well—in that place. The task of the truly wise observer is to record accurately and describe without bias what works and what does not work. Hence, the famous remark quoted at the beginning of this chapter: Man is the measure of all things. Here is how Plato reported Socrates' characterization of what Protagoras meant:

> Well, is not this what [Protagoras] means, that individual things are for me such as they appear to me, and for you in turn such as they appear to you—you and I being "man"?... Is it not true that sometimes, when the same wind blows, one of us feels cold and the other does not? or one feels slightly and the other exceedingly cold?... Then in that case, shall we say that the wind is in itself cold or not cold; or shall we accept Protagoras' saying that it is cold for him who feels cold, not for him who does not?[7]

pragmatism
From the Greek for "deed"; ideas have meaning or truth value to the extent that they produce practical results and effectively further our aims; empirically based philosophy that defines knowledge and truth in terms of practical consequences.

Protagoras predicted a crucial tenet of modern social science: Our values are determined by our culture, our conditioning, our experience, and our particular biopsychology. It is, according to Protagoras, utterly impossible to form a culture-free or context-free belief. For instance, philosophy students born, raised, and educated in Moscow, Russia, cannot help but "see" a different world than do those born, raised, and educated in Moscow, Idaho.

Thus, the useful issue is not what is true, since true always means "true for the believer." If Student A believes something, that alone makes it true from her perspective. The worthwhile issue is what "works" for Student A, not what is universally true or what "works" for Student B. The point of view that beliefs are to be interpreted in terms of "whether they work" (their usefulness) is called **pragmatism**, from the Greek *pragma*, "deed." Pragmatic ideas have meaning or truth value to the extent that they produce practical results and are effective in furthering our aims. (See Chapter 15.)

Plato criticized Protagoras for—in Plato's view—reducing the concept of what is useful to whatever people *think* is useful. Of course, Protagoras could respond to Plato this way: "What is useful if not useful to some particular individual, at some particular place and time? What sense is there in talking about 'useful in general'? Useful always means useful for the specific purposes and desires of an individual. And even for individuals, what is useful changes."

In a speech Plato attributes to Protagoras, the Sophist makes his case that *wisdom is what works:*

> For I maintain that the truth is as I have written; each one of us is the measure of the things that are and those that are not; but each person differs immeasurably from every other in just this, that to one person some things appear and are, and to another person other things...do not lay too much stress upon the words of my argument, but get a clearer understanding of my meaning from what I am going to say. Recall to your mind what was said before, that his food appears and is bitter to the sick man, but appears and is the opposite of bitter to the man in health. Now neither of these two is to be made wiser than he is—that is not possible—nor should the claim be made that the sick man is ignorant because his opinions are ignorant, or the healthy man wise because his opinions are different; but a change must be made from the one condition to the other, for the other is better. So, too, in education a change has to be made from a worse condition to a better condition; but the physician causes the change by means of drugs, and the teacher of wisdom by means of words.... And on the same principle the teacher who is able to train his pupils in this manner is not only wise but is also entitled to receive high pay from them when their education is finished. And in this sense it is true that some men are wiser than others, and that no one thinks falsely, and that you, whether you will or no, must...be a measure. Upon these positions my doctrine stands firm.[8]

Jenny Goodall/Newscom

Protagoras's claim that "each one of us is the measure," because truth is a matter of perception, is dramatically and tragically illustrated in the case of Vikki Hensley, who is twenty-three years old in this photo. Because Hensley began her radical diet before she reached puberty, her body remains that of a twelve-year-old child. In today's fat obsessed world, anorexics see themselves as obese no matter how thin they are and, in the most extreme cases, would rather die than become obese. Do you think our culture suffers from a kind of collective anorexia nervosa, and, if so, does that mean that the individual, not the doctor or scientist, is the measure of health? Are widespread concerns about nutrition, weight, and appearance "reasonable" or just present-day trends and preferences?

PHILOSOPHICAL QUERY

Analyze Protagoras's speech. Has he convinced you? Explain. See if you can identify the trick used by both Protagoras and his pupil in the Wager (see the "Protagoras's Wager" box).

" Protagoras's Wager "

Competitiveness and boldness flourished among the Sophists as they competed for prestige and paying students. This is not surprising given their emphasis on power, winning, and relativism. Moreover, because the Sophists chose to be public figures, seeking fame and influence, they were always eager to show off their abilities. They used their speaking skills to attack one another and attract students. Whenever possible, they spoke to large audiences, whether in the Assembly or in the public square. The average Athenian found these sparring matches entertaining at first. As you will learn, however, Athenians soon regarded the Sophists as disturbing and dangerous. A famous example of sophistic sparring is the story known as *Protagoras's Wager*.

It seems that Protagoras had a pupil named Eulathus, who arranged to take Protagoras's course in rhetoric and sophistry, a kind of law school, for partial tuition. So sure was Protagoras of his abilities as a teacher that he told Eulathus he did not have to pay the balance until Eulathus won his first court case. In fact, Protagoras guaranteed that Eulathus would win his first case.

Time dragged on, and Eulathus neither paid up nor argued any cases in court. Not only was Protagoras out the money, he looked bad to his students and to other Sophists. After all, if winning is what counts, and if appearance is reality, and if the pupil can outmaneuver the old master, why should anyone continue to pay his high fees? Protagoras was compelled to act.

Confronting Eulathus (probably in a public place where he could use his crowd-pleasing skills), Protagoras demanded payment in the form of this dilemma: "Eulathus, you might as well pay me, since I am going to sue you for the rest of the tuition. If I win in court, the court will rule that you owe me the money; if I lose in court, you will have won your first case, and you will owe me the money. Either I win in court or I lose, so either you owe me the money or you owe me the money."

Protagoras, alas, was a good teacher, and Eulathus was ready for him. He shot back with a counterdilemma: "No, sir, you have it backwards. If you defeat me in court, then I have lost my first case and so do not owe the money; if I defeat you, the court will rule that I do not owe you the money. Either I defeat you or you defeat me. In either case, I do not owe you the money."

Who won? The story does not tell us. And besides, Sophists being what they were, neither Eulathus nor Protagoras would have wanted to lose big in a highly publicized trial. Protagoras's Wager gives us an instructive glimpse of sophistry in action. Such encounters were common, as Sophists vied for students and reputation. To the general citizenry, these encounters were sometimes amusing entertainment. Men like Protagoras lived rather mild lives considering what they taught and the reactions their excitable pupils had to their ideas. But when the same kinds of tricks were used for high stakes—say, to convict innocent citizens, to control democracy, to wrest property away from people—no one laughed. Sophistry's reputation grew darker.

> *It is only about things that do not interest one that one can give a really unbiased opinion, which is no doubt the reason why an unbiased opinion is always valueless.*
>
> —Oscar Wilde

Protagoras was a rather tame Sophist. He reasoned that the most intelligent thing to do is to accept the customs and beliefs of your own community. By understanding that the mores of the community are not universal absolutes, you will develop a relaxed, effective attitude about them. This in turn will allow you to use them rather than be controlled by them. Openly flouting convention is most likely to be counterproductive. With the rare exceptions of talented and charismatic individuals, *behaving in a generally conventional way affords us the most social power.*

Dress the way that will get you promoted at work or get you a date at the club. Write the kind of essay your teacher wants, and you'll get a good grade; write your own creative masterpiece, and you might not. Don't attract attention when driving, and you'll most likely avoid legal complications. If you want to get elected in a conservative community, go to church and keep your hair neat and unostentatious.

But what if you want to succeed in a less conservative, or even a radical, community? No matter. Simply conform to your target audience's norms and expectations because customs and norms are just that—particularized, evolving, relative patterns and social expectations. A sophisticated and effective seller of ideas, products, and political practices offers his or her audience whatever it will buy. If your present community prides itself on being unconventional or radical, then by all means conform to the role of being radical. To a sophisticated, pragmatic practitioner of sophistry, there is no contradiction here in conforming to nonconformism. Only naive true believers are lulled into thinking that their beliefs are "true" and "good" and "healthy" without qualification or context.

The spirit of Protagoras is discernable in our own day among paid political consultants who teach their clients to present whatever carefully crafted persona works to further their goals: In a radical community, that persona calls out for social change and attacks "the Establishment" and the power elite—in the name of fairness and common sense. In a conservative community, the effective persona appeals to tradition, faith, and family values—in the name of fairness and common sense. In both communities, today's sophists insist that they—and they alone—represent, care about, and understand what we, the "American people," want, need, and deserve. Just like Protagoras would advise them to—if that is what works.

Tradition has it that Protagoras did not always follow his own advice. The story goes that at the home of a friend, Protagoras gave a reading of one of his own treatises called *On the Gods*. This particular work applied the principle of relativism to religious belief, apparently holding religion to the pragmatic standard. There was no separation of church and state in Athens at this time. Failure to believe in and respect "the gods of the state" was considered a form of treason known as impiety. One of the other guests, a conservative army officer, was so offended by Protagoras's ideas that he consequently had Protagoras indicted for impiety. Protagoras was found guilty. All copies of *On the Gods* were confiscated and burned, and the authorities set out to confiscate Protagoras, too. Facing death or exile, he attempted to escape on a ship headed for Sicily. The ship was wrecked, and Protagoras drowned.

> *As to the Gods I have no means of knowing that they exist or that they do not exist.*
> — Protagoras

Moral Realism: Might Makes Right

In contrast to Protagoras, the next generation of Sophists carried moral relativism to the more radical level of **moral realism**, a pragmatic social philosophy unfettered by any moral considerations.

The laws of every society, says the moral realist, turn out to reflect the interests of those in power. The U.S. Constitution, for example, places great emphasis on property rights and protections because most of its chief architects were landed gentry: persons with property. Hence their view of the "ideal" state reflected and furthered their material interests. Each new Supreme Court reflects the values of the majority of its members, now liberal, now conservative. The "right" view is the view held by those currently in power. The rest of us, says the moral realist, ultimately obey because we have to; we have no other choice: Regardless of whether we believe that what is legal is also right, the average person obeys anyway because he or she lacks sufficient power (and courage) not to obey.

From a certain perspective, history seems to support the view that might and power determine right. But what about counterexamples like the civil rights

moral realism
A pragmatic social philosophy unfettered by moral considerations; expressed in the formula "might makes right."

> *When Aesop's lion was shown a painting in which a man was depicted killing a lion, he commented contemptuously, "The artist was obviously a man."*
> — B. F. Skinner

> *The majority of just acts according to the law are prescribed contrary to nature. For there is legislation about the eyes, what they must see and what not; and about the ears, what they must hear and what not; and about the tongue, what it must speak and what not; and about the hands, what they must do and what not; and about the feet, where they must go and where not. And about the soul, what it must desire and what not.*
>
> —Antiphon

MindTap
Discussing Philosophy

movement of the 1960s? Here "right" finally prevailed, even against centuries of custom and habit that supported racist practices. This example seems to show that moral progress is possible and that not everyone acts from limited self-interest.

A contemporary Sophist could point out, however, that civil rights changes occurred in this country only after members of the powerful white middle class began to support the position of the nonwhite minorities. The view of the most powerful faction of the time won. Civil might made civil rights. The same is true of women's rights. Women's rights have increased in proportion to women's power. African Americans, Hispanic Americans, Asian Americans, and other groups have rights in direct proportion to their might. The elderly will have more rights in the future because they will outnumber members of other age groups for years to come. In recent years, states have increasingly broadened the definition of marriage to include same-sex marriage. Gender rights advocates are calling for the expansion of gender-equity rights for transgendered and transsexual individuals. Medical marijuana advocates are working to extend the right to grow and smoke marijuana. As the number of undocumented or illegal immigrants grows, so do concerns over what constitutes the "right" to vote or have a driver's license. And so it goes. Your philosophy instructor has more power over your philosophy course than you do. Thus—ultimately—her interpretation of your test is more "right" than yours. Her answers are more "useful" than yours. Parents are "right" about many things simply because they have more power than children. Whoever has power gets to be right. Or so it seems.

PHILOSOPHICAL QUERY

Is "might makes right" the only explanation for social changes like the civil rights movement? Could other factors besides self-interest account for a shift in basic social values? What factors? Is anything lost by accepting a might-makes-right interpretation? Is anything gained? Explain.

The Doctrine of the Superior Individual

Not everybody willingly submits to those in power or depends on a group for clout. Those who do not are well represented by a Sophist named **Callicles** (c. 435 B.C.E.). His version of moral realism goes by different names: the doctrine of the superior individual, the true man, the natural man, the superman. You may recognize foreshadowings of Nazism, racism, and religious intolerance in the doctrine of the superior individual. It is always *elitist*, but it is not always a *racial* doctrine. Indeed, in its most compelling form, it is highly individualistic, holding that a person is superior not because of ethnic or cultural background but only because of individual virtues and traits. (We will study one of the most notorious expressions of this view in Chapter 16.)

Callicles distinguished what is right by nature from what is right by convention. In the following selection from Plato's *Gorgias*, Callicles asserts that by nature the strong dominate the weak, whereas conventional morality tries to restrain the superior, strong, truly powerful individual. In nature, the survival of the fittest is the rule. This, said Sophists such as Callicles, shows that power is the ultimate value and that the superior and powerful individual has a natural right to dominate others. All people are no more created equal than all animals are.

> For to suffer wrong is not the part of a man at all, but that of a slave for whom it is better to be dead than alive, as it is for anyone who is unable to come either to his own assistance when he is wronged or mistreated or to that of anyone he cares about. I can quite imagine that the manufacturers of laws and conventions are the weak, the majority, in fact. It is for themselves and their own advantage that they make their laws and distribute their praises and their censures. It is to frighten men who are stronger than they and able to enforce superiority that they keep declaring, to prevent aggrandizement, that this is ugly and unjust, that injustice consists in seeking to get the better of one's neighbor. They are quite content, I suppose, to be on equal terms with others since they are themselves inferior.
>
> This, then, is the reason why convention declares that it is unjust and ugly to seek to get the better of the majority. But my opinion is that nature herself reveals it to be only just and proper that the better man should lord it over his inferior: It will be the stronger over the weaker. Nature, further, makes it quite clear in a great many instances that this is the true state of affairs, not only in the other animals, but also in whole states and communities. This is, in fact, how justice is determined: The stronger shall rule and have the advantage over his inferior. . . .

Even today, with all of our "sophisticated" understanding of the world and our technology, many of us find the natural world haunting, beckoning, awe-inspiring. Just imagine what thoughts and feelings a starry sky might have inspired in the psyche of a Heraclitus, Parmenides, Democritus, or Thales. How could they not help but wonder, not help but begin to philosophize? Is it any wonder that we wonder?

"Darrow's Cigar"

An apocryphal story about the legendary lawyer Clarence Darrow circulates among law students: Darrow had to defend an especially unsavory client. This was a hard case to make. As the prosecutor ranted and raved to the jury about the heinous nature of the crime and the plight of the suffering victims, Darrow paid him close and courteous attention, puffing distractedly on a large cigar. The ash grew, an eighth of an inch, a quarter, a half, an inch or more—yet did not fall. Darrow didn't seem to notice. He just politely concentrated on the prosecutor's words. But the jury noticed. Instead of paying full attention to the prosecutor, they were drawn again and again to Darrow's cigar—into which he had secretly inserted a thin piece of wire.

One sophistry used by contemporary Darrows is having their clients dress "persuasively." Wealthy defendants

Erik and Lyle Menendez often wore "college boy" crewneck sweaters at their trials for killing their parents.

O. J. Simpson testified that he could not pay the $30 million civil judgment against him while uncharacteristically wearing inexpensive shoes—and slacks with a hole in the backside.

Sophists were also notorious for "making the better argument appear the worse" by playing word games. Of course, what's a "word game" and what's "being precise" is itself the sort of issue sophists addressed. In 1998, then-president Bill Clinton came under scrutiny for answering a question about whether or not he was having sexual relations with Monica Lewinsky by stating that the answer "depends on what the meaning of 'is' is." Some commentators accused President Clinton of sophistry. What do you think?

> Now, my dear friend, take my advice: Stop your [philosophy], take up the Fine Art of Business, and cultivate something that will give you a reputation for good sense. Leave all these over-subtleties to someone else. Should one call them frivolities or just plain nonsense? They'll only land you in a house where you'll be the only visitor! You must emulate, not those whose very refutations are paltry, but men of substance and high repute and everything else that is good.[9]

Discussing Philosophy

Aplia

PHILOSOPHICAL QUERY

Is some part of you stirred by all this talk of power and superiority? The Sophists would say that if you can be honest, you'll answer in the affirmative. What might prevent you (in the Sophists' view) from admitting that you agree with them? Are they correct? Even if you personally reject Callicles' position, how common do you think it is? Lastly, what do you think of the Sophists' overall assessment of the way society really operates? Are they onto something or not? What's your evidence?

Commentary

The questions raised by the Sophists are important, not just in the dusty archives of scholarly concerns but also because of the continuing influence sophistic ideas exert on our lives and beliefs. Sophists helped free the Greeks to think on new, less restricted levels. From this beginning emerged a nonreligious (amoral) scientific method as well as a philosophic method of questioning, both of which are free to pursue knowledge for its own sake and wherever it leads. The Sophists laid the cornerstone for the scientific study of human behavior—what would become the social, psychological, political, and anthropological sciences. In other words, the Sophists helped break the shackles of dogma and superstition. For that, we remain in their debt.

The Sophists' emphasis on the individual as determiner of value and the challenges Sophists posed to the possibility of a moral absolute contributed to increased democracy in Athens. Thus, the Sophists were perceived as a direct threat by the "establishment" of privileged aristocrats.

The youth of Athens responded with gusto to these ideas, treating them as a call to unrestrained self-assertion and personal freedom. It was stimulating to challenge the stuffy, square, straight, uptight values of the establishment. The glorification of the "superior individual" or "natural man" appealed to adolescent cravings for power, fame, freedom, and identity.

Logic and the rhetorical devices refined by the Sophists were liberally applied to legal maneuvering, politics, techniques of manipulation, and control of the marketplace. By the third generation, Sophists no longer claimed to be *sophistai*, teachers of wisdom, but advertised shortcuts to guaranteed social, political, financial, and personal success. These Sophists were the forerunners of today's how-to-succeed, you-can-have-it-all books, courses, and techniques. Freed of any moral anchor, the most ruthless Sophists were often deadly and effective. They took no responsibility for the ways people might use their ideas, as the great Sophist Gorgias reminds us:

> And if a man learns rhetoric, and then does injustice through the power of his art, we shall not be right, in my opinion, in detesting and banishing his teacher. For while the teacher imparted instruction to be used rightly, the pupil made a contrary use of it. Therefore, it is only right to detest the misuser and banish and kill him, not his teacher.[10]

Although they were attacked by Plato and others on moral grounds, most Sophists were actually amoral (nonmoral) rather than immoral. Like the caricature of a mob attorney who uses all his persuasive skills to vigorously and lucratively defend known drug dealers and crime bosses, the Sophists made no moral judgments. They were concerned only with "what worked." They saw the world as hard and brutal, a jungle. Because, in their view, the restraints and inhibitions of morality weaken us, the Sophists refused to acknowledge any moral prohibitions. In contemporary terms, they were masters of "effective" thinking, communicating, and acting.

Many sophistic techniques, like Darrow's cigar, are genuinely clever and clearly effective. The Sophists of ancient Athens inspired mixed feelings of awe and admiration, anger and disgust. They raised vital, ongoing questions: When the stakes are high, is playing fair the smart thing to do? Just how important is winning? And how should we be judged? On the conventional morals most of us profess? Or on the values we actually practice and (secretly?) admire: strength, power, daring, attractiveness, social contacts, success? Can we ever have objective knowledge or escape the limits of culture? In the absence of certainty, might it be better to allow more individual choice rather than less?

Throughout this chapter we've noted the Sophists' interest in important social, political, and philosophical matters. Often, such "big issues" don't engage us

---

Go about with your middle finger up and people will say you're daft; go about with your little finger out, and they will cultivate your company.
— Diogenes

Fools shiver with excitement about everything they hear.
—Heraclitus

It is impossible to defeat an ignorant man in argument.
— William G. McAdoo

personally precisely because they are big. It is as if they are "out there," affecting us only now and then, perhaps during philosophy class or political discussions or periods of reflection. They are, as it were, at a distance. From a distance, the Sophists are exciting, daring, brave, and brutally honest. But we've also seen how the Sophists' emphasis on rhetoric, convention, and persuasion attracted individuals whose interests were crudely pragmatic, personally ambitious, short-sighted, socially indifferent, venal, and close to home. These small-s sophists are uninterested in philosophical discussions of might making right or various forms of relativism or justice. No. Their goals are worldly and immediate. Today, when people talk about sophists they usually mean only win-at-any-cost, small-s sophists, the kind who treat their targets—be they customers, voters, jurors, objects of sexual or romantic interest—as mere means to ends. (See Chapter 11 for more about treating persons as means only.)

As you reflect on the philosophical archetype of the Sophist, think about its place in today's world. As you are probably realizing, the similarities between the cultural climate of ancient Athens and that of contemporary America are widespread and deeply rooted. The Sophists represent one side of the timeless struggle between "the world" and wisdom. Because we all face this struggle, we're not just learning about the past, about dead ideas, but we are also learning about living issues.

As the original Sophists grew in numbers and boldness, they attracted more and more enemies. Unable to distinguish sophistic philosophies from other forms, the citizens of Athens began to agree with each other that philosophy itself was unacceptably subversive. Philosophy's reputation for being somehow unpatriotic and dangerous was established. Into this breach stepped perhaps the single most influential and arresting philosopher of all, the first major philosopher of the West: Socrates.

Summary of Main Points

- As Athens grew in influence it attracted more and more people from other city-states and countries. Opportunities for a growing number of Athenians to speak before the Assembly created a demand for specialized education in subjects such as letters, rhetoric, science, statesmanship, and philosophy.

- Those who considered themselves original, true Athenians became increasingly ethnocentric. Ethnocentrism is the tendency to consider one's own customs and values as superior to all others.

- The Sophists were the first professional educators, a group of wandering teachers who charged a fee to teach anyone who wished to study with them. Sophists argued that the difference between a good argument and a bad argument is custom and individual preference.

- The Sophists believed that virtually nothing is good or bad by nature, but only by custom and preference. They argued that truth is relative and that knowledge is determined by specific qualities of the observer. Cultural relativism is the belief that all values are culturally determined. Individual relativism is the belief that even in the same place and time, right and wrong are relative to the unique experiences and preferences of the individual.

- Protagoras of Abdera was one of the most influential of the Sophists. He said that morals are nothing more than the social traditions, or mores, of a society or group and that following local mores is the best way to live successfully and well—in that place. Hence his famous remark: *Man is the measure of all things.*

- Later generations of Sophists carried moral relativism to more radical levels than Protagoras did. Moral realism is the belief that all values reflect the interests of the strong. Certain values dominate because they are the views preferred by the most powerful individual or group, not because they are in some absolute sense "right." Callicles was a Sophist associated with an aspect of moral realism known as the doctrine of the superior individual, which holds that nature dictates that the strong should dominate the weak.

Post-Reading Reflections

Now that you've had a chance to learn about the Sophists, use your new knowledge to answer these questions.

1. If, as Protagoras claimed, all opinions are true, why discuss them? What grounds does a relativist have for being angry when others dispute her beliefs? Does she need any grounds? If not, what follows?

2. Is there any merit to the claim that modern colleges and universities are sophistic in their attempts to compete for students by teaching whatever they will pay to learn? Do you think there is a conflict of interest in charging students tuition *and* grading them honestly? That is, might schools be reluctant to flunk out paying customers—er, I mean, students?

3. Is there any way to refute the idea that "might makes right"? Why is this question more complicated than it might seem at first glance?

4. Suppose it were discovered that Protagoras secretly violated many of his teachings. Would this affect your attitude toward his philosophy? How? Why?

5. Are lawyers Sophists? Are advertisers? In what ways are these professions susceptible to sophistry? Explain.

6. Today, the terms *sophist* and *sophistry* are usually used as criticisms of those whom we distrust for having ulterior motives or a win-at-all-costs attitude. Have the Sophists been given a bad rap? Why or why not? Is sophistry always wrong? If not, when is sophistry warranted and why?

7. Does the fact that politicians carefully craft their messages, speaking styles, clothing, hair, and personae to sell themselves make them sophists— or just practical? Are there social consequences to the *perception* that politicians are sophists?

 MindTap

Experience MindTap through the activities highlighted in this chapter. Further explore this online, personalized learning tool to deepen your comprehension and improve your grades.

4

The Wise Man
Socrates

I do not suppose that I know.
— *Socrates*

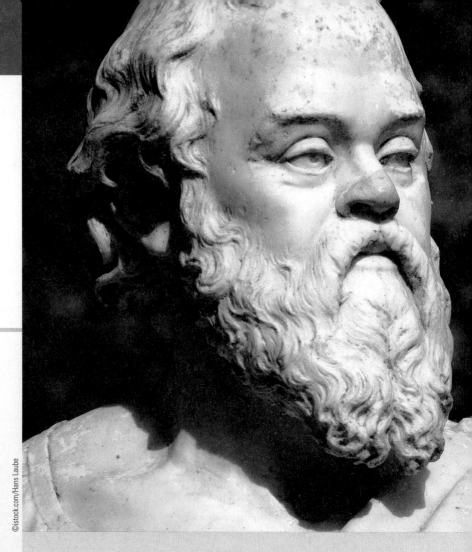

©istock.com/Hans Laube

Learning Objectives

 MindTap

After you complete this chapter, you should be able to:

- Explain the Socratic problem.
- Define the concept of the *paradigmatic individual*.
- Evaluate Socrates' attitude toward social success.
- Summarize the encounter between Socrates and Thrasymachus.
- Describe the Socratic dialectic.
- Identify examples of Socratic irony in his *Apology*.
- Defend the claim that Socrates was a Sophist.
- Criticize the claim that Socrates was a Sophist.
- Justify Socrates' claim of ignorance.
- Differentiate between human wisdom and wisdom.
- Analyze Socratic intellectualism.
- Explain Socrates' last words.

YOU ARE ABOUT TO MEET Socrates (c. 470–399 B.C.E.), one of the most powerful, intriguing, annoying, inspiring, widely known, and yet misunderstood figures in the history of philosophy. He has been called the greatest of philosophers and also the cleverest of Sophists. Stoics, Hedonists, and Cynics (each of whom we shall study in other chapters) have all claimed him as their chief inspiration and model. He was a pagan who is seen by many Jews and Christians as a man of God. His Holiness Tenzin Gyatso, the fourteenth Dalai Lama of Tibetan Buddhism, has expressed respect for him as an enlightened individual. Socrates claimed to have devoted his life to serving his country but was executed as a traitor. He attracted faithful and adoring admirers and was idolized by many young followers, yet the second charge at his trial was "corrupting the youth of Athens." Although he wrote no philosophy himself, he taught and inspired one of the two most influential philosophers in Western history, who in turn taught the other one: Plato and Aristotle.

In his impressive book *Socrates*, the renowned classical scholar W. K. C. Guthrie says, "Any account must begin with the admission that there is, and always will be, a 'Socratic problem.'"[1] In the first place, Socrates wrote nothing. (Or at least nothing philosophical. In *Phaedo*, Plato asserted that Socrates wrote a hymn to Apollo and versified some of Aesop's fables while in prison.)[2] Our two main sources of information about Socrates are the dialogues of his most brilliant and famous pupil, Plato, and the anecdotes and memoirs of a less philosophical soldier, Xenophon. In addition, briefer references to Socrates appear in Aristotle, Aristophanes, and elsewhere. The "Socratic problem" is compounded because Socrates' philosophy was nearly inseparable from the way his whole personality was reflected in his spoken teachings and the conduct of his life. Guthrie says, "In spite of the most scientific methods, in the end we must all have to some extent our own Socrates, who will not be precisely like anyone else's."[3]

What will *your* Socrates be like? Perhaps you too will be "stung" by the man who referred to himself as a gadfly (horsefly) sent by "the god" to keep his drowsy fellows alert. Perhaps you too will give birth to a brainchild with the aid of this ancient *sophos* (wise man) who claimed to "teach nothing" but merely to act as a "kind of midwife," helping others draw out the wisdom hidden within them. Or perhaps you too will be annoyed—even angered—at the sophistic arrogance and logical tricks of a dangerous enemy of conventional morality, democracy, and religion. These are just some of the documented reactions to Socrates.

"The fact is," Guthrie says, "that no one was left indifferent by this altogether unusual character: everyone who has written about him was also reacting to him in one way or another."[4] We can still get a basic picture of Socrates, however. For example, even though Plato and Xenophon present almost completely different views of him, we can treat their accounts as honest reflections of Socrates filtered through the minds and experiences of two completely different admirers. Neither account is "inaccurate" as much as incomplete and perhaps exaggerated. By comparing and evaluating various accounts of Socrates, we can get some idea of the man as well as his philosophy. So, let me introduce you to my Socrates.

Philosophy Timelines

> *But I shall be asked, Why do people delight in continually conversing with you? I have told you already, Athenians, the whole truth about this matter: they like to hear the cross-examination of the pretenders to wisdom; there is amusement in it.*
>
> — Socrates

The General Character of Socrates

Plato presents Socrates as an integrated, essentially unambivalent individual who stood clearly for some values and clearly against others. Then, as now, such personal clarity—strong sense of direction and purpose—were attractive to young people (or to anyone else) confused about who they are or want to be. Then, as now, Socrates' consistent respect for justice, integrity, courage, temperance, decency, beauty, and balance was especially appealing in a cultural climate of dizzy excesses, crass materialism, and cutthroat competition for money, power, and prestige. In a complex, sophisticated society in which old values were under siege, the simplicity and clarity of an individual with Socrates' obvious abilities were intriguing, even when they were upsetting. Socrates' guiding motto of "Know thyself" has been challenging to people all over the world and in all historical periods. Socrates struggled with one of the great problems of our time: Who am I? How can I discover my true identity? How shall *I* live?

Against the popular notion of his time (and ours), Socrates taught that beauty and goodness should be determined by usefulness and fitness of function rather than by mere appearance or personal feelings of delight. An interesting illustration of this can be found in his own appearance. Socrates was universally acknowledged to be "extraordinarily ugly"—so ugly, in fact, that he fascinated people. His most notable physical features were a broad, flat, turned-up nose, protruding, staring eyes, thick, fleshy lips, and a belly that he himself characterized as "a stomach rather too large for convenience"[5] and that he elsewhere announced plans to "dance off." His friends compared him to a satyr or an electric eel, whose penetrating questions stunned his listeners, "shocked" them into higher awareness.

Socrates made his appearance serve him well. His humorous references to it reflect his good nature and modesty, as well as his hierarchy of values. If, as he taught, the true self is not the body but the soul (*psyche*), and if *virtue* implies *excellence of function*, then the appearance of the body is less important than how well it functions. True beauty is inner beauty—beauty of spirit and character. In Plato's

Socrates was universally acknowledged to be "extraordinarily ugly."

> *Many are ruined by admirers whose heads are turned by the sight of a pretty face; many are led by their strength to attempt tasks too heavy for them, and meet serious evils; many by their wealth are corrupted, and fall victims to conspiracies; many through glory and political power have suffered great evils.*
>
> — Socrates

This nineteenth-century sculpture of Socrates teaching in the Agora shows the contrast between Socrates' inner beauty and outer ugliness.

Gorgias, Socrates says that we cannot know whether a person is happy just because his external condition is attractive to us. He insists that happiness, like goodness, is a matter of inner qualities:

> Then doubtless you will say, Socrates, that you do not know that even the Great King is happy.
>
> Yes, and I shall be speaking the truth; for I do not know how he stands in point of interior formation and justice.
>
> Why, does happiness entirely consist of that?
>
> Yes, by my account, Polus; for a good and honorable man or woman, I say, is happy, and an unjust and wicked one is wretched.[6]

Don't think Socrates was a prude. He was not. He was tempted by physical attractiveness, but he governed his life according to "true beauty and goodness," preferring a good and beautiful soul to a pleasing body that housed a lesser self.

PHILOSOPHICAL QUERY

One of my college friends resembled Socrates. I first noticed him in the cafeteria. I thought he was one of the most unfortunate-looking persons I had ever seen. He knew some acquaintances of mine, and so I eventually met him. I initially felt uncomfortable even being around him because of his looks, I'm sorry to say. But, slowly I discovered an intelligent, funny, kind, strong, and courageous man. Over the years of our friendship, I lost the capacity to see him as ugly. Sadly, the converse has been true in my experience as well. A beautiful or handsome countenance that belongs to a slothful or self-centered or shallow or cruel person over time becomes less handsome or beautiful to me. Have you noticed this pattern in yourself? Analyze it, if you have.

An informative and humorous passage from Chapter 5 of Xenophon's *Symposium* illustrates how Socrates could incorporate philosophy into anything, even joking around with friends. Socrates is engaged in a good-natured "beauty contest" with a handsome young man named Critobulus. Critobulus has challenged Socrates to use his famous question-and-answer method (we'll look at this shortly) to prove that Socrates is "more beautiful" than Critobulus.

> *Critobulus:* All right, but which of our noses is the more beautiful?
>
> *Socrates:* Mine, I should say, if the gods give us noses to smell with, for your nostrils point to earth, but mine are spread out widely to receive odours from every quarter.
>
> *Critobulus:* But how can a snub nose be more beautiful than a straight one?
>
> *Socrates:* Because it does not get in the way but allows the eyes to see what they will, whereas a high bridge walls them off, as if to spite them.
>
> *Critobulus:* As for the mouth, I give in, for if mouths are made for biting you could take a much larger bite than I.
>
> *Socrates:* And with my thick lips don't you think I could give a softer kiss?

Critobulus: By your account I seem to have a mouth uglier than an ass's....
I give up. Let's put it to the vote, so that I may know as quickly as possible the forfeit I have to pay.[7]

When the votes were counted, Socrates lost unanimously, prompting him to accuse Critobulus of bribing the judges.

For Deeper Consideration

As you read about Socrates, take seriously the possibility of encountering a truly wise individual—not just a "sort of wise" person or a "really smart" person, but a person who fits the description of a wise person discussed in this chapter. How do you think you would fare in such an encounter? Would it be "enjoyable"? How can those of us who are not wise recognize and evaluate the truly wise? Is recognizing wisdom different from, say, recognizing strength, in that the recognition of strength does not require being strong, whereas the recognition of wisdom might require at least a modicum of wisdom? Be on the lookout for Socrates' solution to this puzzlement.

Barefoot in Athens

Socrates was usually barefoot and apparently had only one tattered coat, about which his friends joked. His enemies accused him of being "unwashed," and even his friends admitted that it was a surprise to see Socrates freshly bathed. One of his most noted characteristics was hardiness, reflected in remarkable self-control, or *temperance. Temperance* in this sense means indifference to both the presence and absence of material pleasures; it does not mean total abstinence from pleasure or extreme asceticism. In Xenophon's *Memorabilia*, Socrates put it like this:

> You seem, Antiphon, to imagine that happiness consists in luxury and extravagance. But my belief is that *to have no wants is divine; to have as few as possible comes next to the divine;* and as that which is divine is supreme, so that which approaches nearest to its nature is nearest to supreme.[8] [emphasis added]

Socrates' self-control included indifference to fear. During a battle at Delium, he is said to have been the last Athenian soldier to give way before the advancing Spartans. In the Potidaean military campaign, Socrates is reported to have walked about barefoot on the icy winter ground of Thrace, dressed as he customarily was back home. In Plato's *Symposium*, Alcibiades claims that this irritated the other soldiers, who, bundled and muffled against the fierce winter with their feet wrapped in felt and sheepskin, thought Socrates was trying to humiliate them.

In Xenophon's *Memorabilia*, Socrates talks about self-control and self-discipline with his friend Euthydemus. He uses the term *incontinence* in its original sense to mean lack of self-control, especially concerning appetites and passions. Socrates argues that self-control—not self-indulgence and weakness of will—leads to pleasure. Lack of self-control, he asserts, prevents us from the finest expressions of pleasure in eating, drinking, resting, and making love. If we gratify every urge as soon as

"The Sophos at Large"

When Socrates prayed, he asked only for "good gifts, for the gods know best what things are good."

According to Diogenes Läertius, Socrates' style of arguing was sometimes so intense that his opponents frequently attacked him with their fists or tore his hair out, "yet he bore all this ill-usage patiently."

When Alcibiades offered Socrates a large site on which to build a house, he replied, "Suppose, then, I wanted shoes and you offered me a whole hide to make a pair, would it not be ridiculous of me to take it?"

Socrates used to say that he most enjoyed the food that was least in need of seasoning and the drink that made him feel the least desire for another drink, adding that he was as the gods because he had few wants.

When someone asked Socrates whether he should marry or not, the *sophos* replied, "Whichever you do you will repent it."

When Socrates invited some rich men to dinner, his wife Xanthippe said she was embarrassed by the meal she had prepared. "Never mind," he said. "If they are reasonable they will put up with it, if they are good for nothing, we shall not trouble ourselves about them."

When someone said, "Socrates, you are condemned by Athens to die," he responded, "So are you, by nature."

it arises, we must often settle for fast food, cheap drink, sleeping all day, and crude sexual encounters. We will be little more than animals. Without self-control, we have no hope of learning how to moderate ourselves and our lives:

> "The delights of learning something good and excellent, and of studying some of the means whereby a man knows how to regulate his body well and manage his household successfully, to be useful to his friends and city and to defeat his enemies—knowledge that yields not only very great benefits but very great pleasures—these are the delights of the self-controlled; but the incontinent have no part in them. For who should we say has less concern with these than he who has no power of cultivating them because all his serious purposes are centered in the pleasures that lie nearest?"
>
> "Socrates," said Euthydemus, "I think you mean that he who is at the mercy of the bodily pleasures has no concern whatever with virtue in any form?"
>
> "Yes, Euthydemus," said Socrates.[9]

Part of Socrates' appeal comes from the fact that he had many of the same desires as the rest of us. They may even have been more intense. So we respond to the effort he must have exerted to keep all his appetites and passions under strict control. His philosophical searching was, consequently, based on a full involvement with life. It was not the product of a withered, passionless mentality. Nor was it based on a naive goody-goody view of the human condition. Socrates knew and loved life at its fullest, wrestling with it and challenging others to join his "enduring quest."

PHILOSOPHICAL QUERY

What do you think of Socrates' views on self-control? Does the current concern with healthy diets, exercise, and so on seem to be in line with what Socrates thought, or are we, perhaps, overdoing it or acting from love of beauty, not self-control? Discuss.

A Most Unusual Father and Husband

Socrates was married to Xanthippe and had three sons. He was seventy years old at the time of his execution; his oldest son was not yet twenty, and the youngest was said to be a small child.[10] We know relatively little of Socrates' home life, but Xanthippe probably had aristocratic connections.

Although he was probably apprenticed as a stonecutter or sculptor by his father, Socrates worked only now and then. He lived off a modest inheritance from his father, consisting of a house and some money, which his best friend Crito invested for him.[11] And while he never took money for teaching (as the Sophists did), he occasionally accepted gifts from his wealthy friends and admirers.

Socrates' well-known contempt for indiscriminate social approval made it a simple matter for him to live comfortably without shoes and with an old coat. But what effect would Socrates' uncommon values have had on his wife and sons? Here was an obviously brilliant, physically powerful man who spent his time wandering about the marketplace asking philosophical questions all day. He seems to have had ample opportunity to eat and drink and mingle with the movers and shakers of Athens, yet he refused to seek political, social, or financial influence.

> *In the world, one cannot have it both ways. If he wants to maintain his good reputation, he must not think of pursuing status and wealth. But if he wants status and riches, he must bear in mind that it will be at the expense of his integrity.*
>
> — Lie Zi

Discussing Philosophy

PHILOSOPHICAL QUERY

How might we explain the fact that many churches and schools are luxurious? Don't both educators and preachers (not to mention gurus and therapists) say that material success does not guarantee happiness? Don't many of them say that the life of the mind or soul is most important? Why, then, do they live as if they don't believe it? There are plenty of famous examples of this inconsistency. Discuss one or two of them. If the Socratic view is wrong, why do so many people give it lip service?

The Archetypal Individual

The combined portraits of Plato and Xenophon reveal Socrates as a master teacher, a man of unusual intellectual force, possessing an integrated self, whose charisma and personal power sprang from more than either mere intellect or personality. In other words, Socrates is a genuine **archetypal individual**, or, in a term coined by philosopher and psychologist Karl Jaspers (1883–1969), a **paradigmatic individual**. Jaspers applied the term to a special class of teachers, philosophers, and religious figures whose nature becomes a standard by which a culture judges the "ideal" human being.

An archetypal or paradigmatic individual is a rare human being whose very nature represents something elemental about the human condition. "The historical reality of [the paradigmatic individual]," says Jaspers, "can be discerned only in [his] extraordinary impact on those who knew [him] and in [his] later echoes."[12] In any encounter with an archetypal individual, the power or force of the whole person is galvanic. This power does not come from a rational argument. It is an experience that almost goes beyond words and cannot be ignored. It triggers not just personal but deep philosophical and spiritual responses in others.

archetypal (paradigmatic) individual
A special class of teachers, philosophers, and religious figures whose nature becomes a standard by which a culture judges the "ideal" human being; a rare human being whose very nature represents something elemental about the human condition.

These human paradigms possess a timeless quality, according to Jaspers. They serve as *archetypal images* for their cultures and usually speak to other cultures as well. Although different cultures and eras produce different archetypes (Jaspers used as his examples Socrates, Confucius, Buddha, and Jesus), *the archetypal individual's very nature demands a response:* What is it to be a human being? What is most important? What is good? How should *I* live?

Jaspers says:

A radical change is experienced and demanded [by paradigmatic individuals]. They are stirred to their depths, by what we do not know. They express what there is no appropriate way of saying. They speak in parables, dialectical contradictions, conversational replies. . . .

Socrates seeks himself and his relation to other men. By his extreme questioning he arouses a real, living certainty that is *not mere knowledge* of something. He transcends the world without negating it. He forges total knowledge, total judgments, contenting himself with a nonknowledge in which truth and reality are actualized.[13] [emphasis added]

In other words, Socrates continued to develop and grow as a person because of his philosophical search. He did not "fragment" himself into two parts, the thinker and the real person. He did not force himself to stick to a rigid theory. He responded anew to each experience. When Jaspers refers to "a nonknowledge," he means that Socrates always insisted that his "wisdom" lay in knowing what he did not know. (We'll look into this important concept shortly.)

Because their very natures "demand response," paradigmatic individuals provoke extreme community reactions: Love and embrace them or reject and exclude them. The paradigmatic individual is more challenging and intense than the mere sage is. We saw in Chapter 2 that the sage was considered "strange" and "alien," *atopos* in Greek. But this kind of strangeness can be trivialized or dismissed as merely odd or eccentric. The paradigmatic individual may be just as "strange" as the sage, but in a manner that is more personally disturbing, more deeply unsettling to our everyday habits and values.

Something about a paradigmatic teacher "shocks" us into a state of uncomfortable, reflective alertness. By actually or very nearly living up to principles that we, too, profess to see as worthy—and by living up to them with remarkable consistency and courage—the mere existence of a "human paradigm" provokes us into wondering how well our own lives reflect our beliefs. In other words, the life and teachings of the paradigmatic individual form a whole, a harmony that precludes the "safe distance" that exists between the lives of more ordinary teachers and their teachings. The paradigmatic figure invites us to close the gap by calling on us to live courageously and honestly according to articulated principles—without excusing ourselves.

For the most part, paradigmatic teachers stand in opposition to moral compromises to our integrity—however that is understood. But living without significant compromise is dangerous and perhaps wrong. In the first place, there is the risk that what appears to be integrity is, in fact, dogmatic rigidity, self-satisfied and self-righteous fanaticism. Then, too, by holding themselves to purportedly high standards, paradigmatic teachers step outside the "norm"—become estranged from the more

> *I found that the men in most repute were all but the most foolish; and that others less esteemed were really wiser and better.*
>
> — Socrates

"What an Extraordinary Effect His Words Have Had on Me"

In Plato's *Symposium*, Alcibiades notes the staggering power of Socrates:

> …when we listen to you, or to someone else repeating what you've said, even if he puts it ever so badly, and never mind whether the person who's listening is man, woman, or child, we're absolutely staggered and bewitched. And speaking for myself, gentlemen, if I wasn't afraid you'd tell me that I was completely bottled, I'd swear on oath what an extraordinary effect his words have had on me—and still do if it comes to that. For the moment I hear him speak I am smitten with a kind of sacred rage…oh, and not only me, but lots of other men.
>
> …He makes me admit that while I'm spending time on politics I am neglecting all the things crying for attention in myself. So I just refuse to listen to him—as if he were one of those Sirens, you know—and get out of earshot as quick as I can, for fear he will keep me sitting listening till I'm positively senile.
>
> And there's one thing I've never felt with anybody else—not the kind of thing you'd expect to find in me, either—and that is a sense of shame. Socrates is the only man in the world that can make me feel ashamed. Because there's no getting away from it, I know I ought to do the things he tells me to, and yet the moment I'm out of his sight I don't care what I do to keep in with the mob. So I dash off like a runaway slave, and keep out of his way as long as I can, and the next time I meet him I remember all that I had to admit the time before, and naturally I feel ashamed. There are times when I'd honestly be glad to hear that he's dead, and yet I know that if he did die I'd be more upset than ever—so I ask you, what is a man to do?

Plato, **Symposium**, 215D–16C, in Edith Hamilton and Huntington Cairns, eds., **Plato: The Collected Dialogues**, trans. Michael Joyce (New York: Pantheon, Bollingen Series 71, 1966), p. 567.

modest or common standards and goals of the community. This "outsider" position is, itself, seen as a threat to conformity and group identity. This threat is amplified whenever a sage or prophet refuses to stop with mere *questioning* and throws down the gauntlet by *living* with fearless integrity.

One contemporary educational philosophy actually advises teachers to admit their failings and "share" their weaknesses with their students to make it easier for the students to "relate" to the teachers. From a certain perspective, it does seem safer (easier) to admire the *lessons* of teachers who are "just like us." The shared weaknesses of teachers who are "just like us" protect us from feeling deeply challenged: We are not confronted by the power of the kind of teacher whose teaching is completely reflected in his or her *being*. By actually "living up to" their teachings, integrated teachers deny us the safety of believing that the standard is set too high to reach, the notion that *no one really lives like that*.

Sometimes, we actually prefer the pastor who humbly admits to—and indulges in—a love of fine automobiles or sailboarding, willingly paid for out of the collection plate; the ethics professor who copies colleagues' new software and uses the schools equipment to play on the Internet; the psychology instructor who lectures while intoxicated and dates students (only "mature" students, of course); the activist professor whose passionate indictments of elitism or racism or sexism are simply virulent forms of the same "isms," only in reverse.

So ingrained is contemporary suspicion of the possibility of healthy expressions of paradigmatic—or pretty much any other kind of—integrity, that I am uncomfortable writing this passage and listing these commonplace examples of apparent gaps between teachers and what they teach. So let's engage in a bit of sophisticated, contemporary snarkiness for a moment: The historical Socrates was probably not such a fine fellow, anyway. Plato probably just invented him to get back at the Sophists (Chapter 3). Once we grow up, we see through these romanticized, Sunday-school-type heroes. Nobody could really live like Socrates today. But what if....

PHILOSOPHICAL QUERY

Can you think of other paradigmatic individuals? Remember, a paradigmatic individual is more than a merely influential teacher, adviser, social reformer, or significant religious figure. Do you think that contemporary America, with its present encouragement of personal liberty and diversity combined with suspicion of even a hint of authoritarianism can produce archetypal philosophers? Or must each community or ethnic group have its own human paradigms? What qualities do you think a contemporary American sophos must possess?

The Teacher and His Teachings

As presented by Plato, the harmony between Socrates' life and teachings transformed him from a truth-seeker into a sage and from a sage into a paradigm of the teacher-as-more-than-sage. Pierre Hadot says:

> There were several reasons for the fact that my research on the sage as a model gradually became fixed upon Socrates. In the first place, I found in him a figure who exercised a widespread influence of the greatest importance on the entire Western tradition. Secondly, and most importantly, the figure of Socrates— as sketched by Plato, at any rate—had it seemed to me one unique advantage. It is the portrait of a mediator between the transcendent ideal of wisdom and concrete human reality. It is a paradox of highly Socratic irony that Socrates was not a sage, but a "philo-sopher": that is, a lover of wisdom.[14]

For reasons that remain controversial to this day, Socrates' "electric shock" effect on Athens resulted in his indictment, conviction, and execution as a traitorous blasphemer. Speaking for the last time as a public figure, on trial for his life, the seventy-year-old philosopher repeated what he had *always* insisted: "I neither know nor think that I know."

As we learn more about Socrates' teachings and teaching method, let's see if we can gain some understanding of how it came to pass that a philosopher who insisted, under threat of death, that his wisdom consisted of knowing that he did not know still stands as *the* archetypal *wise man* in Western philosophy.

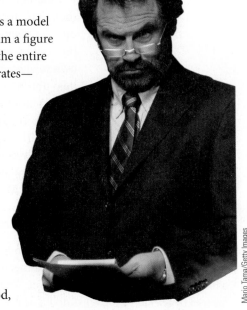

Comedian Dennis Miller often uses a low-key version of Socratic inquiry to cross-examine callers to his radio talk show. The results can be revealing.

The Dialectic

Socrates argued that one of the chief reasons many people cannot think clearly is that they do not even know what they are talking about. Consequently, the first order of business is to define our terms. The early dialogues of Plato reveal a Socrates constantly pushing and searching for clearer and more precise definitions of key terms. Time after time he lures a confused individual from one muddled definition to another. Then, using skillful (some would even say loaded or leading) questions, he attempts to guide his "opponent" closer to the truth by allowing the opponent to experience the logical inconsistencies in his own stated positions. Socrates was so effective with this method of philosophical teaching and inquiry that it came to be known as the **Socratic dialectic**, also known as the **Socratic method**.

The Socratic method begins with the assumption that the function of education is to draw the truth out of the pupil rather than "fill an empty vessel." In practice, it is a series of guided questions known as the *dialectical method of inquiry*. Claims are continually refined, definitions required for all key terms, logical inconsistencies brought to light and resolved. A vital aspect of Socratic teaching is the active involvement of the audience (pupils, listeners), hence the use of questions rather than straight lectures.

The dialectical process as Socrates practiced it was dynamic and hopeful. At worst, the participants learned that although they might not have found *the* answer, *the* meaning of justice, *the* good life, or courage, they were at least a bit clearer than before. At any rate, this was Socrates' experience—others were often angered and frustrated, if not humiliated, as their confusion and ignorance were exposed.

Socrates believed that the truth was somehow in each of us. The teacher's role, then, isn't to put knowledge into an empty mind but to draw wisdom and clarity out of a disordered and confused soul. Just as a midwife does not herself give birth but, rather, aids the mother, Socrates claimed to aid others in giving birth to their own insights by *drawing out what was already there*. And just as a midwife is of no help until the mother has conceived a child, Socrates was of no help until the other person had conceived at least a sketchy idea.

For Socrates, the most important order of business was to *engage* the other person. The Socratic method in full form is more than just questions and answers. It is a highly personal activity, guided by one who knows both the general direction of the inquiry (but not "the answers") as well as the nature and needs of the individual student. It works only if the other participant actively listens and responds.

Socratic Irony

A key element in keeping his pupils engaged, and calling attention to the importance of meaning, was Socrates' use of **irony**, a way of communicating on more than one level. An ironic utterance has at least two levels of meaning: *the literal level*, also known as the obvious level, and *the hidden level*, also known as the real level. As a rule, the two meanings are near opposites, as in the case of the sarcastic professor who writes on a woefully inadequate term paper: "Beautiful job! You've never done better!"

---

socratic dialectic, socratic method
A question-and-answer technique Socrates used to draw truth out of his pupils, often by means of achieving a clearer, more precise definition of a key term or concept.

irony
Communication on at least two levels, a literal or obvious level and a hidden or real level; favored by Socrates as a technique for keeping his listeners alert and involved.

By using words in unexpected ways, by meaning more than one obvious, surface-level thing, Socrates hoped to keep his listeners alert. Further, the use of irony underscored his belief that things are not always as they first appear, that there is a deeper meaning than may be apparent. Socrates used irony to keep his listeners on their toes and to avoid putting answers in their mouths. For instance, he begins his *Apology* (his defense at his trial) by referring to the persuasive abilities of his immediate accusers, who are Sophists. Of course, his remark is actually an ironic way of showing that these Sophists have not persuaded him of anything. His use of irony in his opening remarks gets the audience's immediate attention:

> How you, O Athenians, have been affected by my accusers, I cannot tell; but I know that they almost made me forget who I was—so persuasively did they speak; and yet they have hardly uttered a word of truth. But of the many falsehoods told by them, there was one which quite amazed me;—I mean when they said that you should be upon your guard and not allow yourselves to be deceived by the force of my eloquence. To say this, when they were certain to be detected as soon as I opened my lips and proved myself to be anything but a great speaker, did indeed appear to me most shameless—unless by the force of eloquence they mean the force of truth; for if such is their meaning, I admit that I am eloquent. But in how different a way from theirs! Well, as I was saying, they have scarcely spoken the truth at all; but from me you shall hear the whole truth: not, however, delivered after their manner in a set oration duly ornamented with words and phrases...at my time of life I ought not be appearing before you, O men of Athens, in the character of a juvenile orator—let no one expect it of me.[15]

Ironic communication confuses those who are inattentive or not in on the hidden meaning. For instance, most members of Socrates' jury would have been familiar with his wranglings with Sophists and with sophistic emphasis on the arts of persuasion. A smaller group would have also responded to the irony of Socrates, whose life was devoted to following the command "Know thyself," forgetting who he was. Irony was both a crucial component of Socrates' method and a contributing factor to his ultimate trouble, because to many observers, Socrates' use of irony was just another sophistic trick.

PHILOSOPHICAL QUERY

See how many ironic references to Sophists you can find in the preceding passage from Plato's *Apology*.

Socrates at Work

Before we look further into some specific Socratic doctrines, let's enrich our sense of the dialectic as an interpersonal philosophical method. We can do that by taking an extended look at the kind of dialectical exchange with a Sophist that Socrates became famous for: precisely the sort of explosive encounter that fueled his ambiguous reputation and contributed to the animosity between Socrates and certain Sophists.

Alcibides Reprimanded by Socrates, c.1780 (pastel on paper), Italian School, (18th century)/Private Collection/ © Charles Plante Fine Arts/The Bridgeman Art Library International

Socrates so confounded the brilliant and controversial general Alcibiades that Alcibiades said he would almost be happy to learn that Socrates was dead—and yet Alcibiades loved Socrates.

To some critics, Socrates' entire philosophical career was what vaudeville performers used to call a "shtick," a gimmick that gives a performer a recognizable identity to hide behind and a repertoire of predictable routines. Sophists and other critics saw him as an undemocratic elitist merely pretending to be a simple fellow, poor and modest, on a so-called quest for wisdom. According to this view, Socrates was a Sophist. From this perspective, his "Aw, shucks," seemingly meek demeanor was thought to be a ruse designed to set opponents up for the fall. That is, by lulling people into a false sense of security and trust, Socrates was able to catch them off guard and shock them with sneaky word tricks and leading questions. Whether there is merit to such a picture of Socrates is something you must wrestle with for yourself.

Plato provides one of the most intriguing examples of the Socratic dialectic in action early in his masterpiece, the *Republic* (Chapter 5). The passage concerns a typical encounter between Socrates and a Sophist. Thrasymachus (c. 450 B.C.E.) is the kind of Sophist who is less interested in theories and philosophy than in political and social action. In Book I, section 3 of the *Republic*, Plato paints a vivid portrait of the volatile, aggressive style Thrasymachus used in confronting his opponents.

The *Republic* consists of a series of dialogues between Socrates and various individuals, chiefly about the nature of justice. By skillful questioning, Socrates reveals that conventional notions of morality are confused and muddle-headed. After Socrates has rejected a number of attempts to define justice, Thrasymachus literally bursts onto the scene. With energy and sarcasm, the Sophist categorically denies that any one moral standard can be equally applicable to rich and poor, strong and weak, superior and inferior.

Thrasymachus goes well beyond Socrates' rejection of common conceptions of justice such as repaying debts or giving persons their due and substitutes unabashed self-interest for any other view of justice. He thereby transforms *moral relativism* into a hard-edged *moral realism*, contending that an unsentimental view of life shows quite clearly that *might makes right*.

Whether we like it or not, according to Thrasymachus, the values that prevail in all areas of life—economic, political, racial, educational—reflect the *interests of the strong*. Certain values dominate not because they are in some absolute sense right but because they are the views preferred by the most powerful individual or group. And since nature rewards power, the powerful individual is always the superior individual, the "true individual," gloriously free in his or her indifference to the puny concerns of conventional morality.

Reflecting Socrates' harsh opinion of moral realism, Plato portrays Thrasymachus as loud, offensive, and often on the verge of resorting to force. From the very start, we know we are in for an interesting experience as Thrasymachus disrupts the courteous, philosophical tone of the discussion.

Sophos Versus Sophist

As you read the following extended passage from the *Republic*, look for examples of irony (and sarcasm). Reflect on Thrasymachus' accusations against Socrates and his method. Study Socrates' responses. Note how Socrates manages to draw Thrasymachus into his preferred question-and-answer process—in spite of Thrasymachus' apparent awareness of the dialectic's effects and his own strong assertions that he will not participate. Be alert for the possible psychological consequences that might result from an encounter with Socrates. (And add some zest to your reading by mentally picturing the two protagonists: the volatile, stylish, younger, stronger, hotheaded Thrasymachus and the confident rumpled old master of the cross-examination.)

As our drama opens, Socrates is describing Thrasymachus' impatient interruption of a discussion Socrates was having with a man named Polemarchus:

> Several times in the course of the discussion Thrasymachus had made an attempt to get the argument into his own hands, and had been put down by the rest of the company, who wanted to hear the end. But when Polemarchus and I were done speaking and there was a pause, he could no longer hold his peace; and, gathering himself up, he came at us like a wild beast, seeking to devour us. We were panic-stricken at the sight of him.
>
> He roared out to the whole company: What folly, Socrates, has taken possession of you all? And why, like crybabies, do you so meekly defer to one another? I say that if you really want to know what justice is, you should not only ask but answer, and you should not claim victory just because you have refuted an opponent, but because you have your own answer. For there are many who can ask questions yet cannot answer them. And I will not have you say that justice is duty or advantage or profit or gain or interest, for this sort of nonsense will not do for me. I must have clearness and accuracy.
>
> I was panic-stricken at his words, and could not look at him without trembling. Indeed I believe that if I had not already noticed his growing anger, I would have been struck dumb…
>
> Thrasymachus, I said, with a quiver, don't be hard upon us. Polemarchus and I may have been guilty of a little mistake in the argument, but I can assure you that the error was not intentional. If we were cooperating in a search for gold, you would not be accusing us of "meekly deferring to one another," and in so doing harming our chances of finding it. Why, when we are looking for justice, a thing more precious than gold, do you say that we are weakly yielding to one another and thus not doing our utmost to get at the truth? Nay, my good friend, we are most willing and anxious to get at the truth, but the fact is that we cannot. If we are unable to find it, people like you, who know all things, should pity us and help us and not be angry with us.
>
> How characteristic of Socrates! he replied, with a bitter laugh;—that's your ironical style! Did I not foresee—have I not already told you, that whatever Socrates was asked he would refuse to answer, and would instead try irony or any other shuffle, in order that he might avoid answering?…But what if I give you a better and different definition of justice, he said, than any of these? What do you deserve to have done to you?

Of what value is smartness of speech? Opposing a man with the mouth excites anger.
— Confucius

Socrates is guilty of rejecting the gods acknowledged by the state and of bringing in strange deities; he is also guilty of corrupting the youth.
— Indictment brought against Socrates

Done to me? Why, as best becomes an ignorant man, I must learn from the wise. That is what I deserve to have done to me.

What, and no payment! a pleasant notion!

I will pay when I have the money, I replied.

Don't worry about money, Socrates, said Glaucon. And you, Thrasymachus, need be under no anxiety about money, for we will all make a contribution for Socrates.

Yes, he replied, and then Socrates will do as he always does, refuse to answer himself, and twist and pull to pieces someone else's answer.

Why, my good friend, I said, how can I answer when I do not know, and when I so freely admit that I do not know. Even if I did have some faint notions of my own, I have been told by you, a man of authority, not to utter them. That being so, it makes much more sense for you—someone who professes to know—to tell what he knows. Will you, then, kindly answer, for the edification of Glaucon and company, and of myself?

Glaucon and the rest of the company joined in my request and Thrasymachus, as all could see, was quite eager to speak, for he thought that he had an excellent answer and would distinguish himself by giving it. But at first he made a show of insisting that I do the answering. Eventually, he consented to answer, proclaiming: Behold the wisdom of Socrates! He refuses to teach, instead pretending to learn from others without ever saying thank you.

That I learn from others, I replied, is quite true, but that I am ungrateful I deny. Money I have none, and therefore I pay in praise, which is all I have. And I am eager to praise any one who appears to me to answer well, as you will soon find out, for I have no doubt that you will answer well.

Listen, then, he said: I proclaim that justice, or what is right, is nothing else but whatever is in the interest of the stronger party. And now why do you not praise me? But of course you won't.

Before I can praise you, I must first understand you, I replied. Justice, you say, is the interest of the stronger party. What, Thrasymachus, is the precise meaning of this? You cannot mean to say that because Polydamas, the athlete, is stronger than we are, and finds the eating of beef conducive to his bodily strength, that eating the same things he does is equally good for we who are weaker than he is, and so his athlete's diet is right and proper for us?

That's abominable of you, Socrates. You take my words in the sense which is most damaging to my argument.

Not at all, my good sir, I said. I am trying to understand you, and I wish that you would be a little clearer.

Well, he said, have you never heard that forms of government differ, that there are tyrannies and democracies and aristocracies?

Yes, I know.

And the government is the ruling power in each state?

Certainly.

And the different forms of government make laws with a view to their own particular interests—democracies make democratic laws, tyrannies make tyrannical laws, and aristocracies make aristocratic laws. And these laws, which are made by the ruling classes for their own interests, are the "justice" which they deliver to their subjects, and the rulers punish anyone who breaks their laws for being unjust. And that is what I mean when I say that in every kind of state there is the only one principle of justice, and that principle is to further the interest of the government,

I think that all men have a choice between various courses, and choose and follow the one which they think conduces most to their advantage.

— Socrates

of the ruling class. And because the government is supposed to have power, the only reasonable conclusion is that everywhere there is one principle of justice: justice is that which is in the interest of the strongest party....

Consider further, most foolish Socrates, that the just man is always a loser in comparison with the unjust. First of all, in private contracts, wherever an unjust man is a partner of a just man and the partnership is dissolved, the unjust man always comes out ahead and the just man comes out behind. Secondly, consider their dealings with the State. When there is an income tax, the just man will pay more and the unjust man will pay less on the same amount of income. And when there is anything to be received the just man gains nothing and the unjust man gains much. Observe also what happens when they hold office. There is the just man neglecting his private affairs and perhaps suffering other losses, and getting nothing out of public office, because he is just. Moreover he is hated by his friends and acquaintances for refusing to help them out in unlawful ways. But all this is reversed in the case of the unjust man. I am speaking...of injustice on a large scale where the advantages of being unjust are more apparent...People censure injustice because they are afraid that they may be the victims of it—not because they would not like to get away with it. And thus, as I have shown, Socrates, injustice, when practiced on a sufficient scale, has more strength and freedom and mastery than justice, and, as I said from the first, justice is the interest of the stronger party, whereas injustice is the profit and interest of oneself.

...Now I understand you, I said. Whether you are right or not I will try to discover. But let me remark, that in defining justice you have yourself used the word "interest," one of the words you forbade me to use. It is true, however, that in your definition the words "of the stronger" are added.

A small addition, you must allow, he said.

Great or small, never mind about that. We must first enquire whether what you are saying is the truth. Now we are both agreed that justice is interest of some sort, but you go on to say "of the stronger." About this addition I am not so sure, and must therefore consider further.

Proceed.

I will; and first tell me, do you admit that it is just for subjects to obey their rulers?

I do.

But are the rulers of states absolutely infallible, or are they sometimes liable to err?

To be sure, he replied, they are liable to err.

Then in making their laws they may sometimes make them rightly, and sometimes not?

True.

When they make them rightly, they make them agreeably to their interest; when they are mistaken, contrary to their interest; you admit that?

Yes.

And the laws which they make must be obeyed by their subjects, and that is what you call justice?

Doubtless.

Then justice, according to your argument, is not only obedience to the interest of the stronger but the reverse?

What is that you are saying? he asked.

> *And this, O men of Athens, is the truth and the whole truth; I have concealed nothing, I have dissembled nothing. And yet, I know that my plainness of speech makes them hate me, and what is their hatred but a proof that I am speaking the truth?*
>
> — Socrates

Only what you are saying. Consider: Have we not admitted that the rulers may be mistaken about their own interest in what they command, and also that to obey them is justice? Has not that been admitted?

Yes.

Then you yourself acknowledge that justice is not the interest of the stronger party when the stronger party unintentionally commands things to be done which injure it. In such a case, O wisest of men, is there any escape from the conclusion that the just act is not what is in the interest of the rulers—the stronger party—but what, on the contrary, is against the interest of the stronger party?[16]

PHILOSOPHICAL QUERY

Statistically, poorer, less-educated people make up a disproportionate segment of our prison population. Just how relevant to Thrasymachus' position is it that white-collar and celebrity criminals are often punished less severely than are poor or obscure defendants? Other studies suggest that physically attractive job candidates are most likely to be hired. Have you ever noticed how some students seem to get by mostly on cleverness and charm? Should we draw conclusions about the nature of justice from these cases or just chalk them up to the way things sometimes go? Try to separate our lip-service moral values from those we practice. Try to separate a storybook conception of life from a realistic one. Are moral realists onto something or not? Explain.

The Unexamined Life

Among Socratic teachings, the most persistent command was "Know thyself." The significance to Socrates of this command is underscored by the fact that he stressed its importance to his life and mission during his *Apology*. Facing the end of a long life, Socrates uttered one of the most famous statements in the history of ideas: "The unexamined life is not worth living." By this he meant, among other things, that a life devoid of philosophical speculation is hardly a *human life*. That is, it is incomplete; it is not fully functioning and so lacks virtue or excellence.

Socrates believed that the human **psyche** is the essence of humanness. To him, the psyche was a combination of what we think of as the mind and soul: consciousness, the capacity to reason, and the ability to reflect, known as *reflective thinking*. Giovanni Reale says:

> As has recently come to light, no one prior to Socrates had understood by *soul* what Socrates understood by it, and after Socrates the whole of the West....the soul for Socrates was identified *with our consciousness when it thinks and acts with our reason and with the source of our thinking activity and our ethical activity*. In short, for Socrates the soul *is the conscious self, it is intellectual and moral personhood*.[17]

An unexamined life is a life that takes the psyche for granted. An unexamined life is, in a sense, an unconscious life. It is lived on the minimal level: Thinking never rises above practical concerns; desires are rarely pondered; custom, habit, and unquestioned beliefs substitute for reflection and assessment. Consequently, it is possible for a very

psyche
Greek for "soul"; in today's terms, a combination of mind and soul, including the capacity for reflective thinking.

intelligent, materially successful individual to live an unexamined life. The examined life does not produce all the answers. Instead, it results in a life devoted to knowing more, a life in which progress means shedding false beliefs, a life in which pretense is continually reduced. The examined life is lived in conscious awareness of the human condition; it is not merely spent in an uncritical attempt to satisfy various needs and desires.

PHILOSOPHICAL QUERY

Do some informal research among your friends to get a sense of some contemporary conceptions of the soul. Compare and contrast what you discover with Socrates' conception of the psyche. How might a person's conception of the soul influence his or her response to the issue of the unexamined life?

Socratic Ignorance

When Socrates was probably in his thirties, his friend Chaerephon went to the Oracle at Delphi with a question: Is anyone wiser than Socrates? The Oracle was believed to have the gift of prophecy. Either through divine guidance or cleverness, it gave this famous, ambiguous reply: *No man is wiser than Socrates.* This can be taken to mean either (a) Socrates is the wisest man in Athens, or (b) even though Socrates is not very wise, he is as wise as anybody gets. The first interpretation makes Socrates unique. The second makes him an exemplar of the human condition.

Socrates took the Oracle's reply quite seriously, claiming that it was the turning point in his life. His first reaction to hearing the god Apollo's reply was confusion:

> I said to myself, What can the god mean? and what is the interpretation of his riddle? for I know that I have no wisdom, small or great. What then can he mean when he says that I am the wisest of men? And yet he is a god, and cannot lie; that would be against his nature. After long consideration, I thought of a method of trying the question. I reflected that if I could only find a man wiser than myself, then I might go to the god with a refutation in my hand. I should say to him, "Here is a man wiser than I am; but you said I was the wisest." Accordingly I went to one who had a reputation of wisdom, and observed him—his name I need not mention; he was a politician whom I selected for examination—and the result was as follows: When I began to talk with him, I could not help thinking that he was not really wise, although he was thought wise by many, and still wiser by himself; and thereupon I tried to explain to him that he thought himself wise, but was not really wise; and the consequence was that he hated me, and his enmity was shared by several who were present and heard me. So I left him, saying to myself, as I went away: Well, although I do not suppose that either of us knows anything really beautiful and good, I am better off than he is—for he knows nothing, and thinks that

If, as they say, I am only an ignorant man trying to be a philosopher, then that may be what a philosopher is.
— Diogenes

The Oracle at the Temple of Apollo at Delphi was a priestess thought to deliver messages from Apollo while sitting on a tripod placed over a crevice in the floor, from which gases escaped. In a semi-trance, the Oracle delivered cryptic utterances such as "No man is wiser than Socrates."

he knows; I neither know nor think that I know. In this…, then, I seem to have slightly the advantage of him. Then I went to another who had still higher pretensions to wisdom, and my conclusion was exactly the same. Whereupon I made another enemy of him, and of many others besides him.[18]

What point could Socrates have been making? Clearly—it seems—Socrates possessed some kind of knowledge, if not wisdom. Just as clearly—it seems—he must have believed in his own ignorance, since he alluded to it on many occasions. If we allow for an element of irony in Socrates' language, it then becomes likely that Socrates was challenging our notions of wisdom and knowledge. To certain sorts of people, Socrates' statements will remain clouded, perhaps beyond comprehension. Among them are young people whose "minds have not conceived at all" or older ones whose thoughts are already so firmly set that they can see only a phony technique used to avoid answering questions. Such people cannot conceive of their own ignorance. They are firmly convinced that they know everything important. To the Sophists, Socrates' use of craftily faked ignorance was merely a clever psychological ploy to keep them off balance and on the spot. It's this sort of thing that made Thrasymachus so angry.

Given that the Socratic method employs guided questions, we can reasonably conclude that Socrates *does* have some ideas about the general direction the search for answers will take and the adequacy of certain lines of analysis but refuses to reveal them in dogmatic form. Socrates' ignorance was part of his whole mission, which he saw as bringing home to others *their own* intellectual needs. Once that was accomplished, they were invited to join the search for truth using the dialectical method of question-and-answer. The essence of the Socratic method is to help us realize that, although we thought we knew something, in fact we did not.

Socrates may also have been sharing his own honest doubt. Even if he knew more than he let on, which is likely, he was probably more aware of the uncertain nature and limits of knowledge (his own included) than many of us are. In this, he seems wiser than the average person in two ways. First, many of us tend to think that we know much more than we do. Second, all human knowledge is tentative and limited: We are not gods, though we sometimes act as if we were.

For Deeper Consideration

Socrates said that the unexamined life is not worth living for a human being. Does that strike you as a reasonable assertion? Is there any way to know whether an unexamined life is worth living except by examining it? In other words, can we make any reasonable claims about the quality of an unexamined life—or an unexamined anything? Consider the possibility that Socrates has something up his sleeve when he talks about this.

The Power of Human Wisdom

Perhaps the best way to glimpse the power of Socratic ignorance is to look once more to the *Apology*, this time where Socrates makes tantalizing statements regarding his merely human wisdom:

I dare say, Athenians, that some of you will reply, "Yes, Socrates, but what is the origin of these accusations which are brought against you; there must have been something strange which you have been doing? All these rumours and this talk about you would never have arisen if you had been like other men: tell us, then, what is the cause of them, for we should be sorry to judge hastily of you." Now I regard this as a fair challenge, and I will endeavour to explain to you the reason why I am called wise and have such evil fame. Please to attend then. And although some of you may think that I am joking, I declare that I will tell you the entire truth. Men of Athens, this reputation of mine has come of a certain sort of wisdom which I possess. If you ask me what kind of wisdom, I reply, wisdom such as may perhaps be attained by man, for to that extent I am inclined to believe that I am wise; whereas the persons to whom I was speaking have a superhuman wisdom, which I may fail to describe, because I have it not myself; and he who says I have, speaks falsely, and is taking away my character.[19]

The Socratic distinction between "human wisdom" and "more-than-human wisdom" is a powerful one. Buddha made a similar point in his intriguing discussion of "questions not tending toward edification" (discussed in Chapter 1).

In his effort to understand why the god said no one was wiser than he, Socrates discovered how easy it is to become deluded by our own special skills. The modern tendency to compartmentalize rather than integrate our lives, combined with the respect we have for specialized skills and knowledge, might make us especially susceptible to this delusion. Modern media of all forms offer an endless array of individuals expressing their "insights" and "discoveries" in all areas of life. Psychologists discuss morals, entertainers lecture on food additives, preachers propose legislation, all sorts of people write books generalizing from their own limited experience to the human condition. And what are we to make of the proliferation of blogs, tweets, YouTube rants, anonymous online commenting, and #hashtag philosophizing posted by self-identified experts on current affairs, politics, theology, music, health—every conceivable field of human endeavor? They—and we—seem to assume that if you have a degree, sell lots of books, get rich, have a television or radio show, or become famous, then you *must know what you're talking about no matter what you're talking about.* Things haven't changed:

> At last I went to the artisans, for I was conscious that I knew nothing at all, as I may say, and I was sure that they knew many fine things; and here I was not mistaken, for they did know many things of which I was ignorant, and in this they certainly were wiser than I was. But I observed that even the good artisans fell into the same error as the poets—because they were good workmen they thought that they also knew all sorts of high matters, and this defect in them overshadowed their wisdom; and therefore I asked myself whether I would like to be as I was, neither having their knowledge nor their ignorance, or like them in both; and I made answer to myself and to the oracle that I was better off as I was.
>
> This inquisition has led to my having many enemies of the worst and most dangerous kind, and has given occasion to many calumnies. And I am called wise, for my hearers always imagine that I possess the wisdom which I find wanting in others; but the truth is, O men of Athens, that God only is wise; and by his answer he intends to show that the wisdom of men is worth little or nothing; he is not

If I had engaged in politics, I should have perished long ago . . . for the truth is, that no man who goes to war with you or any other multitude, honestly striving against the many lawless and unrighteous deeds which are done in a state, will save his life; he who will fight for the right, if he would live even for a brief space, must have a private station and not a public one.

— Socrates

speaking of Socrates, he is only using my name by way of illustration, as if he said, He, O men, is wisest, who, like Socrates, knows that his wisdom is in truth worth nothing. And so I go about the world, obedient to the god, and search and make enquiry into the wisdom of anyone, whether citizen or stranger, who appears to be wise; and if he is not wise, then in vindication of the oracle I show him that he is not wise; and my occupation quite absorbs me, and I have no time to give either to any public matter or interest or to any concern of my own, but I am in utter poverty by reason of my devotion to the god.[20]

MindTap

Discussing Philosophy

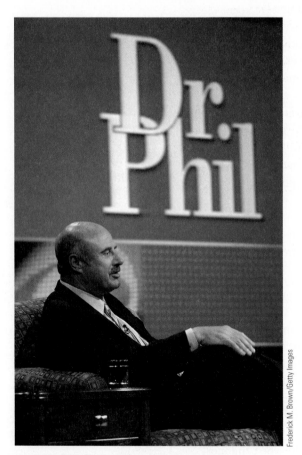

It is fascinating to imagine encounters between Socrates and today's confident "sages" and professional advice-givers such as television talk-show host Dr. Phil. How do you think Dr. Phil (and other celebrity gurus) would fare with Socrates as a guest?

Frederick M. Brown/Getty Images

The Physician of the Soul

Socrates' entire teaching mission centered on his conviction that *we are our souls*. That is, the "real person" is not the body but the *psyche*. Perhaps the most important passage in the *Apology* concerns Socrates' description of himself as a kind of "physician of the soul." In Socrates' sense, "seeking my own welfare" means "seeking the welfare of my soul." Note how in the following passage Socrates implies that he does indeed know something (that the most important thing is care of the soul) and that he views his whole public career as a teacher in light of his expanded notion of the self as the soul:

Men of Athens, I honour and love you; but I shall obey God rather than you, and while I have strength I shall never cease from the practice and teaching of philosophy, exhorting any one whom I meet and saying to him after my manner: You, my friend,—a citizen of the great and mighty and wise city of Athens,—are you not ashamed of heaping up the greatest amount of money and honour and reputation, and caring so little about wisdom and truth and the greatest improvement of the soul, which you never regard or heed at all? And if the person with whom I am arguing, says: Yes, but I do care; then I do not leave him or let him go at once; but I proceed to interrogate and examine and cross-examine him, and if I think that he has no virtue in him, but only says that he has, I reproach him with undervaluing the greater, and overvaluing the less. And I shall repeat

"Oh, the Pure Innocent Child!"

Oh, tell me who was it first announced, who was it first proclaimed, that man only does nasty things because he does not know his own interests; and that if he were enlightened, if his eyes were opened to his real normal interests, man would at once cease to do nasty things, would at once become good and noble because, being enlightened and understanding his real advantage, he would see his own advantage in the good and nothing else, and we all know that not one man can, consciously, act against his own interests, consequently, so to say, through necessity, he would begin doing good? Oh, the babe! Oh, the pure innocent child!

Fyodor Dostoevsky, *Notes from the Underground*, trans. Constance Garnett, in *Existentialism from Dostoevsky to Sartre*, ed. Walter Kaufmann (New York: New American Library, 1975), p. 67.

the same words to everyone I meet, young and old, citizen and alien, but especially to the citizens.... For know that this is the command of the god; and I believe no greater good has happened to this state than my service to the god. For I do nothing but go about persuading you all, old and young alike, not to take thought for your persons or your properties, but first and chiefly to care about the greatest improvement of your soul. I tell you that virtue is not given by money, but that from virtue comes money and every other good of man, public as well as private. This is my teaching.[21]

> *To pretend to know what you do not know is a disease.*
>
> — Lao-tzu

PHILOSOPHICAL QUERY

Compare Socrates' attitude toward the soul with your own—and with that of your religion, if you practice one. What do you see as the main differences? What are some advantages and disadvantages of Socrates' view?

No One Knowingly Does Evil

The fundamental Socratic imperative "Know thyself" takes on special significance in light of Socrates' view that human beings always seek what they believe to be their own welfare and cannot deliberately do otherwise. In the *Gorgias*, Socrates points out that when people do what appear to be bad or distasteful things, it is always with some ultimate good in mind:

So it is for the sake of the good that people do all these [distasteful] actions?
   Yes, it is.
   And we have admitted that when we act for any purpose, we do not desire the action itself but the object of the action?
   Yes.
   Then we do not desire...these [distasteful] actions themselves; but if they are advantageous, we desire to do them; and if they are harmful, we do not. For we desire what is good...but things that are neither bad nor good we do not desire, nor things that are bad either.[22]

For Socrates, the good or harm in question is always determined by what benefits or harms the soul. In order to seek my soul's welfare I have to know myself.

And in order to know myself, I have to know what kind of thing I am. Without this knowledge, I cannot know what is really good for me. In the *Protagoras*, Socrates reinforces his conviction that no one knowingly does evil:

> For no wise man, I believe, will allow that any human being errs voluntarily, or voluntarily does evil or base actions; but they are very well aware that all who do evil and base things do them against their will.[23]

PHILOSOPHICAL QUERY

Do you agree that no one knowingly does evil? Explain. You might want to read the box about the Ring of Gyges in Chapter 3 before you answer.

Virtue Is Wisdom

The Sophists claimed to be teachers of human excellence, with excellence meaning "excellence of function," or **virtue** (*arete* in Greek). Too often, however, the result, as we saw in Chapter 3, was might-makes-right moral relativism and a radical this-worldly egoism—in contrast to Socratic egoism, which centers on the soul as the true self. The Sophists looked outward for markers of well-being and success, whereas Socrates looked inward at character.

Socrates believed that human excellence (virtue for short) is a special kind of knowledge that combines technical understanding with the skill and character to apply that knowledge. One of the words Socrates used for this kind of knowledge was **techne**, the Greek term for practical knowledge of how to do things. At various times, *techne* meant "art," "skill," "craft," "technique," "trade," "system," or "method of doing something." It is the root of English words such as *technique, technical,* and *technology. Techne* is knowledge of what to do and how to do it. It is knowledge of both means and ultimate ends. Plato accused the Sophists of developing persuasive skills (rhetoric) without acquiring a corresponding knowledge of what ought to be done or avoided—that is without knowledge of ultimate ends.

For example, according to Socrates, a knowledgeable physician has both theoretical understanding and practical skill. Her *techne* is manifest by the fact that she makes her patients well. If she made them worse, we would conclude that she was not really a physician, that she lacked medical knowledge. *Techne* is not like merely cognitive knowledge of a cake recipe; it involves the skills needed to actually bake a good cake.

According to Socrates, the Sophists' lack of *techne* was evident because their teachings made people worse. Their own pupils engaged in corrupt business practices and destructive political schemes. Sometimes the Sophists' pupils even attacked their teachers and tried to cheat them out of their tuition, as we saw in the case of Protagoras' Wager (Chapter 3). Thus, the Sophists lacked knowledge of human excellence, or virtue.

Socrates believed that knowledge (wisdom) always produces behavioral results, because behavior is always guided by beliefs. For instance, if I believe that the glass of water in front of me is poisoned, I will not drink it—unless I also believe

virtue
From the Greek *arete*, meaning "that at which something excels," or "excellence of function."

techne
From the Greek for "art," "skill," "craft," "technique," "trade," "system," or "method of doing something"; root of English words such as *technique, technical,* and *technology*; term Socrates used when he asserted that virtue (*arete*) is knowledge or wisdom (*techne*).

that dying will be better for me than living, given my present circumstances (say, terminal cancer of a painful sort). This rationalistic view that behavior is always controlled by beliefs about what is good and the means to that good is sometimes called **intellectualism**. Intellectualism emphasizes cognitive states (beliefs), whereas egoism emphasizes desires.

Socrates' intellectualism was part of his unusual claim that no one knowingly does wrong. According to Socrates, when we merely "admit" (state) that our choices are wrong, we are playing word games. To take an extreme example, a satanist who glories in "choosing" *evil* really believes in the superiority of what he is calling evil. Perhaps, according to Jews, Christians, or Muslims, what he is choosing is wrong, but to the satanist, it is *really good*. If he honestly believed (knew) that *X* was wrong (fatal to his soul), our hypothetical satanist could not choose *X*, according to Socrates.

In other words, there is no such thing as true *weakness of will*. We are, implies Socrates, psychologically incapable of knowing what is good and not doing it. Conversely, we are psychologically incapable of doing what we really know (and believe wholeheartedly) will harm us. Socrates' simple psychology and intellectualism led him to the conviction that all evil is a form of ignorance, because no one knowingly wills harm to herself.[24]

For Socrates, knowledge of virtue is wisdom; it goes beyond theoretical understanding of justice or right and wrong and includes *living* justly, living honorably and well in the highest sense. In the following passage from the *Meno*, Socrates argues that virtue is wisdom and that all things "hang upon" wisdom:

> *Socrates:* The next question is, whether virtue is knowledge or of another species?
> *Meno:* Certainly....
> *Socrates:* Do we not say that virtue is good?...
> *Meno:* Certainly....
> *Socrates:* Then virtue is profitable?
> *Meno:* That is the only inference....
> *Socrates:* And what is the guiding principle which makes [things] profitable or the reverse? Are they not profitable when they are rightly used, and hurtful when they are not rightfully used?
> *Meno:* Certainly.
> *Socrates:* Next, let us consider the goods of the soul: they are temperance, justice, courage, quickness of apprehension, memory, magnanimity, and the like?
> *Meno:* Surely.
> *Socrates:* And such of these as are not knowledge, but of another sort, are sometimes profitable and sometimes hurtful; as, for example, courage wanting prudence, which is only a sort of confidence? When a man has no sense he is harmed by courage, but when he has sense he is profited?
> *Meno:* True.
> *Socrates:* And...whatever things are learned or done with sense are profitable, but when done without sense they are hurtful?
> *Meno:* Very true.

intellectualism
A term used to refer to the claim that behavior is always controlled by beliefs about what is good and the means to that good.

To live is not itself an evil, as has been claimed, but to lead a worthless life is.
— Diogenes

Socrates: And in general, all that the soul attempts or endures, when under the guidance of wisdom, ends in happiness; but when she is under the guidance of folly, the opposite?

Meno: That appears to be true.

Socrates: If then virtue is a quality of the soul, and is admitted to be profitable, it must be wisdom or prudence, since none of the things of the soul are either profitable or hurtful in themselves, but they are all made profitable or hurtful by the addition of wisdom or folly; and therefore if virtue is profitable, virtue must be a sort of wisdom or prudence?

Meno: I quite agree....

Socrates: And is this not universally true of human nature? All other things hang upon the soul, and the things of the soul herself hang upon wisdom, if they are to be good; and so wisdom is inferred to be that which profits—and virtue, as we say, is profitable?

Meno: Certainly.

Socrates: And thus we arrive at the conclusion that virtue is either wholly or partly wisdom?

Meno: I think that what you are saying, Socrates, is very true.[25]

PHILOSOPHICAL QUERY

If all evil is ignorance, can we ever justly punish evildoers? Discuss.

The Trial and Death of Socrates

> *Either acquit me or not; but whichever you do, understand that I shall never alter my ways, not even if I have to die many times.*
>
> — Socrates

For most of his long life, Socrates was able to function as a critic-at-large, questioning Athenian values and occasionally annoying important and powerful people in the process. He acquired a mixed reputation, being viewed on the one hand as a harmless eccentric and on the other as a dangerous social critic and free-thinker—in short, a Sophist. Socrates' philosophic method consisted of raising question after question, calling into doubt cherished, often previously unchallenged, beliefs to see if they were worthy of allegiance. Many Athenians found this skeptical attitude undemocratic, disrespectful, and threatening; they preferred unwavering loyalty to the status quo and to conventional beliefs. To these citizens, the very process of questioning fundamental values was subversive, perhaps even traitorous.

Socrates' status changed from mere annoyance to overt threat because of events associated with the bitter Peloponnesian Wars between Athens and Sparta. One of Socrates' students, Alcibiades, went to Sparta, where he advised the Spartans during the war. In some people's minds, as the teacher, Socrates was responsible for the student's act of betrayal.

Socrates further alienated himself from powerful Athenians when he resisted efforts to judge eight Athenian generals accused of poor military strategy as a group, rather than as individuals, as was their right under the Athenian constitution. Socrates was the *one member* of the Committee of the Senate of Five Hundred *to refuse.* The other 499 members initially agreed with Socrates' position but backed down when aggressive prosecutors threatened to add to the indictment the names of

Committee members who refused to ignore the constitution. The threat worked, the generals were found guilty, and the six who were already in custody were executed on the same day. This is another example of Socrates' willingness to put his principles above all other considerations (including, perhaps, his family's well-being).

Sparta defeated Athens in 404 B.C.E. and set up a Commission of Thirty to form a new Athenian government. The Thirty turned out to be a ruthless dictatorship that executed supporters of the earlier Periclean democracy and greedily confiscated their property. The Thirty lasted about eight months before being removed from power by force. Unfortunately for Socrates, among the Thirty were his close friends Critias and Charmides. Once again, in the minds of many Athenians, Socrates was guilty of treason by association.

Finally, resentment, distrust, and hostility against Socrates grew to such proportions that he was brought to trial for "not worshiping the gods of the state" and "corrupting the young." These were potentially capital offenses, and Socrates' prosecutor, Meletus, demanded death. At the time, it was customary for individuals charged with such crimes to submit to voluntary exile. Had Socrates chosen this option, there would have been no trial. Socrates, however, remained to answer his accuser before a jury of his peers.

Athenian trials consisted of two parts. First, the jury determined whether the accused was guilty as charged. If guilty, the second stage of the trial determined the most appropriate punishment. Socrates' jury consisted of 501 members. There was no way such a large group could reasonably debate various penalty options, so if a defendant was convicted, the prosecutor proposed a penalty and the defendant proposed a counterpenalty. Then the jury voted once more, choosing one or the other. The hope was that both sides would be moderate in their demands.

Socrates defended himself and was judged guilty by a rather close vote. The custom of the time was for those convicted to show some contrition. The greater the prosecutor's proposed penalty, the more remorse the condemned man was expected to express. In cases where death was demanded, the proposed counterpenalty was supposed to be stiff. It might include leaving Athens forever and giving up most or all of one's property as fines. Public humiliation was also part of the price of escaping death. Defendants were expected to tear at their clothes, roll on the ground, and throw dirt on themselves while crying and wailing. They would usually have their wives and children and friends cry and plead for their lives. An important function of the trial involved making peace with those one had offended.

Instead of following custom, Socrates pointed out that it would be undignified at his age to grovel for a little more life. He refused to allow his friends and family to beg either. To make things even worse, he reminded the jury that many of them believed he was not guilty and had been falsely convicted. In this way, Socrates offered to redeem the jury. At one point, he mused that since he had given up opportunities to make money because he was trying to help others, he should perhaps be given free meals for the rest of his life. Ultimately, he made only a modest, inadequate concession to the jury by offering to let his friends pay a fine for him. His conviction did not upset him, for a divine sign had led him throughout:

O my judges—for you I may truly call judges—I should like to tell you of a wonderful circumstance. Hitherto the divine faculty of which the internal oracle is the

In ancient Athens, jurors voted with bronze disks. One type had holes in the round center tubing. The other type had a solid center tubing. Those with the hole indicated "guilty"; those without, "not guilty." Jurors cast them in urns to vote, placing their fingers over the cylinder in order to keep their vote secret. This is an illustration of an acquittal ballot uncovered in Athens. It measures two and one-half inches in diameter.

> *If you think that by killing men you can prevent someone from censuring your evil lives, you are mistaken; that is not a way of escape which is either possible or honorable; the easiest and the noblest way is not to be disabling others, but to be improving yourselves. This is the prophecy which I utter before my departure to the judges who have condemned me.*
>
> — Socrates

source has constantly been in the habit of opposing me even about trifles, if I was going to make a slip or error in any matter; and now you see there has come upon me that which may be thought, and is generally believed to be, the last and worst evil. But the oracle made no sign of opposition, either when I was leaving my house in the morning, or I was on my way to the court, or while I was speaking, at anything which I was going to say; and yet I have often been stopped in the middle of a speech.... What do I take to be the explanation of this silence? I will tell you. It is an intimation that what has happened to me is good, and that those of us who think that death is an evil are in error. For the customary sign would surely have opposed me had I been going to evil and not to good.[26]

Though we cannot know the exact nature of Socrates' "divine sign," we know that he took it seriously. One result was that Socrates himself always had a clear sense of purpose, a vocation. At his trial he said, "My service to the god has brought me into great poverty." For Socrates, real beauty was beauty of soul, real riches were riches of soul. Socrates was poor only by conventional standards. By his own sense of things, his service to the god brought real riches rather than apparent ones.

MindTap
Discussing Philosophy

> ### PHILOSOPHICAL QUERY
>
> Some people argue that Socrates committed suicide by provoking the jury. By insisting that he was right and by refusing to show fear or at least some repentance, he drove the jury members to execute him. He knew they would get carried away, and yet he insulted them. So it is his own fault that he was executed. What do you think? Is there a defense for Socrates' actions? Who is responsible in such circumstances?

When Rabbi Bunam lay dying his wife burst into tears. He said: "What are you crying for? My whole life was only that I might learn how to die."
— Martin Buber

The Death of Socrates

Socrates could not be executed on the day of the trial, as was customary, because the trial had lasted longer than usual, extending into late afternoon, the beginning of a holy period. Socrates was put in prison to await the end of the holy period, in this case about a month. While there, he continued to pursue his philosophical questions. He was offered the opportunity to escape, the officials going so far as to make it clear they would not stop him. He refused, and finally the holy period ended and word came that Socrates must die before sundown.

A number of Socrates' friends visited him in prison on the last day of his life. He discussed the nature of the soul with them and told a mythical story about the soul's immortality. When his friend Crito asked how they should bury him, Socrates jokingly replied, "In any way you like; but you must get hold of *me*, and take care that I do not run away from you." Plato described what happened next:

Then he turned to us and added with a smile: I cannot make Crito believe that I am the same Socrates who has been talking and conducting the argument; he fancies that I am the other Socrates whom he will soon see, a dead body—and he asks, How shall you bury me? And though I have spoken many words in the endeavour to show that when I have drunk the poison I shall leave you and go to the joys of the blessed.... I shall not remain, but go away and depart;... I would not have [you] sorrow at my hard lot, or say at the burial, Thus we lay out Socrates, or, Thus we follow him to the grave or bury him; for false words are not only evil in themselves, but they infect the soul with evil. Be of good cheer then,…and say that you are burying my body only, and do with that whatever is usual, and what you think best.[27]

Socrates went to bathe, while his friends talked about what he had said. Plato reported that his friends felt as if they were losing a father and would be orphans for the rest of their lives. After Socrates' bath, his children and the women of his household were brought in. When he finally sent the women and children away, it was close to sunset—the end of the day, by which time he was officially supposed to be dead. The jailer came in while he was talking and said that it was time.

Most condemned men resisted drinking the hemlock until late into the evening, getting drunk and putting off the inevitable for as long as they could, but Socrates asked that the poison be prepared and brought to him. Socrates' jailer noted how different Socrates was and, weeping, he thanked Socrates for talking with him and treating him as a friend. Crito begged him to delay, but Socrates said that there was nothing to be gained by it. Rather, there was much to lose by degrading himself. To evade and fear death would have made a mockery out of his entire life, for Socrates had long taught that death was not an evil.

When the jailer returned with the cup, Socrates asked what he had to do and was told to just drink it and then walk around a bit. Plato's account continues:

> Then raising the cup to his lips, quite readily and cheerfully he drank off the poison. And hitherto most of us had been able to control our sorrow; but now when we saw him drinking, and saw too that he had finished the draught, we could no longer forbear, and in spite of myself my own tears were flowing fast; so that I covered my face and wept, not for him, but for the thought of my own calamity in having to part with such a friend. Nor was I the first; for Crito, when he found himself unable to restrain his tears, had got up, and I followed; and at that moment Apollodorus, who had been weeping all the time, broke out in a loud and passionate cry which made cowards of us all. Socrates alone retained his calmness: What is this strange outcry? he said. I sent away the women mainly in order that they might not misbehave in this way, for I have been told that a man should die in peace. Be quiet then and have patience. When we heard his words we were ashamed, and refrained our

Wherefore, O judges, be of good cheer about death, and know of a certainty, that no evil can happen to a good man, either in life or after death. He and his are not neglected by the gods.…
— Socrates

" Hemlock "

Conine is the toxic component of the plant commonly known as *hemlock*. Hemlock is a coarse biennial plant that looks like a carrot or parsnip plant when young. Mature hemlock stands four to ten feet tall, has small white flowers, and has small grayish-brown fruit that contains seeds. Native to Europe and Asia, hemlock can be found in waste areas throughout the eastern United States, the Rocky Mountains, southern Canada, and the Pacific coast.

Depending on the dose, initial symptoms can be vomiting, confusion, respiratory depression, even muscle paralysis. Other possible effects include salivating, thirst, double vision, loss of vision, slow heartbeat, seizures, burning sensations of mouth, throat, and abdomen, and kidney failure. Ultimately, hemlock poisoning results in paralysis of the skeletal muscles and intense, diffuse muscle pain.…

Source: *POISINDEX*®, Vol. 86, © 1974–1995 Micromedia Inc.

Francis G. Mayer/Fine Art Value/Corbis

Jacques-Louis David's 1787 painting *The Death of Socrates* is perhaps the most famous artistic depiction of that significant event. Does it reflect your conception of Socrates' death?

> *Socrates needed the hemlock, as Jesus needed the Crucifixion, to fulfill a mission. The mission left a stain forever on democracy. That remains Athens' tragic crime.*
>
> — I. F. Stone

tears; and he walked about until, as he said, his legs began to fail, and then he lay on his back, according to the directions, and the man who gave him the poison now and then looked at his feet and legs; and after a while he pressed his foot hard, and asked him if he could feel; and he said, No; and then his leg, and so upwards and upwards, and showed us that he was cold and stiff. And he felt them himself, and said: When the poison reaches the heart, that will be the end. He was beginning to grow cold about the groin, when he uncovered his face, for he had covered himself up, and said—they were his last words—he said: Crito, I owe a cock to Asclepius [the god of healing]; you will remember to pay the debt? The debt shall be paid, said Crito; is there anything else? There was no answer to this question; but in a minute or two a movement was heard, and the attendants uncovered him; his eyes were set, and Crito closed his eyes and mouth.

Such was the end...of our friend; concerning whom I may truly say, that of all the men of his time whom I have known, he was the wisest and justest and best.[28]

PHILOSOPHICAL QUERY

Although complex political reasons lay behind some of the animosity that led to Socrates' execution, it is likely that bad feelings of a deeper, more primitive nature were also important factors. Whatever reasons there may have been for prosecuting Socrates on capital charges, recall that he was seventy years old at the time of his trial. What is the significance of this fact? Why bother to try, convict, and execute a seventy-year-old man whose behavior had been remarkably consistent and publicly observed for perhaps fifty years? There was nothing new about Socrates. So what was it?

Aplia

Commentary

Socrates was, after all, quite an optimist. He was convinced that knowledge would make us good. The social qualities of the dialectic are predicated on the belief that by working together, two or more honest, well-meaning, and reasonable people can move steadily from ignorance to virtue (goodness and happiness).

Although Socrates was probably correct in his belief that no normally reasonable person willingly does himself harm, he was surely wrong in his rejection of the possibility of weakness of will. His limited knowledge of the complexities of human psychology prevented him from recognizing what is a very common experience for most of us: We lack the will to do the good we know or to resist the bad that tempts us. Jesus' oft-quoted line that "the spirit is willing, but the flesh is weak" probably comes closer to our experiences than does Socrates' intellectualistic optimism.

Perhaps the best way to approach the seeming paradoxes of Socrates' rejection of the weak will and insistence that virtue is knowledge lies in not imposing contemporary values on the ancient *sophos*. Socrates' love of wisdom was rare in his own day, and his indifference to money, property, and prestige flies in the face of the values many of us devote our lives to (or seem to, at any rate). The common counterexamples used to show that we often know what is good but choose what we know is bad (smoking, acts of malice, dishonesty) are only counterexamples when we separate knowledge from wisdom.

If by "know the good," we mean, for example, to understand cognitively that smoking leads to impaired health and that lying corrupts our character, then it is possible to know the good and do the bad. But if by "know the good" we mean to value and love the soul, then perhaps Socrates is correct. Perhaps we choose to smoke or to lie in ignorance of their *qualitative* effects on our souls.

We might also find Socrates' ideas difficult to accept because—like the Sophists and many Greeks of his time—we grant primacy to the external physical and social world rather than to the soul. We more easily recognize harm to our reputations and physical health than we do harm to our souls. Using the physical and deductive sciences as our paradigms of knowledge can make it difficult to recognize even the possibility of wisdom.

By professing his ignorance, Socrates has achieved a kind of immortality. He is one of the few great philosophers to whom people of many cultures, eras, abilities, and interests have looked for wisdom. The Socratic mission has not ended. Socrates' power to provoke, challenge, and awaken lives on.

©iStock.com/Ladida

Asclepius was the Greek god of healing. To this day, his symbol, the snake-entwined caduceus, is still associated with medicine. Why do you think Socrates' last words acknowledged a debt of gratitude to this god? Of what "disease" was Socrates being cured?

Summary of Main Points

- Socrates was the first major Western philosopher. He wrote no philosophy, and what we know of him comes chiefly from his pupils Plato and Xenophon. Socrates challenged the Sophist doctrines of relativism, moral realism, and might makes right. Socrates' teaching and life were so fully integrated that the force of his whole person galvanized others. Individuals of this sort are known as paradigmatic or archetypal individuals, rare human beings whose very nature represents something elemental about the human condition.

- Socrates perfected a style of philosophical inquiry known as the Socratic method or dialectic. Based on the assumption that the function of education is to draw the truth out of the pupil rather than "fill an empty vessel," Socratic dialectic consists of a series of guided questions that continually refine the ideas under scrutiny. Definitions are required for all key terms, and logical inconsistencies are brought to light and resolved. Socrates used irony to encourage active listening by his pupils and dialectical partners.

- An ironic utterance is a way of communicating that has at least two levels of meaning: the literal level, also known as the obvious level, and the hidden level, also known as the real level.

- Among Socratic teachings, the most persistent command was "Know thyself," meaning, among other things, that a life devoid of philosophical speculation is hardly a human life, because only philosophical reflection can help us discover what is real and important from the standpoint of the psyche, the uniquely human soul-mind. Acknowledgment of ignorance, Socrates taught, is a fundamental characteristic of the examined life.

- Socrates saw himself as a kind of "physician of the soul." He believed that the "real person" is not the body, but the psyche.

- For Socrates, human excellence (virtue) is a special kind of knowledge (*techne*) that combines technical understanding with the skill and character to apply that knowledge. According to Socrates, knowledge (wisdom) always produces behavioral results, because behavior is always guided by beliefs. This view is sometimes called intellectualism, the idea that no one knowingly does wrong. According to Socrates, there is no such thing as weakness of will: "To know the good is to do the good."

Post-Reading Reflections

Now that you've had a chance to learn about Socrates, use your new knowledge to answer these questions.

1. What do you see as the *philosophical relevance* of Socrates' life to his teachings? Do you think it is possible to separate a philosopher's life and character from his or her philosophy? That is, does the value of a philosophy of life suffer when its advocate fails to live up to it? Explain.

2. In line with question 1, use Socratic principles to defend Socrates against the charge of being a bad husband and father. Is such a defense persuasive? Does it work for, say, any spouse or parent who does socially valuable work for little money and who puts in long hours but neglects his or her family?

3. Socrates thought it very important not to teach for money. Why? What kind of teaching did he mean? Was he right? Can this principle be extended to priests, rabbis, and preachers? To psychologists? Explain.

4. Suppose it were discovered that Socrates secretly violated many of his teachings. Would this affect your attitude toward his philosophy? How? Why?

5. Use your responses to questions 1–4 to devise a tentative "philosophy of personal relevance for philosophers."

6. How did Socrates use his physical appearance to support his general theory of virtue? Do you think his approach was effective? Did doing so contribute to the notion that Socrates was a Sophist? Was he a Sophist? Make the case that he was and that he was not. Which is the stronger case?

7. Do any individuals or groups fulfill a Socratic function in today's society? If so, explain how. If not, explain that.

 MindTap

Experience MindTap through the activities highlighted in this chapter. Further explore this online, personalized learning tool to deepen your comprehension and improve your grades.

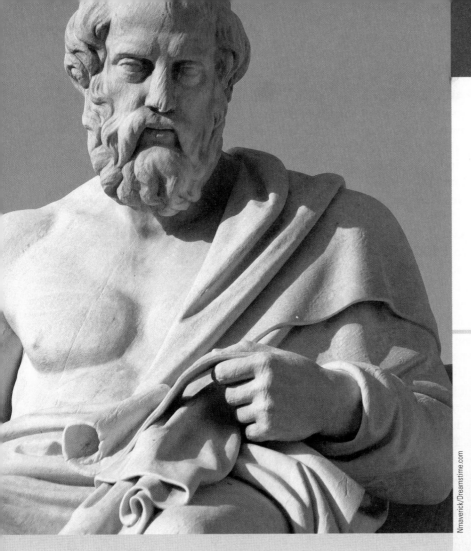

Nmaverick/Dreamstime.com

5

The Philosopher-King
Plato

Until philosophers are kings,
or the kings and princes of this
world have the spirit and power
of philosophy ... cities will never
have rest from their evils ... nor
the human race ... and then only
will our State ... behold the light
of day.

— *Plato*

Learning Objectives

MindTap™

After you complete this chapter, you should be able to:

- Identify the sources of Plato's disillusionment.

- Explain the creation of the Academy and its chief purpose.

- Explain why Plato needed Forms.

- Distinguish between *knowledge* and *opinion*, according to Plato.

- Differentiate between instrumental and functionalist theories of morality.

- Describe the Allegory of the Cave.

- Rank the four cardinal virtues, according to Plato.

- Assess Plato's claim that society consists of three classes of people.

- Analyze Plato's theory of the development and decline of democracy.

- Describe the tyrannical soul, according to Plato.

DEMOCRACY IS THE BEST form of government. Can there be any doubt? One of the great traditions of American history has been that "any boy can grow up to be president." And certainly our history suggests a continuous (if sometimes painfully slow) movement toward extending greater and greater choices and opportunities to all our citizens. Now it's no longer "any *boy* can grow up to be president," but "any *child*." Barriers of skin color, creed, and social class are being removed. The only limits on our dreams are our own. And someday these barriers may disappear as we learn new ways to abolish disadvantages of birth or social status.

As citizens of a democracy, we are free to seek any position we wish in society. The presidency itself has only three requirements: citizenship, age, and a majority of electoral college votes. If in practice our presidents come from the wealthier, more educated classes, they still do not need to meet any stringent requirements of self-discipline, character, or wisdom. Nor do we who elect them. This is the glory of democracy.

Picture now a November morning. A line of voters waits to elect the next president of the United States. You have spent weeks critically assessing a seemingly endless series of speeches and debates (going so far as to annotate written transcripts). You've subscribed to liberal and conservative podcasts, blogs, magazines, and newspapers in order to get as complete a picture of the candidates' records and the issues as you can. You've read long political editorials as well as your voter's pamphlet. Because there are a number of lesser offices, bond issues, and legislative amendments on the ballot, you've brought a written list of your carefully reasoned decisions with you to the polls.

Patiently waiting your turn, you overhear a small group of people standing in line behind you. A woman announces, "I'm voting for X. She's a woman, and that's good enough for me." Someone else says, "My dad always voted Republican, so I'm voting Democrat!" A third person chimes in, "I'm not voting for Y. He's a member of the Tea Party." A fourth voter announces that she will renounce her citizenship before she votes for a progressive socialist." Someone asks about "all those propositions and stuff," and the group laughs. "Who cares?" someone else snaps. "None of that stuff makes any difference." "Yeah," another responds, "there are too many to keep straight anyway. I just vote yes, no, yes, at random." Yet another says, "As a single parent, I'm only interested in Prop. M, since I need money for child care. I'll just guess at the rest."

Disturbed by this, you suddenly notice that the man in front of you is weaving. You ask if he's sick, and he laughingly answers, with the unmistakable smell of beer on his breath: "Heck, no. I'm loaded. It's the only way to vote." You vote anyway but can't shake your anger for a long time. It doesn't seem fair that these irresponsible votes should equal your carefully researched and reasoned decisions. They might even cancel out your vote. It's worse than unfair. It's dumb. It's not *reasonable*, you think. There should be *some* requirement for voting. Not anything unfair or discriminatory, just *reasonable*. And come to think of it, there should be some kind of test or something for politicians. They're a pretty unethical and dumb lot, too.

If you have ever had thoughts like this, your disgust and annoyance at "the way things are run around here" have probably triggered a desire for a "more ideal" society. As we all know, however, no such ideal society exists in this world, so where

How can any man be a democrat who is sincerely a democrat?
— H.L. Mencken

did you get the idea for it? It's as if you have seen beyond the way things are, seen a *higher possibility*.

Anyone who has visualized a fairer, more ideal society has already shared at least some ideas with Plato, perhaps the greatest, and certainly one of the most imposing and influential, philosophers in the Western world.

PHILOSOPHICAL QUERY

As persistent voting controversies make clear, Americans have reason to be wary of requirements for voting. In the past, voting requirements have been used to prevent women and people of certain ethnic groups from voting. On the other hand, a case might be made that by not having some minimal standard of preparedness and awareness, we make a mockery of "choosing." How can an ignorant voter "choose" anything? Does "choosing" matter? Can I be truly free if I am uninformed and ignorant? Discuss from both sides.

MindTap

Discussing Philosophy

Plato's Life and Work

Our chief source of information regarding Plato's philosophy is Plato himself. We still have all the works attributed to him by ancient scholars. The most important of these are philosophical dialogues. We have already seen material from some of these in Chapters 3 and 4: the *Apology, Crito, Phaedo, Theaetetus, Timaeus, Gorgias, Protagoras, Meno*, and the *Republic*. We also have the summaries and analyses of some of Plato's doctrines left by his greatest student, Aristotle. We probably have more biographical information about Plato than about any other ancient philosopher, much of it from Diogenes Läertius's *Life of Plato*. There is also a controversial collection of thirteen letters and some dialogues whose authenticity some scholars dispute. One of these, *Letter: VII*, is of special interest because of its comments regarding the mature Plato's attitudes toward democracy in view of the way Socrates was treated by it.

Perhaps no single work of Western philosophy has been read by as many people as Plato's *Republic*. It is considered by most philosophers to be Plato's most impressive and important work because it presents his overall philosophy in a dramatic, organized, and brilliant form. We'll use the *Republic* as the basis for our introduction to this would-be philosopher-king, but first let us start with a brief sketch of Plato's life.

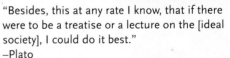

"Besides, this at any rate I know, that if there were to be a treatise or a lecture on the [ideal society], I could do it best."
—Plato

The Decline of the Aristocracy

Plato (c. 427–348 B.C.E.) is actually the nickname of Aristocles, the son of one of the oldest and most elite Athenian families. Through his mother's family he was related to a celebrated lawgiver named Solon. Plato's father's family traced its lineage to the ancient kings of Athens and even further back to Poseidon, the god of the sea. His given name, Aristocles, meant "best, most renowned." He is said to have done well

"Perictione: Plato's Philosopher-Mother"

In *On the Harmony of Women*, **Perictione** (c. 450–350 B.C.E.) calls women to philosophy in terms reminiscent of Socrates (Chapter 4), Epicurus, and Epictetus (Chapter 7). Perictione is believed to have been Plato's mother, and we hear in her work echoes of Socrates' disdain for vanity, his ideal of self-control, and his affirmation of the superiority of inner or essential beauty over mere physical attractiveness. We must wonder about the influence Perictione had on her son, as well as about the influence other forgotten and overlooked women philosophers may have had on their more famous peers. In the passage quoted here, Perictione argues that wisdom and self-control in an individual woman generate other virtues, which in turn lead to harmony and happiness for the entire community:

One must deem the harmonious woman to be full of wisdom and self-control; a soul must be exceedingly conscious of goodness to be just and courageous and wise, embellished with self-sufficiency and hating empty opinion. Worthwhile things come to a woman from these—for herself, her husband, her children, her household, perhaps even for a city....

But one must also train the body to natural measures concerning nourishment and clothing, baths and anointings, the arrangement of the hair, and ornaments of gold and precious stone. Women who eat and drink every costly thing, who dress extravagantly and wear the things that women wear, are ready for the sin of every vice both with respect to the marriage bed and the rest of wrongdoing. It is necessary merely to appease hunger and thirst, even

if this be done by frugal means; in the case of cold, even a goat-skin or rough garment would suffice.... So the harmonious woman will not wrap herself in gold or precious stone from India or anywhere else, nor will she braid her hair with artful skills or anoint herself with infusions of Arabian scent, nor will she paint her face, whitening or rouging it, darkening her eye-brows and lashes and treating her gray hair with dye; nor will she be forever bathing. The woman who seeks these things seeks an admirer for feminine weakness. It is the beauty that comes from wisdom, not from these, that gratifies women who are well-born....

But I think a woman is harmonious in the following way: if she becomes full of wisdom and self-control. For this benefits not only her husband, but also the children, relatives, slaves; the whole house, including possessions and friends, both fellow-citizens and foreign guest friends. Artlessly, she will keep their house, speaking and hearing fair things, and obeying her husband in the unanimity of their common life, attending upon the relatives and friends whom he extols, and thinking the same things sweet and bitter as he—lest she be out of tune in relation to the whole.

Holger Thesleff, "Pythagorean Texts of the Hellenistic Period," *Acta Academiae Aboensis, Humaniora*, trans. Vicki Lynn Harper, in *A History of Women Philosophers*, vol. 1, 600 B.C.–500 A.D., ed. Mary Ellen Waithe (Dordrecht: Martinus Nijhoff Publishers, 1987), pp. 20–21.

at practically everything as a young man: music, logic, debate, math, poetry. He was attractive and made his mark as a wrestler. In the military, he distinguished himself in three battles and even won a prize for bravery.[1] The Greek root of Plato is *Platon*, which means "broad" or "wide"; one story is that he had wide shoulders, another that he had a wide forehead.

Plato was born two years after the death of Pericles, the great architect of Athenian democracy. Athens was fighting Sparta in the Peloponnesian Wars, which lasted more than twenty years. During that time Athens was in a state of turmoil (not unlike America now and during the Vietnam War). Great energy and expense were drained off by the war itself, as well as by disagreements over whether Athens should continue to fight and, if so, how. As we learned in Chapter 4, Athens finally surrendered to Sparta in 404 B.C.E.

Plato

The conquering Spartans supported a group of nobles, known as the Thirty, who overthrew the democracy and ruled Athens for a short time. Plato's family were members of this group. This is the same Thirty that Socrates resisted when he was ordered to condemn and execute Leon of Salamis in violation of the Athenian constitution.

Members of the Thirty failed in their efforts to restore rule by an elite based on bloodlines rather than on character or wisdom. Their reign lasted only about eight months before democracy was restored. It was the restored democracy, however, that tried and condemned Socrates. The impact of these events never left Plato, who was in his early twenties at the time. Looking back on this time, Plato recalled:

> Of course I saw in a short time that [the Thirty] made the former government look in comparison like an age of gold. Among other things they sent an elderly man, Socrates, a friend of mine, who I should hardly be ashamed to say was the justest man of his time … against one of the citizens.… Their purpose was to connect Socrates to their government whether he wished or not.… When I observed all this—and some other similar matters of importance—I withdrew in disgust from the abuses of those days.[2]

The nobles who formed the Thirty had no doubt been disturbed by changes in Athenian society brought about by the long war: the loss of elitist privileges that accompanied increased democracy, the breakdown of tradition, the Sophists' use of debaters' tricks to sway the mob. In a democracy, the cleverest, most persuasive, and most attractive speakers could control the state. Also, the emerging business class had created a power base dependent on money and aggressiveness rather than on tradition and social status.[3]

> *Plato's genius is exhibited in the fact that he succeeded in eliciting from his observations of the Athenian state reflections on society and government that are true everywhere.*
> — Raphael Demos

Plato's Disillusionment

Plato became increasingly discouraged by both the "mob" and the "elite." The mob, represented by the jury at Socrates' trial, was irrational and dangerous; it was swayed by sophistic appeals to emotion, not by reason. Rule by the elite, represented by the behavior of the Thirty, was cruel, self-centered, and greedy. When Plato saw that neither the aristocracy nor the common citizenry was capable of superior rule, his "disillusionment [was] fearful and wonderful to behold."[4]

Plato concluded that most people are unfit by training and ability to make the difficult and necessary decisions that would result in a just society. The "average person" lacks wisdom and self-restraint. As Plato saw things, most people make emotional responses based on desire and sentiment rather than on rational considerations stemming from an objective view of what is genuinely good for the individual and society. What, he wondered, could be clearer proof of the mob's deficiencies than its utter failure to recognize the truth of Socrates' message? The trial and death of Socrates showed Plato what happens when justice is detached from wisdom and self-restraint and reduced to a majority vote.

> Now as I considered these matters, as well as the sort of men who were active in politics, and the laws and the customs, the more I examined them and the more I advanced in years, the harder it appeared to me to administer the government correctly.… The result was that I, who had at first been full of eagerness for a public

career, as I gazed upon the whirlpool of public life and saw the incessant movement of shifting currents, at last felt dizzy, and … *finally saw clearly in regard to all states now existing that without exception their system of government is bad.*[5] [emphasis added]

Plato would see to it that Socrates would be avenged—but by philosophy rather than by political action.

After the revolt of the Thirty and the execution of Socrates, Plato left Athens and wandered for nearly twelve years. He studied with Euclid (the great pioneer of geometry) and possibly with the hedonist Aristippus. He seems also to have gone to Egypt. During his travels he studied mathematics and mysticism, both of which influenced his later philosophy. He studied Pythagorean philosophy and was deeply influenced by its emphasis on mathematics as the basis of all things (see box "The Celestial Music of the Spheres," in Chapter 2).

The Academy

Plato was about forty years old when he founded his Academy (around 388 B.C.E.). Because, in Plato's view, "no present government [was] suitable for philosophy," the Academy was established as a philosophic retreat, isolated from the turmoil of Athenian politics, safe from the fate of Socrates. Its chief purpose was probably to educate people who would be fit to rule the just state. Plato's ideal educational program was a progressive one in which the study of mathematics, geometry, music, and so forth introduced discipline into the student's overall character and order into the student's mind. Only after the mind and soul were disciplined were a select few allowed to study ultimate philosophical principles.

The material ruins of Plato's Academy may have decayed, but, appropriately, his ideas remain potent and timely.

Ironically, considering the importance of the Academy and the influence it was to exert, we have no solid evidence concerning when it was founded, how it was organized, what exactly was studied, or what educational techniques were used. Most of Plato's writing seems to have been finished before he founded the Academy, with the exception of a few works completed when he was an old man. His chief function at the Academy was probably as a teacher and administrator. Here Plato lived for forty years, lecturing "without notes," until he died.[6]

Plato's Epistemology

Socrates' death, the revolt of the Thirty, sophistic abuses, and other factors convinced Plato that a corrupt state produces corrupt citizens. He thus attempted to develop a theory of knowledge that could refute sophistic skepticism and moral relativism. Plato believed that if he could identify and articulate the difference between mere opinion and genuine knowledge, it would then be possible to identify the structure of an ideal state based on knowledge and truth—rather than the mere appearance of truth and personal whim.

Plato correctly understood that before he could provide satisfactory answers to ethical, social, political, and other philosophical questions, he must first tackle the problem of knowledge. We have seen how the conflicting opinions of the Presocratics first led to philosophical confusion and then to ethical and political abuses in the hands of the most extreme of the Sophists. Socrates' heroic effort to refute ignorance and relativism was most successful in its exposure of error and inconsistency. It was less successful in establishing any positive knowledge.

Consequently, Plato could not avoid the challenge of sophistic skepticism or ignore philosophy's reputation for generating ludicrous doctrines that contradicted each other—and themselves. Though the Presocratics, the Sophists, and Socrates had all made use of the distinction between appearance and reality, the exact nature of reality and clear rational criteria for distinguishing reality from appearance had eluded them.

> The feeling of wonder is the touchstone of the philosopher, and all philosophy has its origins in wonder.
> — Plato

Plato's Dualistic Solution

Plato concluded that the solution to the basic problem of knowledge lay in acknowledging that both Heraclitus and Parmenides were partially correct in their efforts to characterize reality (Chapter 2). Heraclitus asserted that the "one" is some kind of orderly cycle or process of change. He said that "change alone is unchanging." Parmenides, in contrast, referred to the "one" as *being*. Parmenides argued that *being* is perfect and complete or whole. It cannot move or change. Parmenidean *being* is material; "it is the *being* of the visible cosmos, immobilized, and to a great extent purified, but still clearly recognizable."

According to Plato, Heraclitus and Parmenides probably thought they were discussing things that could be sensed or perceived as part of the physical world. (We will refer to such things as "sensibles," for short.) The Sophists' skeptical arguments were also aimed at contradictions and difficulties generated by problems of sensation and perception. (See Chapter 3.)

What if, Plato wondered, reality is not a single thing (a monism) but rather a dualism? One reality might be Heraclitean and another Parmenidean—one reality in constant change and the other eternally changeless:

> After an initial critical period during which, with Socrates as spokesperson, Plato called into question his contemporaries' opinions and values, he adopted a more dogmatic approach, staking out a certain number of positions in the fields of ethics, epistemology, and ontology. In all these domains, one idea was stressed above all others: that of transcendence, implying on the one hand the division of reality into two realms—the sensible, the realm of individuals that is continually changing, and the intelligible, the realm of the absolutely immutable—and on the other hand the distinction, within each human being, between a mortal body endowed with five senses and an immortal soul that can grasp the intelligible.[7]

Of course a supposition is not evidence. Plato needed to prove the dual nature of reality. Part of the proof seemed easy enough: It is obvious that a world of "sensibles" exists. And the sensible world certainly seems to be one of change: growth cycles, soil erosion, flowing rivers, the wear and tear of the implements of daily living, and so on. Further, this change is orderly: The same seasons follow the same seasons, dogs do not give birth to stones, objects fall down and not up. So, as far as the world of sensibles is concerned, Heraclitus seems to be correct.

But a completely Heraclitean world of observable change, for all its obviousness, would be a world devoid of the possibility of knowledge and certainty, according to Plato. Such a world would be a world of appearances only, a realm of opinion, not knowledge. Plato called this condition the world of *becoming*.

Knowledge and Being

Attempts to explain how one kind of thing changes into another generated ambiguities and seeming contradictions: How could "one thing" somehow change into something else? In what sense can my twelve-year-old dog Daiquiri be the "same" dog she was five years ago? Does this mean that Daiquiri is both the same dog she was *and* a different dog? In what sense does the same *person* change from an infant into a philosophy student?

Plato recognized the full importance of the questions raised by the Presocratics concerning coherent explanations of how things change, how reality "becomes" appearance, how appearances are related to reality, and other fundamental issues. The relationship between appearance and reality, the problem of "the one and the many," and the nature of change needed to be clarified before any refutation to the sophistic assault on rationality was possible.

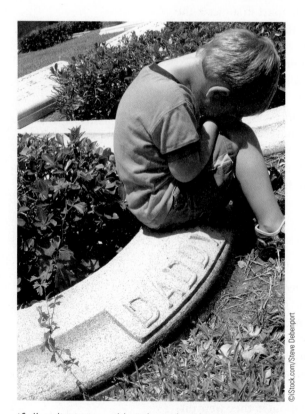

©iStock.com/Steve Debenport

If all reality is "sensible," then what do we miss when a loved one dies? Is profound grief merely a biochemical condition or brain state—or is there more to persons than what can be perceived with the senses? Perhaps something transcendent?

According to Plato, the Sophists could not discover truth because they were only concerned with the Heraclitean world of sensibles, the world of ever-changing perceptions and customs. But the very essence of knowledge is unchanging. What is true is always true. Therefore, whatever is relative and *always changing* cannot be true. Truth and knowledge are found in another realm of reality: the level of *being* that Parmenides tried to characterize.

Plato believed that this second reality, although closely related to the world of *becoming*, exists independently of it. This other reality has many of the qualities Parmenides ascribed to the one (*being*): It is not physical, and it is not affected by space and time. According to Plato, what is eternal is *real*; what changes is only *appearance*. We can have *knowledge* of what is eternal (*being*); of appearances (*becoming*), there can be only *opinions*. Plato insisted that whatever is permanent is superior to whatever is not. Therefore, reality is superior to appearance, and knowledge (reality) is superior to opinion (appearance).

> *Plato … knew that our reason, if left to itself, tries to soar up to knowledge to which no object that experience may give can ever correspond; but which is nonetheless real, and by no means a cobweb of the brain.*
> — Immanuel Kant

The Theory of Forms

In Plato's metaphysics, the level of *being* consists of timeless essences or entities called *Forms*. Such a metaphysics is sometimes called transcendental because it asserts that there is a plane of existence "above and beyond" our ordinary existence. To transcend anything is to go so far beyond it as to reach a qualitatively different level.

The **Platonic Forms** are independently existing, nonspatial, nontemporal "somethings" ("kinds," "types," or "sorts") that cannot be known through the senses. Known in thought, these Forms are not ideas in the usual sense. Knowledge is always about Forms.

It may be helpful to think about other meanings of the word *form*. "Form" sometimes refers to the shape, manner, style, or type of something. We make forms from which to mold dishes or statues, for example. We fill in business forms. The very notion of form implies something that provides general or essential order, structure, or shape for a particular instance. Thus, the form of something is sometimes called its structure or essence, or even its basic nature. Many of these everyday meanings involve the essence of a thing, the quality that makes it what it is. In Platonic terms, a thing's Form is what it uniquely and essentially is.

However, *exactly what Plato meant* by "Forms" has remained a subject of intense philosophical debate and disagreement from Plato's time to ours. For over the past fifty years, the theory of Forms has been one of the most discussed parts of Plato's philosophy among English-speaking philosophers. And, still, philosophers cannot agree on exactly what Plato meant. The complexity of the problem is further compounded by the fact that although Plato places great importance on the Forms, he does not seem to have a very well worked out theory of Forms.[8]

Nevertheless, because Plato's theory of Forms is central to the rest of his philosophy, and thus the basis for his theory of the ideal state, we need to take the time to develop a general sense of what Plato hoped to show with his theory of Forms, always keeping in mind that philosophers are still arguing over precisely what Plato meant.

platonic forms Independently existing, nonspatial, nontemporal "somethings" ("kinds," "types," or "sorts") known only through thought and that cannot be known through the senses; independently existing objects of thought; that which makes a particular thing uniquely and essentially what it is.

What Are Forms?

The Greek root for "form" (*eidos*) is sometimes translated as "idea." Thus it is tempting to think of Forms as mental entities (ideas) that exist only in our minds. But Plato insists that the Forms are independent of any minds (real).[9] To avoid this confusion, some philosophers translate *eidos* as "archetype" or "essence."

According to Plato, each Form actually exists—pure and unchanging—regardless of continuous shifts in human opinions and alterations in the physical world of sensibles. Each Form is a pure, unmixed essence that exists independently of human consciousness. It is important to be very clear about this: Although the Forms actually exist, they are not physical objects.

Forms are universal types or kinds that somehow exist outside of space and time. The physical world contains particular *instances* of the various universal Forms. Today we might call Forms abstract objects. Plato considers such abstract objects more real than concrete physical objects.

The sorts of things Plato refers to as Forms include geometrical, mathematical, and logical relationships (triangularity, equivalence, identity); virtues (goodness, wisdom, courage); and sensible properties (roundness, beauty, redness). Note that the physical sensations we associate with such qualities as roundness and redness are not the same thing as *roundness* and *redness* in and of themselves.

Particular things differ in terms of what Plato variously refers to as their "participation in," "sharing in," "resembling," or "reflecting" the Form *roundness* or the Form *redness*. There is only one Form of *redness*, for instance, although there can be a virtually infinite number of particular things that "share" some element or degree of *redness*, that "resemble" or "reflect" the essence of pure *redness*. But *redness* (the Form) is always the same regardless of any changes that occur in some particular object. When, for example, a red flower fades to pale pink, its participation in the Form *redness* decreases. There is, however, no decrease in the Form *redness* itself.

What might Plato have meant by saying that particular things "resemble," "share in," "participate in," or "reflect" different Forms? Consider two apparently identical glass beads, each "reflecting" *roundness* and *identity*. Yet no sensible object is ever absolutely, truly, perfectly round, because sensible objects always contain "mixtures," "impurities," even "opposites." Under microscopic scrutiny, we would expect to find that the surface of the smoothest, purest glass bead ever discovered was minutely pitted or uneven—microscopically imperfect—yet imperfect nonetheless. At most, it might be "as round as physically possible."

According to Plato, no two beads are, or ever can be, identically round. "Aha!" you may think, "but two glass beads can be identical—especially given today's computerized technologies and sophisticated manufacturing techniques."

Stop and think a little further, though. What would it mean for two physical objects to be genuinely, absolutely, perfectly *identical*? In the strictest sense, "two things are identical if all the characteristics of one are also possessed by the other and vice versa."[10] Is it possible for two glass beads to be *absolutely identical*? No, because in order to be identical—not just very, very similar—they would have to contain exactly the same silica molecules, atoms, quarks, neutrinos, and in exactly the same place at exactly the same time. Of course, they cannot do so, for if that were the case, there would be only one glass bead. Two very, very similar glass beads

I had a dream, and I heard in my dream that the primeval letters or elements out of which you and I and all other things are compounded have no reason or explanation; you can only name them, but no predicate can be either affirmed or denied of them ... if you mean to speak of this or that thing by itself alone.

— Plato

must be in two distinct places. By being in two distinct places at precisely the same moment, they are different from each other in respect to location. Thus, they are not—strictly speaking—identical.

Finally, consider the kinds of reasons Plato might offer to support the claim that Forms exist independently of human consciousness: We have good reasons to believe that round objects existed before any perceivers (animals or people) did. Hence, roundness is not a property that depends on human minds for existence; *roundness* is more than just a human idea. *Roundness* itself—as distinct from any particular round thing—is unchanging. It cannot change from being *roundness* to, say, *nearly roundness* or *oblongness* or *rectilinearity*. Following basic laws of rationality, *roundness* is either *roundness* or it is not. And so for all Forms. (For a different view of whether objects and properties can exist independently of perceivers, see Chapter 10.)

In general, the truths about mathematical objects exist whether we know those truths or not. Plato thinks the same is true for moral and aesthetic facts.

PHILOSOPHICAL QUERY

Reflect on the following objection to the preceding paragraphs: "The glass bead example is only playing with semantics. When we talk about two physical objects being 'identical', we don't mean literally identical—we mean so similar that human beings are unable to distinguish one object from the other. Obviously we can distinguish different things from each other when they're right next to each other. But if we find no differences when we analyze them one at a time, we are justified in saying that they are identical, 'indistinguishable'! Identical means indistinguishable to human beings; that is, so closely resembling each other that we cannot tell them apart." How might Plato answer this objection?

Why Plato Needed the Forms

Among other things, Plato wanted the theory of Forms to provide a *rational explanation* of how knowledge is possible. The Forms are the foundation of Plato's bold answer to the Sophists' skeptical assault on knowledge and to their relativistic rejection of universal (absolute) truths. Defense of absolute, unchanging truths is difficult under the best of circumstances; it is especially difficult if we wish to move beyond merely heartfelt belief in absolutes. Plato knew that unless he could offer more than *faith* in the existence of absolutes, more than authoritarian and dogmatic pronouncements, he would fail, as a philosopher, to meet the challenge of relativism.

Plato's task here is of more than mere historical interest to us; it bears on important epistemological questions: *Is* everything a matter of opinion? If not: (1) Is there any way to *show* that knowledge is possible? and (2) Is there any way those of us who are not wise or enlightened can identify those who are? That is, if we cannot always grasp the truth, can we at least identify those who can and thereby benefit from their counsel? If the answer to 2 is "no," then we are at the mercy of unverifiable beliefs, rule by force, rhetoric, and seduction. If one opinion is ultimately as good as any other, then one form of government is no better than any other, and there is no point

It is hard, too, to see how a weaver or a carpenter will be benefitted in regard to his own craft by knowing this [a form], or how the man who has viewed the Idea itself will be a better doctor or general thereby. For a doctor seems not even to study health in this way, but the health of man, or perhaps rather the health of a particular man; it is individuals that he is healing.

— Aristotle

in seeking truth or wisdom. All that matters is surviving as comfortably as possible (in my opinion).

On the other hand, if knowledge is possible, and if some opinions really are better than others, how can we justify democracy, a form of government that treats each citizen's opinion as equal? Put more forcefully: If knowledge exists, what would justify ignoring it? Can there be any reasonable justification for ignoring the difference between knowledge and opinion?

In struggling to develop his theory of Forms, Plato was struggling to *refute*—not just *deny*—relativism and thereby preserve the distinction between knowledge and opinion. Plato reasoned that if he could solidly establish that knowledge is possible, and that knowledge exists, then he could also justify and preserve real (objective) distinctions between right and wrong, true and false, better and worse.

PHILOSOPHICAL QUERY

Is it possible to know that no one does know? Is it possible to know that no one does know that no one does know? Is it possible to know that no one can know that no one does know? How do you know? Or, how do you know that you don't know?

Knowledge and Opinion

For Plato, the chief distinction between knowledge and opinion is that knowledge is fixed, absolutely and eternally true (correct), whereas opinions are changeable and "unanchored." According to Plato, *scientific knowledge of particulars is impossible.* That is, fundamental knowledge of reality must always be knowledge of forms. Thus, a "science" consists of necessary and universal truths about the objects (forms) that the science studies. In all scientific subject areas, the physical objects, structural relationships, particular individuals, societies, or governments studied represent Forms. The particular things themselves are never "as real" as the Forms they participate in or resemble.

Remember, too, that for Plato, that which changes is less real than that which does not. That which changes is "lower" than that which does not. And since all particular things change, when Protagoras said that the individual is "the measure," he was, from Plato's view, talking about the level of *becoming*, about the lower level of perceptions of particular things, about the personal and individual rather than the public and universal.

In Plato's metaphysics, the level of change is the level of growth and decay, life and death—*becoming*. Only in the realm of *becoming* can opinions change from true to false. In the *Timaeus* Plato says:

> That which is apprehended by intelligence and reason is always in the same state, but that which is conceived by opinion with the help of sensation and without reason is always in a process of becoming and perishing and never really is.[11]

What Happens When We Disagree?

Granted that people and conditions change, and granted that we disagree among ourselves over what is true and what is real, what happens when we disagree about knowledge?

Suppose, for example, that Michael simply cannot see or understand that 2×3 does not equal 4. In other words, for Michael, $2 \times 3 = 4$. We can say, then, that Michael has a false belief or opinion; we can also say, however, that the product of 2×3 is not a matter of opinion (Michael's or anyone's) but of fixed mathematical properties and relationships. We know this because in order to *understand* concepts such as number, three, two, product, equivalence, and such, we have to "glimpse" their Forms. This glimpse of recognition is what understanding the concept is.

Next, consider the case of Michael's aunt, Patricia. Asked the product of 2×3, Patricia proudly says, "I know the answer. It's six!" Asked how she knows, Patricia explains, "Because mother told me so. And because my mother's mother told her." Michael's friend, Emma, also confidently agrees that $2 \times 3 = 6$. When we ask her to explain why, Emma says, "Teacher told me so."

Emma does not *know* that $2 \times 3 = 6$ any more than Michael "knows" that $2 \times 3 = 4$ or Patricia "knows" that $2 \times 3 = 6$. Unlike Michael's belief, Patricia's and Emma's beliefs are true. But they are still just *beliefs* (opinions). Patricia and Emma are lucky this time—their beliefs are "unanchored," however.

Lacking knowledge, Michael, Patricia, and Emma have no way to *determine* who is right. If they vote, they might end up with the correct answer—but only by chance. What they cannot do is willingly choose the correct answer, because they lack sufficient understanding to make an informed determination: They don't *know* what it is.

Without knowledge, we are like Michael, Patricia, and Emma: We, too, are at the mercy of luck and uninformed preference. We are "unanchored" and so can only act based on habit, tradition, personal preference, and impulse.

Throughout the *Republic*, Plato repeatedly distinguishes between knowledge and opinion, warning against even true opinions that lack grounding in knowledge. Here's a typical passage:

> "But I don't think it's right, Socrates … for you to be able to tell us other people's opinions but not your own, when you've given so much time to the subject."
>
> "Yes, but do you think it's right for a man to talk as if he knows what he does not?"
>
> "He has no right to talk as if he knew; but he should be prepared to say what his opinion is, so far as it goes."
>
> "Well," I [Socrates] said, "haven't you noticed that opinion without knowledge is blind—isn't anyone with a true but unthinking opinion like a blind man on the right road?"
>
> "Yes."[12]

As Socrates' encounters with the Sophists showed, distinguishing between knowledge and opinion can sting when cherished beliefs come under scrutiny. Deeply committed partisans sometimes dismiss opposing views as uninformed opinions rooted in the self-interest and willful blindness of those who disagree with them—while thinking of themselves as well-informed and well-intentioned individuals whose beliefs are based on solid, objective knowledge of all relevant facts. This sort of partiality is easy to recognize when it involves other people heavily invested in intense disagreements we care little about. It is much harder to acknowledge, much less resist, when we are convinced that we are on the side of truth in the controversies of our day—such as the scope of and solutions to climate change or

> *To what purpose is it for philosophy to decide against common sense in this or any other matter? The material world is older, and of more authority, than any principles of philosophy. It declines the tribunal of reason, and laughs at the artillery of the logician.*
>
> — Thomas Reid

whether measles vaccines cause autism or violent videogames cause violent behavior. On what grounds are those of us untrained and inexperienced in the precise areas of expertise at issue justified in dismissing those who disagree with us as *clearly* wrong? If we refer to experts, how do we choose among all those claiming expertise? Looking more closely won't help if we are unsure of our own judgment. And the popularity of a claim won't help either because merely counting always risks multiplying tainted, partial, or irrelevant evidence. We need a qualitatively different approach if we are serious about distinguishing between knowledge and opinion.

According to Plato, the Sophists failed to understand this, confusing opinion with knowledge, perception with understanding, and the realm of *becoming* with the realm of *being*. Plato's task, then, is analogous to "proving" the existence of colors to persons born blind.

When an appeal to direct experience or common understanding is not possible, an indirect approach may prove effective. If we have yet to grasp the Forms, perhaps we can get some indirect idea of them. In the *Republic*, Plato uses three different comparisons to help express various aspects of the theory of Forms: the Divided Line, the Simile of the Sun, and the Allegory of the Cave. We will study each of them. Each comparison clarifies different but interconnected aspects of the theory of Forms. Do not worry if you need to take extra time with this material. Allow each of Plato's similes to help you better grasp the whole.

The Divided Line

> For as all nature is akin, and the soul has [already] learned all things, there is no difficulty in ... learning ... all the rest, if a man is strenuous and does not faint; for all enquiry is but recollection.
> — Plato

Plato used the concept of a divided line to illustrate the relationship of knowledge to opinion, reality to appearance, metaphysics to epistemology, and the world of *being* to the world of *becoming*. The Divided Line shows that both knowledge and opinion deal with Forms, though in different ways.

The Divided Line consists of two basic sections, each unevenly divided into two segments. The four segments illustrate four ways of apprehending four components of reality; two each of being and becoming. Figure 5.1 is a representation of the Divided Line that you can refer to as you read Plato's presentation of it. Note how the four metaphysical levels of reality correspond to four epistemological ways of apprehending the Forms.

With Figure 5.1 as a guide, let's take a look at what Plato said about the Divided Line. In this passage, Socrates is describing a conversation he had with Plato's older brother, Glaucon:

"Well, take a line divided into two unequal parts, corresponding to the visible and intelligible worlds, and then divide the two parts again in the same ratio, to represent degrees of clarity and obscurity. In the visible world, one section stands for images: by 'images' I mean first shadows, then reflections in water and other close grained, polished surfaces, and all that sort of thing if you understand me."

"I understand."

"Let the other section stand for the objects which are the originals of the images—animals, plants and manufactured objects of all kinds."

"Very good."

METAPHYSICS	EPISTEMOLOGY		
Higher forms Example: The Good	**A** Understanding	KNOWLEDGE	INTELLIGIBLE WORLD
Lower forms Example: Form Human	**B** Reasoning		
Sensible objects Example: Nelson Mandela	**C** Perception	OPINION	VISIBLE WORLD
Images Example: Nelson Mandela photograph	**D** Imagination		

(BEING and BECOMING brackets on far left; BEING spans Higher forms/Lower forms, BECOMING spans Sensible objects/Images)

FIGURE 5.1 PLATO'S DIVIDED LINE

A + B = World of Forms (Being)
C + D = Physical World (Becoming)
Segments A, B, C, D represent decreasing degrees of truth. Each degree of truth corresponds to a different kind of thinking and different level of reality.
A: This is the level of pure intelligence or understanding. Here the soul directly apprehends truth at its highest level.
B: This is the level of reasoning; specifically, mathematical thinking and deductive reasoning.
C: This is the level of belief or common opinions about physical objects, morals, politics, practical affairs.
D: This is the level of illusion, dominated by secondhand opinions and uncritical impressions.
(This characterization of the lowest level goes beyond what Plato says in this section but is required considering what he does say in the Allegory of the Cave and Book X about poetry and art.)

"Would you be prepared to admit that these sections differ in their degree of truth, and that the relation of image to the original is the same as that of opinion and knowledge?"

"I would."

"Then consider next how the intelligible part of the line is to be divided. In one section the mind uses the originals of the visible world in their turn as images, and has to base its inquiries on assumptions and proceed from them to its conclusions instead of going back to first principles: in the other it proceeds from assumption back to self-sufficient first principles, making no use of the images employed by the other section, but pursuing its inquiry solely by means of Forms....

"... it treats assumptions not as principles, but as assumptions in the true sense, that is, as starting points and steps in the ascent to the universal, self-sufficient first principle; when it has reached that principle it can again descend, by keeping to the consequences that follow from it, to a final conclusion. The whole procedure involves nothing in the sensible world, but deals throughout with Forms and finishes with Forms."[13]

> *When it is a question of thinking in earnest, … there is something in man that rebels against the rigors of responsible self-clarification. He does not want to wake up but go on sleeping.*
> — Karl Jaspers

Levels of Awareness

The lowest level of awareness, **D** in Figure 5.1, is the level of illusion. Virtually no one inhabits this level all the time, but we can occasionally slip into states of illusion. We slip into **Level D** on purpose and for fun when we go to magic shows or watch movies (which are really just light, shadows, and sound creating the illusion of depth and action). This is known as the "willing suspension of disbelief." But we can also slip into illusion without being aware of it when we hold opinions based solely on appearances, unanalyzed impressions, uncritically inherited beliefs, and unevaluated emotions. The image—opinion—I have of Nelson Mandela is an example of **Level D** awareness. It is based on photographs I have seen, news clips on television, and books about apartheid that I've read.

Level C in Figure 5.1 represents the second or informed level of awareness. It involves a wider range of opinions about what most of us probably think of as reality. At this level of informed awareness, we attempt to distinguish appearance from reality, but in a kind of everyday way. For example, I believe that my desk looks solid, but it is actually made up of countless molecules and atoms in motion. I believe that the sun looks small because of its distance from earth, but in fact, it is much larger.

Strictly speaking, I do not *know* these things. I have had some science classes, and looked through microscopes and telescopes, but I do not have a scientist's sophisticated knowledge built upon rigorous deductive reasoning. At the same time, my **Level C** opinions are based on observations and perceptions of physical objects, not just on photos or representations of them. On this informed level, we realize that the way things appear may not be the way they are. Most of us spend much of our lives dealing with more or less informed opinions about most things. If I had known Nelson Mandela, my **Level D** image of him would have been a **Level C** informed opinion.

The next level of awareness (**B**) takes us out of the realms of becoming and opinion (**D/C**) and into the world of being and the first stage of knowledge acquired through deductive reasoning. As we've learned, Plato believed truth is changeless, eternal, and absolute and that knowledge doesn't grow or decay but just *is*. Nelson Mandela the individual did grow and change, however, so **Level B** knowledge must be of a form, say the Form Human. The Form Human does not change—grow or decay—according to Plato.

At the highest level of reality (**A**), the soul has no need for perception or interpretation. Plato says that it "directly apprehends" the "absolute Form of the Good." At the highest level, reason does not—indeed it cannot—deduce the Forms. The higher Forms are directly understood, apprehended—"glimpsed"—without any mediating process or principles.

The Simile of the Sun

Plato compared the "absolute Form of the Good" to the sun: Just as the sun (light) is necessary for vision and life, so, too, the Good makes Reality, Truth, and the existence of everything else possible. The Good exists beyond becoming at the highest reaches of being. The Good cannot be observed with the five senses and can be known only by pure thought or intelligence. The Good is the source of both the value and the existence of all other Forms. The Good is the Form of the Forms.

Comprehension of the Good is unlike other forms of knowing. It is holistic, not partial. The soul must deliberately work its way up from the lowest level of becoming to enlightenment. Experience of the Good so far transcends all other experiences that it cannot be clearly described, so Plato uses a comparison or simile to allude to the Good. We can represent Plato's comparison of the Good to the sun as shown in Figure 5.2.

In the following passage from the *Republic*, Plato (in the character of Socrates) compares the Good to the sun and apprehension of the Good to seeing. Note how strongly he expresses his ultimate regard for the Good:

> "Well, [the sun] is the child of the Good. … The Good has begotten its own likeness, and it bears the same relation to sight and visibility in the visible world that the Good bears to intelligence in the intelligible world."
>
> "Will you explain that a bit further?"
>
> "You know that when we turn our eyes to objects whose colours are no longer illuminated by daylight, but only by moonlight or starlight, they see dimly and appear to be almost blind, as if they had no clear vision."
>
> "Yes."
>
> "But when we turn them on things on which the sun is shining, then they see clearly and their power of vision is restored."
>
> "Certainly."
>
> "Apply the analogy to the mind. When the mind's eye rests on objects illuminated by truth and reality, it understands and comprehends them, and functions intelligently; but when it turns to the twilight world of change and decay, it can only form opinions, its vision is confused and its beliefs shifting, and it seems to lack intelligence."
>
> "That is true."
>
> "Then what gives the objects of knowledge their truth and the mind the power of knowing is the Form of the Good. It is the cause of knowledge and truth, and you will be right to think of it as being itself known, and yet as being something

With [the Good], it is not the same as with other things we learn: it cannot be framed in words, but from protracted concentration devoted to [it] and from spending one's life with it, a light suddenly bursts forth in the soul as though kindled by a flying spark, and then it feeds on itself.

— Plato

VISIBLE WORLD	INTELLIGIBLE WORLD
(C + D)	(A + B)
The Sun	The Good
Growth	Reality
Light	Truth
Visibility	Intelligibility

FIGURE 5.2 PLATO'S HIERARCHY OF BEING AND KNOWLEDGE

The hierarchy of being and knowledge is reflected in Plato's Simile of the Sun.
A = pure understanding
B = deductive thinking
C = common opinion
D = uncritical impressions

other than, and even higher than, knowledge and truth. And just as it was right to think of light and sight as being like the sun, but wrong to think of them as being the sun itself, so here again it is right to think of knowledge and truth as being *like* the Good, but wrong to think of either of them as being the Good, which must be given still a higher place of honor."

"You are making it something remarkably exalted, if it is the source of knowledge and truth, and yet itself higher than they are. For I suppose you can't mean it to be pleasure?"

"A monstrous suggestion," I replied. "Let us pursue our analogy further.... The sun, I think you will agree, not only makes the things we see visible, but causes the process of generation, growth and nourishment, without itself being such a process.... The Good therefore may be said to be the source not only of the intelligibility of the objects of knowledge, but also of their existence and reality; yet it is not itself identical with reality, but is beyond reality, and is superior to it in dignity and power."[14]

Toward the end of the discussion of the Good, Glaucon remarks that the process of escaping from shadows to enlightenment "sounds like a long job." Plato-Socrates agrees, adding:

> And you may assume that there are, corresponding to the four sections of the line, four states of mind: to the top section [**A**] Intelligence, to the second [**B**] Reason, to the third [**C**] Opinion, and to the fourth [**D**] Illusion. And you may arrange them in a scale, and assume that they have degrees of clarity corresponding to the degree of truth and reality possessed by their subject-matter.[15]

Just as people born blind have different meanings for color words than those who have seen colors, those on one level of reality cannot recognize what is being said by those on a higher level. They have no comparable experience. Those who reach the level of comprehending the Good are forever transformed; they are enlightened—they are wise. And the relationship between the enlightened and the unenlightened is at the heart of Plato's philosophy.

> *There seems to be nothing in the study of chemistry that makes you feel like a superior order of being but you study Plato and you begin to believe you're a philosopher.*
>
> — S. I. Hayakawa

PHILOSOPHICAL QUERY

Compare Plato's use of similes to show that there are levels of knowledge with John Stuart Mill's more "ordinary" argument regarding levels of knowledge in judgments of quality (Chapter 12). Which approach seems most compelling, if either does? Assess.

The Allegory of the Cave

One problem common to any hierarchical enlightenment philosophy involves the gap between what the wise master knows and the pupil's initial ignorance. Different levels of experience can create communication and comprehension gaps.

We see a similar kind of difficulty in interactions between adults and young children. Most of us—at least as we mature—have no difficulty with the concept of degrees of awareness and knowledge between adults and children. We even accept the fact that there are levels of knowledge and experience dividing adults with some form of mental impairment or limit and those of average or better mental capacities.

But what about differences between average and so-called wise or enlightened people? Do such differences really exist? If they do, are they indicators of different levels of what Plato refers to as "intelligence" or "wisdom," or are they just unprovable claims made by people who think they know more than the rest of us? What reasons do we have for believing Plato's claims about levels of being and the Good? Why should we discount the views and experiences of the vast majority of people and listen to the claims of one supposedly wiser person?

Plato responded to this important challenge by telling a story with a lesson—an allegory—in Book VII of the *Republic*. This allegory is offered not as a conclusive proof but as a suggestive possibility. It is the summation of the exposition of Plato's theory of Forms that includes the Divided Line and the Simile of the Sun.

The Divided Line expresses Plato's hierarchical view of reality and wisdom. The Simile of the Sun characterizes the act of apprehending highest truth in the form of the Good. In the Allegory of the Cave, Plato compares the level of becoming to living in a cave and describes the ordeal necessary for the soul's ascent from shadowy illusion to enlightenment—from mere opinion to informed opinion to rationally based knowledge to wisdom. The allegory also alludes to the obligation of the enlightened wise person (say, Socrates) to return to the world of becoming in order to help others discern the Forms.

The levels of awareness identified in the Allegory of the Cave correspond to the segments of the Divided Line referred to in Figure 5.1: Those chained to the wall of shadows are imprisoned in the shadowy world of imagination and illusion (**D**); those loose within the cave occupy the "common sense" world of perception and informed opinion (**C**); those struggling through the passageway to the surface are acquiring knowledge through reason (**B**); the rich surface world of warmth and sunlight is the highest level of reality directly grasped by pure intelligence (**A**).

Plato presents the allegory as part of Socrates' continuing conversation with Glaucon:

> Let me show a picture of whether our nature is enlightened or unenlightened. Imagine human beings living in an underground den or cave, with an opening that faces the light and reaches well into the cave. Here they have been from childhood, with their legs and necks chained so that they cannot move, and can only see in front of them, being prevented by the chains from turning their heads. Above and behind them a fire is blazing at a distance, and between the fire and the prisoners there is a raised way with a low wall built along it, like the screen marionette players hide behind in a puppet show.
>
> I see.
>
> Imagine also men passing along the wall carrying all sorts of vessels, and statues and figures of men and of animals made of wood and stone and various materials, which stick up over the wall. Some of these men are talking, others are silent.
>
> You have shown me a strange image and strange prisoners.
>
> They are like ourselves, I replied. They see only their own shadows, or the shadows of one another, which the fire throws on the opposite wall of the cave, do they not?

The Allegory of the Cave illustrates Plato's vision of the ascent of the mind from illusion (Level D) to opinion (Level C) to reasoned knowledge (Level B) to enlightenment (Level A). These levels of awareness correspond to the segments of the Divided Line illustrated in Figure 5.1.

True, he said; how could they see anything but the shadows if they were never allowed to move their heads? …

And if they were able to converse with one another, would they not assume that they were describing what was actually before them?

Very true.

And if the cave had an echo which came from the opposite wall, would they not be convinced that when one of the passers-by spoke the voice which they heard came from its shadow on that wall?

No question, he replied.

To them, I said, the truth would be literally nothing but the shadows of images of animals and men and other things.

That is certain.

And now look again, and see what will naturally follow if the prisoners are released and cured of their illusions. At first, when one of them is liberated and compelled suddenly to stand up and turn his neck round and walk and look towards the light, he will suffer sharp pains. The glare will confuse him, and he will be unable to see the realities of what in his former state he had seen only shadows of. If someone says to him that what he saw before as reality was merely an illusion, and that he now, in his discomfort, has clearer vision because his eye is turned toward more real existence, what will he reply? Further imagine that his instructor points to objects as they pass and demands that he name them—will he not be perplexed? Will he not remain convinced that the shadows which he saw in the cave are more real than the objects now shown to him?

Far more real.

And if he … were reluctantly dragged out of his cave and up a steep and rugged ascent, and held fast until he is in the sunlight, wouldn't he be pained and irritated? When he looked toward the light his eyes would be dazzled, and at first he would not be able to see anything at all of the things he is now told are real. … He would need to grow accustomed to the sight of the upper world. At first he would see shadows best, next the reflections of men and other objects in the water, and then the objects themselves. Then he would gaze upon the light of the moon and the stars and the spangled heaven. And for a time would he not see the sky and the stars at night better than the sun itself or the sunlight of day?

Certainly.

Finally, he would be able to see the sun, and not mere reflections of it in the water, but the sun in its own proper place, and he would contemplate it as it is.

Certainly.

Would he not then conclude that it is the sun that creates the season and the years, and is the guardian of everything in the visible world, and is, in some way, the cause of all the things he and his fellow prisoners used to behold?

Clearly, he said, he would first see the sun and then he would reason about him.[16]

PHILOSOPHICAL QUERY

The Allegory of the Cave has intrigued students of Plato since it first appeared. Do you think it fairly expresses the way we experience knowledge? For instance, in childhood, everything is black and white, but with experience, we discover rich nuances and hues, as it were. What level are you on? Society in general? The world? Explain. Do you believe in levels of reality? In enlightenment? Why or why not?

The Rule of the Wise

Plato's fundamental vision is deliberately hierarchical and aristocratic rather than egalitarian and democratic. His epistemology and metaphysics reflect and encourage this kind of highly discriminating orientation.

Today, any nondemocratic philosophy is likely to be called elitist. If you believe in the fundamental equality of all people, you may be suspicious of Plato's belief in the superiority of those who have supposedly escaped the Cave and seen the Good. If you are skeptical about the possibility of any human being discovering "the truth," you may have difficulty with the idea that only exceptional, enlightened individuals are fit to govern the rest of us. But, then, aren't you dangerously close to believing that you have discovered that no one—including you—can discover the truth? Now what? This nagging suspicion will haunt philosophy for centuries, returning with a vengeance in the twentieth century. See Chapter 17.

Nonetheless, such concerns are well-founded. We are all aware of the abuses committed by Nazis, racist supremacists, and all sorts of true believers who are convinced that they alone know the truth and are thus superior to the rest of us.

Out of Plato come all things that are still written and debated among men of thought. Great havoc makes he among our originalities. We have reached the mountain from which all these drift boulders were detached.

— Ralph Waldo Emerson

Plato's aristocracy of wisdom, however, is not based on gender, national origin, and the like—at least in theory. It is built on Plato's conviction that enlightenment is real and that it is more than mere intellectual ability. Platonic enlightenment is the product of careful training, directed desire, hard work, and the good luck to live in an environment that does not prevent us from escaping the Cave.

> And when he who escaped the cave remembered his old habitation, and the so-called wisdom of his fellow-prisoners, do you not suppose that he would feel happiness for himself because of his good luck and pity for them?…
>
> Yes, he said, I think that he would rather suffer anything than entertain his previous false notions and live in such a miserable manner.
>
> And if there were a contest in measuring the shadows and he had to compete with prisoners who had never left the cave, while his sight was still weak and before his eyes had adjusted to the dim light—and this might take a long time—would he not seem ridiculous? Men would say of him that his trip to the upper world ruined his eyes. They would say that it were better not even to think of ascending. And if any one tried to free them and lead him into the light, they would put him to death if they could catch him.
>
> No question, he said.
>
> Now this entire allegory, my dear Glaucon, must be added to our previous discussion [of the Divided Line and the Simile of the Sun]. The prison is our world of sight and the light of the fire corresponds to the sun. And you will not misapprehend me if you interpret the journey out of the cave as comparable to the ascent of the soul into the world of understanding, at least according to my poor belief, which, at your request, I have expressed—whether rightly or wrongly only God knows. But, true or false, my opinion is that in the world of knowledge, the form of the Good appears last of all, and is seen only with an effort. And, when seen, it is also inferred to be the universal author of all things good and beautiful and right.… And it is the power upon which he who would act rationally, either in public or in private, must have his eye fixed.[17]

Plato wrote the *Republic* to show that the levels of reality correspond to three types of people. The *Republic* is Plato's answer to what kind of person is qualified to rule the state, based on his theory of reality.

At the beginning of the *Republic*, Socrates and his friend Glaucon have spent the day at a festival and are on their way home when another friend, Polemarchus, stops them. The dialogue begins with good-natured banter among friends:

> "Socrates," said Polemarchus, "I believe you are starting off on your way back to town."
>
> "You are right," I [Socrates] replied.
>
> "Do you see how many of us there are?" he asked.
>
> "I do."
>
> "Well, you will either have to get the better of us or stay here."
>
> "Oh, but there's another alternative," said I. "We might persuade you that you ought to let us go."
>
> "You can't persuade people who won't listen," he replied.[18]

You can't persuade people who won't listen. Plato is no doubt referring in part to the people who executed Socrates. But he may also be giving us a key to the rest of the *Republic*.

Socrates believed in the pursuit of wisdom through the dialectical method of question-and-answer. This required participants willing to listen actively and to respond intelligently. But what about people who cannot or will not listen? What about people who are satisfied with life in the Cave? What good is being reasonable in the face of ignorance? Will a mob listen to reason? Will the lazy?

Plato thought not. He came to believe that there were different types of human beings, with different strengths and weaknesses corresponding to each type. Not everyone is capable of participating in rational discourse. Some people lack the intellect. Some lack the will. Some even lack both. Thus it is that a wise and wonderful individual who has escaped from the Cave, like Socrates, can be brought down by his moral and intellectual inferiors who are still in it. In Plato's view, Socrates made a mistake in going to the Athenian people at all. Socrates himself had even said that in matters of virtue and wisdom, the majority is usually wrong, while only a few are wise.

The Search for Justice

Plato argued that a reciprocal relationship exists between the individual and the kind of society he or she lives in. That means a certain kind of society produces a certain kind of individual, and certain kinds of individuals produce certain kinds of societies. In fact, Plato thought the relationship between the two was so close that a clear understanding of the just (ideal) society would yield a clear understanding of the just (healthy) individual. In the *Republic*, he refers to society as "the individual writ large." The *Republic* is, consequently, a study of Plato's ideal society and, by extension, a study of types of individuals.

The first book of the *Republic* begins with a discussion of justice. But justice in this context does not mean quite what it does today. Philosophical translator H. D. P. Lee says that the Greek roots of what is usually translated as *justice* cover a cluster of meanings that no single English word does. According to Lee, *justice* in the *Republic* is a broad term covering right conduct or morality in general; the verb from the same root can mean to act "rightly" or "justly."[19] For Plato, justice involved much more than fairness under the law; it went beyond a legalistic limit. Historian of ancient Greece B. A. G. Fuller says that what Plato is interested in is nothing less than "the whole sphere of moral action, both external and internal."[20]

Various limited and specific definitions of justice are offered during the course of the *Republic*. The first one is that justice is paying our debts and telling the truth. During the course of the dialogue, a variety of modifications and alternatives are discussed and rejected.

Function and Happiness

The *Republic* contrasts two views of morality. One asserts that right and wrong must be determined by the consequences our acts produce, and the other holds that they can be understood only in terms of their effect on our overall functioning as human beings. The first view is sometimes called an **instrumental theory of morality**. Right and wrong are treated as *means to, or instruments for, getting something else*. Be good, get *X*. Be bad, get *Y*. Plato characterizes the instrumental view:

> For fathers tell their sons, and pastors and masters of all kinds urge their charges to be just not because they value justice for itself, but for the social prestige it brings;

instrumental theory of morality
A moral position that right and wrong must be determined by the consequences of acts; right and wrong viewed as means (instruments) for getting something else.

they want them to secure by a show of justice the power and family connexions and other things which [were] enumerated, all of which are procured by the just man of good reputation.[21]

functionalist theory of morality
A moral position that right and wrong can be understood only in terms of their effect on anything's natural function; each kind of thing has a natural purpose (function).

Plato, by contrast, argues for a **functionalist theory of morality** in which each kind of thing (including human beings) has a "natural purpose or function." Renowned Plato scholar A. E. Taylor says that in the *Republic*, "Happiness depends on conformity to our nature [function] as active beings."[22] In other words, only virtuous people can be happy.

The Greeks viewed happiness as being more than a matter of personal satisfaction. *Happiness was the result of living a fully functioning life.* It involved balance and wholeness. It required being pleased by what is good and being displeased by what is bad. For instance, under such a view, no cigarette smoker can be "happy", regardless of the pleasure derived from smoking. The reason is that no fully functioning, maximally healthy human being will enjoy polluting his or her body. (For a fuller treatment of this view of happiness, see Chapter 6.)

The Philosopher's Republic

The *Republic* reveals Plato's view that a good life can be lived only in a good society because no one can live a truly good life in an irrational, imbalanced society. Nor can one live a truly good life without having some social activities, obligations, and concerns.

Plato said that society originates because no individual is self-sufficient. The just or ideal state meets three basic categories of needs: (1) nourishing needs (food, shelter, clothing); (2) protection needs (military, police); (3) ordering needs (leadership, government). These needs are best met by members of three corresponding classes of people: (1) workers (computer programmer, banker, truck driver); (2) warriors (soldiers, police officers, firefighters); (3) guardians (philosopher-kings).

A state is "just" when it functions fully. An unjust state is dysfunctional; it fails to meet some essential need. Only when all classes of people are virtuous *according to their natures* is the state whole, healthy, balanced, and just. *The good life is nothing more—or less—than each individual functioning well according to his or her own nature, in a state that is well-ordered and wisely ruled.*

Injustice is a form of imbalance for Plato. It occurs whenever a state does not function properly. Some imbalance always results when one part of the state tries to fulfill the function of another part. Justice, happiness, and the good life are interrelated *functional results* of order. Because the essence of a thing determines its proper order, function, and proper care, only those who have seen the Forms and seen the Good know what this essence is for the state or for individuals.

The Parts of the Soul

virtue (platonic)
Excellence of function.

For Plato, **virtue** is *excellence of function* (which reflects form). We must identify a thing's function before we can fully evaluate it. The healthy good, or virtuous, soul is one in which all parts function harmoniously. The human soul resembles the state in that it too is divided into three parts. The three parts of the soul are *reason, spirit,* and *appetite*.

Plato believed in weakness of will; he disagreed with Socrates' belief that "to know the good is to do the good." According to Plato, we most clearly encounter each part of our souls when we're faced with a difficult choice. Suppose, for example, that you are on a date with someone who wants to go dancing and stay out late. You, on the other hand, have an important test early the next morning. Your *reason* says: "Go home, review your notes, rest. You can go dancing another time, but you cannot make up this important test." Your *appetite* says: "I'd love a pizza. I'd love to party." Your *spirit*, which is concerned with honor, says: "This is awful! I hate it! I don't know what to do. I sort of want to study—but I'd really like to go out. Oh my, oh my!" Most of us are intimately familiar with what can be characterized as parts of ourselves. Plato called them parts of the soul.

In the *Phaedrus*, Plato compares the soul to a chariot being pulled by two horses. One horse needs no touch from the whip, responding instantly to whispers and spoken commands. The other horse is full of "insolence and pride" and "barely yields to whip and spur." The charioteer knows where he wants to go but needs the help of both horses to get there. The driver, of course, corresponds to *reason;* the horse that responds to the merest whisper corresponds to *spirit* (or will), and the bad but powerful horse represents *appetite.*

If the charioteer is unable to control both horses, he will be dragged all over the place by the stronger horse. It is the *function* and therefore the *duty* and the *right* of the charioteer to control the horses. In the *Republic*, Plato says:

> So the reason ought to rule, having the ability and foresight to act for the whole, and the spirit ought to obey and support it. And this concord between them is effected, as we said, by a combination of intellectual and physical training, which tunes up the reason by intellectual training and tones down the crudeness of natural high spirits by harmony and rhythm.[23]

> *Bodily exercise, when compulsory, does no harm to the body; but knowledge which is acquired under compulsion obtains no hold on the mind.*
> — Plato

The Cardinal Virtues

Plato identifies four "cardinal virtues" as necessary for a good society and for a happy individual. Cardinal virtues are essential, basic virtues that provide optimal functioning for the human soul.

Temperance is another name for self-control and moderation. It is important for the worker class, but necessary for all three classes of people. The state, too, must control itself, not yielding either to the unjust demands of other states or to a lust for expansion or power. The state must not give in to an excess of liberty or repression. The healthy state resembles the healthy person. Both are moderate, self-disciplined, and guided by reason. The healthy soul is not controlled by appetites.

Courage is the essential virtue of the warrior class. Courage is necessary to protect the community and to enforce the just laws of the guardians. In the individual, courage is a quality of will, an essential drive that provides a person with stamina and energy.

Wisdom is the virtue associated with the guardians who are called the philosopher-kings. In the individual, wisdom is present when the rational part of the soul is healthy and in control. Wisdom is found only in a community ruled by those fit by nature and training to guide it: the philosopher-kings who have seen the Good.

justice (platonic)
Excellence of function for the whole; in a just society, each individual performs his or her natural function according to class; in a just individual, reason rules the spirit and the appetites.

Discussing Philosophy

Justice is the result of the other three cardinal virtues, in much the same way that bodily health is the result of the proper functioning of all organs and systems. **Justice** *is excellence of function for the whole:* Each essential element works well, and together all elements blend into a balanced system in the just state and in the just individual.

For Plato, justice extends far beyond a legal system. The just state is well, whole, vital. It nurtures each individual by providing a lifestyle appropriate to him or her.

PHILOSOPHICAL QUERY

Consider the family as a functional system: If young children are allowed to spend the money, determine bedtimes, and so on, the whole family suffers. If the parents try to live like children, the whole family suffers. If every family member is free to pick and choose what he or she feels like doing or not doing every day, there can be no family. You might try similar analyses of marriages, churches, schools, or factories. Discuss the need for hierarchy, authority, and a governing order.

What would Plato think of our style of democracy, which not only allows, but encourages, individuals to switch from governing to being governed and which encourages us to select ourselves as fit to be philosopher-kings?

The Origin of Democracy

Plato's *Republic* and a later dialogue called *Laws* outline **utopias**—that is, perfect, ideal societies. (Although Plato originated the idea, the word *utopia* was coined by Sir Thomas More in 1516.) A Platonic utopia would be enormously difficult, perhaps impossible, to achieve. But a consideration of Plato's program for a utopia will prove to be worthwhile on many counts.

For Plato, the ideal Form of government is rule by philosopher-kings, not democracy. Because our current culture is democratic and individualistic in so many respects, many of us view democracy as the ideal form of government, without giving any other possibilities serious consideration. For that reason alone, consideration of an elitist alternative can be illuminating. It may help us to better identify the virtues of our own society—and we may get a clearer look at its shortcomings.

In Book VIII of the *Republic*, Plato discusses different kinds of governments and the types of souls each produces. He argues that democracy grows out of a type of government called *oligarchy*, the rule of a wealthy few. Because the chief aim of the oligarchs is to get rich, they create a constitution and type of government that encourage the acquisition of property.

But just having property isn't enough. Plato asks, "Doesn't oligarchy change into democracy because of lack of restraint in the pursuit of its objective of getting as rich as possible?"[24] The seeds of democracy, according to Plato, are the love of property and riches, and a corresponding desire for a free economy: In order to preserve their wealth, oligarchs must encourage trading in real estate, heavy borrowing, and lack of self-control. In order to increase wealth, "money people" need to stimulate irrational but constant consumption by everyone else. Plato declares, "It should then be clear that love of money and adequate self-discipline in its citizens are two things that can't co-exist in any society; one or the other must be neglected."[25]

utopia

Term for a perfect or ideal society derived from Sir Thomas More's 1516 novel of the same name; the word was created from the Greek root meaning "nowhere."

PHILOSOPHICAL QUERY

Do you agree with Plato that democracy is incompatible with self-discipline? What sort of self-discipline do you think Plato was concerned about?

In Plato's diagnosis, as the rich get richer, the poor grow angrier until they somehow overthrow the rich, either through armed revolt or by using social and legal pressure. Resentful over their status, the poor initiate a program of *equality*.

> Then democracy originates when the poor win, kill or exile their opponents, and give the rest equal rights and opportunity of office.... There is liberty and freedom of speech in plenty, and every individual is free to do as he likes.... That being so, won't everyone arrange his life as pleases him best? ... a democracy is the most attractive of all societies. The diversity of its characters, like the different colours in a patterned dress, make it look very attractive.... Perhaps most people would, for this reason, judge it to be the best form of society ... [if they] judge by appearances.[26]

A democratic state, Plato says, will contain every type of human temperament. But the predominant characteristic of democracy is lack of guidance and self-control, lack of wisdom, and lack of temperance. Swayed by opinion rather than grounded in knowledge, the democratic state is in a state of constant flux, always *becoming*. It is hostile to the possibility of a fixed hierarchy of being:

> In a democracy ... there's no compulsion either to exercise authority if you are capable of it, or to submit to authority if you don't want to; you needn't fight if there's a war, or you can wage a private war in peacetime if you don't like peace.... It's a wonderfully pleasant way of carrying on in the short run, isn't it?[27]

Plato says that, in a democracy, "there's no distinction between citizen and alien and foreigner" and warns that "excessive liberty" eventually results in chaos, anger, and distrust. Do the intense feelings aroused by today's "immigration issue" buttress his case, or are they more evidence of democratic liberty?

> *Then the master passion runs wild and takes madness into its service; any decent options or desires and any feelings of shame still left are killed or thrown out, until all discipline is swept away, and madness usurps its place.*
>
> — Plato

Democracy is so pleasant, Plato asserts, that even those convicted of a crime in a democracy can continue "to go about among their fellows." H. D. P. Lee paraphrases Plato's description of the democratic type as versatile but lacking principle.[28]

Most damning of all, Plato says, democracy violates the principle of functional order and rule by reason. He asserts that only very rare and exceptional individuals can grow up to be good people without strict training from infancy, in a good environment. But democracy lacks the order and balance to provide such an environment. At its most extreme, the disordered, democratic soul resists all limits, both internal and social:

> All pleasures are equal and should have equal rights. [Such a character] lives for the pleasure of the moment. One day it's wine, women, and song, the next bread and water; one day it's hard physical training, the next indolence and ease, and then a period of philosophic study.... There's no order or restraint in [this] life and [such a person] reckons [this] way of living is pleasant, free, and happy....
>
> It's a life which many men and women would envy, it has so many possibilities.[29]

For Deeper Consideration

We hear a great deal these days about the virtues of democracy. What might Plato think of our "democratic culture"? As you think about this, consider political, social, and cultural trends that Plato could cite as supporting evidence for his characterization of democracy and the democratic soul. Why does Plato argue that democracy turns into tyranny? Does his prediction seem plausible, or is he overlooking something? If so, what?

According to the American Pet Product Association, in 2013, Americans spent $56 billion on pets during a period of economic decline and social unrest. In his *Republic*, Plato says that one of the symptoms of democratic decadence is a culture-wide leveling among classes of people and even among species, as in "Love me, love my dog (or cat or hamster or ...)." Was Plato on to something? Or did he overlook something?

The Pendulum of Imbalance

Ancient philosophers were aware that one extreme often produces another, nearly opposite, extreme in a never-ending effort to achieve balance. In Plato's view, the chief objective of democracy is "excessive liberty." In one of the more interesting and perhaps prophetic passages in the *Republic*, Plato describes the effects "too much liberty" will produce. As you read what he said so long ago, take note of parallels to our own culture.

> It becomes the thing for the father and son to change places, the father standing in awe of his son, and the son neither respecting nor fearing his parents, in order to assert his independence; and there's no distinction between citizen and alien and foreigner. And there are other more trivial things. The teacher fears and panders to his pupils, who in turn despise their teachers and attendants; and the young as a whole imitate their elders, argue with them and set themselves up against them, while their

elders try to avoid the reputation of being disagreeable or strict by aping the young and mixing with them on terms of easy good fellowship....

You would never believe—unless you had seen it for yourself—how much more liberty the domestic animals have in a democracy. Love me love my dog, as the proverb has it, and the same is true of horses and donkeys as well.... Everything is full of this spirit of liberty....

What it comes to is this, ... that the minds of the citizens become so sensitive that the least vestige of restraint is resented as intolerable, till finally, as you know, in their determination to have no master they disregard all laws, written or unwritten.[30]

One form of *shamelessness* is an exaggerated sense of honor. In this condition, the individual is always ready to take offense. Every restriction or social limit is taken personally: "The least vestige of restraint is resented as intolerable." Consider: In recent years, a *kindergartner* was suspended from school for patting a teacher on the bottom (sexual harassment) and another for bringing a metal nail file to school, and a grade-schooler was sent home for chewing a Pop-Tart into a shape that looked like a gun ("zero tolerance" for anything that "looks like a weapon"). A school reacted to excessive absences and poor grades by requiring students to wear uniforms—and then pressuring the entire staff to wear them, too—so as "not to make the students feel like they're different." In 2014, a number of schools and colleges instituted policies requiring teachers and textbooks to warn of upcoming "triggers" that might make students uncomfortable. Triggers consist of any term or topic that anyone might find disturbing for personal reasons or past experiences.

According to Plato, the spoiled and undisciplined person grows used to playing now and paying later. When he cannot pay his own way, Plato says, he turns to his parents to gratify his desires. He sees their estate as "his due," and "if they don't give in to him, he'll try first to get his way by fraud and deceit." But "if his old mother and father put up a resistance and show fight ... [he will not] feel any hesitation about playing the tyrant with them." What begins as unlimited freedom ends up as the tyranny over reason by the lower parts of the soul.

> *The greatest griefs are those we cause ourselves.*
> — Sophocles

MindTap

Discussing Philosophy

PHILOSOPHICAL QUERY

Can you spot any symptoms in our society of the pattern Plato attributes to injustice in individuals and the state? Can you identify individuals or groups that "fall into sickness and dissension at the slightest provocation"? What—if anything—does justice (or a lack of justice) have to do with these reactions? Explain.

The Tyranny of Excess

The ills of democracy were aggravated for Plato by a pattern of increasing self-indulgence, which he thought would pass from generation to generation, until sooner or later pleasures and excesses would actually tyrannize the soul itself:

> Isn't this the reason ... why the passion of sex has for so long been called a tyrant? ... And isn't there also a touch of the tyrant about a man who's drunk?

According to Plato, "a democracy is the most attractive of all societies. The diversity of its characters, like the different colours in a patterned dress, make it look very attractive.... Perhaps most people would, for this reason, judge it to be the best form of society ... [if they] judge by appearances." Do you think Plato's opinion of democracy is confirmed by such spectacles as the Jon Stewart/Stephen Colbert "Rally to Restore Sanity and/or Fear" (left) and the Glenn Beck "Restoring Honor" rally (right)?

> *No educated man stating plainly the elementary notions that every educated man holds about the matters that principally concern government could be elected to office in a democratic state, save perhaps by a miracle. His frankness would arouse fears, and those fears would run against him; it is his business to arouse fears that will run in favour of him.*
>
> — H. L. Mencken

... And the madman whose mind is unhinged imagines he can control gods and men and is quite ready to try.... Then a precise definition of a tyrannical man is one who, either by birth or habit or both, combines the characteristics of drunkenness, lust, and madness.... And how does he live? ... When a master passion has absolute control of a man's mind, I suppose life is a round of holidays and dinners and parties and girl-friends and so on.... And there will be a formidable extra crop of desires growing all the time and needing satisfaction.... So whatever income he has will soon be expended, and he'll start borrowing and drawing on capital.

... When these sources fail, his large brood of desires will howl aloud.... He *must* get something from somewhere or his life will be torment and agony.[31]

According to Plato, the built-in excesses of democracy already contain the seeds of tyranny. **Tyranny** is a form of government in which all power rests in a single individual, the tyrant. For Plato, the tyrant is the most imbalanced type of personality. A tyrant is always a slave to his own strong passions and desires. An individual who is controlled by drugs or lust is obviously a slave. But so is the politically powerful leader who is a slave to his own lust for power and domination.

tyranny
A form of government in which all power rests in a single individual, known as the tyrant.

PHILOSOPHICAL QUERY

Do you think things like laws against hate speech and fundamentalist reactions against "the excesses of Western democracy" support Plato's argument that the inevitable result of democracy is "too much liberty" and that widespread "abuses" of liberty lead to demands for "law and order" and, ultimately, tyranny? What other examples can you think of to buttress Plato's case? What examples to weaken it? (As you ponder this, note that calls for restrictions on personal freedom come from both liberal and conservative thinkers.)

Once again, things are not as they initially appear. What looks like freedom is in reality lack of control; what looks like power is in truth a form of enslavement.

Aplia

Commentary

The most damning charge that can be leveled at all enlightenment philosophies is that no matter how initially intriguing or appealing they seem, they remain impractical and unrealistic in the world as most of us experience and understand it. In Plato's case, we might ask ourselves whether we have any supportable first-hand evidence for believing in actual levels of reality. Does a story like the Allegory of the Cave help us determine who is enlightened and who is deluded? Do the Divided Line and Simile of the Sun do anything besides reflect certain psychological states?

On the other hand, who can doubt the need for order and balance in both the individual and society? Further, it would not be difficult to make Plato's case against the "excesses of democracy" using trends and events from our own time. We might even find some merit in his claim that letting each individual choose his or her occupation based solely (or even chiefly) on strength of desire and ambition leads to great overall unhappiness.

When we rank occupations by income and prestige, most of the tasks needed for a good society are less desirable than a few glamorous, less useful ones. Which, then, does more lasting harm: letting everyone who wishes scramble for the top of the heap or carefully matching people's basic abilities and personalities with various levels of education and occupation? We might find Plato's three categories of people—guardians, warriors, and workers—too restricting, but does that rule out a more realistic division of opportunities and social roles?

Finally, there is much to be said for living a well-rounded life. That includes, of course, being individually balanced. A society that values specialization and material success to the extent that this society does makes personal growth (well-roundedness), as opposed to self-indulgence, difficult.

Interestingly, even though Plato's great pupil Aristotle turns away from the theory of Forms, he follows the direction in which his great teacher pointed and makes his own case for the fully functioning, whole, balanced human being. Aristotle is the subject of the next chapter.

> *The safest general characterization of the European philosophical tradition is that it consists of a series of footnotes to Plato.*
> —Alfred North Whitehead

Summary of Main Points

- Plato was a member of the Athenian aristocracy and Socrates' most famous and important pupil. Socrates' trial and death convinced Plato that Athenian democracy was irrational mob rule. He founded his famous Academy to educate wise rulers.

- In Plato's metaphysics, the highest level of reality consists of timeless "essences" called ideas or Forms. Plato divided reality into three levels. The highest level of reality is eternal and changeless *being*. The other two levels together make up *becoming*, the level of change. Knowledge is always of essence. Disagreement is only possible on the lower level of becoming.

- According to Plato, knowledge is unchanging. The Sophists could not discover truth because they were only concerned with the world of ever-changing perceptions and customs. Truth and knowledge are found at the level of being. Plato's theory of Forms was part of his refutation of sophistry.

- Plato used the concept of a Divided Line to illustrate the relationship of knowledge to opinion, reality to appearance, and the worlds of being and becoming. The Divided Line consists of two basic sections, each unevenly divided into two segments: (1) pure intelligence or understanding, (2) reasoning, (3) informed belief or ordinary opinions, and (4) illusion and imagination, dominated by secondhand opinions and uncritical impressions.

- Plato compared the "absolute Form of the Good" to the sun; the Good makes the existence of everything else possible. The Good cannot be observed with the five senses and can be known only by pure thought or intelligence. It is the source of both the value and the existence of all other Forms.

- In the Allegory of the Cave, Plato characterized three levels of awareness by referring to three distinct levels of reality: two levels of becoming and one qualitatively unique and ultimate level of being. The lowest level is inhabited by people with little or no imagination. The informed level involves a wider range of basic understanding. On the highest level, the soul has no need for perception or interpretation.

- In the *Republic*, Plato argued that there is a reciprocal relationship between the individual and the kind of society in which he or she lives. The ideal state meets three basic categories of needs: (1) nourishing needs; (2) protection needs; (3) ordering needs. These needs are best met by members of three corresponding classes of people: (1) workers; (2) warriors; (3) guardians or philosopher-kings.

- The *Republic* contrasts two views of morality. The instrumental theory of morality asserts that right and wrong must be determined by the consequences our acts produce, and the functionalist theory of morality holds that right and wrong can only be understood in terms of the way they affect our overall functioning as human beings.

- According to Plato, the just state functions fully; the unjust state is dysfunctional. Only when all classes of people are virtuous according to their natures is the state whole, healthy, balanced, and just. The good life consists of each individual functioning well according to his or her own nature, in a state that is ordered and wisely ruled.

- According to Plato, the human soul resembles the state in that it too is divided into three parts: reason, spirit, and appetite. A just (healthy, good, or virtuous) soul is one in which all parts function harmoniously. The just society is one ruled by guardians in such a way that each class functions at its best.

- Plato identified four cardinal (essential, basic) virtues. The virtue of temperance is important for the worker classes but necessary for all classes of people. Courage is the essential virtue of the warrior class; in the individual, courage is a quality of will that provides a person with stamina and energy. Wisdom is the virtue associated with the guardians and the rational part of the soul. Justice, the result of the other three cardinal virtues, is excellence of function for the whole.

- Plato rejected democracy as unjust because rule by the majority usurps the rightful role of the guardian class. The result is an excess of liberty and rule by impulse, appetite, and emotion in which all classes suffer. Democracy violates the principle of functional order and rule by reason. According to Plato, the excessive liberty found in democracies contains the seeds of tyranny, a type of government in which all power rests in a single individual, the tyrant, the most imbalanced type of personality.

Post-Reading Reflections

Now that you've had a chance to learn about Plato, use your new knowledge to answer these questions.

1. Discuss some of the personal experiences that shaped Plato's overall philosophical idealism.

2. Illustrate the Divided Line and relate each segment to Plato's epistemology as it is characterized in the Allegory of the Cave.

3. How did Plato use the sun to help explain the Good?

4. Identify and explain the three basic levels of reality.

5. Distinguish the realm of being from the realm of becoming.

6. Tell the Allegory of the Cave in your own words. Then carefully explain its purpose in Plato's philosophy.

7. Carefully explain the relationship of the individual to the state in the *Republic*. Why is the relationship significant?

8. What does Plato see as the most unjust type of person and state? Why? Do you agree? Explain.

9. Explain the origin and nature of democracy according to Plato.

 MindTap™

Experience MindTap through the activities highlighted in this chapter. Further explore this online, personalized learning tool to deepen your comprehension and improve your grades.

6

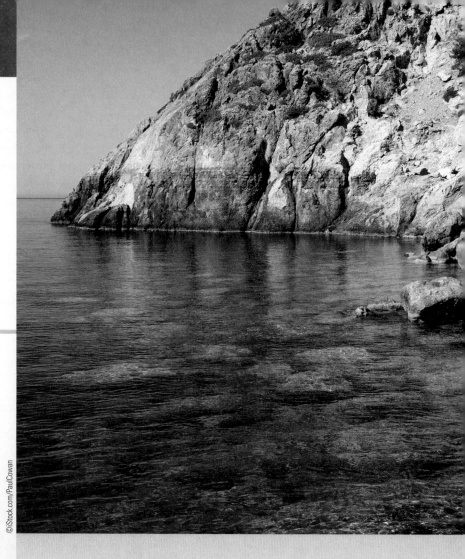

The Naturalist
Aristotle

In all things of nature there is
something of the marvelous.
— *Aristotle*

Learning Objectives

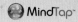

After you complete this chapter, you should be able to:

- Explain why Aristotle accused Plato of mistaking intellectual analysis for ontological status.

- Distinguish between Aristotelian forms and Platonic Forms.

- Define *matter* according to Aristotle.

- Define *entelechy*.

- Distinguish between *eudaimonia* and happiness.

- Criticize the claim that a life governed by *sophrosyne* will be dull, rigid, and boring.

- Explain the relationship of habit to moral virtue for Aristotle.

- Give an example of a character trait for which there is no Aristotelian mean.

- Compare today's widespread understanding of happiness as a subjective state with Aristotle's characterization of happiness as a by-product of a well-balanced life.

ONE OF THE MOST frustrating aspects of college can be choosing a major. Sometimes we are encouraged to decide without having had much exposure to a variety of disciplines, and some of us just may not really know who we are yet. (This condition is not confined to students or persons of any particular age.) As a result, we may change our minds as sophomores or juniors or seniors, when we realize that our initial choice was wrong for the real us. Outside the campus environment, more and more people seem to be making significant career changes at mid-life or later.[1]

What prompts a forty-five-year-old person to leave a secure job, giving up seniority and retirement benefits and company-paid medical insurance, to open a cookie shop? What makes a social worker quit work and go to law school? What drives a middle-aged man or woman to leave his or her family, lose weight, buy a motorcycle, and become a poet? What makes a pre-med major just nine units short of graduation drop out of school and join a Japanese earthquake relief group? There are many reasons, some of which may be unwise, but some of which are good reasons.

Did you ever feel that you weren't really being yourself? What does that mean? Aren't you always yourself, even if that self is confused or inconsistent or phony? Maybe that's just who you are. On the other hand, maybe the "real you" is being denied or starved. Perhaps people who walk away from their jobs or families have been false to their "true selves" for years. Does that seem possible?

Aristotle might have thought so, even though he would not have suggested that we "find ourselves" by returning to adolescence or undertaking a self-indulgent escape from responsibility. But he did believe in a natural development of the soul/self based on an inner essence or goal. He believed that the good life involves balance and fullness. And though each of us may have individually different "selves" to develop, in Aristotle's view, all human beings share a common nature that makes it possible to identify the general outline of a good life.

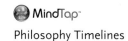 Philosophy Timelines

> *There is perhaps nothing worse than reaching the top of the ladder and discovering that you're on the wrong wall.*
>
> —Joseph Campbell

Works

Aristotle is said to have written twenty-seven dialogues on a level comparable to Plato's, and it is through these dialogues that he was best known in the ancient world.[2] Unfortunately, Aristotle's dialogues were all destroyed when the Visigoths sacked Rome in 400 C.E. What we know today as the "writings of Aristotle" are really a collection of *logoi*—discourses. These apparently include notes Aristotle made for his lectures and possibly notes taken by students who attended his lectures. Of 360 works mentioned by Diogenes Läertius, 40 survive today.

Aristotle's works include *Organon*, a collection of six logical treatises; *Physics; On Generation and Corruption; De Anima (On the Soul); On the Heavens; The History of Animals; On the Parts of Animals; Metaphysics; Politics; Rhetoric; Poetics;* and the *Nicomachean Ethics.*

What remains of Aristotle's work is complex, stiffly written, and often dry. But in spite of that, these notes reflect a genius whose

Aristotle

range of interests, wonder, insight, and effort stands as a most remarkable testament to the human mind and spirit.

Aristotle's Life

Aristotle

The son of a court physician, **Aristotle** (384–322 B.C.E.) was born in Stagira, a Greek community in Thrace. What little we know of him comes primarily through Diogenes Läertius's compilation of the lives of ancient philosophers.

Aristotle probably learned basic anatomy and dissection from his father before he was sent to study at Plato's Academy in Athens at the age of eighteen. When he arrived, practically everyone noticed him, in part because he was something of a dandy. Plato is reported to have said that Aristotle paid more attention to his clothes than was proper for a philosopher. To be fashionable, Aristotle cultivated a deliberate lisp, the speech pattern that the Greek elite used to separate themselves from the masses. (In a similar way, some people today think of an English accent as being "higher class" than a Southern drawl or Brooklyn accent.)

Despite his affectations, Aristotle almost immediately earned a reputation as one of the Academy's finest students. Diogenes Läertius says that on one occasion when Plato read aloud a difficult treatise about the soul, Aristotle "was the only person who sat it out, while all the rest rose up and went away."[3] Aristotle remained with Plato for perhaps twenty years, and Plato is supposed to have humorously remarked that his Academy consisted of two parts: the body of his students and the brain of Aristotle. Although Aristotle disagreed with Plato on important philosophical matters, he built an altar to Plato after his teacher's death.

Thirty-seven years old when Plato died, Aristotle expected to be the next master of the Academy. But the trustees of the Academy picked a native Athenian instead, because they saw Aristotle as a "foreigner." When a former classmate who had become a kind of philosopher-king over a rather large area in Asia Minor invited him to be his adviser, Aristotle accepted.

Apparently, Aristotle had little effect on his friend Hermeias's rulership, but he did manage to marry Hermeias's adopted daughter Pythias in 344 B.C.E. Pythias had a large dowry, which Aristotle happily invested. Aristotle's life was disrupted the same year, however, when his political benefactor offended the king of Persia. Shortly after Aristotle and Pythias fled to the island of Lesbos, Hermeias was crucified by the Persian king. While on Lesbos, Aristotle studied natural history, and Pythias died giving birth to their daughter. Aristotle never forgot Pythias and asked that her bones be buried with him. Aristotle later lived with a woman named Herpyllis. Their long, happy relationship produced Aristotle's son Nicomachus, to whom he dedicated the *Nicomachean Ethics*.

In 343 B.C.E., King Philip of Macedon invited Aristotle to train his thirteen-year-old son Alexander. The boy was wild and crude, but Aristotle was able to smooth his rough edges and instill in him respect for knowledge and science. As Alexander the Great, Aristotle's famous pupil ordered his soldiers to collect specimens of plant, marine, and animal life from faraway places for his old teacher.

In 340 B.C.E., Philip sent Aristotle back to Aristotle's hometown of Stagira, so that he could write a code of laws to help restore the community, which had been

To be sure, the whirl of life and culture in contemporary America is such that we apparently feel little need of, and obviously pay no heed to, such things as the ethical and political observations of an Aristotle. For what is there to human existence, save getting ahead and having a good time?
But Aristotle did not see things this way.
— Henry Veatch

disrupted by a war. He did well enough that Stagira celebrated a yearly holiday in his honor. In 334 B.C.E., Aristotle at last returned to Athens, where he founded his own school, possibly with money from Alexander.

The Lyceum

Aristotle named his school after the god Apollo Lyceus. The Lyceum was built near some of the most elegant buildings in Athens, surrounded by shady groves of trees and covered walkways. Socrates used to visit the same groves, remarking on what a wonderful spot they made for reflection.

Alexander the Great was Aristotle's most famous pupil.

Aristotle's students were known as the *peripatetic* philosophers because he often discussed philosophy while strolling with them along tree-covered walkways called the Peripatos. In addition to philosophy, Aristotle's curriculum included technical lectures for limited audiences and popular lectures of more general interest. Aristotle collected hundreds of maps, charts, and documents, forming the first important library in the West. For instance, he collected and studied 153 political constitutions.

Leadership of the Lyceum rotated among certain members of the school according to rules drawn up by Aristotle. Once a month he held a common meal and symposium at which one of the members was picked to defend a philosophical idea against criticism from everyone else. Aristotle continued to lecture and research for his entire tenure at the Lyceum.[4]

The Lyceum's students tended to be from the middle class, whereas the students at Plato's Academy were more aristocratic. The two schools were bitter rivals for a short while, but as each concentrated on its own particular interests, this rivalry died down. The Academy stressed mathematics and "pure" understanding, while Aristotle's students collected anthropological studies of barbarian cultures, chronologies of various wars and games, the organs and living habits of animals, the nature and locations of plants, and so on.[5]

Alexander the Great died in 323 B.C.E. Athens had smarted under a Greek unification program begun by Philip and continued under Alexander. With Alexander dead, Athens openly expressed its hostility and resentment toward all things Macedonian. Because of his long and favored place under the protection of both Philip and Alexander, Aristotle found himself in an uncomfortable position. He left Athens and the Lyceum the next year, after being legally charged with not respecting the gods of the state—one of the same charges leveled at Socrates. Rather than stand trial like the crusty old *sophos*, Aristotle fled to the island of Euboea (his mother's birthplace), in his words, "lest Athens sin twice against philosophy."

In 322 B.C.E., the man who had created the first important library, tutored the greatest ruler of the ancient world, invented logic, and shaped the thinking of an entire culture died. So great was his influence on later thinkers that for hundreds of years all educated persons knew him simply as *the Philosopher*.

Raphael's famous painting *The School of Athens* depicts Aristotle (right center, blue) conversing with Plato (left center, red) and surrounded by such philosophers as Socrates, Diogenes, Heraclitus, Epicurus, Parmenides, Hypatia, Averroës, and Pythagoras.

The Naturalist

Aristotelian philosophy is so complex in treatment and scope that no introductory survey can do justice to all of it. A good place to begin, however, is with a look at Aristotle's ethics and psychology, for in addition to presenting a powerful and challenging doctrine of happiness as self-realization and personal growth, they rest on Aristotle's naturalistic metaphysics.

In Plato, we saw one significant expression of the search for the good life: evaluating this life by comparing it to some ideal standard and then trying to perfect this world. In a sense, Aristotle brings to full maturity a second major expression of the search for the good life: attempting to acquire facts without bias and then using that information to make this a better world.

Although Aristotle loved and respected Plato, he saw dangers in Plato's rationalistic idealism. Partly as a reaction to Plato, and partly as a consequence of his own temperament, Aristotle is sometimes said to have brought philosophy down to earth. He combined the study of humanity and nature to a degree that was not possible again because, after Aristotle, no single individual could seriously hope to contribute in a major way to so many distinct fields.

Aristotle stands alone as an archetype of the philosophical naturalist. Basically, **naturalism** is the belief that reality consists of the natural world. The naturalist's

naturalism
The belief that reality consists of the natural world; denial of the existence of a separate supernatural order of reality; belief that nature follows orderly, discoverable laws.

Whereas Plato turned inward in his search for truth, Aristotle turned to nature.

universe is ordered in that everything in it follows consistent and discoverable *laws* of nature; everything can be understood in terms of those fundamental laws. Nothing exists outside of space and time. Nature always acts with a purpose, and the key to understanding anything lies in determining its essential purpose.

Philosophical naturalists deny the existence of a separate supernatural order of reality. They believe that *human beings, although special, are part of the natural order and behave according to fixed laws and principles.* Thus a clear understanding of nature is necessary to any clear conception of human behavior. Ethics and political (social) science must be based on the actual facts of life, carefully observed and collected by a scientific method—not on speculative, "otherworldly," rationalistic schemes.

Aristotle based his philosophical positions on scrutiny of particular, actual things, not on the isolated contemplation of mathematical laws or "pure ideas." Let's see what Aristotle discovered when he turned his scientist's eye to the teeming natural world.

Natural Changes

Recall that the Presocratic philosophers struggled to explain how change is possible. In simplified form, the problem of explaining change was generated by a seemingly inescapable contradiction: In order for X to change into Y, then somehow X must be *both* X and Y. If X is Y, then X cannot be said to *become* (change into) Y. For example, water is not ice, yet we say that water "changes into" or "becomes" ice (and the opposite). But until the water becomes ice, it is not ice: It is water. When it is ice, it is no longer water.

A likely impossibility is always preferable to an unconvincing possibility.
— Aristotle

"But," you may ask, "what about the in-between stages, the transitional period when some water molecules are freezing into ice molecules? There we have both ice and water!" Do we? That is, do we have some sort of "ice-water" molecule? If so, then it is not water or ice, but a third—different—thing. Further, we still need some clear explanation of *how* what once *was* water *is* now ice. (You may wish to review the problem of change and "Zeno's Paradoxes" in Chapter 2.)

Aristotle is sometimes called "the father of science" because he was the first Western thinker of record to provide an adequate analysis of a *process* of change based on the claim that form is inseparable from matter.

Form

Aristotle was troubled by Platonic dualism, the division of the universe into two worlds or realms: the realm of *becoming* and the realm of *being*. (You might find it helpful to review the discussion of Plato's theory of Forms in Chapter 5.)

According to Plato, only Forms (with a capital *F*) are truly real; objects of sense perception are mere reflections or diluted copies of Forms. Aristotle worried that dualism leads to "otherworldliness, to a chasm between the actual and the ideal…[which means] that discussion of what is can never amount to more than a 'likely story' and knowledge of what *ought to be* has little or no relevance to pressing moral, political, and social problems."[6] If Aristotle's claim that there is only one world is correct, whatever form is can only be an aspect of *this* world.

Aristotle argued that form can be distinguished from content only in thought and never in fact. For instance, we can make a mental distinction between shape and color, but we never encounter shapeless colors or colorless shapes. We can mentally distinguish between mortality and living things, but we will never encounter mortality of and by itself, any more than we will encounter living things without also encountering mortality. This means that mortality is a formal—or essential—aspect of living things.

Aristotle warned that we must take care not to mistake intellectual analysis for ontological status. Aristotle accused Plato of doing just that by imputing actual existence to the Forms. For Aristotle, form exists *within the natural order* embedded in particular things and *cannot* exist independently.

Aristotle argued that every particular thing, considered at any given time, has two aspects. First, it shares properties with other particulars. For example, you and your philosophy professor share certain properties with each other. You also share properties with Willy the whale, with anything containing hydrogen, and so on. But there is something special, unique, or primary (basic) that you and your professor share with each other and with me. This shared quality consists of whatever answers the question "What is that?" Aristotle characterized this basic essence as the substance of a thing.

So, "What are you, what is your essence?" You are a mammal, an animal, a vertebrate—just like your professor, Willy, and I are. But you, your professor, and I share a common quality that Willy lacks: humanness. All human beings share qualities that Willy lacks, and Willy has qualities that we lack and that he shares with other underwater creatures. The more thorough our list of the shared, common properties that make up a thing's essential nature or form, the fuller our grasp of that form.

According to Aristotle, *form* (with a lowercase *f*) makes a substance what it is. This kind of substance-making form is what is meant by the essence of a thing. So we (you, your professor, and I) share a common "form," "substance," or "essence that makes us human."

After distinguishing among various ways that we talk about *being* (in reference to a thing's size, shape, and such), Aristotle says:

> Although being is used in all these ways, clearly the primary kind of being is what a thing is; for it is this alone that indicates substance. When we say what kind of thing something is, we say that it is good or bad, but not that it is three feet long or that is a man; but when we say what a thing is, we do not say that is white, hot, or three feet long, but that is a man or a god. All other things are said to be only insofar as they are quantities, qualities, affections…so what is primarily—not in the sense of being something, but just quite simply being—is substance.[7]

Could DNA be modern science's version of Aristotelian substance: the essence that makes us human? If so, is that what we "are"—really?

In other words, Aristotle is saying that when we characterize or define *what a thing is*, we are speaking of that thing's substance or essence. Thus, according to Aristotle, *form* is the essence of substance itself, that which makes a substance a substance.

From the Greek word for essence (*ousia*), **Aristotelian form** is that which is *in matter* and makes a thing what it is. Aristotelian form can be abstracted from matter in thought but cannot exist independently of matter. Although knowing what kind of thing a thing is can be useful, merely knowing a thing's form (essence) does not account for its particularness, its individuality. So, according to Aristotle, form is only one basic aspect of reality. The other is matter.

form (Aristotelian) From the Greek word for essence (*ousia*), that which is in matter and makes a thing what it is; can be abstracted from matter but cannot exist independently of matter.

Matter

Navigating wisely through life requires that we recognize the common features of things, their essences, natures, qualities, common characteristics, and such; it also requires dealing with specific things, with particulars. The essence that you, your philosophy professor, and I share is that we are human beings; we are also, however, particular human beings. So we also need to ask about *this* specific human being (or horse, or book, or anything).

In Aristotle's view, when we ask about *this* particular thing, we are asking about the material composition of whatever constitutes that thing, the specific stuff that makes a general form (human being) into a particular instance of that form (you, your professor, me). For Aristotle, **matter**, from the Greek *hyle*, is the common material stuff found in a variety of things; matter has no distinct characteristics until some form is imparted to it or until the form inherent in a thing becomes actualized. Thus, for Aristotle, individual things are "formed matter."

His careful studies of the natural world led Aristotle to posit a *hierarchy of forms*, moving from the simplest kinds of things to the most complex, based on each thing's function or purpose. At the highest levels, form is the "purpose," "goal," or "overall plan" of an object considered as a *whole*, as a *unity*.

matter (Aristotelian) From the Greek *hyle*, the common material stuff found in a variety of things; it has no distinct characteristics until some form is imparted to it or until the form inherent in a thing becomes actualized.

Aristotle did *not* mean that the universe (nature) has been planned by something separate from it like God or Plato's Forms. Rather, he argued, order and purpose are inherent in nature. Nature is purposive. Matter provides "opportunity"; form provides "direction." Form does not—cannot—exist without matter; matter does not—cannot—exist without form. The Aristotelian universe is a continuum of *formed matter*, from the lowest, most inert things to the most complex, autonomous, and active ones. Understanding anything consists of understanding its relationships to other things on this continuum.

Change

> *A great Hasidic rabbi by the name of Zusya once said: When I die, God will not ask me, "Why were you not Moses?" When I die, God will ask me, "Why were you not Zusya?"*

Aristotle thought that his picture of nature as *formed matter* explained how it is that things can change. Consider once more the example of water changing into ice. When water changes into ice, some part of the water itself remains water, and some part of the water changes. The basic matter stays the same, but it changes form. As water becomes progressively colder, the behavior or properties of the molecules that constitute water change from liquid form to crystalline form.

The basic process of change—substitution of forms in stages—is the same from the simplest to the most complex things. As an acorn changes into an oak tree, a progressive succession of shapes occurs: acorn to sprout to sapling to tree. (And the tree stage itself consists of a series of shape changes as the trunk thickens and branches grow out and up.)

Guiding this series of changes, says Aristotle, is movement toward an inherent structure or form (oak tree). The acorn, for instance, contains a potential sprout—a form not yet "materialized." If conditions are right, the acorn's actual form is replaced by its potential form, and the *potential* sprout is *actualized*. The actualized sprout contains within itself the form of a potential sapling. Given the necessary material conditions, the sprout restructures its own matter into a sapling according to this "blueprint" (form of a sapling). The sapling, of course, contains the form of a potential tree, and so on.

So change is really a series of smaller changes in which matter loses and gains form. In complex organisms, change occurs as an orderly series of progressively complex forms. Such structured, systematic change, from simple to complex, accounts for the qualitative distinction between change and *development* or *growth*. Development occurs when changes follow a pattern that leads toward *a goal* or *end* (purpose or function).

The goal or purpose that produces growth unites or unifies the successive changes as *stages* leading to a single goal (actualization of the ultimate form or essence). Aristotle argued that in order to understand something, it is necessary to identify its function or purpose. But there is more to a thing than its function (purpose or end). The most complete analysis or understanding of anything, Aristotle believed, could only come from asking, "What accounts for the existence of this or that thing?"

Aristotle's Hierarchy of Explanations

You may have heard the story of the three bricklayers who are asked, "What are you doing?" The first worker says, "I am laying this brick." The second answers, "I am building an arch." The third says, "I am building a cathedral." In a sense, each worker

According to Aristotle, this acorn realizes its potential as a sprout, which in turn, if it is "happy," will realize its potential as a sapling, which in turn, if it is "happy," will become a sturdy oak.

is correct. He has stated his view of his task, his sense of purpose or primary function. The story is often told to inspire us to set our sights on lofty goals. But it has another lesson, too. This story teaches us that the same thing can be characterized by distinctly different accounts or explanations, depending on the *purpose* of the account—and the purposes that together constitute the thing, process, or activity.

In the story of the bricklayers, each succeeding account includes the essence of the prior account. When the second bricklayer says, "I am building an arch," he implies, "I am laying this brick in order to make an arch." In other words, his goal is the arch. When the third bricklayer says, "I am building a cathedral," he implies, "I am laying this brick in order to make an arch in order to make a cathedral." His goal is "higher" than that of the second worker, whose goal is, in turn, higher than that of the first bricklayer's more modest task.

In this simplistic example, we also see that a number of alternative explanations and accounts could have been given, depending on the focus (purposes) of the account giver. If the first bricklayer is a novice with no knowledge of arches or cathedrals, then he will be unable to grasp the ultimate purpose of his activity as part of a complex, goal-directed process. His view is not incorrect; it is incomplete. He lacks adequate comprehension of the *end* of the construction process, which is only a *means* governed by a plan.

Have you noticed, however, that even the third worker's account can be broadened? We still—naturally—want to ask, "But why are you building a cathedral?" Here, too, a variety of responses will be "correct": "To make money." "To honor God." "To impress my special friend." "Because I enjoy it." The first three answers don't necessarily bring a halt to the inquiry, do they? We may still need to ask, "Why do you want money? What's the money to be used for?" "Why honor God by building a cathedral?" "What's the purpose behind trying to impress your special friend?"

One answer seems somehow different. What kind of answer might we expect to the question, "Why do what you enjoy?" We don't usually ask that question because pleasure (enjoyment) is capable of standing as an *end in itself*. That is, enjoyment is treated as an ultimate goal by many people, a goal that does not look forward toward a yet-higher goal.

Later in this chapter, we'll see what Aristotle has to say about money and other things, including pleasure, as final goals. What's important now is the concept of hierarchical ends, a hierarchy of "whys." Aristotle's hierarchical account of causation serves as a foundation for his moral psychology and greatly influenced subsequent thinkers.

The Four Causes

Aristotle was the first philosopher to understand that not all "why" questions can be answered in the same way because there is more than one kind of *why*. In marked contrast to the single explanation view, Aristotle distinguished among four different kinds of explanations that, together, constitute a complete accounting or understanding of a thing. He referred to them as *causes*.

The Greek word for cause, *aitia*, meant "the reason for something happening." According to Aristotle, complete understanding of a thing must tell us what material the thing is made of, what form the thing takes, what triggered the events that set the thing's existence into motion, and the ultimate purpose for which the thing exists.

Aristotle's Four Causes are thus offered as accounts of (1) the material the thing is made of (*Material Cause*); (2) the form the thing takes (*Formal Cause*); the triggering action or motion that begins the thing (*Efficient Cause*); and the ultimate purpose or goal for which the thing exists (*Final Cause*). After describing the Four Causes, Aristotle says that "it is the business of the natural scientist to know about them all…[and to] give his answer to the question 'why?' in the manner of a natural scientist…[by referring] to them all—to the matter, the form, the mover, and the purpose."[8]

Material Cause

material cause
The material (substance) from which a thing comes and in which change occurs; the first of Aristotle's Four Causes.

The **Material Cause** of a thing refers to the material (substance) from which the thing comes and in which change occurs. What accounts for wood becoming a bed instead of, say, a table? In his *Physics*, Aristotle points out that merely identifying the material out of which, say, a bed or statue is made does not tell us how and why that bed or that statue exists:

> Some people regard the nature and substance of things that exist by nature as being in each case the proximate element inherent in the thing, this being itself unshaped; thus, [according to such a view] the nature of a bed, for instance, would be wood, and that of a statue bronze. [Those who think this way offer] as evidence…the fact that if you were to bury a bed, and the moisture that got into it as it rotted gained enough force to throw up a shoot, it would be wood and not a bed that came into being. [According to this view, the bed's] arrangement according to the rules of an art…is an accidental attribute, whereas its substance is what remains permanently, and undergoes all these changes.[9]

In other words, statues and beds are made of many different things, and some bronze and wood never become statues or beds. Identifying a thing's matter is a necessary part of—but not a complete—accounting for that thing. Aristotle rejects merely identifying a thing's *matter* as a complete understanding of the "how" and "why" of that thing. After all, it is not the nature of wood to become beds or the nature of bronze to become statues.

Formal Cause

Until wood is fashioned into some particular thing—a bed or table—it is *potentially* but not *actually* a bed or table. Wood needs to *be formed* into beds and tables and other crafted objects "according to the rules of an art." It is not just wood (matter), then, that makes a bed or table, but the *form* the wood takes. Therefore, in addition to identifying the Material Cause of a thing, we need to know its **Formal Cause**— the shape, or form, into which "this matter" is changed.

formal cause
The shape, or form, into which matter is changed; the second of Aristotle's Four Causes.

It is easy enough to see how an artisan imposes form on matter; the bed-maker shapes wood into beds or tables. But what about natural things, growing things, and such? What forms natural objects? According to Aristotle, flesh and bone, for example, become flesh and bone only when their substance (matter) *forms* into "that which makes flesh, flesh" and "that which makes bone, bone." Aristotle says:

What is potentially flesh or bone does not yet have its own nature until it acquires the form that accords with the formula, by means of which we define flesh and bone; nor can it be said at this stage to exist by nature. So in another way, nature is the shape and form of things that have a principle of movement in themselves—the form being only theoretically separable from the object in question.[10]

The basic elements that flesh or bone are made from are not—of themselves— flesh or bone. Flesh *is* (essentially and by definition) the precise "formulation" of matter-as-flesh. Bone *is* (essentially and by definition) the precise "formulation" of matter-as-bone.

Together, then, the Material and Formal Causes of a thing tell us what stuff it is composed of and how that stuff is formed. In other words, Material and Formal Causes combine to describe a particular unit of "formed matter."

Efficient Cause

But what explains *why* this bone or flesh or person or tree actually *exists*? What accounts for the potentially "formed matter" *becoming actualized*? What starts the whole process? What gets it going? What "triggers" the sequence that results in this bone or that person? Aristotle answers that a "proximate mover" "causes" a thing's "coming-to-be." Some sort of "motion" is needed to convert potentiality into actuality. Aristotle says:

> Thus the answer to the question "why?" is to be given by referring to the matter, to the essence, and to the proximate mover. In cases of coming-to-be it is mostly in this last way that people examine the causes; they ask what comes to be after what, what was the immediate thing that acted or was acted upon, and so on in order.[11]

Aristotle named a thing's "triggering" cause the **Efficient Cause**: that which initiates activity; the substance by which a change is brought about. Although, for Aristotle, Efficient Causes, like all other causes, are substances, the concept of a triggering action is probably closer to our contemporary notion of cause than the other causes Aristotle discusses.

Final Cause

Aristotle addressed one other why question, a question that still confounds philosophers, scientists, and theologians and that is the basis of certain "ultimate meaning" questions: What is the meaning of life? Does life have purpose? *Why* (not *how*) does this universe exist? Ultimate "why" questions are also asked and (usually) easily answered about crafted objects: "Why do these shoes exist? To keep our feet warm and protected." In the case of the shoes, note that the answer states the *reasons for which* the shoes were made, the *purpose, goal*, or *end* that the shoes exist to serve.

Aristotle called the *ultimate why* of a thing that thing's *telos*, or final goal, the purpose of its very existence. Thus, the very last answer in a series of why questions identifies the final cause needed to complete our understanding of the thing. A thing's **Final Cause** is that for which an activity or process takes place, a thing's very reason for being (*raison d'être*).

efficient cause
The triggering cause that initiates activity; the substance by which a change is brought about; close to the contemporary meaning of cause; the third of Aristotle's Four Causes.

final cause
That for which an activity or process takes place; a thing's very reason for being (*raison d'être*); the fourth of Aristotle's Four Causes.

Another term for final cause is *end*, not in the sense of last event or action, but in the sense of *purpose* or *completed state*. In this sense, a thing is completed or finished in the way that a chair or painting or song is finished when the artisan has accomplished his or her goal. When living things are finished in this sense, they are said to be fully realized, mature, ripe, grown, complete, whole, or perfected. Note that, from a naturalistic perspective, referring to persons as "complete," "whole," and "perfect" does *not* carry religious or moralistic connotations. Rather, the terms connote realization, actualization, or reaching our ultimate stage of development, our end or purpose.

Aristotle claimed to have identified what he called an inner urge in each living thing to realize its end or purpose: a drive to develop, to become its unique self. Speaking this way, we can say that the acorn, for example, has an *inner urge* to become an oak tree, the baby has an *inner urge* to become a fully realized adult, and so forth. Aristotle characterized this inner urge to become what a thing is "meant to be" as "having its end within itself." The Greek word for this is **entelechy**, and Aristotle constructs his theory of human well-being on the concept of *entelechy*.

entelechy
From the Greek for "having its end within itself": according to Aristotle, an inner urge that drives all things to blossom into their own unique selves; inner order or design that governs all natural processes.

Entelechy

Aristotle thought that *entelechy* explained nature as a whole. Certainly the concept frames his entire practical philosophy. *Entelechy means that things do not just happen; they develop according to natural design.* That is, nature is ordered and guided internally. Sometimes Aristotle refers to *entelechy* as a "creative drive." "Such principles" he says, "do not all make for the same goal, but each inner principle always makes for the same goal *of its own [kind]*, if nothing interferes" [emphasis added].[12]

The acorn will become an oak tree if nothing stops it. But the acorn lacks the power to ensure that all its needs are met. It might fall on rocky soil, get too much or too little water, and so forth. It might become a pretty pathetic oak tree—but it will never become any kind of cedar because change occurs only within substances.

Human beings, however, are more complex than acorns. And though we must remain human beings, we may fail (for reasons to be discussed) to follow our own *entelechy*. We may never fulfill our ultimate purpose, to become our "true selves." We may remain incompletely formed, in much the same way that some plants "meant to blossom" never blossom. Malformed, they linger in hostile conditions, spindly, thin, unproductive. Materially, they remain petunias, azaleas, cherry trees; they grow but do not develop.

For Aristotle, life without full development is all too common for human beings, too. Because we are so much more complex than acorns and azaleas, the conditions necessary for fully realized human beings are correspondingly more complex. But before we look into Aristotle's formula for thriving, we need to see how and why Aristotle applied the concept of form to the human soul.

The Hierarchy of Souls

As we have seen, the Greek term for soul is *psyche*. We get the term *psychology* from it. For Aristotle, *psyche is the form of the body*. Just as we cannot even imagine a soul going to Atlanta without a body, so too, one's body is not a human being without a human soul in Aristotle's view. *Soul is entelechy.*

Aristotle believed that it is impossible to affect the body without affecting the soul or to affect the soul without affecting the body. There is no way to reach the soul except through the bodily organs (including the brain), and there is no way for the soul to act or communicate except bodily. Some scientists have lent support to the view that the mind plays a role in altering the course of various autoimmune diseases, that laughter and positive attitudes have healing power. Such ideas seem to be consistent with Aristotle's insistence on the organic, holistic, inseparable union of the body and the natural soul. African, Amazonian, Native American, and other tribal cultures have long accepted this union as a fact.

Human beings are not the only *besouled* (to use one translator's beautiful word) creatures, and each kind of substance requires a different kind of study. Aristotle thought that although various kinds of souls are different enough that no single definition of *soul* can cover them all, they are similar enough that we can still recognize a common nature in all their varieties.[13]

Aristotle taught that there are three kinds of souls, which constitute a hierarchy. Each higher level on the continuum of souls contains elements of the lower levels—but the lower levels do not contain the higher. This hierarchy is based on the capacities or *potentialities* possessed by each level of animal life. The more potentiality a thing has, the higher its place in the hierarchy.

The hierarchy of souls progresses from the simplest life functions to more complicated ones. The lowest type of soul is called the *vegetative*, or *nutritive*, soul. This is the minimal level of life (animate matter). *The nutritive soul absorbs matter* from other things (as food is absorbed and transformed into blood or tissue). The second level of soul is the level of sensation; here we find the *sensitive*, or *sentient*, *soul*. *The sensitive soul registers information* regarding the form of things but does not absorb or become those things (as when we look at or touch something). Human souls include a third, higher level of *entelechy* called the *rational* soul, which includes the nutritive and sensitive souls, as well as capacities for analyzing things, understanding various forms of relationships, and making reasoned decisions (called *deliberation*).

The lowest level of life has the most limited potential; think, for instance, of single cells or worms. At the top of the hierarchy of souls, we observe greater capacities for discriminating among various aspects of the environment and for overriding impulse and instinct with rational deliberation based on goals and ends. We note a capacity for understanding the essence (form) of what's going on and a capacity for creative and self-conscious intelligence. These capacities are lacking in lower life-forms.

Aristotle's ethical philosophy is built on this concept of a hierarchy of souls. It is sometimes classified as an ethic of *self-realization*, but a much better term would be *soul-realization*. A good way to get a basic sense of this kind of ethic is to take a look at the concept of happiness expressed in the *Nicomachean Ethics*.

> For Aristotle, the great philosopher of the classical period, reared to accept slavery and pursue self-centeredness, the Greek was human. The European barbarians were not human, because they were unskilled; nor were Asians human, because they lacked strength and character; women were not human either; women were halfway human and children were only potentially human. The human being par excellence is the free man of the polis of Hellas.
>
> — Enrique Dussel

Natural Happiness

As we've seen, the classical Greeks defined virtue, or *arete*, as excellence of function. Happiness was also understood in terms of function: A thing was happy when it functioned fully and well according to its own nature. In Aristotelian terms, happiness is the state of actualizing or realizing a thing's function, its *entelechy*. A good life is one that provides all the necessary conditions and opportunities for a person to become fully himself or herself—and one in which the person has the character to do so.

As the French classicist Pierre Pellegrin notes, for Aristotle, virtue plays a central, but not self-sufficient, role in the pursuit of human well-being:

> The translation of *arete* by virtue, while it has a long tradition of its own, still remains dangerous because of the connotations of the word. For Aristotle, *arete* is the excellence of some thing. He remarks that we can speak of the *arete* of a tool or a horse. Nonetheless, he uses the term most particularly in the ethical realm. Now "ethical" comes from *ethos*... which means the habitual way to be, the one that results from experience and education. If someone has acquired the habit, from childhood, of being intemperate, intemperance becomes for him a habitual, almost natural way to be. Ethical virtue then will be a state of being virtuous, rooted in the human subject by long experience. But while Aristotle acknowledges that immorality and vice can procure satisfactions, he posits as the basis for his ethics the principle that virtue, which implies moderation of tendencies and self-mastery, is the principal—though not the only—element in happiness (*eudaimonia*).... To be virtuous, then, for human beings, is to give themselves the best opportunity to realize their human nature fully.[14]

For Aristotle, happiness is a quality of life here and now, not something for the hereafter. It is neither entirely material nor entirely spiritual (formal). His is a philosophy of moderation in the fullest sense, based on common experience, stripped of sentimentality: Wealth is not enough to give us happiness, but poverty makes happiness impossible. Mental attitude is important, but so is physical health. No one can be happy *in the fullest sense* who is chronically ill or mentally deficient. Unattractive people are not as happy as attractive ones. No matter how great our efforts, happiness

"The Meaning of Our Existence Is Not Invented But Detected"

What is called self-actualization is, and must remain, the unintended effect of self-transcendence; it is ruinous and self-defeating to make it the target of intention. And what is true of self-actualization also holds for identity and happiness. It is the very "pursuit of happiness" that obviates happiness. The more we make it a target, the more widely we miss.

It may now have become clear that a concept such as self-actualization, or self-realization, is not a sufficient ground for a motivational theory. This is mainly due to the fact that self-actualization, like power and pleasure, also belongs to the class of phenomena which can only be obtained as a side effect and are thwarted precisely to the degree to which they are made a matter of direct intention. Self-actualization is a good thing; however, I maintain that man can only actualize himself to the extent to which he fulfills meaning. Then self-actualization occurs spontaneously; it is contravened when it is made an end in itself....

We have to beware of the tendency to deal with values in terms of the mere self-expression of man himself.... If the meaning that is waiting to be fulfilled by man were nothing but a mere expression of self, or no more than a projection of his wishful thinking, it would immediately lose its demanding and challenging character; it could no longer call man forth or summon him.... I think the meaning of our existence is not invented by ourselves, but rather detected.

Viktor E. Frankl, *Man's Search for Meaning: An Introduction to Logotherapy* (New York: Pocket Books, 1963), pp. 8, 35–36, 156–157.

always contains an element of luck. A person raised well from infancy is a happier person than one who is not. An otherwise good life can be marred by a bad death.

PHILOSOPHICAL QUERY

As an example of the importance of luck in the good life, think about this Aristotelian maxim (derived from Solon): "Count no man happy until he is dead." Aristotle taught that a good life can be marred by a bad death. Discuss this general idea and then tie it to our present attitudes toward death, dying, euthanasia, and the all-too-frequent instances of individuals kept barely alive, condemned to spend their last months or years in nursing homes. Do you agree with Aristotle that a bad death or dying can transform a good life into a bad one? Or do you think that biological life is sacred—period?

Discussing Philosophy

The Good

Whereas Plato believed the Form of Good was the highest form of being, Aristotle believed the good is "that at which all things aim." In other words, the good for anything is the realization of its own nature (essence): *The good at which all things aim is their own entelechy*. When we use the expressions "for your own good" or "that's not good for you," we may have something similar in mind. The good, then, is what's good for something's full functioning. The good encourages the development (realization) of a thing's true nature.

Because human beings are complex, consisting of all three elements of soul, it is possible to develop physically or emotionally or intellectually and still fail to realize our *entelechy*. It is also possible to lack the ability to achieve it, either because the external circumstances of our lives inhibit our full development or because some imbalance in our own characters prevents us from fully developing.

Before we go any further, it's important to be clear about the distinction between "aging" and "developing." We're probably all familiar with people who grow old without growing up. We must not confuse biological growth and maturation with personal development. Aristotle linked the two: A *fully* functioning, *completely* happy person will be mentally, physically, spiritually, financially, professionally, creatively, and socially healthy and well-rounded.

As noted in the Overview of Classical Themes, most classical philosophers included an objective component in their conceptions of happiness. This means that *entelechy* is not determined by the individual. Aristotle's view differs from those self-realization or self-fulfillment theories that claim "you can be anything you want to be." Such a claim would have struck him as ridiculous. It is as irrational and unworthy for a human being to try to live like an animal, for example, as it is for an acorn to try to be an ear of corn—or for us to try to make a dog into a child.

> *"Know thyself" has become "Do whatever you please."*
> — Bruno Bettelheim

PHILOSOPHICAL QUERY

Discuss some of the common obstacles to becoming a fully functioning, balanced individual.

Teleological Thinking

According to Aristotle, observation of the natural world (which includes human behavior) reveals that:

> Every art and every scientific inquiry, and similarly every action and purpose, may be said to aim at some good. Hence the good has been well defined as that at which all things aim....
>
> As there are various actions, arts, and sciences, it follows the ends are also various. Thus health is the end of medicine, a vessel of shipbuilding, victory [is the end] of strategy, and wealth [is the goal] of domestic economy....
>
> ...If it is true that in the sphere of action there is an end which we wish for its own sake, and for the sake of which we wish everything else...it is clear that this will be the good or the supreme good. Does it not follow that the knowledge of this supreme good is of great importance for the conduct of life, and that, *if we know it*, we shall be like archers who have a mark at which to aim, we shall have a better chance of attaining what we want?[15]

The technical name for this kind of thinking is *teleological*, from the Greek root *telos*, meaning end, purpose, or goal. (*Entelechy* comes from the same root.) **Teleological thinking** is a way of explaining or understanding a thing in terms of its ultimate goal, or final cause. For example, in teleological terms, infancy is understood as a stage on the way to mature adulthood. Adulthood is the *telos* of infancy. Teleological thinking also refers to understanding things functionally in terms of the relationship of the parts to a whole—for example, considering a vehicle's transmission in terms of the vehicle's ultimate function: speed, traction, comfort. Both Aristotle's ethic and conception of virtue are teleological.

The Science of the Good

In the first book of the *Nicomachean Ethics*, Aristotle makes a famous and insightful proclamation:

> Our statement of the case will be adequate if it be made with all such clearness as the subject-matter admits; for it would be wrong to expect the same degree of accuracy in all [subjects].... [Due to the nature of our subject] we must be content to indicate the truth roughly and in outline; and as our subjects and premises are true generally *but not universally*, we must be content to arrive at conclusions which are generally true.[16]

Aristotle was aware that moral considerations involve practical judgments of particular circumstances. We might characterize his position as *formal relativism*. That means that even though there is an underlying structure, or form, of happiness for human beings, the specific way in which a particular human being realizes that form varies with his or her circumstances.

Consider an example from Aristotle: A wrestler and a young child do not eat the same kinds of foods or the same amounts; but this does not mean that the laws of nutrition are relative in the Sophists' sense of being radically determined by the individual or group. Indeed, the same natural laws apply to wrestlers and babies: Minimum protein, fat, carbohydrate, and fluid levels must be met for good health.

Why do people feel so crowded? Because each wants to occupy the place of the other.
—Rabbi Abraham Yaakov of Sadagora

teleological thinking A way of explaining things in terms of their ultimate goals; understanding things functionally in terms of the relationship of the parts to the whole.

Appropriate caloric intake should be based on actual energy output, not on a merely theoretical model, and so on. But since individual metabolisms vary, since local temperature affects metabolism, since the quality of food varies, and so forth, we must modify each person's actual diet: "We must be content to indicate the truth roughly and in outline," Aristotle reminds us.

We can identify a general outline of conduct that will lead to the best possible life, but we cannot give a precise prescription for any individual's good life. Still, Aristotle says, we can arrive at a valuable approximation of the "good life" based on human nature and the good we each seek.

According to the *Nicomachean Ethics*, the good to which all humans aspire is happiness:

> As [all] knowledge and moral purpose aspires to some good, what is in our view the good at which the political science aims, and what is the highest of all practical goods? As to its name there is, I may say, a general agreement. The masses and the cultured classes agree in calling it happiness, and conceive that "to live well" or "to do well" is the same thing as "to be happy." But as to the nature of happiness they do not agree, nor do the masses give the same account of it as the philosophers.[17]

The *Nicomachean Ethics* is a careful survey of a variety of opinions regarding what constitutes "living well" in the best, fullest sense. Although Aristotle concludes that the best life is the life of philosophical contemplation, the heart of his ethics is a philosophy of moderation, fulfillment, activity, and balance.

For Deeper Consideration

Increasingly, contemporary philosophers and social scientists are raising questions about the pursuit of happiness, with some suggesting that the pursuit of "happiness" leads to unhappiness and dissatisfaction. Contrast the classical notion of happiness with today's notion in terms of *eudaimonia*. Is *eudaimonia* the same thing as happiness? (Hint: Do not overlook the role of habit as it affects character.) Is today's concept of happiness healthy and reasonable? Might we benefit by modifying it along Aristotelian lines? Use your own expectations and experiences to help you dig into this interesting area of philosophy.

Eudaimonia

The word Aristotle used that is so often translated as "happiness" is **eudaimonia**. The English language does not have a good one-word equivalent for *eudaimonia*. *Happiness* is almost too bland, although it's probably the answer most of us would give if asked what we want from life (or the afterlife, in many conceptions of heaven).

Eudaimonia implies being really alive rather than just existing: fully aware, vital, alert. This is more than being free of cares or worries. Rather, *eudaimonia* implies exhilaration—great suffering and great joy, great passions. It implies a full life, not a pinched, restricted one.

The hell to be endured hereafter, of which theology tells us, is no worse than the hell we make for ourselves in this world by habitually fashioning our characters in the wrong way.

— William James

---

eudaimonia
Often translated as "happiness"; term Aristotle used to refer to fully realized existence; state of being fully aware, vital, alert.

Eudaimonia results when pleasure is the natural companion of a fully functioning life rather than the goal of life. Artisans working at their true calling—such as this eighty-year-old glassblower—combine hard work and happiness in a vital, rich way.

A life devoted solely to pleasure, says Aristotle, is "a life fit only for cattle." Pleasure is not the *goal* of life; it's the natural companion of a full and vigorous life. If you have ever seen an athlete or scholar or artist working very hard at what she loves, you know what Aristotle meant: Deep and satisfying pleasure *accompanies* doing what we are meant to do. But the pursuit of pleasure as an end is shallow:

> Ordinary or vulgar people conceive [the good] to be pleasure, and accordingly approve a life of enjoyment.... Now the mass of men present an absolutely slavish appearance, as choosing the life of brute beasts, but they meet with consideration because so many persons in authority share [such] tastes.[18]

According to Aristotle, a life devoted to acquiring wealth is also a limited one. Its focus is too narrow to nourish the natural soul's full complement of qualities and needs. Think of people who work long, stressful hours to get rich—and then think of how much *living* they miss in the process. They never "stop to smell the roses." The unhappy rich person is common enough to be a stereotype. Even with all the money in the world, a person still needs self-discipline and the knowledge to use his or her riches wisely. Aristotle says:

> The life of money-making is in a sense a life of constraint, and it is clear that wealth is not the good of which we are in quest; for it is useful in part as a means to something else.[19]

Aristotle also rejected fame and public success as leading to *eudaimonia* because he believed that the more self-sufficient we are, the happier we are; and the famous are less self-sufficient than most: They need bodyguards, managers, financial advisers, public adulation, and so forth. There is greater peace of mind, security, and satisfaction in knowing that I can provide for my needs than there is in depending on others, as any adolescent or convalescent knows. If one's happiness depends on fame or Twitter or Facebook followers and likes, it depends on the whims of a fickle, often anonymous, aggregation of individuals whose capacities for assessment may be shallow:

> But [the love of fame] appears too superficial for our present purpose; for honor seems to depend more upon the people who pay it than upon the person to whom it is paid, and we have an intuitive feeling that the good is something which is proper to a man himself and cannot be easily taken away from him.[20]

The Good Life Is a Process

The highest and fullest happiness, according to Aristotle, comes from a life of reason and contemplation—not a life of inactivity or imbalance, but a rationally ordered life in which intellectual, physical, and social needs are all met under the governance of reason and moderation. The reasonable person does not avoid life: He or she engages in it fully. A rich and full life is a social life. Aristotle says that no man would choose to live without friends, even if he could have everything he wanted on the condition that he remain solitary. According to Aristotle, human beings are political (social) creatures "designed by nature to live with others."

The rational person alone knows how to engage in life fully, since he or she alone has fully realized all three souls: the nutritive, sensitive, and rational—according to the basic form or *entelechy* of human beings.[21] *The good life must be lived fully; it is a process, an activity, a becoming, not a static condition.* Not even moral virtue is adequate for happiness by itself, because:

> [Virtue] it appears, lacks completeness; for it seems that a man may possess virtue and yet be asleep or inactive throughout life, and, not only [that], but he may experience the greatest calamities and misfortunes. But nobody would call such a life a life of happiness unless he were maintaining a paradox.[22]

Practicing a philosophy of *fully functioning* moderation is quite difficult, for it often requires that we stretch beyond those talents and areas of life we are currently satisfied with—to stretch, as it were, beyond our present "passion." Aristotle understood this and attempted to present practical advice that could help us come closer to living a richer, more virtuous life:

> The purpose of this present study is not…the attainment of theoretical knowledge; we are not conducting this inquiry in order to know what virtue is, but in order to become good, else there is no advantage in studying it.[23]

> *The happy man lives well and does well; for we have practically defined happiness as a sort of good life and good action.*
>
> — Aristotle

PHILOSOPHICAL QUERY

Consider Aristotle's position carefully here. It might conform more closely to our true feelings about virtue than our sentimental and idealistic platitudes imply. We might be taught that "virtue is its own reward"—but how many of us really think as highly of a "good" person who hides away from the world as we do of someone who has faults and makes mistakes but gets out there and gets involved in life? Is being "good" really enough?

MindTap

Discussing Philosophy

Hitting the Mark

There are, perhaps, two ways to avoid mediocrity. The first is probably the most common today: to excel or fail at something in a big way. The other, it seems, is rarer, probably because it is so difficult for many of us: to live the fullest life possible, developing and nurturing *all* good and necessary qualities while avoiding all character defects.

Now, clearly the second way constitutes an impossible goal for a human being to meet completely. No one seems likely to avoid all defects of character. That does not, however, rule out the desirability of trying to hit this difficult mark. It's one

> *It is possible to fail in many ways…while to succeed is possible only in one way (for which reason also one is easy and the other difficult—to miss the mark easy, to hit it difficult).*
>
> — Aristotle

thing to say "I can't be expected to get perfect scores on all my assignments" and quite another to jump to the conclusion "so there's no point in studying at all." Such a reaction is already extreme.

We saw that temperance was one of the cardinal virtues in Plato's *Republic* and that it was a key virtue for Socrates. Aristotle goes so far as to base his entire moral philosophy on moderation:

> First of all, it must be observed that the nature of moral qualities is such that they are destroyed by defect and by excess. We see the same thing happen in the case of strength and of health...excess as well as deficiency of physical exercise destroys our strength, and similarly, too much and too little food and drink destroys our health; the proportionate amount, however, produces, increases, and strengthens it. The same applies to self-control, courage, and the other virtues: the man who shuns and fears everything becomes a coward, whereas a man who knows no fear at all and goes to meet every danger becomes reckless. Similarly, a man who revels in every pleasure and abstains from none becomes self-indulgent, while he who avoids every pleasure like a boor becomes what might be called insensitive. Thus we see that self-control and courage are destroyed by excess and deficiency and are preserved by the mean.[24]

The Principle of the Mean

sophrosyne
Wisdom as moderation; hitting the mark; quality of finding the mean between excess and deficiency.

The concept of moderation, what the Greeks called **sophrosyne**, seems dull and depriving to many people. It implies a life of rigid rules, no fun, playing it safe and avoiding any risks. As we have seen, however, Aristotle did not regard a narrow, boring, play-it-safe life as good. Indeed, the idea that moderation is boring is itself the product of an extreme view. The attitude that only living on the edge, going for the gusto, abandoning self-restraint, can make life interesting is one-sided.

Aristotelian moderation is based on the concept that wisdom is *hitting the mark* between too much and not enough. If you study a target, you will notice that only a small circle in the center is the bull's-eye. There is more room on the target to miss the mark than there is to hit it.

A life completely devoted to playing it safe would be off the mark—cowardly, boorish, and insensitive in Aristotle's terms. Living that way actually limits opportunities to grow and fully experience life. Living recklessly or self-indulgently, going from extreme to extreme, will not produce a good, full life either. The great artist who lives only for her work is not living a good, full life, since she indulges her work at the expense of other vital parts of herself. The scholar who hides in research does likewise. So, too, the compulsive jogger or bodybuilder. People who spend all their time doing charity work, praying, and

David Reed/Documentary/CORBIS

Compulsive dedication to something may result in excellence at that particular something. But Aristotle cautions that great effort in the service of anything less than the goal of well-balanced thriving results in imbalance and overall dysfunction. Does *specialized* excellence (in any field, not just bodybuilding) inhibit being truly well-rounded? Have we, as a culture, perhaps lost sight of the price we pay for narrowly *specialized* excellence?

reading holy scriptures are not balanced human beings. (Moral virtue, remember, is not enough, according to Aristotle.)

Aristotelian moderation is the crux of becoming a whole person—of actualizing our potentialities, realizing our form. Achieving it may require that we do more of the things that are difficult for us and less of those we presently enjoy. Just as a proper diet is relative (the overeater must eat less than he is used to or wants to; the anorexic must do the opposite), the goal for each is a bull's-eye.

Each person's prescription for self-realization must be determined by his or her own actual condition. Some of us must become more social, others less so. Some students need to study less to become balanced human beings; others need to study more. If we see the call to moderation in terms of *who we are right now* and what it would take to make us fuller, more balanced, more "alive" and vibrant people, it is anything but a call to boring mediocrity:

> But let us first agree that any discussion on matters of action cannot be more than an outline and is bound to lack precision.... And if this is true of our general discussion, our treatment of particular problems will be even less precise, since these do not come under the head of any art which can be transmitted by precept, but the agent must consider on each different occasion what the situation demands, just as in medicine and in navigation. But although this is the kind of discussion in which we are engaged, we must do our best.[25]

Character and Habit

Central to Aristotle's ethics is the notion of character. From the Greek *charakter*, a word derived from *charassein*, "to make sharp" or "to engrave," **character** refers to the sum total of a person's traits, including behavior, habits, likes and dislikes, capacities, potentials, and so on. For Aristotle, *character* referred to the overall nature or tone of a person's habits, the habitual or predictable and usual way a person behaves. A courageous person is *characteristically* brave. A slothful one is *characteristically* lazy. Moral virtues are habits, according to Aristotle, and must be ingrained in us by training. We are not born with them:

> Moral virtue comes to us as a result of habit.... The virtues we first get by exercising them, as also happens in the case of the arts as well. For the things we have to learn before we can do them, we learn by doing them, e.g., men become builders by building.... So too we become just by doing just acts, temperate by doing temperate acts, brave by doing brave acts.... If this were not so, there would have been no need of a teacher, but all men would be born good or bad at their craft.... Thus in one word, states of character arise out of like activities. That is why the activities we exhibit must be of a certain kind; it is because the states of character correspond to the difference between these. It makes no small difference, then, whether we form habits of one kind or another from our very youth; it makes a very great difference, or rather all the difference.[26]

The coward cannot wait for courage, or he will remain a coward. The coward must first act courageously if he wishes to become brave. The poor student cannot wait for motivation but must first *act the way the disciplined student* acts in order

There is no greater misfortune that can befall you than to be stricken from the roster of the living while you are still living.
— Seneca

character
From the Greek *charakter*, a word derived from *charassein*, "to make sharp" or "to engrave," the sum total of a person's traits, including behavior, habits, likes and dislikes, capacities, potentials, and so on; a key element of Aristotelian ethics and psychology, meaning the overall (generally fixed) nature or tone of a person's habits.

to become a better student. Aristotle anticipated a number of contemporary psychological schools with this emphasis on habitual behavior as the prime element in shaping the human character.

Aristotle distinguishes practical wisdom from theoretical understanding and other forms of knowledge. He links practical wisdom to deliberation. Practical wisdom involves choosing the right goals *and* acting on them. Practical wisdom can help those of us lacking good habits to develop them:

> A man fulfills his proper function only by way of practical wisdom and moral excellence or virtue: virtue makes us aim at the right target, and practical wisdom makes us use the right means.[27]

But, Aristotle notes,

> our ability to perform such actions is *in no way enhanced by knowing them*, since the virtues are characteristics [that is, fixed capacities for action, acquired by habit].[28]

Merely knowing what is good and healthy does not—by itself—usually lead to doing what is good and healthy, as most of us realize. This reminds me of a saying a friend uses as a rule of thumb: "You can act yourself into right thinking, but you can't think yourself into right acting." Like all such sayings, this one needs to be taken with the proverbial grain of salt, but it does emphasize an Aristotelian point: *Happiness requires action.*

Aristotle thought that good habits ingrained in childhood produced the happiest, best life. He said it was better to "overtighten the bow string" in youth, because aging would naturally loosen it.

Application of the Mean

A **mean** is the midpoint between two other points. On a line, it is the exact middle. *Aristotle characterized moral virtue as a mean between too little and too much.* In his terms, the mean is located between deficiency and excess. We might visualize it like this:

vice_____virtue_____vice

deficiency_____mean_____ excess

One advantage of a visual aid like this is that it shows us an action can be *more or less* virtuous or vicious (meaning that it's a vice, not that it's necessarily cruel). Depending on the area encompassed by the mean, there is a certain amount of room within the general area of virtue, but there is even more room in the range of the extremes. Thus it is easier to go wrong than right.

Aristotle realized that some actions are excessive by their very nature; they can have no mean. For instance, there is no moderate, appropriate way to commit adultery. Other kinds of actions admit of degree and so can have a mean. Aristotle illustrated his point with a lengthy analysis of courage, which he placed between the deficiency of cowardice and the excess of recklessness or foolhardiness, both of which are vices. Some examples of Aristotelian vices and virtues are shown in Table 6.1.

Assume the virtue, even if you have it not, For use almost can change the stamp of nature.
— Shakespeare

Moderation in temper is always a virtue; but moderation in principle is always a vice.
— Thomas Paine

mean
From the Latin *medius*, the midpoint between two other points; for Aristotle, moral virtue was characterized as a mean between too little (deficiency) and too much (excess).

TABLE 6.1 ARISTOTELIAN VIRTUES AND VICES		
DEFICIENCY/VICE	**MEAN/VIRTUE**	**EXCESS/VICE**
Cowardice	Courage	Foolhardiness
Anorexia	Moderation	Gluttony
Stinginess	Generosity	Profligacy
Standoffishness	Friendliness	Obsequiousness
Shyness	Pride	Vanity
Pessimism	Realism	Optimism
Celibacy	Monogamy	Promiscuity
Dullness	Well-roundedness	Wildness

© Cengage Learning®

Aristotle noted that some vices are closer to the mean than others are, because they reflect more of the virtue. In the case of courage, for instance, foolhardiness is closer to courage and so is less a vice than cowardice is. Nevertheless, foolhardiness is still a vice. This is why the coward—who is further from the mean—is more easily recognized as flawed than is the foolhardy person who takes too many or the wrong kinds of risks. That's why television and movie characters are easily mistaken for being courageous when they are actually foolhardy. In real life, they are not the people to emulate.

We can easily find many other examples of excess or deficiency being mistaken for valuable character traits. If we take an organic view of life, such examples show how great virtue or talent in one or two areas cannot outweigh significant deficiencies in other areas. An Aristotelian analysis of human activity as an organic

> *His own manners will be his punishment.*
> — Cicero

It isn't always easy to distinguish foolhardiness from courage. When does risk-taking become a vice?

complex affected by our characteristic virtues and vices can improve our moral perspective:

> It is moral virtue that is concerned with emotions and actions, and it is in emotions and actions that excess, deficiency, and the median are found. Thus we can experience fear, confidence, desire, anger, pity, and generally any kind of pleasure and pain either too much or too little, and in either case not properly. But to experience all this at the right time, toward the right objects, toward the right people, for the right reason, and in the right manner—that is the median and the best course, the course that is a mark of virtue.[29]

According to Aristotle, we become our best selves in the process of becoming fully functioning human beings.

One possible benefit of thinking of virtue as a mean between excess and deficiency is an enriched sense of virtue. Thinking only in terms of right *or* wrong can lead to a perception of virtues and vices as simple opposites, whereas Aristotle's system treats them as part of an organic whole, in which each element affects the others and the overall functioning of the organism. *Aristotelian self-realization, like happiness, is a by-product of living a well-balanced life.*

MindTap
Discussing Philosophy
MindTap
Aplia

PHILOSOPHICAL QUERY

Study and discuss Table 6.1, Aristotelian Virtues and Vices, using principles from the *Nicomachean Ethics* and the concept of the mean. Then add and discuss your own examples of virtues and vices.

Commentary

For Aristotle, self-realization was part of a natural process that could be understood only in terms of the whole. Self-realization was not directed by a personal God, nor was it a function of free-flowing self-expression. Aristotle saw limits as set by nature, not by the individual. He thought that he had identified a fixed, natural hierarchy within the human soul. The rational soul is "designed" to control and guide—but not crush—emotions and appetites.

Just as some actions (adultery, for instance) cannot hit a mean because their very nature is imbalanced, so, too, some personalities cannot be actualized (full functioning) because their very essences are excessive or deficient. Some lives are such that self-actualization is impossible. An acorn that falls too close to the parent tree might lack sufficient sunlight to burgeon, or it might be carried to a hostile environment by a bird or used by an artist in a collage. Corn infected with disease will lack the material necessary to complete its development. Human beings raised in seriously defective environments or born with major genetic impairments will never fully realize their *entelechies.*

The simple call to "be yourself" may sound appealing, but it proves to be insubstantial without solid philosophical grounding. While it is possible to be too self-controlled, no substantial good can come from realizing whatever limited conception

"They Are Obliged to Become Somebody Else"

The Trappist monk and Roman Catholic philosopher Thomas Merton (1915–1968) expressed an interesting variation of a self-realization ethic in his book *New Seeds of Contemplation*. By tying individual *entelechy* to God's will, Merton avoided the problem of relativism. His position has some of the contemporary feel of humanistic psychology but with the added moral limits of Roman Catholic values. Merton's work is a blend of philosophy, religion, and psychology. The following passage is typical:

> Many poets are not artists for the same reason that many religious men are not saints: they never succeed in being the particular poet or the particular monk they are intended to be by God. They never become the man or the artist who is called for by all the circumstances of their individual lives.
>
> They waste their years in vain efforts to be some other poet, some other saint. For many absurd reasons, they are convinced that they are obliged to become somebody else who died two hundred years ago and who lived in circumstances utterly alien to their own.
>
> They wear out their minds and bodies in a hopeless endeavor to have somebody else's experiences or write somebody else's poems or express somebody else's spirituality.
>
> As long as you have to defend the imaginary self that you think is important, you will lose your peace of heart. As soon as you compare that shadow with the shadows of other people, you lose all joy, because you have begun to trade in unrealities, and there is no joy in things that do not exist.

Thomas Merton, **New Seeds of Contemplation** (New York: New Directions, 1961), p. 98.

of a self we happen to feel like—and this includes a self based only on religious, moral, or personal feelings.

It is difficult to judge Aristotle's conception of the self-realized, superior person today. Clearly, his classical model of human excellence is alien to a culture that encourages the expression of virtually every emotion as healthy. His basic values are alien to a culture that prizes youthful spontaneity and talent over mature self-mastery and self-discipline. The modern, individualistic self is, it seems, set free without a clear direction. The Aristotelian self is crafted according to standards of excellence discovered through philosophical contemplation and careful observation.

Summary of Main Points

- Aristotle was Plato's most illustrious pupil and tutor of Alexander the Great. In contrast to Plato's rationalistic approach, Aristotle brings to full maturity a second major approach to the study of the good life: collecting facts and using factual information to make this a better world.

- Aristotle was a philosophical naturalist. Naturalism is the belief that reality consists of the natural world and that the universe is ordered. Everything follows consistent and discoverable *laws* of nature and can be described in terms of fundamental laws.

- According to Aristotle, form can be abstracted from matter but cannot exist independently of matter; this kind of form is sometimes referred to as essence. Matter is the common material stuff found in a variety of things; it has no distinct characteristics until some form is imparted to it or until the form inherent in a thing becomes actualized. Individual things are "formed matter."

- Aristotle claimed that complete understanding of a thing required identifying its "four causes." The Four Causes are the Material Cause (the material the thing is made of); the Formal Cause (the form the thing takes); the Efficient Cause (the "triggering" motion that begins the thing); and the Final Cause (the *telos*, or ultimate purpose for which the thing exists).

- Aristotle identified what he called an "inner urge" in every living thing, a drive to become its unique self. He called this inner urge *entelechy*, meaning "having its end within itself." Things do not just happen—they develop according to natural design. Nature is ordered and guided "internally." The technical name for this kind of thinking is *teleological*, from the Greek root *telos*, meaning end, purpose, or goal.

- Aristotle taught that there are three kinds of souls and that they constitute a hierarchy. Each higher level of soul contains elements of the lower levels—but the lower levels do not contain the higher. The lowest soul is the vegetative, or nutritive, soul. The second level is the sensitive, or sentient, soul; it registers information regarding the form of things, but does not absorb or become those things. Human souls include a third, higher level of *entelechy* called the rational soul, which includes the nutritive and sensitive souls plus capacities for analysis, understanding various forms of relationships, and making reasoned decisions.

- According to Aristotle, the good is "that at which all things aim." The good at which all things aim is their own *entelechy*. *Eudaimonia*, which is often translated as "happiness," means being really alive rather than just existing. According to Aristotle, happiness requires activity, good habits, and practical wisdom.

- Aristotelian moderation is based on the concept of wisdom as hitting the mark (*sophrosyne*) between too much and not enough. Virtue consists of hitting the mark of moderation, and vice consists of being off by too much (excess) or too little (deficiency). Virtue is the mean between either extreme.

Post-Reading Reflections

Now that you've had a chance to learn about Aristotle, use your new knowledge to answer these questions.

1. What is unusual about the nature of the writings attributed to Aristotle?

2. What do scholars mean by saying that Aristotle brought philosophy down to earth? How does this relate to Plato?

3. Why does Aristotle characterize things as "formed matter"? Explain.

4. Construct and evaluate a teleological explanation of your education.

5. In what sense can Aristotle's position be termed "formal relativism"? Is Aristotle a relativist? Explain.

6. What did Aristotle identify as the highest kind of life? Explain fully.

7. Explain the importance of *sophrosyne* and character to Aristotle's concept of happiness.

8. What is the "principle of the mean"? Give one or two examples of using it to evaluate a course of action or moral choice. Give several examples of activities for which there is no mean.

9. How do character and habit affect happiness and virtue, according to Aristotle?

10. Analyze one or two ranges of activity to show how some vices are more virtuous than others.

 MindTap

Experience MindTap through the activities highlighted in this chapter. Further explore this online, personalized learning tool to deepen your comprehension and improve your grades.

7

The Stoics
Epictetus and Marcus Aurelius

You shame yourself, my soul, you shame yourself, and you will have no further opportunity to respect yourself; the life of every man is short and yours is almost finished while you do not respect yourself but allow your happiness to depend upon...others.

— *Marcus Aurelius, Emperor of Rome*

Learning Objectives

After you complete this chapter, you should be able to:

- Define *Stoicism*.

- Define *hedonism*.

- Define *Cynicism*.

- Construct a dialogue between a contemporary, comfortable cynic and Diogenes to show the difference between cynicism as an attitude and cynicism as a way of life.

- Explain how the radically different lives of Epictetus and Marcus Aurelius led both a slave and an emperor to become Stoics.

- Differentiate between control and influence, according to Epictetus.

- Defend the Stoic claim that we suffer when we take our own lives personally.

- Describe the *cosmopolis*.

- Explain what James Stockdale meant when he said that few of us are ever very far from the world of Epictetus.

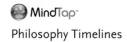

Philosophy Timelines

Stoicism

A philosophy that counsels self-control, detachment, and acceptance of one's fate as identified by the objective use of reason.

Stoic

An individual who attempts to live according to Stoic doctrine.

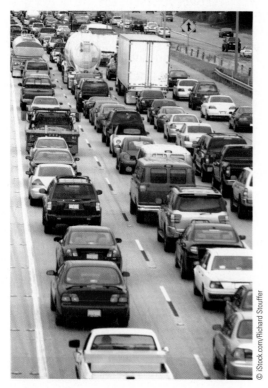

© iStock.com/Richard Stouffer

IT'S THE FRIDAY before a three-day weekend and you are looking forward to a romantic vacation on the beach with your special friend. You get off work a bit late and head for the bank to cash a check that requires in-person proof of identification. Pulling onto the freeway, you're immediately locked into a bumper-to-bumper mass of vehicles, lurching along at fifteen miles per hour. Forty-five minutes later, still a couple of miles from the bank, you notice that you're low on fuel. You begin to steam. Someone tries to cut in front of you, and you explode in a rage, shaking your fist and shouting obscenities.

When you finally get to the bank, there's no place to park. After circling the parking lot for twenty minutes, you find a space. The line in the bank looks endless, and there are only three tellers. The man in front of you has a bag of checks and cash from his business. You continue to steam. It seems like every customer chats with the tellers. And the tellers! It takes them forever to do anything. As you inch along in line, you glare at various bank officers to let them know how angry you are about the inefficient way they run their bank.

By the time you get out of the bank, you're behind schedule, and it's rush hour—pre-holiday, Friday-afternoon rush hour. You race out of the parking lot, squealing your tires as you cut into traffic. Rushing through an intersection at high speed, you catch the attention of a police officer. It's not enough that you get a ticket for reckless driving—the officer takes forever checking out your license and writing the ticket. When you finally get going again, you feel like a bomb about to go off.

If you have ever had an experience anything close to the one just described, you've shared the nearly universal sense of frustration, anger, and anxiety caused by "stupid people" and "events beyond our control." This kind of reaction to external events is so common that a school of philosophy sprang up to deal with just such experiences. Yet its basic tenets go against the grain for most people, at least initially. This philosophy is called **Stoicism**, and those who practice it are called **Stoics**.

Stoicism initially emerged as a reaction against the belief that pleasure is always good and pain is always bad or evil. Rather than pursue pleasure and trying to avoid pain, the Stoic seeks serenity (peace of mind) through self-discipline. Stoicism asserts that seeking anything but self-control results in *avoidable* unhappiness. In the Stoic view, happiness comes only through detachment from all "externals." Put another way: Everything is a matter of attitude. The disciplined, reasonable person can be happy under any and all conditions.

Stoics believe that nothing can make you happy or unhappy without your consent. All unhappiness is the result of bad thinking, poor character, and confusing what we can control with what we cannot control. Regarding the opening story, a Stoic would diagnose your frustration and anger as self-induced. Traffic jams, lines and crowds, and cars nearly running out of gas are normal, common aspects of life. There is nothing new or surprising in anything that happens to you. In fact, nothing "happens to you." *You* are the problem.

Discussing Philosophy

Hedonism

To a considerable extent, Stoicism is a refutation of one of the earliest and most persistent, perhaps even the most basic, theories of happiness: Pursue pleasure (whatever suits you) and avoid pain (whatever causes you suffering and discomfort). The technical name for this kind of philosophy is hedonism. From *hedone*, the Greek root for "pleasure," **hedonism** is the general term for any philosophy that says pleasure = good and pain = evil. Some hedonists stress the pursuit of pleasure, and others emphasize avoiding pain. For a strict hedonist, nothing that provides pleasure can be bad.

Simply put, a hedonist sees the happy life in terms of having the most possible pleasure and the least possible pain. The pursuit of pleasure, says the hedonist, is our birthright. The baby in the cradle coos when it is cuddled, fed, or played with. It cries when it is uncomfortable. No baby has to be taught this; it comes with the territory. We have to learn to be honest, to work hard, to delay gratification, but we do not have to learn to seek pleasure and avoid pain. On the contrary, we have to be forced to go against our basic hedonistic natures.

The difference between *philosophical* hedonism and the instinctive pursuit of immediate pleasure rests, among other things, on the possibility that although most people *think* they know what they need to be happy, a cursory look around makes it clear that many of us don't. We may be able to provide ourselves with *momentary distractions* or *isolated pleasures*, but that's not the same thing as *being happy*. The hedonistic philosopher argues that the pursuit of pleasure and flight from pain may be universal, but genuine happiness is not.

The Meaning of Life Is Pleasure

Aristippus (c. 430–350 B.C.E.) lived in the town of Cyrene on the coast of North Africa in what is now Libya. Cyrene was founded by Greek colonists on the

hedonism
From the Greek root for "pleasure," the general term for any philosophy that says pleasure = good and pain = evil.

In J. W. Waterhouse's romanticized painting, Diogenes ignores the blandishments of civilization from the comfort of his barrel-home. The lantern reminds us of the Cynic's quip that even with a lantern in broad daylight, it is impossible to find an honest man.

edge of a plateau near the Mediterranean coast. The soil and climate made the area rich in flowers, fruits, and lush vegetation. By the time Aristippus was born, Cyrene was a prosperous city, noted for its marble temples, its opulent public square, and the huge, luxurious homes of its wealthiest citizens. Like ancient Athens, Cyrene's strategic location helped make it a wealthy and exciting trading center.

Aristippus was a friendly and clever young man, fond of pleasures of all sorts. He heard about Socrates while attending the Olympic Games with a friend and was so impressed that he rushed to Athens to meet Socrates. Aristippus quickly became a member of the closest, most involved groups of Socrates' followers and eventually did some teaching himself. Aristippus annoyed some of his Socratic friends, who thought he was behaving like a Sophist when he began to travel about teaching and collecting higher and higher fees. Eventually, Aristippus returned home and opened a school of philosophy in Cyrene. His doctrine of unrefined hedonism is known as **Cyrenaic hedonism**, after his hometown.

Aristippus taught that pleasure is the principal motive for living and that pleasure is always good—regardless of its source. He thought it was obvious, to anybody who cared to see it, that all people seek pleasure (whether they are aware of it or not). Aristippus argued that the meaning of life can only be discerned by observing our *actual behavior*. Doing so reveals that the meaning of life is pleasure. The simple, healthy, proper course of life is to follow our natural desires openly, without guilt or apology, and to learn how to most enjoy ourselves. Since pleasure is the natural goal of all life, we should try to have as much intense, sensual pleasure as we can.

Aristippus asserted that because sensory pleasures are more intense than mental or emotional ones, they are the best of all. Therefore, physical pleasure is superior to all other things. Only physical pleasure makes life exciting, dynamic, worth living. Not only that, but actual pleasures of the moment are much more desirable than are potential pleasures that might (or might not) occur in the future. In the first place, we are certain only of the present; the future might not even come. And besides, things may be different for us in the future.

Any distinction between good and bad pleasures was as absurd and contradictory as distinguishing between good and bad sins or good and bad virtues. The only difference among pleasures is their intensity: *Whatever pleases me most at the moment is the highest good there can be.* No pleasure can be "sick" in such a value system. No enjoyment can be wrong. No passion is evil in itself. Only loss of self-control that leads to less pleasure is wrong.

The consequence of such a view is that *whatever feels good is good.* Lacking any objective standard of comparison, the Cyrenaic hedonist concludes that the individual is the measure: of that which is pleasure, that it is pleasure; of that which is pain, that is pain. (See Protagoras, Chapter 3.) And since any pleasure is by definition good, it follows that I *ought* to be doing whatever I enjoy doing. This transforms psychological hedonism into ethical hedonism: Although we are, by nature, predisposed to seek pleasure and avoid pain, some of us become confused, and our instincts and habits get corrupted. We attempt to stifle the pursuit of pleasure because we see it as somehow shameful or immoral. We may even add pain to our lives if we think that by suffering we become purified or ennobled. Our natural hedonism can be subdued by childhood training, religious indoctrination, or a puritanical culture. Thus, the

Cyrenaic hedonism
A philosophy that advocates the unreflective pursuit of intense, immediate pleasure; makes no qualitative distinctions among pleasures.

Aristippus

Being asked what was the difference between the wise man and the unwise, Aristippus said, "Strip them both and send them among strangers and you will know." To one who boasted that he could drink a great deal without getting drunk, his rejoinder was, "and so can a mule."
—Diogenes Läertius

Cyrenaic hedonist argues, it makes sense to advise people that they *ought* to do what they are by nature meant to do: Be happy at all costs.

Epicureanism

Though **Epicurus** (341–270 B.C.E.) was born in the Asia Minor city of Samos, he was an Athenian citizen because his father had moved to Samos as an Athenian colonist. When he was eighteen years old, Epicurus went to Athens to complete the two years of military service required of Athenian males. The Macedonian king of Greece, Alexander the Great, had just died, and the Athenians, who had resented his rule, revolted against the regent he had imposed on them. It took less than a year for this revolt to be crushed, but Epicurus drew an important lesson from it: Political activities and ambitions are pointless.

Epicurus

Epicurus remained in Athens for a time and studied with followers of both Plato and Aristotle. He never accepted Plato's philosophy and came to reject Aristotle's as well. He referred to himself as self-taught and never acknowledged any philosophical teacher or master. He saw himself as a moral reformer who had discovered a brand-new message, one that could save others from unhappiness:

> Vain is the word of a philosopher which does not heal any suffering of man. For just as there is no profit in medicine if it does not expel the diseases of the body, so there is no profit in philosophy either if it does not expel the suffering of the mind.[1]

Epicurus called his school the Garden. A serene retreat from the social, political, and even philosophical turmoil of Athens, Epicurus's Garden became as well known for good living and pleasant socializing as it was for its philosophy. One of the unusual features of the Garden was that it welcomed everyone. It was one of the very few places in Greece where women were allowed and encouraged to interact with men as *equals*. Epicurus's Garden provided a truly unique experience for *both* men and women, since elsewhere men, as well as women, were denied the opportunity to experience equality. Epicurus also made no distinctions based on social status or race. He accepted all who came to learn: prostitutes, housewives, slaves, aristocrats. His favorite pupil was his own slave, Mysis.[2] Epicurus took as his mistress a courtesan (a kind of prostitute) named Leontium, and under his nurturing influence she wrote several books.

Guest, thou shalt be happy here, for here happiness is esteemed the highest good.

— Motto hung over the entrance to the Garden of Epicurus

As you might expect, rumors were rampant about exactly what went on in the Garden. We can lose sight of the truly radical nature of Epicurus's understanding and tolerance if we judge it only in light of today's more enlightened attitudes. In his time, the mere acceptance of all races, sexes, and social classes would have been enough to brand Epicurus as a dangerous and ungrateful rebel, regardless of his philosophical ideas. Yet he went well beyond theoretical tolerance, actively welcoming and encouraging all comers. Even in our own time, such an attitude is often met with fear and criticism when it is put into practice.

Quality of Life

Neither life nor death is good or bad in itself, Epicurus said; only the quality of our pleasures or pains is important. This is a major departure from Aristippus's

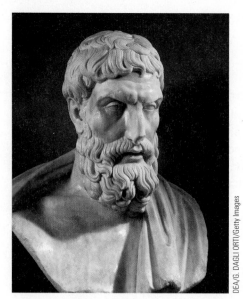

Epicurus said, "We must not make a pretense of doing philosophy, but really do it; for what we need is not the semblance of health but real health."

emphasis on intensity (quantity). Rather than seek to have the most of anything, including the longest possible life span, the wise and sophisticated Epicurean chooses to have the finest:

> Most people, however, recoil from death as though it were the greatest of evils; at other times they welcome it as the end-all of life's ills. The sophisticated person, on the other hand, neither begs off from living nor dreads not living.
>
> Life is not a stumbling block to him, nor does he regard not being alive as any sort of evil. As in the case of food he prefers the most savory dish to merely the larger portion, so in the case of time, he garners to himself the most agreeable moments rather than the longest span.[3]

Practically anything can be *desired* by someone somewhere. But that does not mean that it is *desirable*. This distinction goes beyond Aristippus's simple hedonism to a much more disciplined and subtle concept. In Epicurus's words,

> Because of the very fact that pleasure is our primary and congenital good we do not select every pleasure; *there are times when we forgo certain pleasures, particularly when they are followed by too much unpleasantness. Furthermore, we regard certain states of pain as preferable to pleasures, particularly when greater satisfaction results from our having submitted to discomforts for a long period of time. Thus every pleasure is a good by reason of its having a nature akin to our own, but not every pleasure is desirable.* In like manner every state of pain is an evil, but not all pains are uniformly to be rejected. At any rate, it is our duty to judge all such cases by measuring pleasures against pains, with a view to their respective assets and liabilities, inasmuch as we do experience the good as being bad at times and, contrariwise, the bad as being good.[4] [emphasis added]

Perhaps you associate the term *Epicurean* with expensive tastes, exotic food and drink, elegant clothing, and a life devoted to the pursuit of such pleasures. If so, you are not alone. Even in Epicurus's time, many people mistakenly thought that Epicureanism was a philosophy of expensive self-indulgence. For Epicurus, however, the highest pleasures are intellectual, and the greatest good is peace of mind, not intense or exquisite physical pleasure:

> Thus when I say that pleasure is the goal of living I do not mean the pleasures of libertines or the pleasures inherent in positive enjoyment, as is supposed by certain persons who are ignorant of our doctrine or who are not in agreement with it or who interpret it perversely. I mean, on the contrary, the pleasure that consists in freedom from bodily pain and mental agitation. The pleasant life is not the product of one drinking party after another or of sexual intercourse with women and boys or of the seafood and other delicacies afforded by a luxurious table. On the contrary, it is the result of sober thinking—namely, investigation of the reasons for every act of choice and aversion and elimination of those false ideas about the gods and death which are the chief source of mental disturbances.[5]

"What Would Epicurus Eat?"

In the *Letter to Menoeceus*, Epicurus praises self-sufficiency and easily got satisfactions, noting that "everything natural is easy to obtain and whatever is groundless is hard to obtain." Ironically, the man whose name is inaccurately linked with Epicurean delicacies believed that "simple flavors provide a pleasure equal to that of an extravagant life-style when all pain from want is removed, and barley cakes and water provide the highest pleasure when someone in want takes them."

When Indiana University professors Lisa Keele and Rondo Keele tried to find a recipe for the sort of barley cakes Epicurus might have had in mind, they found that coming up with a "derivation of a truly Epicurean [in the original sense] recipe for barley cakes was no trivial matter." Their research led them to the oldest surviving work of Latin prose, *De agricultura*, or *On Farming*, of the Roman Statesman Marcus Porcius Cato, "the elder" (234–149 B.C.E.). There, the Keeles found a recipe for a simple barley cake called *libum*, which may have been derived from a Greek sacrificial cake.

Here, then, is the Keeles' "reasonably authentic" recipe for the sort of cake Epicurus might have enjoyed—with friends of course.

    2 pounds (or four cups) plain cream cheese
    1/2 pound (or two cups) barley flour
    1 egg
    a good quantity of dry bay leaves (say, 10 or more)

Place the cheese in a clean mixing bowl. Knead the cheese somewhat to soften it. Add the flour; work it in with your hands until well-mixed. Then add the egg; knead it in well too. When all is mixed, the dough should resemble the texture of wet potter's clay; mold it into a loaf shape and place it in a casserole dish, the bottom of which is lined with bay leaves. The bay leaves insure that the cake will not stick to the pan. Because the loaf will rise in the oven, make sure that the casserole dish is larger than the cake loaf. For aesthetic reasons, you may wish to smooth the top of the loaf with your hands. Place the lid on the casserole; bake in a preheated 350° oven. The cake is done when it is golden-brown and the top has cracked. This takes approximately an hour. Remove the cake from the casserole; peel the bay leaves from the bottom and discard; serve immediately or store for later use. Makes about 15 servings. Dribble with honey, if desired. Enjoy!

See Lisa Keele and Rondo Keele, "Let Them Eat (Barley) Cake: An Epicurean Recipe to Share with Your Students," in *Teaching Philosophy*, **APA Newsletter**, Fall 2002, Vol. 2, no. 1, pp. 208–210.

The Cynical Origins of Stoicism

As disciplined and moderate as Epicurus's refined hedonism was, it was still too soft for another important influence on Stoicism. Cynicism was a philosophic "school" only in the loosest sense. Founded by **Antisthenes** (c. 455–360 B.C.E.), its most famous proponent was **Diogenes** (c. 412–323 B.C.E.). As a philosophical school, Cynicism existed from the fourth century B.C.E. until the sixth century C.E., although by the first century its reputation had seriously diminished.

Although the Cynics revolted against the rigidly ordered philosophies of Plato and Aristotle, they admired Socrates. Socrates was the model on which Antisthenes built his Cynicism, and, by extension, Socrates was a model for the Stoics. It is said that Antisthenes walked almost five miles every day to hear Socrates.

Antisthenes was apparently more impressed with Socrates' lifestyle and character than with his philosophical ideas, though Antisthenes, too, sought to base his life on the rule of reason. Socrates' disdain for fashion, his ragged, functional clothing, lack of shoes, ability to not sleep or eat for long periods, physical

Cynicism
A philosophy based on the belief that the very essence of civilization is corrupt and that civilization destroys individuals by making them soft and subject to the whims of fortune.

toughness, and forthright honesty made a tremendous impression on the young Cynic.

After Socrates' death, Antisthenes founded a school called the *Cynosarges* (the Silver Dog). The word **Cynic** comes from the Greek word for "dog," and this label was later given to Diogenes because he "lived like a dog." That is, he was unwashed and rough-looking, he scrounged for food, and he refused to follow conventional standards of dress and behavior.

Because Antisthenes attended some lectures of Gorgias the Sophist and because he stayed so close to Socrates, it is not surprising that he was especially affected by Socrates' stinging attacks on such sophistic values as power, celebrity, prestige, wealth, and clever deception. The Cynics also despised the widespread hedonism and hypocrisy that they saw throughout Athens. They believed that the very essence of civilization is corrupt: Manners are hypocritical and phony; material wealth weakens people, making them physically and morally soft; the desire for success and power produces dishonesty and dependency; flattery, fashion, and convention destroy the individual and make him or her vulnerable to the whims of fortune. And, as the tragic death of Socrates underscored, not even the wisest person can control other people or external events.

So the less an individual needs to be happy, the less vulnerable he or she is. Diogenes, for example, lived in an abandoned wine barrel on the beach and once said, "When I saw a child drinking from his hand, I threw away my cup." The Cynics lived austere, unconventional lives. They distrusted luxury as a hook that always brought complications and ultimately frustration into people's lives. What happiness was possible, according to the Cynics, came from self-discipline, rational control of all desires and appetites, and minimal contact with conventional society.

Even though Epicurus also emphasized a simple life and the avoidance of pain, the Cynics still found Epicureanism too conventional and too encouraging of

Cynic
An individual who lives an austere, unconventional life based on Cynic doctrine.

> *Plato winces when I track dust across his rugs: he knows that I'm walking on his vanity.*
> — Diogenes

"A Socrates Gone Mad"

Diogenes studied under Antisthenes, who, by the way, hated students. Diogenes took his master's teachings to heart and went him one better. Being called a dog was not enough for him; he actually lived with a pack of stray dogs.

Alexander the Great (356–323 B.C.E.), having heard of Diogenes, made a point of meeting him. Diogenes was sitting on the seashore when the magnificent, handsome young king of Greece and future conqueror of the known world rode up on his powerful charger. Looking down on the reclining Cynic, he said,

"I am Alexander the Great."

"I am Diogenes the dog," replied the Cynic.

"The dog?"

"I nuzzle the kind, bark at the greedy, and bite louts."

"What can I do for you?" asked the Ruler of the World.

"Stand aside, you're blocking my light."

So impressed was Alexander with the uncompromising character of Diogenes that he later said, "If I were not Alexander, I would be Diogenes."

This sketch is based on material in Guy Davenport's ***Herakleitos and Diogenes*** (San Francisco: Grey Fox Press, 1979), pp. 35–37.

dependence to suit them. The Cynics believed that the Epicureans relied too much on their friends and certain "proper" pleasures. Cynicism, on the other hand, was rough-and-tumble. Its most famous advocates were sarcastic and hostile toward conventions and institutions. Rejecting Epicurus's high esteem for friendship, Cynics relied only on themselves.

Few Cynics exhibited the moral or intellectual virtues of Antisthenes or Diogenes, however, and eventually Cynicism fell into disrepute. Later Cynics were hostile, arrogant individuals who despised everyone else and hated the society in which they lived. Indiscriminate scorn and contempt for practically everything replaced penetrating social criticism. Today the terms *cynic* and *cynical* are commonly used to refer to a general attitude of basic contempt for people, an excessively hostile or critical stance, or a tendency to distrust other people's motives.

A Scout for Wisdom

The Stoics agreed with the Cynics' admiration of Socrates' sturdy character and wholeheartedly accepted the basic Cynic premise that excessive wanting always leads to unhappiness. The Stoic Epictetus considered the Cynic as a sort of ideal, while acknowledging that most of us are not called to the Cynic's way of life, a way of life that depends on extraordinary moral, philosophical, and physical fitness. Epictetus characterized the "true Cynic" as a "free open-air spirit," saying to himself:

> Henceforth, my mind is the material I have to work on, as the carpenter has his timber and the shoemaker his leather: my business is to deal with my impressions aright. My wretched body is nothing to me, its parts are nothing to me. Death? Let it come when it will, whether to my whole body or part of it. Exile? Can one be sent into exile beyond the Universe? One cannot. Wherever I go, there is the sun, there is the moon, there are the stars, dreams ... conversation with the gods. The true Cynic when he has ordered himself thus ... must know that he is sent as a messenger from God to men concerning things good and evil, to show them that they have gone astray and are seeking the true nature of good and evil where it is not to be found.[6]

Epictetus described the Cynic as a "scout" sent "to find out what things are friendly to men and which hostile," a scout who must first do his scouting accurately, and on returning must tell the truth, not driven by fear. The Cynical roots of Stoicism are apparent in the respect and admiration that flows through Epictetus's portrait of the Cynic, who must, whenever possible, report his findings like Socrates, calling out:

> "Alas! men, where are you rushing? What are you doing, O wretched people? Like blind men you go tottering all

> *I can see Antisthenes' vanity through the holes in his cloak.*
> — Plato

Ocean/Corbis

Do you think you could distinguish a contemporary Diogenes from a street person? To what extent might beliefs about the importance of money, status, material comfort, and the like blind us to accepting the possibility that at least some homeless people (and other social outcasts) are philosophical Cynics?

around. You have left the true path and are going off on another; you are looking for serenity and happiness in the wrong place, where it does not exist, and you do not believe when another points them out to you. Why do you look for [the true path] outside? It does not reside in the body.... It is not in possessions.... It is not in office....

...It is where you do not expect it, and do not wish to look for it. For if you had wished, you would have found it within you, and would not now be wandering outside, nor would you be seeking what does not concern you, as though it were your own possession. Turn your thoughts upon yourselves, find out the kind of preconceived ideas you have.

...Look at me...I am without home, without a city, without property, without a slave; I sleep on the ground; I have neither wife nor children, no miserable governor's mansion, but only earth, and sky, and one rough cloak. Yet what do I lack? Am I not free from pain and fear, am I not free? When has anyone among you seen me failing to get what I desire, or falling into what I would avoid? When have I ever found fault in either God or man? When have I ever blamed anyone? Has anyone among you ever seen me with a gloomy face? And how do I face those persons before whom you stand in fear and awe? Do I face them as slaves? Who, when he lays eyes upon me, does not feel that he is seeing his king and master?"

Lo, these are words that befit a Cynic, this is his character, and his plan of life.... Why, then, are you even laying your hand to so great an enterprise?[7]

"The Cynic," says the Stoic, "has made all mankind his children; the men among them he has as sons, the women as daughters; in that spirit he approaches them all and cares for them all...as a father...as a brother, and as a servant of Zeus, who is father of us all."[8]

Epictetus: From Slave to Sage

Epictetus

Though the philosophical school known as Stoicism was founded in Greece by **Zeno** (c. 334–262 B.C.E.) around 300 B.C.E., it flourished in Rome. Because Zeno lectured at a place called the *stoa poikile*, or painted porch, his followers were known as "men of the porch"—Stoics.

Under Alexander the Great, Greece conquered the Persian Empire (what is now Iran and Iraq) and established Greek rule over a large area of the Near East and Egypt. As a result, Greek culture became more sophisticated and cosmopolitan, absorbing ideas and customs from the cultures it conquered. As the Greek Empire expanded, the importance of individual city-states such as Athens and Sparta diminished, and people identified themselves as part of a larger, more international community.

Alexander's empire was unstable, however, and began to fall apart almost immediately after his death. For most of the third century B.C.E., no single dominant power emerged in the Mediterranean region. By the middle of the second century B.C.E., Rome had destroyed what was left of Alexander's kingdom and annexed Greece as a Roman province called Achaia. By 100 B.C.E., Rome essentially controlled the entire Mediterranean area.

The Romans were not particularly interested in abstract, speculative thinking. Pragmatic and religiously tolerant, they borrowed heavily from Greek culture, including philosophy. Given their interest in establishing social order, the Romans were especially attracted to the Stoics' emphasis on duty and self-control.

The two most philosophically influential Stoics are a Roman slave and a Roman emperor: Epictetus and Marcus Aurelius. The Roman senator Seneca, although not a particularly original thinker, was one of the finest Stoic writers. We will be using some of his *Discourses* and *Moral Letters* to supplement our two main sources. For centuries, Stoic literature has been some of the most popular of all philosophical writings. Let's see why as we encounter the archetype of the Stoic in two radically different forms: a slave and an emperor.

Stoicism appealed to Romans living in times of great uncertainty, under emperors of widely differing abilities and virtues. It spread throughout the Roman world because it was advocated by three important public figures: **Cicero** (106–43 B.C.E.), **Cato** (95–46 B.C.E.), and **Seneca** (c. 4 B.C.E.–65 C.E.). Ironically, however, one of the most important Stoic philosophers was a former slave named **Epictetus** (c. 50–130 C.E.). Perhaps because a slave's life is not his own, Epictetus acquired special insight into the major issue of Stoicism: controlling what we can and accepting what is beyond our control.

We do not know much about Epictetus's early life. His mother was a slave living in Hierapolis, a city in the Asia Minor province of Phrygia. Epictetus was brought to Rome as the slave of a former slave named Epaphroditus, who seems to have been Nero's administrative secretary. Epictetus must have demonstrated unusual abilities, for Epaphroditus sent the youth Epictetus to study with Musonius Rufus, the most powerful Stoic since the days of Zeno. Even so, Epictetus never lost sight of the fact that he could be bought or sold, pampered or tortured, at his owner's whim. As a slave, he was constantly reminded that what happened to him had no bearing on his own wishes or behavior. As a slave, the only absolute control Epictetus had was over his own reactions to what happened. His motto was *Anechou kai apechou:* Bear and forbear.

Epictetus was once so badly tortured—for another slave's mistake—that his broken leg did not heal properly, and he limped for the rest of his life. The story goes that as his leg was being twisted, Epictetus reminded his master that a person's leg was likely to break under such torture. Epaphroditus ignored this, and when his leg finally broke, Epictetus said, "See, it's just as I told you." He later said, "I was never more free than when I was on the rack." He had learned that he could control his attitude but that fate controlled his life:

> If the captain calls, let all those things go and run to the boat without turning back; and if you are old, do not even go very far from the boat, so that when the call comes you are not left behind.[9]

"Soldiers have gone without everything and eaten roots and things we may not name, in order that someone else may not reign over them. . . . Liberty never comes *gratis*."—Seneca

Freed sometime after Nero's death in the year 68 C.E., Epictetus became a well-known teacher. Sometime around the year 90, all the philosophers were ordered out of Rome by the emperor Domitian, who was angry about the encouragement certain Stoics had given to his opponents. Epictetus fled to Nicopolis in northern Greece, where he taught until he was very old. He was a popular teacher, and his schools in both Rome and Nicopolis throve during his lifetime.

A modest man, famed for his sweetness and simplicity, Epictetus lived in a sparely furnished house, content with a straw mat and pallet for a bed and a clay lamp (after his iron one was stolen). He was especially loving toward children, and he was charitable toward all those who came to him for advice and guidance. Following the example of Socrates, he published nothing. His ideas have come down to us in the form of the class notes of his student Flavius Arrianus, called the *Discourses*, and as a truly remarkable set of excerpts from them called the *Enchiridion*, also known as the *Manual* or *Handbook* (because it was made into books that were carried "at hand" into the field by Roman soldiers).[10]

Marcus Aurelius: Philosopher-King

Marcus Aurelius Antoninus

Marcus Aurelius Antoninus (121–180 C.E.) was bound by duty. By temperament a scholar and a recluse, he lived surrounded with commotion, deception, and crowds. Marcus so impressed the emperor Hadrian that he advised Marcus's uncle Aurelius Antoninus (commonly known as Antoninus Pius) to adopt Marcus. When Marcus was forty years old, Antoninus Pius, then emperor, appointed Marcus heir over Pius's other adopted son, Lucius Verus.

When Pius died in 161, Marcus generously named his stepbrother Verus the co-emperor—against the wishes of the senate—but got little help from him. All the serious work of governing was done by Marcus. As emperor, he was obliged to contend with flatterers, liars, and enemies. He was regularly dragged away from Rome to deal with uprisings and barbarian invasions along the frontiers. He was betrayed by a trusted general and spent the last years of his life away from home, on a difficult military campaign. He suffered through the deaths of four of his five sons, and he even endured unsubstantiated rumors that his wife took many lovers in and that his sole surviving son was not his own. To himself, he wrote:

> Everywhere and at all times it is in thy power piously to acquiesce in thy present condition, and to behave justly to those who are about thee, and to exert thy skill upon thy present thoughts, that nothing shall steal into them without being examined.[11]

Marcus was loved by many Romans for his kindness and mercy. He refused to turn away from his incompetent stepbrother, choosing instead to carry out both their duties until Verus died in 169, after which Marcus ruled alone. He convinced the Senate to pardon the family of the traitorous general when other emperors would have destroyed it. He stood by his wife as cruel rumors about her virtue spread everywhere and his own soldiers mocked his masculinity. He went so far as to promote those accused of being her lovers when doing so was good for Rome:

Emperor Marcus Aurelius

© iStock.com/piola666

Let it make no difference to thee whether thou art cold or warm, if thou art doing thy duty; and whether thou art drowsy or satisfied with sleep; and whether ill-spoken of or praised; and whether dying or doing something else. For it is one of the acts of life, the act by which we die: it is sufficient then in this act also to do well what we have in hand.[12]

The last truly great figure of imperial Rome, Marcus combined classical philosophy with a spiritual quality that foreshadowed the Christian-influenced Scholasticism of the Middle Ages. He was also one of the kindest, wisest, and most virtuous of philosophers:

> Only attend to thyself, [Marcus,] and resolve to be a good man in every act which thou doest; and remember.... Look within. Within is the fountain of good, and it will ever bubble up, if thou wilt ever dig.[13]

Marcus's last years were hard and lonely, spent on a military campaign along the Danube. Yet rather than succumb to bitterness or lash out at others, he sought solace in philosophy. Late at night, after his public duties were done, he did his duty to his soul, sitting alone in his tent writing what are popularly known as his *Meditations*, but which he addressed "To Myself." This journal is one of the finest, most widely read examples of both Stoic thought and personal reflection in Western literature.

On this last campaign, Marcus Aurelius, a man once described as "by nature a saint and sage, by profession a warrior and ruler," died at the age of fifty-nine, worn down by fatigue and toil.[14]

Begin the morning by saying to yourself, I shall meet with the busy-body, the ungrateful, arrogant, deceitful, envious, unsocial. All these things happen by reason of their ignorance of what is good and evil. But I who have seen the nature of the good that it is beautiful, and of the bad that it is ugly, and the nature of him who does wrong, that it is akin to me . . . I can neither be injured by any of them, for no one can fix on me what is ugly, nor can I be angry with my kinsman, nor hate him. For we are made for co-operation, like feet, like hands, like eyelids, like the rows of the upper and lower teeth. To act against one another then is contrary to nature; and it is acting against one another to be vexed and to turn away.

— Marcus Aurelius

The Fated Life

Though fate is an important aspect of their philosophy, the Stoics were rather imprecise about what fate meant in specific terms. In some mysterious way, the actual course of our lives is directed by the *Logos*, which the Stoics thought of as World

"Why Should Anywhere I Go Not Be All Right?"

One of the great joys of learning is the discovery of common themes and threads. This is especially so in matters of wisdom. The great sages are at their most powerful when they speak of acceptance in the face of great hardship. Sometimes, it seems as if one spirit speaks with many voices and accents. Consider this beautiful passage from Marcus Aurelius: "Out of the universal substance, as out of wax, Nature fashions a colt, then breaks him up and uses the material to form a tree, and after that a man, and next some other thing: and not one of these endures for more than a brief span. As for the vessel itself, it is no greater hardship to be taken to pieces than to be put together." See if you don't detect a similar spirit in Chuang-tzu's story about a master sword maker:

> Tzu-lai fell ill, was gasping for breath and was about to die. His wife and children surrounded him and wept.... He said, "Don't disturb the transformation that is about to take place." Then, leaning against the door, he continued, "Great is the Creator! What will he make of you now? Where will he take you? Will he make you into a rat's liver? Will he make you into an insect's leg?"

> Tzu-lai said, "Wherever a parent tells a son to go, whether east, west, south, or north, he has to obey. The yin and yang are like a man's parents. If they pressed me to die and I disobeyed, I would be obstinate. What fault is theirs? For the universe gave me the body so I may be carried, my life so I may toil, my old age so I may repose, and my death so I may rest. Therefore, to regard life as good is the way to regard death as good.

> "Suppose a master foundryman is casting his metal and the metal leaps up and says, 'I must be made into the best sword....' The master foundryman would certainly consider the metal as evil. And if simply because I possess a body by chance, I were to say, 'Nothing but a man! Nothing but a man!' the Creator will certainly regard me as evil. If I regard the universe as a great furnace and creation as a foundry-man, why should anywhere I go not be all right?"

Chuang-tzu, in *A Source Book in Chinese Philosophy*, trans. and comp. Wing-Tsit Chan (Princeton, N.J.: Princeton University Press, 1963), p. 197.

Reason or Cosmic Mind (see Chapter 2). Sometimes the *Logos* is referred to as God, Zeus, Nature, Providence, Cosmic Meaning, or Fate. Seneca says:

> We are all chained to [fate].... All of us are in custody, the binders as well as the bound... some are chained by office, some by wealth; some weighed down by high birth, some by low; some are subject to another's tyranny, some to their own; some are confined to one spot by banishment, some by a priesthood. All life is bondage.[15]

The Stoics learned, as many of us do, that our lives are not entirely our own. This discovery did not, at least in the cases of Epictetus and Marcus Aurelius, lead to despair or escapist indulgence but, rather, to a shift in the focus of responsibility. Rather than complain about what they could not control, the Stoics chose to master what they could: their own minds. By mastering their thoughts, they believed, they could master their feelings.

Stoics believed that serenity comes to that individual whose will is in accord with the World Reason, the *Logos*, for right thinking leads to a reduction of frustration and anxiety. In the words of Epictetus,

Marcus Aurelius pardoning defeated Barbarians

> Remember that thou art an actor in a play, of such a kind as the author may choose: if short, a short one; if long, a long one: if he wishes you to act the part of a poor man, see that you act the part naturally: if the part of a lame man, of a magistrate, of a private person (do the same). For this is your duty, to act well the part that was given to you; but to select the part belongs to another.[16]

The Stoic Logos

Under the guidance of the **Logos**, the universe remains rational and ordered. Seneca said, "Events do not just happen, but arrive by appointment." Everything that occurs is connected to everything else. Everything that exists is connected to the *Logos*. Our individual minds are "emanations" or "sparks" from the *Logos*, which is sometimes characterized as "fire." (The Stoics borrowed this idea from Heraclitus.) Our finite human reason is, thus, a small reflection of divine reason. Seneca puts it like this:

> We do not need to lift our hands to heaven... God is near you, with you, inside you. Yes... there is a holy spirit abiding within us.... No man is good without god.[17]

Faith in a rationally ordered universe and our intimate relation to the *Logos* are central aspects of Stoicism. If the universe is divinely ordered, then there is a plan. Things happen to us for a reason—a divinely ordained reason.

If this is true, then nothing that happens can be wrong or bad, since everything that happens is part of God's rational plan. When I truly grasp this, I will no longer fear for the future nor complain about the past or present, but can remain as calm as Zeno did when he heard that all his possessions were lost in a shipwreck and said, "Fortune bids me philosophize with a lighter pack."

Logos (Stoic)
According to Stoic doctrine, World Reason, also referred to as Cosmic Mind, God, Zeus, Nature, Providence, Cosmic Meaning, and Fate; force that governs the universe; also see Chapter 2.

What can I do, then, if the course of my life's events is beyond my control? The Stoic answers that I can concentrate on developing an attitude of courageous acceptance. My efforts should be directed toward that part of my life over which I can exert absolute control: my attitudes, or my will.

> **PHILOSOPHICAL QUERY**
>
> Do you agree that the test of faith is anxiety? Are the Stoics correct in insisting that one who truly realizes that everything is governed by a divine plan will lose all fear and anxiety? Justify your position.

The Disinterested Rational Will

If we are "bits" of the *Logos*, it follows that our virtue and happiness will consist in being as much like the *Logos* as possible. Being perfectly rational, the *Logos* is not partisan; that is, the *Logos* is objective. It is calm and serene, viewing events with "disinterest." Seneca says:

> Just as the rays of the sun do indeed warm the earth but remain at the source of their radiation, so a great and holy soul is lowered to earth to give us a nearer knowledge of the divine; but though it is in intercourse with us, it cleaves to its source…it looks toward it, it seeks to rejoin it, and its concern with our affairs is superior and detached.[18]

Everything that happens is as normal and expected as the spring rose or the summer fruit; this is true of sickness, death, slander, intrigue, and all the other things that delight or trouble foolish men.
— Marcus
   Aurelius

To be *disinterested* is to have no *personal* attachments or motives. For example, a judge or a teacher should be disinterested when he passes sentence or grades papers—he should not play favorites. Marcus Aurelius was disinterested when he promoted the men accused of being his wife's lovers.

The Stoics make an intriguing case that our best chance for happiness is to adopt a disinterested attitude toward our own lives, as well as toward all life. The Stoics thought such a perspective would result not in a world of self-centered isolationists but in a sense of universal communion and duty. Why? Because turning to the *Logos* means looking beyond the particular laws, customs, and prejudices of one's self and society and rejecting them if they deviate from Nature/Logos. Unlike the hedonists, who evaluated the welfare of others only in terms of one's own happiness, the Stoics viewed all humans as citizens of a universal city, a *cosmopolis*. Whereas the hedonist tends to be indifferent to others, the Stoic is indifferent to self (ego). When our duties are dictated by disinterested reason rather than by custom or personal preference, we become members of a community, a human fellowship. Marcus Aurelius alludes to this in a beautiful passage:

> It is man's peculiar distinction to love even those who err and go astray. Such a love is born as soon as you realize that they are your brothers; that they are stumbling in ignorance, and not willfully; that in a short while both of you will be no more; and, above all, that you yourself have taken no hurt, for your master-reason has not been made a jot worse than it was before.
>
> Out of the universal substance, as out of wax, Nature fashions a colt, then breaks him up and uses the material to form a tree, and after that a man, and next

Reflect on the precarious nature of the human condition by reading the box "Why Should Anywhere I Go Not Be All Right?" and study these two photographs of the late actor-director Christopher Reeve. It is all too easy to think that science, good habits, and technology can give us control over our lives. Reeve's public courage and lack of self-pity remind us of Epictetus's doctrine that although the role we play in life's saga may not be up to us, how we play it is. The picture on the right shows Reeve at a dinner for the American Paralysis Association, one of a number of organizations and causes that he supported.

some other thing: and not one of these endures for more than a brief span. As for the vessel itself, it is no greater hardship to be taken to pieces than to be put together....

Only a little while, and Nature, the universal disposer, will change everything you see, and out of their substance will make fresh things, and yet again others from theirs, to the perpetual renewing of the world's youthfulness.[19]

PHILOSOPHICAL QUERY

Discuss the advantages and disadvantages of disinterestedness. When is it a virtue? When is it not? Give some examples and explain them.

Whereas other philosophies used various criteria to distinguish between good and bad emotions, the Stoics rejected emotion to the extent it was humanly possible. The best attitude, they claimed, was rational, detached acceptance.[20] Seneca says:

Philosophers of our school reject the emotions; the [Aristotelian] Peripatetics keep them in check. I, however, do not understand how any half-way disease can be either wholesome or helpful....

"But," you object, "it is natural for me to suffer when I am bereaved of a friend; grant some privileges to tears which have the right to flow! It is also natural to be affected by men's opinions and to be cast down when they are unfavourable; so why should you not allow me such an honorable aversion to bad opinion?"

There is no vice which lacks some plea....we are in love with our vices; we uphold them and prefer to make excuses for them rather than shake them off. We mortals have been endowed with sufficient strength by nature, if only we use this strength....The real reason for failure is unwillingness, the pretended reason, inability.[21]

Stoic Wisdom

By the time of Marcus Aurelius, Stoicism had a religious quality that made it especially attractive to the growing Christian community in the Roman world. As we have seen, classical philosophies were naturalistic: They placed rational humanity at the center of things. By contrast, Christian values place a personal God at the center. Though the Stoics were classical in their emphasis on the impersonal *Logos* as being material and on reason and self-control of the human will as the means to salvation, they also anticipated Christianity in their emphasis on the divine will and on our submission to it. As you will see, many of the Stoics' specific lessons also have a decidedly Judeo-Christian flavor to them. Thus, Stoicism stands as the most influential transitional philosophy between classical and Christian values. Even so, Augustine (Chapter 8) rejected Stoicism as man-centered, not God-centered.

Control Versus Influence

All wisdom can be stated in two lines: What is done for you—allow it to be done. What you must do yourself—make sure you do it.
— Khawwas

Given the Stoic position that our lives are fated but that our wills remain free, our first task must be to distinguish what we can control from what we cannot control. Because Stoic literature is sometimes imprecise and inconsistent, it is important to be sensitive to the distinction between *control* and *influence*.

Even though the Stoics believed in destiny, or fate, they also talked about choosing appropriate actions, in addition to just controlling our attitudes. This suggests that a given individual's fate is painted in broad strokes: *X* will not get into medical school; *Y* will marry *Z*. But *X* may have the freedom to apply to medical school, and *Y* may be free to break up with *Z* two or three times. There appear to be gaps in our fate. For instance, in the first section of the *Enchiridion*, Epictetus says:

If then you desire...great things, remember that you must not (attempt to) lay hold of them with small effort; but you must leave alone some things entirely, and postpone others for the present.[22]

Later he says:

When you are going to take in hand any act, remind yourself what kind of act it is. If you are going to bathe, [remind] yourself what happens in the [public] bath; some splashing the water, others pushing against one another, others abusing one another, and some stealing.[23]

Elsewhere, Epictetus talks about choosing to be a philosopher or deciding to train for the Olympics. This implies that we have at least some degree of influence over our actions. So the Stoics must have thought that we have influence over more than just our attitudes; otherwise, such advice is illogical. Advice makes sense only where there is some choice.

Although the Stoics are theoretically inconsistent when they counsel accepting fate on the one hand and then advise us to live moderately and wisely on the other, their position contains merit because *it is consistent with common experience.* A careful survey of the human condition reveals that many of us expend a great deal of effort trying to control things that we cannot control while nearly ignoring those areas over which we do have control.

A common example will make the point. Technically speaking, you cannot *control* your grades in school, although you have considerable *influence* over them. No matter how carefully you listen to instructions, no matter how good your notes, how thorough your studying and grasp of the material, you cannot *guarantee* a passing grade in any course. Your professor might have a personal grudge against you or be depressed or ill while grading your work. A clerical error might alter your grade in a class, and the school might refuse to correct it. By the same token, you cannot even guarantee a failing grade. Another clerical error might result in an A for a class you haven't attended for weeks, or the professor might confuse your name with that of another student.

We are foolish when we exert no effort on our own behalf. We all know that. But, the Stoic reminds us, we are also foolish to believe that we *control* our GPAs. Rather than try to control our grades, we should work wisely to *influence* them and should make sure to *control our attitudes* toward them.

This difference can be difficult to grasp in a culture that believes that "you can be anything you want to be if you work hard enough." From the Stoic point of view, it is misleading to talk about controlling our lives (or grades); we can only influence them up to a point. And we must remember this warning: *The results of our efforts are out of our hands.*

Off campus we see this as well. Jim Fixx, a well-known running enthusiast, ate sensibly and exercised regularly yet died in his forties of an inherited heart condition. The film genius Orson Welles ate what he wished, never exercised, smoked cigars, and weighed over four hundred pounds when he died—at age seventy. Such an example is not an excuse for self-indulgence but a hard fact of life: We do not control our destinies; we influence them just enough so that we should do our best to behave responsibly.

This is the crux of Stoicism. The inconsistencies in Stoic writing are due, in part, to our ignorance of precisely when influence becomes control in a particular case. There are ways to learn what to try and what to avoid, but in all cases, the Stoic remains aware that the *Logos* ultimately rules the universe. The individual's task is to identify the will of the *Logos* and then put his or her will in harmony with it. While we may not have control over the events in our lives, we do have control over our happiness. The wise person is the serene individual who lives courageously and responsibly, who knowingly accepts everything that happens, be it good or bad, without becoming bitter or broken—and without resorting to distortion or denial. (See what Augustine says about this in Chapter 8.)

> *Which of you by worrying can add a moment to his life-span?*
> — Jesus,
> Matthew 6:27

> *Do to me what is worthy of Thee And not what is worthy of me.*
> — Saadi

Some Things Are Not in Our Control

To achieve serenity and wisdom, we must remain clear about what is not in our control:

> Not in our power are the body, property, reputation, offices…and in a word, whatever are not our own acts…the things not in our power are weak, slavish, subject to restraint, in the power of others. Remember that if you think the things which are by nature slavish to be free, and the things which are in the power of others to be your own, you will be hindered, you will lament, you will be disturbed, you will blame both the gods and men.[24]

"Not in our power" means not under our control. If I realize that these things are not under my control, I can adopt a healthy attitude toward them. For instance, since my reputation is not totally up to me, I can quit trying so hard to make everyone like me. I cannot *make* anyone like me—or dislike me. My family likes me even when I'm a fool, and some people don't like me no matter how hard I try to be likable. Instead of directing my efforts where they are ineffective, I can devote them to what I have more control over: myself. In practical terms, this means that I take appropriate action and then mentally let go of the results.

Once I realize that how long I live, who likes me or doesn't, and my social status are beyond my total control, I can quit being obsessively fearful. I can manage my health with moderation but will not be bitter if after watching my diet and exercising daily I develop cancer. Bitterness will not get me well. Bitterness, or envy, or resentment are never my fate; they are always my choice. Not getting into the university of my choice might be my fate. Resenting it for the rest of my life is not—it's my choice. I can ask you to marry me and marry you if you say yes, but I cannot make you happy. I cannot make you stay with me. If you leave, my anger and despair are not my fate—they are my choice.

PHILOSOPHICAL QUERY

Reflect on letting go in the sense of doing what seems right and then relaxing. Provide a few of your own examples of how fear of consequences and an obsession with control can affect us. Discuss ways for identifying and striking a balance between letting go in a wise way and in an irresponsible way.

Some Things Are in Our Control

What is in our power is our free *will*. Epictetus insists, contrary to what we may believe, that we alone control our feelings. We control our feelings because we control our thinking. We can also reason out that other people's likes and dislikes are beyond our total control. This should free us from depending on other people's opinions of us for self-esteem or happiness:

> In our power are opinion, movement towards a thing, desire, aversion; and in a word, whatever are our own acts. And the things in our power are by nature free, not subject to restraint or hindrance…if you think that only which is your own to

be your own, and if you think of what is another's, as it really is, belongs to another, no man will ever compel you, no man will hinder you, you will never blame any man, you will accuse no man, you will do nothing...against your will, no man will harm you, you will have no enemy, for you will not suffer any harm.[25]

I wonder how many hours of human suffering can be chalked up to trying to control how others feel about things. I also wonder if we really try to control our own thoughts. For example: Mike suffers and worries every time Helon is annoyed with him. He buys her flowers, is distracted at work, agonizes until she likes him again. If he had control over how she felt, he would never let her be annoyed. Since she gets annoyed and he doesn't want her to be annoyed, it follows logically (and causally) that he *cannot* control her feelings. But—irrationally—he tries to, again and again.

Suppose that Mike reads Epictetus. Now, instead of trying to make Helon feel a certain way, he tries to control his own thoughts and behavior. When he starts to worry, he consciously, and with great effort at first, forces himself not to dwell on Helon. He may not be able to stop fears about her from popping into his mind, but he can stop himself from dwelling on them. He can exert his *will* over his own thinking. He is not responsible for his first thoughts, but he is responsible for his second thoughts.

This is a difficult lesson. It may be especially difficult to accept today, when we place so much importance on relationships and when we have been told that inadequate parents, genetics, environment, social conditions, and abusive individuals are responsible for our unhappiness.

PHILOSOPHICAL QUERY

By some estimates, 60 percent of Americans are overweight or obese. Some 95 percent of those who try to lose and maintain a clinically healthy weight will fail. Could being obese be part of a person's fate? Could being an alcoholic? Sexually promiscuous? Lazy? As more and more behaviors are linked to genetics, how can we distinguish between defects of character and things not in our control?

MindTap
Discussing Philosophy

Relationships

According to the Stoics, we suffer to the extent that we take our own lives personally. Consequently, relationships must be evaluated with the same disinterested detachment as everything else:

Duties are universally measured by relations. Is a man a father? The [duty] is to take care of him, to yield to him in all things, to submit when he is reproachful, when he inflicts blows. But suppose he is a bad father. Were you then by nature [guaranteed] a good father? No; [just] a father. Does a brother wrong you? Maintain then your own position towards him, and do not examine what he is doing, but what you must do [in order] that your will shall be [in accord with] nature. For another will not damage you, unless you choose; but you will be damaged when you shall think that you are damaged. In this way then you will discover your duty from the relation of a neighbor, from that of a citizen, from that of a general, if you are accustomed to contemplate [your relationships].[26]

This passage is an excellent example of applying disinterested reason to daily affairs. The Stoics believed that a disinterested study of life shows that no one is *entitled* to good, healthy parents; loving, supportive brothers and sisters; obedient children; or sexy, interesting, loyal boyfriends, girlfriends, or spouses. If the *Logos* provides *everything we need* to be happy, then it is clear that no one needs good parents, and so on. The reason is obvious: Not everyone gets them. Thus, these are not things to which we are entitled, or the *Logos* would have provided them.

The only way to grasp this point is to set aside our *feelings* and apply *disinterested reason* to relationships. For example, a popular marriage vow commits each spouse to the other "for richer or poorer, in sickness and in health." This means that as a husband—not as an individual—I have obligations that stem from the nature of the marital relationship, regardless of how my wife behaves. Duties are not based on the personalities or preferences of the individuals involved. Similarly, as a son, I have duties toward my father whether or not I "like" him and whether or not he is a good father.

In Epictetus's time, social roles were less flexible than they are now. We have more sophisticated psychological knowledge of the damage that bad, abusive relationships can cause. So it will be necessary to modify Epictetus's strict position. But even today, I can still be a Stoic without being a martyr. I can remind myself that as long as I am in this marriage or have this job, *I* have duties that are not contingent on other people fulfilling *their* duties. What kind of teacher, what kind of person, would I be if I did not prepare my lessons carefully just because many of my students come to class unprepared? What kind of student, what kind of person, would you be if you whispered and checked your email and texted your friend just because your teacher was unprepared or you were bored?

> *"These sons belong to me, and this wealth belongs to me"—with such thoughts a fool is tormented. He himself does not belong to himself; how much less sons and wealth?*
> — Buddha

PHILOSOPHICAL QUERY

Discuss the preceding passage from Epictetus about relationships. What lessons might it offer regarding our relationships and the things that make us unhappy?

Everything Has a Price

One reason we might be frustrated by events is that we tend to focus on the object of our desire while ignoring its cost. Yet everything has a clearly marked price tag. The athlete with a fine physique has paid the price of training and discipline, perhaps by giving up a broad education or full social life. The ambitious character at the office has paid the price of flattering the boss and working late while you did not have to "kiss up" and were home enjoying your family life. The A student has paid the price of missing many parties and other kinds of socializing. According to Epictetus, we suffer unnecessarily when we try to have things without paying the price:

Bernd Thissen/dpa/Landov

Olympic champion swimmer Michael Phelps and the happy graduate (below) have paid the price of training and self-discipline. As Epictetus said, "You will be unjust and insatiable if you do not part with price in return for which…things are sold." Perhaps if we remember this Stoic principle, we will not envy or resent those who have paid a price that we have not.

You will be unjust then and insatiable, if you do not part with the price, in return for which…things are sold, and if you wish to obtain them for nothing. Well, what is the price of lettuces? An obulus perhaps. If then a man gives up the obulus and receives the lettuces, and if you do not give up the obulus and do not receive the lettuces, do not suppose that you receive less than he who has got the lettuces; for as he has the lettuces, so you have the obulus which you did not give…you have not been invited to a man's feast, for you did not give the host the price at which the supper is sold; but he sells it for praise (flattery), he sells it for personal attention. Give him the price, if it is for your interest, for which it is sold. But if you wish both not to give the price, and to obtain the things, you are insatiable and silly. Have you nothing then in place of the supper? You have indeed, you have the [satisfaction of] not flattering…him…whom you did not choose to flatter; you have [not had to put up with him].[27]

What would you think of someone who screamed and turned red with rage when asked to pay for a

© Douglas J. Soccio

"For What Matters Above All Is the Attitude We Take Toward Suffering"

Perhaps the most philosophical and Stoic psychology today is Viktor E. Frankl's logotherapy. During World War II, Frankl (1905–1997), an Austrian Jew, was imprisoned for three years in the Nazi concentration camp at Auschwitz. Upon his release he discovered that his whole family had been destroyed. Based on his personal experience and subsequent clinical experiences with suffering, Frankl developed logotherapy, based on the definition of *Logos* as "meaning." Frankl's most famous book is *Man's Search for Meaning*. If you have not read it, I recommend it to you. Here's an extract to whet your appetite:

Whenever one is confronted with an inescapable, unavoidable situation, whenever one has to face a fate that cannot be changed, e.g., an incurable disease, such as inoperable cancer, just then one is given a last chance to actualize the highest value, to fulfill the deepest meaning, the meaning of suffering. For what matters above all is the attitude we take toward suffering, the attitude in which we take our suffering upon ourselves.... Suffering ceases to be suffering in some way at the moment it finds a meaning, such as the meaning of a sacrifice.... It is one of the main tenets of logotherapy that man's main concern is not to gain pleasure or avoid pain, but rather to see a meaning in his life. That is why man is ready to suffer, on the condition, to be sure, that his suffering has a meaning.

From *Man's Search for Meaning: An Introduction to Logotherapy* (New York: Pocket Books, 1963), pp. 178–179.

Stop for a moment to study this photo of a concentration camp prisoner burned to death by Nazi soldiers to prevent him from being freed after the war. It is no wonder that Stoicism appeals to us when we're obviously *in extremis*. Yet at every moment we are each only a fall or an accident or a sudden loss away from great suffering. Thus, Epictetus said, "The lecture-room of the philosopher is the hospital; students ought not to walk out of it in pleasure, but in pain."

basket of groceries at the market? He or she would be silly, to say the least. How is this different from the couple who once eagerly desired a baby and now resent the infant's demands? Or the married man who chafes at his obligations? Or the woman who has a job, a social life, and three children and is surprised that she feels tired and run-down? As obvious as the notion of a price seems, many of us seem to be stunned when we are expected to pay up.

Suffering and Courage

Stoicism is a "mature" philosophy in that its appeal seems to increase with experience—that is, with frustration and disappointment. Growing up emotionally and philosophically involves adopting realistic expectations and accepting one's limits. The challenge of maturity is how to do this without becoming overly negative or giving in to inertia. How can I develop an attitude of Stoic detachment and acceptance and still have hopes and take action?

The Stoics sometimes compared the *Logos* to a parent or teacher. They pointed out that hardship and suffering can be viewed as gifts, if we understand that the best teachers are strictest with those pupils in whom they see the most ability. They also noted that suffering cannot be bad by nature, or else good men like Socrates would not have suffered. In other words, who am I that I should escape the ordinary trials of life? The goal isn't to avoid them but to use them to become a good person. Seneca said, "The greater the torment, the greater shall be the glory." He adds:

> Prosperity can come to the vulgar and to ordinary talents, but to triumph over the disasters and terrors of mortal life is the privilege of the great man.
>
> To be lucky always and to pass through life without gnawing of the mind is to be ignorant of the half of nature. You are a great man, but how can I know, if Fortune has never given you a chance to display your prowess? You have entered the Olympic games but have no rival; you gain the crown but not the victory. . . . I can say . . . "I account you unfortunate because you have never been unfortunate. You have passed through life without an adversary; no man can know your potentiality, not even you." For self-knowledge, testing is necessary; no one can discover what he can do except by trying.[28]

Since there is really no way to avoid pain, it is especially tragic to see those who try, for not only are they doomed to failure, but they suffer additionally because they lack character. They live at the whim of circumstances. Seneca says:

> So god hardens and scrutinizes and exercises those he approves and loves; but those he appears to indulge and spare he is only keeping tender for disasters to come. If you suppose anyone is immune you are mistaken. . . . Why does god afflict every good man with sickness or grief or misfortune? Because in the army, too, the most hazardous duties are assigned to the bravest soldiers. . . . In the case of good men, accordingly, the gods follow the plan that teachers follow with their pupils; they demand more effort from those in whom they have confident expectations. . . . What wonder, then, if god tries noble spirits with sternness? The demonstration of courage can never be gentle. Fortune scourges us; we must endure it. It is not cruelty but a contest.[29]

Thus, the Stoics say, our misfortune on this earth is not a result of God's disfavor but possibly the result of His respect or understanding of what we need to endure but would avoid if left to our own devices. Certainly faith in a divine will seems to obligate us to reach such a conclusion. Even without belief in God, we can still ask the Stoic's question: Which is more reasonable: to endure inescapable hardship and to suffer mental torment or to endure inescapable hardship but accept it with courage and magnanimity? As I have framed the question, it answers itself. Without trivializing it, we can say that Stoicism comes down to this: *While making reasonable efforts to get what we want, it is wise to learn to be happy with what we get.*

> *Discourse on virtue and they pass by in droves; whistle and dance the shimmy, and you've got an audience.*
>
> — Diogenes

The World of Epictetus

Perhaps the greatest testimonies to the merit of Stoicism come from those who have suffered greatly, as Frankl reminds us. One of the most interesting and compelling arguments for the practical value of a good philosophical education came from an unexpected source: a highly trained United States Navy fighter pilot.

What we know as the *Enchiridion* of Epictetus can be a powerful consolation and support to people undergoing the severest trials. In fact, **James Bond Stockdale** (1923–2005), a vice admiral (retired) in the United States Navy, credited his education in the humanities—and Epictetus in particular—with helping him survive seven and

James Bond Stockdale

one-half years as a prisoner of war in North Vietnam, including four years in solitary confinement. Stockdale was awarded the Congressional Medal of Honor after his release.

In April 1978, the *Atlantic Monthly* published a remarkable article by this unusual warrior-philosopher called "The World of Epictetus." Stockdale describes the brutal conditions that POWs were kept in and his own fear and despondency. As he reviewed his life from his solitary cell, Stockdale "picked the locks" to the doors of his past experiences. He recalled cocktail parties and phony social contacts with revulsion as empty and valueless. "More often than not," he said, "the locks worth picking had been old schoolroom doors."

In this passage, Stockdale testifies to the real-life value of Epictetus's *Enchiridion:*

The messages of history and philosophy I used were simple.

The first one is the business about life not being fair. That was a very important lesson and I learned it from a wonderful man named Philip Rhinelander....He said, "The course I'm teaching is my personal two-term favorite—The Problem of Good and Evil—and we're starting our second term." He said the message of his course was from the Book of Job. The number one problem in this world is that people are not able to accommodate the lesson in the book.

He recounted the story of Job. It starts out by establishing that Job was the most honorable of men. Then he lost all his goods. He also lost his reputation, which is what really hurt. His wife was badgering him to admit his sins, but he knew he had made no errors. He was not a patient man and demanded to speak to the

> *I consider it a dangerous misconception of mental hygiene to assume that what man needs in the first place is equilibrium or . . . a tensionless state. What man actually needs is not a tensionless state but rather a striving and struggling for some goal worthy of him.*
> — Viktor E. Frankl

Bettmann/CORBIS

Courtesy of Sybil Stockdale

"Lameness," said Epictetus, "is an impediment to the leg, but not to the Will. Say this to yourself with regard to everything that happens. For you will find such things to be an impediment to something else, but not truly to yourself." Twenty centuries later, after his own leg was broken by torturers, James Bond Stockdale used Epictetus's teachings to help endure seven and one-half years in a North Vietnamese prison camp. Sometimes, as Ernest Hemingway wrote, we are indeed stronger at the broken places.

Lord. When the Lord replied in the whirlwind, he said, "Now, Job, you have to shape up! Life is not fair." That's my interpretation and that's the way the book ended for hundreds of years. I agree with those of the opinion that the happy ending was spliced on many years later.... People couldn't live with the original message.

Cell door in Hanoi Prison where Stockdale spent seven and one-half years.

Rhinelander also passed on to me another piece of classical information which I found of great value. On the day of our last session together he said, "You're a military man, let me give you a book to remember me by. It's a book of military ethics." He handed it to me, and I bade him goodbye with great emotion. I took the book home and that night started to read it. It was the *Enchiridion* of the philosopher Epictetus, his "manual" for the Roman field soldier.

As I began to read, I thought to myself in disbelief, "Does Rhinelander think I'm going to draw lessons for my life from this thing? I'm a fighter pilot. I'm a technical man. I'm a test pilot. I know how to get people to do technical work. I play golf; I drink martinis. I know how to get ahead in my profession. And what does he hand me? A book that says in part, 'It's better to die in hunger, exempt from guilt and fear, than to live in affluence and with perturbation.'" I remembered this later in prison because perturbation was what I was living with. "When I ejected from the airplane on that September morn in 1965, I had left the land of technology. I had entered the world of Epictetus, and it's a world that few of us, whether we know it or not, are ever far away from.[30]

The lessons that the old Roman slave learned on the rack gave comfort and courage to a solitary prisoner of war two thousand years later in the rice paddies of Southeast Asia.

Aplia

Commentary

This summary glance at Stoicism points out some inconsistencies and difficulties. The nature of fate remains ambiguous: How detailed is my life script? Has the *Logos* determined that I drop a pencil or make a typing mistake as I write this? Or is my fate painted in broader strokes? If so, in what sense is it fate? Are all emotions "bad"? Is it *reasonable* to be so detached, if it's even possible? Can a disinterested person have a motive, or are motives emotional?

Such obvious problems result partly from the Stoics' near indifference to everything except the issue of how to live the least disturbed life possible. They were not concerned with providing a completely worked-out philosophical *system*. Even so, Stoicism retains an appeal that rests on genuine insights into the causes of much suffering and unhappiness. The Stoics were highly practical moral psychologists whose chief interests were ethics and psychology. As such, the most insightful of them offer sage counsel and inspiration that is as pertinent and helpful today as it was when first presented over two thousand years ago.

> *In this day and age, the greatest devotion, greater than learning and praying, consists in accepting the world exactly as it happens to be.*
> — Rabbi Moshe of Kobryn

When I first encountered Stoicism as an undergraduate, I found it annoying. The ideal Stoic seemed to be a bland, emotionless vegetable—certainly not the kind of person I wanted to be. I needn't have worried. Stoic self-control and discipline were unable to stifle my great emotions. And so I spent too many years fuming over traffic, long lines, the way the world behaved, my teachers, my students, being alone, not being alone—life.

Today, I recognize the depth of passion behind the words of Marcus Aurelius and Epictetus. They certainly were not bland, unfeeling people. I understand how much of my own frustration has come from not looking carefully for the price tag before I rushed to the checkout.

Given the seemingly perpetual flux of social conditions and common human responses to them, today I see enough merit in Stoic wisdom to compensate for certain ambiguities and inconsistencies in its expression. If nothing else, it *sometimes* helps me sit through time-wasting and mind-numbing traffic jams and crowded waiting rooms. More importantly, reading Stoic works inspires me to look beyond my own immediate comfort (or discomfort), to strive for self-discipline, courage, and serenity.

Stoicism provides a counterbalance of sorts to today's love affair with instant gratification and emotional expressiveness. In its lessons on relationships and suffering, Stoicism wisely reminds us that what cannot be changed must be accepted graciously if we are ever to be happy. We live in a time when people seek external solutions to nearly every sort of predicament. Many solutions will be found. But no external solution can make us happy or unhappy, for, as a late friend used to remind me, "Happiness is an inside job."

> *Let others practice lawsuits, others study problems, others syllogisms; here you practice how to die, how to be enchained, how to be racked, how to be exiled.*
> — Epictetus

After his 1973 release from prison, Admiral Stockdale served as president of the Naval War College in Newport, Rhode Island; president of the Citadel, the military college of South Carolina; and a senior research fellow at the Hoover Institution, located at Stanford University. In 1992, third-party presidential candidate Ross Perot asked Stockdale to be his vice presidential running mate. During an election-year debate among the three vice presidential candidates, Stockdale began, as Socrates might have, with two timeless questions: "Who am I? Why am I here?" Though the philosophical thrust of the questions was missed by most people, Stockdale's philosophical vision attracted national attention to Stoicism in general and Epictetus in particular. In 1999, Stoicism played a central role in Tom Wolfe's best-selling novel *A Man in Full*, which involved a character based loosely on Stockdale. On May 10, 2008, Stockdale's wife, Sybil, christened the *USS Stockdale*—perhaps the only U.S. Navy destroyer ever named in honor of an American philosopher.

Stockdale remains one of our most remarkable contemporary philosophers in the original sense. The lessons of wisdom he learned are particularly compelling because they come from as broad a spectrum of experiences as is humanly possible—the extremes of defeat, degradation, torture, and isolation on the one hand, and the heights of influence, national prominence, and academic recognition on the other. Few of us experience such extremes in either direction; fewer yet in both. Thus, Stockdale's life and writings provide us with a rare contemporary example of the Stoic sage. Who better to have the last word in our survey of one of the most influential archetypes of wisdom?

Stoicism is certainly not for everybody, and it is not for me in every circumstance, but it is an expression in philosophical terms of how people find purpose in what they have every right to see as a purposeless world.... [Stoicism] speaks to people everywhere who persist in competing in what they see as a buzz-saw existence, their backs to the wall, their lives having meaning only so long as they fight for pride and comradeship and joy rather than capitulate to either tyranny or phoniness....

...We who are in hierarchies—be they academic, business, military, or otherwise—are always in positions in which people are trying to manipulate us, to get moral leverage on us. The only defense is to keep yourself clean—never to do or say anything of which you can be made to feel ashamed....

Am I personally still hooked on Epictetus's Principle of Life? Yes, but not in the sense of following a memorized doctrine. I sometimes become amused at how I have applied it and continue to apply it unconsciously. An example is the following story about myself.

As the months and years wear on in solitary confinement, it turns out each man goes crazy if he doesn't get some ritual into his life. I mean by that a self-imposed obligation to do certain things in a certain order each day. Like most prisoners, I prayed each day, month after month, continually altering and refining a long memorized monologue that probably ran to ten or fifteen minutes. At some point, my frame of mind became so pure that I started deleting any begging of God and any requests that would work specifically for my benefit. This didn't come out of any new Principle of Life that I had developed; it just suddenly started to seem unbecoming to beg. I knew the lesson of the book of Job: life is not fair. What claim had I for special consideration? And anyway, by then I had seen enough misery to know that He had enough to worry about without trying to appease a crybaby like me. And so it has been ever since.[31]

Summary of Main Points

- Hedonism is the general term for any philosophy that says that pleasure is identical with good and pain is identical with evil. Hedonists stress either the pursuit of pleasure (Cyrenaic) or the avoidance of pain (Epicurean). Cyrenaic hedonists believe that all pleasures of the same intensity are equal. They deny the possibility of qualitative differences among pleasures. Epicurean hedonism is the more refined doctrine that there are qualitative differences among pleasures.

- Antisthenes was the founder of a philosophical school known as Cynicism, and Diogenes was its most famous advocate. The Cynics believed that the very essence of civilization is corrupt, that manners are hypocritical, that material wealth weakens people, and that civilization destroys the individual and makes him or her vulnerable to the whims of fortune. According to the Cynics, the death of Socrates showed that not even the wisest person can control other people or external events. They concluded that the less an individual needs to be happy, the less vulnerable he or she will be. Cynics lived austere, unconventional lives.

- Founded in Greece by Zeno, Stoicism grew out of Cynicism and achieved widespread influence in first-century Rome, ultimately spreading throughout Christianized Europe. The Roman slave Epictetus, the Emperor Marcus Aurelius, and the senator

Seneca are the most influential Stoic writers. Stoics recommended accepting whatever circumstances we are in without resentment. They believed that the cosmos is wisely governed by the *Logos* (World Reason) and that everything happens as part of a divine plan.

- According to the Stoics, human beings are bits of the *Logos* because we have rational souls. Happiness comes from the effective use of reason to alter the will. Based on their concept of a disinterested World Reason, the Stoics taught that it is wise to minimize personal attachments and motives. They rejected emotion to the extent it was humanly possible, favoring detached, rational acceptance over personal, emotional involvement.

- Though the Stoics believed that life is fated, they understood this in a loose sense. Because we cannot know precisely what our fate is, we must take reasonable action without pinning our happiness on a particular result. According to the Stoics, we can control our ideas and attitudes, but we cannot control "externals" such as reputation, social status, relationships, health, and wealth.

- Stoic virtues include strength of will, courage, dignity, and maturity. According to Stoic doctrine, everything has a price that reason can reveal. The price of happiness is personal detachment from external conditions; peace of mind comes from indifference to everything except accepting the will of the *Logos*. Stoics taught that only great struggle could produce greatness of character.

- The philosopher-warrior James Bond Stockdale refined Epictetus's Principle of Life and communicated it to a growing audience.

Post-Reading Reflections

Now that you've had a chance to learn about the Stoics, use your new knowledge to answer these questions.

1. Explain the role hedonistic thinking played in the origins of Stoicism.

2. How did Cynicism influence Stoicism? Be specific.

3. What is the relationship of Socrates to Cynicism and Stoicism?

4. How are the *Logos* and fate related in Stoicism?

5. Identify and discuss possible problems with the Stoic notion of fate.

6. Stoicism was quickly absorbed into Christianity. Identify and comment on any similarities you are aware of.

7. What is the disinterested rational will, and why is it important to Stoic doctrine?

8. What do the Stoics think falls under our control? What do the Stoics think does not fall under our control? Do you agree? Why or why not?

9. Discuss the difference between avoidable and unavoidable suffering. How can we tell which is which? Why does it matter?

10. Explain the Stoic attitude toward relationships. How does it differ from today's attitudes? What do you see as important strengths and weaknesses of each perspective?

11. What does Seneca mean when he says "I account you unfortunate because you have never been unfortunate"? How do the Stoics interpret suffering? What do you think of this view?

12. What do you think of James Stockdale's claim that a good philosophical education is highly practical? Give his position and then comment on it.

 MindTap

Experience MindTap through the activities highlighted in this chapter. Further explore this online, personalized learning tool to deepen your comprehension and improve your grades.

8

The Scholar
Thomas Aquinas

Now, among the inquiries that we must undertake concerning God in Himself, we must set down in the beginning that whereby His Existence is demonstrated, as the necessary foundation of the whole work. For, if we do not demonstrate that God exists, all consideration of divine things is necessarily suppressed.

— *Thomas Aquinas*

Learning Objectives

 MindTap

After you complete this chapter, you should be able to:

- Define *theology*.
- Describe what is meant by a *principle of reason*.
- Define *Scholasticism*.
- Critique the argument from motion.
- Critique the cosmological argument.
- Explain the importance of the principle of sufficient reason and the principle of plenitude to the argument from necessity.
- Critique the argument from gradation.
- Describe the teleological argument.
- State the problem of evil.
- Analyze Thomas Aquinas's argument that no one can knowingly choose evil.
- Critique Thomas's claim that the real possibility of evil is necessary for the good of the whole universe.

MindTap

Philosophy Timelines

> *And, now and then,
> an amiable person…
> believes in a pistareen-
> Providence, which,
> whenever the good
> man wants a dinner,
> makes that somebody
> shall knock at his door,
> and leave a half-dollar.*
> —Ralph Waldo
> Emerson

I ONCE WATCHED A TELEVISION NEWS reporter interview a weeping woman who sat on the pile of rubble that had been her small mobile home. Everything she owned had been destroyed by a tornado. Through her tears, the victim expressed her gratitude to God for saving her life. As she explained it, she was preparing supper when she mysteriously had the urge to go to the corner market for a loaf of bread. She was gone for only a few minutes, but in those minutes the tornado struck. "If I hadn't gone for that bread," she said into the camera, "I would be dead now. God told me to go get that bread in order to save my life."

Does this mean that God *wanted* those people who were not warned to die? Suppose the woman's neighbor had been planning to go to the store but got a phone call just as he started for the door. Should we conclude that God arranged the timing of the call to make sure he didn't escape the tornado?

After all, if God is the cause of *everything* that happens, *everything* includes tornadoes and torture, as well as salvation and joy. If God knows *everything*, does He know your grade on your philosophy final right now? But if God knows things before they happen, how can *we* be held responsible for them? If God knew before you were born that you would get a C minus in philosophy, isn't *He* the "cause" of your grade, not you? But if there is even one thing that He does not know, even one thing, how can He be all-wise?

These and related questions are of more than just academic interest. They are vitally important to anyone who attempts to reconcile faith with reason. One solution to such problems has been to hold a *dual-truth point of view*. This is the position that there is one small-t truth on the finite, human level and another, superior, capital-T Truth for God. Another strategy is to declare that these problems demonstrate that the ways of God are a "mystery" to human beings. In both cases, inconsistencies and ambiguities are not so much resolved as they are evaded.

Many believers and nonbelievers alike feel cheated when asked to accept inconsistent beliefs or simply to dismiss the most vital questions of faith. If you doubt this, wander through the sections of your college library's stacks dealing with theology and religious philosophy or conduct a Google search focused on reconciling faith and reason or the problem of evil. You will find a large number of books and articles attempting to reconcile faith with reason. If you have ever seriously wrestled with the problem of evil (How can a good, loving, wise, powerful God allow evil?) or the problem of moral responsibility (If God gave Adam and Eve a corrupt nature, how can they—and we—justly be held responsible?), you have entered a timeless struggle.

Our culture has been heavily influenced by an ongoing clash between Christian values and the values established in classical Greece. In the classical view, human beings, despite our many faults, represent the most important life-form. The classical philosophers believed that objective knowledge and logic could unlock the keys to the universe, improving our lives in the process.

When we thank God for deliberately saving us from some disaster, do we imply that God deliberately caused others to perish?

The good life was seen as being a product of reason. Reason was valued over faith because knowing was thought to be more useful than believing.

The Christian view presents a completely different picture. Human beings are seen as fallen and corrupt creatures, finite and ignorant. Christian theology teaches that we are incapable of avoiding sin and the punishment of hell through our own efforts. Only the undeserved grace and sacrifice of a loving God can save us. Obedience to the revealed word of God is also necessary for salvation. Faith is valued more highly than reason because salvation is more important than worldly success in a life that is relatively brief compared with the afterlife—where we will spend eternity in heaven (if we are saved) or hell (if we are not). As a result of its emphasis on the afterlife, Christian theology is sometimes characterized as *otherworldly*.

Whereas the classical mind was predominantly secular, the medieval mind was chiefly theological. **Theology**, from the Greek *theos* (God) and *logos* (study of), means "talking about God" or "the study or science of God." The Middle Ages saw philosophers turn from the study of man and nature to otherworldly inquiries and the study of God.

> **theology**
> From the Greek *theos* (God) and *logos* (study of); "talking about God" or "the study or science of God."

The Seeds of Change

The Christian religion arose after the death of Jesus Christ, through the efforts of the early apostles and disciples, especially Paul. Christianity originally consisted of scattered groups of believers who anticipated the Second Coming of Christ, which would signal the end of the world. Thinking that they would soon be in heaven, early Christians saw no need to develop political interests. Similarly, they were uninterested in science and philosophy and remained indifferent to much of what went on around them. Their chief concern was salvation through faith. Expecting that the risen Christ would return at any moment, they were understandably impatient with the affairs of this world. Thus, the first Christians devoted themselves to converting non-Christians and to preparing their own souls for judgment. In a major contrast with the classical view of life, they saw no time or need to fashion philosophical, social, or moral theories.

As time passed and the world did not end, Christians found it increasingly difficult to avoid dealing with problems of the here and now. Principles and rules for interpreting the basic teachings of Christ, collected as the New Testament, became necessary when it grew clear that the Second Coming might not occur until well into the future.

Interpreting revealed sacred dogma is always dangerous, however, for once the inevitability of interpretation is accepted, the door is open to competing interpretations. If *every* claimed interpretation is reliable, God's revealed will is going to appear chaotic, inconsistent, contradictory, and capricious. There must be criteria for distinguishing revelation from delusion and dogma from error. And there must be criteria for choosing criteria. And criteria for choosing criteria for choosing criteria…

Some reinterpretation of Christian teachings was clearly called for, if the Second Coming might be generations away. Giving all our goods to the poor is one thing when we expect to be in heaven in the immediate future; practical considerations complicate matters if the final judgment may be years away. As the centuries passed and

> *A person who says he has faith in God's goodness is speaking as if he had known God for a long time and during that time had never seen him do any serious evil. But we know that throughout history God has allowed numerous atrocities to occur. No one can have justifiable faith in the goodness of such a God.*
> — B. C. Johnson

the Second Coming did not occur, Christianity continued to expand: As Christian doctrine increased in complexity theological issues added to practical complications.

Augustine: Between Two Worlds

Aurelius Augustine

Aurelius Augustine (354–430) has been described as "a colossus bestriding two worlds" for his efforts to synthesize early Christian theology with his own understanding of Platonic philosophy and Manichean dualism, the belief that God and Satan are nearly evenly matched in a cosmic struggle and that human beings must choose sides.

Augustine's struggle to "choose sides" began at home. He was born in the North African city of Tagaste, in the province of Numidia. His mother, Monica, was a devout Catholic Christian, while his father, Patricius, regularly strayed from the straight and narrow. For all of her life, Monica fought to bring Augustine into the Christian church. Meanwhile, Augustine lived it up. He had a son, Adeodatus ("gift of God"), with one mistress—he had others—and by his own account lived a wanton, worldly life until he was thirty-three years old:

> I was so blind to the truth that among my companions I was ashamed to be less dissolute than they were. For I heard them bragging of their depravity, and the greater the sin the more they gloried in it, so that I took pleasure in the same vices not only for the enjoyment of what I did, but also for the applause I won....I gave in more and more to vice simply in order not to be despised....I used to pretend that I had done things I had not done at all, because I was afraid that innocence would be taken for cowardice and chastity for weakness.[1]

Augustine's influence, like his life and work, emanates from the fearless way he pursues "something missing," looking for it in sex, glory (he was a fierce and effective debater), and companions, but also searching his heart and soul, his "interior teacher":

> Bodily desire, like a morass, and adolescent sex welling up within me exuded mists which clouded over and obscured my heart, so that I could not distinguish the clear light of true love from the murk of lust. Love and lust together seethed within me. In my tender youth they swept me away over the precipice of my body's appetites and plunged me into the whirlpool of sin.[2]

Eventually, under the prodding of his mother and at the bidding of Ambrose (c. 339–397), the Bishop of Milan, Augustine turned to the Bible. Sitting in a garden one day with his friend Alypius, Augustine heard the "sing-song voice of a child" saying over and over, "Take it and read, take it and read." He did, and the first passage his eyes fell upon seemed written just for him:

> Let us behave with decency as befits the day; no drunken orgies, no debauchery or vice, no quarrels or jealousies! Let Christ Jesus himself be the armour that you wear; give your unspiritual nature no opportunity to satisfy its desires.[3]

On Easter Sunday, 387, as Monica watched, Augustine, Adeodatus, and Alypius were baptized in Milan by Ambrose. Full of faith, the four left for Africa, where they planned to live ascetic lives, but Monica died before they reached Tagaste. In

THE SCHOLAR: THOMAS AQUINAS

"The Need to Reconcile Faith and Reason"

The great paradoxes of faith are sometimes superficially dismissed by people who have never really grappled with them. Their religious training may have given them simple answers to problems such as free will, evil, predestination, and God's nature. Or they may have been taught to "exalt faith" by condemning reason. It is easy to say that faith surpasses understanding until you fully grasp the complex depths and significance of these problems. Whatever our individual religious beliefs, most of us are also rational creatures for whom it is somehow unsatisfying to accept contradictions and serious inconsistencies concerning something as important as our religious faith. We are uncomfortable when we learn that we are violating rational principles.

The basic **principles of reason**—also called **rules of inference**—define the limits of rationality. That is, consistently violating them moves us to the realm of the irrational or illogical. They are true by their very structure (by definition). They cannot be rationally refuted since we rely on them in order to reason. Contemporary logicians recognize several rules of inference. One of the most important is the law of contradiction.

The **law of contradiction** (sometimes known as the law of noncontradiction) means that no statement can be both true and false at the same time and under the same conditions. Or to use symbols (as philosophers who study logic often do), p cannot be both p and *not-p* at the same time. For example: Either this is a philosophy book or it is not a philosophy book. It cannot be both a philosophy book and not a philosophy book. It can, however, be a philosophy book and a doorstop at the same time. There is no contradiction involved in asserting that it is a philosophy book and more. The contradiction occurs in the mutually exclusive assertions "This is a philosophy book" and "This is not a philosophy book."

Take a moment to reflect on the law of contradiction. See if you can get a sense of just how basic it is to rationality. Because it is a fundamental principle of reasoning, we are usually disturbed to discover that our ideas are contradictory, for such awareness commits us to resolving the contradiction or holding seemingly irrational ideas.

In matters of faith, trying to avoid the possibility of contradiction by claiming that the human mind is finite and unable to understand God and God's ways is ultimately unsatisfying, for it removes us from meaningful communication with God. If we can never fully comprehend God, if we must trust that things are not at all what they seem (for instance, that evil only appears to be evil from our level but is really good from God's), then our "solution" may not be what it appears to be, either.

Tagaste, Augustine sold his inheritance, gave the money to the poor, and, with the help of friends, founded the Augustinian Order, the oldest Christian monastic order in the West. In 391, Augustine was ordained a priest by Valerius, the Catholic Bishop of Hippo, a Roman coastal city in North Africa. In 396, Augustine succeeded Valerius as Bishop of Hippo, a post he held for thirty-four years.

Augustine was a daring and active Christian bishop, just as he had been a daring and active anti-Christian Manichean. In both roles, he challenged doubters and nonbelievers to public debates, first defending Manicheanism against Christianity and then defending Christianity against Manicheanism.

After his conversion, Augustine produced more than 230 treatises, two of which, the *Confessions* (c. 400) and the *City of God* (413–426), remain important philosophical works for Christians and non-Christians alike.

In his writings, Augustine anticipates major philosophical and theological ideas concerning doubt and certainty, the divided self, consciousness, time, and free will and God's foreknowledge of history. The *City of God* details the fall of Rome in terms of a full-fledged philosophy of history, the first *philosophy* of history ever. By arguing that the fall of Rome was part of the Christian—not pagan—God's plan, the *City of God* signals the end of the ancient worldview.

principles of reason (rules of inference) Principles (such as the law of contradiction) that define the limits of rationality by their very structure and that cannot be rationally refuted since we rely on them in order to reason.

law of contradiction A rule of inference that says that no statement can be both true and false at the same time and under the same conditions; sometimes known as the law of noncontradiction.

"For the sake of a laugh, a little sport, I was glad to do harm and anxious to damage another....And all because we are ashamed to hold back when others say, 'Come on! Let's do it!'"—Augustine

Augustine's *Confessions* is considered by some scholars to be the first true autobiography, a claim challenged by other scholars. Whether autobiography or something else, the *Confessions*, like the *Meditations* of the pagan emperor Marcus Aurelius, engages readers from divergent backgrounds. Like Marcus, Augustine takes the measure of his own soul in remarkably direct language and thereby speaks to almost anyone who has ever struggled to reconcile the longings of the heart with the demands of the mind, appetite with order, and resolve with repeated failures to live up to that resolve:

> I was held fast, not in fetters clamped upon me by another, but by my own will, which had the strength of iron chains....the new will which had come to life in me...was not yet strong enough to overcome the old [will], hardened as it was by the passage of time. So these two wills within me, one old, one new, one servant of the flesh, the other of the spirit, were in conflict and between them they tore my soul apart.[4]

Augustine died shortly after the Vandals, who were at war with Rome, reached Hippo. He left no will, having no property. He did, however, write his own epitaph: "What maketh the heart of the Christian heavy? The fact that he is a pilgrim, and longs for his own country."

Pride and Philosophy

Combined with his Christian faith, Augustine's training in rhetoric and philosophy led him to reject Platonism, Epicureanism, and Stoicism (Chapters 5 and 7) as ways of life. Of particular concern to Augustine was the emphasis the classical Greeks, from Socrates through the Stoics, placed on human reason and the pride of place given to the human will.

Typically, the Greek philosophers held that reason is capable of distinguishing between truth and error and between reality and illusion. Even the Epicureans, with their emphasis on human happiness, stressed the importance of reason as the key to happiness in the here and now. In spite of their individual differences, the classical philosophers believed that human understanding (wisdom and knowledge) could and naturally would lead to proper emotions and proper behavior—to happiness here and now.

By Christian standards, classical humanism was too human or, rather, merely human in its indifference to the need for God's grace and guidance in the application of reason and moderation of the will. Augustine argued that, by itself, reason is powerless—even perverse—without the right will, without a will grounded in grace, love, and proper longing. Faith must precede education, for faith alone makes true understanding possible. Thus it is that faith is a necessary condition for productive philosophical inquiry.

Without faith, reason—the ground of so much classical philosophy—is, by Christian standards, unreliable, even dangerous. Left to its own devices, reason does not guide the will but is guided—pulled hither and yon—by the will, especially if the will itself is corrupt, fallen, unsaved. The will cannot redeem itself, nor can it think itself well. To believe otherwise is to lapse into pride and ignorance.

Although Augustine may have misinterpreted some of the teachings of the Stoics and Epicureans, his uneasiness with their emphasis on the natural world and on self-willed self-control is understandable. Because Epicurus taught that the soul is physical and cannot survive in immaterial form, Augustine accuses the Epicureans of advocating the pursuit of physical pleasure to the exclusion of all else: "Eat, drink, and be merry, for tomorrow we may die."

According to Augustine, Epicureanism is fit only for swine, not for human beings. Besides debasing human beings, the Epicureans, in Augustine's view, make what God intended only as a means (appetites) into the be-all and end-all of life (satisfaction, pleasure). In so doing, Epicureans, in their retreat into the earthly Garden, satisfy themselves at the expense of the poor. In their rejection of an afterlife, they ignore their own souls.

Augustine had more respect for the Stoics. He admired their emphasis on virtues, particularly courage and integrity, but mocked the way they made serenity and detachment their chief goals, asking sarcastically, "Now is this man happy, just because he is patient in his misery? Of course not!" A steady state of serenity, regardless of what condition the world is in, strikes Augustine as an insubstantial goal. Worse yet, the Stoic's faith, like the Epicurean's, is in himself, not in God:

> By which thing it seems to me to be sufficiently proved that the errors of the Gentiles in ethics, physics, and the mode of seeking truth, errors many and manifold, but conspicuously represented in these two schools of philosophy [Epicureanism and Stoicism], continued even down to the Christian era, notwithstanding the fact that the learned assailed them most vehemently, and employed both remarkable skill and abundant labour in subverting them. Yet these errors…have been already so completely silenced, that now in our schools of rhetoric the question of what their opinions were is scarcely ever mentioned; and these controversies have been now so completely eradicated or suppressed…that whenever now any school of error lifts up its head against the truth, i.e., against the Church of Christ, it does not venture to leap into the arena except under the shield of the Christian name.[5]

Augustine took note of Paul's encounter with the Stoics and Epicureans described in the Acts of the Apostles:

> While Paul was…at Athens…some of the Epicurean and Stoic philosophers joined issue with him. Some said, "What can this charlatan be trying to say?"… And when they had heard of the raising of the dead, some scoffed; others said, "We will hear you on this subject some other time." So Paul left the assembly.[6]

Augustine's misgivings notwithstanding, late Stoicism, especially in the *Meditations* and *Letters* of Marcus Aurelius, marks the beginning of the shift from purely pagan to Christian philosophy. Though pagan himself, Marcus in the *Meditations* expresses values and interests that become hallmarks of Christian philosophy: devaluing of this life and its temporary nature, a strong sense of duty, and the idea that human beings are related to the *Logos* (see Chapter 7).

But Marcus, like Plato and Epicurus, differed from his Christian successors, in his emphasis on human reason and his focus on this world. Augustine understood this and took up Paul's crusade against the errors of Greek philosophy. In so doing,

> *We see then that…the earthly city was created by self-love reaching the point of contempt for God…the earthly city glories in itself.*
>
> — Augustine

he set in motion a major shift from the human-centric classical worldview to the God-centered medieval worldview.

The Life of Thomas Aquinas

Thomas Aquinas

Thomas Aquinas (c. 1225–1274) was born near Naples.[7] His father, who was related to the count of Aquino, planned for Thomas to achieve a position of importance in the Catholic Church. To this end, he enrolled Thomas in the Benedictine abbey school at Montecassino when Thomas was about five. The Benedictines are Roman Catholic monks famed for their modest lifestyle, which involves physical labor as well as spiritual discipline. As a general rule, Benedictines remain in one monastery for life. The monks of Montecassino taught close scrutiny of Scripture, careful reading and writing, and rote memory of long and complicated passages. While under their care, Thomas acquired basic religious knowledge, academic skills, and good study habits.

The Dominican

In 1239, Thomas was sent to study at the Imperial University of Naples, where he befriended some Dominican friars. Dominicans were dedicated to education and to preaching to common people. They took vows of poverty, chastity, and obedience. Unlike the Benedictines, who tended to establish their monasteries in the country, the Dominicans established themselves in the towns. As the spiritual authority of the Benedictine monasteries was declining, in part due to their wealth and prosperity, the Dominicans were emerging as the intellectual elite of the thirteenth century.[8]

Thomas was so attracted to the Dominican way of life that he decided to join the order. This decision disturbed his family, who had been looking forward to enjoying the advantages of being related to a powerful priest or bishop. That Thomas would become a poor friar was not in their plans.

Nonetheless, in 1243 or 1244, Thomas entered the Order of Preachers, as the Dominicans are known. His mother was so unhappy about it that she sent a distress message to his older brothers, who were soldiers. Thomas was traveling with other Dominicans when his brothers tracked him down and ordered him to remove his Dominican habit. When he refused, they kidnapped him. His family held Thomas captive for several months. They applied various arguments and pressures but did allow him to wear his Dominican habit and to study—though they kept him confined to his room.

One biographer reports the interesting but unlikely story that his family sent a provocatively dressed girl into his room one night while Thomas slept: "She tempted him to sin, using all the devices at her disposal, glances, caresses and gestures."[9] The saint in Thomas proved stronger than temptation, and he prayed until the girl left. In any event, Thomas managed to write the treatise *On Fallacies* while in family captivity. Finally, convinced of Thomas's sincerity and strength, his family released him. Soon after, the Dominicans sent him first to Cologne to continue his studies with the acclaimed teacher Albertus Magnus and then to the University of Paris.

> *You can say that you trust God anyway— that no arguments can undermine your faith. But that is just a statement describing how stubborn you are; it has no bearing whatsoever on the question of God's goodness.*
>
> — B. C. Johnson

Albertus Magnus: The Universal Teacher

While at Cologne, Thomas was encouraged in the search for philosophical unity by his teacher Albertus Magnus (Albert the Great) (c. 1200–1280), who was among the first scholars to realize the need to ground Christian faith in philosophy and science. If this were not done, the church would lose influence in the face of great advances in secular and pagan knowledge. Rather than ignore the huge quantity of learning made available by the Crusades, Albert chose to master it. He read most of the Christian, Muslim, and Jewish writers and wrote continuously about what he read. Albert was called the "Universal Teacher" because of the breadth of his knowledge and because he tried to make Aristotle accessible by paraphrasing many of his works.

Although Albert has been criticized for not being creative and consistent, his efforts at synthesis laid a foundation for Thomas Aquinas. Albert quoted extensively and without alteration, and from this Thomas learned the value of broad knowledge and extensive documentation.

In his own work, however, Thomas went beyond his teacher by using his sources to construct a coherent philosophy of his own. Still, his scholarly skills owe a great deal to Albert, who recognized his ability while Thomas was still a young man, as a famous anecdote reveals: When Thomas first arrived in Paris, his rural manners, his heavyset, farm-boy physique, and slow, quiet ways earned him the nickname "the Dumb Ox," and his handwriting was so bad that others could barely read it. Yet he studied hard and remained good-natured as the other students laughed at him— until the day he answered one of Albert the Great's questions with such stunning brilliance that the master said to the others: "We call this man the Dumb Ox, but someday his bellow will be heard throughout the whole world."

A philosopher is a blind man in a dark room looking for a black cat that isn't there. A theologian is the man who finds it.
— H. L. Mencken

The Task of the Scholar

Shortly before Thomas was born, the church had forbidden the teaching of Aristotle's natural science and *Metaphysics*. His Unmoved Mover was an impersonal, natural force—not a loving, personal God. *Entelechy* (soul) was part of nature, inseparable from the body that housed it, and so it seemed that Aristotle's naturalism denied the possibility of personal immortality. (See Chapter 6.)

Yet the thorough, systematic quality of Aristotle's work on scientific thinking, logic, and nature gradually won more and more medieval converts. As Aristotle's influence spread throughout the University of Paris, questions arose regarding both the relationship of Aristotle's classical naturalism to orthodox Christianity and the accuracy of newly arrived Arabian commentaries on Aristotle. The faculty realized that Aristotle would have to be integrated into Christian theology. This task became the great, courageous accomplishment of Tommaso d'Aquino, "the Dumb Ox of Sicily."

In 1252, Thomas received his master's degree from the University of Paris, where he was also lecturing. He taught theology at the papal court in Rome in 1259, and from 1268 to 1272 lectured in Paris once more. During the twenty years that he was an active teacher, Thomas wrote disputations on various theological questions, commentaries on books of the Bible, commentaries on twelve works of Aristotle and others, and nearly forty other miscellaneous notes, sermons, lectures, poems, and treatises. His crowning achievements are the multivolume summaries of arguments and theology known as the *Summa Theologica* and *Summa contra Gentiles*.

Thomas was sent to Naples to establish a Dominican school in 1272, and in 1274 he was commanded by Pope Gregory X to attend the Council of Lyons. He died on the trip to Lyons on March 7, 1274. As reported by Brother Peter of Monte San Giovanni, his last hours reflected his submission to the authority of the church.

The Wisdom of the Scholar

scholasticism
A Christian philosophy dominating medieval Europe from about 1000 to 1300 that stressed logical and linguistic analysis of texts and arguments in order to produce a systematic statement and defense of Christian beliefs.

The term **Scholasticism** refers to mainstream Christian philosophy in medieval Europe from about 1000 to about 1300, just after the death of Aquinas. It comes from the Greek *scholastikos*, meaning "to enjoy leisure" or "to devote one's free time to learning."

Scholastic philosophy rested on a strong interest in logical and linguistic analysis of texts and on arguments producing a systematic statement and defense of Christian beliefs. As the revealed word of God, the Bible was central to this project but always was interpreted in accord with the authority of the church and the wisdom of selected earlier Christian writers.

A central effort of Scholastic philosophers was the attempt to reconstruct Greek philosophy in a form that not only was consistent with but also supported and strengthened Christian doctrine. An important aspect of this effort was the imposition of a hierarchy of knowledge, in which the highest place was held by revelation, as interpreted by the church; next were faith and theology; philosophy came last, subordinated to both faith and revelation.[10]

Medieval scholars were the first *professors of philosophy*; their task was to teach, to expound on texts, to write about them, to debate in class and in public, and to publish great educational summations of official doctrine.[11] Generally viewed as the most complete realization of medieval Scholasticism, Thomas Aquinas is the archetype of the scholar. Unlike modern professional philosophers, Thomas was not free to *pursue* the truth wherever it led; he *started from the truth*—always ultimately supporting Christian doctrine.

In Scholastic philosophy, the *way* a case was made and analyzed became an integral part of what was being claimed, and method remains an important concern to today's scholars. Logic and linguistic analysis were vital elements in proving a case—as they are today. Scholarly, intellectual standards were developed for documenting an argument with citations from approved sources—standards that any student who has ever written a research paper will recognize. In fact, in the first twelve questions of the *Summa Theologica*, Thomas refers to other authors 160 times.

Scholastic philosophers had to present their arguments publicly and defend them against all comers—a precursor to the modern professor's obligation to publish, present, and defend papers. Subject matter became specialized, and a universal impersonal, technical, scholarly style of writing was developed to communicate with a select audience of students and teachers devoted to mastering an elaborate professional technique.[12]

The emergence of the Scholastic *professor of philosophy* reflects a move away from the importance of a particular philosopher, away from the *sophos* whose work closely reflected his life, to a less personal view of the individual thinker as a part of a scholarly community. Thus, although Thomas's work reflected his life, the

Science has not killed God—quite the contrary. It is clearer now than ever that what we can learn from science is limited to what is abstract and quantifiable. Because of what science has achieved…God is needed now more than ever.

— René J. Muller

product of his work is scholarly and technical in ways unlike anything produced before. He says:

> That which a single man can bring, through his work and his genius, to the promotion of truth is little in comparison with the total of knowledge. However, from all these elements, *selected and coordinated and brought together*, there arises a marvelous thing, as is shown by the various departments of learning, which by the work and sagacity of many have come to a wonderful augmentation.[13] [emphasis added]

Why Do People Argue About Spiritual Matters?

Absent some sort of objective proof or rational argumentation, all we have to offer those who disagree with us about spiritual and religious matters are appeals to bald assertions of our sincerity, insistent claims that we are "saved" or happier than they are, and other "bits of autobiography." Although we may believe that we are discussing the content of our beliefs, we are actually reporting information about ourselves (hence, "autobiography"). As a result, those who already believe what we do continue to believe what we do. And while those who do not believe what we do may have learned something about *us*, we have provided them with no evidence demonstrating the actual merits of the beliefs themselves.

But, clearly, our great and persistent disagreements over matters of faith are not meant to be reduced to assertions of personal feelings (subjective states) but, rather, are intended to be about claimed realities, about *what is true*, about whether or not God actually exists—objectively, really. Otherwise, there is nothing to dispute.

Consider the hypothetical case of Ross, who believes that only God *X* exists; Dean, who believes that only God *Y* exists; and Joe, who believes that no god whatsoever exists. If Ross, Dean, and Joe were simply reporting subjective states, they would not need argumentation, because they would each be right. "Right" would be equivalent to "reporting present beliefs accurately." But Ross, Dean, and Joe think that they are doing more than reporting products of thinking. And, hence, as reasoning creatures, as rational agents, they are compelled to apply "laws of reason" to their beliefs. If the phrase "laws of reason" seems too authoritarian or dated to you, try the more expansive and less-imposing term "standards of evidence." The main point here is to note that, for the most part, we agree with Ross, Dean, and Joe: Our religious questions are about what is real, what exists, what is true. They are not just about what people feel or think is true.

In Thomas's time, as in our own, there were conflicting claims about what constituted proper standards of evidence for evaluating matters of theology, church authority, and religious faith in general. One view held that all truth claims must be tested against *revealed* truths. From this perspective, *revelation* was the chief and only reliable source of knowledge of God and God's ways. At the opposite extreme were those philosophers and scientists who argued that truth could only be *discovered through concrete experience and deductive reasoning*.

God and Natural Reason

Thomas approached this problem from an Aristotelian, naturalistic position. This is sometimes referred to as *natural theology* because it appeals to what Thomas

> The creationist, whether naive Bible-thumper or an educated bishop, simply postulates an already existing being of prodigious complexity. If we are going to allow ourselves the luxury of postulating organized complexity without offering an explanation, we might as well make a job of it and simply postulate the existence of life as we know it!
> — Richard Dawkins

calls *natural reason*, or *natural intelligence*. By "natural" here, Thomas means "of this world"—not sloppy or undisciplined. Natural reason is, thus, reason unaided by divine revelation, and natural theology is theology based on appeals to natural reason. Although Thomas had great respect for, and submitted to, church authority, his efforts to prove God's existence begin with appeals to concrete experience and empirical evidence rather than with revelations or dogma—an argument style favored by Aristotle. (You may wish to review the material concerning Aristotle's ideas regarding form, matter, change, and cause in Chapter 6.)

As we review selected passages from Thomas, keep in mind that no introductory survey can do justice to the complexity of Thomas's thought. So although what follows is a plausible interpretation of some of the most studied and disputed arguments in the history of philosophy, it cannot serve as a definitive account.

Thomas's Five Ways are so influential and persuasive that I am sure you've already thought about some of them, at least in simplified form. You may even think of them as your own since popularized versions of them have become staples of Christian "apologetics," the offering of reasons to justify the divine origin of faith. To get the most out of your efforts, I recommend approaching the Five Ways as a whole, focusing on what Thomas is arguing and why it matters, before accepting or rejecting the individual arguments. That being accomplished, you'll be in a good position to assess not only this particular version of Thomas's arguments but also more general issues of faith and evidence.

Proving the Existence of God

Although Thomas believed in God, he also thought God's existence could be demonstrated by natural reason. To this end, he offered his famous five proofs for the existence of God. Each proof follows a basic pattern, beginning with some natural effect with which we are all familiar, such as movement or growth. Thomas then tries to show that the only possible explanation for this effect is God. *The Five Ways are cause–effect arguments, beginning with our experience of effects and moving toward their cause, God.*

The Five Ways are most effective if viewed as parts of a single argument. The first three ways deal with avoiding an infinite chain of causes in nature. Their conclusion is that an Unmoved Mover/Uncaused Cause must exist—that is, a being whose existence depends only on its own essence and not on anything external to itself. But Aristotle said much the same thing without concluding that a personal god exists; such an impersonal cause could just as easily be basic matter and energy. The Fourth and Fifth Ways are thus crucial. They are needed to introduce some hierarchical quality into the overall description of causes and effects that can transform them into a personal god.

The First Way: Motion

The Five Ways begin with the argument Thomas thought was the easiest to understand, the **argument from motion**. Starting with the indisputable observation that things are moving, the argument points out that motion must be given to each object by some other object that is already moving. (By "motion," Thomas means

argument from motion
An attempt to prove the existence of God based on the reasoning that to avoid an infinite regress, there must be an Unmoved Mover capable of imparting motion to all other things; Aristotelian argument that forms the basis for the first of Thomas Aquinas's Five Ways.

both linear motion and more complex "life-motion," animating motion.) For instance, the suspended steel balls in a Newton's Cradle do not move until some external force—a finger flick, an earthquake, a gust of air, a cat's playful swipe—sets them in motion. Only after being moved by something *already in motion* does the first ball swing and strike the second and so on until the tethered balls swing back and forth as long as they have sufficient energy—energy supplied by something else *already in motion* that must itself have first been set in motion by something else already in motion. So too with you and I, who have been set in motion, as it were, by our parents who were…You get the picture.

Gregor Schuster/Getty Images

"Therefore, whatever is moved must be moved by another. If that by which it is moved be itself moved, then this also must needs be moved by another, and that by another again. But this cannot go on to infinity…."

It *might* be possible to keep imagining an infinite chain of things already in motion moving other things. But no such infinite regress can account for the fact that things are *actually in motion*. Given that things are moving, we know that some *first already-moving thing* had to move other not-yet-moving things. Thomas reasoned that some "first mover" had to exist outside the series of *becoming*—some force or being with the ability to move other things without itself needing to be moved by any outside force. God is just such an Unmoved Mover. Here is Thomas's argument:

> Therefore, whatever is moved must be moved by another. If that by which it is moved be itself moved, then this also must needs be moved by another, and that by another again. But this cannot go on to infinity, because then there would be no first mover, and, consequently, no other mover, seeing that subsequent movers move only inasmuch as they are moved by the first mover; as the staff moves only because it is moved by the hand. Therefore it is necessary to arrive at a first mover, moved by no other; and this everyone understands to be God.[14]

PHILOSOPHICAL QUERY

Is there any other explanation for present motion besides a previously "unmoved mover"? If so, what is it? If not, is Thomas's conclusion sound? Convincing?

The Second Way: Cause

The explanation just given for the movement of balls in a Newton's Cradle and the birth of children is incomplete. We can still ask what accounts for the very existence of Newton's Cradles and tethered balls and parents giving birth to children who grow up to become parents giving birth to children…and to everything else already in motion. Thomas answered with a second argument, similar in pattern to his first, but based on the Aristotelian concept of cause. Because the second argument

cosmological argument

From the Greek word *kosmos*, meaning "world," "universe," or "orderly structure"; argument for the existence of God that because it is impossible for any natural thing to be the complete and sufficient source of its own existence, there must be an Uncaused Cause capable of imparting existence to all other things; Aristotelian argument that forms the basis for the second of Aquinas's Five Ways.

concerns the initiating cause of the existence of the universe, it is called the **cosmological argument**, from the Greek word *kosmos*, meaning "world," "universe," or "orderly structure."

In a nutshell, the cosmological argument asserts that it is impossible for any natural thing to be the complete and sufficient source of its own existence. In order to cause itself, a thing would have to precede itself. Put another way, in order for me to be the source of my own existence, I would have to exist before I existed. This is as absurd as it is impossible.

In broad strokes, my existence is explained by my parents' existence, and theirs by my grandparents' existence, and so on. But if *every* set of parents had to have parents, there could never be any parents at all. At least one set of parents must not have had parents. In the Bible, this is Adam and Eve. But even Adam and Eve did not cause their own existence. They were created by God, who creates but is uncreated. This is why it is said that "God always was, is, and will be."

In Thomas's understanding of things, any series or system of causes and effects requires an originating cause. In order to avoid an infinite regress of causes, which he thought was impossible, there had to be an Uncaused Cause.

The cosmological argument is based on Aristotle's concept of *Efficient Cause*. (See Chapter 6.) Efficient cause is the force that initiates change or brings about some activity. The efficient cause in the development of a human fetus, for example, is the entire biochemical process of changes in the mother's womb that nurtures the growing fetus. In the case of an acorn, the efficient cause that produces an oak tree consists of rain, sun, soil, and temperature interacting to initiate growth and development. Thomas argues:

> In the world of sensible things we find there is an order of efficient causes....Now in efficient causes it is not possible to go on to infinity, because in all efficient causes following in order, the first is the cause of the intermediate cause, and the intermediate is the cause of the ultimate cause, whether the intermediate cause be several, or one only. Now to take away the cause is to take away the effect. Therefore, if there be no first cause among efficient causes, there will be no ultimate, nor any intermediate, cause....Therefore it is necessary to admit a first efficient cause, to which everyone gives the name God.[15]

Discussing Philosophy

PHILOSOPHICAL QUERY

Think carefully about the cosmological argument. Is Thomas's reasoning sound? Are you comfortable with the possibility that there is no "first cause"? If there isn't, can we explain the existence of the universe at all? Discuss.

The Third Way: Necessity

Thomas's third proof, the **argument from necessity**, may seem odd to you. It is based on the difference between two classes of things: those whose existence is only contingent, or *possible*, and those whose existence is *necessary*. Contingent things might or might not exist, but they do not have to exist, and they all eventually cease to exist. You and I do not exist of necessity: We just happen to exist given the particular history of the world. Our existence is contingent, dependent on something else. This is true, in fact, of every created thing in the universe. It is even possible and imaginable that the universe itself never existed or that someday it will cease to exist. In other words, the universe is also contingent.

But, Thomas pointed out, it is not possible to conceive of a time in which nothing whatsoever existed. There would be no space; time itself would not exist. There would be no place for something to come into existence from or move to. There would be nowhere for anything to move, if there were anything to move, which there would not be. Without movement, there would be no passage of time. If no time passes, nothing happens. *Thus, if nothing had ever existed, nothing would always exist.* But all around us we see things in existence. Therefore, there was never no-thing. Getting rid of the double negatives, this becomes: There was always something—or there is something that always existed and always will. (See Democritus, Chapter 2.)

The logic of Thomas's Third Way relies on the principle of sufficient reason and the principle of plenitude. According to the **principle of sufficient reason**, nothing happens without a reason. Consequently, no *adequate* theory or explanation can contain any brute, crude, unexplained facts. The **principle of plenitude** is the metaphysical principle that given infinity and the richness of the universe, any real possibility must occur—at least once. Based on these two principles, Thomas concluded that there must be something whose existence is necessary and not just possible. There needs to be some reason that what is possible actually happens. In short, God's existence is necessary. As Thomas puts it,

> We find in nature things that are possible to be and not to be, since they are found to be generated, and to be corrupted, and consequently, it is possible for them to be and not to be. But it is impossible for them always to exist, for that which can not-be at some time is not. Therefore, if everything can not-be, then at one time there was nothing in existence. Now if this were true, even now there would be nothing in existence, because that which does not exist begins to exist only through something already existing.... Therefore, we cannot but admit the existence of some being having of itself its own necessity, and not receiving it from another, but rather causing in others their necessity. This all men speak of as God.[16]

PHILOSOPHICAL QUERY

Scholastic arguments often hinged on whether something was conceivable (clearly imaginable). One cardinal principle held that no one could even conceive of absolute nothingness. Do you agree? Explain. Whether or not you agree, do you find the argument from necessity convincing?

The Fourth Way: Degree

The first three arguments for the existence of God fail to establish the existence of a good and loving being. They only deny the possibility of an infinite series of causes and effects, an infinity of *becomings*. Even if some element or entity functions as an

argument from necessity
An argument for the existence of God based on the idea that if nothing had ever existed, nothing would always exist; therefore, there is something whose existence is necessary (an eternal something); Aristotelian argument that forms the basis for the third of Aquinas's Five Ways.

principle of sufficient reason
The principle that nothing happens without a reason; consequently, no adequate theory or explanation can contain any brute, crude, unexplained facts. First specifically encountered in the work of the medieval philosopher Peter Abelard (1079–1142), it is usually associated with the rationalist philosopher Gottfried Wilhelm Leibniz (1646–1716), who used it in his famous "best of all possible worlds" argument.

MindTap
Discussing Philosophy

principle of plenitude
The name given by American historian of ideas Arthur O. Lovejoy (1873–1962) to the metaphysical principle that, given infinity, any real possibility must occur (at least once).

ever-existing Prime Mover or Uncaused Cause, these characteristics alone do not describe God. In the fourth and fifth arguments, Thomas makes a qualitative shift in his proofs.

The Fourth Way rests on the idea of qualitative differences among kinds of beings. Known as the **argument from gradation**, it is based on a metaphysical concept of a hierarchy of souls. (See Chapter 6.) In ascending order, being progresses from inanimate objects to increasingly complex animated creatures. (For instance, a dog has more being than a worm and a person more than a dog.) Thomas believed that what contemporary philosopher Arthur O. Lovejoy called "the great chain of being" continued upward through angels to God.

This chain of being, Thomas thought, is reflected in the properties of individual things, as well as in the kinds of things that exist. For example, there are grades of goodness, going from the complete lack of goodness (evil) to pure goodness (God), from the complete lack of honesty to complete honesty, from utter ugliness to sublime beauty, and so forth. In very general terms, existence flows downward from perfection and completeness to varying lower stages, each descending level possessing less being.

Of the Five Ways, the significance of this argument can be especially difficult for contemporary thinkers to grasp because it rests on a metaphysical worldview that is alien to many of us today. Yet we cannot just dismiss it as a quirk of the medieval mind-set. The Five Ways form a cumulative argument. The first three arguments cannot establish the existence of a *qualitatively different kind of being*. The fifth argument, as we shall see, only establishes that the universe is ordered. Without the argument from gradation, Thomas can make a case only for an eternal something that follows orderly patterns. But this "something" is almost a contemporary scientist's description of the universe; it is certainly not a description of God. Without the introduction of qualitatively different kinds of entities, Thomas cannot establish the existence of God by rational argument. Here is Thomas's argument from gradation:

> Among beings there are some more and some less good, true, noble, and the like. But *more* and *less* are predicated of different things according as they resemble in their different ways something which is the maximum, as a thing is said to be hotter according as it more nearly resembles that which is hottest; so that there is something which is truest, something best, something noblest, and, consequently, something which is most being, for those things that are greatest in truth are greatest in being.... Therefore there must also be something which is to all beings the cause of their being, goodness, and every other perfection; and this we call God.[17]

PHILOSOPHICAL QUERY

Do you have any sense of grades of being? Is there anything in your own experience that supports Thomas's argument? Discuss the argument from gradation.

The Fifth Way: Design

Thomas's **teleological argument**, also called the argument from design, is one of the most widely known and used arguments for the existence of God. Teleological

---

argument from gradation
An argument for the existence of God based on the idea that being progresses from inanimate objects to increasingly complex animated creatures, culminating in a qualitatively unique God; Aristotelian argument that forms the basis for the fourth of Aquinas's Five Ways.

© Douglas J. Soccio

According to the principle of gradation, the little girl and her grandfather in this photo have more "being" than the dogs, which have more than the trees. Does such a view reflect reality or does it foster a kind of arrogance in which we see ourselves as superior to—rather than a part of—the natural world? Does the way the dogs and humans are engaged with one another tell us anything significant about the principle of gradation?

thinking, as we learned in Chapter 6, is a way of understanding things in terms of their *telos*, or end. For example, infancy is understood in relationship to adulthood: The adult is the *telos* of the infant; the oak tree is the *telos* of the acorn. When archaeologists uncover some ancient artifact unlike anything ever seen before, they often recognize that it was made for a purpose, a *telos*, even if they do not know what specific purpose. In other words, they infer the existence of a designer who shaped the mysterious object.

Thomas asserts that the entire natural world exhibits order and design. Water behaves in orderly ways, as do rocks, crabs, clouds, reindeer, and people. Today, we are even more aware of the complex interrelatedness of the natural world than Thomas was: Rain forests in the Amazon basin scrub the atmosphere in ways that affect the whole earth; this is their *telos*. Cells and chromosomes, molecules, atoms, and subatomic particles exhibit order, with each performing a specific function, a *telos*. On inspection, the universe reveals order; otherwise, we could not quantify scientific laws.

Order, Thomas argued, implies intelligence, purpose, a plan. Here again he follows the pattern of starting with common observations and searching for principles to explain them. In this case, Thomas held that the order we observe in inanimate nature cannot come from matter itself, since matter lacks consciousness and intelligence. Design, by its nature, implies conscious intent. Thus, if

teleological argument
Also called the argument from design, a widely known argument for the existence of God that claims that the universe manifests order and purpose that can only be the result of a conscious intelligence (God); Aristotelian argument that forms the basis for the fifth of Aquinas's Five Ways.

the world exhibits evidence of design, it follows logically that there must be a designer:

> We see that things which lack knowledge, such as natural bodies [matter and inanimate objects], act for an end, and this is evident from their acting always, or nearly always, in the same way, so as to obtain the best result. Hence it is plain that they achieve their end, not fortuitously, but designedly. Now whatever lacks knowledge cannot move towards an end, unless it is directed by some being endowed with knowledge and intelligence; as the arrow is directed by the archer. Therefore some intelligent being exists by whom all natural things are directed to their end; and this being we call God.[18]

PHILOSOPHICAL QUERY

Is order the same thing as design? Does the universe seem to be ordered and "intelligently" designed? (For more on this intriguing topic, see Chapter 10.)

Commentary on the Five Ways

Thomas's arguments begin with empirical observations and then attempt to show that the only logically consistent, adequate explanation for them requires the existence of God. If other equally plausible arguments can account for these observations, then Thomas has not conclusively proved the existence of God; he has at best shown that God's existence is possible or probable.

Supposing science ever became complete so that it knew every single thing in the whole universe. Is it not plain that the questions, "Why is there a universe?" "Why does it go on as it does?" "Has it any meaning?" would remain just as they are?

— C. S. Lewis

Thomas's teleological argument posits both order and design. Does the ability to identify a causal sequence imply "order"? Consider global warming: Who, or what, is the designer (orderer) of climate change, if, indeed, it has been correctly and thoroughly explained?

Underlying Thomas's first three arguments is his conviction that an infinite series of events (motions or causes) is impossible, even inconceivable. But is it? Not according to modern science and mathematics. The simplest example of an infinite series is the positive numbers. No matter what number you reach, you can always add 1. If one infinite series is possible—and it is—then another is possible. So to the extent that Thomas's arguments rely on the impossibility of any infinite series, they fail.

But *is* Thomas merely denying the impossibility of *any* infinite series? Probably not; it is more likely that he is denying the possibility of an infinite series of *qualitatively identical* finite series. Recall that Thomas is attempting to establish the metaphysical grounding for all natural existence, all contingent or dependent existence. Simply adding to the *same kind* does not account for the very existence of the kind.

It is certainly possible to argue that nature exhibits as much ugliness and disorder as it does design and purpose. What's the *telos* of starving children or freak accidents? Where is the hand of the most good, most noble designer in poverty and inequity? Perhaps Thomas only *projected* his own sense of order onto the world rather than *observing* order in it. Other observers simply deny the presence of design; they fail to see the world as consciously and deliberately ordered.

But don't be too quick to reject Thomas's proofs. The historian of philosophy W. T. Jones points out that the force of Thomas's arguments rests on whether they "account for" motion, cause, goodness, and design. Jones distinguishes between explanations *inside* a system and explanations that account for the system *as a whole*.[19] Ignorance of this difference is a chief source of conflict between science and religion. Scientific explanations are explanations within systems; Thomas, on the other hand, was attempting to account for the universe as a whole. Let's examine this difference.

In 1953, Stanley Miller, a biochemist at the University of Chicago, provided the first empirical evidence for the possibility that organic life could evolve from inorganic matter. Miller tried to replicate conditions as they could have been soon after the earth formed. He put methane, ammonia, and hydrogen—elements believed to have been present in the early atmosphere—into a glass container. As the chemicals were mixed with steam from boiling water, they passed through glass tubes and flowed across electrodes that were constantly emitting a spark. At the end of a week, a soupy liquid had formed in the container. This liquid contained organic compounds and amino acids—building blocks for organic matter and life-forms. In the decades since Miller's experiment, many of these building-block chemicals have been produced in laboratory conditions thought to mimic conditions during various stages of the earth's history.

Such experiments might explain the origins of life *within* the universe, understood as a system composed of basic matter and energy. But they cannot address certain kinds of questions regarding the universe *as a whole*. Where did the matter and energy come from? In his experiment, Miller *acquired* matter and energy; he did not *create* them from nothing. He "created" only in

In 1953, Stanley Miller provided the first empirical evidence for the possibility that organic life could evolve from inorganic matter.

DAVID MCNEW/Reuters/Landov

the sense that an artist creates—by transforming what is already there. Interestingly, experiments like Miller's can be used to support Thomas's arguments. Miller had to design his experiment, being careful in his selection of gases. Then he had to provide a fitting environment and introduce motion/cause in the form of electrical impulses. The existence of the experimenter and the need for carefully controlled conditions can be interpreted as demonstrating the need for the intervention of the Designer. If the analogy is carried further, the scientist represents the need for God to get the whole thing going.

Which interpretation is correct—the Thomistic or the scientific? The question cannot be answered without qualification. Scientific explanations enable us to understand and control events within the natural order. Even if all scientists were to agree on the steps that produced the universe, such explanations cannot account for the existence of matter and energy themselves. All they can account for is the behavior of matter and energy, *given their existence and given how they exist.*

Discussing Philosophy

PHILOSOPHICAL QUERY

In 1999, the Kansas Board of Education attracted national attention when it ruled against mandating the teaching of evolution in science classes. This sparked an ongoing national debate concerning, among other things, the adequacy of explanations of the origins of life. Do you think distinguishing between explanations inside a system and explanations that account for the system as a whole could help avoid controversies regarding science versus religion in our schools? Why?

Complications for Natural Theology

If Thomas's arguments are unconvincing to you, keep in mind that he was applying what he called "natural reason" to a complex theology. Part of the difficulty he faced, as does any philosopher who attempts such a task, is that various articles of faith seem to contradict each other and appear inconsistent with common experience. Had Thomas been able to follow *either* faith *or* reason, he could have avoided certain inconsistencies and confusions more easily. Instead, he struggled with the most difficult questions facing a Christian philosopher. (Similar difficulties face Jewish and Muslim philosophers as well.)

If God is the wise and good First Cause, it follows that God wills everything that happens, including the existence of each individual. Nothing occurs by chance. Chance is merely the name we give to events that occur in a causal sequence that is unclear or unknown to us. Since *all* causal sequences lead back to the First Cause, everything happens "for a reason" or, more accurately, "nothing happens unless God causes it." It would seem to follow, then, that because of God's foreknowledge and the fact that He causes everything to happen, every event *must* occur exactly as it does.

In Thomas's language, every event that occurs does so out of *necessity*—nothing that happens can be merely *possible.* If everything that happens must happen exactly as it does, how can humans be free? Yet free will—the freedom to choose our own actions—is a necessary condition for moral responsibility. We cannot *justly* be held responsible for events over which we have no control.

The Problem of Evil

I think the **problem of evil** is the most important theological question for any religion or philosophy that asserts the existence of an all-powerful, all-wise, all-good God. It is a question that confronts nearly every thinking person sooner or later and is often cited by agnostics and atheists as a barrier to faith in the Judeo-Christian-Islamic God. Here's the problem: *If God can prevent the destructive suffering of the innocent yet chooses not to, God is not good. If God chooses to prevent the suffering but cannot, He is not omnipotent. If God cannot recognize the suffering of the innocent, He is not wise.*

Quick answers to the problem of evil are usually worse than no answers because they involve obvious absurdities or suggest a callousness that's inconsistent with charity. If someone answers that suffering builds character, I offer you the starvation, molestation, or torture of children. Modern psychology has clearly shown that the damage caused by childhood suffering is often severe enough to last a lifetime. If someone answers that we are unable to understand the ways of God, I remind you that this gap of comprehension must apply to *everything else* about God if we are to be consistent. But these are distractions.

The real force of the problem of evil always comes back to justifying preventable evil and suffering. Given the qualities attributed to the Judeo-Christian God, how can He not be responsible for evil? Thomas himself deplored contradictions. Is it not contradictory to assert that God is the cause of everything and then to say that He is not responsible for the existence of evil (just everything else)?

Thomas reasoned that God willed the universe in order to communicate His love of His own essence, in order to "multiply Himself." Now of course this does not mean that God created other gods, for as we have seen, God must be a unique essence. It means that God created the universe as a reflection of His love.

problem of evil
If God can prevent the suffering of the innocent yet chooses not to, He is not good. If God chooses to prevent the suffering but cannot, He is not omnipotent. If God cannot recognize the suffering of the innocent, He is not wise.

Has all this suffering, this dying around us, a meaning? For, if not, then ultimately there is no meaning to survival; for a life whose meaning depends upon such a happenstance— whether one escapes [suffering] or not— ultimately would not be worth living at all.
— Viktor E. Frankl

Andrew Holbrooke/Historical/Corbis

Perhaps the greatest theological question of all is the problem of evil. Is there any way to reconcile the suffering of the innocent (such as this child begging for food) with the existence of an all-wise, all-good, all-powerful God?

Evil, in Thomas's view, is not a positive, created entity, however. Rather, it is a lack of goodness, which he calls a "privation," and as such, it is not "creatable." Instead, evil is a kind of *necessary by-product* of free will. But it is not a product of the informed human will: *No one can deliberately will evil who fully recognizes it as evil.* For example, Thomas points out that an adulterer is not *consciously willing a sin* but is willing something that appears to be good—say, sensual pleasure. In this case, however, the pleasure is sought in a way that lacks goodness. To lack goodness is to be evil.

Even the most deliberate, diabolical willing of evil—the most blatant defiance of God—is not really *chosen as evil*. Even if the person uses the word *evil* to describe an action, it is misperceived as being something desirable, something good. Satan himself thought it was bad to be second to God and viewed his rebellion as *good for himself*. No one can knowingly choose evil as evil. (Compare this to Socrates' similar belief, discussed in Chapter 4.)

But God surely foresaw the evil that would occur in His creation. Evil is not all that God foresaw, however. Augustine noted that it would be contradictory and pointless for God to *command* us to do anything if we lack the power to obey or to disobey. Yet we are commanded to love one another, to do good. As for the issue of God's foreknowledge, Augustine said that there is a difference between being *fated*, preordained to live out an unchangeable future that is independent of our willing, and *foreknowledge*, God's foreseeing of the future that we make for ourselves through our own free choices. Among the things that God foresees is the fact that we exercise free will:

> God knows all things before they come to pass, and...we do by our free will whatsoever we know and feel to be done by us only because we will it. But that all things come to pass by fate, we do not say; nay, we affirm that nothing comes to pass by fate....for our wills themselves are included in that order of causes which is certain (known) to God, and is embraced by his foreknowledge, for human wills are also causes of human actions; and He who foreknew all the causes of things would certainly among those causes not have been ignorant of our wills....for He whose foreknowledge is infallible foreknew that they would have the power (free will and ability) to do it, and would do it. ...
>
> ...For a man does not therefore sin because God foreknew that he would sin....But if he shall not will to sin, even this did God foreknow.[20]

Thomas argued that God willed the creation of a universe in which His love could be multiplied. In His wisdom, He chose to do this through a rich natural order that allowed for the possibility of physical defect and suffering. Physical suffering is not the same as moral evil. God did not directly will suffering, He willed sensitive, rational creatures. In *Summa contra Gentiles*, Thomas says:

> Now it is necessary that God's goodness, which in itself is one and simple, should be manifested in many ways in His creation; because creatures in themselves cannot attain the simplicity of God. Thus it is that for the completion of the universe there are required diverse grades of being, of which some hold a high and some a low place in the universe. That this multiformity of grades may be preserved in things, God allows some evils, lest many good things should be hindered.[21]

This is an interesting point. It means that the inescapable price for awareness and feeling is the possibility of pain. The eye that is exquisitely sensitive to beauty,

The claim could be made that God has a "higher morality" by which his actions are to be judged. But it is a strange "higher morality" which claims that what we call "bad" is good and what we call "good" is bad. Such a morality can have no meaning to us....God's "higher morality" being the opposite of ours, cannot offer any grounds for deciding that he is somehow good.

— B. C. Johnson

"Would You Consent?"

The morality of torture is a topic in ongoing discussions of the ethics of gathering vital information in attempts to prevent acts of terrorism. Here the question is raised on a more basic level:

> "Tell me yourself, I challenge you—answer. Imagine that you are creating a fabric of human destiny with the object of making men happy in the end, giving them peace and rest at last, but that it was essential and inevitable to torture to death only one tiny creature—the baby beating its breast with its fist, for instance—and to found that edifice on its unavenged tears, would you consent to be the architect of those conditions? Tell me, and tell me the truth."
>
> "No, I wouldn't consent," said Alyosha softly.

Fyodor Dostoevsky, **The Brothers Karamazov**, trans. Constance Garnett (London: Heinemann, 1912).

for example, will be equally sensitive to ugliness. The only way we could suffer less is if we loved less. It is the nature of love to experience both happiness and sadness. To use Thomas's logic, love without concern for our loved ones is contradictory. Is it possible to love others and not suffer when they suffer? No, love without suffering is impossible. Feeling and awareness, Thomas argued, involve both pleasure and pain, which are inseparable.

According to Thomas, God could not have fully manifested His nature if He had created a universe of limited choices in which we were forced to love Him and do His will. God, Thomas says, is worthy of love freely given. If we had no choice but to love God, it would no longer be love. It would not be worthy of God. Besides, love under coercion is one of those contradictions Thomas said could not exist. Therefore, since God chose to create a universe in which we could love, He *had* to give us the freedom necessary for love. "Freedom" that prohibits certain choices is not freedom; it is another contradiction.

This, then, is Thomas's solution to the problem of evil: *Though God did not deliberately will evil, He willed the real possibility of evil: Evil must always be possible when love and goodness are free choices.* God wills the good of the whole universe. From the standpoint of the whole, a universe containing free moral choices is better than a restricted universe without love and responsibility. We are more like God with freedom than without it.

According to Thomas, the overall perfection of the universe requires a range of beings, some of which get sick, decay, and die. By virtue of being human, as a union of body and soul, we are subject to physical pain and suffering. God could have created beings that do not suffer physical death and pain (like angels), but they would not be human. He could not create *humans* who do not suffer.

God willed us freedom that we might love Him in this world, not so we could use it for moral evil. But He could not give us the freedom to choose good without also letting us choose evil. God wills our free choice of good by allowing us the free choice of good or evil. Mature parents understand this. At some point, the child's greatest good must be purchased at the risk of letting him or her make bad decisions. Some of these can have terrible consequences. But love of the child requires the risk.

For Deeper Consideration

Reflect on the idea that God chose to allow evil in order to allow free will and love. Do you think freedom with the real possibility of abuse is better than forced limitation, no matter how good the reasons for limitations? What might this imply about forms of government? About censorship? About banning books or music or drugs? Which is more godlike: protecting people for their own sakes or letting them risk harm in the name of freedom? Has Thomas provided a satisfactory solution to the problem of evil?

These are intriguing and complex arguments (and there is much more to both Augustine's and Aquinas's positions than can be addressed here), and it is not clear that they "solve" the problem of evil. Isn't God still responsible for creating a universe in which so much evil is chosen, in which so much suffering occurs? Is it not still reasonable, even necessary, to ask whether we would not be better off with less "freedom" if that means less overall suffering? But what if, in exchange for less freedom and less suffering, we must do without love?

Aplia

Commentary

Perhaps you find Thomas's arguments not quite convincing. Why doesn't God make His existence clearly indisputable to everyone? Why require proofs anyway? Why didn't God use His wisdom and omnipotence to create us so that we do not suffer or do wrong? These are always unanswerable questions, for they amount to asking why did God create *this* universe?

As a Christian philosopher, Thomas pursued his natural theology as far as he could, but he refused to speculate on God's ultimate motives. In the end, he accepted the limits of the human mind when it confronts the infinite. There's even a tradition that Thomas turned toward mysticism late in his life. He is supposed to have said that everything he had written was "as straw"—but he wouldn't say what he "saw" that taught him that.

Thomas's philosophy is alive today as a vital component of Roman Catholicism, but the impact of his great efforts extends beyond the church. He is the first philosopher to have actually produced a comprehensive, logically ordered synoptic (holistic) science, when science is understood as *organized knowledge*. That is, he fulfilled the promise of Aristotle and actually produced a cohesive *system* that included all the known sciences of his time.

Of course, the fragmentation and specialization of knowledge today almost certainly make such an achievement impossible. That does not reduce the desirability, and perhaps the need, for a cohesive, consistent, all-encompassing philosophy, even if it must be less grand. From Thomas we can learn more than the Scholastic method. In his great effort, we see that faith need not be a substitute for philosophical rigor. We see that in spite of the confusions and problems in his arguments, it is still preferable to balance faith with reason rather than to believe not in humility but in ignorance.

The logical and theoretical questions Thomas faced still confront basic Christian doctrine. Questions about ultimate causes remain beyond the scope of science, but they do not disappear just because scientists cannot answer them. In Thomas Aquinas we encounter a rare, magnificent attempt to blend faith, reason, and experience into wisdom. If so comprehensive a system is no longer possible, it does not follow that no comprehensive vision is possible. The very effort to construct a consistent, coherent philosophy may be worth more than any risk to our faith in science or religion.

Thomas squarely faced the tension between reason and faith and, without abandoning either, gave faith his ultimate allegiance. The next major figure in the history of philosophy, René Descartes, faced the same tension but gave himself to reason. In so doing, he ushered in the modern era.

> *Religions are the great fairy-tales of the conscience.*
> — George Santayana

Summary of Main Points

- Augustine's efforts to synthesize early Christian theology with his own understanding of Greek philosophy and Manichean dualism anticipate major philosophical and theological ideas concerning doubt and certainty, the divided self, consciousness, time, free will and God's foreknowledge of history, and the philosophy of history.

- Augustine rejected Epicureanism and Stoicism for placing too much value on human reason and will. According to Augustine, reason is powerless and perverse without a will grounded in grace, love, and proper longing. For Augustine, faith alone makes understanding possible; faith is a necessary condition for productive philosophical inquiry.

- Scholastic philosophy was a product of a hierarchical society based on a God-centered view of the universe. Scholastic philosophy developed out of efforts to reconcile Aristotle's naturalism with the increasingly complex theological problems that developed when it became clear the Second Coming of Christ might not occur for generations.

- Scholastic philosophy rested on logical and linguistic analysis of texts and arguments for the ultimate purpose of producing a systematic statement and defense of Christian beliefs. The reconciliation of faith and reason was based, in part, on the law of contradiction: No statement can be both true and false at the same time and under the same conditions.

- Thomas Aquinas introduced new levels of thoroughness, scholarship, and methodical rigor to philosophy in the form of his massive summaries known as *summae*. Thomas's efforts to prove the existence of God using the Five Ways are among the most widely studied examples of Scholastic thinking. The Five Ways are the argument from motion, the cosmological argument, the argument from necessity, the argument from gradation, and the argument from design.

- Thomas's logic relies on two principles: The principle of sufficient reason is the idea that nothing happens without a reason, that no *adequate* theory or explanation can contain any brute, crude, unexplained facts. The principle of plenitude is the metaphysical principle that given infinity and the richness of the universe, any real possibility must occur—at least once.

- The problem of evil derives from the apparently inescapable conclusion either that God cannot prevent evil, and is therefore not all-powerful, or that God will not prevent evil, and is therefore not all-good. Thomas answers the problem of evil from two directions: First, he argues that evil is not a positive thing, but a lack of goodness. Hence, it cannot come from God. Second, Thomas returns to the importance of love, asserting that God created the universe in order to multiply His love. Because love cannot be forced, it always requires freedom of choice. Genuine freedom of choice includes the real possibility of evil. God does not will evil; He wills freedom and love.

Post-Reading Reflections

Now that you've had a chance to learn about the Scholar, use your new knowledge to answer these questions.

1. Compare and contrast the classical worldview with the medieval.

2. What basic conditions led to the development of Christian philosophy? Where did the need for interpretation come from?

3. In your own words, describe the chief characteristics of Scholastic scholarship.

4. In what ways is the medieval scholar the forerunner of the modern professor?

5. Which of the Five Ways do you think is the weakest? Explain why.

6. Which of the Five Ways do you think is the most convincing? Explain why.

7. In general terms, compare and contrast scientific attempts to explain the origin of the universe with theological or philosophical ones.

8. What is evil, according to Thomas?

9. According to Thomas, what is the relationship of free will to love?

 MindTap

Experience MindTap through the activities highlighted in this chapter. Further explore this online, personalized learning tool to deepen your comprehension and improve your grades.

Overview of Modern Themes

Good sense is of all things in the world the most equally distributed . . . is by nature equal in all men.

— *René Descartes*

'Tis not contrary to reason to prefer the destruction of the whole world to the scratching of my finger.

— *David Hume*

Learning Objectives

After you complete this overview, you should be able to:

- Utilize the concept of authority to contrast the medieval worldview with the modern worldview.

- Describe Martin Luther's role in the Reformation.

- Describe the cultural significance of Luther's claim that every believer is a priest.

- Describe the philosophical significance of the grounds upon which Nicolaus Copernicus challenged the geocentric worldview.

- Compare the strengths and weaknesses of a God-centered worldview with the strengths and weaknesses of an individual-centered worldview.

Sapere aude!—Dare to reason! Have the courage to use your own minds!— is the motto of the enlightenment. . . . If I have a book which understands for me, a pastor who has a conscience for me, a doctor who decides my diet, I need not trouble myself. If I am willing to pay, I need not think. Others will do it for me.

— *Immanuel Kant*

IT IS GENERALLY AGREED that the modern era, also known as the *Enlightenment* or the Age of Reason, began in the first half of the seventeenth century with the publication of two seminal texts: Sir Francis Bacon's *Novum Organum* (1620) and René Descartes's *Discourse on Method* (1637). This does not mean that Bacon and Descartes—by themselves—created a new philosophical era. Their ideas were, of course, reactions and responses to the ideas of both earlier and contemporary writers and thinkers.

In the realm of philosophy, Descartes challenged and ultimately rejected the cumbersome and complex disputations and speculations of Scholastic philosophy in favor of his own simpler, more "natural" appeals to "common reason"—written in ordinary French rather than in scholarly and obscure Latin. Our look at the origins of modern philosophy includes Descartes (Chapter 9), David Hume (Chapter 10), and Immanuel Kant (Chapter 11).

Reason, Reformation, and Revolution

Together, what we now refer to as the *Reformation* and the *Copernican Revolution* signaled a major shift away from the medieval worldview, with its organic emphasis on a God-centered, Earth-centered universe in which everything had an allotted place in a fixed hierarchy. The modern worldview, in stark contrast, moved Earth from the center of the universe and put the reasoning *individual* at the forefront of philosophy. Objective and methodical reason replaced faith as the path to truth.

In the medieval worldview, everything was understood in terms of its place in the whole scheme of things. God ruled the universe, the pope ruled the church, the king ruled the state, and so on down through lords, merchants, craftsmen, and serfs. In such a worldview, social order was transformed into a divine purpose that was reflected in a hierarchy of authority that permeated the entire universe. Throughout the Middle Ages, most Europeans accepted that this hierarchy came from God—and therefore accepted the authority of God's church and pope as legitimate.

The Reformation

By the fourteenth century, the authority of the Roman Catholic Church and of the pope had eroded. The credibility of the papacy was severely damaged by a series of disputes and scandals as popes began to keep church offerings for their own use and to sell offices and ecclesiastical titles. These abuses led to cries for reform.

What is known today as the Protestant Reformation began in Germany on October 31, 1517, when **Martin Luther** (1483–1546), a Roman Catholic Augustinian monk and professor at the University of Wittenberg, nailed ninety-five theses (criticisms of church teachings and practices) to the church door. The papacy viewed this as a gesture of rebellion rather than a call for debate and labeled Luther a heretic. Luther persisted, and in 1520 he published three significant treatises: *An Open Letter to*

Portrait of Martin Luther as an Augustinian Monk, c.1623-24 (oil on vellum on panel), Cranach, Lucas, the Elder (1472-1553)/Germanisches Nationalmuseum, Nuremberg, Germany/The Bridgeman Art Library

North Wind/North Wind Picture Archives

Martin Luther took advantage of the invention of the printing press to advocate that scripture be read in local vernacular languages like German and English rather than Latin.

the Christian Nobility of the German Nation Concerning the Reform of the Christian Estate, The Babylonian Captivity of the Church, and *A Treatise on Christian Liberty*.

On April 18, 1521, Luther stood before the Holy Roman Emperor Charles V and an assembly of German nobility at the Diet at Worms. Luther refused to recant unless he could be proven wrong by the Bible *or by clear reason*. Luther's bold words of refusal to bow to institutional or civic authority in matters of truth still ring: "Here I stand; I can do no other." Although Luther and his ideas generated popular support, he was formally excommunicated in 1521.

Church authorities realized Luther's ideas and actions constituted a public challenge to the entire medieval and Scholastic worldview. By asserting that the individual's channel to God was "justification by faith" rather than by "works" (that is, living a good life in accord with the teachings of the church), Luther made the individual believer his or her own authority.

In addition to rejecting "works," Luther rejected the sacraments of the Eucharist (the transubstantiation of bread and wine into Christ's body and blood) and confession of one's sins to a priest—two important Catholic practices that made the institutionalized church an essential part of salvation. Moreover, if, as Luther claimed, the institution and *authority* of a church are unnecessary, then "every believer is a priest." Despite having been labeled a heretic, Luther had enough political support in Germany that the church was reluctant to use force against him. He went on to establish his own church—which, ironically, very quickly institutionalized its own rigid requirements and began ejecting heretics.

The Bancroft Library, University of California at Berkeley

This illustration from Martin Luther's Bible shows God as the orderer of the Ptolemaic universe. So convinced was Luther of the accuracy of this picture of the heavens that he called Copernicus "that fool [who would] reverse the entire art of astronomy. . . . Joshua bade the sun and not the earth to stand still."

The philosophical significance of Luther's move lay in its implication that individual experience and interpretation are more truly Christian than unquestioning acceptance of an official, authoritative position. Luther's revolt against institutionalized authority is one of the major markers of the decline of the medieval worldview.

As doubts grew about the legitimacy or necessity of an authoritarian, institutionalized church hierarchy, reliance on individual reasoning and experience increased. And since the reach of the medieval church extended into the teachings and practices of science, challenges to authoritarian and archaic science paralleled challenges to theology.

The Copernican Revolution

In the Middle Ages, it was commonly believed that the universe was carefully created by a God of harmony and design and that human beings were the very purpose of creation. The heavens themselves, so it was believed, reflected this: God made the sun and moon to shine upon *us* and placed Earth so that the rest of the universe revolved around *us*. As part of this divine harmony, the natural (physical) world was also thought to reflect spiritual order.

This *geocentric* worldview, with Earth at the center of the universe, can be both comforting and reassuring: If the universe physically manifests a sense of divine order and purpose, then each of us is assured that we "belong" where we are, socially and geographically. The universe is our neighborhood, and Earth is "home"; the universe is not a cosmic accident of such immensity that it lacks a fixed center and reduces the entire Earth to less than a speck.

But as it became clearer and more widely known that Earth is a sphere, with no fixed up or down, the old worldview began to totter. Once Luther's contemporary Nicolaus Copernicus mapped the heavens, it toppled.

Some ancient Greek astronomers—in particular, the philosopher Aristarchus of Samos (third century B.C.E.)—had concluded that Earth revolves around the sun. Most of Aristarchus's writings were lost, however, and later astronomers rejected his ideas, partly because they seemed contrary to common experience and partly because they conflicted with Aristotle's teachings. Aristotle believed that Earth was the unmoving center of the universe and that the sun, moon, and planets moved in semiregular "epicycles" around it. Ptolemy, an astronomer of the second century C.E., gave Aristotle's ideas even more weight by designing a mathematical model that seemed to predict planetary motions quite well.

By the fifteenth century, however, calculations using the Ptolemaic model no longer matched the observed positions of the planets. This inspired the Polish astronomer **Nicolaus Copernicus** (1473–1543) to look for a more accurate model. His proposal that the sun is the center of the solar system set in motion a revolution in thinking. He made his case in such a way that knowledgeable astronomers realized the entire Ptolemaic model had to be revised.

Copernican astronomy directly refuted Aristotle, who believed that Earth was the center of the universe. Because Thomas Aquinas and the church were so closely tied to Aristotelian philosophy and science, any major threat to Aristotle threatened church authority. If the church—guided by God— was in error here, where else might it be in error? Copernicus was sensitive enough to the church's attitude toward criticism

As Copernicus's ideas spread, so did doubts about the significance of human beings living on one planet among many in a vast solar system.

Imagno/Hulton Archive/Getty Images

and unofficial doctrines that he withheld publication of his discoveries until shortly before he died.

Once Copernicus's work was known, Earth was "cut loose" from its central place of honor, both physically and psychologically, and became just one more planet revolving around the sun. If Earth was reduced in significance, what about humans? This major change in perspective did not *feel right* to either Catholic or Protestant theologians. Thus, Martin Luther called Copernicus "that fool [who would] reverse the entire art of astronomy.... Joshua bade *the sun* and not the earth to stand still."[1]

Luther's opinion notwithstanding, Copernicus was no fool. Although the details of his model were inaccurate (for instance, he thought Earth's path around the sun was a circle, but it really is an ellipse), his hypothesis that Earth is part of a sun-centered system was correct. Copernicus developed this hypothesis by applying careful calculations to careful observations. The danger in his position can be clearly observed if we speak bluntly: Copernicus rendered both church authority and the consensus of unqualified nonastronomers irrelevant. His careful application of reason and observation began revolutions in both astronomy and philosophical thought.

Where Are We Then?

The struggle for authority, for the right to determine truth, between the church and science that began in the early Enlightenment continued until God was reduced to the role of spectator. Faith in God was replaced by faith in the orderly discovery of laws of nature and in the power of human reason to ensure continuous progress and improvement of the human condition.

It was taken for granted that the scientific method could and would unlock all the mysteries of the universe. Given the wealth of scientific discoveries in physics, optics, astronomy, biology, and so on, it was but a simple step to conclude that God (if there is a God) has created a universe of such regularity and order that He no longer need bother running it. Further, having imbued us with reason, God has no need to govern or rescue us.

For almost three centuries, many "enlightened" thinkers remained convinced that, with the exception of "idiots," people possessed an innate, virtually equal capacity for rational thinking that could be nurtured, developed, and tapped to produce progressively better lives for each generation. Out of this optimism emerged modern anti-authoritarian democratic principles, founded on unalienable "natural rights" and rational self-interest.

You might recognize this optimistic faith in science and rational self-interest as a fundamental element of American thinking. Indeed, the framers of our Constitution were children of the Enlightenment who believed that science and universal reason would combine to produce a rational, free, ever-progressing society.

A major task of the Enlightenment was to start anew—just like America, just like each new wave of immigrants—and to use reason to accomplish a kind of individual and cultural *rebirth*, uncluttered by past superstitions and unprovable beliefs, to create a "new world" based on objective, universal knowledge.

9

The Rationalist
René Descartes

But what then am I?
A thing which thinks.
— *René Descartes*

Learning Objectives

After you complete this chapter, you should be able to:

- Describe the problem of authority that triggered the emergence of modern philosophy.

- Define *rationalism*.

- Define the *coherence theory of truth*.

- Give an example of an innate idea.

- Differentiate between *a priori* and *a posteriori* knowledge.

- Critique the ontological argument.

- Apply René Descartes's clear and distinct standard of truth to his own idea of God.

- Define *materialism*.

- Explain how Cartesian dualism generates the mind–body problem.

- Summarize Susan Bordo's critique of Cartesian rationalism.

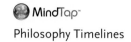

Philosophy Timelines

BY THE SEVENTEENTH CENTURY, developments in modern science, combined with a decline in the authority of a single (Roman Catholic) church, signaled the end of the medieval era and the beginning of what we now refer to as the modern worldview. In philosophy, the result of these changes was a shift away from metaphysics toward epistemology.

As remarkable as it may seem, René Descartes was the first philosopher to study the *process of thinking* itself. In so doing, he began what philosophers refer to as the *epistemological turn*, a major transformation in the character of philosophy that would ultimately require a century and a half to complete, culminating with Immanuel Kant's *Critique of Pure Reason* (Chapter 11).

Whereas earlier philosophers sought knowledge about the good life, nature, the soul, God, the ideal society, and so forth, from Descartes forward, modern philosophers increasingly devoted themselves to acquiring knowledge about knowledge. The power of Descartes's original insight becomes clear once it is articulated: *Before we can reasonably evaluate any beliefs about reality, we must inquire into the nature of the "instrument" we use to observe it.*

The Problem of Authority

Modern philosophy emphasizes methodology, technique, and personal, social, and historical *detachment*. Its origins lie in the decline of a stable social order, the loss of central authority by the Roman Catholic Church, and the proliferation of scientific advances. More sophisticated mathematics and improved scientific instruments had resulted in discoveries that challenged and contradicted Aristotelian naturalism. Scientists were able to move beyond metaphysical speculations to careful observations. No authority—religious or political—could refute what the individual observer *saw* or the individual mind *calculated* for itself.

Descartes was a Catholic, but his argument that each individual possesses the "natural light of reason" and needs no intervening authority to interpret "the great book of the world" may remind you of Luther's claim that each person can go directly to God, without the church as an intermediary. In other words, Descartes, like Luther, set aside the so-called accumulated wisdom of the past, insisting that each person must examine what is true and false afresh.

Descartes's scientific interests led him to observe and experiment for himself, and he soon discovered that Aristotle's authoritative writings on nature contained many errors:

> But so soon as I had achieved the entire course of study at the close of which one is usually received into the ranks of the learned,...I found myself embarrassed with so many doubts and errors that it seemed to me that the effort to instruct myself had no effect other than the increasing discovery of my own ignorance. And yet I was studying at one of the most celebrated schools in Europe.[1]

In Descartes's time, the distinction between science and philosophy was not clear. His interests and abilities in philosophy, mathematics, and science made this confusion especially intolerable to him. He expected scientific claims to be provable by appeals to observation and clear thinking. So he made a radical proposal: Let's start fresh, throwing out everything we think we know, and build a system of knowledge based entirely on ideas whose truth can be clearly and distinctly known—to us, firsthand.

René Descartes: The Solitary Intellect

René Descartes (1596–1650) was born into an old and respected family in the French province of Touraine. His mother died of tuberculosis a year after his birth, and Descartes believed he inherited a frail constitution from her. His father was a famous lawyer, whose career kept him away from home for months at a time.

René Descartes

When he was approximately nine years old, Descartes was sent to the Jesuit college at La Flèche, where his physical weakness and mental strength were both acknowledged, and he was allowed to sleep later than the other students (a lifelong habit). At La Flèche, Descartes studied Greek, Latin, history, liberal arts, science, mathematics, and philosophy, in addition to music, dancing, and fencing.

After completing his studies at La Flèche, Descartes spent the next few years living the life of the young gentleman he was. He practiced fencing, rode horses, and—already in love with mathematics—briefly took up gambling to see if he could devise a system to break the bank. At the University of Poitiers, he earned degrees in civil and canon law.

In 1618, when Descartes was twenty-two years old, the Thirty Years' War broke out. To the surprise of his friends, a strong, healthy Descartes enlisted in the army of the Prince of Nassau and later joined the army of the Duke of Bavaria. It is not clear whether he ever saw combat.

On November 10, 1619, Descartes had a revelation that transformed him and ultimately changed the direction of Western philosophy. As he later wrote, "I remained the whole day shut up alone in a stove-heated room, where I had complete leisure to occupy my thoughts."[2] There, Descartes says, he "discovered the foundations of a wonderful new science." The next night, full of excitement and anticipation over his discovery, he had three dreams, in one of which he heard a clap of thunder. He took it to be "the Spirit of Truth descending to take possession" of him. Descartes believed he had been divinely encouraged to establish a universal method of reasoning, based on mathematical principles, which, if followed carefully enough, would guarantee the absolutely certain truth of its results.

After this remarkable experience, Descartes's outward life seemed little changed. His inheritance, first from his mother and then from his father, had freed him from the need to make a living, so he traveled, studied, conversed, and wrote. He lived alone most of his life, except for his servants, and during a twenty-year period lived in twenty different houses.

Solitary and secretive, Descartes preferred to avoid the distractions and commotion of city life and social involvements. Most of his philosophical discourse took the form of letters. There were times when he didn't want his friends to know where he was; he even asked them not to write to him for a while. Descartes thought he worked better this way, completely free to devote all his energy, at his own pace, to his

As soon as age permitted me to emerge from the control of my tutors, I quitted the study of letters... resolving to seek no other science than that which could be found in myself, or at least in the great book of the world.

—René Descartes

> *Descartes'*
> *metaphysics, as he so*
> *clearly sees himself, is*
> *the natural product of*
> *a precious ingredient*
> *of the past which*
> *today is in danger of*
> *rapid extinction—*
> *privacy—that*
> *marvelous compound*
> *of withdrawal,*
> *self-reliance,*
> *quiet, solitude,*
> *contemplation, and*
> *concentration which*
> *seems the exclusive*
> *possession of a bygone*
> *age.*
> — A. W. Levi

studies. In a letter to a friend, Descartes wrote from Amsterdam: "And thus in this large city where I now am, since I seem to be practically the only one here who is not a merchant or in trade; all are so bound up in their profitable business transactions that I could remain here my entire life without being noticed by anyone."[3] Living this way, Descartes was able to study philosophy, geometry, physics, optics, circulation, and other subjects. Conducting experiments and dissections, as well as making important discoveries in mathematics, he rejected the Scholastic model of science and philosophy, turning instead to firsthand observations and deductions.

In 1635, Descartes had an illegitimate daughter (who died at the age of five) with a servant girl. Later, he referred to the episode as "a dangerous commitment" from which he had "extricated" himself. He was not entirely immune to the charms of women, however. He had a close six-year correspondence with Princess Elizabeth, daughter of the dethroned queen of Bohemia. When she was nineteen, the princess read his *Discourse on Method* and was surprised and delighted to discover philosophy written in clear, everyday language.

Through a friend who had become the French ambassador to the court of Queen Christina of Sweden, Descartes was ultimately convinced in September 1649—against his better judgment—to join her court in Stockholm. He was not happy there. He had little time for his experiments, and the queen forced him to break his lifelong habits of sleeping late and working at leisure—she wanted to be tutored in philosophy at five in the morning! This forceful woman even managed to get Descartes to write a ballet. The cold weather and austere conditions weakened his already frail health. By the end of January 1650, he was ill with pneumonia. He died February 11, two months before his fifty-fourth birthday.

René Descartes stands not only as the father of modern philosophy but also as the original archetype of the modern rationalist: He boldly relied on the disciplined use of his own reason; he refused to accept as true anything that did not square with what he had personally verified as true; he exalted the thinking, conscious self as the foundation of all certainty.

Rationalism

rationalism
An epistemological position in which reason is said to be the primary source of all knowledge, superior to sense evidence. Rationalists argue that only reason can distinguish reality from illusion and give meaning to experience.

Rationalism is an epistemological position in which reason is said to be the primary source of all knowledge, superior to sense evidence. Rationalists argue that only reason can distinguish reality from illusion and give meaning to experience.

In general, rationalists believe that abstract reasoning can produce undeniable, absolutely certain truths about nature, existence, and the whole of reality. Many of these ultimate truths can be discovered without observation, experiment, or even experience. These are called *a priori* **ideas** or, sometimes, **innate ideas**. Thus, to the rationalists, reason—not empirical observation—is the ultimate test of truth.

According to the **coherence theory of truth**, new or unclear ideas are evaluated in terms of rational or logical consistency and in relation to already established truths. The ultimate criteria for basic, originating truths are clarity and distinctness. Once fundamental truths are established, the rationalist uses a deductive, mathematical/logical method to test and establish other, more complex ideas. True ideas are coherent (rationally consistent) with each other, and the rationalist's aim is to

Queen Christina of Sweden watches a demonstration by Descartes (standing at right).

achieve absolute certainty of the sort possible in mathematics. "My method," said Descartes, "contains everything which gives certainty to the rules of arithmetic."

The coherence theory of truth is in direct opposition to the correspondence theory of truth (Chapter 10) and differs from the other major theory of truth, the pragmatic theory of meaning (Chapter 15).

Against Disorganized Thinking

Descartes's first philosophical work was *Rules for the Direction of the Mind*. The twenty-one principles contained in *Rules* reappear in Descartes's major philosophical works, *Discourse on Method* and *Meditations on First Philosophy*.

Rule 3 advises: *Once we have chosen a subject to study, we should confine ourselves to what we can clearly intuit and deduce with certainty for ourselves.* We must not rely on what others have thought or on our own as-yet-untested beliefs. We must look for ourselves, with new eyes and new understanding. Referring to the Scholastics, among others, Descartes cautions that "in a too absorbed study" of the works of earlier thinkers, we become "infected with their errors, guard against them as we may."

This is a general caution against authoritarian thinking, in which we give more weight to the opinions of others than to our own experience and clear thinking. When we accept views *solely* on the weight of the authority or prestige of those who hold them, or because of loyalty to a cause or belief structure, we become nonrational at best. We become memorizers, not thinkers.

a priori **ideas (innate ideas)**
Truths that are not derived from observation or experiment, characterized as being certain, deductive, universally true, and independent of all experience.

coherence theory of truth
A truth test in which new or unclear ideas are evaluated in terms of rational or logical consistency and in relation to already established truths.

"Beyond Intellect There Is Yet Another Stage"

In 1091, the Persian philosopher **Abu Hamid Muhammad al-Ghazali** (1058–1111) was appointed professor of Islamic theology at the Nizamiyah College in Baghdad. In 1095, al-Ghazali, by then a man of great influence, suffered a spiritual crisis and nervous breakdown that resulted in a speech impediment that prevented him from lecturing. He left the college and ultimately embraced a mystical form of Islam known as *sufism*. Al-Ghazali briefly returned to teaching but eventually quit for good and founded a monastic community in Tus, the city of his birth.

The passage that follows is from his work *The Deliverance from Error*. Note how al-Ghazali's work anticipates Descartes's first meditation by five hundred years. Whereas Descartes exalted reason over faith, al-Ghazali "transcended" reason with the mystic's direct and immediate experience of God (Allah).

To thirst after a comprehension of things as they really are was my habit and custom from a very early age....as I drew near the age of adolescence the bonds of mere authority...ceased to hold me and inherited beliefs lost their grip upon me, for I saw that Christian youths always grew up to be Christians, Jewish youths to be Jews and Muslim youths to be Muslim....

I therefore said within myself: "To begin with, what I am looking for is knowledge of what things really are, so I must undoubtedly try to find what knowledge really is." It was plain to me that sure and certain knowledge is that knowledge in which the object is disclosed in such a fashion that no doubt remains along with it, that no possibility of error or illusion accompanies it, and that the mind cannot even entertain such a supposition. Certain knowledge must also be infallible....Thus, I know that ten is more than three. Let us suppose that someone says to me: "No, three is more than ten, and in proof of that I shall change this rod into a serpent": and let us suppose that he actually changes the rod into a serpent and that I witness him doing so. No doubts about what I know are raised in me because of this. The only result is that I wonder how he is able to produce this change. Of doubt about my knowledge there is no trace.

After these reflections I knew that whatever I did not know in this fashion and with this mode of certainty is not reliable and infallible knowledge; and knowledge that is not infallible is not certain knowledge....

Thereupon I investigated the various kinds of knowledge I had, and found myself destitute of all knowledge with this characteristic of infallibility except in the case of sense-perception and necessary truths....

I proceeded therefore with extreme earnestness to reflect on sense-perception and on necessary truths, to see whether I could make myself doubt them. The outcome of this protracted effort was that I could no longer trust sense-perception either....

..."Do you not see," [my ego] said, "how, when you are asleep, you believe things and imagine circumstances, holding them to be stable and enduring, and, so long as you are in that dream-condition, have no doubts about them?...Why then are you confident that all your waking beliefs, whether from sense or intellect, are genuine? They are true in respect of your present state; but it is possible that a state will come upon you whose relation to your waking consciousness is analogous to the relation of the latter to dreaming. In comparison with this state your waking consciousness would be like dreaming! When you are in this state, you will be certain that all the suppositions of your intellect are empty imaginings...."

It became clear to me...that what is most distinctive about mysticism is something which cannot be apprehended by study, but only by immediate experience...by ecstasy and by a moral change. What difference between *knowing* the definition of health and satiety...and *being* healthy and satisfied!...

Beyond intellect there is yet another stage. In this another *eye* is opened, by which he beholds the unseen, what is to be the future, and other things which are beyond the ken of intellect.

Abu Hamid Muhammad al-Ghazali, *The Deliverance from Error, in The Faith and Practice of Al-Ghazali*, trans. W. Montgomery Watt (London: George Allen and Unwin, 1953), pp. 21–68.

Descartes points out that it is common to overlook clear, simple truths (intuitions) when we do encounter them. We quickly complicate them with cloudy but elaborate "explanations." He speculates that we surround the truth with ambiguities because we are afraid that the simplicity of our discoveries will make them seem unimportant. He adds:

> For we shall not, e.g., turn out to be mathematicians though we know by heart all the proofs others have elaborated, unless we have an intellectual talent that fits us to resolve difficulties of any kind. Neither, though we may have mastered all the arguments of Plato and Aristotle, if yet we have not the capacity for passing solid judgment on these matters, shall we become Philosophers; we should have acquired the knowledge not of a science, but of history.[4]

PHILOSOPHICAL QUERY

Use Descartes's distinction between memorizing ideas and understanding them to examine your own education. Describe the distinction between learning to love psychology or literature and becoming a *historian* of psychology or literature, in Descartes's terms. Speculate on ways this distinction might be used to reform education.

Addressing the fact that we are bombarded with conflicting knowledge claims, Rule 4 succinctly states: *There is need of a method for finding the truth.*

> So blind is the curiosity by which mortals are possessed, that they often conduct their minds along unexplored routes, having no reason to hope for success.... it were far better never to think of investigating truth at all, than to do so without a method. For it is very certain that unregulated inquiries and confused reflections of this kind only confound the natural light and blind our mental powers.... In [method] alone lies the sum of all human endeavour, and he who would approach the investigation of truth must hold to this rule.[5]

For Deeper Consideration

Descartes says that "it were far better never to think of investigating the truth at all, than to do so without a method." Why was he so troubled by disorganized thinking and blind curiosity? What do you think he might say to us about basing our opinions regarding climate change, creation versus evolution, gun control, sexual identity, balancing the federal budget, the Constitution, and other controversial matters on what we "learn" from movies, TV, the Internet, bloggers, politicians, and even our professors? What methods do you use to choose among competing "experts" and positions? Is Descartes suggesting that we must become experts in choosing experts? Or is he arguing for something else entirely, and if so, what and why?

I shall not say anything about Philosophy, but that, seeing that it has been cultivated for many centuries by the best minds that have ever lived, and that nevertheless no single thing is to be found in it which is not the subject of dispute, and in consequence which is not dubious.

— René Descartes

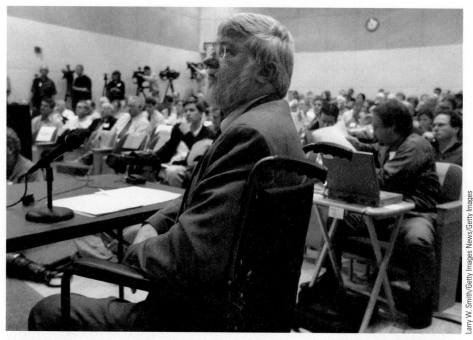

A scientist with a Ph.D. in physical chemistry is questioned by the members of the Kansas State Board of Education about teaching evolution. What expertise is required to evaluate his claims?

In order to reach a wider audience of European intellectuals, Descartes wrote in everyday French rather than in Latin, the "universal language of scholars."

The Method of Doubt

Descartes believed that a mathematically precise method is the only reliable way to discover the truth about the universe. He proposed to use the new spirit of scientific inquiry and mathematical rigor to reexamine everything! His effort not only marks the beginning of an entirely new philosophical orientation but also remains fascinating and relevant.

Descartes attacked earlier philosophy on the grounds that it did not demand rational comprehension from the individual intellect. It did not rest *solely* on ideas known through "the clear light of natural reason":

> I thought that the sciences found in books—and those at least whose reasonings are only probable and which have no demonstrations, composed as they are of the gradually accumulated opinions of many different individuals—do not approach so near to the truth as the simple reasoning which a man of common sense can quite naturally carry out respecting the things which come immediately before him.[6]

"Common sense," which Descartes also referred to as *natural reason*, is the ability to think that is found in all normal humans. It does not depend on divine revelation or formal education—at least according to Descartes. Though not everyone has the talent for or interest in refined thinking, Descartes believed all reasoning individuals could apply his method to basic questions concerning human nature, truth, and the existence of God:

> Good sense is of all things in the world the most equally distributed, for everybody thinks himself so abundantly provided with it, that even those most difficult to please in all other matters do not commonly desire more of it than they already possess. It is unlikely that this is an error on their part; it seems rather to be evidence in support of the view that the power of forming a good judgment and of distinguishing the true from the false, which is properly speaking what is called Good Sense or Reason, is by nature equal in all men. Hence too it will show that the diversity of our opinions does not proceed from some men being more rational than others, but solely from the fact that our thoughts pass through diverse channels and the same objects are not considered by all. For to be possessed of good mental powers is not sufficient; the principal matter is to apply them well. The greatest minds are capable of the greatest vices as well as of the greatest virtues, and those who proceed very slowly may, provided they always follow the straight road, really advance much faster than those who, though they run, forsake it.[7]

PHILOSOPHICAL QUERY

Comment on the preceding passage. Do you agree with Descartes? Why? Is common sense the same thing as good sense? Analyze the notion of common sense. Do you really think there is such a thing? What is your evidence either way?

The Cartesian "I" and Methodic Doubt

Descartes did not write in Latin, the "universal language of scholars," but in everyday French. His aim was to reach beyond the confines of the university and church to a wider audience of European intellectuals. Consequently, Descartes cast all his works in the first person to describe both his *conclusions* and his *thinking process*. He wanted to call our attention to the actively reasoning mind itself. Until Descartes, philosophers tended to focus on the content of ideas and on their logical relations to each other, not on the mind. Although "reason" was discussed and referred to, and often cited as the guide by which we should live, the "reasoning thing" itself was not directly studied.

As you study Descartes's ideas, don't always interpret the "I" as referring to Descartes; allow it also to refer to you while you are reading (and, I hope, thinking along with) the words Descartes wrote. By occasionally becoming the "I" yourself, you can participate in the *conscious flow* of Descartes's reasoning in a way that will help you evaluate his arguments as if they were your own. You will be reflecting and meditating on your own conscious mind.

Descartes was convinced that he could apply a mathematically oriented method to the most fundamental problem of all: How can I know that I know anything? In geometry, he pointed out, we begin with self-evident truths such as "A straight line is the shortest distance between two points." More complex theorems based on these truths are then called upon to prove less-evident truths. Descartes proposed

For those who like a dramatic and specific date, the simple but far-reaching phrase of Descartes, "I think, therefore I am" will do very well for the beginning [of the Age of Reason]: 1657.
—Crane Brinton

applying this basic method to philosophy. In his *Rules*, he stated that *we must not accept anything we can doubt at all.*

In his effort to base his philosophy on an absolutely certain foundation, Descartes had a culture-altering insight. He discovered **methodic doubt**. Simply put, *methodic doubt involves deliberately doubting everything it is possible to doubt in the least degree. Whatever remains will be known with absolute certainty.* In order to apply methodic doubt, Descartes had to rely on a standard of truth that could tell him whether it was reasonable to doubt something.

methodic doubt
A cartesian strategy of deliberately doubting everything it is possible to doubt in the least degree so that what remains will be known with absolute certainty.

Standard of Truth

No matter what method we employ in a search for truth, we must have some criterion for distinguishing truth from falsity. Descartes proposed that we "might assume as a general rule that the things which we conceive very clearly and distinctly are all true." He defined *clear* as "that which is present and apparent to an attentive mind" and *distinct* as "that which is so precise and different from all other objects that it contains within itself nothing but what is clear." We might say that for Descartes, knowledge requires precision and detail.

Throughout his philosophical writings, Descartes appeals to clear and distinct knowing as the ultimate standard to be used in accepting or rejecting ideas. To produce the most certain conclusions possible, he rejected *anything* he did not know "clearly and distinctly." He also believed that certain very basic propositions *need only to be understood* to be recognized as true. To understand something clearly and distinctly, according to Descartes, is a matter of perceiving that there are no reasonable grounds on which it can be doubted. In other words, *to recognize something clearly and distinctly is to know that it is true.*

Some philosophers are troubled by Descartes's standard of truth. They claim that *the standard itself is* ambiguous and subjective and thus cannot be known with clarity and distinctness. They accuse Descartes of basing his rationalism on the subjective states of the perceiver; they interpret this to mean that, in spite of his talk about reason, Descartes actually bases much of his philosophy on his feelings and moods. Their point is that "clear and distinct" vary from individual to individual; I might be convinced I know something clearly and distinctly and still be wrong about it.

PHILOSOPHICAL QUERY

A common criticism of Descartes's standard of truth is that he failed to apply it to itself. *Do we know with clarity and distinctness that only what we know with clarity and distinctness is true?* Can we know it? Not if, as critics claim, Descartes's standard is itself unclear and ambiguous. Do you have a clear and distinct idea of Descartes's criterion? How can we tell when an inability to perceive something clearly and distinctly is the fault of the individual or of the quality of the idea?

Innate Ideas

As you wrestle with these issues, keep in mind that getting started is the most difficult part of establishing a new or original philosophical orientation. We must begin with initially unquestioned assumptions and basic principles. To a certain extent, some ideas must be known before we can know anything else. These ideas must be first or occur *prior* to knowing everything else. *A priori* ideas are characterized as being certain, deductive, universally true, innate, or independent of all experience. *A priori* knowledge is derived from reason without reference to sense experience. Truths of reason and laws of logic are usually thought to be *a priori*. Examples include "All triangles contain 180°" and "Every event has a cause."

In contrast to *a priori* knowledge, *a posteriori* knowledge is empirical knowledge derived from sense experience. This kind of knowing comes from the accumulation of experience. It is not regarded as certain or necessary, because the conditions under which it is acquired change, perceivers vary, and factual relationships change. For example, the statement "My shirt is white" can be true for a particular set of circumstances today and false tomorrow. "My shirt is white" is not universally or eternally true in the way that "Every event has a cause" is. *A posteriori* truths are also called factual truths or truths of fact, as opposed to rational truths. (Not all philosophers agree that *a priori* truths exist. For example, the empiricists, whom we will meet in Chapter 10, insist that all knowledge comes from sense experience.)

As a brilliant geometer, Descartes was familiar with the axioms for geometric proofs, which he characterized as *a priori* ideas. He believed we are born with certain ideas "implanted" in us by God. For example, we are born with the idea of a triangle in our minds. When we see triangles or triangular-shaped objects, we are reminded of this innate idea. Descartes often appeals to the standard of clarity and distinctness as if its truth should be obvious to us with a bit of reflection. All we need is to be "reminded" of it to recognize its truth.

a priori knowledge
Knowledge derived from reason without reference to sense experience. Examples include "Alltriangles contain 180°" and "Every event has a cause."

a posteriori knowledge
Empirical knowledge derived from sense experience and not regarded as universal because the conditions under which it is acquired change, perceivers vary, and factual relationships change.

PHILOSOPHICAL QUERY

Is Descartes correct? What about seemingly sincere, rational, and intelligent people who say they do not, perhaps cannot, see the truth of this idea about innate ideas? Compare Descartes's problem here with Plato's problem of accounting for ignorance of the Forms. Do you think Forms are innate ideas? Are innate ideas Forms? (See Chapter 5.)

The Cartesian Genesis

To summarize: Descartes wanted to find an absolutely certain, indubitable starting point for his philosophy. He chose a form of deliberate, methodological skepticism that we have labeled *methodic doubt*. As we will see from the work of David Hume (Chapter 10), there are degrees of skepticism, progressing from total doubt about everything to temporary or particular doubt invoked just for the process of analysis. Descartes's skepticism is part of his method and is, consequently, of the temporary—but still serious—sort. He does not really doubt everything he challenges in his *Meditations;* rather, systematically doubting is the *process* of Cartesian inquiry, not the end result. Descartes hoped to use skepticism to establish complete certainty.

Descartes' success is indicated by the extent to which the central notions of his philosophy became the common conception of man and the universe for nearly three centuries.

—Alexander Sesonske and Noel Fleming

> *Consciousness is a disease.*
> — Miguel de Unamuno

In the *Meditations*, Descartes begins by asking if it is rationally possible to doubt everything. He reasons that by doing this, he will quickly discover if there is any certain, undoubtable truth. In the course of this inquiry, Descartes tears down the old world of Scholastic philosophy, unquestioned beliefs, and ambiguous ideas and attempts to replace it with a brand-new, certain, clearly proved, rational order. He suggests that his readers reflect on one meditation a day, reading carefully and leisurely. After six days, Descartes, like God in the biblical book of Genesis, will have finished with his own creation. The attentive, rational reader, by becoming the Cartesian "I" in the manner noted earlier, will also have torn down and rebuilt his or her previously unquestioned house of beliefs on a solid, rational foundation.

Descartes begins the *Meditations* by giving his methodic doubt the widest possible scope. He calls Meditation I *Of the things which may be brought within the sphere of the doubtful*. In the first two paragraphs, Descartes invokes the skeptical method and introduces the standard of clarity and distinctness and immediately points out that it would be impossible to examine every belief he currently holds. Instead, he will examine the origins and foundations of basic kinds of beliefs. If there is *any* possibility, however remote, that they could be mistaken, Descartes will reject them and every idea that depends on them:

> It is now many years since I detected how many were the false beliefs that I had from my earliest youth admitted as true, and how doubtful was everything I had since constructed on this basis; and from that time I was convinced that I must once and for all seriously undertake to rid myself of all the opinions which I had formerly accepted, and commence to build anew from the foundation if I wanted to establish any firm and permanent structure in the sciences....
>
> Now for this object it is not necessary that I should show that all of these are false—I shall perhaps never arrive at this end. But inasmuch as reason already persuades me that I ought no less carefully to withhold my assent from matters which are not entirely certain and indubitable than from those which appear to be manifestly false, if I am able to find in each some reason to doubt, this will suffice to justify my rejecting the whole. And...owing to the fact that the destruction of the foundations of necessity brings with it the downfall of the rest of the edifice, I shall only in the first place attack those principles upon which all my former opinions rested.[8]

PHILOSOPHICAL QUERY

How carefully have you examined your own fundamental beliefs? What—if anything—is wrong with trusting beliefs handed down by others? Why not rely on the testing of others, trusting their conclusions? Also consider the widespread tendency to believe something if it could possibly be correct. What is the relationship between possible and plausible, and what might it have to do with this entire issue? Explain.

Maybe It's All a Dream?

Like most of us, prior to his investigations, Descartes had uncritically assumed that the most true and certain things known come from the senses. For example, it seems "obviously true" that my computer exists as I type this sentence, and it seems "obviously true" that the book you are reading exists. What could be more certain than simple, direct sensations and perceptions of our immediate environment?

Ah, but our senses sometimes deceive us. For example, we may think we are looking at an airplane and later discover that it is a bird. Witnesses to crimes disagree over descriptions of perpetrators, and we sometimes think we recognize the figure coming down the sidewalk, only to be wrong. Even so, aren't we always sure of immediate sensations? Though our senses may deceive us about distant events, there are many other things we know through our senses "as to which we cannot reasonably have any doubt." Descartes reflects:

> At the same time I must remember that I am a man, and that consequently I am in the habit of sleeping, and in my dreams representing to myself the same things or sometimes even less probable things, than those who are insane do in their waking moments. How often has it happened to me that in the night I dreamt that I found myself in this particular place, that I was dressed and seated near the fire, whilst in reality I was lying undressed in bed! At this moment it does indeed seem to me that it is with eyes awake that I am looking at this paper; that this head which I move is not asleep, that it is deliberately and of set purpose that I extend my hand and perceive it; what happens in sleep does not appear so clear and distinct as does all this. But in thinking over this I remind myself that on many occasions I have in sleep been deceived by similar illusions, and in dwelling carefully on this reflection I see so manifestly that there are no certain indications by which we may clearly distinguish wakefulness from sleep that I am lost in astonishment. And my astonishment is such that it is almost capable of persuading me that I now dream.[9]

With this example, Descartes rejects sense knowledge as a sufficient foundation for certainty. In so doing, he also rejects the primacy of the external, physical world because it is *possible* that the whole so-called real world is nothing but an elaborate mental construct, a hallucination. Remember, in the interest of constructing a flawless philosophy, Descartes is being ultracautious. He will not settle for degrees of probability, no matter how "virtually certain" they may be. Whether or not you consider it *probable* that your world is a dream, Descartes points out that it is at least *possible*.

But even if the world is a dream, it still has regularity and predictability, doesn't it? Maybe the world is just a dream implanted in the mind by God.

> *It seems to me that the greatest lesson of adult life is that one's own consciousness is not enough.*
> — Sir Fred Hoyle

PHILOSOPHICAL QUERY

How do we know the difference between a dream or hallucination and reality? Seriously consider how a confused person might verify that he or she is or is not dreaming.

The Evil Genius

Perhaps, like Descartes, you are having some trouble seriously doubting your experiences of the real world. Descartes says, "These ancient and commonly held opinions [that I am not dreaming] still revert frequently to my mind." To better test his most persistent beliefs, Descartes decides to allow himself deliberately "to be deceived, and for a certain time pretend that all these opinions are entirely false and imaginary." Descartes is in no danger of losing his bearings; this is still methodic doubt, not real confusion or delusion. He even says not to worry about giving in to too much doubt and distrust, since he is "not considering the question of action, but only of knowledge."

At this point, Descartes introduces one of the most intriguing figures in the history of philosophy, the *evil genius:*

> I shall then suppose, not that God who is supremely good and the fountain of truth, but some evil genius not less powerful than deceitful, has employed his whole energies in deceiving me; I shall consider that the heavens, the earth, colours, figures, sound, and all other external things are nought but the illusions and dreams of which this genius has availed himself in order to lay traps for my credulity; I shall consider myself as having no hands, no eyes, no flesh, no blood, nor any senses, yet falsely believing myself to possess all these things; I shall remain obstinately attached to this idea, and if by this means it is not in my power to arrive at the knowledge of any truth, I may at least do what is in my power [i.e., suspend my judgment], and with firm purpose avoid giving credence to any false thing, or being imposed upon by this arch deceiver, however powerful and deceptive he may be.[10]

This cold possibility of ultimate delusion concludes the first Meditation. Descartes has reduced his world to himself and one all-powerful, all-evil source of deception. He reasons that if he can find one anchor point of undoubtable certainty in the midst of the possibility of error in *all* quarters of his life, he will have found his unshakable foundation.

PHILOSOPHICAL QUERY

Before reading any further, stop for a moment and play with Descartes's idea of an evil genius. Try to get into the spirit of doubting as much as you can. Do not be limited by what you actually doubt; this is an intellectual exercise, not a personal confession. See if you can extend the range of what might on the remotest possibility be false or other than what you think it is. Can you be absolutely sure that there is no evil genius?

Cogito, Ergo Sum

Could the evil genius so arrange things that nothing is as I think it is? In the physical realm, he could. He could trick me into thinking that I have a body when I don't, that things have shapes, colors, and so on that they really don't. Descartes says that—as difficult as it is to imagine—he might even be able to deceive me regarding certain innate, *a priori*, ideas so that maybe 7 + 5 does not really equal 12 or triangles don't have three sides. If I can be tricked into thinking things exist that do not exist, and if I can be fooled into thinking things do not exist when they really do, then maybe I am being deceived about my own existence. Is there anything the evil genius cannot trick me about? Maybe I don't really exist?

Frank and Ernest reprinted by permission of Bob Thaves.

Not at all; of a surety I myself [must] exist since I persuaded myself of something [or merely because I thought of something]. But [what if] there is some deceiver or other, very powerful and very cunning, who ever employs his ingenuity in deceiving me. Then without doubt I exist also if he deceives me, and let him deceive me as much as he will, he can never cause me to be nothing so long as I think that I am something. So that after having reflected well and carefully examined all things, we must come to the definite conclusion that this proposition: I am, I exist, is necessarily true each time that I pronounce it, or that I mentally conceive it.[11]

This is the famous "cogito," from the Latin sentence *Cogito, ergo sum*, meaning *I think, therefore I am*. In some ways, this Cartesian insight, more than anything else, marks the beginning of the modern worldview.

Cogito, ergo sum
Latin for "I think,
therefore I am."

Note the difference between "Descartes thinks, therefore Descartes exists" and "I think, therefore I exist," where the "I" refers to whoever speaks or thinks the sentence. The cogito must be understood in the first person. In that form, it meets Descartes's conditions for being utterly unshakable. No rational person can doubt his or her own existence as a conscious thinking entity—while being aware of thinking about anything.

Descartes interprets this to mean that while bodily existence may seem more solid and certain than ideas, mental existence is in actuality more certain. He goes on:

I find here that thought is an attribute that belongs to me; it cannot be separated from me. I am, I exist, that is certain. But how often?...to speak accurately [at this stage of the Meditations] I am not more than a thing which thinks, that is to say a mind or soul, or an understanding, or a reason, which are terms whose significance was formerly unknown to me. I am...a real thing and really exist; but what thing? I have answered: a thing which thinks.

...What is a thing which thinks? It is a thing which doubts, understands, [conceives], affirms, denies, wills, refuses, which also imagines and feels.[12]

Descartes argues that we identify and know everything—including bodily and material things—through the mind. He grounds all knowledge in mental states, in awareness. Thus the foundation of Descartes's philosophy and, to a considerable extent, of the modern worldview is the thinking self. Although Descartes was a rationalist, the thrust of the cogito is not *reasoning but self-awareness*. Augustine had a similar formula: "I doubt, therefore I am," and in *Nausea* Jean-Paul Sartre wrote, in effect, "I am nauseated, therefore I exist."

Hamlet did think a great many things; does it follow that he existed?
— Jaako Hintikka

"Quod Si Fallor, Sum: *If I Am Mistaken, I Exist*"

More than twelve centuries before Descartes's attempt to refute skepticism with the certain knowledge of his own existence (the cogito), Augustine (Chapter 8) used a remarkably similar argument for the same purpose in *The City of God:*

> The certainty that I exist, that I know it, and that I am glad of it, is independent of any imaginary and deceptive fantasies.
>
> In respect of these truths I have no fear of the arguments of the [Skeptics]. They say, "Suppose your arguments are mistaken?" I reply, "If I am mistaken, I exist." A non-existent being cannot be mistaken; therefore I must exist, if I am mistaken.

> …Since therefore I must exist in order to be mistaken, then even if I am mistaken, there can be no doubt that I am not mistaken in my knowledge that I exist. It follows that I am not mistaken in knowing that I know. And when I am glad of those two facts, I can add the fact of that gladness to the things I know, as a fact of equal worth. For I am not mistaken about the fact of my gladness, since I am not mistaken about the things which I love. Even if they were illusory, it would still be a fact that I love the illusions.

Augustine, ***The City of God***, trans. Henry Bettenson (Harmondsworth, England: Penguin, 1972), 11.26.

So far, Descartes has established that the thinking thing possesses absolute certainty of its own existence as a consciously thinking thing. Thus there is one rather limited fact I know with certainty. Do any other insights follow from this bedrock experience of self-consciousness? Can Descartes move from it to re-create the external world?

Discussing Philosophy

PHILOSOPHICAL QUERY

When I was a student I felt compelled to challenge anything presented to me as being irrefutable. As soon as I heard about the cogito, I assumed I would be able to refute it, to show that it was not necessarily true. That proved easier said than done. Try for yourself; it is interesting, and it is the only way to grasp Descartes's point. Discuss your efforts.

The Innate Idea of God

Descartes begins the third Meditation still treating everything he thinks of as part of himself, as merely "perceptions and imaginations" from his own mind. That being so, his next step is to survey his own thoughts, to see whether there might be something he has overlooked or been unaware of so far. He reasons that the most important issue is the existence of God:

> I must inquire whether there is a God as soon as the occasion presents itself; and if I find that there is a God, I must also inquire whether He may be a deceiver; for without a knowledge of these two truths I do not see that I can ever be certain of anything.[13]

In other words, if Descartes can establish the existence of God rationally, he will have a foundation for truth concerning other ideas. If God is not an evil deceiver, Descartes argues, He will have created the reasoning mind to seek and know the truth. Rationally verifying the existence of God will not only guarantee the possibility of knowledge with certainty but also bridge the gaps between religion and science and between the imagination and reality. If God is the source of reason, then it follows that He wills the use of reason in pursuit of truth. If so, then God is the impetus behind science. If God is not a deceiver, then He will have given Descartes the ability to distinguish the real from the merely imagined. Thus the issue of God's existence and nature is crucial to Descartes's entire rationalistic enterprise.

The Perfect Idea of Perfection

As a rationalist, Descartes cannot appeal to Aquinas's arguments for the existence of God (Chapter 8) because they are based on claims about the external world, the existence of which Descartes has yet to establish. Indeed, Descartes needs to establish the existence of God in order to establish the existence of the external world. Descartes can—at this point—only examine the nature and quality of his own ideas:

> I shall now close my eyes, I shall stop my ears, I shall call away all my senses, I shall efface even from my thoughts all the images of corporeal things, or at least (for that is hardly possible) I shall esteem them as vain and false; and thus holding converse only with myself and considering my own nature, I shall try little by little to reach a better knowledge of and a more familiar acquaintanceship with myself.[14]

Clearly, Descartes says, the *idea* of God exists. He notes the obvious: Such an idea does exist—he has it. But does it follow that an *object* corresponding to this idea exists?

> Hence there remains only the idea of God, concerning which we must consider whether it is something which cannot have proceeded from me myself. By the name of God I understand a substance that is infinite [eternal, unchangeable], independent, all-knowing, all-powerful, and by which I myself and everything else, if anything else does exist, has been created. Now all these characteristics are such that the more diligently I attend to them, the less do they appear capable of proceeding from me alone; hence, from what has been already said, we must conclude that God necessarily exists.[15]

Descartes's position amounts to this: I have in me the clear and distinct idea of a perfect, infinite being. Where could I, an imperfect, finite creature, ever get the idea of infinite perfection? A perfect being is not just a bigger, stronger, quantitatively improved Descartes. If my idea of God were merely of a kind of superhuman being, then I might have created it out of wishful thinking. But how could I even have a notion of infinite perfection, or want to be more perfect myself, "unless I had within me some idea of a Being more perfect than myself, in comparison with which I should recognize the deficiencies of my nature?"[16] In other words, because of its very uniqueness, the idea of an infinite, perfect being must come from just such a being: God.

Note that Descartes has ruled out the idea of an infinite regress of causes. He is also appealing to a version of the principle of sufficient reason (Chapter 8). No matter

©iStock.com/ivan-96

Does your idea of God include a body, a gender, a location like those in this eighteenth-century engraving by Julius Schnorr von Carolsfeld? If you have any specific ideas of God's properties, are they "perfect" ideas of perfect properties?

how far the chain of causes extends, nothing is sufficient to explain (cause) the idea of a perfect, infinite being but a perfect, infinite being:

> And although it may be the case that one idea gives birth to another idea, that cannot continue to be so indefinitely; for in the end we must reach an idea whose cause shall be so to speak an archetype, in which the whole reality [or perfection] which is so to speak objectively [or by representation] in these ideas is contained formally [and really]. Thus the light of nature causes me to know clearly that the ideas in me are like [pictures or] images which can, in truth, easily fall short of the perfection of the objects from which they have been derived, but which can never contain anything greater or more perfect.[17]

In other words, Descartes's mind cannot be the cause of this one special idea. If Descartes were the cause of Descartes, then he would have given himself all the perfections associated with God. So ultimately something other than Descartes must be its cause. The same is true of any so-called evil geniuses or angels or other not-perfect, finite beings.

Descartes, for all his dislike of Scholastic philosophy, follows a Scholastic line in his analysis of these matters. He seems to be saying that not only is God a perfect being, but the idea of God is also a "perfect idea." If it is, he reasons, where could it come from? Imperfect creatures such as ourselves can imagine only imperfect ideas; we could not come up with the idea of a *perfect* anything without help. Where could the idea of perfection come from? Only from a mind more perfect than ours:

> It is perfectly evident that there must be at least as much reality in the cause as in the effect; and thus since I am a thinking thing, and possess an idea of God within me, whatever in the end be the cause assigned to my existence, it must be allowed that it is likewise a thinking thing and that it possesses in itself the idea of all the perfections I attribute to God.... But if it derives its existence from some other cause than itself, we shall again ask, for the same reason, whether this second cause exists by itself or through another, until from one step to another, we finally arrive at an ultimate cause, which will be God.[18]

Descartes determines that he cannot have "received" the idea of God through the senses, nor has it suddenly burst upon his consciousness. He cannot have imagined it, for he lacks the ability to improve upon or to detract from it. Consequently, he says, "the only alternative is that it is innate in me, just as the idea of myself is innate in me."[19]

Descartes's conception of God as a perfect being includes the qualities of all-knowing, all-powerful, all-loving, all-good. Descartes posits that such a God would not let him be constantly deceived by either himself or some evil genius. If, the argument goes, God gave us reason and faculties of perception, they must be basically accurate and reliable. God's existence is crucial to the Cartesian Genesis:

> And the whole strength of the argument which I have here made use of to prove the existence of God consists in this, that I recognize that it is not possible that my nature should be what it is, and indeed that I should have in myself the idea of a God, if God did not veritably exist—a God, I say, whose idea is in me, i.e., who possesses all those supreme perfections of which our mind may indeed have some idea but without understanding them all, who is liable to no errors or defect [and who has none of all those marks which denote imperfection]. From this it is manifest that He cannot be a deceiver, since the light of nature teaches us that fraud and deception necessarily proceed from some defect.[20]

Descartes's Ontological Argument

In the fifth Meditation, Descartes presents an argument for the existence of God based on the claim that it is impossible to conceive of or even imagine God without also thinking of existence. The very essence of the idea of God includes "all perfections," and certainly existence is a perfection. This line of reasoning is known as an ontological argument. The term *ontology* derives from the Greek roots *onta*, "truly real," and *logos*, "study of." An **ontological argument** is an attempt to prove the existence of God by referring either to the meaning of the word *God* when it is understood a certain way, or by referring to the purportedly unique quality of the concept of God.

The purest form of the ontological argument first occurs in the *Proslogion* of St. Anselm (1033–1109). A Benedictine monk who eventually became the archbishop of Canterbury, Anselm attempted to provide a rational basis for Christian doctrine. He asserted that the very idea of God "contains existence" because *by definition* God is "that than which nothing greater can be conceived." And of any two things, a real one

ontological argument
An attempt to prove the existence of God either by referring to the meaning of the word *God* when it is understood a certain way or by referring to the purportedly unique quality of the concept of God.

is "greater" than an imaginary one. Hence, an existing God is greater than a merely imaginary God. Therefore, by definition, the term *God* refers to a real, existing being. When we use *God* to refer to a fantasy being, we have changed its meaning.

For Descartes, the idea of God (infinite perfection) is unique. It is an idea that can only be caused by something external to Descartes. More than that, it is an idea that must resemble the being that it is an idea of. That is not to say that our limited grasp of this privileged idea is adequate. Of course we cannot comprehend God. But we can, Descartes believes, clearly and distinctly grasp the uniqueness of the idea of God, and in so doing, we understand that existence is part of God's essence. He writes:

> This indeed is not at first manifest, since it would seem to present some appearance of being a sophism. For being accustomed in all other things to make a distinction between existence and essence, I easily persuade myself that the existence can be separated from the essence of God, and that we can thus conceive God as not actually existing. But, nevertheless, when I think of it with more attention, I clearly see that existence can no more be separated from the essence of God than can its having its three angles equal to two right angles be separated from the essence of a [rectilinear] triangle, or the idea of a mountain from the idea of a valley; and so there is not any less repugnance to our conceiving a God (that is, a Being supremely perfect) to whom existence is lacking (that is to say, to whom a certain perfection is lacking), than to conceive of a mountain which has no valley.
>
> But although I cannot really conceive of a God without existence any more than a mountain without a valley, still from the fact that I conceive of a mountain with a valley, it does not follow that there is such a mountain in the world; similarly although I conceive of God as possessing existence, it would seem that it does not follow that there is a God which exists; for my thought does not impose any necessity upon things, and just as I may imagine a winged horse, although no horse with wings exists, so I could perhaps attribute existence to God, although no God existed.
>
> But a sophism is concealed in this objection; for from the fact that I cannot conceive a mountain without a valley, it does not follow that there is any mountain or any valley in existence, but only that the mountain and the valley, whether they exist or do not exist, cannot in any way be separated one from the other. While from the fact that I cannot conceive God without existence, it follows that existence is inseparable from Him, and hence that He really exists; not that my thought can bring this to pass, or impose any necessity on things, but, on the contrary, because the necessity which lies in the thing itself, i.e. the necessity of the existence of God determines me to think in this way. For it is not within my power to think of God without existence (that is of a supremely perfect Being devoid of a supreme perfection) though it is in my power to imagine a horse either with wings or without wings.[21]

Discussing Philosophy

PHILOSOPHICAL QUERY

Some philosophers doubt that we really do have a clear and distinct (precise) idea of God. Reflect on the idea of God. Is it clear and distinct? Do you have a clear and distinct idea of perfection—in beings or automobiles or marriages or anything? Does Descartes's argument?

Reconstructing the World

Having shown that at least one mind (his own) and God exist, Descartes concludes his project by reestablishing knowledge of the objective existence of the external world:

> Nothing further now remains but to inquire whether material things exist.... And certainly I at least know that these may exist.... For there is no doubt that God possesses the power to produce everything that I am capable of perceiving with distinctness.[22]

Descartes reasons that since he has a clear and distinct idea of himself *both as a mind and as having a body*, he must of necessity be both a mind and a body. But the idea of being both mind and body is neither innate nor known to be true with deductive certainty. Thus, the idea of the body must originate outside Descartes's mind:

> And...because I know that all things which I apprehend clearly and distinctly can be created by God as I apprehend them, it suffices that I am able to apprehend one thing apart from another clearly and distinctly in order to be certain that one is different from the other, since they may be made to exist in separation at least by the omnipotence of God.... On the one side, I have a clear and distinct idea of myself inasmuch as I am only a thinking and unextended thing, and as, on the other, I possess a distinct idea of body, inasmuch as it is only an extended and unthinking thing, it is certain that this I [that is to say, my soul by which I am what I am], is entirely and absolutely distinct from my body and can exist without it.
>
>   ...But, since God is no deceiver, it is very manifest that He does not communicate to me these ideas immediately and by Himself.... I do not see how He could be defended from the accusation of deceit if these ideas were produced by causes other than corporeal objects. Hence we must allow that corporeal things exist.[23]

Descartes reasoned that his own ideas of body and mind must be basically sound, since God allowed him to know clearly and distinctly that he is both. At this point, the Cartesian Genesis is essentially complete. All that remains are the details of reconstructing knowledge of the world on a solid base by carefully following the rules of method.

The Cartesian Bridge

Descartes was a devout Catholic who took his religion seriously. He was aware of the challenge to religion posed by advances in physics and astronomy and the reemergence of **materialism** (also known as **behaviorism, mechanism,** or **reductionism**). Other philosophers, most notably Thomas Hobbes (1588–1679), were arguing that everything is composed of matter (and energy) and can be explained by physical laws. This means all human activity can be understood as the natural behavior of matter according to mechanical laws. Thus, thinking is merely a complex form of behaving, and the body is a fleshy machine. The so-called mind can be reduced to the brain, and thinking and acting can be reduced to biochemical brain states and stimulus–response reactions. Since the laws of physics are universal, there can be no

materialism (behaviorism, mechanism, reductionism) The belief that everything is composed of matter (and energy) and can be explained by physical laws, that all human activity can be understood as the natural behavior of matter according to mechanical laws, and that thinking is merely a complex form of behaving: The body is a fleshy machine.

such thing as a free will. If everything is material, there can be no such thing as an immaterial soul. (This point of view, which is held by many scientists and philosophers today, will be discussed more fully in Chapter 10.)

Like the theologians, Descartes was alarmed by the amoral, secular nature of this particular view of the universe. Yet, as we have noted, he was a scientist himself, and his philosophy was designed to bridge the growing gap between the "new science" and religion. By showing that the mind is different in kind from the body, Descartes hoped to prove that the discoveries of the physicists posed no threat to free will or the existence of an incorporeal soul. The laws of physics apply only to matter, but the mind (soul) is an incorporeal thinking substance. Mind and body are two completely different kinds of substances. Thus, science turns out to be the language of bodies; it cannot address minds or souls, so it is no threat to the church or basic Christian theology.

Cartesian Dualism

Any philosophical position that divides existence into two completely distinct, independent, unique substances or kinds of things is a form of **dualism**. The distinction can be between mind and body, natural and supernatural, spirit and matter, soul and body, good and evil, and so on. (**Monism** is the general name for the belief that everything consists of only one, ultimate, unique substance, such as matter; **pluralism** is the name for the belief in more than one substance.)

Cartesian dualism refers to Descartes's conviction that human beings are a mysterious union of mind (soul) and body, of incorporeal substance and corporeal substance, with each realm operating according to separate sets of laws. The mind follows the laws of reason but otherwise is free. The body is governed by the laws of physics and falls under the rule of cause and effect: The human body is no freer than any other material thing. The soul is somehow dispersed to all parts of the body, but thinking enters the brain through the pineal gland:

> And as a clock composed of wheels and counter-weights no less exactly observes the laws of nature... if I consider the body of a man as being a sort of machine so built up and composed of nerves, muscles, veins, blood, and skin, that though there were no mind in it at all, it would not cease to have made the same motions as at present, exception being made of those movements which are due to the direction of the will, and in consequence depend upon the mind.[24]

If we can understand thinking without ever referring to the body, and if we can understand the body without ever referring to the mind/soul, then minds and bodies are essentially independent of each other. Science can study bodies and the natural world without ever treading in theology. Initially, this rationale seems satisfactory. Indeed, it fits the commonsense view of Christian theology and ordinary experience. Thus, Cartesian dualism allows for the doctrine of the soul's continued existence after the body's death. Further, by defining himself as *thinking substance* rather than corporeal, Descartes reaffirms the primacy of the soul over the body. Human beings are essentially spiritual beings who happen to inhabit bodies. As a devout believer, Descartes appears to have found a way to salvage his faith from the

dualism
Any philosophical position that divides existence into two completely distinct, independent, unique substances.

monism
The general name for the belief that everything consists of only one, ultimate, unique substance such as matter or spirit.

pluralism
The belief that more than one reality or substance exists.

threats of purely materialistic science. As a scientist, he has freed science to progress without church interference, since scientific discoveries are about the body and have no real bearing on the nature of the soul.

The Mind–Body Problem

Dualism generates one of the most tenacious of philosophical questions: What is the relationship of the mind to the body? Yet so appealing is dualism to philosophers, preachers, psychologists, and most of the rest of us that in his influential and controversial book *The Concept of Mind*, contemporary philosopher Gilbert Ryle refers to it simply as "the official doctrine." Ryle says:

> The official doctrine, which hails chiefly from Descartes, is something like this. With the doubtful exceptions of idiots and infants in arms every human being has both a body and a mind. Some would prefer to say that every human being is both a body and a mind. His body and his mind are ordinarily harnessed together, but after the death of the body his mind may continue to exist and function.[25]

Corollaries of the official doctrine are found in beliefs about the immortality of the soul and reincarnation. Corollaries are implicit in psychological theories that view the mind as something other than the brain and that differentiate mental states from bodily conditions and behavior. The official doctrine is reflected in ordinary language when we talk about *having* a body and in common experience when we feel as if "we" are somehow *in* our bodies.

Religious and metaphysical versions of the official doctrine sometimes compare the soul to a driver and the body to a car. At death, we get out of the car or—if you believe in reincarnation—trade in the old body for a new one. Descartes rejects the car–driver type of analogy and unites mind and body into "one whole":

> Nature also teaches me by these sensations of pain, hunger, thirst, etc., that I am not only lodged in my body as a pilot in a vessel, but that I am very closely united to it, and so to speak so intermingled with it that I seem to compose with it one

"Darrow's Trip to Goofville"

If I am told that next week I shall start on a trip to Goofville; that I shall not take my body with me; that I shall stay for all eternity: can I find a single fact connected with my journey—the way I shall go, the part of me that is to go, the time of the journey, the country I shall reach, its location in space, the way I shall live there— or anything that would lead to a rational belief that I shall really take the trip? Have I ever known anyone who has made the journey and returned? If I am really to believe, I must try to get some information about all these important facts.

Clarence Darrow, "The Myth of the Soul," *The Forum* 80 (October 1928).

Hulton Archive/Getty Images

A sketch from Descartes's *Treatise on Man* depicting brain function and the anatomy of the eyeball. According to Descartes, the pineal gland (H) is the crucial link between mind and body.

whole. For if that were not the case, when my body is hurt, I who am merely a thinking thing, should not feel pain, for I should perceive this wound by the understanding only, just as a sailor perceives by sight when something is damaged in his vessel; and when my body has need of drink or food, I should clearly understand the fact without being warned of it by confused feelings of hunger and thirst. For all these sensations of hunger, thirst, pain, etc., are in truth none other than certain confused modes of thought which are produced by the union and intermingling of mind and body.[26]

(The "union" or "intermingling" occurs, as noted earlier, in the pineal gland. Descartes apparently devoted some time to dissecting animal carcasses in order to study this mysterious gland.)

Dualism *feels consistent* with certain common experiences but inconsistent with others: If I hit my thumb with a hammer, I experience no mind–body split. Yet there are serious consequences if we reject dualism in favor of a materialistic, behavioristic monism: When we reduce mental states to physical states, do we lose the possibility of free will, moral responsibility, and the possibility of survival after death? Such beliefs are important to the very meaning of life for many people, real enough and important enough so that any difficulties of *explaining* mind–body interaction pale beside the consequences of rejecting dualism.

But the fact that millions of people believe something does not make it true. Cartesian dualism—indeed, metaphysical speculation itself—stands in direct opposition to another major modern philosophical archetype: the skeptical questioner who turns to experience rather than to the mind for knowledge. The skeptic is the subject of Chapter 10. Chapters 14–18 deal with existential and postmodern rejection of abstract metaphysics.

PHILOSOPHICAL QUERY

How plausible is this "official doctrine"? On Descartes's own terms, how "clearly and distinctly" do we understand the relationship of the mind to the body? How can a completely nonphysical thing interact with a completely physical thing? To ask Mark Twain's insightful question, How come the mind gets drunk when the body does the drinking? Why does my mind react to what happens to my body with such intensity if it's not part of my body?

From Cosmos to Machine

As noted in Chapter 2, ancient Greek philosophy developed in a series of increasingly abstract steps, until growing concern with logical consistency and rules of thinking led to theories that, though logically consistent, did not match observed facts.[27] One result of this split between common experience and the claims of early philosophers was the alienation of philosophy from the life concerns of most people. Historian of philosophy Amaury de Riencourt says, "The absolute predominance of the dissociating, analytical masculine principle in Greek thought is obvious—hence its strength and its weakness."[28]

As the early Greeks developed and refined rational skills, they increasingly valued personal detachment and the suppression of traits that today we associate with maternal and caring qualities. Objectivity and emotional detachment—qualities traditionally associated with masculinity—were considered essential aspects of knowledge, and subjectivity and emotional involvement were considered hindrances.

According to feminist philosopher of culture Susan Bordo (b. 1947), this "masculinizing" of philosophical thought reached a watershed at the beginning of the modern period. In "The Cartesian Masculinization of Thought," Bordo argues that "Cartesian modernity is inherently linked to the repression of nature and women."[29] This repression, she suggests, is motivated by revulsion and uneasiness that modernity has traditionally associated with the daily lives of women.[30] Women's lives are circumscribed by menstruation, childbirth, nursing, caring for others. In short, women's experiences are *embodied* experiences that cannot be abstracted into distinct mental and physical substances. Bordo's point is that the daily lives of women do not reflect Cartesian dualism.

Bordo's critique of modern philosophy adds a feminist perspective to the radical sorts of criticisms brought to bear on objectivity and rationality by Marx, Kierkegaard, James, and Nietzsche. (See Chapters 13–16.)

PHILOSOPHICAL QUERY

Do you think that Cartesian dualism reflects men's lives more than women's? Do you think Cartesian dualism reflects anyone's life?

MindTap

Discussing Philosophy

According to Bordo, modernity rests on Descartes's attempt to *reconstruct the world* based solely on his own clear and distinct ideas. She says, "We are all familiar with the dominant Cartesian themes of starting anew, alone, without influence from the past or other people, with the guidance of reason alone."[31] The result, Bordo argues, is that *objectivity*, rather than *meaning*, became the chief philosophical issue. But as long as human beings are "embedded in nature," embodied and subject to its rhythms, such detachment is impossible.

In Bordo's view, Descartes's particular genius was the way in which he laid a philosophical foundation for transforming the initial experience of alienation and loss that accompanied the Copernican Revolution into an optimistic, objective method for understanding, dominating, and managing nature. (See the Overview of Modern Themes.) According to Bordo, Cartesian rationalism required sundering the organic ties between the person (subject) and the world (object). As Bordo sees it, starting with Descartes, modern philosophy reacted to the new cosmic order with an exaggerated emphasis on objectivism and mechanism. As a result,

Susan Bordo

> *If a kind of Cartesian ideal were ever completely fulfilled, i.e., if the whole of nature were only what can be explained in terms of mathematical relationships—then we would look at the world with that fearful sense of alienation, with that utter loss of reality with which a future schizophrenic child looks at his mother. A machine cannot give birth.*
>
> — Karl Stern

the modern vision of the universe is one of a complex machine, not an organic whole (cosmos):

> This re-visioning of the universe as a *machine*—most often, a clockwork—was not the work of philosophers alone. Astronomy and anatomy had already changed the dominant picture of the movements of the heavens and the processes of the body by the time the *Meditations* were written. But it was philosophy…that provided the cosmology that integrated these discoveries into a consistent and unified view of nature.… Nature became *defined* by its lack of affiliation with divinity, with spirit. All that which is god-like or spiritual—freedom, will, and sentience—belong entirely and exclusively to *res cogitans* [the thing that thinks]. All else—the earth, the heavens, animals, the human body—is merely mechanically interacting matter.[32]

Bordo goes on to suggest that the masculinization of science involves more than just the historical fact of male dominance of the sciences, noting that "the most interesting contemporary discussions of the 'masculinist' nature of modern science describe a…characteristic cognitive style, an epistemological stance which is required of men *and* women working in the sciences today."[33] Bordo does not, however, see modernity as entirely negative:

> Inspired by the work of [Carol] Gilligan, [Nancy] Chodorow, [Susan] Harding, and [Evelyn Fox] Keller, feminist theory has been systematically questioning the historical identification of rationality, intelligence, "good thinking," and so forth, with the masculine modes of detachment and clarity, offering alternative models of fresher, more humane, and more hopeful approaches to science and ethics.[34]

The Cartesian Fantasy

In a series of articles and essays collected in her influential book *Unbearable Weight: Feminism, Western Culture, and the Body*, Susan Bordo analyzes what she and other philosophers identify as hurtful, real-life consequences of what Bordo describes as "the Cartesian fantasy." Bordo is particularly interested in important, widespread, and, until recently, unrecognized, cultural limits and expectations that Cartesian dualism has exerted on gender and women's self-concepts. In the process, Bordo conducts an intriguing philosophical inquiry into the far-reaching effects that seemingly technical and academic philosophical arguments and doctrines can have on an entire culture.

Bordo makes effective use of mundane examples from contemporary culture that include references to pop music, movies, commercials, and clothing to buttress her contention that we are all affected by Cartesian dualism. We don't have to be philosophers or even to have ever heard of Descartes or modernity to be dualists, at least some of the time. According to Bordo, modern dualism reinforces a culture-wide mechanistic, technologized view of the human body that has destructive consequences for the lives, aspirations, and self-concepts of women (and men and children).

The problem, as Bordo describes it, is a Cartesian fantasy built on the possibility of pure objectivity—a delusion that pure objectivity is attainable with sophisticated, rational, scientific effort. Herein lies our contemporary quest to observe and manage life from an idealized God's-eye perspective, or if reference to God offends us, from a pure, scientific, data-based perspective. We seek to transcend partiality, ethnocentrism, sexism, racism, particularity in short. We seek a "view from nowhere."

Descartes, Bordo reminds us, believed that the mind could achieve the view from nowhere by adopting his rationalistic philosophical method. The careful, methodical Cartesian mind attempts to transcend the body and thereby escape the limited perspective of the material world. In this sense, the Cartesian mind philosophizes from nowhere.

But, Bordo suggests, in addition to freeing philosophers to reason afresh, dualism also contributes to our culture's extraordinary goals of "defying aging, our various 'biological clocks,' and even death itself." When we think of our bodies as objects, as out there, we treat them as things to sculpt, trim, and maintain (like automobiles and healthy GPAs) according to cultural expectations and "objective" scientific standards of wellness and desirability. We observe and try to control, from a distance, as it were, our BMIs, our cholesterol levels, waistlines, wrinkles, crooked teeth, and biceps. We become rational ghosts inside of messy, embodied machines:

> Clearly, then, mind/body dualism is no mere philosophical position, to be defended or dispensed with by clever argument. Rather, it is a *practical* metaphysics that has been deployed and socially embedded in medicine, law, literary and artistic representations, the psychological construction of the self, interpersonal relationships, popular culture and advertisements, a metaphysics which will be deconstructed only through the concrete transformation of the institutions and practices that sustain it.
>
> ...But it is not easy to "go beyond dualism" in this culture...[35]

If Bordo and other critics of depersonalization are generally correct (see Chapters 13–18), the scientific, technological, and cultural advances generated by modern science and philosophy carry a high price. This price includes widespread alienation from the natural world; fear and revulsion in the face of "messy" aspects of life such as birthing, caring, and dying; and the trivialization of the family in the name of "justice" and "objectivity."

Dualism...cannot be deconstructed in culture the way it can be on paper. To be...culturally accomplished requires that we...legitimate and nurture...marginalized ways of knowing, speaking, being.
— Susan Bordo

MindTap
Aplia

Commentary

Descartes's rationalism was inspired by a vision and three dreams, which he interpreted as a divine calling to establish his method of rational inquiry. Through the innovative use of methodic doubt, he established one irrefutable certainty, the cogito. Descartes claimed that God's existence was the foundation for all knowledge and for the general reliability of the "natural light" of reason, yet, for the contemporary observer, the cogito is more solidly grounded than the proof for God.

To a considerable extent, the modern era is grounded in Cartesian self-consciousness, self-reflection, and self-analysis. In its emphasis on an individual's inquiry after truth rather than official answers, Cartesian rationalism seems to pave the way for social and political democracy. The irony in this is that we note a kind of cool, analytic detachment as Descartes makes himself the subject of study in a new way. As the modern era develops, purity of method ultimately takes precedence over the search for wisdom. This trend might be a consequence of the detached, depersonalized quality of rationalistic analysis that emerged in the work of Descartes.

The benefits of the Cartesian revolution include the use of clearer, simpler, ordinary language (an idea that significantly influenced subsequent philosophers). Descartes paved the way for psychological studies by showing that the "thinking thing" is not a neutral "window" but a dynamic entity whose very nature affects its observations and conclusions. He initiated the study of knowledge and the sources of knowledge that continues to this day. Even the rationalists' great epistemological opponents, the empiricists, found themselves responding partly to issues raised by rationalism.

Unlike others of his time (and ours), Descartes refused to bow before authority, choosing to accept only what he knew for himself. He stands out as an archetype of the rationalist for his unwillingness to settle for inconsistencies and contradictions between his faith and his intellect. If his notion of "clear and distinct" is itself cloudy, if his introduction of God is suspicious, and if his attempt to account for mind–body interaction is unsatisfying, he is nonetheless remarkable for squarely facing up to the need to reassess his belief system for himself. Descartes tried not to believe what he could not clearly understand. That in itself is a remarkable achievement.

Summary of Main Points

- Descartes's scientific and mathematical interests demanded clear, provable evidence of a sort lacking in Scholasticism's cumbersome reliance on authority and resulted in a radical proposal: Start fresh; throw out everything we think we know and build a system based entirely on ideas whose truth can be clearly and distinctly known to us firsthand. Rationalists rely on the coherence theory of truth: New or unclear ideas are evaluated in terms of rational or logical consistency and in relation to already established truths.

- Reliance on reason as the ultimate source of knowledge is a form of rationalism, the notion that abstract reasoning can produce absolutely certain truths about reality and that some important ultimate truths can be discovered without observation, experiment, or experience. Such truths are known as innate ideas or *a priori* ideas. Ideas derived from experience are known as *a posteriori* ideas.

- Descartes's interest in the "thinking thing itself" was the first major step in a shift in emphasis in modern philosophy from metaphysics to epistemology. He recognized the need for orderly thinking, which he called

method. This paved the way for the modern emphasis on technique (method) and marks a major change from metaphysical, authoritarian medieval thinking to epistemological, technical modern thinking.

- Descartes employed *methodic doubt* in his effort to find one absolutely certain and undoubtable idea. Methodic doubt is a form of skepticism that rejects any idea that could possibly be false, no matter how remote that possibility. Methodic doubt coupled with the concept of the evil genius led Descartes to raise questions about whether or not he was dreaming and about the existence of his own body and of the entire external world.

- Even an evil genius could not shake one fundamental idea: "I think, therefore I am." This is known as the cogito. Having found an undoubtable truth, Descartes tried to build a reliable foundation for knowledge on the innate idea of God. He did this by appealing to an argument that attempts to prove the existence of God by showing that the idea "God" cannot be derived from human experience; it can only come from the actual existence of God.

- Having established the existence of God to his satisfaction, Descartes believed he had clearly and distinctly demonstrated the reliability of reason and the possibility of certain knowledge, since if God is all-knowing, all-good, and all-powerful, He would not let us live in constant ignorance.

- Descartes rejected the materialists' challenge to the notion of free will with Cartesian dualism, the belief that two completely different kinds of things exist, bodies and minds, and that human beings are a mysterious union of both. Dualism, however, generates the mind–body problem: What is the relationship of the mind to the body? How can a nonmaterial thing (mind) affect a material thing (body)?

- According to Susan Bordo, a "masculinizing" of modern philosophical thought reached a watershed at the beginning of the modern period. Bordo asserts that Cartesian modernity is inherently linked to the repression of both nature and women. Bordo argues that the daily lives of women do not reflect Cartesian dualism because women's experiences are embodied experiences that cannot be abstracted into distinct mental and physical substances.

Post-Reading Reflections

Now that you've had a chance to learn about the Rationalist, use your new knowledge to answer these questions.

1. What was Descartes's proposal, and how did his Scholastic education influence it?
2. Give a brief summary of the role methodic doubt plays in Descartes's overall effort to discover certain knowledge.
3. How is skepticism important to Cartesian philosophy?
4. What is the evil genius, and what is its significance to the Cartesian Genesis?
5. Can the Evil Genius refute the cogito? Is there any way to "refute" the cogito?
6. Give Descartes's argument for the existence of God in your own words and then analyze it. Is it convincing? Why or why not?
7. How did Descartes answer the materialists' rejection of free will?
8. What is the mind–body problem? How does Descartes deal with it? Is he successful? Why or why not?
9. What is the "view from nowhere" and why is Susan Bordo troubled by its cultural pervasiveness?

 MindTap™

Experience MindTap through the activities highlighted in this chapter. Further explore this online, personalized learning tool to deepen your comprehension and improve your grades.

10

The Skeptic
David Hume

I am uneasy to think I approve
of one object, and disapprove of
another; call one thing beautiful,
and another deform'd; decide
concerning truth and falsehood,
reason and folly, without knowing
upon what principles I proceed.
— *David Hume*

Learning Objectives

After you complete this chapter, you should be able to:

- Describe a philosophical skeptic.

- Define *empiricism*.

- Define the *correspondence theory of truth*.

- Define *epistemological dualism*.

- Describe John Locke's egocentric predicament.

- Define the *empirical criterion of meaning*.

- Critique David Hume's claim that, strictly speaking, there is no empirical evidence for the existence of cause and effect.

- Analyze Hume's critique of the argument from design.

- Explain Hume's assertion that reason is, and ought only to be, the slave of the passions.

- Differentiate between facts and values, according to Hume.

- Critique Hume's rejection of egoism.

A FRIEND OF MINE ONCE told me that her third cousin could move objects by psychokinesis—that is, by mind power. She insisted that she had seen him send ashtrays and glasses across a room, without touching them or leaving his chair, merely by concentrating very deeply. I was intrigued, because I had known this woman for years, and she seemed intelligent and sane to me—yet I had never seen such a phenomenon for myself. I asked to be allowed to witness this amazing feat but was told that, sadly, this remarkable individual had died some years before. This did not surprise me, and I may have been too blunt in saying so. "You don't believe me, do you?" my friend said, obviously annoyed with me. "You never believe anything! You're too skeptical."

A **skeptic** is a person who demands clear, observable, *undoubtable* evidence—based on experience—before accepting any knowledge claim as true. The word *skepticism* (from the Greek *skeptesthai,* "to consider or examine") refers to both a school of philosophy and a general attitude. Originally, a skeptic was a special kind of doubter, one who withheld judgment while waiting for better evidence. Sextus Empiricus (c. 200) even devised a *skeptical grammar,* which ends every proposition with "so it seems to me at the moment." There are variations of skepticism, progressing from total doubt about everything to temporary or particular doubt invoked just for the process of analysis—what Descartes called "methodic doubt" (Chapter 9).

My friend's reaction was common: She took my demand for firsthand evidence personally. That is, she interpreted it as an attack on her integrity. She would have preferred that I accept her claim as true simply because we were friends. I have reacted to requests for evidence the same way myself. Yet if we are seriously interested in the pursuit of truth in general, or in the truth of a specific claim, we must demand more than the personal testimony of others, no matter how sincerely they may give it or how much we may care for them.

 MindTap

Philosophy Timelines

© Pepe Ramirez/Shutterstock.com

The New Testament story of the disciple Thomas's refusal to believe that Jesus had returned from the dead until he had examined Jesus for himself—rather than taking the claim on faith—is the source of the expression "Don't be a Doubting Thomas." Suppose, instead, that Thomas were thought of as skeptical, careful, scientific Thomas?

PHILOSOPHICAL QUERY

Have you ever been angry or insulted when someone pressed you for evidence? Or has anyone ever gotten angry with you for asking for evidence? Why do you suppose that is? Is it rude to ask "How do you know that?" or "Can you prove that?" when people make claims about important, or even not so important, things? Analyze this question and see if you can justify not asking for evidence.

MindTap

Discussing Philosophy

skeptic
From the Greek *skeptesthai,* "to consider or examine"; a person who demands clear, observable, undoubtable evidence before accepting any knowledge claim as true.

Standards of evidence vary with conditions. The more important the issue is, the stricter our standards must be. And the more important the issue is, the greater is our obligation to demand evidence. Expertise and training—as well as time, interest, and ability—also matter when we are justifying our beliefs. Ideally, we should accept as true only what we can verify for ourselves. Often, however, we must rely on the testimony of qualified experts, but this differs considerably from relying on unverified testimony. My friend was not qualified to determine the genuineness of psychic experience. Accepting her claim at face value would have been unreasonable; it would require discounting my own experience without ever having seen the phenomenon for myself or having read about incontrovertible, repeatable, carefully controlled cases of similar powers.

Yet consider how rarely we demand good evidence for beliefs and knowledge claims. We buy so-called health foods on the recommendation of neighbors and fellow students. Political candidates make claims about education, the environment, even moral values. Automobile manufacturers make claims for the reliability and safety of their vehicles. Political action groups make claims concerning abortion racial prejudice, toxic effects, crime rates, drugs, and other hot-button topics. How often have you asked for verification of such claims? When a salesperson makes claims about this refrigerator or that smart phone, do you ask for unbiased supporting data? If you do, how do you, a nonexpert, determine its validity?

All these issues involve knowledge claims. In technical language, they are *epistemological issues*. The study of the theory of knowledge, **epistemology**, is the branch of philosophy concerned with the origins, quality, nature, and reliability of knowledge. Beginning with Descartes, Western philosophy has been dominated by epistemological issues.

epistemology
A branch of philosophy that studies the nature and possibility of knowledge.

> **PHILOSOPHICAL QUERY**
>
> Who is a qualified expert in areas such as psychic phenomena, miracles, nutrition, or philosophy? What is the relationship between the reports of experts and your own experience? When the two conflict, which should you trust? Why? How do you know?

John Locke

Attempts to answer fundamental epistemological questions gave rise to the two major orientations of modern philosophy. The first, as we learned in Chapter 9, is rationalism. The other is known as **empiricism**, from the Greek root *empeiria*, meaning "experience."

Empiricists believe that all ideas can be traced back to *sense data*. Abstractions and complex beliefs are said to be combinations and mental alterations of original impressions and perceptions, as when, for example, we imagine a man with a horse's head. Empiricists believe that reason is unable to provide knowledge of reality; such knowledge can only be derived from experience. The strictest empiricists believe that even mathematical and logical principles are derived from experience. A potent form of empiricism emerged with the advent of modern philosophy. Because its three founding philosophers were all British, it has come to be called *British empiricism*.

The earliest of the three British empiricists, **John Locke** (1632–1704), was disturbed by the confusion and uncertainty surrounding seventeenth-century

empiricism
The belief that all knowledge is ultimately derived from the senses (experience) and that all ideas can be traced to sense data.

philosophy and theology. Like Descartes, he was troubled by Scholastic philosophy (Chapter 8), which he had encountered as a student at Oxford. He was especially critical of its emphasis on formal disputations and debates, which he said were "invented for wrangling and ostentation, rather than to discover the truth." Locke's *An Essay Concerning Human Understanding*, published in 1690, established the groundwork for empiricism as it is generally understood today.

John Locke

Educated as a physician, Locke was aware of the great changes and progress being generated by science. Trained to rely on his own powers of perception, he pointed out that as a physician, you cannot "wait until you have reached mathematical certainty about the correct treatment" before helping a patient. You have to observe and act based on what you perceive. You must turn to the facts.[1]

In the winter of 1670, Locke had a series of philosophical discussions concerning morality and religion with some friends. It wasn't long before the friends found themselves confused and puzzled. Their inability to reach clearly right or wrong answers—in the way a chemist or baker often can—had a profound effect on Locke. He realized he had to take a step back and examine the nature and limits of knowledge before trying to sort out the truth or falsity of specific ideas:

> After we had awhile puzzled ourselves, without coming any nearer a resolution of those doubts which perplexed us, it came into my thoughts that we took a wrong course; and that before we set ourselves upon inquiries of that nature, it was necessary to examine my own abilities, and see what *objects* our understanding were, or were not, fitted to deal with.[2]

Without some clear idea of the ultimate source of knowledge in a given area, we have little hope for resolving philosophical agreements. If you have ever been involved in a nearly endless and unsettled disagreement over social, moral, political, or religious issues at some casual gathering, you know what Locke experienced. Each person seems to have an unstated set of rules and assumptions regarding what is obviously true and what is ridiculous, which sources of information are reliable and which are not. Without a clearly stated and agreed-upon set of basic principles, such discussions often amount to nothing more than each person repeatedly affirming a set of favored beliefs and denouncing all others.

Locke's solution was to study the origins of our ideas to better understand the nature and process of acquiring knowledge. He hoped he could thereby find a way to settle difficult issues. Although his philosophy contains its own inconsistencies, Locke initiated an emphasis on logical rigor and analytic precision that would shake the foundations of many of our most cherished beliefs. He began by calling for philosophers to refocus their attention "outward," on experience.

Experience Is the Origin of All Ideas

According to Locke, all *ideas* originate in *sensation* and *reflection*. Specifically, he says we can think about things only *after we have experienced them*. In other words, all ideas originate from sense data. For example, no one born blind can ever have an idea of color, according to this theory. Those of us who are sighted "abstract" the *idea of color* from specific sense data by reflecting on, say, red, green, yellow, and blue circles. In doing so, we note that they have two common qualities, circularity

> *Scepticism, while logically impeccable, is psychologically impossible, and there is an element of frivolous insincerity in any philosophy which pretends to accept it.*
> — Bertrand Russell

and color. Our blind friend can trace their shape and thus acquire sensations of circularity, but color, which is only perceived through sight, will remain unknown.

As part of his empirical inquiry into the nature of human understanding, Locke attempted to explain and classify different kinds of ideas and the ways we arrange sense data from simple into increasingly complex and abstract ideas. He insisted that all ideas are *copies* of the things that caused the basic sensations on which they rest. Ideas are less intense copies, or images, of sensations. Your idea of a baseball, for example, is a copy of the set of sensations and impressions you have received from seeing and handling actual baseballs. If your idea of a baseball includes the shape of a cube, it is a poor copy. It does not *correspond* to reality.

This position is known as the *copy theory* or *representation theory* or **correspondence theory of truth**, a term attributed to contemporary philosopher Bertrand Russell. The correspondence theory of truth is a truth test that holds that an idea (or belief or thought) is true if whatever it refers to actually exists. In other words, an idea is defined as true if it corresponds to a fact. The procedure for checking the truth of an idea is called *confirmation* or *verification* (see Chapter 17).

Favored by empiricists, the correspondence theory of truth is in direct contrast with the *coherence theory of truth* favored by rationalists (see Chapter 9) and differs from the other major truth theory, the *pragmatic theory of truth* (see Chapter 15).

Locke's Rejection of Innate Ideas

In Chapter 9, we learned that Descartes, as a rationalist, believed in a special class of ideas known as *a priori* or **innate ideas**. So-called innate ideas are truths that are not derived from observation or experience; they are characterized as being certain, deductive, universally true, and independent of all experience. Examples of innate ideas include mathematical equivalences, such as "2 + 3 = 5" and deductive principles of reason, such as "Every event has a cause" and "All triangles contain 180°."

In the *Meditations*, Descartes based a major part of his case for the certainty of reason—as well as for general reliability of the senses and knowledge of the existence of an external world—on the clarity and distinctness of "the innate idea of God" (see Chapter 9). But if Locke's view proves to be the correct one, Descartes's entire project collapses. Whereas Descartes's prototype of reason was modeled after mathematical (deductive) reasoning, Locke's model was fashioned from his experiences as a physician.

In Locke's estimation, Cartesian-style speculation (abstract thinking modeled after geometric method) can at best "amuse our understanding with fine and useless speculations." It cannot, however, adequately deal with concrete problems. When used for more than amusement, Cartesian-type reasoning is dangerous because it distracts "our inquiries from the true and advantageous knowledge of things." All that can result from such "idle speculation," suggests Locke, is "to enlarge the art of

correspondence (copy or representation) theory of truth
A truth test that holds that an idea (or belief or thought) is true if whatever it refers to actually exists (corresponds to a fact).

innate ideas (*a priori* ideas)
Truths that are not derived from observation or experiment; characterized as being certain, deductive, universally true, and independent of all experience.

Locke said that it is as irrational to believe that we can see with other people's eyes as it is to think that we can know things with other people's understandings.

talking and perhaps [lay] a foundation for endless disputes." It cannot provide useful knowledge, the way, say, Isaac Newton's new scientific reasoning could.[3]

Locke accused the rationalists of labeling their pet ideas "innate" in order to convince others to accept them secondhand, without question:

> We may as rationally hope to see with other men's eyes, as to know by other men's understandings. So much as we ourselves consider and comprehend of truth and reason, so much we possess of real and true knowledge. The floating of other men's opinions in our brains, makes us not one jot the more knowing, though they happen to be true.
>
> When men have found some general propositions that could not be doubted of as soon as understood, it was, I know, a short and easy way to conclude them innate. This being once received, it eased the lazy from the pains of search, and stopped the inquiry of the doubtful concerning all that was once styled innate. And it was of no small advantage to those who affected to be masters and teachers, to make this the principle of principles,—*that principles must not be questioned....* [This] put their followers upon...[a] posture of blind credulity.[4]

From Locke's point of view, Descartes's attempt to introduce a method of inquiry that would free us from the dogmatic shackles of Scholasticism merely results in another dogmatism—a rationalistic one.

Locke argued that without appealing to the ultimate test of experience, reason has no "ground," or standard, for distinguishing truth from fantasy. Modifying a characterization used by some rationalistic philosophers, who compared the mind to a pantry well stocked with "innate ideas," Locke suggested that the mind is better compared to an empty pantry, waiting to be stocked by experience.[5] But Locke's most famous comparison was to describe the mind at birth as a completely blank tablet, or clean slate, a *tabula rasa*, to use the Latin equivalent:

> *All ideas come from sensations or reflection*—Let us then suppose the mind to be, as we say, white paper, void of all characters, without any ideas:—How comes it to be furnished?... Whence has it all the *materials* of reason and knowledge? To this I answer, in one word, from EXPERIENCE. In that all our knowledge is founded; and from that it ultimately derives itself.[6]

Locke's Dualism

Although Locke rejected Descartes's theory of innate ideas, he did agree with Descartes that "something substantial" underlies and holds together the sensible qualities of experience (color, taste, size, shape, location, sound, motion, and such). This substantial something is *substance*, a complex idea according to Locke:

> The mind being, as I have declared, furnished with a great number of simple ideas, conveyed in by the senses as they are found in exterior things, or by reflection on its own operations, takes notice also that a certain number of these simple ideas go constantly together; which being presumed to belong to one thing, and words being suited to common apprehensions...are called, so united in one subject, by one name; which, by inadvertency, we are apt afterward to talk of and consider as one simple idea, which indeed is a complication of many ideas together: because...not

tabula rasa
Latin expression for a "clean slate" used by John Locke to challenge the possibility of innate ideas by characterizing the mind at birth as a blank tablet or clean slate.

imagining how these simple ideas *can* subsist by themselves, we accustom ourselves to suppose some *substratum* wherein they do subsist, and from which they do result, which therefore we call *substance*.[7]

Locke proceeds to argue that we have only an obscure idea of substance "in general" He claims that upon analysis, we have no clear, distinct idea of substance itself but only a notion of "such qualities which are capable of producing simple ideas in us." Locke says that if pressed to explain "what is the subject wherein colour or weight inheres," all we can offer is "the supposed, but unknown, support of those qualities we find existing, which we imagine cannot subsist ... without something to support them."[8]

Having affirmed the general idea of substance, Locke next inquires into *kinds of substances*. He reports that observation and experience reveal that certain sorts of simple ideas seem to cluster together. From these clusters of simple ideas, we form ideas of "a man, horse, gold, water," and so on. According to Locke, although philosophers might have trouble describing it, our everyday experiences confirm the existence of substance:

> I appeal to every one's own experience. It is the ordinary qualities observable in iron, or a diamond, put together, that make the true complex idea of those substances, which a smith or a jeweler commonly knows better than a philosopher; who, whatever *substantial forms* he may talk of, has no other idea of those substances, than what is framed by a collection of those ideas which are found in them.[9]

According to Locke, the substance that holds "extended things" together, things known through sensible qualities, is *matter*. Locke claims that upon reflection, the "same thing happens concerning the operations of the mind, viz. thinking, reasoning, fearing, &c." That is, we identify a "thinking substance":

> ... some other *substance*, which we call *spirit;* whereby ... supposing a substance wherein thinking, knowing, doubting, and a power of moving, &c., do subsist, we have as clear a notion of the substance of spirit, as we have of body; the one being supposed to be (without knowing what it is) the *substratum* to those simple ideas we have from without; and the other supposed (with a like ignorance of what it is) to be the *substratum* to those operations we experiment in ourselves within.[10]

Thus, Locke affirms the existence of two substances: *matter* and *mind*. So, although Locke rejected Descartes's rationalism and theory of innate ideas, he accepted a Cartesian-type of *dualism*, in which mind and matter are viewed as different kinds of substance.

Primary and Secondary Qualities

In addition to distinguishing between two kinds of substance, Locke distinguished between two kinds of qualities. **Primary qualities** are sensible qualities that exist independently of any perceiver. Shape, size, location, and motion are examples of primary qualities. **Secondary qualities** are qualities whose existence depends on a perceiver. Examples of secondary qualities include color, sound, taste, and texture. Thus, we can say that primary qualities are *objective* properties of things; they exist

---

The world of explanations and reasons is not the world of existence.
— Jean-Paul Sartre

primary qualities
According to Locke, objective sensible qualities that exist independently of any perceiver; shape, size, location, and motion are examples of primary qualities.

secondary qualities
According to Locke, subjective qualities whose existence depends on a perceiver; color, sound, taste, and texture are examples of secondary qualities.

in the *object*. Secondary qualities depend on—"exist in"—a knowing or perceiving *subject;* thus, they are said to be *subjective* properties.

We have seen the importance of this basic objective–subjective distinction many times. It is at the heart of the quarrels between the Sophists and Plato, as well as the earliest efforts of philosophers to identify reality and to distinguish it from appearance. Locke's distinction between primary qualities (located in independently existing material objects) and secondary qualities (located in subjective mental acts and perceptions) is important because so much is riding on it.

If primary qualities do not exist, then what of the possibility of objective knowledge? What can we know of the existence of an independent reality? In other words, some real distinction between primary and secondary qualities *seems* necessary for confirmation of the "world of common sense." The "world of common sense" is simply a term for the widely held view that an objective world exists independently of our perceptions and that it exists "out there" and not simply as a figment of our imaginations or mental construct.

Locke's Egocentric Predicament

Locke holds a position known as **epistemological dualism**, the view that knowing contains two distinct aspects: the knower and the known. Given the basic empiricist premise that all knowledge comes from our own ideas, which in turn are based on our own sensations and perceptions, epistemological dualism presents us with a fundamental problem: If all knowledge comes in the form of my own ideas based on sense data, how can I verify the existence of anything external to the sensations that constitute sense data? That is, won't the very process of verification take place within the realm of my own ideas?

This problem has been termed Locke's **egocentric predicament** because Locke's copy theory seems to put us in the egocentric position of being able to know only a world of our own mental construction, a self-limited world. Indeed, if there is no external world, can there be any mind other than my own? How could I know? How could I distinguish another mind from my own if I only know my own subjective perceptions?

And if, as Locke suggests, all true ideas are based on sense data that correspond to something else, how can we ever verify the objective, independent existence of an external reality? How can we ever apply Locke's own standards of verification to his notion of primary qualities?

epistemological dualism
The view that knowing consists of two distinct aspects: the knower and the known.

egocentric predicament
A problem generated by epistemological dualism: If all knowledge comes in the form of my own ideas, how can I verify the existence of anything external to them?

"If Physics Is to Be Believed"

We think that the grass is green, the stones are hard, and the snow is cold. But physics assures us that the greenness of the grass, the hardness of the stones, and the coldness of snow are not the greenness, hardness, and coldness that we know in our own experience, but something very different. The observer, when he seems to himself to be observing a stone, is really, if physics is to be believed, observing the effects of the stone upon himself.

Bertrand Russell, *Our Knowledge of the External World as a Field for the Scientific Method in Philosophy* (Chicago: Open Court, 1915).

> *Suppose that a [plain] man meets a modern philosopher, and wants to be informed what smell in plants is. The philosopher tells him that there is no smell in plants, nor in anything but the mind; that it is impossible there can be smell but in a mind; and that all this hath been demonstrated by modern philosophy. The plain man will, no doubt, be apt to think him merry.*
>
> — Thomas Reid

At this point, it seems as if all I can know are my own perceptions (secondary qualities). As soon as I am *aware* of them, I have labeled and organized them. That is, even if external objects exist, the process of perceiving sense data is a process of becoming aware of *my ideas*. I don't ever seem to be able to actually experience *things-in-themselves*. If, as Locke claims, my ideas are "messages" from my senses, how can I—or anyone else—verify that the messages come from *independently existing things*? Locke himself asks, "How shall the mind, when it perceives nothing but its own ideas, know that they agree with things themselves?"

Locke tries to avoid the egocentric predicament by asserting that we "somehow know" that mental and physical substances—and an objective external reality— exist. We just don't have a clear idea of the *difference* between minds and bodies or other aspects of ultimate reality:

> Sensation convinces us that there are solid extended substances [matter and bodies]; and reflection that there are thinking ones [minds, souls]; experience assures us of the existence of such beings; and that one has the power to move body by impulse, the other by thought; this we cannot have any doubt of. Experience, I say, every moment furnishes us with clear ideas both of one and of the other. But beyond these ideas, as received from their proper sources, our faculties will not reach.[11]

In other words, Locke holds on to both a commonsense view of reality *and* his copy theory of truth, even though he cannot verify either by appealing to the copy theory. In spite of his major differences with Descartes, Locke draws surprisingly similar conclusions for similar reasons.

Both Locke and Descartes shied away from pursuing the logical consequences of their basic premises. Descartes was able to establish the momentary certainty of the cogito but had difficulty moving beyond his own mind when he attempted to provide a certain foundation for the external world and God's existence. Locke was able to demonstrate the importance of experience as an element of knowledge and show that many of our ideas are based on sensation and experience. He was also able to show the inadequacy of pure reason as a foundation for all knowledge. But, like Descartes, Locke was unable to move from direct knowledge of his own ideas to direct knowledge of external reality.

Pursued to its logical conclusion, Locke's empiricism does seem to end in the egocentric predicament. If it does, not only are we denied knowledge of an external, independent reality, but we are also denied the possibility of knowing God, for what simple sensations and experiences can there be on which the idea of God rests? Locke chose, in the end, to affirm certain beliefs at the expense of philosophical consistency. The second of the British empiricists tried to be more consistent.

PHILOSOPHICAL QUERY

Reflect on the claim that ideas are copies of sensations by considering these ideas: love, God, perfection, wisdom. Can you identify the *precise* sensations to which they correspond?

George Berkeley

George Berkeley

George Berkeley (1685–1753) was an Anglican bishop who posed one of the most quoted and least understood questions in the history of ideas: Does a tree falling in the forest make a sound if no one is there to hear it? Berkeley's answer is no, and it is based on a clear sense of the predicament Locke's empiricism generated.

From a commonsense point of view, it may seem absurd to deny the existence of a material world, but Berkeley pointed out that on closer examination, it makes more sense to deny the existence of matter than it does to affirm it. Don't pass over this point too quickly. Taking empiricism a logical step further than Locke, Berkeley argues that the material world does not exist. Only ideas exist, and ideas are mental states, not material objects. This makes Berkeley an **idealism** or **immaterialist**. The idea of matter existing without mental properties is self-contradictory, for there is no way to conceive of what an unperceived, unexperienced existence would consist of. We can conceive of things only in terms of the perceptions (ideas) we have of them.

Berkeley challenged Locke's copy theory of truth by pointing out that the so-called objects Locke thought our ideas correspond to lack any fixed nature. They are constantly changing. There is no "thing" to copy, Berkeley said, only a cluster of constantly changing perceptions:

> [Some hold that] real things, it is plain, have a fixed and real nature, which remains the same notwithstanding any change in our senses or in the posture and motion of our bodies; which indeed may affect the ideas in our minds, but it were absurd to think they had the same effect on things existing without the mind.
>
> …How then is it possible that things perpetually fleeting and variable as our ideas should be copies or images of anything fixed and constant? Or, in other words, since all sensible qualities, as figure, size, color, etc., that is, our ideas, are continually changing upon every alteration in the distance, medium, or instruments of sensation—how can any determinate, material objects be properly represented or painted forth by several distinct things each of which is so different from and unlike the rest? Or, if you say it resembles some one only of our ideas, how shall we be able to distinguish the true copy from all the false ones?[12]

According to Berkeley, all the qualities we assign to material objects are relative to the perceiver, what Locke called "secondary" qualities. For example, the coffee I am drinking is hot or cold depending on my perception of it. It is absurd to ask if it is *really* hot or cold. But, you might point out, it has an objective temperature, say 120° Fahrenheit—only, however, when someone measures it, that is, only when someone perceives a thermometer registering 120° Fahrenheit. Even so, you're probably tempted to respond, it *does have* a certain temperature, regardless of whether someone is aware of it.

Does it? What kind of temperature is it if no one anywhere is aware of it? And how can we ever—*in fact* or *in theory*—verify the existence of a thing's temperature *when no one is aware of it?* If there is an "objective, real" temperature, we will never know it.

We can know things only in terms of some perception of them through the senses, or as ideas perceived by the mind. And this being so, Berkeley argued, we

idealism (immaterialism) The belief that only ideas (mental states) exist; the material world is a fiction—it does not exist.

No sooner do we depart from sense and instinct to follow… reason… but… we are insensibly drawn into uncouth paradoxes, difficulties, and inconsistencies, which multiply and grow upon us as we advance in speculation; till at length, having wandered through many intricate mazes, we find ourselves just where we were, or, which is worse, sit down in a forlorn Scepticism.

— George Berkeley

know only perceptions—not *things-in-themselves*, only *things as perceived*. What difference does it make to insist that things exist independently of perceptions? If they do, we have no awareness of them, and they have no effect on us, so they are of no importance to us. When they do affect us, we perceive them. Thus, if no one or no thing were around to perceive the famous tree falling all alone in the forest, it would be absurd to say that it made a sound.

In *Three Dialogues Between Hylas and Philonous*, written in 1713, Berkeley points out that there is no difference between sound as perceived by us and sound as it is in itself. We may define sound in terms of what is perceived: sensations, atmospheric disturbances, decibels, waves, marks on a graph, or whatever, but in all cases sound remains *something that is perceived*:

> *Philonous:* It should follow then, that, according to you, real sounds may...never [be] heard.

> *Hylas:* Look you, Philonous, you may, if you please, make a jest of my opinion, but that will not alter the truth of things...sounds too have no real being without the mind.[13]

Berkeley takes the radical—but logically correct—step of concluding that this is true of everything. We know things only as different kinds of ideas about them. Berkeleian ideas imply consciousness, perception. It is self-contradictory to discuss ideas we do not know we have.

PHILOSOPHICAL QUERY

Think about the notion of *mind* as contrasted to the *brain* and *brain states*. It seems clear that our behavior, moods, and even thoughts can be influenced by factors we are unaware of. These might include fatigue, hunger, the effects of medication, allergies, neurological disorders, and so on. Could we also have ideas, motives, and emotions we are unaware of? That is, could we have an unconscious *mind*?

It is equally absurd to posit an independent, external reality, for if it exists, we cannot have anything to do with it. If we accept Locke's starting point that all knowledge derives from experience, Berkeley reasons, we must conclude that all knowledge is limited to ideas, because *we experience things only as ideas*. So-called material or physical *states* are perceptions, mental acts. Pain is a perception; sweet and sour are perceptions; the moon is a perception; my own body is known to me only as a series of perceptions. ***Esse est percipi***: To be is to be perceived.

As Descartes pointed out, there can be no doubt about my existence while I am aware of it: To think is to exist. Berkeley adds that to exist is to be thought about; nothing, not even an unthinking thing, can exist unless something perceives it:

> The table I write on I say exists; that is, I see and feel it: and if I were out of my study should say it existed; meaning thereby that if I was in my study I might perceive it, or that some other spirit actually does perceive it.... This is all that I can understand by these and the like expressions. For as to what is said of the *absolute*

Esse est percipi
Latin for Berkeley's belief that "to be is to be perceived."

existence of unthinking things [matter], without any relation to their being perceived, that to me is perfectly unintelligible. Their *esse* is *percipi*; nor is it possible they should have any existence out of the minds or thinking things which perceive them.[14]

Had Berkeley continued working out the logical consequences of his position, he would have had to accept a disturbing picture of reality: Only particular, immediate perceptions can be known to exist.

Berkeley stopped short of the skeptical conclusions implied by his premises. He introduced God as a guarantee that he had a continuing self, that he existed during deepest sleep, and that there was indeed an external world, safely encapsulated in the never-resting, all-perceiving mind of God. His successor, David Hume, did not stop but pursued skeptical logic to unsettling consequences.

David Hume: The Scottish Skeptic

David Hume (1711–1776) stands out in the history of ideas for the fearless consistency of his reasoning. I am aware of few other philosophers who so relentlessly and thoroughly follow the premises and principles on which his or her philosophy rests to such chilling and disturbing conclusions. Many great thinkers ultimately shied away from the logical conclusions of their ideas for personal, social, or religious reasons. Hume refused to do so. So powerful is his analysis that it effectively destroyed many important philosophies that went before it and much of the philosophy, science, and commonsense beliefs that follow it. Ironically, the wielder of perhaps the sharpest philosophical ax was one of the sweetest, most accessible figures in Western philosophy.

David Hume

Hume was born in Edinburgh, Scotland, and raised by his mother under a strict Presbyterian regimen. He attended three-hour morning services, went back for an hour in the afternoon, and joined in family prayers every evening. His father died the year after he was born, leaving his son a small income. Hume enrolled in the University of Edinburgh when he was twelve years old but, after three years, dropped out without a degree, planning to devote himself to philosophy and literature. A short time later, Hume admitted he had lost the faith of his childhood, writing that once he read Locke and other philosophers, he never again "entertained any belief in religion."[15]

The small income his father left allowed him only the barest existence, and Hume's family tried to persuade him to do something more practical and profitable than just study literature and philosophy. He studied law from 1726 to 1729, but the experience was so unpleasant that he had a breakdown and for a time lost interest in everything. In his own words, "The law appeared nauseous to me."[16]

Hume moved to London "to make a very feeble trial for entering into a more active scene of life" though he must have had a somewhat active social life in Scotland, for on March 5 and again on June 25 of 1734 he was accused of being the father of Agnes Galbraith's child. Hume escaped censure by the church because he was out of Scotland, but poor Agnes was required to wear sackcloth in front of the congregation and be put on public display in the pillory for three consecutive Sundays.

> *Upon the whole, I have always considered [David Hume], both in his lifetime and since his death, as approaching as nearly to the idea of a perfectly wise and virtuous man as perhaps the nature of human frailty will permit.*
>
> — Adam Smith

Meanwhile, Hume was working for a merchant in Bristol, but "in a few months I found that scene totally unsuitable to me." He moved to France, where living expenses were lower, finally settling near Descartes's old college at La Flèche. There the Jesuits allowed him full access to their first-rate library. Already his skeptical, questioning mind and discomfort in the face of any authority not supported by clear evidence stood out. One of the Jesuits described Hume as "too full of himself...his spirit more lively than solid, his imagination more luminous than profound, his heart too dissipated with material objects and spiritual self-idolatry to pierce into the sacred recesses of divine truths."[17]

The Skeptical Masterpiece

The Jesuits were correct in one aspect of their assessment of Hume, for they recognized a mind given to no allegiance but its own experiences, interpreted in an unforgiving rational light. While in France, Hume had what contemporary philosopher Richard Watson calls a "skeptical crisis." In six weeks he gained sixty pounds, and he remained a "fat, jolly fellow for the rest of his life."[18] He also completed the first two books of his powerful and disturbing *Treatise of Human Nature*.

In 1737, Hume returned to England, hoping to publish the *Treatise* and immediately ran into objections from publishers. In December 1737 he wrote, "I am at present castrating my work, that is, cutting out its noble parts,...endeavoring it shall give as little offense as possible."[19] Hume found most resistance to his analysis of miracles. He agreed to remove the most offensive passages but did not destroy them. In this censored form, the two-volume *Treatise* was published anonymously in January 1739. Hume received fifty pounds and twelve copies as his total payment. At the age of twenty-seven, he had written one of the major works of modern philosophy.

In the *Treatise*, Hume makes compelling arguments *against* materialism, the possibility of a spiritual, supernatural reality, and personal immortality—this in the watered-down version! Pushing beyond Locke and Berkeley, Hume argued that neither matter nor mind exists. (A standing joke at the time referred to Berkeley and Hume with the slogan "No matter; never mind.")

The uncensored version of the *Treatise* does not stop there. Hume ultimately reduces reason to the "slave of the passions" and alters the conventional picture of the nature of science by denying cause and effect as they are generally understood. Thus Hume challenged established religious beliefs, moral judgments, reason and rationalism, earlier forms of empiricism, and the certainty of science. He denied the existence of a "fixed self," the possibility of personal immortality, and the possibility of miracles. It would not be surprising if such a book provoked a great storm of controversy. Ultimately, Hume's book did just that, but not

David Hume (1711–76) 1766 (oil on canvas), Ramsay, Allan (1713-84)/Scottish National Portrait Gallery, Edinburgh, Scotland/The Bridgeman Art Library International

Even in Hume's time being overweight was subject to scorn. But as the philosopher Richard Watson notes in his delightful book *The Philosopher's Diet*, "Hume was a wonderful man. He and Benjamin Franklin used to have grand times together in Paris, eating and drinking and playing whist, and pulling bluestocking ladies down to sit on their fat laps."

among the general public and not right away. The second, uncensored, edition of the *Treatise* was not published until after Hume's death.

An Honest Man

Unable to earn his living as a writer, Hume applied for a professorship at the University of Edinburgh but was rejected. He took a somewhat humiliating job as the tutor of a young nobleman, who shortly went insane. Hume was ultimately dismissed and had to sue for his salary. He eventually secured a position as secretary to a general who was on a mission to Turin, Italy. Hume, having apparently gained more weight, began wearing a scarlet uniform. His appearance unsettled the young Earl of Charlemont, who wrote as follows: "His face was broad and fat, his mouth wide, and without any other expression than that of imbecility.... The corpulence of his whole person was far better fitted to communicate the idea of a turtle-eating alderman than that of a refined philosopher."[20]

Hume returned to London in 1748 and published *An Enquiry Concerning Human Understanding*. In 1749 he went back to Edinburgh and in 1751 published *An Enquiry Concerning the Principles of Morals*. These works reach the same conclusions as the *Treatise* but in a softer tone.

The softer tone was not to last, for in about 1751 Hume wrote the most devastating, direct, and irreverent of his works, the *Dialogues Concerning Natural Religion*. In it Hume mounts an unrelenting attack on the argument from design (see Chapter 8) and other attempts to demonstrate the existence of or understand the nature of God. At the urging of friends, Hume withheld the *Dialogues* from publication. They were finally published in 1779, three years after his death.

Hume wearied of the heated discussion his philosophical reasonings provoked and turned to politics and history. He finally achieved some success as an author with *Political Discourses* (1751) and *Essays on Various Subjects* (1753). The theory of economics discussed in the *Essays* was substantial enough to influence the great economist Adam Smith.

In 1752, Hume was elected keeper of the library for the Faculty of Advocates in Edinburgh. The pay was low, but Hume was delighted with the job because it gave him control of thirty thousand volumes. Taking advantage of this opportunity, he researched and wrote *History of England*. He was a competent enough historian that Edward Gibbon, the author of *The Decline and Fall of the Roman Empire* (1776), cited him as an influence.

Hume published his *History* in six volumes, in reverse order, beginning with the years 1603–1649 and ending with the period from Julius Caesar to Henry VII in 1485. His attitudes toward Parliament and Bonnie Prince Charlie were unorthodox, and the controversy aroused by the first volume was so intense that Hume grew depressed and planned to move back to France. But France and England were at war, and the second volume was nearly done. So Hume revised the first volume and continued with the others. By the publication of the sixth volume, Hume's popularity as a writer had soared. James Boswell referred to him as "the greatest writer in Britain," and Voltaire said Hume's work was "perhaps the best history ever written in any language."[21] (Today, hardly anyone reads Hume's *History of England*, but no truly educated person fails to read something of Hume's philosophy.)

> As a philosophical critic Hume has few peers. No one has challenged more sharply rationalism's central thesis that matters of fact can be known without recourse to experience; nor has anyone revealed more clearly the severe problems raised by insisting that all factual claims be empirically verified.
> — John W. Lenz

In spite of his success, Hume remained troubled by the unrelenting attacks from ecclesiastical and other sources. Relief arrived in the form of an appointment as deputy secretary to the Earl of Hertford, ambassador to France. Hertford also arranged that Hume should receive a pension of two hundred pounds for life.

Hume's writing was more popular in France than in England, and by the time he returned to France he was almost a cult figure. The aristocracy loved him (the ladies most of all), and he loved them (the ladies most of all). The Earl of Hertford found that Hume was more popular and respected than the earl was. Once, at a party, an envious French intellectual made fun of Hume's weight, quoting the Gospel verse "And the word was made flesh." One of Hume's many lady admirers quickly countered, "And the word was made lovable."

After Britain appointed a new ambassador to France in 1765, Hume worked for a time as undersecretary at the Foreign Office in London. He retired to Edinburgh in 1769, being, in his own words, "very opulent (for I possessed a revenue of £1,000 a year), healthy, and though somewhat stricken in years, with the prospect of enjoying long my ease, and of seeing the increase of my reputation."[22]

Hume's home (on, fittingly, St. David Street) became an intellectual salon for Scottish celebrities, including Adam Smith. Hume was a friendly, supportive, encouraging mentor, despite the rigor and iconoclasm of his intellect. He remained a popular guest, even if he occasionally broke a host's chair.[23] He once proposed a tax on obesity but thought its passage unlikely because it might put the church in danger, and he blessed Julius Caesar for preferring fat men.

Part of Hume's charm came from his personal modesty. These days celebrities and television "personalities" in their teens think nothing of writing a two- or three-hundred-page autobiography, yet one of the finest minds ever to have written considered it sufficient to pen an eight-page one—and then only shortly before he died. In it he wrote:

> In the spring of 1775 I was struck with a disorder in my bowels, which at first gave me no alarm, but has since, as I apprehend it, become mortal and incurable. I now reckon upon a speedy dissolution.
>
> I have suffered very little pain from my disorder; and what is more strange, have, notwithstanding the great decline of my person, never suffered a moment's abatement of my spirits; insomuch that were I to name the period of my life which I should most choose to pass over again, I might be tempted to point to this later period. I possess the same ardor as ever in my study, and the same gaiety in company. I consider, besides, that a man of sixty-five, by dying, cuts off only a few years of infirmities.[24]

In 1775, Hume lost seventy pounds due to his illness. In 1776, he was prepared to die "as fast as my enemies, if I have any, could wish, and as easily and cheerfully as my best friends could desire."[25]

Even in his last hours, Hume was not spared the attentions of the devout. James Boswell was troubled that the agnostic Hume, whom many erroneously believed to be an atheist, could be so cheerful in the face of death. But Hume did not deny the existence of God, a position known as *atheism;* rather, he adopted the agnostic view that we do not know enough to assert or deny the existence of God.

Happiness in the face of death was thought to be a virtue of the devout believer, not the skeptical agnostic. Unrelenting even at the end, Boswell asked the dying Hume if he did *now* finally believe in an afterlife. Hume answered, "It is a most unreasonable fancy that we should exist forever." Asked if he didn't at least think the possibility of another plane of existence was desirable, the dying skeptic answered, "Not at all; it is a very gloomy thought." A small parade of women visited Hume, begging him to believe, but he distracted them with humor.[26]

David Hume died free of much pain on August 25, 1776. The story goes that a large crowd attended his burial, despite heavy rain. Someone was heard to say, "He was an atheist." "No matter," a voice answered from the crowd. "He was an honest man."

Hume's Skeptical Empiricism

Hume's philosophy rests on the rejection of overly abstract, obscure, bloated speculations. Hume found most metaphysical speculation irrelevant to the lives of ordinary people. It was poorly worded, unclear, and based on unverified assumptions; it was also, he observed, never-ending. No metaphysical issue was ever clearly and thoroughly settled. For each theory about the soul or nature or reality, there were opposing theories and modifications, apparently infinite in number.

Hume thought such "abstruse speculation" was useful only to individuals with some theological motive, who, "being unable to defend [their views] on fair grounds, raise these entangling brambles to cover and protect their weaknesses." The only way to rid ourselves of these pointless excursions, he claimed, is to inquire seriously and thoroughly into the nature of human understanding, "and show, from an exact analysis of its powers and capacity, that it is by no means fitted for such remote and abstruse subjects."

In other words, Hume continued the "epistemological turn" moving further away from metaphysics than Locke and Berkeley had. Although he said we must "cultivate true metaphysics with some care in order to destroy the false," Hume moved modern philosophy firmly into the realm of epistemology:

> Accurate and just reasoning is the only catholic remedy, fitted for all persons and all dispositions; and is alone able to subvert that abstruse philosophy and metaphysical jargon, which, being mixed up with popular superstition, renders it in a manner impenetrable to careless reasoners, and gives it the air of science and wisdom.[27]

One has no knowledge of the sun but only of an eye that sees a sun, and no knowledge of the earth but only of a hand that feels an earth.

— Arthur Schopenhauer

Impressions and Ideas

In *An Enquiry Concerning Human Understanding*, Hume set out to modify Locke's theory of ideas in a way that removed any metaphysical residue. He began by pointing out the very obvious difference between, say, the painful perception of excessive heat or the pleasure of comforting warmth and the memory of such perceptions. There is also, he noted, a difference between anticipating a perception in the imagination and actually perceiving it. He says, "The most lively thought is still inferior to the dullest sensation." This kind of distinction also applies to "mental perceptions," such as anger and hate.

Hume thought Locke was correct in claiming that thought is a "faithful mirror, and copies objects truly." But he reminds us not to overlook a vital fact: The copies are always duller and fainter than the original perceptions on which they are based. Hume proposes that we distinguish "ideas" from "impressions":

> Here therefore we may divide all perceptions of the mind into two classes or species, which are distinguished by their different degrees of force and vivacity. The less forcible and lively are commonly denominated *Thoughts* or *Ideas*. The other species wants a name in our language, and most others.... Let us, therefore, use a little freedom, and call them *Impressions*; employing that word in a sense somewhat different from the usual. By the term *impression*, then, I mean all our more lively perceptions, when we hear, or see, or feel, or love, or hate, or desire, or will. And impressions are distinguished from ideas, which are the less lively perceptions, of which we are conscious, when we reflect on any of those sensations or movements above mentioned.[28]

More careful analysis of ideas, no matter how fanciful, creative, or original, reveals that "all this creative power of the mind amounts to no more than the faculty of compounding, transposing, augmenting, or diminishing the materials afforded us by the senses and experience." In other words, all ideas can be traced to impressions and, thus, are derived from experience, even if they become so abstracted and diluted that they no longer resemble any identifiable impressions. If you doubt this, Hume says the only way to refute him is to produce an idea not derived from impressions or from combining and altering the ideas that impressions generate. Modifying Locke's copy theory of ideas, Hume developed an empirical test of meaning:

> When we entertain, therefore, any suspicion that a philosophical term is employed without any meaning or idea (as is a bit too frequent), we need to enquire, *from what impression is that supposed idea derived?* And if it be impossible to assign any, this will serve to confirm our suspicion. By bringing ideas into so clear a light we may reasonably hope to remove all dispute, which may arise, concerning their nature and reality.[29]

The **empirical criterion of meaning** holds that all *meaningful* ideas can be traced to sense experience (impressions). Beliefs that cannot be reduced to sense experience are technically not "ideas" at all: They are *meaningless utterances*.

empirical criterion of meaning
Meaningful ideas are those that can be traced back to sense experience (impressions); beliefs that cannot be reduced to sense experience are not "ideas" at all but meaningless utterances.

Discussing Philosophy

PHILOSOPHICAL QUERY

Apply the empirical criterion of meaning to such concepts as God, love, justice, creativity, and intelligence. What, in general, do you see as the strengths and weaknesses of this criterion?

The Self

As we have seen, Descartes based modern philosophy on the thinking thing, the self. What could be more certain than the existence of my self? But what exactly does the word *self* refer to? Applying his empirical criterion of meaning, Hume argues that we do not have any idea of self as it is commonly understood:

> For from what impression cou'd this idea be deriv'd? This question 'tis impossible to answer without a manifest contradiction and absurdity; and 'tis a question, which necessarily must be answer'd, if we wou'd have the idea of self pass for clear and intelligible. But self or person is not any one impression, but that to which our several impressions and ideas are suppos'd to have a reference. If any impression gives rise to the idea of self, that impression must continue invariably the same, thro' the whole course of our lives; since self is suppos'd to exist after that manner. But there is no impression constant and invariable. Pain and pleasure, grief and joy, passions and sensations succeed each other, and never all exist at the same time. It cannot, therefore, be from any of these impressions, or from any other, that the idea of self is deriv'd; and consequently there is no such idea.[30]

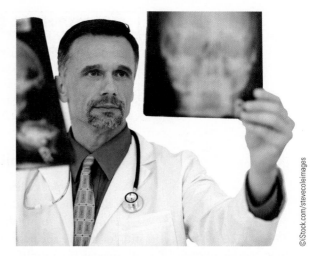

Where is "the self" located? Where is the mind? Is there any empirical evidence for their existence?

If we have no specific *impression* of self, then what are we? Hume gives one of the most intriguing, yet elusive, answers in modern philosophy:

> For my part, when I enter most intimately into what I call *myself*, I always stumble on some particular perception or other, of heat or cold, light or shade, love or hatred, pain or pleasure. I never can catch *myself* at any time without a perception, and never can observe any thing but the perception. When my perceptions are remov'd for any time, as by sound sleep; so long am I insensible of *myself*, and may truly be said not to exist. And were all my perceptions remov'd by death, and cou'd I neither think, nor feel, nor see, nor love, nor hate after the dissolution of my body, I shou'd be entirely annihilated, nor do I conceive what is farther requisite to make me a perfect non-entity. If any one upon serious and unprejudic'd reflexion, thinks he has a different notion of *himself*, I must confess I can reason no longer with him. All I can allow him is, that he may be in the right as well as I, and that we are essentially different in this particular. He may, perhaps, perceive something simple and continu'd, which he calls *himself*; tho' I am certain there is no such principle in me.
>
> But setting aside some metaphysicians of this kind, I may venture to affirm of the rest of mankind, that they are nothing but a bundle or collection of different perceptions, which succeed each other with an inconceivable rapidity, and are in a perpetual flux and movement.[31]

In such passages, Hume sounds very much like a Buddhist or Hindu. He has dissolved the self into a flickering series of perceptions with no underlying, constant *thing* to unite them. What has come to be known as Hume's **bundle theory of the self** is difficult for most of us to accept. Yet Hume's position is more consistent than are some that are more comforting and popular.

bundle theory of the self A Humean theory that there is no fixed self but that the self is merely a "bundle of perceptions"; a self is merely a habitual means for discussing certain perceptions.

Personal Immortality

If we cannot speak clearly about the self, what happens to the common belief that the self (or the soul) survives after bodily death?

Hume says, in his straightforward fashion, that there can be no persistent identity for us. We speak of "the oak tree" in the backyard, but, in fact, each time we see it, "the oak tree" is different. It may have a different number of leaves, and certainly it has changed in some ways, even when we cannot discern these changes. Any change in a thing changes its identity. In what sense can a two-hundred-pound man who has been married twice and fathered children be the same person who was once a fifty-pound third-grader? In what sense are you the same person who began reading this book? Your mind—or brain—has different ideas. Your body has different cells. As Heraclitus noted, "We cannot step twice into the same river, for the water into which we first stepped has flowed on."

In other words, identity is not a property of things but a mental act. Our minds *confer* identity on things; we do not perceive it. A self is merely a habitual way of discussing certain perceptions:

> The whole of this doctrine leads us to a conclusion, which is of great importance in the present affair, *viz.* that all the nice and subtle questions concerning personal identity can never possibly be decided, and are to be regarded rather as grammatical than as philosophical difficulties.... We have no just standard, by which we can decide any dispute concerning the time, when [things] acquire or lose a title to the name of identity. All the disputes concerning the identity of connected objects are merely verbal, except so far as the relation of parts gives rise to some fiction or imaginary principle of union, as we have already observ'd.[32]

Strictly speaking, Hume is correct. We do not *perceive* identity. Yet something gives order and continuity to our experiences, and Hume does not deny that. Rather, he insists on clearer, more precise talking, reasoning, and thinking about this and other important matters. In the process, Hume challenges the limits of reason and, perhaps, of knowledge.

The sceptic wishes, from considerations of humanity, to do all he can with the arguments at his disposal to cure the self-conceit and rashness of the dogmatists.
— Sextus
    Empiricus

The Limits of Reason

In a sense, Hume stops at the first part of Berkeley's position:

> The mind has never anything present to it but the perceptions, and cannot possibly reach any experience of their connexion with objects. The supposition of such a connexion...is, therefore, without any foundation in reasoning.[33]

We have no way of empirically establishing the independent existence of an external world, or of what many of us mean by "reality." We can only know our own perceptions, ideas, and experiences:

> As several impressions appear exterior to the body, we suppose them also exterior to ourselves. The paper, on which I write at present, is beyond my hand. The table is beyond the paper. The walls of the chamber beyond the table. And in casting my eye towards the window, I perceive a great extent of fields and buildings beyond my chamber. From all this it may be infer'd, that no other faculty is requir'd, besides the senses, to convince us of the external existence of body. But to prevent this inference, we need only weigh the three following considerations. *First*, That, properly speaking, 'tis not our body we perceive, when we regard our limbs and members, but certain impressions, which enter by the sense; so that in ascribing a real and corporeal existence to these impressions, or to their objects, is an act of the mind as difficult to explain, as that which we examine at present. *Secondly*, Sounds and tastes, and smells, tho' commonly regarded by the mind as continu'd independent qualities, appear not to have any existence in extension, and consequently cannot appear to the senses as situated externally to the body.... *Thirdly*, Even our sight informs us not of distance or outness (so to speak) immediately and without certain reasoning and experience, as is acknowledg'd by the most rational philosophers.[34]

If, as Hume thought, there is no rational evidence whatsoever for belief in an external reality, then why is the notion so popular? Hume suggests that the imagination accounts for the universal notion of the independent existence of an external world. It is the nature of the imagination to complete and fill in gaps between perceptions. If we regularly experience very much the same perceptions—say, of the oak tree in the yard or our own face—we overlook the gaps between different perceptions. Hume says we "feign," or fabricate, continuity. I assume that because my face looks "the same" this morning as yesterday morning, it has existed continuously all night (and at other times) when I had no perception of it.

Further, our experiences tend to occur with a kind of pattern or regularity, which Hume refers to as *coherence*. That is, when I turn my head to the left, my view in the mirror is a particular perception. When I tilt forward, I have a completely different perception, and so on. When I turn around and use a hand mirror to examine the thinning hair on the back of my head, I have yet another perception. What I never have is an impression of my whole head—and neither do you have an impression of my whole head. No one does. But because my various views always follow a pattern, my imagination feigns, or fabricates, an idea of my whole head.

According to Hume, this process explains our belief in an external world. This "natural quality" of the mind is much more powerful than logical reasoning; it always reasserts itself after being challenged on logical grounds:

> There is a great difference betwixt such opinions as we form after a calm and profound reflection, and such as we embrace by a kind of instinct or natural impulse, on account of their suitableness and conformity to the mind. If these opinions become contrary, 'tis not difficult to foresee which of them will have the advantage. As long as our attention is bent upon the subject, the philosophical and study'd principle may prevail; but the moment we relax our thoughts, nature will display herself, and draw us back to our former opinion....[35]

It is easier to indulge in abstract thought than it is to exist.
— Søren Kierkegaard

If Hume is correct, nature and reason are adversaries: "Nature is obstinate, and will not quit the field, however strongly attack'd by reason; and at the same time reason is so clear in the point, that there is no possibility of disguising her."

A completely nonrational life would be barely human, however. Even the most primitive, nontechnical, "natural" cultures depend on reason. What Hume suggests is a kind of fluctuating balance between reason and nature, or between logic and emotion. His skepticism indicates that a completely rational view of reality is not possible, or at least not for more than brief, concentrated periods. It suggests that reason, the great ideal of so many philosophers, is, in fact, the slave of emotions, shaped by psychology and biology.

PHILOSOPHICAL QUERY

Have you been able to take Hume's strictest claims seriously? That is, have you seriously considered the possibility that we lack knowledge of the external world? Discuss some factors that make taking this idea seriously so difficult. Can you spot any errors in Hume's reasoning?

The Limits of Science

inductive reasoning
A reasoning pattern that proceeds from the particular to the general or from "some" to "all" and results in generalized rules or principles established with degrees of probability.

Scientific reasoning rests on a pattern of **inductive reasoning**, which results in generalized rules or principles. Simplistically, induction reasons from the particular to the general, or from "some" to "all." Scientific principles are never based on experience with *all* things of a certain kind. Newton did not have to observe the behavior of all bodies to conclude that they are subject to gravity. He based his conclusion on the behavior of just some bodies.

Scientists assume that such inferences are reliable because they identify *causal patterns*. In Hume's time, cause and effect were defined in terms of a *necessary connection*. That is, *A* was said to cause *B* if the occurrence of *A* *always and without exception* was followed by the occurrence of *B*. But if Hume's epistemology is correct, how can we perceive the actual connection, the causal relationship? Strictly speaking, all we actually observe is *A* followed by *B*. We observe constant conjunction. That is, a perception of *A* is always (or so far) followed by a perception of *B*. But that is a temporal sequence, not a necessary connection. If Hume is correct, there is no empirical evidence for the existence of cause and effect:

> We have sought in vain for an idea of power or necessary connexion in all the sources from which we could suppose it to be derived. It appears that, in single instances of the operation of bodies, we never can, by our utmost scrutiny, discover anything but one event following another, without being able to comprehend any force or power by which the cause operates, or any connexion between it and its supposed effect. The same difficulty occurs in contemplating the operations of mind on body—where we observe the motion of the latter to follow upon the volition of the former, but are not able to observe or conceive the tie which binds together the motion and volition, or the energy by which the mind produces this

effect. The authority of the will over its own faculties and ideas is not a whit more comprehensible: So that, upon the whole, there appears not, throughout all nature, any one instance of connexion which is conceivable by us. All events seem entirely loose and separate. One event follows another; but we can never observe any tie between them. They seem *conjoined*, but never *connected*. And as we can have no idea of any thing which [is not based on an impression], the necessary conclusion *seems* to be that we have no idea of connexion or power at all, and that these words are absolutely without any meaning, when employed either in philosophical reasonings or common life.[36]

What *do we observe* that we call cause and effect? Hume answers that we observe a series of recognizable impressions and that we come to expect the first part of the series to be followed by the second part. When we are correct, we assume that the connection is causal. But we cannot observe that one event *must* follow the other. All we *know* is that one event *happens* to follow another. We may have observed this pattern countless times, but that does not logically justify inferring any sort of necessity.

In other words, the mind creates the ideas of causality and necessity; we do not observe them. The best we can do is take for granted that the future will resemble the past: There is no way to prove that it must. We are psychologically constructed so that we have no choice but to *believe in* cause and effect. And for the most part, our inferences regarding the predictability and uniformity of experience have been borne out. But, Hume cautions, we should not forget that the real origin of science lies in the operation of the human mind. We believe in an independent, external reality because we cannot help it.

The Limits of Theology

Given his radical view of cause and effect, it is not surprising that Hume rejected all efforts to use causality to prove the existence of God. The cosmological argument and the argument from motion (Chapter 8) were meaningless for him. The ontological argument (Chapter 9) was meaningless as well, because the very qualities ascribed to God—perfection, omniscience, omnipotence, and so forth—do not correspond to specific impressions. They are empty noises.

Besides rejecting these arguments, Hume wrote perhaps the most devastating and complete critique of the argument from design, also known as the teleological argument (see Thomas Aquinas's fifth way in Chapter 8). After taking the briefest look at this compelling bit of logical analysis, we can understand why Hume withheld publication of his *Dialogues Concerning Natural Religion* during his lifetime.

Recall that the core of the argument from design is the belief that all about us we see evidence of God's handiwork. We perceive order and harmony and beauty throughout the universe. We sense divine purpose in a beautiful sunset or an

It follows from this definition of cause, that night is the cause of day, and day the cause of night. For no two things have more constantly followed each other since the beginning of the world.

— Thomas Reid

"This is not…what we expect from infinite power, infinite wisdom, infinite goodness," Hume declares. "Look round this universe. What an immense profusion of beings…hostile and destructive to each other…contemptible or odious to the spectator! The whole presents nothing but the idea of a blind nature…pouring forth from her lap, without discernment or parental care, her maimed and abortive children."

ocean breeze; we feel God's presence in the miracle of childbirth or the renewing of the seasons. But as Hume points out, that's not the whole picture:

> But were this world ever so perfect a production, it must still remain uncertain, whether all the excellences of the work can justly be ascribed to the workman. If we survey a ship, what an exalted idea must we form of the ingenuity of the carpenter, who framed so complicated, useful, and beautiful a machine? And what surprise must we feel, when we find him a stupid mechanic, who imitated others, and copied an art, which, through a long succession of ages, after multiplied trials, mistakes, corrections, deliberations, and controversies, had gradually been improving? Many worlds might have been botched and bungled, throughout an eternity, ere this system was struck out: Much labor lost: Many fruitless trials made: And a slow, but continued improvement carried on during infinite ages in the art of world-making....
>
> Did I show you a house or palace, where there was not one apartment convenient or agreeable; where the windows, doors, fires, passages, stairs, and the whole economy of the building were the source of noise, confusion, fatigue, darkness, and extremes of heat and cold; you would certainly blame the contrivance, without any farther examination.... If you find many inconveniences and deformities in the building, you will always, without entering into any detail, condemn the architect.[37]

There is even less reason to infer the existence of a good God once one takes a thorough, objective look at life:

> But allowing you, what never will be believed; at least, what you never possibly can prove, that animal, or at least human happiness, in this life, exceeds its misery; you have yet done nothing: For this is not, by any means, what we expect from infinite power, infinite wisdom, infinite goodness. Why is there any misery at all in this world? Not by chance surely. From some cause then. Is it from the intention of the Deity? But he is perfectly benevolent. Is it contrary to his intention? But he is almighty. Nothing can shake the solidity of this reasoning, so short, so clear, so decisive....
>
> Look round this universe. What an immense profusion of beings, animated and organized, sensible and active! You admire the prodigious variety and fecundity. But inspect a little more narrowly these living existences, the only beings worth regarding. How hostile and destructive to each other! How insufficient all of them for their own happiness! How contemptible or odious to the spectator! The whole presents nothing but the idea of a blind nature, impregnated by a great vivifying principle, and pouring forth from her lap, without discernment or parental care, her maimed and abortive children.[38]

Based solely on our observations of human experience, we find insufficient evidence to assume the existence of a good, all-wise, all-powerful God. Imagine what kind of argument Hume could have made had he known of the Holocaust or Darfur.

At this point in the dialogue, Hume has the person representing orthodox belief object, asking, "What *data* have you for such extraordinary conclusions?" Hume makes his most important and devastating point:

Christianity does not—and cannot—explain how a God who is infinitely powerful and infinitely loving came to create a universe which turned out to be not very good.
— Arnold
      Toynbee

This is the topic on which I have all along insisted. I have still asserted that we have no *data* to establish any system of cosmogony [theory of the origins of the universe]. Our experience, so imperfect in itself, and so limited both in extent and duration, can afford us no probable conjecture concerning the whole of things.[39]

Strictly speaking, our own little corner of the universe is too small to permit useful generalizations about the whole. To conclude yea or nay about God's existence and nature is beyond the limits of both reason and experience.

In a note added to the *Dialogues* just before his death, Hume stated that "*the cause or causes of order in the universe probably bear some remote analogy to human intelligence.*" But he insisted that this analogy does not suggest that God exists, at least not the God of Judeo-Christian-Islamic religions.

For Deeper Consideration

When he died, there was a commonly held belief that David Hume was an atheist. Why did so many people believe that he was an atheist (a notion that is still widely held by those who know only a smattering of his philosophy)? What did he assert that might lead to such a conclusion? If Hume wasn't an atheist, what position did he hold in regard to God's existence and nature? In what sense might Hume's position be even more troubling to a theist than atheism?

> *I said that I could not imagine being an atheist any time before 1859, when Darwin's* Origin of Species *was published. "What about Hume?" replied the philosopher. "How did Hume explain the organized complexity of the living world?" I asked. "He didn't," said the philosopher. "Why does it need any special explanation?"*
> — Richard Dawkins

The Limits of Ethics

As we have seen, reason has played a dominant role in Western philosophy. Plato argued that reason's function is to rule the appetites and emotions. The Stoics attempted to control their passions through reason. Descartes attempted to replace the authority of the church with the authority of reason. Descartes was not alone in his vision of reason as the ground of all knowledge, including moral knowledge. The seventeenth and eighteenth centuries are sometimes characterized as the Age of Reason. Attempts to ground morals in reason continue in the present. Hume, in contrast, challenged the role of reason in morality in an unprecedented way and achieved results similar to his critiques of theology and metaphysics.

Hume insisted that morality is grounded in sentiment, not reason. His devastating attack on any "metaphysic of morals" has had an enormous influence on modern and postmodern conceptions of morality, value judgments, and the possibility of moral knowledge. Immanuel Kant (Chapter 11) would ultimately refer to Hume's work as a "scandal in philosophy."

In his *Treatise of Human Nature*, Hume asserts that "reason alone" can never provide a motive for any action:

Nothing is more usual in philosophy, and even in common life, than to talk of the combat of passion and reason, to give the preference to reason, and to assert that men are only so far virtuous as they conform themselves to its dictates. Every rational creature, 'tis said, is oblig'd to regulate his actions by reason; and if any other

Douglas J. Soccio

Consider the ongoing controversy surrounding gay marriage. To what extent do you think the persistence and intensity of this matter involves moral "sentiment"? Take a close, thoughtful look at the happy couple in this photograph and reflect on the extent to which *feelings* influence our moral values. According to Hume, what we call "virtues" are traits of character that we find agreeable, and what we call "moral judgments" are matters of taste, feeling, or "sentiment." If there is more to morality than sentiment and taste, what is it? If Hume is right, what is the best way to approach moral disagreements?

motive or principle challenge the direction of his conduct, he ought to oppose it, 'till it be entirely subdu'd, or at least brought to a conformity with this common principle. On this method of thinking the greatest part of moral philosophy, ancient and modern, seems to be founded; nor is there an ampler field, as well for metaphysical arguments, as popular declamations, than this suppos'd pre-eminence of reason above passion....

In order to shew the fallacy of all this philosophy, I shall endeavour to prove *first*, that reason alone can never be a motive to any action of the will; and *secondly*, that it can never oppose passion in the direction of the will.[40]

Hume did not deny that reason plays a role in making moral judgments. Rather, he argued that reason's role is secondary to the role of moral feelings or *sentiments*, because reason can never provide ultimate ends:

It appears evident that the ultimate ends of human actions can never...be accounted for by *reason*, but recommend themselves entirely to the sentiments and affections of mankind, without any dependence on the intellectual faculties. Ask a man *why he uses exercise;* he will answer, *because he desires to keep his health.* If you then enquire, *why he desires health*, he will readily reply, *because sickness is painful.* If you push your enquiries farther, and desire a reason *why he hates pain*, it is impossible that he can ever give any. This is an ultimate end, and is never referred to any other object.[41]

According to Hume, although reason has a useful role to play in moral discernment, moral judgments themselves ultimately rest on "some internal sense or feeling which nature has made universal in the whole species."[42] Reason helps us clarify experience. It helps us identify facts. It does not, however, evaluate them: "Reason is, and ought only to be the slave of the passions, and can never pretend to any other office than to serve and obey them."[43]

The Facts, Just the Facts

Hume's analysis of moral judgments resembles his analysis of causality. Recall that, according to Hume, we do not actually perceive "necessary connection" but, rather, associate the feeling of necessity with certain related events (events constantly conjoined). Moral judgments are like causal judgments: They are mental associations or projections, not *perceptions* of facts. When we like a certain quality, we call it a virtue or label it "good" or "right." When we dislike something, we call it a vice or label it "wrong" or "bad." These evaluations are not derived from reason but from experience. It is "just a fact" that a certain combination of conditions produces cold or heat; likewise, it is "just a fact" that we associate some experiences with good feelings (these are desired) and some with bad feelings (these are disliked). In other words, through experience, we learn to associate certain facts with positive sentiments (being good or desired) and other facts with negative sentiments (being bad or disliked). The facts themselves are value neutral.

In the important and influential Part I of Book III of his *Treatise*, Hume makes a crucial distinction between *facts* and *values* (evaluations of facts). According to Hume, *facts themselves are valueless*. Moral judgments (like all other evaluations) are not judgments of facts but reports of moral sentiments or feelings. Hume's fact–value distinction has exerted tremendous influence on all moral philosophy since. In the *Treatise* he says:

> But can there be any difficulty in proving, that vice and virtue are not matters of fact, whose existence we can infer by reason? Take any action allow'd to be vicious: Willful murder, for instance. Examine it in all lights, and see if you can find the matter of fact, or real existence, which you call *vice*. In whichever way you take it, you find only certain passions, motives, volitions and thoughts. There is no matter of fact in the case. The vice entirely escapes you, as long as you consider the object. You can never find it, till you turn your reflexion into your own breast, and find a sentiment of disapprobation, which arise in you towards this action. Here is a matter of fact; but 'tis the object of feeling, not of reason. It lies in yourself, not in the object. So that when you pronounce any action or character to be vicious, you mean nothing, but that from the constitution of your nature you have a feeling or sentiment of blame from the contemplation of it. Vice and virtue, therefore, may be compar'd to sounds, colours, heat and cold, which according to modern philosophy, are not qualities in objects, but perceptions in the mind.[44]

To fully grasp what Hume is saying, it helps to distinguish between *descriptive language* and *normative language*. Descriptive language—as the name suggests—is devoid of all subjective, evaluative characterizations. Using Hume's example of "willful murder" we might expect to find descriptive language in a police report: "Dean Fetters shot J. Scott Vargas in the chest six times. Vargas fell to the floor. He lost three quarts of blood and died at 6:15 P.M." and so on. No matter how precise and elaborate a purely factual description of the circumstance is, it will contain no moral judgments. Indeed, the moral judgment of murder is like the legal judgment of murder. Although we base both judgments on our beliefs about the facts, murder (in either the moral or legal sense) is an interpretation of the facts—not a description or observation. No one sees murder. We see Fetters shoot Vargas. We do not see murder. In a court of law, we *decide* murder (or not). In the moral case, we react subjectively to the facts and feel murder (or not). Moral judgments, according to Hume, are like judgments about art or food—matters of moral taste or sentiment.

Discussing Philosophy

PHILOSOPHICAL QUERY

Hume's point here is very important. Don't rush by it. Take a moment and try to write a purely factual description of something you believe is immoral. Do you agree with Hume that the facts are value-neutral and that all moral judgments are reports of feelings associated with certain facts? Explain why or why not.

Moral Sentiments

Hume believed that the task before him was a "question of fact, not of abstract science" and that success was possible only by "following the experimental method, and deducing general maxims from a comparison of particular instances." Using the fact–value distinction, he attempted a reformation of moral philosophy, announcing that it was time to "reject every system of ethics, however subtle or ingenious, which is not founded on fact and observation."

Hume's efforts did, indeed, launch a revolution in moral philosophy. He helped establish a method of "ordinary language analysis" that became especially influential in the early part of the twentieth century and whose influence is still significant. (See Chapter 17.) Notice how the empirical criterion of meaning affects Hume's language analysis in the following passage. Also note the role he gives reason:

> The very nature of language guides us almost infallibly in forming a judgment of [matters of Personal Merit]; and as every tongue possesses one set of words which are taken in a good sense, and another in the opposite, the least acquaintance with the idiom suffices, without any reasoning, to direct us in collecting and arranging the estimable or blamable qualities of [people]. The only object of reasoning is to discover the circumstances on both sides, which are common to these qualities; to observe that particular in which the estimable qualities agree on one hand, and the blamable on the other; and thence to reach the foundation of ethics, and find those universal principles, from which all censure or approbation is ultimately derived.[45]

In all cases of moral judgment, what we call virtues are the traits that we, in fact, find agreeable. The feeling of agreeableness is what makes them virtues to us. We do not find them agreeable because they are virtues. We call them virtues because we find them agreeable. That's an important distinction.

We sometimes lose sight of the fundamental nature of all value judgments because we use different terms to distinguish among variations of experience. Put another way, different pleasures are like different flavors; all the good flavors are pleasing, yet we call some sweet, some sour, some chocolate, some lime, some fruity, some salty. Similarly, all unpleasant sentiments are alike, yet we call some disgusting, some ugly, some evil, some bad, some cowardly, and so forth.[46]

What, then, is unique to that "peculiar kind" of sentiment that Hume calls moral? Hume says that *moral sentiment is a disinterested reaction to character (motive)*. Moral virtue is *disinterested approbation* (liking or approval) of character or motive. Moral vice is *disinterested disapprobation* (disliking or disapproval) of character or motive. According to Hume, careful language analysis reveals that, *as a matter of fact*, moral judgments are disinterested judgments of character.

Rejection of Egoism

By asserting that moral judgments are disinterested, Hume rejected egoism. (See Chapters 3, 4, 11, 12, 16, and 17 for more about the relationship of self-interest to morality.) In his forceful attack, he refers to egoism as "a principle...supposed to prevail among many." Hume characterizes egoism as the belief that

…all *benevolence* is mere hypocrisy, friendship a cheat, public spirit a farce, fidelity a snare to procure trust and confidence, and that while all of us, at bottom, pursue only our private interest, we wear these fair disguises, in order to put others off their guard, and expose them the more to our wiles and machinations.[47]

Hume argues that egoism is utterly inadequate as an account of real life. A clear look at the facts makes it plain that we have other motives than these. He rejects egoism as factually inaccurate and overly simplistic, warning that the love of such contrived simplicity "has been the source of much false reasoning in philosophy." He says:

The most obvious objection to the selfish hypothesis is that, as it is contrary to common feeling and our most unprejudiced notions, there is required the highest stretch of philosophy to establish so extraordinary a paradox. To the most careless observer there appear to be such dispositions as benevolence and generosity; such affections as love, friendship, compassion, gratitude.[48]

Hume's attack on egoism is withering in its clarity and appeal to everyday experience. He rejects and ridicules the complications implicit in the belief that our real motives are always some form of narrow self-interest. Consider, Hume suggests, feelings of grief. Which is more absurd: to assume that all feelings of grief over the deaths of our loved ones are really disguised self-interest or to accept them as we experience them? Are we, Hume asks, ready to believe that our loving pets are really motivated solely by self-interest? Obviously not. The most cursory glance at our actual experiences with animals shows that conditioning (or even instinct) does not adequately describe all acts of animal loyalty and affection. Does this mean that animals can express disinterested benevolence but human beings cannot? Hume thought such an idea was preposterous.

According to Hume, pure self-love is another of the fictions that results from rationalistic thinking that loses touch with actual experience because it is not based on empirical facts. When we take our actual experience into account, self-love is not an adequate explanation of human motivation:

Where is the difficulty in conceiving, that…from the original frame of our temper, we may feel a desire of another's happiness or good, which by means of that affection, becomes our own good, and is afterwards pursued, from the combined motives of benevolence and self-enjoyments? Who sees not that vengeance, from the force alone of passion, may be so eagerly pursued, as to make us knowingly neglect every consideration of ease, interest, or safety; and, like some vindictive animals, infuse our very souls into the wounds we give an enemy; and what a malignant philosophy it must be, that will not allow to humanity and friendship the same privileges which are indisputably granted to the darker passions of enmity and resentment.[49]

> *Even an act performed out of love is supposed to be "unegoistic"? But you blockheads!*
> — Friedrich Nietzsche

Emotions Are Also Reasons

To nonphilosophers, Hume's refusal to ignore moral and other sentiments may seem trivially obvious. After all, what moderately aware person doesn't realize that people are not, cannot, and should not be, pure reasoning machines? But before we succumb to easy, historically naive cynicism in this regard, let us keep in mind why modern philosophers were so interested in objectivity and rationality. The search for objective rules of reason that apply to everyone was part of a major cultural shift away from a medieval, faith-based, God-centered worldview toward a modern, science-based worldview. The hope was to find a universal way to settle epistemological disagreements buttressed by more than customs, or feelings, or the strength of our convictions. Without some universal, objective standards and methods, how, the early modern philosophers wondered, can we move beyond mere belief? How can we transcend the perpetual discord grounded in mere subjective preferences?

Encouraged by early scientific discoveries and wary of the sorts of perpetual faith-based conflicts that plagued medieval thinkers, modern philosophers focused on the advantages promised by the development of an impartial—objective and universal—epistemology. In their search for epistemological neutrality, modern philosophers tended to ignore—when they did not outright reject—emotions and sentiments as important sources of knowledge and insight. But as we have already seen, the most well-intentioned human endeavors to correct one imbalance risk generating an opposing imbalance. In this instance, a narrow focus on rationality and objectivity tended to discount or overlook other important factors at play in the search for knowledge. (See Susan Bordo's comments regarding Cartesian dualism in Chapter 9 and Carol Gilligan's characterization of the different voice in philosophy in Chapter 18.)

Today, a substantial body of cross-disciplinary work challenges the exclusive status of the rationalistic model of detached, objective knowing. We've seen some of these challenges already. In succeeding chapters we will encounter a new intensity in the way certain questions are raised by existentialist and postmodern critiques of the pursuit of pure rationality and objectivity (Chapters 14–18): Can knowledge be divorced from social conditions? Is there only one correct way of thinking? To what extent, if any, are personal detachment and objectivity possible? What, if any, contributions do emotions make to knowledge? Perhaps most intriguing: Are personal detachment and objectivity *desirable*?

In contrast to a one-size-fits-all exclusive epistemology, "nontraditional" (more on this in Chapter 18) contemporary philosophers answer these questions with an inclusive model of thinking that does not reject logical reasoning and objectivity. Rather, the inclusive model of knowing complements and balances logical reasoning and objectivity—humanizes them—by including life experience, subjective responses, and empathy as necessary sources of knowledge.

As the term suggests, an *inclusive* model of knowing resists the depersonalized, disembodied language that Susan Bordo associates with the "masculinization" of epistemology and metaphysics (Chapter 9). Rather than treat epistemology as a purely cognitive or historical exercise, feminist philosophers expect philosophy to make a difference in people's lives, individually and by way of social action.

The contemporary philosopher Alison Jaggar reminds us that emotions are vital aspects of anyone's picture of reality because they influence what we notice or ignore, and, thus, add value (degrees of interest and importance) to experience. According to Jaggar, emotions select, direct, and even help define what we acknowledge as observations and experiences. If we don't care about something, we tend to trivialize

> [A] man, being just as hungry as he is thirsty, and placed between food and drink, must necessarily remain where he is and starve to death.
> — Aristotle

it. We may even not notice or remember it. In a sense, then, without some emotional interest, without caring, we can fail to experience all of our experiences. Yet, Jaggar notes, more often than not, traditional Western philosophy has viewed emotion as inferior to reason and often treated emotions as subversive hindrances to knowledge. The facts are otherwise, Jaggar suggests. There is no gap between emotion and knowledge:

> From Plato until the present, with a few notable exceptions, reason rather than emotion has been regarded as the indispensable faculty for acquiring knowledge....Empirical [objective] testability became accepted as the hallmark of natural science; this, in turn, was viewed as the paradigm of genuine knowledge....Because values and emotions had been identified as variable and idiosyncratic, [the objective standard of knowing] stipulated that trustworthy knowledge could be established only by methods that neutralized the values and emotions of individual [thinkers].[50]

Jaggar points out that traditional, supposedly impersonal epistemology has given short shrift to the emotional acumen women have developed over centuries due to their socially assigned roles as caretakers and household managers. She suggests that these roles require a specially refined *emotional acumen* that consists of an intuitive ability to recognize, assess, and empathize with the unspoken or overlooked pain of others. Jaggar also raises the possibility that oppressed people may have an especially clearer understanding of life because oppression provides a strong motive for paying attention, for observing, for finding out what is wrong.

This does not mean, however, that emotional acumen is just a "women's issue." Emotional acumen is a human issue because it helps each of us more accurately and fairly manage the social, legal, and political aspects of our lives. According to Jaggar, emotional sensitivity is often anyone's "first indication that something is wrong with the way alleged facts have been constructed, with the accepted understanding of how things are," eloquently reminding us that:

> Emotion is necessary for human survival. Emotions prompt us to act appropriately, to approach some people and situations and to avoid others, to caress or cuddle, fight or flee.[51]

Should two courses be judged equal, then the will cannot break the deadlock. All it can do is suspend judgment until circumstances change, and the right course of action is clear.

— Jean Buridan

In other words, we need not just reason (rationality) but reasons (motives, desires) to live. We need emotions to survive. We need to care about things to see them clearly—without becoming so entangled in what we're looking at that we distort it. That's why knowledge is social as well as rational or scientific.

If there is a caution here, it is to avoid the error that the early modern rationalists made in the direction of exclusivity, the error of over-esteeming inclusivity. We want to resist deifying or demonizing one way of knowing or one kind of knower at the expense of others. Just as the goal of pure objectivity may be a fantasy, as Susan Bordo described modern Cartesian epistemology in Chapter 9, so too, the notion that our particular personal experiences, intuitions, and emotional responses are somehow privileged may be another kind of fantasy. We don't want to deify either reason or emotion in the abstract. Like David Hume, Alison Jaggar resists this error and calls on us all, women and men, to live the kind of life that expands our interests and our concerns, a life of the mind and reason, certainly, but also a life of the heart.

 Aplia

Commentary

In the end, Hume compared full-blown skepticism to doubting the existence of an external reality, pointing out that the issue cannot be settled logically and rationally. No one can actually live as a skeptic:

> To whatever length anyone may push his speculative principles of scepticism, he must act…and live, and converse like other men.…It is impossible for him to persevere in total scepticism, or make it appear in his conduct for a few hours.[52]

Having reasoned carefully and thoroughly, without shying away from what he discovered, no matter how alien to common sense or established knowledge and custom, no matter how foreign to his heart's desire, the great archetype of the skeptic expresses a timeless lament in his own fashion:

> Where am I, or what? From what causes do I derive my existence, and to what condition shall I return? Whose favour shall I court, and whose anger must I dread? What beings surround me? and on whom have I influence, or who have influence on me? I am confounded with all these questions, and begin to fancy myself in the most deplorable condition imaginable, inviron'd with the deepest darkness, and utterly depriv'd of the use of every member and faculty.
>
>   Most fortunately it happens, that since reason is incapable of dispelling these clouds, nature herself suffices to that purpose, and cures me of this philosophical melancholy and delirium.…I dine, I play a game of backgammon, I converse, and am merry with my friends; and when after three or four hours' amusement, I wou'd return to these speculations, they appear so cold, and strain'd and ridiculous, that I cannot find in my heart to enter them any farther.[53]

What, then, is the point of these difficult and frustrating skeptical inquiries if, in the end, not even Hume takes them seriously? Ah, but he does take them seriously. Using careful observation and analysis, Hume raises important points about both the limits of reason and the needs of the human heart.

Hume exposes cloudy and meaningless language and bogus theorizing. He shows clearly the ultimate inadequacy of rational and empirical efforts to prove God's existence or infer His nature. In Hume's own time, a great scientific revolution had already established the force and usefulness of the scientific method. His analysis of cause and effect, as he acknowledges, does not destroy science but, rather, modifies a bit of what some see as its arrogance. Neither science nor theology can explain the ultimate origins of life or the ultimate nature of reality.

Hume has shown us how little we actually *know* of the most important and most common aspects of existence: self, personal identity, cause and effect, reality, the external world, the universe, and God. Read correctly, I think, Hume reveals that the power of logic and reason are, nevertheless, not all-powerful. He also shows that many of the great theological and metaphysical beliefs to which so many are devoted are barely intelligible. In other words, Hume teaches us that neither the scientist nor the philosopher nor the priest has *the* method and *the* answer to timeless questions.

Hume reminds us that there is no absolute certainty in life, only enough uniformity to live reasonably well, if we are lucky. He also shows that belief without reason is often meaningless but that a life based solely on reason is not possible. We live and

Scepticism is…a form of belief. Dogma cannot be abandoned; it can only be revised in view of some more elementary dogma which it has not yet occurred to the sceptic to doubt; and he may be right in every point of his criticism, except in fancying that his criticism is radical and that he is altogether a sceptic.

— George Santayana

act on what George Santayana calls *animal faith:* a force within us that *trusts something* in spite of the limits of our experience and reason.

Hume, the archetypal skeptic, suggests that a person will always be more than philosophy, religion, or science can hope to know:

> It seems, then, that nature has pointed out a mixed kind of life as the most suitable to the human race, and secretly admonished them to allow none of these biases to *draw* too much, so as to incapacitate them for any other occupations and entertainments. Indulge your passion for science, says she, but let your science be human, and such as may have a direct reference to action and society. Abstruse thought and profound researches I prohibit, and will severely punish, by the pensive melancholy which they introduce, by the endless uncertainty in which they involve you, and by the cold reception which your pretended discoveries shall meet with, when communicated. Be a philosopher; but amidst all your philosophy, be still a [human being].[54]

> *The refutation of skepticism is the whole business of philosophy.*
> — Rush Rhees

Summary of Main Points

- A skeptic is a person who demands clear, observable, undoubtable evidence based on experience before accepting any claim as true. Empiricism is the belief that all knowledge is ultimately derived from the senses (experience). Empiricists believe that all ideas can be traced to sense data. There are no innate ideas. At birth the mind is a clean slate, or *tabula rasa*.

- John Locke claimed that all ideas are copies of the things that caused the basic sensations on which they rest. Today, Locke's copy theory is known as the correspondence theory of truth, and according to this theory, an idea is true if whatever it refers to actually exists. The copy theory generates what is called the egocentric predicament: If all knowledge comes in the form of my own ideas, how can I verify the existence of anything external to them? Locke distinguished between *primary qualities* and *secondary qualities*. Primary qualities are sensible qualities that exist independently of any perceiver. Secondary qualities are qualities whose existence depends on a perceiver. Although he rejected Descartes's rationalism and theory of innate ideas, Locke accepted a Cartesian type of *dualism*, in which mind and matter are viewed as different kinds of substances.

- Locke's successor, George Berkeley, rejected the correspondence theory, pointing out that there is no fixed "thing" to copy; we know only perceptions. Berkeley's formula is *esse est percipi:* To be is to be perceived. This view is known as idealism or immaterialism. Berkeley shied away from the logical consequences of immaterialism and posited the existence of a universal perceiver (God) to account for the existence of the external world and regularity of nature.

- David Hume rejected metaphysical speculation as meaningless and irrelevant to the lives of ordinary people. He asserted that no metaphysical issue was ever clearly and thoroughly settled. Hume modified Locke's theory of ideas by distinguishing between two kinds of perceptions: ideas and impressions. All ideas can be traced to the impressions on which they are based. All ideas are derived from experience.

- Hume established an empirical criterion of meaning: All meaningful ideas can be traced to sense experience (impressions). Beliefs that cannot be traced to sense experience are technically not ideas at all; they are meaningless utterances. Strict application of the empirical criterion of meaning led Hume to skeptical conclusions regarding some of our most fundamental beliefs. Hume thought that imagination, rather than reason or experience, accounts for the persistence of our belief in the independent existence of an external world and that imagination ultimately overrides reason.

• Hume argued that the self is only a bundle of impressions and that identity is a mental act, not a property of things. Therefore, personal immortality is a meaningless concept. He also argued that cause and effect are products of imagination and that the argument from motion and the ontological argument are meaningless. According to Hume, the argument from design fails because human experience cannot provide sufficient evidence of order on earth, much less order in the universe. Hume denied the possibility of rationalistic ethics and claims that all moral judgments are based on sentiments.

• Building on an analysis of the emotional acumen that women have had to develop over centuries in their historical roles as caretakers and household managers, the contemporary feminist philosopher Alison Jaggar notes that traditional, male-dominated Western epistemology has ignored emotions as sources of knowledge or treated them as hindrances. She argues that if we don't care about something, we trivialize or ignore it. Emotions focus our attention on what matters and help us care enough to observe, study, and understand. Jaggar proposes a more inclusive theory of knowledge, one that respects both reason and emotional acuity as necessary sources of knowledge.

Post-Reading Reflections

Now that you've had a chance to learn about the Skeptic, use your new knowledge to answer these questions.

1. Outline the development of the "epistemological turn" from Descartes through Locke and Berkeley to Hume.

2. In your own words, reconstruct the basic empirical critique of rationalism.

3. What is the *tabula rasa*? What is its significance to Locke's empiricism?

4. Explain the philosophical significance of the question "Does a tree falling in the forest make a sound if no one is there to hear it?" Then answer it as Berkeley would.

5. Why is the distinction between impressions and ideas important to Hume's philosophy?

6. Apply the empirical criterion of meaning to an example of your own choosing.

7. How does Hume's bundle theory of the self affect his reasoning regarding personal identity and immortality.

8. How does Hume account for the external world?

9. Sketch Hume's analysis of cause and effect.

10. Summarize and analyze Hume's critique of the argument from design.

11. Construct a Humean analysis of some contemporary moral issue. What are the advantages of Hume's approach? The disadvantages?

12. Why does Hume say "I am ready to throw all my books and papers into the fire, and resolve never more to renounce the pleasures of life for the sake of reasoning and philosophy"?

 MindTap

Experience MindTap through the activities highlighted in this chapter. Further explore this online, personalized learning tool to deepen your comprehension and improve your grades.

11

The Universalist
Immanuel Kant

Two things fill the mind with ever new and increasing admiration and awe...the starry heavens above me and the moral law within me.

— *Immanuel Kant*

©iStock.com/Alex Potemkin

Learning Objectives

 MindTap

After you complete this chapter, you should be able to:

- Define *moral*.

- Distinguish between amorality and immorality.

- Describe the good will according to Immanuel Kant.

- Distinguish acts of will from inclinations and wishes according to Kant.

- Give an example of a moral maxim.

- State the categorical imperative.

- Describe Kant's kingdom of ends.

- Explain the relationship between moral dignity and reason, according to Kant.

- Identify what Susan Moller Okin saw as the chief oversight in most contemporary theories of justice.

- Defend Kant from the charge that, as long as our intentions conform to the categorical imperative, we are not responsible for the consequences of our actions.

moral
From the Latin *moralis*, meaning "custom," "manner," or "conduct"; refers to what people consider good or bad, right or wrong; used descriptively as a contrast to *amoral* or *nonmoral* and prescriptively as a contrast to *immoral*.

nonmoral (amoral)
Not pertaining to moral; a value-neutral descriptive claim or classification.

immoral
Morally wrong, bad, or not right; a moral value judgment or prescriptive claim.

> *It is precisely in knowing its limits that philosophy consists.*
> — Immanuel Kant

MORAL ISSUES CONFRONT US DAILY. We live in a time troubled by intense moral controversies concerning abortion, euthanasia, affirmative action, terrorism, capital punishment, substance abuse, monetary fraud, governmental deception, the environment, aid to the homeless, welfare, the rights of disabled persons, parental influence in the schools, pornography, copying of digital media, gender reassignment, smoking in public, and sexual conduct. Such issues have political, financial, legal, religious, technological, and psychological aspects. But in their *moral dimensions*, they touch upon our most fundamental values concerning good and bad, personal worth and character, respect for ourselves and others—in sum, what it means to be a human being.

The word **moral** comes from the Latin *moralis*, meaning "custom," "manner," or "conduct." Moral refers to what people consider good or bad, right or wrong. There are two contrasting words: **nonmoral (amoral)** and **immoral**. The *moral–nonmoral* distinction is *descriptive*. It makes no value judgment and only distinguishes moral concerns from nonmoral ones, such as economic, mechanical, nutritional issues. The *moral–immoral* distinction is *prescriptive;* it makes a value judgment about what we ought to do. The distinction between moral and immoral is equivalent to that between right and wrong or good and bad.

The moral dimension confronts us in courtrooms, in classrooms, at work, and at home, as we try to determine who is or is not *responsible* for this or that act. Moral responsibility is different from the factual issue of determining who did what. It has to do with punishment or forgiveness; it affects whether we see a sexual offender as bad or sick, whether we scold a child or hug her, whether a criminal defendant is imprisoned, hospitalized, or released. Morality seems to be inseparable from responsibility.

Responsibility, in turn, implies freedom of choice, the ability to decide on one course of action over another, to think and behave one way instead of another way. For example, a person unwillingly drugged is not held morally accountable for actions performed under the influence of the drug, but a person who willingly gets drunk and then drives probably is.

Lawyers, theologians, psychologists, and parents continually wrestle with issues of free, responsible choice. Yet scientific evidence of causal patterns suggests that more and more conduct once labeled immoral may be beyond our control. Biopsychologists and geneticists continue to discover physical and biochemical "causes" of behavior.

But if all nature is *governed* by laws of chemistry and physics, laws that admit of no exceptions, then I can no more be held responsible for helping you across the street than you can be held responsible for striking me with an ax because you're bored. If our behavior is determined by genetic influences, how can we ever hold anyone responsible for anything? And if we cannot, how do we justify moral sanctions? Stripped of the possibility of moral choice, how different am I from any other animal?

Troubled by scientific and philosophic arguments against the possibility of human freedom and responsibility, Immanuel Kant completed the epistemological turn begun by René Descartes (Chapter 9) by challenging Hume's skepticism (Chapter 10).

Discussing Philosophy

PHILOSOPHICAL QUERY

Think for a moment about a nonmoral world, a world in which no one is held morally accountable. In such a world, every action would be viewed as the inevitable result of genetic, social, and historical causes. What are the advantages of such a view? The disadvantages? Think about some time when you made an excuse for yourself, claiming that you "couldn't help" doing or not doing something. What is gained and lost by making such excuses?

The Professor

Immanuel Kant (1724–1804) was born in Königsberg in what was then known as East Prussia (now Kaliningrad in the former Soviet Union). His parents were poor but devout members of a fundamentalist Protestant sect known as Pietism. Pietists rejected the idea of imposing a church and priests between the individual and God, preferring to rely on immediate personal appeal to God. They emphasized faith and repentance and lived severe, puritanical lives.

When he was eight years old, Kant was sent to a school founded by a local Pietist preacher. The regimen was exceptionally strict, beginning daily at five-thirty in the morning. Students received an hour's instruction in Pietism, and each class period concluded with a prayer. Sundays were devoted almost completely to religious activity. Later in life, Kant said that he resented the school's heavy emphasis on a theology of terror and piety—fear of hell and trembling before a vision of a wrathful God. Yet he never lost his regard for righteousness and moral severity. As an old man, Kant spoke respectfully of his parents' faith, saying, "People may say what they will of Pietism. Those in whom it was sincere were worthy of honor. They possessed the highest thing that man can have—the quiet, the content, the inner peace, which no suffering can disturb."[1]

At the age of sixteen, Kant entered the University of Königsberg, where he studied for six years. Upon leaving the university, he refused a lucrative offer to become a Lutheran minister, but he chose instead to continue his studies. For the next nine years he supported himself with meager earnings as a private tutor. In 1755, Kant received the equivalent of today's doctoral degree. This earned him the privilege of lecturing at the university as a *Privatdozent*, a private teacher whose salary was paid directly by his students. The more students he attracted and retained, the more money he earned. Kant became a popular lecturer, and in 1770, when he was forty-six, the university hired Kant as a professor of logic and metaphysics. Though the salary was small, Kant was pleased with his improved status.

Immanuel Kant

The Solitary Writer

For the most part, Kant's life is noteworthy for not being noteworthy. He probably never traveled more than sixty miles from his birthplace during his entire life. One biographer said, "Kant's life was like the most regular of regular verbs," to which another added, "But it was not a *conjugated* verb. For Kant never married."[2]

> The life of Immanuel Kant is hard to describe; he had neither life nor history in the proper sense of the words.
>
> — Heinrich Heine

"A Beloved Teacher"

I have had the good fortune to know a philosopher who was my teacher. In the prime of his life he possessed the joyous courage of youth, and this also, as I believe, attended him to extreme old age. His open, thoughtful brow was the seat of untroubled cheerfulness and joy, his conversation was full of ideas most suggestive. He had at his service jest, witticism, and humorous fancy, and his lectures were at once instructive and most entertaining.... No cabal or sect, no prejudice or reverence for a name, had the slightest influence with him in opposition to the extension and promotion of truth. He encouraged and gently compelled his hearers to think for themselves.... This man, whom I name with the greatest gratitude and reverence, is Immanuel Kant; his image stands before me, and is dear to me.

Johann Gottfried Herder (1744–1803), quoted by Will Durant and Ariel Durant in **Rousseau and Revolution**, vol. 10 of **The Story of Civilization** (New York: Simon & Schuster, 1967), p. 532.

Kant lived most of his life on a rigid schedule. The poet Heinrich Heine described Kant's penchant for routine:

> I do not believe that the great cathedral clock of this city accomplished its day's work in a less passionate and more regular way than its countryman, Immanuel Kant. Rising from bed, coffee-drinking, writing, lecturing, eating, walking, everything had its fixed time: and the neighbors knew that it must be exactly half past four when they saw Professor Kant, in his gray coat, with his cane in his hand, step out of his housedoor, and move toward the little lime tree avenue, which is named after him, the Philosopher's Walk. Eight times he walked up and down that walk at every season of the year, and when the weather was bad, or the gray clouds threatened rain, his servant, old Lampe, was seen anxiously following him with a large umbrella under his arm like an image of providence.[3]

Kant is reported to have missed his walk only once, when he became so absorbed in reading Rousseau's *Émile* that he forgot to take it.

Kant was a prolific writer. His works include the difficult but revolutionary *Critique of Pure Reason* (1781 and a second edition in 1787), *Prolegomena to Any Future Metaphysics* (1783), *Foundations of the Metaphysics of Morals* (1785), *Critique of Practical Reason* (1788), *Critique of Judgment* (1790), and *Religion Within the Limits of Reason Alone* (1793).

The *Critique of Pure Reason* is one of the most difficult books ever written. Philosophy majors approach it with dread and then forever after boast proudly if they manage to read the entire thing. Kant once said that he did not fear being refuted; he feared not being understood. He had good reason to fear. On August 16, 1783, he wrote that his work was "the result of reflection which occupied me for at least twelve years":

> I brought it to completion in the greatest haste within four or five months, giving the closest attention to its contents, but with little thought of the exposition, or of rendering it easy of comprehension by the reader—a decision which I have never regretted, since otherwise, had I longer delayed and sought to give a more popular form, the work would probably never have been completed at all.[4]

Kant admitted that he deliberately left out illustrative examples because they would just add length to an already massive work. Besides, he added, examples are only necessary for popular appeal, "and this work can never be made suitable for popular consumption."[5] When he sent the metaphysician Marcus Herz the manuscript of the *Critique of Pure Reason*, Herz sent it back only half read, saying, "If I finish it I am afraid I shall go mad."[6]

Kant's work was made difficult by another factor: Because he was trying to express new concepts, he felt that he had to invent new meanings for Latin terms or coin new phrases in German; he also gave his own unusual meanings to common terms and sometimes used the same term to mean different things. All of that notwithstanding, the little professor's big, difficult books forever altered Western thinking.

Kant retired from public lecturing in 1797, and although he declined physically, he remained a prolific writer. Immanuel Kant died a lonely old man who had never seen a mountain or the sea. Yet he shook the foundations of Western philosophy to such an extent that it has been said that whether or not philosophers agree or disagree with Kant, they must face him. Above his grave in the Königsberg Cathedral, his own words are inscribed: "The starry heavens above me; the moral law within me."

The philosopher-poet Friedrich Schiller, referring to the richness, complexity, and importance of Kant's philosophy, as well as its impact on the many philosophers whose work is in one way or another a response to Kant's, said, "See how a single rich man has given a living to a number of beggars."[7]

Kant's work was important and troubling, for it included devastating critiques of rationalism and empiricism (the dominant philosophical schools of the day), as well as popular theology. It is said that some clergymen called Immanuel Kant a dog, and others called their dogs Immanuel Kant.

Heinrich Wolff/Popperfoto/Getty Images

The regularity of Kant's daily walks captured the interest of his neighbors enough to be noted by his many biographers, although commentators disagree as to precisely when the precise philosopher took his famed walks.

A Scandal in Philosophy

In Chapter 10, we saw how radical Hume's skepticism was. Hume was one of the most troublesome philosophers of his or any other time. His critique of empiricism led him to such disturbing conclusions as we can never know cause and effect, the self, or the external world. He also argued that moral judgments are somehow like matters of taste. Hume's withering *Dialogues Concerning Natural Religion* applied a strictly rational analysis to cherished arguments for the existence of God and showed them to be illogical and unpersuasive. With his strict understanding of knowledge and reason, Hume concluded that reason is and ought to be "the slave of the passions." Hume's philosophy made the external world unknowable and rendered

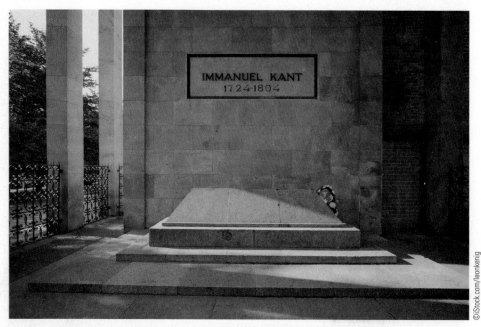

©iStock.com/leonkenig

Above his grave in the Königsberg Cathedral, Kant's own words are inscribed: "The starry heavens above me; the moral law within me."

reason impotent to unlock the secrets of nature. His critique of rationalistic ethics seemed to show that reason was utterly incapable of motivating people. In other words, Hume undercut the very essence of optimistic Enlightenment thinking.

Kant was one of the first thinkers to realize the consequences of Hume's relentless attack on the scope of reason. In the preface of his *Prolegomena to Any Future Metaphysics*, Kant wrote:

> Since the origin of metaphysics so far as we know its history, nothing has ever happened which could have been more decisive to its fate than the attack made upon it by David Hume. He threw no light on this species of knowledge, but he certainly struck a spark by which light might have been kindled had it caught some inflammable substance and had its smouldering fire been carefully nursed and developed.
>
> …However hasty and mistaken Hume's inference may appear, it was at least founded upon investigation, and this investigation deserved the concentration of the brighter spirits of his day as well as determined efforts on their part to discover, if possible, a happier solution of the problem in the sense proposed by him.
>
> But Hume suffered the usual misfortune of metaphysicians, of not being understood. It is positively painful to see how utterly his opponents…missed the point of the problem; for while they were ever taking for granted that which he doubted, and demonstrating with zeal and often with impudence that which he never thought of doubting, they so misconstrued his valuable suggestion that everything remained in its old condition, as if nothing happened.[8]

The seeds of what Kant referred to as a "scandal" in philosophy were planted when Descartes doubted his own existence and divided everything into two completely distinct substances: minds and bodies. Descartes was never able to account satisfactorily for mind–body interaction or to establish with certainty the existence of an external, material world. Although Descartes refused to follow his rationalistic premises to their logical conclusions, the Continental rationalists who came after him did. Because their model of certainty was mathematical and geometric, they moved further and further away from experience. As a result, they established grand systems of logical relationships ungrounded in observation or perception.

The British empiricists chose another tack, viewing the human mind as the passive receiver of impressions and experiences. But this view leads to the unfortunate conclusion that all certain knowledge is confined to ideas. Ironically, though they began with experience, the empiricists were unable to get back to it. The result was Hume's admission that we must believe in an external world, in selves, and in causes and effects, without ever knowing them.

As it has so often in history, scientific progress challenged the dominant philosophies of the day. As Kant noted, something was drastically wrong with philosophy if between them the two major philosophical schools at the time denied the importance of perception, denied the possibility of knowledge of cause and effect, denied the verifiable existence of the external world, and rendered reason impotent as a motivator in human affairs, while science—not to mention common sense and everyday experience—clearly showed otherwise.

Why didn't Kant abandon philosophy if it was so out of touch, so bizarre? Why not just accept the supremacy of science and let philosophy die of irrelevance? Kant found this course unsatisfying, for science was unveiling a mechanistic universe in which everything (at least once fully understood) would ultimately be shown to follow universal, unchanging laws of nature. If such a picture is complete and accurate, then God is unnecessary, free will is an illusion, and morality is impossible. If we have no choice but to follow "laws of nature," then values as they are usually understood disappear. Our behavior is only more complex than that of rocks or worms—it is not different in kind. The murderer and the saint are both following inescapable patterns of cause and effect.

How, Kant asked, could science, which was clearly making progress, be headed for conclusions that reduced human life to blind mechanism? How could two radically different philosophies each reach such odd, unacceptable results? Was it possible to synthesize science with the good parts of rationalism and empiricism in a way that would give a rational account of the world without stripping us of moral worth and dignity? Surely there had to be better alternatives than the cold, unfree world of science or the unverifiable, impractical worlds of rationalistic and skeptical philosophy.

> *I have therefore found it necessary to deny knowledge in order to make room for faith.*
> — Immanuel Kant

For Deeper Consideration

Do you think morality must disappear if everything we do can be explained according to scientific laws and patterns? Could there be another kind of morality based on laws of behavior and biopsychology? Why or why not? What is lost in the purely scientific view of humanity, of personhood? Anything important? Explain.

regulative ideas
(transcendental ideas)
In Kantian philosophy,
a special class of ideas,
also known as catego-
ries, that bridges the
gap between the phe-
nomenal and noumenal
worlds: self, cosmos,
and God.

Kantian idealism
Kant's theory that knowl-
edge is the result of the
interaction between the
mind and sensation and
is structured by regula-
tive ideas called cat-
egories; also known as
Kantian formalism and
transcendental idealism.

Kant's Copernican Revolution

In response to the "scandal in philosophy," Kant turned to an analysis (which he called a "critique") of *how* knowledge is possible. In the process, he posited an underlying *structure* imposed by the mind on the sensations and perceptions it encounters. We can think of this structure as the *formal* component of knowing. For this reason, Kant is known as a formalist. Kant theorized that neither reason by itself nor sensation by itself can give us knowledge of the external world. Knowledge is the result of the interaction between the mind and sensation. Knowledge and experience are shaped, structured, or formed by special **regulative ideas** called *categories*. This theory is known as *Kantian formalism*, **Kantian idealism**, or *transcendental idealism*.

Kant noted that Descartes's principal error began with a failure to understand scientific method. Galileo had changed science by establishing a "common plan of procedure," a method for studying phenomena. Though Descartes had understood the importance of method, he had not fully understood that the *scientific* method is *both* empirical *and* rational. Kant realized that the empiricists were guilty of a similar error of incompleteness by discounting the importance of reason. Knowledge, as the scientific method shows, consists of both a rational and a perceptual (empirical) component. It requires both a subject (a knowing mind) and an object (that which is known).

The common belief during Kant's time, however, was that truth occurs when ideas in the mind agree with external conditions or objects, the "copy theory"

A Diderot Pictorial Encyclopedia of Trades & Industry, Dover Publications

This illustration of a print shop from Denis Diederot's *Encyclopédie* illustrates the Enlightenment's optimistic faith in the spread of knowledge through free exchange of ideas. Does today's interest in the Internet reflect similar faith in the spread of knowledge through free exchange of ideas?

(see Chapter 10). For example, if I think this book has a red cover, my idea is true if the cover actually is red. But as Kant realized, if all knowledge fits that model, we could never discover general laws of nature. We could discover only that *this* apple falls, not that all bodies are subject to gravity—because we never experience all bodies. Hume understood this but was willing to limit the domain of knowledge to particulars, in the end asserting that we could *only believe* in the most important aspects of our existence: the regularity of experience, the existence of an external world, the existence of a unified self, cause and effect, and a moral order.

If we accept Hume's initial premises, his conclusions follow. However, close inspection of the way science is actually done shows that scientists make precisely the kinds of generalizations Hume's theory says we cannot make. Kant said that *when a theory results in conclusions that are clearly inconsistent with experience, real-world evidence must outweigh theoretical consistency*. And everyday experience shows that knowledge of causes and effects, the external world, and the self exists.

According to Kant, the scientific method is obviously more reliable and complete than Hume's philosophy. How do they differ? Kant pointed out that scientific thinking involves the *activity* of asking questions and framing hypotheses. Scientific thinking is not merely the passive recording of whatever happens; it requires the *active* setting up of controlled experimental conditions.[9] And this suggests that knowledge is a kind of *interaction*, a two-way street between the knower (the subject) and the known (the object).

Kant realized that he was proposing to change fundamental assumptions about the structure of knowledge, much as Copernicus had changed our assumptions about the structure of the universe. After astronomers had failed for centuries to make consistent sense of an earth-centered universe, Copernicus proposed a revolutionary hypothesis: that the sun is at the center, that the earth is part of a solar system. This assumption dissolved the great difficulties of the past and produced new, predictable knowledge. Kant was advocating a Copernican revolution in philosophy: He would reverse the course of his philosophical predecessors and assume that *instead of the mind having to conform to what can be known, what can be known must conform to the mind*.

> *[T]he demand for intellectual honesty is itself dishonest.... Rather, knowledge comes to us through a network of prejudices, opinions, innervations, self-corrections, presuppositions and exaggerations.*
> — Theodor Adorno

Critical Philosophy

Descartes began the epistemological turn by focusing on the mind as a rational substance. But by concentrating on the mind's rational function, he ignored its *organizing function* and so was unable to avoid generating conclusions that do not square with experience. The British empiricists, culminating with Hume, took the second step and demonstrated both the importance of experience and the limits of *a priori* reason. So strict was Hume's emphasis on experience as the sole source of knowledge that, coupled with the empiricists' view of the mind as a passive, neutral blank tablet, he was forced to conclude we cannot "know" that anything happens of necessity or even that we have a self.

Kant proposed a radical alternative, which we can think of as the third and final step of the epistemological turn: a critical analysis of what kind of knowledge we actually have, based on a new view of the mind as actively interacting with impressions and perceptions.

Hume had insisted that all knowledge begins in experience with sense impressions. But Hume confused knowledge that is *triggered* by experience with knowledge that is *based* on experience. Kant raised the possibility that our "faculty of knowledge" (mind, for short) might add something to the raw data of experience. Because experience *triggers* and hence *accompanies* all knowledge, we may fail to notice the effects the mind has on experience:

> But though all our knowledge begins with experience, it does not follow that it all arises out of experience. For it may well be that even our empirical knowledge is made up of what we receive through impressions and of what our own faculty of knowledge (sensible knowledge serving merely as the occasion) supplies from itself. If our faculty of knowledge makes any such addition, it may be that we are not in a position to distinguish it from the raw material, until with long practice of attention we have become skilled in separating it.
>
> This, then, is a question which at least calls for closer examination, and does not allow of any off hand answer:—whether there is any knowledge that is thus independent of experience and even of all impressions of the senses. Such knowledge is entitled *a priori*, and distinguished from the *empirical*, which has its sources *a posteriori*, that is, in experience.[10]

Kant asked a basic question: *Is metaphysics possible?* Can we know things beyond immediate experience? That is, does the human mind have the capacity for *a priori* knowledge, knowledge derived from reason without reference to sense experience? (See Chapters 9 and 10.) In answer, Kant proposed a critical reexamination of metaphysics. Metaphysics, as distinct from science, is an attempt to acquire and systematize knowledge derived by reason, not experience. Kant referred to earlier metaphysical philosophies as *dogmatic*, by which he meant, among other things, that they were *uncritical efforts* to understand the nature of whatever lies beyond immediate experience.

Critical philosophy is Kant's term for his effort to assess the nature and limits of "pure reason" (reason unadulterated by experience) in an effort to identify the actual relationship of the mind to knowledge. "Pure knowledge" is not morally pure but refers, rather, to *independent reasoning* (*a priori* reasoning)—that is, to knowledge *not derived from* the senses.

Phenomena and Noumena

According to Kant, our knowledge is *formed* by two things: our actual experiences and the mind's faculties of judgment. If Kant is correct, then we cannot know reality as it is. We can know reality only as it is organized by human understanding. **Phenomenal reality** is Kant's term for the world as we experience it. **Noumenal reality** is his term for reality as it is, independent of our perceptions, what we commonly call "objective reality." All we can know is perceived reality. This is not the same thing as saying that we each have our own private, subjective reality. All other things being equal, Kant says, the human mind imposes uniform categories on reality. Because the faculty of understanding is uniform, all functioning minds impose the same basic order on experience. We might think of Kant's distinction as between *human reality* and *pure reality*.

critical philosophy
Kant's term for his effort to assess the nature and limits of "pure reason," unadulterated by experience, in order to identify the actual relationship of the mind to knowledge.

phenomenal reality
Kant's term for the world as we experience it.

noumenal reality
Kant's term for reality as it is, independent of our perceptions; what is commonly called "objective reality."

Although we never experience pure reality, we can nonetheless know (understand) that our minds do not just invent the world. In Kant's language, the mind imposes order on a world of things-in-themselves. Things-in-themselves are *noumena*, things as they exist independently of us. We know *that they exist*, but we can never know them, because in the act of imposing order, the mind changes things-in-themselves to a comprehensible form.

For example, the human ear cannot hear the noumena—the full spectrum of air vibrations known as sound. We cannot hear the highest-pitched sounds a dog hears or the lowest pitches an elephant hears. Human beings would not know that these other wavelengths of sound exist without the help of dog and elephant ears or sensitive instruments. We can experience only what our human faculty of understanding is capable of processing.

Why make such a distinction, since we will never experience noumena? Kant's response is twofold. First, the distinction shows us the limits of human understanding. Second, such a distinction is necessary in order to establish a foundation for a moral philosophy capable of preserving our moral autonomy and sentiments in light of the onslaught from science and Humean philosophy. But to accomplish this second goal, Kant must first somehow connect human reality to pure reality.

Transcendental Ideas

Kant argues that although we cannot directly experience noumena, a special class of *transcendental ideas* bridges the gap between the phenomenal and noumenal worlds. Empirical ideas are validated by sense data (experience). Transcendental ideas are "triggered" by experience when we rely on them to impose unity on the totality of our experiences. They "unify" or "make possible" having experience in the first place. Without some sort of unifying structure, Kant argues, the mind could not "experience" raw sense data. It would be meaningless, undifferentiated—unexperienced. Transcendental ideas do not correspond to any specific experience, but they "make experience possible."

Kant identified three transcendental ideas: *self, cosmos* (totality), and *God*. Kant also called them *regulative ideas* because they regulate and synthesize experience on a grand scale:

> Everything that has its basis in the nature of our powers must be appropriate to, and consistent with, their right employment—if we can only guard against a certain misunderstanding and so discover the proper direction of these powers. We are entitled, therefore, to suppose that transcendental ideas...have an excellent, and indeed indispensably necessary, regulative employment, namely, that of directing the understanding towards a certain goal upon which the routes marked out by all its rules converge.[11]

According to Kant, pure reason synthesizes all our psychological activities into a unity by positing the idea of *self*:

> The first [regulative] idea is the "I" itself, viewed simply as thinking nature or soul...; in a word, the idea of a simple self-sustaining intelligence. [Reason operates] to represent all determinations as existing in a single subject, all powers, so far as possible, as derived from a single fundamental power, all change as belonging to the states of one and the same permanent being.[12]

Pure reason also attempts to lend unity to experience by synthesizing all events into a single totality, or *cosmos*. Although the idea of cosmos helps organize and frame our experience, we cannot establish (prove) its actual existence. The idea of cosmos remains, for Kant, a deep instinctive need that reason satisfies. But it remains a "mere idea"—though a most important one:

> The second regulative idea of merely speculative reason is the concept of the world in general.... The absolute totality of the series of...conditions...is an idea which can never be completely realised in the empirical employment of reason, but which yet serves as a rule that prescribes how we ought to proceed in dealing with such series.... Cosmological ideas are nothing but simply regulative principles, and are very far from positing...an actual totality.[13]

God, or "the highest intelligence," is Kant's third regulative idea:

> The third idea of pure reason, which contains a merely relative supposition of a being that is the sole and sufficient cause of all cosmological series, is the idea of *God*. We have not the slightest ground to assume in an absolute manner [the existence of] the object of this idea.[14]

By "mere" or "pure" idea, Kant means that God is not the kind of thing that can be verified by an appeal to experience. We know that some people don't believe in God and that others dismiss the idea of God as being unimportant. Kant, however, claims that it is not possible to dismiss the *idea of God*, since it forms one of the organizing structures or categories of reason.

Kant goes on to say that we must act as if self, cosmos, and God refer to existing things but that, as in the case of all noumena, there is no way empirically to verify that they do. God, self, and cosmos are nonetheless real. They refer to universal ideas that regulate human understanding. But if the rest of Kant's epistemology is correct, God, self, and cosmos remain, like other things-in-themselves, known only through the operations of reason rather than through experience.

The Objectivity of Experience

In very simple terms, Kant's complex project attempts to show that experience is possible only under a certain general condition: objectivity. Kant argues that there must be a real—objective—distinction between how the world seems to me and how the world is *in order for me to have any experience at all*.[15]

Crudely put, if there were no difference between the world and me, I could not even have an idea of "having an experience." But I do have experience. Indeed, the skeptical arguments of Hume make sense only if Hume (or any skeptic) understands that he has experience. But experience itself presupposes precisely what the skeptic doubts: his own independent existence as a unified, continuing self that is part of an objective order, subject to causal laws.[16]

Although commentators on Kant understandably disagree over the precise nature of his *argument* here, the disagreement seems to center on the concept of the unity of self that allows me to say (and experience) that this thought or this sensation belongs to *me*, belongs to *one thing*, belongs to a unity that exists prior to *any* empirical verification. For Kant, such a transcendental sense of unity is necessary in order for *me* to have any experience—and, of course, without "me," the whole world ceases to exist.

This awareness of transcendental unity is possible because I *am aware of my own existence and identity through time*. And I can only be aware of my identity through time because I situate or locate myself in a world of actually existing things, things that endure through time. These things have the capacity to be other than I perceive them. They are not merely my perceptions. Thus, they must exist objectively.

You may need to study the preceding passages more than once and may wish to do additional reading to get a better grasp of Kant's complicated, but influential, critical philosophy. And your philosophy instructor might have other interpretations of Kant. That's not surprising given both the complexity of Kant's subject matter and his complex treatment of it.

Kant himself is inconsistent in his treatment of the noumenal world and regulative transcendental ideas, sometimes talking about them as mental constructs and other times suggesting that they are existing entities. That's not surprising either, since, if he is correct, the human need for unity and transcendence is very strong. One defense of Kant's inconsistencies might be the force and power of regulative ideas. They may not give us new empirical knowledge, but they allow us to meet our persistent metaphysical longings for an ordered, objective world.

For many people, one of the great weaknesses of the strictest empirical theories of knowledge is that by ruling out knowledge of the existence of God, mind (soul), and other transcendental metaphysical beliefs, these theories fail to satisfy deep, nearly universal needs. Kant deserves credit for recognizing and respecting these

> *In this enquiry I have made completeness my chief aim, and I venture to assert that there is not one single metaphysical problem which has not been solved, or the solution of which the key at least has not been supplied.*
>
> — Immanuel Kant

needs and for offering a rigorous and sustained explanation and defense of the kind of thinking that springs from them. (Of course, longing for something to be true does not mean that it is true. And as philosophers, we do not want to accept as true whatever we deeply long for just because we long for it.)

Having at least a rudimentary sense of Kant's critical project and methods, we are ready to turn to a more accessible, and equally influential, aspect of Kantian philosophy—his categorical imperative and the universalist moral philosophy on which it rests.

The Metaphysics of Morals

If I am asked "What is good?" my answer is that good is good, and that is the end of the matter. Or if I am asked "How is good to be defined?" my answer is that it cannot be defined, and that is all I have to say about it.
— G. E. Moore

You may have identified a basic strategy throughout Kant's philosophy so far. Kant shows great respect for powerful and persistent ways of thinking, even if they seem difficult to justify philosophically. I have in mind, for example, the persistence of belief in cause and effect, self-identity, the external world, and God. To establish his "metaphysics of morals," Kant starts with the hypothesis that somehow such ideas can be justified *because we keep relying on them*. Given how they work in our lives and their apparent universality, such ideas must have more than just the psychological value Hume assigned them.

Using the distinction between the phenomenal world and the noumenal world, Kant asserts that it is possible to be both determined, or unfree (in the phenomenal world), and free (in the noumenal world). We have a phenomenal self that falls under the laws of nature and behavior and a noumenal self that is free. Thus, free will exists in the noumenal world. This means we are free and morally responsible even though from the empirical, scientific view of life, we cannot *experience* our freedom but only *think* of it. It is a mistake to attempt an empirical proof of human freedom. Science describes the phenomenal world, but it cannot deal with the noumenal world.

Although there is only one reason, one faculty of understanding, Kant distinguishes two functions of reason, which he called theoretical reason and practical reason. **Theoretical reason**, including scientific reasoning, is confined to the empirical, phenomenal world. Interaction with the world of experience produces laws of behavior that force reason to view everything mechanically. Theoretical reason thus concludes that human beings, like all other phenomena, are governed by cause and effect in the form of inescapable laws of nature. Limited by the way the mind can understand the phenomenal world, we must accept that there is no freedom on that level. If freedom is necessary for morality, we must find our freedom elsewhere.

According to Kant, we use **practical reason** to move beyond the phenomenal world to the moral dimension. Practical reason begins with knowledge about moral conduct and produces religious feelings and intuitions. Practical reason helps us deal with the moral freedom provided by free will. In his *Critique of Practical Reason*, Kant says that no matter how many natural causes and sensations might "drive" a person, "they cannot produce [a state of] *being under obligation*, they cannot account for moral duty."[17] The feeling of duty comes from within; it comes from being rational.

Kant uses the term *practical* reason to indicate that we do not act on impulses and desires alone. We also act from *conscious choice* based on our general principles.

theoretical reason According to Kant, a function of reason confined to the empirical, phenomenal world.

practical reason According to Kant, a moral function of reason that produces religious feelings and intuitions based on knowledge of moral conduct.

"Metaphysical Moments"

The name metaphysics is apt to suggest something difficult, unusual, and remote. Yet it has its familiar side. Most of us have times at which, in reflection, we seem to be confronted not with any particular isolated problem or any particular aspect of our experience, but with experience, or life, or existence, *as a whole*. These might be called our metaphysical moments. It is not easy to give a detailed description of them and for our purpose it is not necessary. Indirectly and roughly, however, it is possible to identify them by saying that if they did not occur there would be no point in religion and little in many works of art and philosophy.

S. Körner, **Kant** (Baltimore: Penguin, 1955), p. 13.

In direct opposition to Hume's claim that reason cannot be a motivator, Kant argues that we can consciously act when no desire is involved at all.[18] Consider, for example, the kind of inner conflict you might experience between a strong desire to buy a new smart phone and your awareness of your duty to repay a friend from whom you borrowed money. You can *choose* to repay your friend because you ought to, even though you do not want to. (This is not the same thing as doing something to avoid feeling guilty: That does involve desire.)

PHILOSOPHICAL QUERY

What would a person be like who could choose only what he or she desired? Do you think it is possible to choose to do something if no desire whatsoever is involved? Would you criticize an exceptionally good and kind person who is unable to choose to be cruel? Is desiring the main issue, or is it something else?

The Moral Law Within

For Kant, morality is a function of reason. Specifically, morality is based on our consciousness of necessary and universal moral laws (or rules, as Kant calls them). Moral rules of behavior differ from other, pragmatic rules because moral rules alone have the quality of being thought of as universal and necessary. And since only *a priori* judgments are universal and necessary, moral judgments must be *a priori*. This is why the empiricists could not discover them.

Thus the moral law cannot be discovered in actual behavior. It is a function of reason, a component of how we think. From this it follows that only rational creatures can be moral and held morally accountable. It also follows that any and all rational creatures are moral beings. The capacity for reason is the source of morality. Reason imposes moral obligation.

Imagine a world in which *no one* had any moral obligations. Would any rational creature desire to live in it? Kant answers with a resounding no! Therefore, he reasoned, morality is absolutely necessary for human relationships. Empirical studies can identify only what people *actually do;* they cannot identify what we *ought to do*. Whereas Hume (Chapter 10) dealt with the is/ought (fact/value) issue by denying

To those who look at the rich material provided by history . . . it will become clear that there is only one principle that can be defended under all stages of human development. It is the principle: anything goes.

— Paul Feyerabend

that "ought" refers to any fact, it seemed obvious to Kant that the very essence of moral judgments involves *duty*, what we ought to do. Again, Kant begins his inquiry with awareness of and respect for the way we actually think. He notes that very few people consistently think of their own moral judgments as mere matters of custom or taste. Whether we actually live up to our moral principles or not, we think of moral judgments as concerned with how people ought to behave.

Thus, if we begin with the *actual form* of moral judgments as they occur in our lives, we see that they are judgments of duty. As an example, Kant offered the moral judgment "We ought to tell the truth," which he said has the same status as "Every change must have a cause." (Hume rejected the idea of cause.) Just as we cannot begin to think of or even experience anything without already assuming the principle of cause and effect, Kant thought that we cannot function without a sense of duty. Practical reason *imposes* the notion of *ought* on us.

Morality and practical reason rely on concepts that transcend particular facts and immediate experience. Practical reason deals with human behavior and relationships by continually monitoring how we ought to behave. Further, practical reason goes beyond merely addressing how we ought to behave in particular circumstances and generates universal principles that apply to everyone's behavior in similar circumstances at all times.

PHILOSOPHICAL QUERY

Psychologists have identified a character disorder that is labeled as either "sociopathic" or "antisocial personality disorder." One component of this diagnosis is that such people are amoral, lacking any conscience. Do you know people without any sense of moral duty? What are they like? Does the existence of such people mean there is no such thing as a necessary, universal moral law?

The Good Will

For Kant, goodness depends not on our behavior but on our will, on what we intend to do if circumstances do not prevent it. Kant insisted that morality was entirely a matter of reason and good will, not, as some believe, a matter of consequences or action.

It's important to note that Kant conceives of the good will as a component of rationality. He argues that "ought implies can," by which he means it must be possible for human beings to live up to their moral obligations. Yet circumstances sometimes prevent us from doing the good we want to do. I may sincerely wish to minister to the sick but be physically or financially unable. I may diligently try to love my neighbor, only to be rebuffed by him. Thus, Kant reasons, I must not be judged on the consequences of what I actually do but on my reasons. Put another way, morality is a matter of motives:

> A good will is good not because of what it performs or effects, not by its aptness for the attainment of some proposed end, but simply by virtue of the volition, that is, it is good in itself, and considered by itself is to be esteemed much higher than all that

Morality is not properly the doctrine of how we should make ourselves happy, but how we should become worthy of happiness.
— Immanuel Kant

can be brought about by it in favour of any inclination, nay, even of the sum-total of all inclinations. Even if it should happen that, owing to special disfavour of fortune, or the niggardly provision of a step-motherly nature, this will should wholly lack power to accomplish its purpose, if with its greatest efforts it should yet achieve nothing, and there should remain only the good will (not, to be sure, a mere wish, but the summoning of all means in our power), then, like a jewel, it would still shine by its own light, as a thing which has its whole value in itself. Its usefulness or fruitlessness can neither add to nor take away anything from this value.[19]

We must not, of course, confuse a good will with rather halfhearted good wishes. After all, "The road to hell is paved with good intentions." I have the will to do something, in Kant's words, only when I "summon all the means within my power." This is much more than merely wishing to be good. It is certainly more than a cheerful expression of moral platitudes.

PHILOSOPHICAL QUERY

Does the idea of a good will help our analysis of the sociopath in the preceding Philosophical Query?

Inclinations, Wishes, Acts of Will

In Kantian terminology, decisions and actions based on impulse or desire are known as *inclinations*, and Kant was convinced that morality could not be "reduced to" inclinations because inclinations are notoriously unreliable and inconstant. Inclinations are not products of practical reason; indeed, they are not products of reason at all. We can see this clearly when we consider the behavior and motivations of dogs, cats, and infants. Dogs, cats, and infants have very strong inclinations: to eat this but not that, now but not later, and so on. But in Kant's sense of the term, they do not have "a will"; they cannot *act from a will*.

> *The majesty of duty has nothing to do with the enjoyment of life.*
> — Immanuel Kant

It is important to be clear here. "Having a will" and "acting from a will" have a precise meaning for Kant, a meaning connected to acting from "internal commands" or maxims that are the result of rational deliberation. So, although we sometimes call infants or pets "willful," from a Kantian point of view, they are merely manifesting powerful inclinations, not a will. *Willing X* requires consciously and deliberately committing ourselves to bringing about *X*. There is something "wholehearted" and conscious about willing.

We can see that Kant's strong sense of willing is not so far from everyday language as it might first appear if we consider what we mean by "willpower." We often lament lacking the willpower to stop smoking, start exercising, stop overeating, study for philosophy class. We say, "She meant well" and "If wishes were horses, then beggars would ride." In other words, we distinguish between merely wanting, wishing, or being inclined and actually *willing* something, seriously committing ourselves wholeheartedly, consciously, and consistently—regardless of our inclinations and desires. We do not ordinarily talk about "wish power" or "want power."

In contrast to inclinations, acts of will reflect autonomy, the capacity to choose clearly and freely for ourselves, without "outside" coercion or interference.

With inclinations, it is as if "one part of me wants to be healthy but another part of me wants to enjoy a smoke now." Rather than make a focused, unified, wholehearted commitment not to smoke, I make a "halfhearted gesture."

When we *will* something, we issue ourselves a kind of internal command, or order, of the type: "I refuse to eat meat" or "I will not lie." These *subjective intentions* can be framed as *maxims*, the reason or rule according to which an act is done (or not done). In these two examples, maxims might be framed as "Do not eat meat" and "Do not lie." In a sense, when I will something, I pass a law, framed as my maxim—and I obey my own law. I am both a lawgiver and a servant of the law.

Kant's moral philosophy is his attempt to distinguish morally proper maxims and motives from morally unacceptable ones. Ultimately, Kant thought that he was able to identify the "supreme moral principle," the moral motive that distinguishes the good will from all other motives.

Moral Duty

Kant thought it was crucially important to distinguish moral motives from other kinds of motives. I might tell the truth to impress you or to avoid going to jail for perjury. Obviously, such considerations (motives) are not moral. I may give money to charity in order to cut my tax bill. I might do what I think God commands in order to go to heaven or to escape hell, but then my motive is self-interest. Only when I do a thing solely because it is my duty do I have a good will.

What, then, is duty? Kant says, "*Duty is the necessity of acting from respect for the [moral] law.*"[20] He goes on to explain that duty does not serve our desires and preferences (he calls these "inclinations") but, rather, *overpowers* them. Put another way, duty excludes considerations of personal preference or profit and loss from moral calculation. For example, suppose I have criticized my boss to others. When she asks me whether I've done this, I decide to tell her the truth because I am not sure what my co-workers have already told her. Even though I do my duty, I cannot get moral credit for it, according to Kant, because my decision is based on something other than moral duty—it's based on not getting fired:

> Thus the moral worth of an action does not lie in the effect expected from it, nor in any principle of action which requires to borrow its motive from its expected effect. For all these effects—agreeableness of one's condition, and even the promotion of the happiness of others—could have been also brought about by other causes so that for this there would have been no need of the will of a rational being; whereas it is in this alone that the supreme and unconditioned good can be found. The preeminent good which we call moral can therefore consist in nothing else than *the conception of law* in itself, which certainly is only possible in a rational being, in so far as this conception, and not the expected effect, determines the will.[21]

If this seems unduly strict (and it has to many philosophers), keep in mind that decisions based on "inclinations" are often inconsistent and always relative. My inclination might be to renege on a loan or to be rude to a dirty, smelly customer. How can anyone rely on me if I only follow my inclinations? My inclination on the day I asked you to dinner might have been to keep our date, but by Friday my inclination might be to stay home alone. And I might not be inclined to call and inform you of this, either. Imagine the chaos of a world in which our obligations were tied to our moods.

According to Kant, moral obligations cannot be grounded in whims and personal taste. Moral duty must be confined to considerations of the form: *What are the universal obligations of all persons in similar circumstances?* My duty cannot be based on what I want to do, what I like or don't like, whether or not I care about the people involved. Kant's next step was to devise a way to determine exactly what our duty is in this or that case, to ask, *What is the moral law?* Kant's answer is one of the most intriguing and widely debated principles in all moral philosophy.

PHILOSOPHICAL QUERY

Do you think it is possible to have only one motive for an action? Is it common to have only one motive? Is it important to distinguish moral motives from pragmatic ones? Why? Compare Kant with Hume on the issue of moral sentiments.

Hypothetical Imperatives

Kant argues that the moral quality of an act is determined by the *principle* to which the will consciously assents. If, for instance, I resolve to feed the hungry and mistakenly serve tainted meat at a charity dinner, my intention is praiseworthy even though my action results in sickness or death. If, on the other hand, I intend to poison my sick wife in order to inherit her fortune and mistakenly give her a chemical that cures her, I am morally guilty of murder, for that was what I consciously willed.

Since they affect behavior, moral principles are always framed as commands, according to Kant. He refers to commands by their grammatical designation as *imperatives*. Examples of imperatives are "Shut the door," "Always brush your teeth after eating," "Love your neighbor as yourself," and "Double-space your term paper."

Imperatives that tell us what to do under specific, variable conditions are called **hypothetical imperatives**. In logic, a hypothetical proposition takes the form "*If* this, *then* that." These are also called conditional propositions because they set up a *conditional* relationship: *If* it rains, *then* postpone the picnic. The imperative "Postpone the picnic" is binding only in the condition of rain. According to Kant, all empirical or factual imperatives are hypothetical because they are binding only so long as certain conditions apply.

There are a variety of *kinds* of hypothetical imperatives. Some are technical, applying to chemists or surgeons or bakers. Others are social, telling us how to be popular or get dates. Some are legal, and so on. No hypothetical imperative is binding on everyone or even on one person all the time. When factual conditions change, so do hypothetical imperatives. No hypothetical imperative is *a priori*. All are relative.

In fact, Kant says, "the imperatives of prudence do not, strictly speaking, command at all."[22] No one has a necessary obligation to be practical, to make money, to eat wisely. Thus, though hypothetical imperatives can help us deal with life, they cannot be a basis for determining moral duty.

hypothetical imperatives Propositions that tell us what to do under specific, variable conditions.

The Categorical Imperative

According to Kant, what is needed is a **categorical imperative**, a command that is universally binding on all rational creatures. This alone can guide the good will. Indeed, the good will is precisely that which summons all its powers in order to obey just such an imperative.

Moral duty must be universally—not conditionally—binding. What principle can we follow that is not conditional? After considering the difference between telling the truth because it is a duty and telling it because it might yield some payoff, Kant concludes that acting from duty is always based on the principle of a "conception of the law in general."

What Kant means can be characterized as *acting on the principle of acting on principle*. In the case of telling the truth, I tell the truth because I have a basic, general obligation to tell the truth—period. This obligation is general in the sense that I must not base it on particular considerations at all. I must not be partial to myself and my fears or my wants. Kant thus strips the good will of every Humean sentiment, every impulse, appetite, fear, preference, or other practical or person-specific consideration. What's left?

> There remains nothing but the universal conformity of [the will's] actions to law in general, which alone is to serve as its principle, *i.e.*, I am never to act otherwise than *so that I could also will that my maxim should become a universal law*. Here, now, it is the simple conformity to law in general, without assuming any particular applicability to certain actions, that serves the will as its principle, and must so serve it, if duty is not to be a vain delusion and a chimerical notion.[23]

Kant formulated the categorical imperative as "*Act as if the maxim of thy action were to become a universal law of nature*." In other words, we must act only according to principles we think should apply to everyone. Because a free will is a necessary condition of morality, Kant reminds us that the "universal law" in question comes from our own rational, willing assent; it is not imposed on us from the outside. Obeying God or nature or any other *overpowering force* out of fear or necessity is not moral. If we obey out of fear, our motive is partial and pragmatic; if we have no choice but to obey, we are not free. Moral law is obligatory because it springs from our own rational nature and becomes law only when we willingly assent to it.

> *The way to appraise a "way of life" may well be by considering what's in it for you; the way to appraise the moral value of a course of action is by considering what's in it for everyone.*
>
> — Jan Narveson

MindTap
Discussing Philosophy

PHILOSOPHICAL QUERY

To get a clearer sense of the power of the categorical imperative to clarify the nature of various forms of behavior, formulate and then analyze the maxims that are required to justify the following: charging things on credit without being sure you can pay them off on time; enrolling in two different high-demand courses so that you can check them both out and drop the one you don't like; having unprotected sex without knowing if you are HIV positive; texting in a darkened theater; forcing schools to teach the values of your religion—or insisting that there be no mention of God because you are an atheist.

The Kingdom of Ends

Kant believed that as conscious, rational creatures, we each possess intrinsic worth, a special moral dignity that always deserves respect. Kant uses a beautiful expression to describe the moral universe, the universe of all moral beings, of all creatures possessing intrinsic worth. He refers to it as the *kingdom of ends*, a kingdom in which everyone is an end in himself or herself, and no one is just a means to be used and tossed aside. In other words, we are more than mere objects to be used to further this or that end. We are *persons*, reasoning creatures capable of monitoring and guiding our own behavior according to principles. Thus, the ability to reason carries with it an obligation to respect the rights of others to reason for themselves.

Moral dignity is not contingent on anything. It is not a function of how likable we are, how attractive, talented, clean, or even good we are. It is not contingent on how well we use our reason or on whether we use it at all. We possess intrinsic worth (moral dignity) just because we *can* reason.

We have seen that, according to Kant, our basic obligations to one another cannot rest on inclinations or sentiments (desires), for that amounts to saying we have no moral obligations. Imagine a wedding in which the bride or groom promised to love, cherish, and respect the other "as long as I feel inclined to." The very concept of duty implies acting in an appropriate way regardless of our sentiments, convenience, comfort, or other personal factors. In Kant's terms, this is an objective duty toward other rational beings—exactly what Hume denied:

> Man and generally any rational being *exists* as an end in himself, *not merely as a means* to be arbitrarily used...but in all his actions, whether they concern himself or other rational beings, must be always regarded at the same time as an end. All objects of inclination have only a conditional worth; for if the inclinations and the wants founded on them did not exist, then their object would be without value....Rational beings...are called *persons*, because their very nature points them out as ends in themselves....These, therefore, are not merely subjective ends whose existence has a worth *for us* as an effect of our action, but *objective ends*, that is, things whose existence is an end in itself: an end moreover for which no other can be substituted...for otherwise nothing whatever would possess *absolute worth*; but if all worth were conditional and therefore contingent, then there would be no supreme practical principle of reason whatever.
>
> If then there is a supreme practical principle or, in respect of the human will, a categorical imperative, it must be one which, being drawn from the conception of that which is necessarily an end for everyone because

> *We do not need science and philosophy to know what we should be to be honest and good, yea, even wise and virtuous.*
>
> — Immanuel Kant

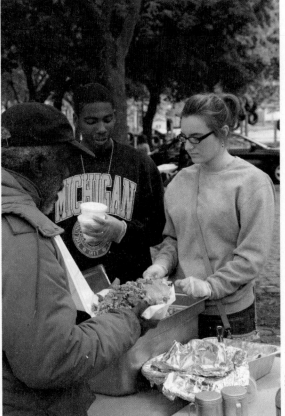

Kant held that, as conscious, rational creatures we each possess dignity that deserves universal respect and that is not contingent on how likable we are, how attractive, successful, and so forth. Note how these caregivers' expressions and body language reflect patience and concern as signs of respect for the dignity of the hungry man they are feeding—as well as respect for their own dignity.

Jim West/AGE Fotostock

it is *an end in itself*, constitutes an *objective* principle of will, and can therefore serve as a universal practical law. The foundation of this principle is: *rational nature exists as an end in itself*.[24]

Kant formulates the categorical imperative around the concept of dignity in a way that is sometimes referred to as the **practical imperative** or **principle of dignity**: "*Act in such a way that you always treat humanity, whether in your own person or in the person of another, never simply as a means but always at the same time as an end*."[25] I confess I'm partial to this particular principle. It has, I believe, much to teach us.

If, for example, I view my students only as a way to make a living, or only as a captive audience to indoctrinate with my views, I treat them as a means to an end without honoring their basic dignity as persons. We violate this principle of dignity when we hurl ethnic or gender insults at one another, for then we are treating other persons as means of venting rage or expressing feelings. No abusive parent or spouse treats the objects of his or her abuse as *persons*. In the kingdom of ends, there are no slaves, no sweatshops, no terrorists, no bullies, no rude clerks or surly customers, no unprepared teachers or students, no sophistic politicians cleverly manipulating their constituents—only respectful and respected *persons*.

Yet in fact, my students *are a means* to an income for me. I *am a means* to a degree or meeting a requirement for them. A boss and an employee are each a *means* and an *end*. Note that Kant's principle does not preclude this. Rather, it adds a dimension of universal respect to all human relationships: We are means *and* ends.

practical imperative (principle of dignity)
Kant's formulation of the categorical imperative based on the concept of dignity: "Act in such a way that you always treat humanity, whether in your own person or in the person of another, never simply as a means but always at the same time as an end."

MindTap
Discussing Philosophy

PHILOSOPHICAL QUERY

Consider the actual case of the parents who conceived a child for the express purpose of producing a bone marrow donor for their teenaged daughter who had leukemia. Doctors advised the parents that a bone marrow transplant was the only hope of saving their daughter's life. Unable to find a compatible donor match, the parents took the desperate step of having another child. When the specially conceived child was a year old, her bone marrow was transplanted to her nineteen-year-old sister. Can the parents' action be morally justified? Does it make any difference that, twenty years later, the baby whose bone marrow was used says that she is glad she was part of saving her sister's life? Would the parents' decision have been worse if the younger sister resented "being used"?

A Kantian Theory of Justice

In 1971, Harvard professor **John Rawls** (1921–2002) published *A Theory of Justice*, which became one of the most significant philosophical books of the twentieth century. Rawls's attempt to refine Kant's moral philosophy continues to influence political scientists, economists, and moral philosophers.

According to Rawls, the fundamental principles of justice are those principles to which "free and rational" persons would agree if they were in an "original position" of equality. Of course, Rawls continued, we are not in and cannot create a position of perfect equality. How, then, he asked, can we ever determine what

John Rawls

justice is, since any inquiry into justice will be influenced by our actual—and unequal—circumstances?

One way to deal with the limits imposed by our actual circumstances is known as a thought experiment. A **thought experiment** is a way of using our imaginations to test a hypothesis that cannot be tested in fact. During a thought experiment, we think rather than field-test a hypothesis, using reasoned imagination to provide the necessary conditions for the experiment and then reasoning out the most likely consequences according to our hypothesis.

Kant had already tried to overcome the limits of personal circumstances and bias with the categorical imperative, which is supposed to overlook all merely personal considerations and inclinations. Rawls used a thought experiment as part of an attempt to improve upon Kant's efforts to overcome the limits of personal concerns in ethical deliberations.

The **original position** of equality is Rawls's term for an imaginary setting in which we can identify the fundamental principles of justice from an *objective, impartial* perspective—as "rational agents," rather than as "interested parties." And this is where the thought experiment comes in. We "enter into the original position" by imaginatively placing ourselves behind what Rawls terms a "veil of ignorance." The **veil of ignorance** is a problem-solving device that prevents us from knowing our social status, what property we own, what we like and don't like, how intelligent we are, what our talents and strengths are, "and the like." In other words, the veil of ignorance is a way of adopting an objective (or at least disinterested) perspective. In the following passage, Rawls introduces the veil of ignorance and the original position:

> The original position is not, of course, thought of as an actual historical state of affairs, much less as a primitive condition of culture. It is understood as a purely hypothetical situation characterized so as to lead to a certain conception of justice.... Among the essential features of this situation is that no one knows his place in society, his class position or social status, nor does any one know his fortune in the distribution of natural assets and abilities, his intelligence, strength, and the like. I shall even assume that the parties do not know their conceptions of the good or their special psychological propensities. The principles of justice are chosen behind a veil of ignorance. This assures that no one is advantaged or disadvantaged in the choices of principles by the outcome of natural chance or the contingency of social circumstances.[26]

Rawls goes on to argue that persons in the original position "would all agree"— being rational and mutually disinterested—to principles of equal political liberty and opportunity. That is, any *rational agent* looking out for his own self-interest would agree to two basic principles: (1) Everyone has an equal right to "the most extensive basic liberty compatible with a similar liberty for others," and (2) any social and economic inequalities must be such that "they are both (a) reasonably expected to be to everyone's advantage and (b) attached to positions and offices open to all."[27] When the two principles conflict, reason directs us to defer to the first.

According to Rawls, "whenever social institutions satisfy these principles those engaged in them can say to one another that they are cooperating on terms to which they would agree if they were free and equal persons whose relations with respect to one another were fair."[28]

thought experiment
A way of using our imaginations to test a hypothesis; we think rather than field-test a hypothesis, using reasoned imagination to provide the necessary conditions for the experiment, and carefully reasoning out the most likely consequences according to our hypothesis.

original position
John Rawls's imaginary setting in which we can identify the fundamental principles of justice from an objective, impartial perspective, as rational agents rather than as "interested parties": similar to the "state of nature" in the social contract theories of Thomas Hobbes, Jean-Jacques Rousseau, and John Locke.

veil of ignorance
John Rawls's mechanism for imaginatively entering into the original position by avoiding all personal considerations in the process of determining principles of justice; the veil of ignorance is a problem-solving device that prevents us from knowing our social status, what property we own, what we like and don't like, how intelligent we are, what our talents and strengths are, and so on.

PHILOSOPHICAL QUERY

Conduct your own thought experiment by using the concept of a veil of ignorance to write a code of conduct for college courses. Imagine that you do not know if you are a pupil or professor, or any other personal factors. Does the veil of ignorance aid in such tasks, or is something overlooked?

Susan Moller Okin

© Cengage Learning®

The traditional canon is elitist... concerned with the writing primarily of privileged white men. Women's writing, writing of people of color, people of the working class— these voices need to be brought into... study.

— Sue Howard

What About Family Justice?

In *Justice, Gender, and the Family*, **Susan Moller Okin** (1946–2004) analyzes Rawls's theory of justice, with special attention to issues of gender and the family. Okin points out that no adequate theory of justice can fail to include an analysis of justice within the family, since the family—in whatever form—is still the primary shaper of personality, as well as of basic attitudes of self-respect (self-esteem), gender, and ethnicity. In sum, justice cannot be separated from considerations of justice for each specific member of the family. Clearly, in our present society, wealth, equality, and liberty are not evenly or justly apportioned. Okin continues:

> Yet, remarkably, major contemporary theorists of justice have almost without exception ignored the situation I have just described [the status of all family members]. They have displayed little interest in or knowledge of the findings of feminism. They have largely bypassed the fact that the society to which their theories are supposed to pertain is heavily and deeply affected by gender, and faces difficult issues of justice stemming from its gendered past and present assumptions. Since theories of justice are centrally concerned with whether, how, or why persons should be treated differently from one another, this neglect seems inexplicable.[29]

Okin argues that Rawls's analysis of justice is "ambiguous" regarding gender because she says, he rarely indicates "how deeply and pervasively gender-structured" this society is. Further, Okin points out, Rawls fails to mention that *Kant did not intend for his moral theory to apply to women*. Okin asserts that in his discussion of Sigmund Freud's theory of the formulation of the male superego, Rawls simply ignores the fact that Freud thought that women's moral development was *psychologically deficient*. Okin concludes that

> Thus there is a blindness to the sexism of the tradition in which Rawls is a participant, which tends to render his terms of reference more ambiguous than they might otherwise be. A feminist reader finds it difficult not to keep asking, Does this theory apply to women?[30]

According to Okin, Rawls's work is "ambiguous" rather than flatly sexist because he does acknowledge that sex is one of the morally relevant contingencies that are to be hidden behind the veil of ignorance. But reconsider Rawls's language regarding these contingencies in light of Okin's observations:

> Among the essential features of this situation is that no one knows *his* place in society, *his* class position or social status, nor does any one know *his* fortune in the distribution of natural assets and abilities, *his* intelligence, strength, and the like.[31] [emphasis added]

Rawls had hoped that the veil of ignorance could be used to "correct for" the "arbitrariness of the world" by putting people in a position to reason independently of "morally relevant contingencies" such as actual social status, talent, ethnicity, *and the like*. As "pure rational agents," they would think from an identical standpoint. Each one's perspective would be the perspective of all. Okin notes that "one might think that whether or not they knew their sex might matter enough to be mentioned." "Perhaps" she suggests, "Rawls meant to cover it by his phrase 'and the like,' but it is also possible that he did not consider it significant."[32]

Aplia

Commentary

Kant remains *the* major figure in modern philosophy. His effort to understand how the mind *knows* has shaped a significant portion of the field. Kant is also a major influence in modern psychology. In fact, many of the epistemological issues he raised are now being addressed by the cognitive sciences, which are devoted to unraveling the mysteries of perceiving, learning, knowing, and thinking.

In the field of ethics, three imposing visions dominate modern philosophy. One is Kantian formalism, the second is Humean subjectivism (Chapter 10), and the third is utilitarianism (the subject of Chapter 12). We will address some criticisms of Kantian ethics in the process of understanding the major alternative to it in the next chapter. Even so, some general remarks are in order here.

In spite of the difficulty of his arguments and writing style, Kant's moral philosophy has proved to be influential beyond philosophical circles. Part of its power lies in a deep sense that it is wrong to make ourselves the exception in moral matters. If something is right (or wrong) for one person, it seems only fair that it be right (or wrong) for other persons in similar circumstances. We are offended when others make themselves or their loved ones exceptions to their own purported moral rules. This sense of offense may stem from a glimmer of a "moral law within."

Kant's categorical imperative is a more refined and sophisticated version of the Golden Rule: "Do unto others as you would have them do unto you." Kant understood that a sloppy formulation of the Rule can be interpreted as saying "Treat others as you would *like* to be treated." Such a formulation generates what I call the Sadomasochistic Paradox, from an old joke in which a masochist says to a sadist, "Hurt me!" and the sadist replies, "No." The point, of course, is that how we *want* to be treated varies and is often determined by our individual tastes, background, personal beliefs, and temperament. This is certainly not a very reliable standard for treating others. If we lack self-respect or have some psychological quirk, we might want to be treated very poorly indeed. Kant's insistence that duty rise above inclination is meant to prohibit such individualistic interpretations of the Rule.

A common criticism of Kant's moral philosophy is that it promotes rash and irresponsible behavior by exempting us from responsibility for the consequences of our actions. After all, if the only truly good thing is a good will or motive, then all that matters morally is my intention—not the results of my behavior. Sophisticated Kantians point out, however, that any universalizable maxim must include concern for and consideration of the likely consequences of action. No defensible moral duty can condone indifference to what happens to others.

> *The notion of happiness is so indefinite that although every man wishes to attain it yet he never can say definitely and consistently what it is that he really wishes and wills.*
>
> — Immanuel Kant

Another intriguing problem has to do with the conscience of a fanatic. By stressing the rational aspects of morality, Kant might have given too little weight to important psychological factors. A famous example involves a Nazi who is willing to universalize this maxim: "Always annihilate those whom you judge to be inferior and impediments to human progress." When it is pointed out that the Nazi could become the target of annihilation if he turns out to be an impediment to human progress, he is expected to see the "unreasonableness" of his maxim. If he still holds to it, knowing that it could result in his own destruction, he is said to be a fanatic. But isn't this judgment based on our own inclinations (sentiments) and beliefs about what is reasonable? Yet how else can we determine what's rational? Did Kant merely use his own Western European Christian background to define "reasonable"? Is he, perhaps, guided by moral sentiment after all—as Hume thought? This is a complex and important problem, one even the finest moral philosophers still struggle with.

Being "rational" is clearly not all that matters, as the harm caused by "rational" criminals, frauds, toxic polluters, and others clearly demonstrates. Experience offers countless examples of dangerous, immoral schemes hatched by rational individuals lacking good will. Equally dangerous is the well-intentioned but shortsighted or incompetent individual whose motives are unassailable yet whose actions generate harm. The best will must be combined with a certain minimum of intelligence, insight, and ability. Just as being rational is not a sufficient condition for being moral, neither is having a good will.

Because we lack the ability to frame moral rules so clearly that they do not generate problems, attempting to apply the categorical imperative to specific cases is often quite difficult. Suppose, for instance, that you promise a friend to repay borrowed money whenever he requests it. One evening your friend and a drug dealer show up. Your friend demands the money to buy an ounce of heroin. Should you repay it? Which is more important: keeping a promise or looking out for a friend's welfare when he or she is unable to? Can a drug user be rational when compelled by a powerful addiction? Does treating my friends as ends entail protecting them from themselves or letting them make their own choices no matter how harmful the consequences?

Can I frame a moral maxim to guide me in choosing between conflicting moral rules in such a case? I could add qualifications to my rules, but what is the purpose or benefit of having rules if they require so many qualifications that they cease to function as moral maxims? It is not clear there is *any* maxim that can be universalizable without qualification and still function as more than a very loose guideline.

In spite of such difficulties, I remain especially impressed by Kant's pattern of starting with commonly accepted ideas like causality, the unitary self, and free will and then trying to determine how the mind can know them. The result is certainly not a simplistic epistemology or moral philosophy. Kant presented a radically new picture of the mind as an active organizer and questioner of sensation. He identified important limits of empiricism and rationalism and identified vital questions that wait to be answered. His insistence that "reason demands" a noumenal world beyond immediate experience and the reach of science remains a profound expression of a moral sense shared by many people.

> *Deficiency in judgment is just what is ordinarily called stupidity, and for that there is no remedy.*
> — Immanuel Kant

How often we seem to forget that others are *persons* when we use them as status symbols or see only their outward appearance or religious or political beliefs. Imagine a world in which clerks and medical doctors and parents and children and spouses and students and teachers and politicians and police officers and everyone else followed this principle. If I can remember that I live in a kingdom of ends, I can transform my relationships from a sort of bartering for favors or competing for power and success. I can elevate my life to something beyond a contest in which I and mine must struggle against a "different" and "inferior" them. In the kingdom of ends, it is always *us*.

Summary of Main Points

- Kant fully understood the serious implications of the "scandal in philosophy" that resulted from Hume's devastating use of the empirical criterion of meaning and the failure of rationalism and empiricism to adequately account for knowledge of the external world, cause and effect, and knowledge in general while science clearly showed otherwise.

- Kant developed a special kind of analysis called a critique, which combined reason and experience in order to avoid the errors of rationalism and empiricism. Critical philosophy attempts to discover whether *a priori* knowledge and metaphysics are possible. Kant claimed that knowledge is formed by actual experience and faculties of judgment called categories of understanding. We know reality only as it is organized by human understanding (phenomenal reality), not reality as it is (noumenal reality).

- Kant distinguished between theoretical reason and practical reason. Theoretical reason is confined to the phenomenal world; practical reason moves beyond the phenomenal world to the moral dimension. Practical reason reveals a moral dimension based on our consciousness of necessary and universal moral laws, which Kant calls rules or maxims.

- Moral rules cannot be discovered empirically; reason imposes moral obligation. Reason reveals that morality is a matter of moral duty (good will) rather than consequences. Moral duty must be confined to considerations of the form: What are the universal

obligations of all persons in similar circumstances? The moral quality of an act is determined by the principle to which the will consciously assents. Moral obligations are not hypothetical and dependent on individual circumstances but, rather, categorical, universally binding on all rational beings.

- Kant called the universal command that infuses all moral obligations the categorical imperative: Act as if the maxim of thy action were to become a universal law of nature. A special formulation of the categorical imperative acknowledges this worth: Act in such a way that you always treat humanity, whether in your own person or in the person of another, never simply as a means but always at the same time as an end.

- John Rawls, an influential modern philosopher, constructed a theory of justice designed to overcome the limits of personal bias that prevent us from basing our moral and social values on objective and impartial rational principles.

- Susan Moller Okin argues that overlooked gender bias remains present in both the language and choice of examples Rawls employed in his influential attempt to refine Kant's modern moral philosophy. Okin analyzes Rawls's theory of justice with special attention to issues of gender and the family, arguing that Rawls's position is "ambiguous" regarding gender because he rarely indicates how deeply and pervasively gender-structured this society is.

Post-Reading Reflections

Now that you've had a chance to learn about the Universalist, use your new knowledge to answer these questions.

1. Why did Kant think it necessary to posit the existence of the noumenal world?

2. How does Kant answer Hume's bundle theory of the self? Do you think he is successful?

3. Describe the moral dimension as Kant understood it.

4. Explain the reasoning behind Kant's efforts to make morality a matter of motives, not consequences.

5. What is a good will, according to Kant, and why does he claim that the only thing good in itself is a good will?

6. For Kant, how does *willing X* differ from *wanting X*, and why is this distinction important?

7. What is a maxim? What makes a maxim *moral* in Kantian terms?

8. What is the basis of our intrinsic worth, according to Kant? How does this Enlightenment conception of moral (human) dignity differ from today's broader understanding of human worth?

9. What Kantian problem was Rawls addressing with his theory of justice? What did Rawls offer as an alternative?

10. What oversight did Susan Moller Okin identify in modern theories of justice, including Rawls's? Why does she say that Rawls's theory of justice is ambiguous?

 MindTap·

Experience MindTap through the activities highlighted in this chapter. Further explore this online, personalized learning tool to deepen your comprehension and improve your grades.

12

The Utilitarian
John Stuart Mill

If all mankind minus one were of one opinion, and only one person were of the contrary opinion, mankind would be no more justified in silencing that one person than he, if he had the power, would be justified in silencing mankind.

— *John Stuart Mill*

Learning Objectives

After you complete this chapter, you should be able to:

- State the principle of utility.
- Apply Jeremy Bentham's egoistic hook to a current social issue.
- Identify the basis of Bentham's attribution of moral rights to animals.
- Describe Harriet Taylor's role in John Stuart Mill's life and thought.
- Distinguish between simple utilitarianism and refined utilitarianism.
- Distinguish between happiness and contentment, according to Mill.
- Critique the assertion that utilitarianism is nothing more than majority rule and, as such, is nothing more than a philosophy based on quantity, on the force of numbers.
- Contrast Mill's defense of liberty with Sarah Conly's defense of coercive paternalism.

> It is vain to talk of
> the interest of the
> community, without
> understanding what
> is in the interest of the
> individual. A thing
> is said to promote
> the interest, or to be
> for the interest, of
> an individual when
> it tends to add to
> the sum total of his
> pleasures; or, what
> comes to the same
> thing, to diminish the
> sum total of his pains.
> — Jeremy
>   Bentham

TWO COMPETING IMPULSES struggle to control the general direction of any society: a desire for change and progress and a desire for security and order. To do justice to both tendencies, free societies struggle to balance individual rights and freedoms with the general social welfare, what's best for everyone. The problem is, not everyone agrees about what's best for everyone.

As contemporary life grows more complex and the world more populous, competing interests, limited resources, and conflicting beliefs make dealing with all sorts of issues increasingly touchy. What seems obvious, fair, and just to one group often seems unfair and unjust to other groups. The wants of the privileged appear to conflict with the wants—and needs—of the many.

If you traveled to work or school today on a major roadway, you may have benefited from someone else's loss. Suppose that when the community decided to build the highway that now benefits you and thousands of others, engineers determined that the best route for most people cut straight through a family farm. Based on that information, the local government, on behalf of the majority of citizens, would try to buy the land. Such an offer is technically only a courtesy, for virtually every community in this country can appropriate private land—at a "fair market price"—under what is called the right of eminent domain. If the owners don't want to sell, they can be forced to on the grounds that the general welfare takes precedence over individual preferences.

The use of eminent domain to promote the "greater good" is an application of a philosophical principle that's become so entrenched in our culture that many of us take it for granted. It is the principle that, although individual rights and desires must be respected, the good of the majority ultimately takes precedence over the happiness of any one individual or small group of individuals. Greatest-happiness reasoning limits when we can run our loud leaf blowers; it also prevents us from refusing to rent apartments to people of ethnicities, gender orientations, or ages we may not like.

Immediately after the events of September 11, 2001, the federal government initiated time-consuming and annoying security checks at airports. A year later, security procedures were modified in an effort to balance security and convenience for the largest number of travelers while jeopardizing the smallest number. From matters of the gravest concern to mundane decisions about what to have for dinner, groups almost instinctively try to make as many people as possible as happy as possible.

In this chapter, we'll look at utilitarianism, a modern application of hedonism that was first formulated by the British philosopher Jeremy Bentham. Bentham's simple utilitarianism was refined by his friend and student John Stuart Mill into one of today's most influential moral and social philosophies. (Hedonism is discussed in Chapter 7.)

Social Hedonism

Modern utilitarianism developed as a response to social conditions created by the Industrial Revolution—which in Britain ran roughly from 1780 to 1835. As the term implies, this era was characterized by massive social change and upheaval generated by new scientific manufacturing techniques that, in turn, produced

The advantages of the Industrial Revolution came at a high price for many of the working poor, who found themselves crowded into slums and tenements near the great factories and workhouses that sprang up as labor became increasingly centralized and standardized. The Field Lane Refuge pictured here was founded in 1842 to provide shelter for homeless men.

geographic, familial, spiritual, and economic disruption as a newly created class of "workers" competed for jobs that were often repetitive, dangerous, and poorly paid—degrading and dehumanizing.

The advent of efficient steam and water power made large factories practical. Cloth weaving, for example, had once been a cottage industry, but the textile mills could make cloth much more cheaply. Hordes of workers sought jobs in the mill towns and cities, creating large slums. Between 1800 and 1831, the English cities of Leeds, Sheffield, Manchester, and Liverpool nearly doubled in population. Shabbily constructed buildings rented at such high prices that they paid for themselves in five years. Of course, such high rents resulted in overcrowding, as poorly paid workers lived two and three families to an apartment. In Manchester in 1845, for example, twenty-seven cases were documented of up to seven people trying to sleep in one bed.[1]

In 1798, **Thomas Malthus** (1766–1834), an Anglican minister, published a work titled *An Essay on the Principle of Population as It Affects the Future Improvement of Society*. In it, Malthus expressed grave doubts about the feasibility of social reform:

> I have read some…speculations, on the perfectibility of men and society, with great pleasure. I have been warmed and delighted with the enchanting picture which they hold forth. I ardently wish for such happy improvements. But I see great and, to my understanding, unconquerable difficulties in the way to them.[2]

It is clear that any society where the means of subsistence increase less rapidly than the numbers of the population is a society on the brink of an abyss.…Destitution is fearfully prolific.
— M. Louis Blanc

The "great difficulties" Malthus feared were overpopulation and underproduction of food. He argued that although food production increases arithmetically (1 to 2 to 3 to 4 to 5 to 6, and so on), unchecked population growth progresses geometrically (1 to 2 to 4 to 8 to 16 to 32, and so forth). Thus, according to Malthus, unchecked population inevitably outgrows the food supply.

Troubled by both the growing slums in the cities and efforts to improve living conditions for the poor, Malthus concluded that there could be no justification for helping the disadvantaged. Raising wages would only enable the poor to marry younger and have even more children; the population would outgrow the food supply, and poverty would return anyway. Welfare programs would only result in increased "idleness" and encourage large families—with the same result.

Malthus argued that the only way to avoid such harsh "natural cures" as epidemics and the "historical cure" of war or rebellion was to stop helping the poor and remove all restraints on the free enterprise system. Buyers, sellers, bosses, workers, and owners must be left to their own struggle. The law of supply and demand would make it more difficult for the poor to afford to marry early or support very many children, thereby checking the geometric rise of population.

The conservative British ruling class eagerly embraced Malthusian principles. Factory owners and businessmen were able to justify low wages as their "duty." The evils of the Industrial Revolution could be rationalized away by blaming the miserable living and working conditions of the poor on the poor themselves. And certainly these conditions were discouraging.

In such a context, Jeremy Bentham's insistence that legislators consider the greatest happiness of the greatest number of people can be seen as the radical philosophy that it was.

MindTap

Discussing Philosophy

PHILOSOPHICAL QUERY

Think carefully about Malthus's arguments. Can you think of any current evidence to support Malthus's view? Can you think of any evidence against it?

Philosophy and Social Reform

Jeremy Bentham

Jeremy Bentham (1748–1832) directly challenged the owners, bosses, and ruling classes when he insisted that "each counts as one and none more." Bentham blasted those in power for pursuing their own narrow, socially destructive goals instead of pursuing happiness for everyone.

Bentham's solution was to establish democratic rule by the whole people rather than by a select class. If "the rulers are the people," as Bentham believed, then "all government is in itself evil," and the only justification for government is to prevent worse evils. For Bentham, the legitimate functions of government are social reform and the establishment of the conditions most conducive to promoting the greatest happiness for the greatest number of people. This proved to be a nearly irresistible philosophy for many.

Although much nineteenth-century philosophy had been a response to Kant's work, with the notable exceptions of G. W. F. Hegel and Arthur Schopenhauer, many philosophers rejected Kant's elaborate systems and transcendental meta-physics. They viewed metaphysics as cumbersome, irrelevant, and meaningless—unverifiable by science and unclear according to the empirical criterion of meaning (see Chapter 10). Philosophers' interest shifted from the search for transcendental truth or systemic coherence to practical remedies for the pressing problems of society. They explored social and political philosophy, empirically based ethics, and the application of scientific knowledge to immediate problems of human happiness.

Predictably, this secular, fact-oriented approach revived interest in the cultural relativity of values and beliefs. Philosophers no longer felt obliged to produce elaborate theories or systems, since they thought even their own theories were culturally limited. By contrast, particular strategies and factual information were thought to be reliable, provided that they were "scientific" and "objective."

Moreover, the new scientific view of an evolving universe made elaborate metaphysical theories seem irrelevant. If the universe and everything in it is slowly changing, then any fixed "grand theory" would apply for a brief time at best. Growing belief in evolution resulted in efforts to identify an evolutionary view of ideas rather than a search for *the* static truth.

Lastly, the social change and turmoil generated by the Industrial Revolution, the French Revolution, and the Napoleonic Wars cast serious doubts on the adequacy of Kant's ethic of *good will*. Looking about them, philosophers noted that *what actually happens to people* is of supreme importance. A clear need for fact-based, humanistic reform emerged.

> *I would have the dearest friend I have to know that his interests, if they come in competition with those of the public, are as nothing to me. Thus I would serve my friends—thus I would be served by them.*
>
> — Jeremy Bentham

In his will, Jeremy Bentham donated his body to the public good. After a public autopsy, his skeleton and head were preserved. In 1850, Bentham's remains were acquired by the University of London, where his skeleton is on display dressed in his own clothes and with a wax head. For some years, Bentham's mummified head was kept in a box at his feet. The replica is referred to as the Auto-Icon.

Bruce Dale/National Geographic Creative

Science became the new hope for this reform, replacing Enlightenment conceptions of reason. Scientists and reformers believed that the application of scientific methods of inquiry could identify and eliminate poverty, crime, ignorance, and other sources of widespread misery. Social and political issues eventually dominated metaphysical concerns. Epistemology was important only to the extent that it related to verifiable, immediate improvements in society. If the Enlightenment was the Age of Reason, the nineteenth century began as the Age of Reform. (How it ended is another story.)

The Principle of Utility

In contrast to Kant, who would have dismissed Bentham's work as "anthropology," Bentham attempted to base his philosophy on careful consideration and observation of social conditions and actual human behavior. Like Aristippus before him (Chapter 7), Bentham declared that careful observation of actual behavior makes it crystal clear that pain and pleasure shape all human activity. As he says in the famous opening passage of *An Introduction to Principles of Morals and Legislation*:

> I. Nature has placed mankind under the governance of two sovereign masters, *pain* and *pleasure*. It is for them alone to point out what we ought to do, as well as determine what we shall do. On the one hand the standard of right and wrong, on the other the chain of causes and effects, are fastened to their throne. They govern us in all we do, in all we say, in all we think: every effort we can make to throw off our subjection will serve but to demonstrate and confirm it. In words man pretends to abjure their empire; but in reality he will remain subject to it all the while. The *principle of utility* recognizes this subjection and assumes it for the foundation of that system, the object of which is to rear the fabric of felicity by the hands of reason and of law. Systems which attempt to question it deal in sounds instead of sense, in caprice instead of reason, in darkness instead of light.[3]

psychological hedonism
The belief that all decisions are based on considerations of pleasure and pain because it is psychologically impossible for human beings to do otherwise.

ethical hedonism
The belief that although it is possible to deliberately avoid pleasure or choose pain, it is morally wrong to do so.

In other words, Bentham espouses both **psychological hedonism** (pain and pleasure "determine what we shall do") and **ethical hedonism** (pain and pleasure "alone…point out what we ought to do"). Thus, the principle of utility is sometimes referred to as the *pleasure principle*.

The term *utility* has two related meanings. Utility can refer to a thing's usefulness, to how well it performs a specific function. In this sense, a strictly utilitarian automobile might have standard wheels and only the most practical accessories, such as rear-window defrosters or antilock brakes. Although this no-frills notion of utility enters into Bentham's meaning, he generally uses the term to mean *pleasure-producing* or *pain-avoiding*. We might simplify that to *pleasure-maximizing*, if we remember that sometimes the best we can do to maximize pleasure is minimize pain.

Having asserted both ethical and psychological hedonism, and having described what he meant by utility, Bentham made a move that revolutionized the concept of hedonism: He enlarged the ethical interests of the hedonist. And since he thought we are all hedonists, whether we know it or not, this amounted to enlarging everyone's general ethical obligation. Bentham transformed personal hedonism into a potent social and ethical philosophy, using the **principle of utility**: *Act always to promote the greatest happiness for the greatest number.*

Although Bentham's successor John Stuart Mill coined the term *utilitarianism*, philosophers sometimes also refer to Bentham's philosophy as utilitarianism. To avoid confusion, we'll refer to Bentham's philosophy as *simple utilitarianism* to distinguish it from Mill's more refined and elaborate version, which we'll refer to as *utilitarianism*.

> **principle of utility**
> A principle that says to always act to promote the greatest happiness for the greatest number.

The Hedonic Calculus

Bentham wanted to make ethics a science. To that end, he tried to base his philosophy on observations of actual conditions and to derive principles of behavior from facts. Bentham thought he had found a scientific way to calculate the proper course of action for any circumstance. He called his technique the *hedonic calculus.* John Stuart Mill sometimes referred to the calculus as Bentham's "method of detail," because it considered various factors.

To introduce mathematical precision to the difficult task of weighing alternative courses of action, Bentham proposed the notion of "units" of pleasure or pain, which he called *hedons* or *lots*. (Some contemporary philosophers use the term *utiles*.) Thus, when contemplating an action, we add units of pleasure or subtract units of pain. Bentham identified four elements that affect pleasure or pain themselves, two that affect action related to pleasure or pain, and one based on the number of people affected. The seven elements are:

1. *Intensity.* How strong is the pleasure?
2. *Duration.* How long will the pleasure last?
3. *Propinquity.* How soon will the pleasure occur?
4. *Certainty.* How likely or unlikely is it that the pleasure will occur?
5. *Fecundity.* How likely is it that the proposed action will produce more pleasure?
6. *Purity.* Will there be any pain accompanying the action?
7. *Extent.* How many other people will be affected?

Positive units of pleasure or negative units of pain can be attached to each of these seven elements. The resulting unit totals can then be compared, and if the balance is on the positive (pleasure) side, the proposed choice is good; if the balance is on the negative (pain) side, the choice is bad. If a hedonic calculation results in more units of pleasure, we should perform the contemplated action; if more units of pain, we should not. Bentham believed that each of us already uses hedonic calculation on a commonsense, intuitive level; in his view, he was simply adding scientific rigor to our informal methods of choosing pleasure and avoiding pain.

The Egoistic Foundation of Social Concern

Like Aristippus, Bentham claimed that psychological egoism is natural and universal. Psychological egoism asserts that we are always interested chiefly in our own welfare, whether or not we admit it. That's not to say we don't care about anyone or anything else, but this caring is based on how things affect our own happiness. People we love give us pleasure, and pleasure is in our self-interest. People we hate cause us pain, which is not in our self-interest. To those who cause us neither pain nor pleasure, we remain indifferent.

If the psychological egoist is correct, all ethical systems, regardless of their terminology, attempt to maximize pleasure and minimize pain. They may speak of right and wrong, good and bad, and so forth, but these terms all reduce to pleasure and pain. Reason is simply a tool that helps us determine whether our actions will result in more pain or more pleasure. Bentham's calculating concept of reason contrasts significantly with Kant's concept of the good will (Chapter 11).

Building on this egoistic foundation, Bentham thought that if people could be shown how a better society for others would result in less pain and more pleasure for *them*, genuine social reform would occur. That is, natural self-interest provides an *egoistic hook* that shows how our individual welfare is inseparable from social welfare. Thus, the proper role of government must be to ensure that the *enlightened self-interest* of each individual is allowed to develop. Further, to promote the greatest possible happiness for the greatest number, laws and regulations must be not only fair and effective but also designed to motivate people to consider others' welfare as well as their own.

Bentham, along with other liberal laissez-faire reformers, made a revolutionary connection between the welfare of the individual and the welfare of the community by trying to *show* how clear-thinking "selfishness" could produce a better world. Rather than chastise us for being self-interested, Bentham sought to take advantage of it.

> *Have I a genius for anything? What can I produce?... What, of all earthly pursuits, is the most important? Legislation. Have I a genius for legislation? I gave myself the answer, fearfully and tremblingly: "Yes."*
> — Jeremy Bentham

Let's examine Bentham's egoistic hook by considering an actual issue. During a heated debate over a severe cut in tax money available for schools, a number of letters to the editor of a local newspaper made this basic point: "I have paid my dues. My children are grown and I've paid taxes for years. Why should I pay to send someone else's children to school? Let their families pay." These letters reflected a disappointing lack of enlightened self-interest. It is in every individual's self-interest—even individuals who don't have children themselves—to see that all children get a good education. Poorly educated people are much more likely to be unemployed or dependent on government assistance than are adequately educated ones. Moreover, if poorly educated people turn to crime for survival, the rest of us will have to live in fear and to pay for more judges, district attorneys, police officers, and jails; we'll see a general decline in our own social services. Thus, it is clearly in every individual's interest for as many children as possible to grow up to be well-educated, productive (happy) members of society.

Bentham's move was motivationally brilliant. In one fell swoop he found a way to link individual self-interest and the good of the community. Egoistic utilitarian logic is concrete and practical, based on everyday concerns and foreseeable consequences. We need not be able to reason abstractly to understand the basic appeal of the greatest happiness principle. Such reasoning, however, remains egoistic and potentially destructive, for whatever sense of community it creates is based chiefly on selfish concerns, not compassion or empathy.

The Question Is, Can They Suffer?

By appealing to the egoistic hook, Bentham extended the ethical reach of the pleasure principle beyond the merely human community to include any creature with the capacity to suffer.

Although the *Introduction to Principles of Morals and Legislation* begins with the ringing announcement that nature has placed *mankind* under the governance of pain and pleasure, Bentham used the fact of suffering to push the moral domain well beyond Kant's kingdom of ends and beyond other Enlightenment philosophies that treat rationality as the source of morality. As far as Bentham was concerned, suffering makes moral claims on us whether or not the sufferer can reason.

In this, Bentham disagreed with René Descartes (Chapter 9), whose dualism led him to conclude that bodies are soulless, unself-conscious objects and that, consequently, animals are meaty machines, bodies without souls. Shortly after reading Descartes's ideas about animals in the posthumously published *Treatise on Man*, the French philosopher **Nicolas Malebranche** (1638–1715) put Descartes's dualistic thinking into practice as he was walking along with some friends. When a friendly dog came up to them, eagerly looking for attention, Malebranche knelt down and patted it. Then, when he was sure that his friends were watching, he stood up and kicked the poor creature in the stomach as hard as he could. As the dog yelped off, the philosopher noted that it was just a machine.[4]

The Dutch rationalist **Baruch de Spinoza** (1632–1677) admitted that animals suffer but argued that we are within our moral rights to "use them as we please, treating them in the way which best suits us; for their nature is not like ours, and their emotions are naturally different from human emotions."[5]

Immanuel Kant, recall, argued that moral dignity is a function of rationality. Kant, like Spinoza, understood that animals suffer but insisted that they lack any moral worth or dignity. Animals are excluded from the kingdom of ends because they cannot reason from moral maxims. According to Kant, even though we have *no duties toward the animals themselves*, we should treat them humanely, because treating animals humanely is good practice for treating people humanely:

> So far as animals are concerned, we have no direct duties. Animals are not self-conscious and are there merely as means to an end. That end is man. . . . Our duties towards animals are merely indirect duties toward humanity. . . . Thus, if a dog has served his master long and faithfully, his service, on the analogy of human service, deserves reward, and when the dog has grown too old to serve, his master ought to keep him until he dies. Such action helps to support us in our duties towards human beings. . . . Tender feelings towards dumb animals develop humane feelings towards mankind.[6]

Bentham rejected any notion that animals lack moral worth simply because they cannot reason, comparing such thinking to racist thinking. Note how far Bentham seems to have moved beyond simple, egoistic hedonism in the following passage:

> The day may come when the rest of animal creation may acquire those rights which never could have been witholden from them but by the hand of tyranny.

This, then, is our Bentham. He was a man both of remarkable endowments for philosophy, and of remarkable deficiencies for it: fitted, beyond almost any man, for drawing from his premises conclusions not only correct, but sufficiently precise and specific to be practical: but whose general conception of human nature and life furnished him with an unusually slender stock of premises.

— John Stuart Mill

The French have already discovered that the blackness of the skin is no reason why a human being should be abandoned without redress to the caprice of a tormentor. It may one day come to be recognized that the number of the legs, the villosity of the skin, or the termination of the os sacrum [tailbone], are reasons equally insufficient for abandoning a sensitive being to the same fate. What else is it that should trace the insuperable line? Is it the faculty of reason, or perhaps the faculty of discourse? But a full-grown horse or dog is beyond comparison a more rational, as well as more conversable animal, than an infant of a day, or even, a month old. But suppose they were otherwise, what would it avail? The question is not, Can they reason? nor Can they talk? but, Can they *suffer*?[7]

For all Bentham's personal empathy and kindness, his *philosophy* remained egoistic at base. Its full moral force did not emerge until John Stuart Mill's suffering produced a more refined, clearly altruistic application of it.

John Stuart Mill

John Stuart Mill

Few but those whose mind is a moral blank, could bear to lay out their course of life on the plan of paying no regard to others except so far as their own private interest compels.

— John Stuart Mill

John Stuart Mill (1806–1873), one of the most interesting figures in philosophy, began life with nearly equal doses of favor and misfortune. A lucid defender of individual liberty, his childhood was severely restricted, his emotional needs virtually ignored.

Mill's parents were estranged—in his words, living "far apart, under the same roof, as the north pole from the south." Mill's contemporary biographer, A. Bain, described John Stuart Mill's father, James Mill, as unfeeling. James Mill believed that the best way to love his children was by identifying and prohibiting their "vices."[8]

John Stuart Mill's destiny was sealed when Jeremy Bentham befriended his father, who became one of Bentham's younger disciples. From Bentham, James Mill came to believe that all minds are the same at birth and that proper education—begun early enough—would produce a healthy, rational child. Bentham and James Mill decided to use little John Stuart to show just how effective Bentham's ideas were. They gave him a rigorous education, carefully planned to produce a champion of utilitarianism.

Basing their program in part on Bentham's own experiences as a child prodigy, the experimenters saw to it that John Stuart learned Greek and arithmetic at three; Latin, geometry, and algebra at eleven; and logic and philosophy at twelve. Though not everything went smoothly (young John Stuart had some trouble with Plato's *Theaetetus*), he was such a whiz at math that he had to teach himself once he had surpassed his father's abilities.[9] In an effort to refine John Stuart's thinking and to prevent "the mere cramming of the memory," James Mill forced John Stuart to try to learn everything for himself before James would even consider explaining it. In his touching *Autobiography*, John Stuart Mill characterized his education:

> Most boys or youths who have had much knowledge drilled into them have their mental capacities not strengthened, but overlaid by it. They are crammed with mere facts, with the opinions and phrases of other people, and these are accepted as a substitute for the power to form opinions of their own; and thus the sons of

eminent fathers, who have spared no pains in their education, so often grow up mere parroters of what they have learnt, incapable of using their minds except in the furrows traced for them. Mine…was not an education of cram. My father never permitted anything that I had learnt to degenerate into a mere exercise of memory. He strove to make the understanding not only go along with every step of teaching, but, if possible, precede it. Anything which could be found out by thinking, I never was told, until I had exhausted my efforts to find it out for myself.[10]

Because John Stuart Mill ultimately proved to be brilliant, Bentham and James Mill "produced" not just a champion of utilitarianism but a true genius. John Stuart Mill said his education gave him a quarter of a century advantage over others his age—but added that any average, healthy boy or girl could achieve the same results with the same training.[11] The personal cost, however, was high: Mill's education robbed him of his childhood. His father's strict control, though typical of the time, stifled any expression of emotion or spontaneity:

I was so much accustomed to expect to be told what to do, either in the form of direct command or of rebuke for not doing it, that I acquired a habit of leaving my responsibility as a moral agent to rest on my father, my conscience never speaking to me except by his voice.[12]

Later, a friend would say of Mill, "He had never played with boys; in his life he never knew any."[13] In an early version of his *Autobiography*, Mill said: "Mine was not an education of love but of fear.…My father's children neither loved him, nor, with any warmth of affection, anyone else."[14] This is not true of Mill himself, for as we'll see, Mill dearly loved one woman his entire adult life.

Mill's Crisis

When he was twenty, Mill began to pay the high price of his hothouse education in earnest with a depression or breakdown he described as a "dry heavy dejection":

I seemed to have nothing left to live for. At first I hoped that the cloud would pass away of itself; but it did not. A night's sleep, the sovereign remedy for the smaller vexations of life, had no effect upon it. In vain I sought relief from my favourite books, those memorials of past nobleness and greatness from which I had always hitherto drawn strength and animation. I read them now without feeling, or with the accustomed feeling *minus* all its charm; and I became persuaded that my love of mankind, and of excellence for its own sake, had worn itself out.[15]

Mill blamed the strict, critical, analytic environment he was raised in for robbing him of his feelings by conditioning him to believe that only facts and reasons, only the objective, mattered. But a finely honed analytic mind, unaided by emotion, cannot provide life with meaning:

I was…left stranded at the commencement of my voyage, with a well equipped ship and rudder, but no sail; without any real desire for the ends which I had been so carefully fitted out to work for; no delight in virtue or the general good, but also just as little in anything else.[16]

Mill was eventually able to pull himself out of his depression and begin the process of becoming a more integrated person by studying music and Romantic poetry. After reading a passage about the way a father's death affected his son in the memoirs of a French writer, Mill had an emotional catharsis that opened him to a wider range of experience. Aided by his superior intellect, Mill developed a fuller and deeper insight into the human condition than his two teachers knew. Although he had bouts of depression for the rest of his life, and although he is reported to have remained rather serious, John Stuart Mill became a compassionate champion of the oppressed and a brilliant defender of classical liberal principles.

Redemption and Balance

Mill's rigid training was also balanced and softened by his remarkable relationship with Harriet Taylor. The couple fell in love when Mill was twenty-four and Harriet was married to a merchant quite a bit older than she was. The relationship began with discussions of Mill's writings and Harriet's plans (she wanted to be a writer also). As Mill began to spend all his free time at the Taylors' house, it eventually became obvious to Harriet's husband that the relationship was more than simple friendship.

Ultimately, an arrangement was worked out so that Mill could stay with Mrs. Taylor when her husband was away, and she could stay with Mill during the summer and on weekends. This arrangement lasted more than fifteen years. Two years after Harriet's husband died, she and Mill were finally married. After seven years of marriage, Harriet Taylor Mill died suddenly, while the couple was in Avignon. A grieving Mill said, "The spring of my life is broken." Mill credited his wife with influencing his work for the better, saying:

John Stuart Mill credited his wife Harriet Taylor (1819–1887) with helping him add a "human element" to his philosophy and writing and with enriching his life.

What was abstract and purely scientific was generally mine; the properly human element came from her: in all that concerned the application of philosophy to the exigencies of human society and progress, I was her pupil. . . . Her mind invested all ideas in a concrete shape, and formed to itself a conception of how they would actually work: and her knowledge of the existing feelings and conduct of mankind was so seldom at fault that the weak point of any unworkable suggestion seldom escaped her.[17]

Those who knew them both suggested that Mill's vision of Harriet was more loving than it was objective. There may be some truth to that, but there can be no doubt that her relationship with Mill was beneficial and encouraging. Mill insisted that Harriet gave him a better sense of what truly mattered—and what did not—than he had on his own.

Mill's writings show the breadth and balance he worked so hard to develop: *System of Logic* (1843), *Principles of Political Economy* (1848), *On Liberty* (1859), *Representative Government* (1861), *Utilitarianism* (1863), the posthumous

"Mill on Women's Rights"

As I have already said more than once, I consider it presumption in anyone to pretend to decide [what] women are or are not, can or cannot be, by natural constitution. They have always hitherto been kept, as far as regards spontaneous development, in so unnatural a state that their nature cannot but have been greatly distorted and disguised; and no one can safely pronounce that if women's nature were left to choose its direction as freely as men's, and if no artificial bent were attempted to be given to it except that required by the conditions of human society, and given to both sexes alike, there would be any material difference, or perhaps any difference at all, in the character and capacities which would unfold themselves.

John Stuart Mill, "On the Subjection of Women," in **Human Worth**, eds. Richard Paul Janaro and Darwin E. Gearhart (New York: Holt, Rinehart & Winston, 1972), p. 53.

Autobiography (1873), and *Three Essays on Religion* (1874). His "On the Logic of the Moral Sciences" has been described as "the most enduring essay on the method of the social sciences which has ever been written."[18]

In 1873, a fatigued Mill went to Avignon, where Harriet had died so suddenly in 1858. After an especially strenuous day, he developed a high fever and died at sixty-seven on May 7, 1873. John Stuart Mill was buried in Avignon beside his beloved Harriet. So ended the remarkable life of this archetypal utilitarian, a lover of liberty and equality, reason and feeling, who worked tirelessly to improve the lot of all people.

MILL'S LOGIC; OR, FRANCHISE FOR FEMALES.
"PRAY CLEAR THE WAY, THERE, FOR THESE—A—PERSONS."

Hulton Archive/Getty Images

Refined Utilitarianism

Mill could not accept Bentham's simple version of hedonism, for Bentham, like Aristippus, leveled all pleasures. He did not assign higher importance to moral, intellectual, or emotional pleasures. His only criteria are those included in the hedonic calculus. All other factors being equal, for Bentham, the crucial difference between two pleasures is merely intensity. "Prejudice apart, the [child's] game of push-pin is of equal value with the arts and sciences of music and poetry. If the game of push-pin furnish more pleasure, it is more valuable than either."[19]

Bentham even referred to a "moral thermometer," implying that the only difference among various kinds of behavior was the "degree" of pleasure they produced.

Mill, who had been salvaged and made whole by love, music, and poetry, knew better. He knew from personal experience that pleasures differ in *kind* as well as in *degree* and identified with the Epicurean hedonists: "There is no known Epicurean theory of life which does not assign the pleasures of the intellect, of the feelings and imagination, and of the moral sentiments, a much higher value as pleasure than those of mere sensation."[20]

By introducing the notion of *quality* into utilitarianism, Mill refuted the orthodoxy he had been raised to defend. In his analysis of this crucial issue, Mill offers a most persuasive solution to a question we have encountered before: *Is there any way to prove that supposedly "enlightened" opinions and judgments are more than mere opinions?* Mill doesn't address the issue directly in terms of wisdom and enlightenment, but he does address the heart of the matter: *Is there an objective way to settle disagreements involving "levels" of knowledge and value disputes?*

Having inherited a dislike of abstract theories and systems and having been trained as a social empiricist, Mill approached this ancient problem in a straightforward way. He included an objective component in the assessment of pleasure. In *Utilitarianism*, Mill writes:

> If I am asked what I mean by difference of quality in pleasures, or what makes one pleasure more valuable than another merely as a pleasure, except its being greater in amount, there is but one possible answer. Of two pleasures, if there be one which all or almost all who have experience of both give a decided preference, irrespective of any feeling of moral obligation to prefer it, even though knowing it to be attended with a greater amount of discontent, and would not resign it for any quantity of the other pleasures which their nature is capable of, we are justified in ascribing to the preferred enjoyment a superiority in quality, so far outweighing quantity as to render it, in comparison, of small account.[21]

In other words, only those fully acquainted with two pleasures can decide which, if either, is better. If there is no consensus among them, then there is no objective difference in quality, only difference in taste or preference. For example, only people well enough versed in two (or more) kinds of music actually know whether one is qualitatively better than another. This is a necessary, *empirical criterion*. Many of us can only (honestly) say, "I don't like such and such, but then I've never really tried to understand it." If we really want to compare various kinds of music, we must either listen widely and carefully or ask those who know a great deal about music. If a consensus exists among those familiar with the types being compared, then on Mill's criterion, we have discovered a qualitative difference. Of course, the same pattern applies to comparing the competing pleasures/values of reading Shakespeare or romance novels or playing basketball or playing checkers.

> *Among the great social thinkers of the nineteenth century... Mill alone tried to do justice to all the competing drives and motives of human nature; he would never banish from his consciousness the many-sidedness and many-leveledness of social reality.*
> — Lewis S. Feuer

PHILOSOPHICAL QUERY

Can you identify any pleasures "which all or almost all who have experience of both give a decided preference, irrespective of any feeling of moral obligation to prefer it, even though knowing it to be attended with a greater amount of discontent, and would not resign it for any quantity of the other pleasures which their nature is capable of"?

©Douglas J. Soccio

©Douglas J. Soccio

Mill claimed that some pleasures are qualitatively better than others. How did Mill make his case? What method did he provide for ranking pleasures? Compare playing video games to playing classical music using Mill's method for assessing the relative qualities of various pleasures.

Higher Pleasures

Mill argued that there are *empirical grounds* for asserting that what we might call "refined pleasures" are preferable to and hence better than the "cruder pleasures:"

> Now it is an unquestionable fact that those who are equally acquainted with, and equally capable of appreciating and enjoying, both, do give a most marked preference to the manner of existence which employs their higher faculties. Few human creatures would consent to be changed into any of the lower animals, for a promise of the fullest allowance of a beast's pleasures; no intelligent human being would consent to be a fool, no instructed person would be an ignoramus, no person of feeling and conscience would be selfish and base, even though they should be persuaded that the fool, the dunce, or the rascal is better satisfied with his lot than they are with theirs. They would not resign what they possess more than he for the most complete satisfaction of all the desires which they have in common with him. If they ever fancy they would, it is only in cases of unhappiness so extreme that to escape from it they would exchange their lot for almost any other, however undesirable in their own eyes. A being of higher faculties requires more to make him happy, is capable probably of more acute suffering, and certainly accessible to it at more points, than one of an inferior type; but in spite of these liabilities, he can never really wish to sink into what he feels to be a lower grade of existence.[22]

This is an interesting argument. Consider typical reactions to individuals with diminished mental or emotional capacities. We love and, perhaps, pity those who are developmentally disabled, but we do not wish to join them. Techniques to control emotional disturbances by removing the possibility for emotion are properly seen as a last resort. Though we may jokingly claim that ignorance is bliss, few of us would consciously choose bliss if the price is ignorance.

Discussing Philosophy

PHILOSOPHICAL QUERY

What would we make of someone who did choose ignorance? Could such a person be sane and rational? Reflect on the following: To be considered sane and rational, a person must recognize the value of both sanity and reason. If so, then by definition no sane or rational person can choose a radical diminishment of an essential capacity such as knowledge. What do you think of this argument?

Not everyone agrees with Mill that the "higher" faculties and their pleasures are superior, however. Many people live as if their values regarding pleasures are just the opposite from Mill's. Not only are their lives not devoted to the use and development of their higher faculties, but these people also seem actively to discourage their higher faculties. Why are the "higher" pleasures unpopular if they are objectively superior?

Lower Pleasures

Mill argues that there is no inconsistency between an appreciation of the superiority of the higher pleasures and succumbing to the temptation of more easily secured lesser pleasures. He recognizes that character and habit are major components of our judgment and behavior:

> Men often, from infirmity of character, make their election for the nearer good, though they know it to be the less valuable; and this no less when the choice is between two bodily pleasures than when it is between bodily and mental. They pursue sensual indulgences to the injury of health, though perfectly aware that health is the greater good. It may be further objected that many who begin with youthful enthusiasm for everything noble, as they advance in years sink into indolence and selfishness. But I do not believe that those who undergo this very common change voluntarily choose the lower description of pleasures in preference to the higher. I believe that before they devote themselves exclusively to the one, they have already become incapable of the other. Capacity for the nobler feelings is in most natures a very tender plant, easily killed, not only by hostile influences, but by mere want of sustenance; and in the majority of young persons it speedily dies away if the occupations to which their position in life has devoted them, and the society into which it has thrown them, are not favorable to keeping that higher capacity in exercise. Men lose their high aspirations as they lose their intellectual tastes, because they have not time or opportunity for indulging them; and they addict themselves to inferior pleasures not because they deliberately prefer them, but because they are either the only ones to which they have access or the only ones which they are any longer capable of enjoying. It may be questioned whether anyone who has remained equally susceptible to both classes of pleasures ever knowingly and calmly preferred the lower; though many, in all ages, have broken down in an ineffectual attempt to combine both.[23]

When Mill speaks of character, he refers to socially conditioned habits. Though there are always exceptions, consider the enormous social pressures that can interfere with nurturing "higher" sentiments: Can we reasonably expect children raised in extreme poverty, violence, turmoil, and instability to develop their higher faculties in school, if every afternoon they return to an empty apartment or social jungle? Can we reasonably expect working parents to find time to work extra hours, raise healthy children, maintain their homes, and *then* develop and nurture their own higher faculties? Compare the numbers of people flocking to inane but easily understood movies with those trickling into museums or art houses. Bombarded on all sides by seductive chemicals and toys, fatigued from self-imposed and inescapable pressures, we find that the lure of philosophy or literature or poetry can pale beside the temptations of a new mountain bike, escapist movie, relationship, or basketball game.

Altruism and Happiness

Having added the notion of quality to utilitarianism, Mill expands Bentham's appeal to enlightened self-interest into a full-fledged altruistic social philosophy. We have seen the general utilitarian connection between our own happiness and the happiness of others expressed in Bentham's conception of enlightened self-interest. Mill's argument in this regard is less problematic than Bentham's because it is based on

To the person with a toothache, even if the world is tottering, there is nothing more important than a visit to the dentist.
— George Bernard Shaw

The only part of the conduct of anyone for which he is amenable to society is that which concerns others. Over himself, over his own body and mind, the individual is sovereign.
— John Stuart Mill

altruism
From Latin for "other"; the capacity to promote the welfare of others; opposed to egoism.

a more solid relationship between the individual and the group. Mill asserts that, ultimately, utilitarianism rests on "the social feelings of mankind; the desire to be in unity with our fellow creatures." **Altruism**, from the Latin *alter*, "other," is the capacity to promote the welfare of others; altruism stands in clear contrast to egoism. According to Mill's altruistic utilitarianism, no individual's self-interest is *more* or *less* important than any other's self-interest:

> I must again repeat, what the assailants of utilitarianism seldom have the justice to acknowledge, that the happiness which forms the utilitarian standard of what is right in conduct is not the agent's own happiness, but that of all concerned. As between his own happiness and that of others, utilitarianism requires him to be as strictly impartial as a disinterested and benevolent spectator.[24]

Mill wanted to show that as civilization advances, the social spirit grows. In the effort, he made an eloquent defense of the importance of universal education to general happiness.

For Mill, the function of education is twofold: to instill the skills and knowledge necessary for an individual to live well and productively and to create healthy, altruistic citizens. But to fulfill the second mandate, education must become a lifelong activity. People must be given opportunities to grow as part of their daily lives. They must be given fulfilling work and sufficient leisure to nurture more than their belly or bank account. The heart of such reform efforts must be widespread, ongoing, high-quality education.

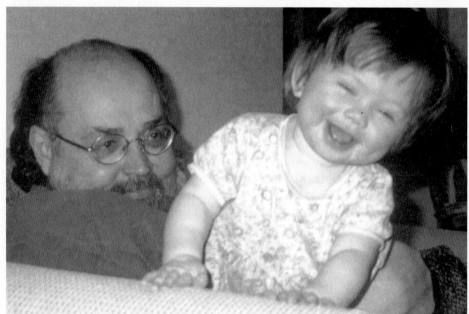

"I sometimes think what a terrible punishment it would be for a ghost or an angel to have no body.... Terribly sad it would be if we should one day return to this earth as ghosts and move silently into our children's bedroom, to see a child lying there in bed and have no hands to fondle him and no arms to clasp him, no chest for his warmth to penetrate to, no round hollow between cheek and shoulder for him to nestle against, and no ears to hear his voice."
— Lin Yutang

Next to selfishness, Mill says that the principal cause of an inability to be happy for an extended period is a lack of mental cultivation:

> A cultivated mind (and I do not mean that of a philosopher, but any mind to which fountains of knowledge have been opened, and which has been taught, in any tolerable degree, to exercise its faculties) finds sources of inexhaustible interest in all that surrounds it; in the objects of nature, the achievements of art, the imaginations of poetry, the incidents of history, the ways of mankind, past and present, and their prospects in the future. It is possible, indeed, to become indifferent to all this, and that too without having exhausted a thousandth part of it; but only when one has had from the beginning no moral or human interests in these things, and has sought in them only the gratification of curiosity.[25]

Mill was convinced that science and clear utilitarian thinking could produce a better environment, one conducive to altruism as well as the mental, emotional, and physical development and well-being of individuals.

Utilitarian Social Logic

An excellent example of enlightened utilitarian reasoning can be found in a brief examination of the rationale behind school desegregation and busing, which caused so much controversy beginning with the civil rights movement of the 1950s and lasting into the 1970s. At the time, some people argued for "separate but equal" schooling for black and white children. Close analysis of actual conditions showed that "separate but equal" was not possible, because most entirely black schools were in communities with inadequate tax bases to support good schools. Wealthier communities attracted the best teachers because they could offer better salaries, facilities, equipment, and teaching conditions.

How could utilitarian social reformers use empirical information to improve education for all children? One utilitarian solution to school integration was to take advantage of the self-interest of those parents with the most social and political influence. How could this be done? By sending *their children* to schools in other neighborhoods. The corollary to this, of course, involved busing black children to white schools. Even if many families resented school busing and integration, in the long run their unhappiness would be balanced against a greater good for society as a whole.

What is utilitarian about this? Recall that Mill argued that we must be dispassionate, impartial spectators to everyone's interest, our own included. When I am not thinking exclusively of my own child, for example, it's clear that everyone is better off if all children go to good schools. But if I cannot—or will not—think dispassionately and objectively, I must be given a *personally effective motive*, an egoistic hook. One way to hook me is to send my child to an inferior school, so that my self-centered interest *in my own child* can be tapped to improve that school's quality, which will benefit other people's children as well as my own.

Until we all possess the "nobler sentiments" Mill praised, we may need to be moved to act for the general good by considerations of narrow self-interest. Believing that *consequences* matter at least as much as motives, a utilitarian might be satisfied (at least initially) with getting me to help improve the school system even if I am

One of the great drawbacks to the self-centered passions is that they afford so little variety. The man who loves only himself cannot, it is true, be accused of promiscuity in his affections, but he is bound in the end to suffer intolerable boredom from the invariable sameness of the object of his devotion.

— Bertrand
   Russell

coerced to do so by law. This kind of forced stretching of my concerns also falls under the heading of ongoing social education.

Discussing Philosophy

Happiness and Mere Contentment

Mill, however, was not satisfied with merely modifying behavior. He wanted to reform character, too. In this regard, he distinguished between what he called happiness and "mere contentment." Mere contentment, as Mill understood it, is a condition of animals and those unfortunate people limited to enjoying lower pleasures. A major goal of Mill's utilitarianism is to make as many people as possible as *happy* as possible, not as *content* as possible:

> The ultimate end, with reference to and for the sake of which all other things are desirable (whether we are considering our own good or that of other people), is an existence exempt as far as possible from pain, and as rich as possible in enjoyments, both in point of quantity and quality...secured to all mankind; and not to them only, but so far as the nature of things admits, to the whole sentient creation.[26]

Mill argued that the principal cause of unhappiness is selfishness. He believed that happiness requires a balance between tranquillity and excitement, and selfishness robs us of both. It robs us of tranquillity because it is never satisfied, and it diminishes our possibilities for excitement (or stimulation) by narrowing our range of interests. Could that be why so many people seem to need artificial or extravagantly orchestrated excitement?

> When people who are tolerably fortunate in their outward lot do not find in life sufficient enjoyment to make it valuable to them, the cause generally is, caring for nobody but themselves. To those who have neither public nor private affections, the excitements of life are much curtailed, and in any case dwindle in value as the time approaches when all selfish interests must be terminated by death; while those who leave after them objects of personal affection, and especially those who have also cultivated a fellow-feeling with the collective interests of mankind, retain as lively an interest in life on the eve of death as in the vigor of youth and health.[27]

For Deeper Consideration

How does Mill distinguish between happiness and contentment? Why is this distinction vital to his utilitarian philosophy? What role does education play in Mill's philosophy? Has your education lived up to Mill's hopes? If yes, in what ways? If no, why not?

Mill's Persistent Optimism

Mill thought that no insurmountable reasons or conditions existed to prevent the emergence of a truly healthy society:

> Genuine private affections, and a sincere interest in the public good, are possible, though in unequal degrees, to every rightly brought up human being. In a world in which there is so much to interest, so much to enjoy, and so much also to correct and improve, everyone who has this moderate amount of moral and intellectual requisites is capable of an existence which may be called enviable; and unless such a person, through bad laws, or subjection to the will of others, is denied the liberty to use the sources of happiness within his reach, he will not fail to find this enviable existence, if he escape the positive evils of life, the great sources of physical and mental suffering—such as indigence, disease, and the unkindness, worthlessness, or premature loss of objects of affection.[28]

According to Mill, the chief task of all right-thinking, well-intentioned people is to address those causes of social misfortune that can be avoided or altered. Mill argued that liberties of thought and speech are absolutely necessary for the general happiness, since we can determine the truth only by an ongoing clash of opinions. He worried about what has been called "the tyranny of the majority" and warned against the very great, and often ignored, dangers of assigning too much weight to majority beliefs. (When we succumb to rule by majority rule, we elevate considerations of quantity over more substantial qualitative matter.)

In the end, Mill remained an optimist who believed that by applying reason and good will, the vast majority of human beings could live with dignity, political and moral freedom, and harmonious happiness. He believed that "the wisdom of society,

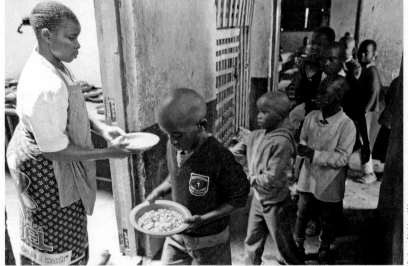

Andrew Aitchison/Alamy

John Stuart Mill argued that, for our own peace of mind, we need to provide social support for those in need—because we never know when we will need help. The quality of life without general assistance would diminish for all of us, Mill insisted.

combined with the good sense and providence of individuals," could extinguish poverty completely and that scientific progress, along with "good physical and moral education," could alleviate the scourge of disease:

> As for the vicissitudes of fortune, and other disappointments connected with worldly circumstances, these are principally the effect of either gross imprudence, of ill-regulated desires, or of bad or imperfect social institutions. All these grand sources, in short, of human suffering are in a great degree, many of them almost entirely, conquerable by human care and effort; and though their removal is grievously slow—though a long succession of generations will perish in the breach before the conquest is completed, and this world becomes all that, if will and knowledge were not wanting, it might easily be made—yet every mind sufficiently intelligent and generous to bear a part, however small and inconspicuous, in the endeavor will draw a noble enjoyment from the contest itself, which he would not for any bribe in the form of selfish indulgence consent to be without.[29]

Mill's optimism is based on his view of a social human nature and a deep, nearly universal, sense of connectedness. It is a vision that sees no *inevitable* competition between my needs and yours, between ours and everyone else's:

> The deeply rooted conception which every individual even now has of himself as a social being tends to make him feel it is one of his natural wants that there should be harmony between his feeling and aims and those of his fellow creatures. If differences of opinion and mental culture make it impossible for him to share many of their actual feelings—perhaps make him denounce and defy those feelings—he still needs to be conscious that his real aim and theirs do not conflict; that he is not opposing himself to what they really wish for, namely, their own good, but is contrary, promoting it.... This conviction is the ultimate sanction of the greatest happiness morality.[30]

In so many ways, our lives, and those of people in many other countries, have directly benefited from the seed Jeremy Bentham and James Mill planted in John Stuart Mill—in my opinion the finest archetype of a utilitarian social reformer so far.

Against Liberty

Today, John Stuart Mill remains a signally influential political and social philosopher even though, according to some contemporary critics, *On Liberty* is outdated and has been for some time. In *Against Autonomy: Justifying Coercive Paternalism*, the philosopher Sarah Conly argues that Mill's defense of personal liberty needs to be rethought. According to Conly, our liberties need to be curtailed in light of new knowledge about our limits as rational thinkers and agents. Conly rejects the liberal principle that respect for our dignity as individuals rests on the freedom to make poor, even irrational, choices. In place of Mill's liberal approach to utilitarianism, she advocates restrictive laws to "nudge" us to do—according to those who know best—whatever is necessary to improve the well-being of society and individuals (ourselves included).

Intriguingly, Conly argues that, misled by his belief that paternalistic laws always result in monolithic, conservative (totalitarian) societies, Mill failed to recognize our "natural, even biological, tendency toward social conformity." Mill, she argues, placed too much faith in our ability to take full, rational, advantage of our liberties. In so doing, he overestimated our individual capacities to act autonomously and to do what we "need" to do to improve our situations. So we need help from those who know better than we do; we need nudges to do what wiser souls recommend. Bluntly put, we need coercion because, "Left to our own devices, free of pressure to do otherwise, we often continue to dig ourselves into a deeper and deeper pit, wondering the while why we haven't yet succeeded in getting out."[31]

According to Conly, despite what Mill and other Enlightenment thinkers said, we are not always rational when it comes to making the best life choices and even when we are rational, we are often unable to do what we know is good for us. That being the case, Conly argues for a reconsideration of Mill's optimism because it is too expensive socially. She argues that even though our foolish and unhealthy choices may not bother us, may even please us, added together they detract from the general welfare. In the real world, autonomy is too expensive, economically, legally, morally, and physically because, according to Conly:

> The truth is that we don't reason very well, and in many cases there is no justification for leaving us to struggle with our own inabilities and to suffer the consequences. Those who say we should respect autonomy by letting people hurt themselves irreparably do not, on my view, show as much respect for human value as they purport to. The common rationale for letting people choose poorly is that autonomy requires that people suffer the results of their own actions, for good or ill, but here respect becomes a justification for inhumanity: the principle that those who fail deserve to fail isn't one that is geared to support equality and mutual respect. What we need to do is to help one another avoid mistakes so that we may all end up where we want to be.[32]

For Deeper Consideration

Consider the preceding words from Conly as you reflect on these questions: Who should decide what counts as a mistake for you in regard to your own well-being? Is it more humane to treat people who make choices we see as unreasonable and unhealthy as children in need of parental guidance or as adults entitled to be imperfect? Is there a limit to paternalism? That is, should certain types of music, certain books, television shows, and movies be illegal? Should we establish risk committees to determine which risks are tolerable?

Conly's work addresses one of the great, persistent dilemmas at the heart of all philosophically liberal social theories, striking a balance between liberty and order and between respect for individual rights and social welfare. In recent years, many communities and social institutions have adopted paternalistic policies limiting the size of soft drinks, placing salt shakers on restaurant tables, and prohibiting sugary snacks in lunches children bring to school, all in the name of individual and common well-being. In one way or another, autonomy is being challenged as unrealistic and costly. Conly says:

> That we should respect autonomy is taken as obvious—it is taken to be the only way to manifest our belief that all people have intrinsic value. While we may interfere with people when they harm others—when they interfere with others' autonomy by imposing actions on them that they don't want—we are held, for the most part, to be morally bound to allow people to choose when it comes to determining how they themselves want to live.... There is ample evidence, however, from the fields of psychology and behavioral economics, that in many situations this is simply not true. The incidence of irrationality is much higher than our Enlightenment tradition has given us to believe, and keeps us from making the decisions we need to reach our goals. The ground for respecting autonomy is shaky.[33]

Of course it is one thing for us, as philosophers in our studies or as social scientists in our labs, to agree in principle, with both Mill and Conly, that accidents of birth, social conditions, and personal idiosyncrasies impede the emergence of a truly healthy society—assuming that such a society can be more than an ideal. It is another, far more difficult, thing to identify those who "know best" where the line between liberty and coercion should be drawn. Then, too, we must be aware of objectifying the very people we see as needing a nudge or two. Consider, for example, what some critics decry as nudgers' elitist characterizations of individuals who resist doing what is best for themselves (according to those who know better), in passages such as this:

"It is better to be a human being dissatisfied than a pig satisfied; better to be Socrates dissatisfied than a fool satisfied. And if the fool, or the pig, is of a different opinion, it is because they only know their own side of the question. The other party to the comparison knows both sides."
— John Stuart Mill

> Some of those who ignore the nudge towards the fruit and go for the pork rinds will be wedging unhealthy, cholesterol-ridden bodies under the cafeteria table, because after years of such food they have a craving for fat and salt that no nudge will override, even while such a diet will give them shorter, more painful lives.[34]

Conly's suggested corrective to Mill strikes some philosophers as evidence that Mill was right to distrust paternalism, even in the form of impeccably well-intentioned nudges. Critics wonder if there isn't at least an element of precisely the sort of monolithic totalitarianism that Mill feared running through Conly's and other nudge-arguments against autonomy. To "know best" implies *knowing* what is best for other people, no matter what they may *believe* to the contrary. And in this case, it also means requiring other people to live as we think *they* should.

As we have seen again and again, the lines between reasons and desires, sentiments and facts, rationalists and empiricists keep shifting as philosophers wrestle with and refine perennial problems. Granting that both Mill and Conly want us all to live the best possible lives, want happiness for the greatest possible number, we're still faced with the contradictions that plague attempts to improve society without sacrificing either individual liberty or the general welfare (according to those who know best). And so, as a society, we wax and wane between political conservatism and political liberalism, between riding free with the wind in our hair and riding safely according to mandatory helmet laws, between free speech and laws against hate speech, between salted peanuts and no salt shakers on restaurant tables.

Conly, like other critics of Enlightenment optimism, has an altogether different vision of our rational capabilities and the path to a better society. She advocates taking away most freedom of choice because, left to our own devices, we simply don't choose well:

> What we need is a democratically elected government, but one in which the government is allowed to pass legislation that protects citizens from themselves, just as we now allow legislation to protect us from others. I argue for the justifiability of coercive paternalism, for laws that force people to do what is good for them.[35]

Mill, as we know, was an optimist who favored liberty over coercion, even as he recognized that a "long succession of generations" would perish in the effort to alleviate the suffering caused by social conditions. He believed that happiness eludes us when we are coerced and when we make it our direct goal. Both Mill and Conly wrestle with what may be *the* dilemma at the heart of every free society.

MindTap

Aplia

Commentary

Although the basic appeal of Bentham's utilitarianism is obvious, Bentham's failure to consider the quality of pleasures is, I think, a fatal flaw. Moreover, the hedonic calculus is arbitrary and subjective, not scientific, as Bentham claimed. It is also probably unworkable. Yet Bentham's attempt to construct a fact-based social ethic is important and generally helpful. It saves both Bentham and Mill from what some philosophers see as Kant's overemphasis on the good will at the expense of actual consequences. It also may provide a more feasible moral code for the average person than does Kant's, since it relies less on abstract reasoning and more on such common practices as calculation of self-interest and desire for basic, identifiable happiness.

The difficulties with Mill's philosophy, as might be expected, are more subtle. He fails to completely resolve the tension between hedonism and altruism, though his "altruistic hedonism" is truly different from Bentham's more egoistic hedonism—if indeed Mill's position is hedonistic. Mill's consideration of quality is important and necessary if utilitarianism is to be anything more than another appeal to pleasure. His attempts to rate the quality of pleasures according to the judgment of those who have experienced them is intriguing but probably cannot be empirically supported. After all, couldn't there be some people well versed in, say, both art movies and slasher movies who prefer the latter?

And let's not overlook the possible influence of social class and training involved in ranking pleasures. It may be tempting to say that the general public has low taste, but is this anything but the opinion of an educated, culturally conditioned elite? Mill was an aristocrat—by influence, intellect, and training. Today, postmodern philosophers claim that distinguishing between higher and lower pleasures reflects an inbred, elitist cultural bias.

Other contemporary moral philosophers have uncovered interesting and troubling problems with utilitarianism in general. Some of these stem from the possibility that an emphasis on the greatest happiness of the greatest number can result in immoral actions. Suppose, for instance, that the vast majority (the greatest number) of a community derives great pleasure (the greatest happiness) from harassing a small minority. There seem to be no clearly utilitarian grounds on which to condemn them. If enough Nazis derive enough pleasure from exterminating a Jewish minority, aren't they thereby generating the greatest happiness for the greatest number? Mill could argue (as he did, in effect, in his essay *On Liberty*) that the rights of minorities must be protected from what Alexis de Tocqueville called "the tyranny of the majority," since everyone is likely to be in a minority on some issue. But that's a factual prediction. What if the present majority doesn't believe Mill, or care?

Problems also arise when we treat the principle of utility as a way of averaging out "units" of happiness. Is there no difference between a community of fifty persons in which one hundred units of pleasure are distributed among twenty people and another fifty-person community in which everybody has two units? In both cases the "totality of pleasure" remains the same.

Even if we know an action will result in the greatest possible happiness for the greatest number, we can—and should—still ask, "But is it right?" The fact that such a question is meaningful suggests that morality is based on more than just considerations of happiness, even the happiness of everybody. Indifference to our own or others' happiness violates the Kantian principle of dignity, but so does a strictly utilitarian exclusion of everything but considerations of happiness.

All that being so, Bentham and Mill have given us one of the most important ethical philosophies of the modern era. If we look beyond their philosophies, we see two diligent social reformers whose lives certainly transcended hedonism. Both lived altruistically. In their efforts to make philosophy matter, both reaffirm the pursuit of wisdom. And time after time, Mill's strongest arguments move well beyond strictly defined utilitarian principles. Without directly referring to wisdom, Mill's educational philosophy is nonetheless a call to wisdom.

Consider, in closing, the following passage from Mill's *Autobiography*. Referring to the time of his crisis, it reveals that early on, Mill's wisdom was deeper than his utilitarianism could accommodate:

I never, indeed, wavered in the conviction that happiness is the test of all rules of conduct, and the end of life. But now I thought that this end was only to be attained by not making it the direct end. *Those only are happy* (I thought) *who have their minds fixed on some object other than their own happiness;* on the *happiness of others*, on the *improvement of mankind*, even on some art or pursuit, followed not as a means, but as itself an ideal end. *Aiming thus at something else, they find happiness by the way.* The enjoyments of life (such was now my theory) are sufficient to make it a pleasant thing, when they are taken *en passant*, without being made a principal object. Once make them so, and they are immediately felt to be insufficient. They will not bear a scrutinizing examination. Ask yourself whether you are happy, and you cease to be so. The only chance is to treat, not happiness, but some end external to it, as the purpose of life.[36]

Summary of Main Points

- Jeremy Bentham resurrected hedonism, adding a social component. He reasoned that if pleasure is good, more pleasure is better. This led him to introduce the greatest happiness principle (also known as the principle of utility): That action is best which produces the greatest happiness for the greatest number. The greatest happiness principle was a direct challenge to the conservative ruling class in Britain, since, according to Bentham, "each counts as one and none more," worker and owner alike.

- Known today as simple utilitarianism, Bentham's philosophy was an attempt to avoid the errors of irrelevant metaphysical theories by basing moral and social policies on experience and scientific principles. Bentham's hedonic calculus was a crude method of reducing issues to simple calculation of units of pleasure versus units of pain. Bentham attempted to take advantage of our "natural" egoism by using reason to show that each individual's welfare ultimately depends on the welfare of the community. The appeal to self-interest as a way of improving overall social conditions is known as the egoistic hook.

- Bentham extended the ethical reach of the pleasure principle beyond the human community to any creature with the capacity to suffer, arguing that the notion that animals lack moral worth simply because they cannot reason is akin to racist thinking. According to Bentham, suffering makes moral claims on us whether or not the sufferer can reason.

- John Stuart Mill coined the term *utilitarianism* and refined Bentham's principle of utility by distinguishing between pleasures on the basis of quality as well as quantity. Mill's concept of happiness is more complex than Bentham's and extends beyond simple concern with pleasure. Mill believed that there is an empirical basis supporting his claim that refined pleasures are objectively better than crude ones: Those familiar with both consistently prefer refined pleasures (philosophical speculation, classical music, poetry) to crude pleasures (eat, drink, and be merry).

- Mill disagreed with Bentham's insistence that all motives are egoistic and based his more refined philosophy on "the social feelings" of all people for unity with each other. Mill believed in the possibility of altruism, the capacity to promote the welfare of others. He argued that lack of altruistic feelings and ignorance of the higher pleasures were products of poor education and harsh conditions, not qualities of human nature. According to Mill, selfishness and lack of mental cultivation are the chief causes of unhappiness, and both can be cured with a proper education and legislation.

- Sarah Conly rejects Mill's faith in individual liberty, arguing that we too often make poor choices that are collectively and individually destructive. In place of liberty, Conly advocates coercive paternalism in the form "nudges" that prohibit foolish and unhealthy choices. Like other critics of Enlightenment optimism, Conly advocates taking away most freedom of choice because, left to our own devices, we simply don't choose well.

Post-Reading Reflections

Now that you've had a chance to learn about the Utilitarian, use your new knowledge to answer these questions.

1. Identify and discuss some of the social and economic factors that influenced Bentham's development of simple utilitarianism.

2. What is "the Malthusian universe"?

3. Apply Bentham's hedonic calculus to a problem in your own life. Does doing so help you deal with it in a "scientific" way—or does it complicate the problem? If it complicates things, is this due to some flaw in the calculus or to its novelty?

4. What role does psychological egoism play in Bentham's simple utilitarianism?

5. Did Bentham include animals in the moral domain? Why or why not?

6. What was Mill's crisis? How did it affect his subsequent philosophizing?

7. How does Mill account for the predominance of lower pleasures? Do you agree? Why?

8. How does Mill account for the rarity of higher pleasures in so many lives? Do you agree? Why?

9. Express Mill's vision in your own words.

10. Is Mill a utilitarian? Why is the question raised at all? Answer it based on what you have just learned about this issue.

11. On what grounds does Sarah Conly justify replacing individual liberties with coercive paternalism?

 MindTap

Experience MindTap through the activities highlighted in this chapter. Further explore this online, personalized learning tool to deepen your comprehension and improve your grades.

13

The Materialist
Karl Marx

The philosophers have only
interpreted the world in various
ways: The point is to change it.
— *Karl Marx*

Learning Objectives

 MindTap™

After you complete this chapter, you should be able to:

- Define *Zeitgeist*.

- Describe mystification.

- Explain the deterministic basis of Marxian materialism.

- Contrast the Marxian meaning of *economic* with today's common understanding of the term.

- Differentiate between the superstructure and substructure of society.

- Define *capitalism*.

- Define *surplus value*.

- Critique Karl Marx's argument that under capitalism, the bourgeoisie co-opts the proletariat.

- Analyze Marx's claim that an increase in the value of things always corresponds to a decrease in the value of human existence.

- Contrast species-life with alienated life.

Philosophy Timelines

HAVE YOU EVER really resented your job, or where you live, yet felt trapped by economic circumstances, unable to improve the basic conditions of your life? Or perhaps your education is uninspiring, something you feel pressured to do in order to get a good—or just an adequate—job? Most of us probably have felt such frustration occasionally. Sometimes, our lives seem to be controlled by our jobs and the need to earn a decent living. It seems as if money determines everything.

In Chapter 12, we learned how Jeremy Bentham and John Stuart Mill hoped to reform society by applying the greatest happiness principle and an empirically based social hedonism to social problems. Mill and Bentham were not the only social reformers inspired by the great inequities of the nineteenth century's fast-moving industrialization, however. Reform movements under the general banners of socialism and communism spread throughout France and Germany. What all these reformers had in common was a clear sense of injustice and increasing inequality. Where they differed, and often significantly, was on the exact causes (and cures) of the dismal living conditions of the working class.

Besides utilitarianism, another influential theory emerged at roughly the same time. We know it today as Marxism, after its founder Karl Marx. The social and political impact of Marxism warrants a careful look. But, as you will discover, *philosophical Marxism* is not at all what most people think of as Marxism (communism)—and it is not what today's Marxists or communists practice, either. Let's see, then, what philosophical Marxism is and what has made it so attractive to so many people.

The Prophet

Karl Marx

© Cengage Learning®

All I know is that I am not a Marxist.
— Karl Marx

Karl Marx (1818–1883) was born in Trier, Germany. His father was a respected lawyer, and both parents were Jewish. Marx's father eventually distanced himself from the local Jewish community, however, and changed the family name from Levi to Marx, most likely for social and business reasons.

Early on, Karl Marx proved to be highly intelligent and obsessively interested in nearly everything. He was also very independent and hard to control. At seventeen, Marx entered the University of Bonn to study law. He enjoyed himself, writing romantic poems, socializing, spending more money than he had, even fighting in a duel—not to mention getting arrested once for disorderly conduct. His conventional father was not at all happy with his son's behavior and insisted that Marx transfer to the more serious and prestigious University of Berlin.

Marx's stay at Berlin proved to be crucial to his later philosophical growth. Big, busy, and ugly, Berlin epitomized the nineteenth-century idea of a modern city. It was a magnet for social agitators, radicals, and other intellectuals. Imagine the impact such an environment would have on a bright, curious, somewhat rebellious young man from a conservative small-town background.

Marx's Hegelian Roots

Georg Wilhelm Friedrich Hegel (1770–1831) was clearly the dominant thinker being read in every major German university when Marx was a student. Though

Hegel was primarily a philosopher, his influence spread across intellectual and artistic disciplines. In those days, one was either a Hegelian or an anti-Hegelian, but no serious German intellectual could ignore Hegel's philosophy. Hegel's works include *The Phenomenology of Mind (or Spirit)* (1807), *Science of Logic* (1812, 1816), *Encyclopedia of the Philosophical Sciences in Outline* (1817), and *Philosophy of Right* (1821).

Hegel was influenced by Kant's attempt to answer Hume's assault on reason. Hegel pushed Kant's claim that the mind imposes categories (concepts) on experience to a different conclusion. Rather than appeal to unknowable *noumena* to avoid slipping into Humean skepticism, Hegel argued that Kant's *categories of thought* are actually *categories of being*. (See Chapter 11.) According to Hegel, it is contradictory to assert that noumena are unknowable because to do so, we must somehow know that noumena exist—and whatever exists is knowable.

For Hegel, Kant's categories exist independently of any specific individual's mind. They are mental processes *and* objective realities. In Hegelian philosophy, Reality is referred to as Absolute Thought, Mind, Spirit, or Idea. Hegel believed that it is the unique task of philosophy to discover the relationships of particular aspects of Reality to the Whole, which is a single, evolving substance known as Absolute Spirit or Absolute Mind. "History" is the all-encompassing Absolute Spirit self-actualizing into perfection.

Known as **absolute idealism**, Hegel's philosophy holds that the only way Mind can be recognized is as "continuously developing consciousness." The pattern that all consciousness follows constitutes a "dialectical process." As Hegel uses the term, **dialectic** refers to a three-step pattern in which an original idea (thought or condition) known as a *thesis* is opposed by a contrary idea (thought or condition) known as an *antithesis*. The interaction or struggle between the thesis and antithesis produces a new idea (thought or condition) that combines elements from the others, known as the *synthesis*.

Once established, the synthesis becomes the thesis for a new cycle until everything is realized in the infinite synthesis of Absolute Spirit. Each resulting level of consciousness includes its predecessors. According to Hegel, the ongoing dialectic represents the actual structure of reality: the unfolding thought of the cosmic *Geist* (Mind, or Spirit).

Hegel believed that it was possible to construct a complete picture of reality, a grand system that would incorporate all of philosophy, science, theology, art, history, and such. In fact, he insisted that it is impossible to understand anything except as it relates to the Whole. Thus, for Hegel, everything is always developing according to the dialectical process.

According to Hegel, previous philosophers were unaware that they were working with a particular stage of the development of Reason as it unfolds in history or that they themselves were products of the *Zeitgeist*, the "spirit of the age." Failing to recognize the *dialectical process* of which they were a part, earlier philosophers mistook something "abstracted" from the Whole for a fixed, independent entity. But things

G. W. F. Hegel was the dominant German intellectual of his time and a major influence on Marx's thinking.

absolute (Hegelian) idealism
Term used to identify Hegel's particular form of German idealism; a monistic philosophy that is based on an all-encompassing Absolute Spirit that is self-actualizing into perfection; Reality (Absolute Mind or Absolute Spirit) is independent of any individual's mind; not to be confused with Berkeleian idealism (immaterialism), in which objective reality is said to exist in the individual's mind.

dialectic (Hegelian)
According to Hegel, a three-step pattern in which an original idea, known as a thesis, struggles with a contrary idea, known as an antithesis, to produce a new synthesis that combines elements of both.

> *To be sure, labor produces marvels for the wealthy, but it produces deprivation for the worker. It produces palaces, but hovels for the worker. It displaces labor through machines, but it throws some workers back into barbarous labor and turns others into machines. It produces intelligence, but for the worker it produces imbecility and cretinism.*
>
> — Karl Marx

can only be understood when they are experienced in relationship to the Ultimate Synthesis toward which all history is unfolding. History does not "just happen." It is the rational development of progressively inclusive stages toward realization in Absolute Spirit.

Hegel was a grand systematizer—some would say *the* grand systematizer. He thought of history as the unfolding of the Absolute Idea of God (Absolute Spirit). He saw philosophy as the attempt to construct a comprehensive picture of *everything as it relates to everything.*

The young Marx was deeply influenced by Hegel, from whom he derived the crucial concept of alienation and the notion of historical evolution as an ongoing struggle.

Other Influences

During this time, Marx became acquainted with a number of radical "freethinkers." These excited young people spent hours arguing the finer points of Hegelian philosophy. Marx thrived on the heady combination of intellectual stimulation and radicalism. Despite all the time spent in coffeehouses and beer halls, Marx completed his doctoral work in philosophy with a dissertation on the materialistic philosophy of Democritus and Epicurus. He planned to be a professor of philosophy.

Life had other plans, however. Marx had been living on money from his father. When his father died about the time of Marx's graduation, he left only enough to support Marx's mother and younger siblings. This would have been no real problem if Marx had been able to secure an appointment as a professor. But by now the Prussian government had grown wary of the young, radical Hegelians and issued a decree prohibiting them from university employment.

Fortunately, Marx was offered a job by a liberal publisher named Moses Hess. Hess, himself a Hegelian, wanted Marx to help him edit a new, vocal "democratic journal" called *Rheinische Zeitung.* Even at this early age, Marx was an impressive figure. Writing about Marx to a friend, Hess said:

> He is the greatest, perhaps the one genuine philosopher now alive and will soon draw the eyes of all Germany. Dr. Marx is still very young (about twenty-five at most) and will give medieval religion and politics their *coup de grace.* He combines the deepest philosophical seriousness with the most biting wit. Imagine Rousseau, Voltaire, Holbach, Lessing, Heine, and Hegel fused into one person—I say fused, not thrown in a heap—you have Dr. Marx.[1]

Marx's admiration for Hegel was altered by an article called *Theses on the Hegelian Philosophy* by Ludwig Feuerbach (1804–1872). Feuerbach was a materialist who challenged Hegel's notion that the driving force behind historical eras was their *Zeitgeist.* Feuerbach argued that any given era was the accumulation of the actual, concrete material conditions of the time—not some abstract "spirit of the age." So important were material conditions, according to Feuerbach, that they controlled not just the way people behave but also *how they think* and *what they believe.* Different material conditions result in what we think of as different cultural eras. After reading Feuerbach, Marx retained Hegel's belief in the dialectics of history and a single reality but concluded that reality was material, not spiritual.

A chance combination of events in a thinker's life sometimes has a lasting and profound effect on his or her later theories. In Marx's case, a series of articles he had been doing for Hess on the exploitation of peasants in the wine-growing Moselle Valley crystallized his understanding of Feuerbach's thesis. Observing the way the landowners repressed the workers, actively inhibiting and even punishing their efforts at self-improvement, Marx concluded that material conditions did indeed dominate all others.

The Wanderer

Like many other social reformers and agitators, Marx paid a price for his outspoken concern for the downtrodden and his vehement attacks on those he saw as their oppressors. After Marx wrote a series of bitter editorials criticizing the Russian government, the rulers of Prussia—afraid of offending their powerful neighbor—shut down Hess's journal. This was April 1843, the same year Marx married Jenny von Westphalen.

Having a wife and no job, and no longer a Hegelian, Marx sought what he hoped would be a freer intellectual climate: He and Jenny moved to Paris. One of the social and political hubs of Europe at the time, Paris attracted thinkers and doers from around the world with its unique atmosphere of openness and encouragement. Naturally, such a climate attracted the most intense and talented freethinkers and radicals. It was not long before Marx felt right at home.

In Paris, Marx discovered another congenial group of radical thinkers, this time centered on the economic ideas of the **Comte de Saint-Simon** (1760–1825). Saint-Simon was especially interested in the emergence of a powerful new middle class, known as the bourgeoisie. He concluded that *economic conditions determine history.* More specifically, Saint-Simon argued that historical change is the result of *class conflict*: Those who control the material necessary for production are in a perpetual struggle with those who do not. This idea, as we shall see, had a major impact on Marx's thinking.

Marx also befriended various revolutionary groups of exiled German workers. These workers were influenced by an organized group of French laborers who agitated for radical changes in the conditions of workers and in the relationship between workers and owners. Because they demanded that property be held in common and shared by all, they were known as *communists*. Members of this group helped Marx develop a keen sense of the proletariat, or working class. He now possessed the seeds of his own philosophy.

Within a year of moving to Paris, Marx was expelled from the city, and from 1845 to 1848, he and his family lived in Brussels. While there, he helped organize the German Workers' Union, which became part of an international Communist League in 1847. Its first secretary was Marx's friend and collaborator Friedrich Engels. Marx and Engels wrote the official statement of beliefs and doctrines of the Communist League, which was published in 1848 as the *Manifesto of the Communist Party* (now known simply as *The Communist Manifesto*). It may be the most important and influential revolutionary tract ever written.

Marx next went to Cologne to help agitate for a revolt in Germany. His timing was poor, however, as a more conservative tide was sweeping across France and

The very idea of distributive justice, or of any proportionality between success and merit, or between success and exertion, is in the present state of society so manifestly chimerical as to be relegated to the regions of romance.

— John Stuart Mill

Rosemary Matthews/Hulton Archive/BIPs/Getty Images

41 Maitland Park Road, Haverstock Hill, Hampstead, England, where Marx spent the last years of his life.

The Communists disdain to conceal their views and aims. They openly declare that their ends can be attained by the forcible overthrow of all existing social conditions. Let the ruling classes tremble at a Communist revolution. The proletarians have nothing to lose but their chains. They have a world to win. Working men of all countries unite!

— The Communist Manifesto

Germany. Marx was formally expelled from Germany by the government, and he returned to Paris. Not yet thirty-two years old, he was already perceived as a dangerous revolutionary. He had barely returned to Paris when the French government again made him leave.

In August 1849, Marx's friends gave him enough money to move to London. Despite the flaws Marx and Engels would find in its class structure and capitalist economy, England proved a haven of freedom of thought and expression. Thus, in one of the ironies of history, the great critic of capitalism found the freedom to criticize capitalism only in a capitalistic environment.

Marx never left London. For almost a decade, he spent long days in the reading rooms of the British Museum, researching some but mostly writing. After returning home, he often continued working late into the night. He and his family lived a hand-to-mouth existence, moving from one shabby apartment to another, unable to pay rent. One time they were evicted without anything when the landlord confiscated their few possessions in lieu of rent. Food and medicine were always scarce. Their poverty was so dire that two sons and a daughter died in childhood.

Friedrich Engels

Friedrich Engels

Friedrich Engels (1820–1895), the son of a wealthy German textile manufacturer, went to Paris to meet Marx, after sending him some articles Engels had written criticizing English economists. The meeting changed forever the lives of both men and the shape of the world. They remained friends and collaborators until Marx's death.

In 1844, Engels published *The Condition of the Working Class in England*. His writing was strong, practical, and effective. He went on to write a series of attacks on the most important English economists of the day, accusing them of rationalizing and justifying the abuses the middle and upper classes heaped upon the poor. He saw their economic theories as capitalistic propaganda rather than honest economic or historical research. As he and Marx discussed these essays, each realized that he had finally found someone who understood the power of economic and material conditions. It has been said that Marx was the deeper thinker, but Engels added breadth and fire to Marx's ideas.

Engels had a gift for acquiring the hard facts Marx needed to support his philosophical arguments and for making Marx's often difficult and obscure thinking easier to follow. Thus Engels played a crucial role in the spread and acceptance of Marxist thinking. Engels and Marx worked together for over forty years, and Engels supported Marx and his family through the long years of poverty in London. When Marx died, Engels protected, advocated, and interpreted Marx's philosophy for the rest of the world.

Vindication

At forty-two, Marx was considered an old man. Poverty and exile had worn him down, and his influence over revolutionary thinkers had begun when he was so young that he was seen as a member of the old guard. His influence grew, however, with the emergence of the militant German Social Democracy party. After Marx became their authority on socialist theory, his financial condition improved. Then, in 1864, the International Workingmen's Association was established by revolutionaries in France and England. They, too, turned to Marx, and he came to dominate their general council. He tolerated no deviance from his views and used any means necessary to defeat those who dared challenge him.

During this time Marx began *Das Kapital*. The first of its three volumes appeared in 1867. This massive work established Marx's reputation as a philosopher. It eventually became what is sometimes referred to as "the Communist Bible," probably because of its nearly mythical status, and possibly because more people claim to give their allegiance to it than have actually read it.

As his health declined, Marx was unable to devote the same care and attention to the two remaining volumes of *Das Kapital* that he had to the first. In fact, he never finished them. What we know as the second and third volumes were extensively edited by Engels in 1885 and 1894, after Marx's death. In many ways, they are inferior to the first volume. (What is called the fourth volume was ultimately compiled later.)

In 1881, Marx's wife Jenny died after a long and painful bout with cancer. The death of the woman who had stood by the exiled, reviled philosopher through poverty and the loss of three children broke his spirit. He lived for fifteen more months in a state of grief and despair. Karl Marx died sleeping in a favorite

> *The society of money and exploitation has never been charged, so far as I know, with assuring the triumph of freedom and justice.*
>
> — Albert Camus

armchair on March 14, 1883, two months after the death of his oldest daughter. His funeral was attended by his family and a few friends. At the funeral of his old friend, Engels said:

> Just as Darwin discovered the law of development of organic nature, so Marx discovered the law of the development of human history: the simple fact that man must first of all eat, drink, have shelter and clothing, before he can pursue politics, science, art, religion, etc.; that therefore the production of the immediate means of subsistence, and consequently the degree of economic development of a given epoch, form the foundation on which state institutions, legal conceptions, art and even religious ideas have evolved and in the light of which they must, therefore, be explained.
>
> Marx was before all else a revolutionist. His real mission in life was to contribute, in one way or another, to the overthrow of capitalistic society, and to the liberation of the proletariat, which he was the first to make conscious of its own position and needs. Fighting was his element. And he fought with a passion, a tenacity, and a success few could rival.
>
> His name will live through the ages, and so also will his work.[2]

Dialectical Materialism

From Hegel, Marx took the ideas that there is only one uniform reality and that history is an evolutionary cycle governed by an internal **dialectical process**, in which progress occurs as the result of a struggle between two opposing conditions. From Feuerbach, Marx concluded that reality is material and that consequently the material conditions of life control reality. And from Saint-Simon, Marx learned to observe the relationship between the owning/governing class and the producing/exploited class. Combining these elements with a deep concern for the conditions of workers and a keen awareness of the importance of economic conditions to other aspects of life, Marx constructed a social-political-economic philosophy known variously as Marxism, communism, historical materialism, Marxian dialectics, historical dialectics, or dialectical materialism.

According to Marx's dialectical materialism, history is the ongoing result of a constant tension between two classes, an upper class of rulers/owners and a ruled and exploited underclass. From the struggle between different economic interests emerges a brand-new economic structure. Marx saw conflicting economic interests in terms of two classes, the **bourgeoisie**, or middle class, and the **proletariat**, or working class. The bourgeoisie consists of those who do not produce anything yet who own and control the means of production. The proletariat consists of all those whose labor produces goods and provides essential services yet who do not own the means of production.

Marx took Hegel's concept of the dialectical process and applied it to historical stages, which he called "the five epochs of history." Named after their dominant economic system, these epochs are (1) primitive/communal, (2) slave, (3) feudal, (4) capitalist, (5) socialist/communist. Marx argued that as each epoch develops, its basic economic structure matures. Changes in the economic structure change the material conditions of people's lives. These altered material conditions eventually amount to new social structure:

The state is not abolished, it withers away.
— Friedrich Engels

---

dialectical process (Hegelian)
An internally governed evolutionary cycle in which progress occurs as the result of a struggle between two opposing conditions.

bourgeoisie
All those who do not produce anything yet own and control the means of production.

proletariat
All those whose labor produces goods and provides essential services yet who do not own the means of production.

The German workers depicted grinding silverware in this 1887 engraving were typical of the alienated proletarians championed by Marx and Engels. Could they even afford to own the very utensils they worked so hard to produce?

Then begins an epoch of social revolution. With the change of the economic foundations, the entire immense superstructure is more or less rapidly transformed. In considering such transformation a distinction should always be made between the material transformation of the economic conditions of production, which can be determined with the precision of natural science, and the legal, political, religious, esthetic, or philosophic—in short, the ideological forms, in which men become conscious of the social conflict and fight it out.

No social order ever perishes before all the productive forces for which there is room in it have developed; and new higher relations of production never appear before the material conditions of their existence have nurtured in the womb of the old society itself. Therefore mankind always sets itself only such tasks as it can solve; since, looking at the matter more closely, it will always be found that the task itself arises only when the material conditions for its solution already exist, or are at least in the process of formation.[3]

> *Socialism will never destroy poverty and the injustice and inequality of capacities.*
> — Leo Tolstoy

According to Marx, since the great injustices of capitalism (thesis) result from the private ownership of property, a new socialistic economy (antithesis) will eventually emerge in which private property is abolished. Society will at last be able to provide decent, meaningful lives to virtually everyone (synthesis). As a result, no one will need private property or wealth. Instead of having to compete for a good life, we will live harmoniously, doing creative, satisfying work that benefits us individually at the same time it benefits society collectively. There will be only one class, hence no class conflict. The economy will reach a state of balance, and history as such (not the world, just history as class struggle) will end.

Economic Determinism

Marx radically transformed Hegel's dialectic by confining it to the material world. He objected to excessively abstract philosophy, referring to it as **mystification**: the use of cloudy abstractions to create elaborate metaphysical systems that distract us from concrete material reality. Marx thought that instead of clarifying ideas, Hegel and other "abstractionists" and idealists make them "mysterious" and vague.

Mystifying logic, like money, does not *produce* anything, it merely alters relationships. Hegel's great error, and that of philosophers in general, according to Marx, is *abstraction*. That is why, according to Marx, most philosophy lacks substance. Like Bentham and Mill, Marx believed sweeping metaphysical systems and grand-sounding statements about human dignity and virtue pale beside the actual, concrete, *existing conditions* under which the poor barely survive.

In the *Manifesto*, Marx asserts that "man's ideas, views and conceptions, in one word, man's *consciousness*, changes with every change in the conditions of his material existence, his social relations, and his social life." When Marx talks about "material conditions," he means more than just natural physical and biological conditions. He includes economic and social relationships.

Thus Marxian materialism should not be confused with scientific materialism (Chapters 9 and 10), which leads to the conclusion that all behavior is governed by strict laws of cause and effect. Marx is a *social determinist*, not a *hard determinist*. Hard determinists deny the possibility of free will or free action. **Marxian materialism**, by contrast, sees a reciprocal relationship between individuals and their environment.

Marx criticized other forms of materialism for failing to understand just how important the role of human consciousness is in shaping society:

> The distinctive character of social development as opposed to the natural process of development lies in the fact that human consciousness is involved.... *Intelligent social action is creative action....* By acting on the external world and changing it, man changes his own nature.... The material doctrine that men are products of circumstances and a changed upbringing forgets that it is men that change circumstance, and that the educator himself needs educating.[4]

This reciprocity between individuals and their circumstances is, of course, a dialectical relationship. Marx believed that his brand of economic materialism avoids

mystification
Use of cloudy abstractions to create elaborate metaphysical systems that distract us from concrete material reality.

Marxian materialism
A form of social determinism based on a reciprocal relationship between individuals and their environment; distinguished from strict materialism and hard determinism.

the futility and degradation he saw in scientific materialism, while still acknowledging the importance of the material conditions of our lives.

Engels referred to Marx's philosophy as *dialectical materialism*, but Marx himself referred to it as *naturalism*. Both characterizations express its overall thrust. Marx's emphasis, like that of his great utilitarian contemporary John Stuart Mill, is on the here and now. Like Mill, Marx refers to what he is doing as "social science." He believed his unique mixture of idealistic (Hegelian) and materialistic principles was the *only way* to understand and predict the course of history:

> We see here how consistent naturalism or humanism is distinguished from both idealism and materialism, and at the same time constitutes their unifying truth. We see also that only *naturalism* is able to comprehend the process of world history.[5]

According to Marx, the process of human history is shaped by inseparable social and economic conditions, much more so than by ideas. Unlike philosophers and other intellectuals who attribute great power to ideas such as democracy or truth, Marx proposed a radical view of ideas, namely, that *the economic structure of a culture creates and forms its ideas*. For Marx, the term **economic** refers to the complete array of social relationships and arrangements that constitutes a particular social order. He assigns a crucial role to the material base of society.

Collectively, this material base is known as the **substructure of society**. Specifically, the substructure of society consists of three components: (1) **means of production** (natural resources such as water, coal, land, and so forth); (2) **forces of production** (factories, equipment, technology, knowledge, and skill); and (3) **relationships of production** (who does what, who owns what, and the effects of this division on each group).

The material substructure determines the nature of all social relationships (parent–child, boss–employee, ruler–citizen, and so on), as well as religions, art, philosophies, literature, science, and government. According to Marx, the material substructure of any society produces ideas and institutions that are compatible with it. Because ideas and institutions emerge from and depend on the economic structure of society, Marx refers to them as the **superstructure of society**. In other words, economics (the substructure) drives ideas, art, religion, and philosophy (the superstructure):

> In the social production which men carry on they enter into definite relations that are indispensable and independent of their will; these relations of production correspond to a definite stage of development of their material powers of production. The sum total of these relations of production constitutes the economic structure of society—the real foundation on which rise legal and political superstructures and to which correspond definite forms of social consciousness. The mode of production in material life determines the general character of the social, political, and spiritual processes of life.[6]

The relationship between the economic structure of a society and the kinds of people, ideas, and institutions it produces will become clearer as we take an extended look at Marx's critique of capitalism.

economic
In philosophical Marxism, the complete array of social relationships and arrangements that constitutes a particular social order.

substructure of society
In philosophical Marxism, the material substructure or base of society that determines the nature of all social relationships, as well as religions, art, philosophies, literature, science, and government.

means of production
In philosophical Marxism, natural resources such as water, coal, land, and so forth; a part of the substructure of society.

forces of production
In philosophical Marxism, the factories, equipment, technology, knowledge, and skill; a part of the substructure of society.

relationships of production
In philosophical Marxism, who does what, who owns what, and how this affects members of both groups; a part of the substructure of society.

superstructure of society
According to philosophical Marxism, the ideas and institutions (religious beliefs, educational systems, philosophies, the arts, and such) compatible with and produced by the material substructure of the society.

PHILOSOPHICAL QUERY

Analyze your education from the standpoint of relationships of production. What—and whose—values does public education really serve? Why are you getting an education? For economic reasons only, chiefly, or marginally, or not at all?

Critique of Capitalism

Given the importance Marx placed on the economic structure of society, it is not surprising that he developed a detailed critique of the prevailing nineteenth-century relationship of production, **capitalism**. Although many of Marx's ideas are clearly revolutionary, and although he did predict a violent overthrow of capitalism, Marx never actually made a moral judgment of capitalism. He thought of his analysis as "pure social science." His aim was to describe current social and economic conditions objectively, identifying their causes and predicting the next historical change.

In Marx's opinion, tension under capitalism increases as *inequities of distribution* destroy any correlation between how much an individual contributes or produces and how much he or she receives. There is a fundamental contradiction at the heart of capitalism: The law of supply and demand determines prices, yet the large pool of workers keeps wages low. Manufacturers keep prices higher than the actual cost of production; thus, over time, workers get less and less for their effort. The result is **surplus value**, which the owners accumulate in the form of capital. Those who contribute the least profit the most.

The bitter irony, Marx says, is that most of the people who suffer under capitalism have been conditioned by it to support a system that favors the rich, dreaming of the day when they, too, will be rich enough to benefit from it. Yet the laws determining who is allowed to own what, and who gets to keep what, are written by those who already own. Education is controlled by that same class, so even the most deprived children grow up believing in free enterprise and "fair competition" only to be condemned to lives of poverty,—or at least constant financial anxiety.

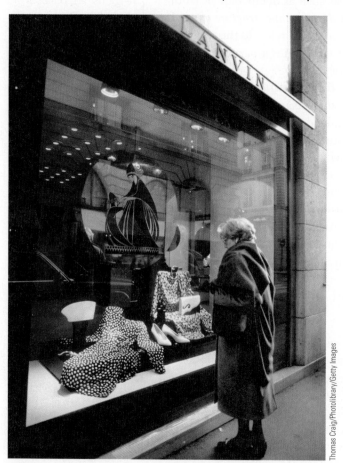

According to Marx, one of the bitterest ironies of capitalism is that those who suffer the most under capitalism have been conditioned to value it. The old woman in this picture may have worked very hard her entire life yet remained unable to purchase expensive clothes like those in the store window. Would Marx find that appalling? What do you think?

Thomas Craig/Photolibrary/Getty Images

The Bourgeoisie and the Proletariat

Marx's critique of capitalism rests on an analysis of the two classes that have emerged under capitalism. In *The Communist Manifesto*, he characterizes the bourgeoisie as disdainful of everything but capital. The government is nothing but "a committee for managing the common affairs of the whole bourgeoisie." In other words, the government is not "of, by, and for the people," but "of, by, and for the important people." The bourgeoisie reduces everything to crude calculations of self-interest and personal wealth:

> [The bourgeoisie] has left no other nexus between man and man than naked self-interest, than callous "cash payment." It has drowned the most heavenly ecstasies of religious fervour, of chivalrous enthusiasm, of Philistine sentimentalism, in the icy water of egotistical calculation. It has resolved personal worth into exchange value, and in place of the numberless indefeasible chartered freedoms, has set up that single, unconscionable freedom—Free Trade. In one word, for exploitation, veiled by religious and political illusions, it has substituted naked, shameless, direct, brutal exploitation.
>
> The bourgeoisie has stripped of its halo every occupation hitherto honoured and looked up to with reverent awe. It has converted the physician, the lawyer, the priest, the poet, the man of science, into its paid wage earners.
>
> The bourgeoisie has torn away from the family its sentimental veil, and has reduced the family relation into a mere money relation.[7]

Some of the complaints people express about today's health care crisis seem to support Marx's concerns. We lament the demise of the family doctor who made house calls. We resent arriving on time for appointments only to be kept waiting and then having to pay high fees for a cursory examination or a battery of tests whose chief purpose is to protect the doctor from a malpractice suit. Could these be examples of what Marx said happens when a profession is reduced to a "mere money relation"?

capitalism
An economic system in which the means of production and distribution are all (or mostly) privately owned and operated for profit under fully competitive conditions; tends to be accompanied by concentration of wealth and growth of great corporations.

surplus value
The term Marx used to refer to the capital accumulated by owners; the result of keeping prices higher than the costs of production at the expense of workers.

For Deeper Consideration

In 2010, the U.S. Congress attempted to reduce what many saw as intolerable inequities in American health care by passing the Affordable Care Act. Almost immediately, controversy arose over whether the new regulations were a form of socialized (Marxist-socialist) medicine or merely long-overdue reforms. Why do you suppose the terms *socialistic* and *socialized medicine* incite such heated disagreements? Do you think it is possible to discuss political and cultural concerns free from class bias?

What else does the history of ideas prove than that intellectual production changes character in proportion as material production is changed? The ruling ideas of each age have ever been the ideas of its ruling class.

— The Communist Manifesto

Marx and Engels claim that the bourgeoisie, with its hunger for more, cannot rest, cannot leave any corner of the world unexploited and unspoiled:

> Constant revolutionising of production, uninterrupted disturbance of all social conditions, everlasting uncertainty and agitation distinguish the bourgeois epoch from all earlier ones. All fixed, fast-frozen relations...are swept away, all new-formed ones become antiquated before they can ossify....
>
> The bourgeoisie has through its exploitation of the world market given a cosmopolitan character to production and consumption in every country....It compels all nations, on pain of extinction, to adopt the bourgeois mode of production; it compels them to introduce what it calls civilisation into their midst, i.e., to become bourgeois themselves. In one word, it creates a world after its own image.[8]

MindTap

Discussing Philosophy

PHILOSOPHICAL QUERY

Do you think that the growth of complex, international corporations, multinational trade alliances, and Internet commerce that are fueling what some observers refer to as the "global economy" or "world village" are signs of a spreading bourgeoisie? Is the "capitalist class" creating "a world after its own image"?

The bourgeoisie cannot actually produce all that it needs and wants, Marx pointed out. Its enormous wealth and comfort have resulted from the exploitation

As modern capitalism develops, it is increasingly difficult to distinguish "professions" from "jobs." This confusion became strikingly apparent (no pun intended) in recent years as civil servants, teachers, laborers, and students from France to Greece to America protested against wage, pension, and student aid cuts. Here, members of the Los Angeles branch of the American Postal Workers Union picket against efforts to privatize the U.S. Postal Service, another in a series of efforts to resist changes to union bargaining rights for state and public employees.

ZUMA Press, Inc./Alamy

of a great underclass, the proletariat. These are the people who actually provide the goods and services society requires to function. Controlled by the bourgeoisie, they are even compelled to produce frivolous luxuries whose real purpose is to generate ever-escalating production. Not only are the workers paid as little as the bourgeoisie can get away with in order to maximize profit, but they are also seduced by bourgeoisie controlled education and media to consume these overpriced, useless products. Thus, the proletarians are trapped in a never-ending cycle of debt, denied significant influence over their own work, and tricked and coerced into furthering the power and advantage of their own exploiters. As *The Communist Manifesto* explains it:

> In proportion as the bourgeoisie, i.e., capital, is developed, in the same proportion is the proletariat, the modern working class, developed—a class of labourers, who live only so long as they find work, and who find work only so long as their labour increases capital. These labourers, who must sell themselves piecemeal, are a commodity, like every other article of commerce, and are consequently exposed to all the vicissitudes of competition, to all the fluctuations of the market.
>
> …But the price of a commodity, and therefore, also of labour, is equal to the cost of production. In proportion, therefore, as the repulsiveness of the work increases, the wage decreases.…The more openly this despotism proclaims gain to be its end and aim, the more petty, the more hateful and the more embittering it is.[9]

If you have ever worked on an assembly line, or at picking fruits and vegetables, or in meat- or fish-packing plants, you will instantly understand the relationships of production that Marx and Engels are describing. Some of the most difficult and "repulsive" jobs are the most necessary to society—yet those who perform them are paid little and often respected less. Those who produce the least in Marxian terms work in air-conditioned offices, are supported by hard-working staffs, and may receive salaries, bonuses, and stock options worth hundreds of thousands—or even millions—of dollars.

Co-Option and Class Struggle

Marx and Engels were among the first modern philosophers to recognize the plight of women in modern society. When physical strength became less important, employment opportunities expanded for women and for men unable to do strenuous manual labor. But the work available and the pay offered were often substandard. Garment factories, for example, paid (and still pay) low piecework wages:

> The less skill and exertion of strength implied in manual labour, in other words, the more modern industry becomes developed, the more is the labour of men superseded by that of women. Differences of age and sex no longer have any distinctive social validity for the working class. All are instruments of labour, more or less expensive to use, according to their age and sex.[10]

According to philosophical Marxism, workers are exploited, even if *they* do not realize it. The fact that a powerless group submits to economic exploitation "willingly" does not alter the nature of the exploitative relationship. Just as abused spouses or children may lose the ability to perceive reality and hence mistakenly see themselves as somehow causing or deserving abuse, so too exploited workers, after

> *Not only has the bourgeoisie forged the weapons that bring death to itself; it has called into existence the men who are to wield those weapons—the modern working class—the proletarians.*
>
> — The Communist Manifesto

generations of capitalistic conditioning through schools and the media, may fail to recognize their actual social condition.

We have already seen how working-class and middle-class people can come to identify with the *possibility* of acquiring wealth rather than with their *actual chances* of doing so. In other words, we may identify with the *system* rather than with our true role in it. Marxists refer to this as being **co-opted**. You are co-opted when you are tricked, seduced, or somehow convinced to further interests that are to your ultimate disadvantage—and think that you do so willingly.

All history, according to Marx and Engels, is the history of a class struggle in which the bourgeoisie forges the instrument of its own destruction as it grows smaller but richer and more powerful. In our own time, social scientists are discussing the "shrinking middle class," the growing disparity between the haves and the have-nots. Unstable housing prices keep more and more working-class families from owning property. Two-income families alter childrearing practices and family interactions. As the divorce rate remains high, people suffer the economic (not to mention psychological) cost of supporting two separate households. Unmarried mothers of young children face the dilemma of working and paying high child-care costs or not working and living at or below the poverty level on state assistance or often inadequate child-support payments. Despite recent efforts to alleviate the problem, medical insurance is likely to remain costly or limited for so many working- and middle-class people that many observers still despair of ever finding a fair, affordable way to provide adequate care to all Americans.

Marx and Engels predicted that such conditions will not change until the proletariat becomes *fully aware* of itself, until people whose class interests are identical see that they are identical. Presently, however,

> ...the labourers still form an incoherent mass scattered over the whole country, and broken up by their mutual competition. If anywhere they unite to form more compact bodies, this is not yet the consequence of their own active union, but of the union with the bourgeoisie, which class, in order to attain its own political ends, is compelled to set the whole proletariat in motion, and is moreover yet, for a time, able to do so. At this stage, therefore, the proletarians do not fight their enemies, but the enemies of their enemies...every victory so obtained is a victory for the bourgeoisie.[11]

Under capitalism, it is in the bourgeoisie's short-term interest for different ethnic, gender, age, and religious groups to distrust and despise one another, Marx and Engels point out. So, for instance, a Marxist might argue that the bitter debate over racial, ethnic, age, and gender inequality serves the bourgeoisie by obscuring the fact that *most people of all backgrounds are being kept out of the wealthy classes*. Indeed, for the bourgeoisie as a class, nothing could be better than for "token" members of all disadvantaged groups to become publicly successful through education and hard work. This will co-opt others in those groups to "behave" and work hard while dreaming of "making it." Real change will come only when the exploited identify with one another and not with their ethnicity, religion, gender, or age, say Marx and Engels in *The Communist Manifesto*:

> This organisation of the proletarians into a class, and consequently into a political party, is continually being upset again by the competition between the workers themselves. But it ever rises up again, stronger, firmer, mightier. It compels

---

co-opted

In Marxian social analysis, co-option occurs when workers identify with the economic system that oppresses them by confusing the remote possibility of accumulating wealth with their actual living and working conditions; being co-opted also refers to anyone who is somehow convinced to further interests that are to her or his ultimate disadvantage.

The oppressed are allowed once every few years to decide which particular representatives of the oppressing class are to represent and repress them.

— Karl Marx

legislative recognition of particular interests of the workers, by taking advantage of the divisions among the bourgeoisie itself.... The bourgeoisie itself, therefore, supplies the proletariat with its own elements of political and general education, in other words, it furnishes the proletariat with weapons for fighting the bourgeoisie.[12]

PHILOSOPHICAL QUERY

Discuss the possibility that efforts to "honor" racial, ethnic, age, and gender diversity actually serve the interests of an exploitative class by creating increased consciousness of difference and division. Are efforts to "honor diversity" aiding or hindering class consciousness? Is there a better solution to social inequality? If so, what?

MindTap

Discussing Philosophy

As capitalism becomes increasingly efficient, it produces more than it can consume, and its technological progress renders large numbers of workers obsolete. Marxists say the result is an overburdened welfare state that provides barely enough sustenance—and no dignity—to its displaced workers:

> The modern labourer, on the contrary, instead of rising with the progress of industry, sinks deeper and deeper below the conditions of existence of his own class. He becomes a pauper, and pauperism develops more rapidly than population or wealth. And here it becomes evident that the bourgeoisie... is unfit to rule because it is incompetent to assure an existence to its slave within his slavery, because it cannot help letting him sink into such a state, that it has to feed him, instead of being fed by him. Society can no longer live under the bourgeoisie; in other words, its existence is no longer compatible with society.... The development of modern industry, therefore, cuts from under its feet the very foundation on which the bourgeoisie produces and appropriates products.[13]

Marx and Engels predicted that more and more workers would suffer as the bourgeoisie acquired capital at their expense, and that the workers' unhappiness, frustration, and indignation would erupt in violent revolution. After the revolution a new social order would emerge, from which all class distinctions, private ownership of the means of production, and exploitation would disappear forever.

For Deeper Consideration

As you analyze Marx's critique of capitalism, reflect on the complexities of "class consciousness." Some of the most vocal champions of the proletariat and critics of capitalism make enormous (bourgeoisie?) incomes. In 2012, for instance, the president of the AFL-CIO labor union earned $558,218; the president of the American Federation of Teachers earned $556,981; and in 2014, the head of the Laborers' International Union earned $618,000. Is there any inconsistency in this? If capitalism corrupts, does the personal accumulation of capital corrupt? Must advocates for the proletariat be poor? What about proletarians who support capitalism?

All previous historical movements were movements of minorities, or in the interest of minorities. The proletarian movement is the self-conscious, independent movement of the immense majority, in the interest of the immense majority.

— The Communist Manifesto

What happened? Is the revolution behind schedule, or is it not going to come at all? To address this issue, we need to look at one of the most important aspects of Marxist theory, one that is often overlooked by capitalistic critics of Marxism.

Alienation

alienation
According to Marx, the condition of workers separated from the products of their labor; primarily an objective state but can also refer to not feeling "at one" with the product of labor.

One of Marx's most interesting and compelling notions centers on the concept of **alienation**, a term he derived from Hegel. Marx thought of alienation as the most destructive feature of capitalism. Indeed, he thought it revealed an inherent irrationality, an inherent evil in the very basis of capitalism. Alienation occurs when the worker no longer feels at one with the product of his or her labor. An alienated individual rarely feels at home with himself or herself, or with others. Alienation is a state of powerlessness, frustration, repressed resentment, and despair. It results from the transformation of a human being into a commodity.

Marx was convinced that we are happiest not when we are idle but when we are engaged in meaningful work. Meaningful work can be work of virtually any kind so long as the worker has control over its products. This is necessary psychologically, not just morally. Imagine the suffering of a designer whose boss controls what brushes, pens, and colors the designer can use; how much time can be devoted to each project; what is good enough (or not); and what happens to the designs. No matter how much such a designer produces, he or she will suffer. Being detached from the work, prevented from exercising personal judgment and applying personal standards, the artist is alienated from his or her own work.

According to Marx, under capitalism, we believe that money, rather than the natural world, provides our means of life. Rather than see ourselves as part of nature, we are alienated from nature and, hence, from ourselves.

Anyone who takes a job *solely* on the basis of what it pays becomes alienated, in Marx's sense, by reducing himself or herself to a money-making machine. Possessions and money to buy them become more important than time to do things right, than the experience itself, and than the people involved. Soon, the alienated worker sees those he or she works for or provides services to as the means to a paycheck, not as full human beings. This is what Marx meant when he said, "The *increase in value* of the world of things is directly proportional to the *decrease in value* of the human world." And, of course, full functioning and *eudaimonia* are impossible in such conditions; this is a "kingdom of means," not a "kingdom of ends."

According to Marx, alienation even extends to our relationship with nature (as environmentalists remind us today). Nature provides the material basis for all work. Yet unchecked capitalism uses up nature, because the capitalist does not feel part of nature. The alienated worker sees money, rather than the natural world that provides bread and milk and fruit and wood, as the means of life. Alienated from nature, we cannot see what we really depend on:

> The more the worker *appropriates* the external world and sensuous nature through his labor, the more he deprives himself of the *means of life* in two respects; first, that the sensuous world gradually ceases to be an object belonging to his labor, a *means of life* of his work; secondly, that it gradually ceases to be a *means of life* in the immediate sense, a means of physical subsistence of the worker.[14]

PHILOSOPHICAL **QUERY**

Discuss some of the ways that alienation spreads from the workplace into society at large and into the home in particular. Has it affected your life? Your church? Your classes? Then identify and discuss activities in which you participate in species-life. What can you do to decrease periods of alienation and increase your own species-life?

Because so many of us must work to live, most of us spend a high percentage of our lives at our jobs. If we are alienated there, we are likely to be alienated elsewhere, for we cannot avoid being shaped by all those hours at work. Marx describes alienation as *externalization:* Work is seen as something I *do*, not as an expression of who I *am*. When I am in a state of alienation, I develop a habit of separating myself from nature and other people. I lose touch with myself, becoming alienated from who I really am, or at least from who I *ought to be*:

> What constitutes the externalization of labor?
>
> First is the fact that labor is *external* to the laborer—that is, it is not part of his nature—and that the worker does not affirm himself in his work but denies himself, feels miserable and unhappy, develops no free physical and mental energy but mortifies his flesh and ruins his mind. The worker, therefore, feels at ease only outside work, and during work he is outside himself. He is at home when he is not working and when he is working he is not at home.... External labor, labor in which man is externalized, is labor of self-sacrifice, of penance. Finally, the external nature of

eudaimonia
Often translated as "happiness"; term Aristotle used to refer to fully realized existence; state of being fully aware, vital, alert.

Discussing Philosophy

Under capitalism man exploits man; under socialism the reverse is true.
— Polish proverb

work for the worker appears in the fact that it is not his own but another person's, that in work he does not belong to himself but to someone else...the activity of the worker is not his own spontaneous activity. It belongs to another. It is the loss of his own self.

The result, therefore, is that...the worker...feels that he is acting freely only in his animal functions—eating, drinking, and procreating, or at most in his shelter and finery—while in his human functions he feels only like an animal. The animalistic becomes human and the human becomes animalistic.[15]

To the extent that Marx is correct, it is no wonder we are so interested in our weekends and vacations, no wonder that we text during class and surf the Web when we're at work, no wonder we seek escape. Only there do we feel fully free to be ourselves. We are alienated when we sell our bodies and souls out of necessity: The capitalist machine demands that we work. Marx did not believe humans are by nature lazy. Quite the contrary; he believed we *want* and *need* meaningful work. Our obsessions with leisure, our malingering and absenteeism, our efforts to strike it rich or retire as early as possible testify to the deep degree of alienation we must be experiencing in our work.

Species-Life

species-life
Fully human life lived productively and consciously; not alienated.

alienated life
Unconscious, unspontaneous, and unfulfilled life; deprived of fundamental conditions necessary for self-actualization.

Marx distinguishes alienated life from species-life. **Species-life** is fully human life, life lived productively and consciously. **Alienated life**, in contrast, creates a sense of distance from nature and renders people unconscious of precisely how unhappy, unspontaneous, and unfulfilled they really are. In other words, alienation prevents us from being fully human. Thus alienation is anti-species or anti-human.

Marx, we see at last, is propounding not just an economic theory but a sophisticated philosophy of *self-actualization*. He thinks that in the next historical stage, people will work to fulfill themselves, for the creative, self-actualizing joy of it. If that is difficult to believe, Marx says, it is because we are so alienated from human nature (our species) that we can conceive of work only in distorted, alienated terms.

What makes something "work" is not whether it is difficult or easy but *how we relate to it*. If we are involved in and care about it, if, in Marx's expression, we are "at home," we do not look upon a task as work. If we have significant say over how we do something, and do it for reasons we understand and for values we hold, we may not like what we do, but we are not alienated from it. If we act from love when we cut the grass for our parents or help a friend move furniture, we are not alienated:

> The animal is immediately one with *its life activity*, not distinct from it. The animal is its life activity. Man makes his life activity itself into an object of will and consciousness. He has conscious life activity. It is not a determination with which he immediately identifies. Conscious life activity distinguishes man immediately from the life activity of the animal. Only thereby is he a species-being. Or rather, he is only a conscious being—that is, his own life is an object for him—since he is a species-being. Only on that account is his activity free activity. Alienated labor reverses the relationship in that man, since he is a conscious being, makes his life activity, his *essence*, only a means for his *existence*.[16]

All of Marx's major predictions have turned out to be wrong.

— Roger Kimball

"Automatons Cannot Love"

Psychologist and socialist humanist philosopher Erich Fromm (1900–1980) wrote in a Marxian vein about self-actualization and love in his influential book *The Art of Loving*. Specifically, Fromm attempted to show how the structure of capitalistic society shapes our personal relationships. Fromm argued that alienated people cannot really love—themselves, one another, or God. Along the way he raised some disturbing questions about our society:

> Modern capitalism needs men who co-operate smoothly and in large numbers; who want to consume more and more; and whose tastes are standardized and can be easily influenced and anticipated....who can be guided without force, led without leaders, prompted without aim—except the one to make good, to be on the move, to go ahead.
>
> What is the outcome? Modern man is alienated from himself, from his fellow man, from nature. He has been transformed into a commodity, experiences his life forces as an investment which must bring him the maximum profit obtainable under existing market conditions. Human relations are essentially those of alienated automatons....man overcomes his unconscious despair by the routine of amusement, the passive consumption of sounds and sights offered by the amusement industry; furthermore by the satisfaction of buying ever more things, and soon exchanging them for others....
>
> The situation as far as love is concerned corresponds, as it has to by necessity, to this social character of modern man. Automatons cannot love; they can exchange their "personality packages" and hope for a fair bargain....

Erich Fromm, ***The Art of Loving*** (1956; reprint, New York: Perennial Library, 1974), pp. 70–71, 72–73.

If capitalism were destroyed, Marx thought, we would revert to species-life. Once freed from the irrational, destructive pressure to survive only at the expense *of* others, we would be free to develop as human beings, to actualize ourselves as productive workers who find joy and fulfillment in personally meaningful work. If we are unable to accept that vision of ourselves right now, Marx would say it is because we are living alienated lives to one degree or another. Our distrust of Marx's utopia becomes a symptom of our distorted view of human nature. What we think of as human nature—people hustling for a buck, scheming to strike it rich, and looking forward to the day they can quit working—is not *human* nature at all. It is alienation.

For Deeper Consideration

The concept of alienation is a central component of Marx's critique of capitalism. How does Marx link alienation to capitalism? How does alienated life differ from species-life? If you are not convinced by his arguments, does that mean that you are living in a state of alienation? That is, is there a way to reject Marx's argument that does not open you up to a charge of failing to grasp what Marx is saying because you have been co-opted by a capitalistic culture and education?

MindTap

Aplia

Commentary

Although Marx may have confused the evils of industrialization with capitalism, his critique of the excesses of capitalism has much to teach us about the relationship of the material conditions of people's lives to the ideas and beliefs they hold. His assessment of the evils of "the bourgeoisie" reminds us of the dangers of class disparity and the harm that can come from separating reward from performance and from determining human worth in monetary terms. Overall, his cultural critique raises important questions about the meaning of work and human dignity that are, if anything, as pressing in this era of downsizing and global conglomerates as they were in Marx and Engels's time.

I confess that I am conflicted about the strong strain of resentment and bitterness that runs through contemporary political Marxism and its socialistic cousins. On the one hand, a certain amount of resentment is understandable, given the disparities between the laboring classes of the world and the nonlaboring classes that control enormous pockets of wealth. But anger alone—even righteous, justified anger—cannot construct a healthy or just society.

On the other hand, I am dismayed at the lack of sustained "middle-class" anger about inequitable social conditions and the egregious disparities between the treatment of corporate CEOs and their workers. One only needs to think of the scandals of recent years involving financial institutions and the collapse of the housing

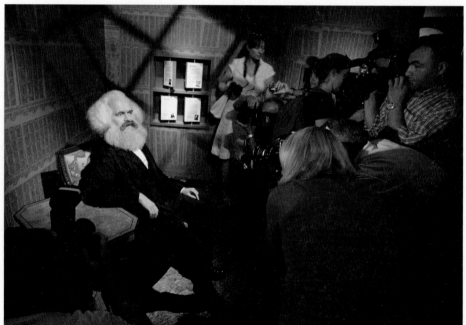

Steffen Kugler/Getty Images

Ironically, but predictably, since his death, Karl Marx has become a successful commercial product whose image, like those of Elvis Presley and Lady Gaga, adorns posters, coffee mugs, and T-shirts. In 2008, a wax effigy of the great critic of capitalism went on display at the Berlin branch of Madame Tussauds's wax museum—where, for the cost of a few euros, he could be seen along with effigies of Gaga, Shrek, and Britney Spears.

market and the declining percentages of fully employed citizens. Losses are anything but evenly distributed across the workforce.

Marx did not allow for the possibility of societal self-correction, serial social revolutions, and consciously guided change, nor could he fully anticipate the shape of the modern economy or the positive features of postindustrial capitalism. Nor did he, nor could anyone, imagine the effects of the great technological revolution we are living through. Indeed, its full effects are probably beyond our comprehension, too.

Finally, despite his genuine concern for the alienated, degraded worker, Marx himself seems to rob individuals of any significant capacity for self determination. Marx's emphasis on classes and class struggle does not, it seems to me, pay enough respect to the individual. One of the major problems with political Marxism is its tendency to sacrifice the individual for the good of the collective. In his zeal to stress the causal properties of the material substructure of society, Marx grants too little importance to the role of ideas and individuals as agents of social progress. It seems to me that in the final analysis, Marx romanticized the proletariat and vilified the bourgeoisie, thereby oversimplifying relations between those two classes. Treating human consciousness and behavior as inevitably determined by economic and material forces absolves one class (the proletariat) at too a high cost for me. But then again, if Marx is correct, my thinking is typical of co-opted members of a doomed class (the bourgeoisie).

Still, Marx's vision of a fuller, better life places him among the champions of the oppressed and exploited. Like a prophet, Marx calls us to account for our sins; like a prophet, he indicates a general direction for our future. Perhaps that is enough. The rest, in any event, is up to us.

> *The philosopher, who is himself an abstract form of alienated man, takes himself as the yardstick of the alienated world. The whole history of alienation…is…nothing but the history of the production of abstract thought.*
> — Karl Marx

Summary of Main Points

- Marx combined Hegel's dialectical view of history with Feuerbach's concept of a materialist *Zeitgeist* (spirit of the age) to produce historical materialism, the view that history is the ongoing result of a dialectical process that consists of an interaction between an original condition (thesis) and a contrary condition (antithesis) to produce a new condition containing elements of the thesis and antithesis (synthesis). Each synthesis becomes the thesis for a new dialectical cycle driven by constant tension between two classes: the exploiters and the exploited.

- Marx identified five epochs of history that constitute the dialectical development of history: (1) primitive/communal, (2) slave, (3) feudal, (4) capitalist, (5) socialist/communist. As each epoch develops, its basic economic structure matures and the material conditions under which people live change. According to Marx, ideas, values, and thinking itself are shaped by material conditions and social relations.

- Marx argued that the economic structure of a culture creates and forms its own ideas. Most important is the material substructure, which consists of three components: (1) the means of production (natural resources); (2) the forces of production (factories, equipment, technology, and knowledge); (3) the relationships of production, which constitute a complex system that shapes everything else. The material substructure produces ideas and institutions compatible with it. These comprise the culture's superstructure and include art, science, philosophy, religion, and government.

- Marx was sharply critical of capitalism, which he saw as a stage on the way to a classless socialistic economy. In his view, the capitalist substructure contains a fundamental contradiction in the tension between the owners' desire to keep wages low while prices fluctuate according to the law of supply and demand.

- Under capitalism, the two struggling classes are the bourgeoisie and the proletariat. The bourgeoisie consists of those who own the means of production but do not produce anything; it views everything in terms of money and self-interest. The proletariat consists of those who produce things but do not own the means of production (including their own time and labor).

- Marx predicted that the demands of the bourgeoisie would result in an ever-growing proletariat whose living conditions would continue to decline until the proletariat would rise up in violent revolt and destroy the bourgeoisie and capitalism, leading to the next historical epoch, socialism.

- The most destructive feature of capitalism, according to Marx, is alienation, which occurs when the worker no longer feels at one with the product of his or her labor; it is a state of powerlessness, frustration, and despair. Capitalism alienates people from one another, from nature, and from work. Marx distinguished alienated life from species-life, which is lived productively and consciously. Species-life is fully human life, a product of self-actualization (which capitalism inhibits).

Post-Reading Reflections

Now that you've had a chance to learn about the Materialist, use your new knowledge to answer these questions.

1. Describe the social conditions that led Marx and Engels to write *The Communist Manifesto*.
2. What was Feuerbach's influence on Marx?
3. What was Hegel's influence on Marx?
4. Explain why Marx's philosophy is sometimes called "historical materialism."
5. Give one or two examples of Marxian mystification.
6. Describe capitalism in terms of the relationships of production.
7. What is the significance of the bourgeoisie to philosophical Marxism?
8. What is the significance of the proletariat to philosophical Marxism?
9. Explain the importance of class consciousness and class struggle to Marxism. What role does consciousness play in species-life, according to Marx?
10. Are Marx's two categories of social class (the bourgeoisie and the proletariat) adequate to describe today's economic conflicts? Are there additional social classes that Marx does not address, and if so, what are they?
11. Is class conflict an outmoded way of understanding current economic conditions, given what we now know about ethnic and gender disparities?

 MindTap

Experience MindTap through the activities highlighted in this chapter. Further explore this online, personalized learning tool to deepen your comprehension and improve your grades.

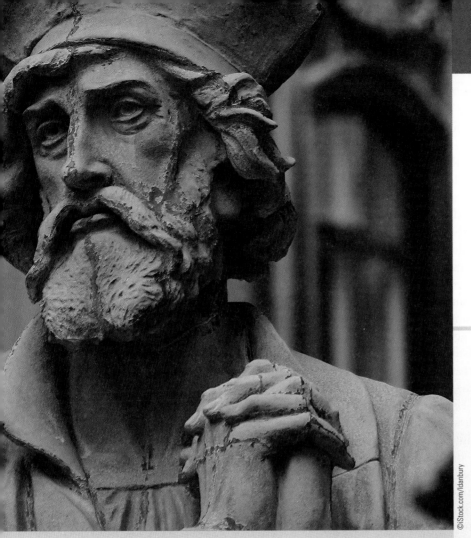

14

The Existentialist
Søren Kierkegaard

The question is not what am I to
believe, but what am I to do?

— *Søren Kierkegaard*

Learning Objectives

 MindTap™

After you complete this chapter, you should be able to:

- Define the concept of existentialism.

- Analyze the role that Søren Kierkegaard's sacrifice of Regine
  Olsen played in his subsequent philosophy.

- Explain the existential significance of Kierkegaard's use of
  pseudonyms.

- Defend Kierkegaard from the accusation that, for him, being a
  Christian is reduced to the mere feeling that one is a Christian.

- Contrast today's use of the word *passion* with Kierkegaard's
  understanding of the term.

- Explain why becoming a subject matters so much to Kierkegaard.

- Describe the leap of faith in terms of the teleological suspension
  of the ethical.

- Identify the existential lesson Kierkegaard discovers in the story
  of Abraham and Isaac.

Philosophy Timelines

HAS IT PERHAPS OCCURRED to you that something fundamentally important seems to be missing from most (or all) of the philosophies we have studied so far? Has the ancient challenge to philosophy been answered for *you*: "Philosophy, what practical difference do you make to *me*?" Perhaps you've wondered what, if any, bearing the categorical imperative has on your actual, day-to-day moral *living*. Do "proofs" for the existence of God, such as those offered by Thomas Aquinas, provide you with a living faith? Do they enhance your relationship with a living God? What do the rigorous inquiries of Hume or Descartes have to do with the concrete and immediate choices facing you as an "existing individual"? As a seeker of wisdom, do you wonder whether a utilitarian calculus or Marxian assessment of history makes any real difference to the daily sufferings of real people?

If it sometimes seems to you that philosophy has passed over the genuine (real-life) concerns of individuals, you are not alone. One of the most influential, intriguing, and arresting responses to the massing of society and the resultant loss of genuine respect for the individual goes under the name **existentialism**. Existentialism refers to any philosophy that asserts that the most important philosophical matters involve fundamental questions of meaning and choice as they affect actual—existing—individuals. Existential themes include choice, freedom, identity, alienation, inauthenticity, despair, and awareness of our own mortality. Existentialists point out that objective science and rationalistic philosophy cannot come to grips with the real problems of human existence: "What am *I* to do?" "To what can *I* commit myself?" "What does *my* life mean?" Existentialists believe that general answers, grand metaphysical systems, and supposedly objective and rational theories cannot address the existential (living, concrete) concerns of individuals.

The early existentialists were among the first to identify major issues unique to postindustrial, highly specialized, technical, sophisticated societies: increased loss of individuality, increased pressure to conform, the threat to human freedom and dignity from science and bureaucracy. Philosopher of history Samuel Enoch Stumpf says:

> Existentialism was bound to happen. The individual had over the centuries been pushed into the background by systems of thought, historical events, and technological forces. The major systems of philosophy had rarely paid attention to the uniquely personal concerns of individuals. Although Aristotle, for example, wrote a major treatise on ethics, Montaigne could say that "I can't recognize most of my daily doings when they appear in Aristotle." Nietzsche also wrote that "to our scholars, strangely enough, the most pressing question does not occur: to what end is their work…useful?"…[Traditional] philosophy for the most part dealt with technical problems of metaphysics, ethics, and the theory of knowledge in a general and objective manner, which bypassed the intimate concerns of [people] about their personal destiny. Historical events, particularly wars, showed a similar disregard for the feelings and aspirations of individuals. And technology…soon gathered a momentum of its own, forcing [people] to fit their lives into the rhythm of machines.
>
> Everywhere [people] were losing their peculiarly human qualities. They were being converted from "persons" into "pronouns," from "subjects" into "objects" from an "I" into an "it."[1]

existentialism
A term used to refer to philosophy that emphasizes fundamental questions of meaning and choice as they affect existing individuals; existential themes include choice, freedom, identity, alienation, inauthenticity, despair, and awareness of our own mortality.

Technological progress creates more problems than it solves. Efficiency experts or social engineering will not redeem humanity. Important as their contributions may be, they do not reach the heart of the problem.
— Abraham
Joshua Heschel

Ironically, today many people talk about existentialism as if it were a clearly defined school of philosophy. It is not. Let's resist reducing the existentialists to an abstraction, to a category, by acknowledging that there is no such thing as an existentialist school of philosophy.

In this chapter, we take a look at one of the most important, intriguing, and controversial thinkers first associated with that label, Søren Kierkegaard, a fierce champion of the real, the concrete, the existing individual.

PHILOSOPHICAL QUERY

Reflect back over your philosophical studies so far. Can you recognize yourself in the philosophies you've studied? In which ones?

Søren Kierkegaard

The most important work of **Søren Kierkegaard** (1813–1855) was virtually ignored during his lifetime, partly because he wrote in Danish, partly because of what he wrote, partly because of his brilliant use of sarcasm and irony. For this reason, and because of the issues he dealt with, Kierkegaard is an "untimely" philosopher who seems more contemporary than his chronological place in history. Some 160 years later, Kierkegaard's journals and essays have a living quality that still engages and disturbs many a reader. His work is not easy to fathom, but it is well worth the struggle.

Søren Kierkegaard

Because he rebelled against "the system" and against objectivity, Kierkegaard's work confounds easy classification (which would delight him). His "unscientific" and "unsystematic" attacks on conventional Christian theology and dogma, on science, and on professional philosophy took the form of satirical essays, parables, anecdotes, and real and fictional journals. What are scholars and philosophers to make of a writer who asserted that "truth is subjectivity" and "the System is a lie"? How can we assess the inconsistencies and lack of a coherent philosophy in a writer who boldly denounced both systematic consistency and coherence?

As we shall see, Kierkegaard's work represented a radical shift in philosophers' orientation from objectivity to subjectivity, from efforts to impose rational consistency to a search for authentic existence. Kierkegaard said, "The question is not what am I to *believe* [think, understand], but what am I to *do*?"

> *Had I to carve an inscription on my grave I would ask for none other than "the individual."*
> — Søren Kierkegaard

The Family Curse

Kierkegaard saw himself as a disciple of Socrates. And in the vein of Socrates, Kierkegaard's life and work make a seamless whole. We cannot know Kierkegaard the existentialist without meeting Kierkegaard the individual. Born in Copenhagen, Denmark, this youngest of seven children was deeply and permanently influenced by his father, Michael, a strict and devout Lutheran. One day, while herding sheep, young Michael cursed God over the conditions of his life. Until his death, he never forgot what he had done and never forgave himself for his youthful

Mario Anzuoni/Reuters/Landov

Compare your first impression of these Miss Teen USA contestants with your impression of Lady Gaga at the Grammy Awards. Is your initial reaction the common one among college students—dismissive of the Miss Teen USA contestants as robotic clones who have "sold out" while seeing Lady Gaga as somehow more authentic and individualistic?

Lucy Nicholson/Reuters/Landov

What, if anything, makes Lady Gaga and the women performing with her "cool" or more "authentic"? Is there something artificial—contrived—about worrying about not being phony? Is authenticity an authentic goal? Can there be such a thing as a crowd of true individuals? An identifiable type of individual?

outburst. Though he grew up to become a successful merchant, Michael Kierkeg-aard remained consumed by what he saw as his unforgivable blasphemy. Years later, weakened by grief and loneliness, he had sexual relations with a housemaid imme-diately after his first wife died. Overwhelmed with guilt and sadness, consumed by these two "great sins," Michael lived without peace of mind or genuine hope, seeing himself only as a sinner.

As the youngest son of an elderly father, Søren was his father's favorite, and to him went Michael's legacy: a sense of despair and melancholy, an obsession with the nature and possibility of a finite individual's relationship with an infinite God. Unusually intelligent and sensitive, Søren had few close friends as a child and spent most of his formative years in the company of his father.

In 1830, Kierkegaard enrolled in the University of Copenhagen to study theology. The "unforgiven" father wanted his son to become a minister. Kierkegaard soon dis-covered, however, that theology did not interest him as much as philosophy and literature. He spent the next ten years living a collegiate life devoted primarily to drinking and attending the theater. He became known for his good taste in food, clothes, and other aesthetic delights. During this time, he lost interest in religion and became estranged from his father.

Father and son made peace before Michael died in 1838, and Michael confessed the two sins of his past to his son. Kierkegaard referred to the confession as "a great earthquake" and became consumed by its implications. He returned to the study of theology, passing his exams with honors in 1840. The next year he preached his first sermon and submitted a master's thesis on Socratic irony.

> *I owe everything I am to the wisdom of an old man and the simplicity of a young girl.*
> — Søren Kierkegaard

The Universal Formula

At about the same time, at age twenty-seven, Kierkegaard fell in love with Regine Olsen, the attractive fourteen-year-old daughter of an important government official. When Regine turned seventeen, the couple became formally engaged, but almost immediately Kierkegaard broke the engagement. For the rest of his life, he struggled to understand, explain, and justify this action. In his *Journals* he wrote, "It was a time of terrible suffering to have to be so cruel and at the same time to love her as I did. She fought like a tigress. If I had not believed that God had lodged a veto, she would have been victorious."[2]

Kierkegaard might have had more than one motive for breaking up with Regine. He might have been afraid of committed marriage. He might have found her cheery temperament incompatible with his somber melancholy. He might have feared that his depressions would harm her. He might have been a cad, as the popular opinion in Copenhagen had it. Perhaps all these motives played a part.

But of special interest to us is Kierkegaard's later interpretation of his "sacrifice" of Regine. Two weeks after he broke the engagement, Kierkegaard fled to Berlin, where he wrote *Either/Or: A Fragment of Life* (1843), his first important work, and *Repetition: An Essay in Experimental Psychology* (1843), through which he hoped to reestablish his relationship with Regine. But before he could publish *Repetition*, Kierkegaard learned of Regine's engagement to a former boyfriend. Stunned, hurt, and despairing, Kierkegaard destroyed the last ten pages of his original manuscript, which addressed his hope of a reconciliation with Regine.

> *All logical thinking employs the language of abstraction.... It is easier to indulge in abstract thought than it is to exist.*
> — Søren Kierkegaard

For the rest of his short life, Kierkegaard claimed he had "offered up" his love for Regine Olsen as a sacrifice to God, just as Abraham offered Isaac in the Old Testament story (Genesis 22). Kierkegaard had thought he had to choose *either* God *or* "the world," and that choosing one excluded the other entirely. Torn between a career as a minister and a comfortable, middle-class life with Regine, he thought he had discovered a way to have both. Kierkegaard's solution was his discovery of what he saw as the "universal formula" revealed in the story of Abraham and Isaac: Having finally blessed Abraham and Sarah with a son in their old age, God then tested Abraham's faith by sending an angel to him, demanding the blood sacrifice of Isaac. Abraham submitted to God's will in a supreme act of faith, resisting the pull of his love for Isaac and resisting the moral code of his time that forbade such human sacrifice. At the last moment, God stopped Abraham and returned Isaac to him. Kierkegaard interpreted this story to mean: If you give something up for God, you get it back *plus* the love and salvation of God. In other words, by giving something up, you get to keep it! Applying this "formula" to his predicament of "*Either* devote my life to God *or* live in comfort with Regine," Kierkegaard "reasoned" a way to have both. He was consequently stunned when he lost her. What went wrong? Didn't Kierkegaard do just what Abraham had done? Was his reasoning somehow flawed?

In his later works, Kierkegaard wrestled with the basic existential problems exemplified in this episode from one individual's life: What am I to *do* when confronted with the awesome finality of any choice? Can I objectively and scientifically model my relationship with God after Abraham's? Or Paul's? Or Christ's? How can I know what God wants *me* to do? Can I *reason* it out? What do *universal principles* have to do with *this choice*? Kierkegaard concluded that universal principles must give way to individual predicaments.

I Can't Help But Smile When I See Her

As with so much else in Kierkegaard's life, his breakup with Regine was not the end of his relationship with Regine—nor of hers with him. It seems as if, for years, they deliberately and openly, but without acknowledging as much, arranged their daily walks so that they passed by one another. And on Kierkegaard's 39th birthday Regine showed up on his front porch without warning. Kierkegaard tipped his hat, and the former sweethearts smiled without speaking and went on with their lives. "As often happens to me of late," he wrote, "I can't help but smile when I see her."[3]

Three years later, on March 17, 1855, Regine and her husband, J. F. Schlegel, left Copenhagen for the West Indies. On that day, as she was preparing to leave, Regine suddenly went out into the city. Eventually she spotted the stooped figure she knew so well and said, softly it seems, "God bless you—may good things come your way!" The forlorn figure tipped his hat but did not speak.

Søren Kierkegaard and Regine Olsen Schlegel never met again. Kierkegaard died eight months later, leaving his entire estate to Regine, writing that "for me an engagement was and is just as binding as a marriage." Regine only asked for some personal effects and the engagement letters between her and Kierkegaard. Sadly, she was also sent some journal entries ("My Relation to 'Her'") and a letter Kierkegaard had, unbeknownst to her, sent to her husband six years earlier.

For a time, Regine wondered if she had somehow let Kierkegaard down, but she eventually realized that Kierkegaard's own internal conflicts and struggles accounted for his "innate tendency toward self-torment." When Kierkegaard's journals were published, Regine had a physical reaction upon discovering just how personal the references to her were. After her husband died, she donated the letters and diaries she inherited from Kierkegaard to Copenhagen University, asking only that they not be made public until her death. Regine Olsen Schlegel died at 82 in 1904.

Kierkegaard's? Works

Interestingly, ironically, and characteristically, Kierkegaard tweaked the noses of his fellows by writing about authenticity and identity under various pseudonyms. Unlike more conventional pseudonymous writers, he was not trying to hide. There was no point to that in a provincial little city like Copenhagen, where he was widely known. The various and odd characters he presents as the "authors" of his writings are existential personas for modes of existence, ways of living, that many of us experience. They are part of a Socratic program designed to prevent Kierkegaard's readers from keeping a safe distance, designed to prevent objective responses. It would not do for Kierkegaard to challenge abstract, detached philosophizing and thinking with his own abstract, detached arguments and analyses. Better to assume the stance and, most importantly, the voice of one who actually lives this way or that way.

Kierkegaard's "authors" and their works can be confusing to sort out, much as our real selves can be difficult to sort out. The authors sometimes appear in more than one essay, intermingling like parts of a single self-in-progress. Kierkegaard sometimes lists himself as editor or "responsible for publication" of the pseudonymous works. He also credits some work to himself.

Kierkegaard's pseudonyms are particularly clever considering his interest in identity, meaningfulness, and authenticity and his efforts to engage his readers in a dialectical "conversation": Nicolaus Notabene (N.N. was a Danish abbreviation indicating anonymity, and *nota bene* is Latin for "note well"; in other words, pay attention); Virgilius Haufniensis (Watchman of Copenhagen); A. B. C. D. E. F. Godthaab, also known as A. B. C. D. E. F. Resenblad; Inter et Inter (Latin for "between and between"); Procul (Latin for "from a distance").

Johannes de Silentio (John the Silent) is the "silent" author who has so much to say in *Fear and Trembling: A Dialectical Lyric* (1843). Frater Taciturnus (Brother Who Keeps Silent) is the author of the third (religious) section of *Stages on Life's Way*. Victor Eremita, the Victorious Hermit, is the "publisher" of volumes 1 and 2 of *Either/Or: A Fragment of Life* (1843). The Either part of *Either/Or* is "authored" and also "edited" by an aesthete known only as A, who claims to have been given the famous *Diary of a Seducer* by someone named Johannes, "nicknamed the Seducer." The *Diary* is part of *Either/Or*.

The Or part of *Either/Or* is, naturally, by B, also known as Judge William. Judge William is also the author of part two (the ethical part) of *Stages on Life's Way* (1845), which was "collected, forwarded to the press and published by" one Hilarius Bookbinder, *Hilarius* being Latin for "merry" or "joyful." The first (aesthetic) section of *Stages on Life's Way* is credited to William Afham. Afham means "by him," and William Afham says his work is "by himself."

> *The story is told (by Kierkegaard) of the absent-minded man so abstracted from his own life that he hardly knows he exists until, one fine morning, he wakes up to find himself dead.*
> — William Barrett

Johannes Climacus, a philosophical character named after a Greek monk, is listed as the author of *Philosophical Fragments, Or a Fragment of Philosophy* (1844). The *Concluding Unscientific Postscript to the "Philosophical Fragments"* (1846) is characterized as "An Existential Contribution" by Johannes as well, with Søren Kierkegaard said to be "responsible for publication." *Sickness Unto Death* (1849) and *Training in Christianity* (1850) are by Anti-Climacus. Unlike Johannes Climacus, who cannot ascend higher than reason and logic can take him, Anti-Climacus can and does. In his journals Kierkegaard writes that "Climacus is lower, denies he is a Christian. Anti-Climacus is higher, a Christian on an extraordinarily high level....I would place myself higher than Johannes Climacus, lower than Anti-Climacus."

By "hiding in plain sight," by playing games about serious matters and devoting minute scrutiny to mundane ones, Kierkegaard dares us to look for the "reasons" behind the poses. If we do, he hopes to engage us in a Socratic exchange that results in deep reflection and change on our part.

The Christian

Struggling with the existential predicament of choice and commitment, Kierkegaard grew increasingly interested in what it means to be a Christian. He became convinced that institutionalized Christianity suffers from the same inauthenticity as other institutions. **Inauthenticity** results when the nature and needs of an individual are ignored, denied, obscured, or made less important than institutions, abstractions, or groups. **Authenticity** is the subjective condition of an individual living honestly and courageously in the moment without refuge in excuses and without reliance on groups or institutions for meaning and purpose. Given the stakes—salvation or damnation—Kierkegaard turned his penetrating wit and scathing criticism to the task of distinguishing inauthentic "institutionalized Christianity" from authentic Christianity.

Kierkegaard published three important attacks on the Danish Church: *The Sickness Unto Death* (1849), *Training in Christianity* (1850), and *For Self-Examination* (1851). When his "attacks on Christendom" were largely ignored, Kierkegaard decided to take a clear, dramatic existential step: He had to break officially with the church. At the time of this decision, the head of the Danish Church was Bishop J. P. Mynster, who had been a close friend of Michael Kierkegaard. Because Søren himself respected and cared for the old man, he delayed his break until Mynster died, whereupon he published a vehement attack on "false Christianity" in an article titled "Was Bishop Mynster a Witness for the Truth?" Kierkegaard's answer was an unequivocal "No!" He argued that the bishop was a witness to an error, a witness to false Christianity.

Both the clergy and the general public rose to the defense of the beloved bishop. Kierkegaard continued to hammer away at what he saw as false Christianity, hypocrisy, inauthenticity, and "mere living." As a contrast to inauthentic Christianity, Kierkegaard countered with his famous "leap of faith," a *blind* commitment to God made each instant, made without guarantees, made alone, made in fear and trembling. The leap of faith is completely "existential," made with absolutely no assurance of any kind, no support, no "reason." Consequently, Kierkegaard strenuously rejected any institutionalized religion of formulas, guarantees, security, and "group salvation."

On October 2, 1855, Kierkegaard was nearly broke. He visited his banker brother-in-law to withdraw the last of his money. On his way home, he fell to the

inauthenticity
A condition that results when the nature and needs of an individual are ignored, denied, and obscured or sacrificed for institutions, abstractions, or groups.

authenticity
A subjective condition of an individual living honestly and courageously in the moment, refusing to make excuses, and not relying on groups or institutions for meaning and purpose.

What I really lack is to be clear in my own mind what I am to do. The thing is to understand myself, to see what God really wants me to do; the thing is to find a truth that is true for me, to find the idea for which I can live and die.
— Søren Kierkegaard

street, paralyzed from the waist down. Destitute, helpless, and weak, Kierkegaard died quietly November 11, 1855. He was only forty-two years old. Today, the bodily remains of Søren Kierkegaard and Regine Olsen are buried 50 yards apart, in Assistens Churchyard—two souls never quite together, never truly apart.

Truth as Subjectivity

Perhaps the major existential issue is "What am I to *do*?" –not "How is an individual to live?" but "How am I to *exist*?" As Kierkegaard pointed out, any choice, once made, rules out *all* other possibilities. To be fully conscious of this is to experience what Nietzsche (Chapter 16) called *fatefulness*, the fact that our actions and choices create our individual destiny. Deciding to take a philosophy class—or deciding not to take one; deciding to marry that person—or not to marry that person; checking the air in a car's tires— or not checking it: On such inescapable daily choices hang the quality and shape of individual lives. The basic fact of Kierkegaard's *project*, as he referred to his existentialism, is the dilemma of lived choices:

The Sacrifice of Abraham, 1635 (oil on canvas), Rembrandt Harmensz. van Rijn (1606-69)/Hermitage, St. Petersburg, Russia/The Bridgeman Art Library

Rembrandt's powerful depiction of the angel staying Abraham's hand just before the sacrifice of Isaac captures the moment of "infinite resignation" that Kierkegaard imagined he could duplicate in his own relationship with his beloved Regine Olsen. Where did Kierkegaard go wrong—if he did go wrong?

> What I really lack is to be clear in my mind *what I am to do*, not what I am to know, except in so far as a certain understanding must precede every action. The thing is to understand myself, to see what God really wishes *me* to do; the thing is to find a truth which is true *for me*, to find *the idea for which I can live and die*. What would be the use of discovering so-called objective truth, of working through all the systems of philosophy and of being able, if required, to review them all and show up the inconsistencies within each system;—what good would it do me to be able to explain the meaning of Christianity if it had *no* deeper significance *for me and for my life*;—what good would it do me if the truth stood before me, cold and naked, not caring whether I recognised her or not, producing in me a shudder of fear rather than a trusting devotion? I certainly do not deny that I still recognise an *imperative of understanding* and that through it one can work upon men, *but it must be taken up into my life*, and *that is* what I now recognise as the most important thing. That is what my soul longs after, as the African desert thirsts for water. That is what I lack, and that is why I am left standing like a man who has rented a house and gathered all the furniture and household things together, but has not yet found the beloved with whom to share the joys and sorrows of his life.[4]

> *Our culture is superficial today, and our knowledge dangerous, because we are rich in mechanisms and poor in purposes.*
> — Will Durant

For all their power, allure, and effectiveness, it is not clear that must-have technological marvels, such as ubiquitous Internet access and trend-setting iPhones, help us live more meaningful lives, lives grounded in what Kierkegaard described as an "idea for which I can live and die." Do these devices, perhaps, have an opposite effect and sink us deeper into "the crowd," thereby distracting us from ourselves?

PHILOSOPHICAL QUERY

How do you make life choices? Do you make them clearly and consciously, or do things just somehow happen? Is it possible to choose without being fully engaged? Does your religion or philosophy help you make concrete choices? Does a psychological theory?

Kierkegaard insisted that no amount of objective, systematic, abstract knowledge could ever provide a meaning for life. He did not deny the value of objective knowledge, which he refers to as an *imperative of understanding*, but he pointed out that the "objective facts" of a life cannot account for its existential quality. In *Either/Or*, he tells the story of a man who decides to scientifically and objectively study a Christian, in order to understand what it is to "be a Christian." Following his subject about, the observer notes what he eats, where he goes, when he reads the paper, what paper he reads, what brand of tobacco he smokes, and so on. After amassing quite a quantity of factual, objective data, the observer laments, "But he does just what I do!"

Kierkegaard's point, made ironically, is that objective information reveals facts or truths, not truth. What makes one individual a Christian and another a non-Christian, Kierkegaard claims, cannot be reduced to the objective conditions of their lives but is a quality of their *inner condition: Truth is a subjective condition, not an objective one.*

The implications of this claim—that scientific, or objective, impersonal, understanding can never pass beyond factual description—are radical. According to Kierkegaard, objective understanding cannot reveal truth; it cannot give Kierkegaard—or any other existing individual—reasons to live; it cannot answer the most important question: What am I to do? Objective, scientific, philosophical, and theological systems and arguments cannot provide "*the idea for which I can live and die.*" In an era seduced by faith that science (or "technology") inevitably leads to "progress," Kierkegaard's existential critique challenges "science" ("the system" or "the establishment") to answer: Give *me* a reason for which *I* can live and die.

Kierkegaard wanted to pass from fragmentation to integration. In his terms, he wanted to alter his life from a "chance assemblage of mere details" into an existence with a "focus and center." But the modern age, with its drive toward massive institutions, infatuation with objectivity, and reliance on the scientific understanding of human behavior, inhibits personal integration. Neither scientific, objective understanding nor elaborate, abstract Hegelian philosophical systems can deal with "*that individual.*" Systems and theories only identify patterns and abstractions. They never even see "the existing individual."

Objectivity as Untruth

As we have seen again and again, for the most part, philosophers have traditionally agreed that arguments and evidence should be evaluated rationally and objectively. Until relatively recently, evidence of partiality or bias has been seen as a serious weakness in a philosopher's or scientist's arguments.

Kierkegaard vehemently disagreed. He considered objectivity, impersonality, and impartiality as dangerous, insulting, and ugly delusions. Not only is impartiality impossible, but claims of objectivity and disinterest are always lies. In the first place,

> *Just as desert travellers combine into great caravans from fear of robbers and wild beasts, so the individuals of the contemporary generation are fearful of existence, because it is God-forsaken; only in great masses do they dare to live, and they cluster together* en masse *in order to feel that they amount to something.*
>
> — Søren Kierkegaard

> *Mass society, with its demand for work without responsibility, creates a gigantic army of rival siblings.*
> — Alexander Misterlich

preferring objectivity and impartiality to subjective involvement is itself a bias: *Favoring objectivity is a form of partiality.* Worse, our desire for objectivity deceives us by obscuring our individual (subjective) responsibility for our evaluations. The philosopher who says, "Reason demands that we must reject *X* because it is inconsistent" has herself *subjectively chosen* certain values: objectivity and consistency. Moreover, "reason" is a mere abstraction, a noble-sounding term that conceals an individual, subjective choice. But anything that obscures the existing individual interferes with authenticity, honesty, and passionate commitment—existence.

To complicate matters, the impersonal quality of objective language reduces the uniqueness of individual existence to generalizations, abstractions, and features in common. But the vital issues of existence confront the complex, individually existing self, not the general self of psychologists and philosophers; not Descartes's "thing which thinks"; not Kant's "rational being"; not Hume's "bundle of perceptions." (See Chapters 9–11.) Objectivity, by its very nature, is cool, detached, impersonal. Existence, however, is not:

> The difficulty that inheres in existence, with which the existing individual is confronted, is one that never really comes to expression in the language of abstract thought, much less receives an explanation....
>
> ...Existing is ordinarily regarded as no very complex matter, much less an art, since we all exist; but abstract thinking takes rank as an accomplishment. But to really exist...that is truly difficult.[5]

Descartes, and all those who followed his lead, reduced existence to believing: "I *think,* therefore I am." Abstract, rationalistic philosophies ignore the real

Roger L. Wollenberg/UPI Photo/Landov

Thousands of *American Idol* contestants wait to audition. Does it strike you as odd that so many of them say, "Music is my passion," regardless of how much of a role music plays in their lives, regardless of how much they sacrifice for this "passion"? What does it mean for music, or anything else, to be a fifteen- or sixteen-year-old's "passion"? A sixty-year-old's?

predicament of actual existence: deciding what to do. Actual decisions are not the neat, reasonable calculations of philosophers, nor are they the products of systematic scientific thinking. Existential decisions can never be satisfied by appealing to surveys or studies. Enlightenment philosophies and all metaphysical systems merely observe life from a distance; they do not take part in it.

The Present Age

Kierkegaard viewed the mid-nineteenth century as an era of passionless mediocrity and conformity. He lamented the *massing of society*, by which he meant the diminution of the individual's role in the face of mass production, the pernicious influence of the press (mass media), and the loss of truth in the face of objectivity and abstraction. Kierkegaard included what he saw as the inflated reputation of science and technological solutions to human problems as factors contributing to the massing of society. In *Either/Or*, Kierkegaard began a profound and eloquent analysis of conformism and mediocrity:

> Let others complain that the age is wicked; my complaint is that it is wretched, for it lacks passion. Men's thoughts are thin and flimsy like lace, they are themselves pitiable like lacemakers. The thoughts of their hearts are too paltry to be sinful. For a worm it might be regarded as a sin to harbor such thoughts, but not for a being made in the image of God. Their lusts are dull and sluggish, their passions sleepy. They do their duty, these shopkeeping souls, but they clip the coin a trifle…; they think that even if the Lord keeps ever so careful a set of books, they may still cheat Him a little. Out upon them! This is the reason my soul always turns back to the Old Testament and to Shakespeare. I feel that those who speak there are at least human beings: they hate, they love, they murder their enemies, and curse their descendants throughout all generations, they sin.[6]

In an essay called *The Present Age* (1846), which, according to philosopher William Barrett, "has become the source of nearly all the Existentialist criticisms of modern society," Kierkegaard continued his attack on conformity.[7] "The crowd," he points out, overwhelms the individual, yet the individual feels frightened and lost without "the crowd." The mediocre, alienated individual needs a group to identify with, to provide "peer approval." Yet, Kierkegaard insists, a collective identity is always somehow false; in order to belong, to fit in, we must betray some part of ourselves, must cease living our own lives and begin living "a kind of life."

> *Because the contemporary individual has no comprehensive picture of the social universe within which he lives and of the structure of modern society, he pays the price of meaninglessness and insignificance in his daily work and even a spiritual isolation from his fellows.*
> — A. W. Levi

For Deeper Consideration

Why did Kierkegaard insist that the "present age" lacked authentic passion? Is our age any more authentic? For example, does the widespread contemporary use of the word *passion*—"Music is my passion," "My kids are my passion," "Writing is my passion"—suggest that he was on to something? Or are we, indeed, more passionate, more authentic today and, thus, Kierkegaard's critique of inauthenticity is outdated?

An Age of Virtual Equality

According to Kierkegaard's view of "the crowd," modern people are anonymous creatures who depend on experts to point the way to salvation or personal growth. As you read the following passage, think about the many coalitions, committees, and other groups that continue to spring up in our own times:

> The present age tends toward a mathematical equality in which it takes so and so many to make one individual. Formerly the outstanding individual could allow himself everything and the individual in the masses nothing at all. Now everyone knows that so and so many make an individual, and quite consistently people add themselves together (it is called joining together, but that is only a polite euphemism) for the most trivial purposes. Simply in order to put a passing whim into practice a few people add themselves together, and the thing is done—they dare to do it....
>
> The individual no longer belongs to God, to himself, to his beloved, to his art or to his science; he is conscious of belonging in all things to an abstraction to which he is subjected by reflection.[8]

If Kierkegaard is correct, rather than being ourselves, we tend to conform to an image or idea associated with being a certain *type* of person. That's what Kierkegaard means by belonging to an "abstraction" (an image or idea) created by "reflection" (self-conscious thinking). Thus, for example, a woman consciously tries to be "a Christian" or "a lawyer" based on some collective abstraction, some image or idea. She attempts to conform to a pattern. In an age of image bombardment, it can be difficult to know what's authentic and what's typecasting. Sometimes, it does seem as if many of us do indeed govern our lives by abstractions based on age, ethnicity, and gender.

To the extent that we do see ourselves and others as *abstract types*, we deal with generalizations rather than with concrete specifics; we overlook individual qualities. Certainly no one disputes the usefulness of generalizations. They provide us with the ability to identify patterns, to recognize principles of behavior, and so forth. What they do not—and cannot—do is recognize *existing individuals*. From an existentialist perspective, all acts of generalizing and abstracting require *leveling*. And for Kierkegaard, leveling, as the word itself suggests, is not a process of exaltation but of reduction to mediocrity—reduction to numerical equality at the expense of authenticity:

> The abstract principle of leveling...like the biting east wind, has no personal relation to any individual, but has only an abstract relationship which is the same for everyone. There no hero suffers for others, or helps them; the taskmaster of all alike is the leveling process, which itself takes on their education. And the man who learns most from the leveling and himself becomes greatest does not become an outstanding man or hero—that would only impede the leveling process, which is rigidly consistent to the end; he himself prevents that from happening because he has understood the meaning of leveling: he becomes a man and nothing else, in the complete equalitarian sense.[9]

We do not err because truth is difficult to see. It is visible at a glance. We err because this is more comfortable.
— Alexander Solzhenitsyn

This picture of Muslim school girls attending the funeral of a friend is a hauntingly beautiful reminder that underneath the particularities of culture and ritual lurk profound human longings for meaning, belonging, and significance, longings Kierkegaard expressed in a cry *de profundis*, from the depths: "It must be terrible on the day of judgment, when all souls come back to life—to stand there alone, *alone* and *unknown* to all."

In courtrooms and classrooms, we use abstractions and utilitarian calculations to level ourselves so that "everyone is treated the same." The press levels presidents and celebrities through exposés of their personal lives. The underlying message is "They're no different from us." Indeed, they are not, but the leveling nature of these exposés, coupled with the sameness and mediocrity of so many of the people we elect to office and turn into celebrities, lends support to a Kierkegaardian conclusion that ours remains an era of increasing dullness, conformity, and lack of genuine individuals.

PHILOSOPHICAL QUERY

Identify some current examples of leveling and discuss the effects of leveling. Must efforts at furthering equality result in leveling? Is equality possible without leveling? Is leveling possibly desirable?

 MindTap
Discussing Philosophy

Philosophers and critics offer a variety of interpretations of Kierkegaard's writings. This is not surprising, given Kierkegaard's penchant for irony, "indirection," and Socratic engagement. I suspect that he would be delighted with the *fact* of these myriad interpretations, even if he should object to their content. One point seems clear, however: Kierkegaard identified and addressed one of the crucial issues of our time: How can we be our "true selves" in an age dominated by ever more sophisticated ways of influencing our thoughts, feelings, and actions? How can we find sufficient passion and clarity of focus to become ourselves in a world seduced by objectivity and conformity and run by ever more massive institutions? (If we aren't careful, even our attempts to be unique, to be authentic, begin to feel phony and contrived.)

Becoming a Subject

> *Philosophy teaches that the way is to become objective, while Christianity teaches that the way is to become subjective, i.e., to become a subject in truth.*
> — Søren
>   Kierkegaard

According to Kierkegaard, my life is the proof that I believe: If I am to be anything, really be something—that is, if I am to *exist*—my life must be a different kind of life than it would be if I believed otherwise. If, for instance, I truly believe that something is sinful or that some practice is morally obligatory, my life must reflect that belief. It won't do to say and think and feel one way but live another:

> Everyone with some capacity for observation who seriously considers what is called Christendom, or the conditions in a so-called Christian country, must surely be assailed by profound misgivings. What does it mean that all these thousands and thousands call themselves Christians as a matter of course? These many, many, many men, of whom the greater part, so far as one can judge, live in categories quite foreign to Christianity! ...
>
> If, then, according to our assumption, the greater number of people in Christendom only imagine themselves to be Christians, in what categories do they live? They live in aesthetic, or at the most aesthetic-ethical categories.[10]

In Kierkegaard's language, I *exist*—as a Christian, specifically, but, to an extent, as anything—only when I *appropriate* my belief by taking it up subjectively, inwardly. I must believe *in it* not merely believe it. I must be faithful to my faith by living it. "Only when reflection comes to a halt can a beginning be made, and reflection can only be halted by something else," Kierkegaard says, "and this something else is something quite different from the logical, being a resolution of the will."[11]

Mere cognitive assent, objective understanding, will not do because objectivity demands so little of me. Objectively, I can know things without caring about them. Indeed, the essential feature of objectivity is lack of passion. Objective truths are not about *us*. Using Kierkegaard's term, they are not *present*. They are detached, "out there." Detachment blinds us to existence, makes us into "persons of a sort," living, as it were, "lives of a sort":

> It is impossible to exist without passion, unless we understand the word "exist" in the loose sense of a so-called existence. Every Greek thinker was therefore essentially a passionate thinker. I have often reflected how one might bring a man into a state of passion. I have thought in this connection that if I could get him seated on a horse and the horse made to take fright and gallop wildly, or better still, for the sake of bringing passion out, if I could take a man who wanted to arrive at a certain place as quickly as possible, and hence already had some passion, and could set him astride a horse that can scarcely walk—and yet this is what existence is like if one has become consciously aware of it. Or if a driver were otherwise not especially inclined toward passion, if someone hitched a team of horses to a wagon

Sophie Elbaz/Sygma/Corbis

Sophie Elbaz/Sygma/Corbis

How can we deny that life is absurd when we look into the face of this little girl and at the solitary figure of the little boy, bonded slaves forced to extract slate from mines and toil in unsafe workshops to produce boxes of fifty pencils for meager pay, so meager that many of them will die of malnutrition or injury without ever earning release from their parents' debts? Alas, relentless poverty, hardship, and suffering are the daily lot of millions of children—and adults. For what purpose?

for him, one of them a Pegasus and the other a worn-out jade, and told him to drive—I think one might succeed. And it is just this that it means to exist, if one is to become conscious of it. Eternity is the winged horse, infinitely fast, and time is a worn-out jade; the existing individual is the driver. That is to say, he is such a driver when his mode of existence is not an existence loosely so called; for then he is no driver but a drunken peasant who lies asleep in the wagon and lets the horses take care of themselves. To be sure, he also drives and is a driver; and so there are perhaps many who—also exist.[12]

PHILOSOPHICAL QUERY

Why do you think Kierkegaard makes one of the horses "a Pegasus" and the other "a worn-out jade"? Who was Pegasus? What is a worn-out jade? (Hint: This has something to do with Kierkegaard's profound interest in his and our relationship to God.)

There is a qualitative difference between what we often call existence and what Kierkegaard means by truly existing. So-called existence is the half-conscious routine of going about our daily affairs, conforming to the conventions of the day, or robotically rebelling against them, rejecting one crowd in favor of another, merely "switching places," living what we sometimes characterize as horizontal, flat lives.

Objective approaches to philosophy fail us when it comes to learning how to exist because they try to instruct us, to inform us. Kierkegaard's philosophy, in contrast, aims to edify us, to change us. It is not, nor does it aim to be, neutral, systematic, and speculative; it is deliberately and necessarily passionate, practical, and subjective—existential, in the full sense of the word. Kierkegaard is not trying to prove something in the ordinary sense of proving via appeals to logic and reason. He is trying to edify us, to engage and encourage us to become more conscious of the extent to which we exist—as opposed to merely live. He cannot do that by way of generalizations and "proofs." No one can.

The most crucial task for Kierkegaard, and, he believes, for anyone, is living "in the truth" by *becoming a subject*, a proper, authentic self or person.[13] If we do not, then we remain, in Kierkegaard's caustic phrase, "a subject of sorts."

This is a long way from Descartes's "I think, therefore I am," grounded as it is in rational reflection. Not for Kierkegaard, Descartes's genteel meditations in a cozy study. Kierkegaard's "I am" suffers and struggles, faces the "predicament" of decision at every moment. Eternity is always at stake, not rational certainty, not the conclusion of some tidy syllogism. The Kierkegaardian self wants desperately to do what is right, yet lacks—and will always lack—sufficient information, sufficient objective knowledge upon which to act. To act is not merely to behave but rather to assent with my whole being. This is the difference between being an observer or a participant.

To Kierkegaard, objectivity is "easy" because it is superficial, blind, and unresponsive to inner reality, to human be-ing, to our existential predicament. Kierkegaard was, of course, affected by his own interior struggles to make sense of his father, the family curse, guilt, and his conflicted feelings regarding Regine Olsen as an impediment to living a religious life. Objectively, these may not seem like "real" problems, and, perhaps, objectively, they were not. But subjectively, personally, "in truth," they were genuine predicaments, the sorts of predicaments any of us face when we dig deep and reflect on what really faces us.

From a child I was under the sway of a prodigious melancholy, the depth of which finds its only adequate measure in the equally prodigious dexterity I possessed of hiding it under an apparent gaiety and joie de vivre.

— Søren Kierkegaard

PHILOSOPHICAL QUERY

Compare Kierkegaard's claims about the limits of objectivity and reason with Hume's assertion that "reason is, and ought only to be the slave of the passions" and Alison Jaggar's assertion that knowledge is grounded in emotions (Chapter 10).

In his writings, Kierkegaard left a record of his own "becoming a subject" through conflict, self-recrimination, accusation, guilt—all the messy stuff that constitutes the foundation of any self's existence:

> Then it was that the great earthquake occurred, the terrible revolution.... Then I suspected that my father's great age was not a divine blessing but rather a curse; that the outstanding intellectual gifts of our family were given in order that we should rend each other to pieces: then I felt the stillness of death ground around me when I saw in my father an unhappy man who was to outlive us all, a cross on the tomb of his hopes. There must be guilt upon the whole family, the punishment of God must be upon it.[14]

> I have just returned from a party of which I was the life and soul; wit poured from my lips, everyone laughed and admired me—but I went away—and the dash should be as long as the earth's orbit _____

> _____ and wanted to shoot myself.[15]

> I was so completely shaken that I understood perfectly well that I could not possibly succeed in striking the comforting and secure *via media* in which most people pass their lives: I had either to cast myself into perdition and sensuality [by choosing Regine Olsen], or to choose the religious absolutely as the only thing—either the world in a measure that would be dreadful, or the cloister.... I had become thoroughly aware how impossible it would be for me to be religious only up to a certain point.[16]

> It must be terrible on the day of judgment, when all souls come back to life—to stand there alone, *alone* and *unknown* to all.

> I am a *Janus bifrons;* I laugh with one face, I weep with the other.[17]

When we approach Kierkegaard objectively, he appears almost pitiful. His obsession with the family curse and decision to abandon Regine Olsen have been a rich vein for armchair psychologists to mine, easy to trivialize as self-delusions, rationalizations, symptoms of neurosis. But when we think back to our own existential struggles about romantic relationships, career choices, getting a divorce, abandoning or joining a church, having a baby or an abortion, we realize that objective advice, information, facts, studies, experts, and statistics are beside the point. We cannot move, cannot choose by being objective and rational; living is not a simple, zero-sum, clear, obvious best-choice game.

To objective observers, our waffling, tortured yes-no-maybe-I-don't-know-okay-wait-not-yet-maybe struggles can seem trivial, not worth the agony; so they present their objective solutions to our subjective predicaments as if they were obvious. We know better. Kierkegaard insists that all such cases are similar, at least in the sense

I am left standing like a man who has rented a house and gathered all the furniture and household things together but has not yet found the beloved with whom to share the joys and sorrows of his life.

— Søren Kierkegaard

of the anxiety and agony that they bring with them—or ought to bring if we are paying attention. Every decision we make rules out all other possibilities. Either Regine Olsen or not; either God or not. Either *we exist* or not.

PHILOSOPHICAL QUERY

Think back to the example of a cart being hauled by a Pegasus and a worn-out jade. Is Kierkegaard's reason for choosing those two horses getting perhaps a bit clearer?

Stages on Life's Way

According to Kierkegaard, existing, becoming a subject, is possible only when we have the—not a—God-relation: "Without God [a man] is never essentially himself (which one is only by being before God) and therefore never satisfied with being himself."[18]

In a secular age, this seems unnecessarily provincial. Isn't it possible to become one's authentic self without relating to the God of the Bible, without becoming a Christian (in Kierkegaard's sense), say by way of a passionate commitment to an ethical or social ideal or even by living passionately and authentically as an atheist? Not for Kierkegaard, who insists that anyone who truly knows himself thereby knows that the need for God is real. Living as if the God-relation is one optional choice among many *equally plausible* and possible choices is delusional, a kind of living (nonexistence) disguised as a life.

Can Kierkegaard "prove" this, prove that God exists, that the Christian way is authentic? No, and recall that he is not interested in proving anything in the ordinary sense of proving. "One is deluded," he says, in "thinking that [one] could demonstrate that God exists":[19]

> (A)ssume that the critics have succeeded in proving about the Bible everything that any learned theologian in his happiest moment has wished to prove about the Bible. These books and no others belong to the canon; they are authentic…—one may well say, that it is as if every letter were inspired….
>
> Well, then, everything being assumed in order with respect to the Scriptures— what follows? Has anyone who previously did not have faith been brought a single step nearer to its acquisition? No, not a single step. Faith does not result simply from scientific inquiry; it does not come directly at all. On the contrary, in this objectivity one tends to lose that infinite personal interestedness in passion which is the condition of faith.[20]

Discussing Philosophy

PHILOSOPHICAL QUERY

Contrast Kierkegaard's approach to theological arguments to Aquinas's Five Ways and Descartes's ontological argument. (See Chapters 8 and 9.)

THE EXISTENTIALIST: SØREN KIERKEGAARD

In lieu of arguments, Kierkegaard offers a series of sketches and descriptions of a dialectical process that involve what David E. Cooper calls "*intimations* of a self-reflective kind that indicate, however inchoately, something about themselves."[21] If we have somehow escaped from or not yet given ourselves over entirely to "the crowd," we may be receptive to these intimations of despair, "the sickness unto death" that afflicts so many of us.

According to Kierkegaard, we are in despair whether we know it or not because we have a "double nature" composed of the infinite and finite, the temporal and the eternal. This is not some sort of Cartesian dualism. Our dual nature does not consist of two substances but of one "self" struggling to exist between the pull of the world and eternity:

> Man is a synthesis of the infinite and the finite, of the temporal and the eternal, of freedom and necessity, in short a synthesis. A synthesis is a relation between two factors. So regarded, man is not yet a self.[22]

Ironically, the despair that I try so hard to deny becomes my gateway to salvation. It is the spring that sets in motion three explicit ways of choosing to live that Kierkegaard refers to as *stages on life's way*. In ascending order, they are aesthetic, ethical, and religious ways of living.[23]

The Aesthetic Stage

We have already seen what life is like at the crowd stage of living, the stage of crude, utilitarian "mathematical equality" and personal inauthenticity. When we are sunk far into the crowd, absorbed by it, we are too unaware of ourselves as selves to exist. We are too unreflective to *be* an individual person in any meaningful sense at all. Most of us, however, are not sunk so far into the crowd that we are utterly without some intimation that our lives remain "far…from what a man's life ought to be."[24] This nagging intimation is a sign that we are not totally in thrall to the crowd but, perhaps, at what Kierkegaard calls the aesthetic stage of life.

The aesthetic stage is characterized by the pursuit of pleasure, not just in art and music but especially in the pursuit of sensuous pleasure. The aesthete is crafty, seductive, and energetic in his or her efforts to find meaning in aesthetic experience. This is a way of life that cultivates easy, uncommitted enjoyment, a life of whim and caprice, focused on the here and now. Its enemies are boredom, frustration, and dissatisfaction.

Although the aesthete chooses, choosing is taken lightly because, well, what difference does any particular choice make? I mean, nothing fateful hangs in the balance, does it? The important point is to avoid getting entangled in tedious, boring decisions. As Kierkegaard characterizes him, the aesthete tends to be either superficially easygoing or superficially cynical.

The aesthetic stage on life's way is amoral, and the legendary seducer Don Juan is an exemplar. Don Juan lives for the sensuous romantic moment and uses whatever crafty strategies he thinks will get him what he wants. His lovers are never real to him, not existing individuals but tokens. As a result, there is a drab sameness to Don Juan's life in spite of its apparent colorful variety. The seducer is doomed to ceaselessness, because, ultimately, he is bored or cynical no matter how many conquests he has. On the surface, the sophisticated aesthete is the life of the party—but—and here, as Kierkegaard wrote, the dash ought to be as long as the orbit of the earth. An aesthete whom Kierkegaard refers to only as A presents his worldview in stark, cynical terms:

> (T)he world goes from bad to worse, and…its evils increase more and more, as boredom increases, and boredom is the root of all evil.
>
> The history of this can be traced back to the very beginning of the world. The gods were bored, and so they created man. Adam was bored because he was alone, and so Eve was created. Thus boredom entered the world, and increased in proportion to the increase of population. Adam was bored alone; then Adam and Eve were bored together; then Adam and Eve and Cain and Abel were bored *en famille;* then the population of the world increased, and the peoples were bored *en masse.* To divert themselves, they conceived the idea of constructing a tower high enough to reach the heavens. This idea itself is as boring as the tower was high, and constitutes a terrible proof of how boredom gained the upper hand….
>
> All men are bores….Those who bore others are the mob, the crowd, the infinite multitude of men in general. Those who bore themselves are the elect, the aristocracy; and it is a curious fact that those who do not bore themselves usually bore others, while those who do not bore themselves entertain others.[25]

The aesthetic stage is, Kierkegaard implies, where most of us live most of our lives. At this stage, we flit from this to that without ever wholeheartedly and consciously committing to anything, not really committing. We toss aside marriages, families, and careers because we are bored. We set off on quests to "find ourselves" in ways that are "congenial," but not authentic. We resist submitting to something higher than ourselves and struggle, futilely, to stay in control. Kierkegaard's aesthete wants an interesting life above all, and on his terms:

> If I had a humble spirit in my service, who, when I asked for a glass of water, brought me the world's costliest wines blended, in a chalice, I should dismiss him, in order to teach him that pleasure consists not in what I enjoy but in getting my own way.[26]

The aesthetic way of living is, ironically, boring—and worse: "every aesthetic life view is despair."[27] It has about it a fundamental sameness and sadness. Aesthetic satisfactions are subject to whims of circumstance. Thus, the aesthete is never *a* self but only a *multiplicity* without the "unifying power of personality."[28] The synthesis of spirit and the world fails. What can a poor, bored, fatigued aesthete do to find relief? Kierkegaard says that the aesthete must consciously choose despair and face up to his predicaments as predicaments. He must stop distracting himself and stop living only for himself.

The Ethical Stage

The next step on life's way is the ethical stage, a way of life that involves making a commitment to the norms, principles, and customs of society. The ethical life is devoted to general principles. It moves beyond the narcissistic motives of the aesthete. Here, one plants oneself via principled commitment. In this way, Kierkegaard says, I "infinitize" myself; that is, I move upward to the level of universalized ethical behavior that, ironically, serves my "finite" aesthetic nature better than the uncommitted aesthetic life does. A faithful, happy marriage, for instance, is more satisfying than the pursuit of ceaseless, increasingly meaningless seduction after seduction.

The ethical man or woman is earnest. He or she seriously chooses an ethical code by which to live. In so doing, the ethical person achieves a degree of unity that the aesthete does not. The ethical person accomplishes this by forcing an either/or option: either a moral life or an amoral life. Kierkegaard's ethical man, the Judge, says:

> It is not so much a question of choosing the right as of the energy, the earnestness, the pathos with which one chooses. Thereby the personality announces its inner infinity, and thereby, in turn, the personality is consolidated....
>
> My either/or does not in the first instance denote the choice between good and evil; it denotes the choice whereby one chooses good *and* evil/or excludes them. Here the question is under what determinants one would contemplate the whole of existence and would himself live. That the man who chooses good and evil chooses good is indeed true, but this becomes evident only afterwards; for the aesthetical is not the evil but the neutrality.... It is, therefore, not so much a question of choosing between willing the good *or* the evil, as of choosing to will.... Here you see again how important it is that a choice be made, and that the crucial thing is not deliberation but the baptism of the will which lifts up the choice into the ethical.[29]

In other words, at this stage what matters is an ethical will. Do not be surprised if the Judge reminds you of Kant (Chapter 11). Kant's moral philosophy centers on the will, on having a moral motive and making a deliberate, rational commitment to universal moral laws and treating all persons as ends-in-themselves. Kantian morality exemplifies the ethical stage. And that, for Kierkegaard, is why Kant's philosophy and essentially any modern (Enlightenment), purely humanistic philosophy fails. It exalts human reason and makes man his own lawgiver, which he never can be:

> Kant held that man was his own law (autonomy), *i.e.*, bound himself under the law which he gave himself. In a deeper sense that means to say: lawlessness or experimentation. It is no harder than the thwacks which Sancho Panza applied to his own bottom.... There [must be] some third and compelling factor, which is not the individual himself....
>
> Not only is the law which I give myself... not a law; but there is a law which is given to me by one higher than I. And not only that; but that lawgiver takes the liberty of joining in at the same time in the character of education and applies the compulsion.
>
> Now if during the whole of his life a man never acts in so decisive a way that the educator [God] can get a hold on him: well, then the man is certainly allowed to live complacently in a state of illusion, imagination, experimentation—but that also connotes: the greatest lack of grace.[30]

Modern faith in mankind, Kierkegaard insists, turns everything upside down, giving man—not God—the final say, making man—not God—the arbiter of good and evil. Yet we cannot reason out how we ought to act any more than a man can determine for himself by himself if he is being reasonable. To what part of himself

> *When I think of*
> *something good that*
> *I intend to do, is*
> *this identical with*
> *having done it? By no*
> *means. But neither*
> *is it the external*
> *that constitutes the*
> *criterion of action; for*
> *the human being who*
> *does not own a penny*
> *can be as charitable as*
> *one who gives away a*
> *kingdom.*
> — Søren
>   Kierkegaard

can he turn to decide which of two contradictory options is true? Will he not then have to assess *that part of himself* with yet another himself *ad infinitum?*

Ultimately, nothing can be resolved on the ethical level. To get beyond it, to get *somewhere*, we must make a leap of faith. We must move beyond the merely ethical stage to the religious stage.

The Religious Stage

Kierkegaard believed that Kantian (and Enlightenment) notions of human autonomy result in despair because, in the end, everything hinges on our human judgment, and human judgment is always subject to doubt. No matter how carefully we think and analyze, we can never be sure that we are right. Our ethics are constantly being challenged and revised—by us. We give ourselves ethical "laws" but ignore and repeal them as our moods and circumstances change. In our never-ending effort to construct perfect, fair, equitable systems, rules, and laws, we exhaust ourselves, never seeming to see the futility of such efforts. Consequently, we live without authenticity, security, and stability. Although we may put on a good front, we are shadowed by a sense of unease, even, perhaps, dread and despair. We have intimations of arbitrariness, partiality, and falsity.

This is not to say that we do not make intense, passionate commitments to ethical (and spiritual) principles. We do. But in the end, our commitments are really to ourselves. The more serious we are about doing what is right, the less sure we are about what we are doing. If we are sure, we cannot, in Kierkegaard's sense, be right, for such certainty is inhuman—or more than human (as Socrates understood).

Nor will it do to say that we have done the best we can. The best we can do is never enough to alleviate our anxiety about our existence—if we take existing seriously, that is:

> No earnest doubt, no really deep concern, is put to rest by the saying that one does what one can. If a man is sometimes in the right, sometimes in the wrong, to a certain degree in the right, to a certain degree in the wrong, who, then, is to decide this except a man; but in deciding it may he not be to a certain degree in the right, to a certain degree in the wrong? . . . We have, then, only the choice of being nothing before God, or the eternal torture of beginning over again every instant, but without being able to begin.[31]

> *How terrible about*
> *the man who once*
> *as a little boy, while*
> *herding sheep on the*
> *heaths of Jutland,*
> *suffering greatly, in*
> *hunger and want,*
> *stood upon a hill and*
> *cursed God—and the*
> *man was unable to*
> *forget it even when he*
> *was eighty-two years*
> *old.*
> — Søren
>   Kierkegaard

It is necessary to "leap" toward the religious, and specifically toward God, if one is ever to escape the despair that Kierkegaard thought was ever present in other ways of living: the crowd life, the aesthetic life, and the ethical life.

The Kierkegaardian leap of faith is controversial theologically and philosophically, involving, as it does, a tricky double-movement, a paradox, and what Kierkegaard calls the *teleological suspension of the ethical.* Consider the case of Abraham once more, this time from what it must be like to be in Abraham's shoes.

Had Abraham been an ethical man, he would not have considered sacrificing his son Isaac for the *possibility* that God had ordered him to do so. As an ethical man, a thinker, Abraham would have concluded that God does not command us to murder and not to murder. What categorical imperative could a Kantian Abraham will: If you believe that God wants you to kill your son, you must kill him? That will not do; "believe" is too vague, too psychological to be the basis of such an imperative.

Okay, then how about: If you are certain that God wants you to kill your son, you must do it? But what kind of human being can ever be certain of such a thing? Don't we, as reasonable observers of the human scene, see all sorts of evil things done by individuals who are certain that God has commanded them to do them? Yet we do not grant their subjective certainty the status of moral duty. Truth may be subjectivity, but beliefs are not true just because they are subjective.

To see what Kierkegaard is trying to express, imagine, as best you can, that you are in Abraham's shoes, that you believe that you have received a message from God to violate what you believe is a fundamental, universal moral principle. Recall that "in his heart" Abraham does the deed: He was in motion when the angel stopped his arm. Kierkegaard writes (thinking, no doubt, also of himself and Regine Olsen):

> With Abraham the situation was different. By his act he overstepped the ethical entirely and possessed a higher *telos* outside of it, in relation to which he suspended the former [the ethical]. For I should very much like to know how one would bring Abraham's act into relation with the universal, and whether it is possible to discover any connection whatever between what Abraham did and the universal... except the fact that he transgressed it. It was not for the sake of saving a people, not to maintain the idea of the state, that Abraham did this.... Abraham's whole action stands in no relation to the universal, is a purely private understanding. Therefore, whereas the tragic hero is great by reason of his moral virtue, Abraham is great by reason of his personal virtue. In Abraham's life there was no higher expression of the ethical than this, that the father shall love his son. Of the ethical in the sense of morality there can be no question in this instance. Insofar as the universal was present, it was indeed cryptically present in Isaac, hidden, as it were, in Isaac's loins, and must therefore cry out with Isaac's mouth, "Do it not! Thou art bringing everything to naught."
>
> Why then did Abraham do it? For God's sake, and (in complete identity with this) for his own sake. He did it for God's sake because God required this proof of his faith; for his own sake he did it that he might furnish the proof. The unity of these two points of view is perfectly expressed in the word which has always been used to characterize the situation: it is a trial, a temptation.... in this case the temptation is itself the ethical—which would keep him from doing God's will....
>
> Therefore, though Abraham arouses my admiration, he at the same time appalls me.... he who gives up the universal in order to grasp something still higher which is not the universal—what is he doing?... And if... the individual was mistaken—what can save him?... Him the beholder cannot understand nor let his eye rest confidently upon him....
>
> ... As the individual he became higher than the universal; that is the paradox which does not permit of mediation.... To him who follows the narrow way of faith no one can give counsel.[32]

From any perspective but that of faith, what Abraham did was *absurd*. He made a choice in a paradoxical state of tension. Objectively, there were no grounds to justify his choice and—this is important—Abraham knew it. He could not consult with his fellow tribesmen nor with his wife, Sarah. He knew in advance what they would say. No universal moral code could help him. He faced an individual predicament:

> When the question is treated in an objective manner it becomes impossible for the subject to face the decision with passion, least of all in an infinitely interested passion. It is a self-contradiction and therefore comical, to be infinitely interested in that which in its maximum still always remains an approximation. If, in spite of this, passion is nevertheless imported, we get fanaticism.[33]

For Kierkegaard, the ethical is the universal and is its own end and fulfillment (*telos*). "Its task," Kierkegaard says, "is to…abolish its particularity in order to become universal."[34] This Abraham refused to do. He transcended the ethical plane by teleological suspension of the ethical:

> (F)aith is this paradox, that the particular is higher than the universal—yet in such a way, be it observed, that…the individual, after having been in the universal, now as the particular isolates himself as higher than the universal. If this be not faith, then Abraham is lost, then faith has never existed in the world.…[35]

Kant is wrong. The Enlightenment is wrong. Universal, generalized humanistic ethics are inadequate. They cannot deal with the existing individual. Only faith (the religious stage) allows us to be our authentic, existing selves. If we are to *exist*, we must be willing (in the strong sense of willing) to suspend the ethical. Individually, objectively, and ethically, this is dangerous, unacceptable, absurd. From a rational, human, and humane perspective, it is absurd that God would ask me (were I Abraham) to kill my son. The whole history of man's relation to God is ethically absurd.

Dangerous Stuff

If I had not been a penitent,…had not been melancholy, my union with [Regine Olsen] would have made me happier than I had ever dreamed of being. But in so far as I was what, alas, I was, I had to say that I could be happier in my unhappiness without her than with her.

— Søren Kierkegaard

One problem with the Abraham example is its "bigness." If we are not careful, we might conclude that for Kierkegaard, religion involves that kind of big, socially dangerous decision. Not so. Kierkegaard takes pains to remind us in different ways that the small particularities of everyday life also involve the God-relation and that any decision we are trying to make—to go to the park, say, or buy a cup of coffee—can generate an irresolvable series of questions if we try to choose objectively. There will be no stopping point.

If I buy this coffee, am I selfish for not giving the money to the poor? Which poor? Is it universally good to give money to "the poor"? How much? How do I know? If I don't buy this coffee, might the barista lose his job, the coffee shop owner her shop? Silly questions? Maybe, from the outside. But not if I am earnest about doing the right thing—rather than merely doing my best.

I cannot think my way out of these predicaments—and once I am conscious of my dual nature, time-bound and facing eternity, they seem to be everywhere. If I am to exist, to "become a subject," I must somehow unite these two natures by obeying God while admitting that I will never know for sure that I am obeying God. I must, paradoxically, know that I do not know—yet believe anyway. Does this "make sense"? Not really. But Kierkegaard is not trying "to make sense." He is trying to edify us:

> I am not a Christian, and unfortunately, I cannot make it apparent that the others are not either—indeed, that they are even less so than I. This is because they imagine themselves to be, or they lie their way into being [Christian].... My task is a Socratic task, to revise the definition of being a Christian. I myself do not call myself a Christian (keeping the ideal free), but I can make it apparent that the others are even less so.[36]

This is precisely the sort of claim that makes many philosophers and theologians uneasy. Once we throw out, or set aside, appeals to ethics, objectivity, and reason, are we not so far into the realm of the subjective that we are back to the Sophists? Isn't Kierkegaard's view of "existing" and authentic Christianity just one more opinion among others, no "truer" than any other? Why should we accept it?

No *reason*—but perhaps there is something—an intimation, perhaps—that Kierkegaard has a valuable lesson to teach us, even if we cannot, or will not, go all the way with him. Perhaps the lesson is that present-day America resembles Kierkegaard's Copenhagen in that a vast majority of Americans claim to "believe in God," and most of those identify themselves as Christians. But what does that mean existentially, in the living? Whatever it means, for Kierkegaard, being a Christian does not—cannot—mean living comfortably:

> All "humanity's" shrewdness is directed toward one thing, toward being able to live without responsibility. The significance of the priest for our society ought to be to do everything to make every person eternally responsible for every hour that he lives, even in the least things he does, because this is Christianity. But, his significance for society is to guarantee hypocrisy, while society pushes off the responsibility from itself onto "the priest."[37]

Are we not, then, priest and nonpriest, our own religious authority, our own self-created church? And if we are, are we not but one very small step away from being our own god? Kierkegaard would not disagree:

> Whoever you are, whatever your life might be, my friend, by ceasing to participate, (if you do) in public worship as it presently is (with its claim to being the Christianity of the New Testament) you will continually have one sin fewer, and a great sin: You are not taking part in making a fool of God.[38]

For Deepest Consideration

Sketch and analyze Kierkegaard's critique of "false Christianity" by contrasting Kierkegaard's existentialist idea of faith with more common conceptions of faith as belief. What, for Kierkegaard, constitutes "being a Christian"? Why did—and do—so many people who see themselves as Christians find Kierkegaard's point of view offensive and wrongheaded? What do you think? Or is this a matter of thinking?

MindTap

Aplia

Commentary

Other philosophers write as well as or better than Kierkegaard. Other philosophers address important issues more consistently and less personally. But few speak to certain important problems of our time as pointedly as Kierkegaard does. He understands the dangers of deferring choices to outsiders, to experts, to "the crowd," and the pressures caused by the massing of society.

Despite our many freedoms, increased leisure, and psychological sophistication, authenticity seems rare in all walks of life, not the least of which is religion. Kierkegaard's great virtue is his reclamation of the existing individual from philosophical, theological, political, and scientific abstraction as he or she struggles to make life meaningful amid a bombardment of answers and options. Kierkegaard's critique of abstract philosophy and Enlightenment reasoning reminds us that individuals construct philosophies, individuals interpret revelations, individuals draw scientific conclusions, and individuals decide what is objective and reasonable.

Yet Kierkegaard seems to swing too much in the direction of subjectivity and individuality. For all his insight and prophetic power, he was unable to overcome his own alienation from science and objectivity. Surely, not even the leap of faith can completely ignore ethical considerations and objective reality. Even though a lack of passion is deadly, the presence of passion is no guarantee of authenticity. Blind, uncontrollable passion can destroy individuality as surely as excessive abstraction. Anyone who has been "consumed" or "swept away" by authentic passion knows that it is possible to lose ourselves in passion as in crowds.

Yet perhaps our biggest danger today is not too much passion but too much resentment, envy, narcissism, and sentimentality masquerading as passion; not the risky leap of faith but the false-faith of mass-movement, fanatical religion, or salad-bar spirituality; not too much subjectivity but too much self-centeredness and too little honest reflection. One might even say that in spite (or because?) of our knowledge of the biology of the human psyche, we still encounter few authentic individuals.

Modern science continues to discover knowledge of many things; nonexistentialist philosophy continues to refine and clarify our capacities for understanding. But should they achieve every one of their goals this minute, we would still have no answer to the profoundest existential questions for ourselves: What is it to be a human being? Is our suffering and struggling worth living for? Has it a meaning? Has *my life* a meaning?

With or without God; with or without loving families; with or without wise advisers; with or without children; with or without jobs; with or without formal education; of whatever age, race, gender—Kierkegaard's question haunts all of us, tracks us like a Socratic hound: What are we—you and I and they—to *do?* Sometimes, when I am in a certain frame of mind, I think I can hear the tortured Dane who tried so hard to mend the rend between the self and the world: "(E)verything goes on as usual, and yet there is no one who believes in it."[39]

Summary of Main Points

- Søren Kierkegaard claimed that truth is subjectivity, and the crowd is untruth. He rejected the view that science and objective truth could provide meaning for the individual. He criticized conformity and the degradation that he claimed results when theories and systems are used to explain and define individuals.

- For Kierkegaard, the most important issue facing any individual is how to relate to God. He criticized efforts to reduce that relationship to a performance contract and rejected as "false Christianity" all efforts to objectify faith or base belief on facts (science).

- Kierkegaard criticized what he saw as the inflated reputation of science and the massing of society, which he thought combined to alienate individuals from themselves by leveling everyone "toward a mathematical equality." People are pressured to conform to types, becoming abstractions rather than authentic individuals. Both mass movements and objective knowledge fail to address the individual.

- According to Kierkegaard, we exist only when we appropriate our beliefs by taking them up subjectively and passionately by "becoming a subject." Rationality and objectivity are hindrances to authenticity because they distance us from our existential predicaments. Existing, becoming a subject, is possible only when we have the God-relation. For Kierkegaard, nothing else suffices.

- Rather than present proofs for his views, Kierkegaard presents a series of edifying sketches and discourses describing three stages on life's way. In ascending order they are the aesthetic, ethical, and religious stages. The aesthetic stage is a futile fight against boredom, characterized by the pursuit of pleasure, especially sensuous pleasure. It is the most common stage. Next is the ethical stage, a way of life that involves making commitments to the norms of society; it is devoted to general (universal) principles that are continually revised according to changing humanistic values.

- For Kierkegaard, the religious stage of life is the highest. It is the only authentic way of living. Only the religious life acknowledges our dual nature and provides a way for the individual to transform the particular into the universal. This is accomplished by a teleological suspension of the ethical, a leap of faith.

Post-Reading Reflections

Now that you've had a chance to learn about the Existentialist, use your new knowledge to answer these questions.

1. Explain what Kierkegaard meant when he said that "truth is subjectivity." Is this the same as "truth is relative"?

2. How did Kierkegaard's application of the universal formula to his particular predicament influence his subsequent thinking? That is, what did he learn about love, faith, and the "God-relation" from his own experience?

3. Why is "becoming a subject" so important to Kierkegaard's philosophical enterprise?

4. Characterize the aesthete and the aesthetic stage on life's way.

5. Characterize the ethical individual and the ethical stage on life's way.

6. Characterize the religious individual and the religious stage on life's way.

7. How are the stages on life's way related?

8. What is the paradox at the heart of the leap of faith?

9. Why does Kierkegaard think that subjectivity is truth but objectivity is untruth? And what does this imply regarding efforts to scientifically and factually ground faith?

10. What role does edification play in Kierkegaard's writing? How does his extensive use of pseudonyms further this project?

11. Was Kierkegaard a Christian? Is this a trick question? Is asking if it is a trick question a trick question? Explain.

 MindTap

Experience MindTap through the activities highlighted in this chapter. Further explore this online, personalized learning tool to deepen your comprehension and improve your grades.

15

The Pragmatist
William James

As a rule we disbelieve all facts
and theories for which we have
no use.

— *William James*

Learning Objectives

After you complete this chapter, you should be able to:

- Define the concept of *pragmatism*.

- Explain what William James means by the cash value of an idea.

- Defend James against the charge that pragmatism, as he presents it, is another form of sophistic relativism.

- Assess the advantages and disadvantages of what has been described as pragmatism's crudeness and lack of philosophical precision.

- Explain what James means by the expression living at home in the universe.

- Critique James's claim that truth happens to an idea.

- Critique James's reliance on feelings of regret to defend our right to believe in free will.

- Describe the heroic life, according to James.

- Explain what a self-fulfilling prophecy is.

- State the pragmatic paradox.

Philosophy Timelines

IN THE INTRODUCTION we saw that philosophy has a reputation for being dangerous and subversive, for destroying people's beliefs without replacing them. We also noted that it has the almost contradictory reputation of being irrelevant, of making no real difference in our lives. "Philosophy bakes no bread," it is said. We have seen very powerful minds disagree about the most fundamental things: Does the "mind" exist? Do we have free will? Do the consequences of our actions matter if the motives are good? What is knowledge? Is reason more reliable than experience, or is it the other way around? Is there only one reality? Is there a God? What is virtue? Can we know anything? Is objectivity possible?

What can a reasonable person, a person of so-called common sense, make of all this? It seems as if each of the great philosophers builds a whole system around one or two insights. These systems can appear farfetched and bizarre compared with life as most of us experience it; though intellectually stimulating and interesting, they hardly seem *useful*. Isn't life too short to waste on philosophical arguments full of abstract terms that have no practical use except perhaps to provide philosophers with jobs?

The first truly great American philosopher demanded that philosophy answer these kinds of questions. **William James** (1842–1910) was the most original and influential advocate of **pragmatism**, an empirically based philosophy that defines knowledge and truth in terms of practical consequences. Like Mill, Marx, and Kierkegaard, James believed that philosophy must be more than a mere academic or intellectual enterprise. For James, philosophy's true purpose is to help us live by showing us how to discover and adopt beliefs that fit our individual needs—and temperaments. James thus shifted the focus of inquiry from the search for objectively true universal beliefs to the search for *beliefs that work for us*. His philosophy is provocative, enthusiastic, optimistic, and vigorous; it speaks to the nearly universal need for ideas and truths that matter to individuals. Voicing the lament of the common person—"What difference does this or that philosophy make to my life?"—James offers an uncommonly rich answer.

pragmatism

From the Greek for "deed"; belief that ideas have meaning or truth value to the extent that they produce practical results and effectively further our aims; empirically based philosophy that defines knowledge and truth in terms of practical consequences.

An American Original

William James was both a product and shaper of his time. The last half of the nineteenth century was a period of great confidence in science. People believed in continuous progress, influenced in part by a social interpretation of Darwin's theory of evolution that promised never-ending growth and improvement. This was also an age of bold action, as the Rockefellers and Carnegies and Vanderbilts carved up the land and established great industrial empires. People were impatient, wanting to move on, to get things done. In America, especially, this was an era of expansion, of strength. James captured this spirit so well and expressed himself in such a clear, powerful, "anti-intellectual" way that he became one of the best-known, most popular, and most influential American philosophers so far.

William James

© Cengage Learning®

The Education of a Philosopher

William James's father was a restless man, so William spent a considerable part of his childhood moving about. In 1855, James's father lost faith in American education

Apic/Hulton Archive/Getty Images

In spite of—or because of—their unconventional childhoods, Henry and William James emerged as two of the most talented and influential writers and thinkers of the nineteenth and early twentieth centuries.

and moved the entire family to Europe. They left America in June; in August, James's father sent William and his younger brother Henry (who became the famous novelist) to school in Geneva; by October the entire family had moved to England. Later they moved to France. In Boulogne, sixteen-year-old William started college and for the first time managed to attend the same school for an entire year.

That spring, however, the Jameses moved to Rhode Island. William wanted to continue his college studies, but his father was unimpressed with American colleges and prevented him from attending. A year and a half later, the family moved back to Switzerland. By this time, William's early interest in science had been replaced by a desire to be an artist, but after a year of art study, he turned back to science.

In 1861, William James entered Harvard as a chemistry major. His interests shifted to biology, anatomy, and ultimately physiology. James was so impressed by Jean Louis Agassiz (1807–1873), one of Harvard's most influential faculty members, that he accompanied him on an expedition to the Amazon. After eight months, James had had enough. He said, "When I get home I'm going to study philosophy all my days," but what he actually did was return to Harvard Medical School, where he had already taken some classes.

During his years as a student, James suffered mentally and physically. He described himself as being "on the continual verge of suicide." Unable to continue his medical studies because his hospital work put too much strain on his back, he went to Germany for the mineral baths. His letters home were funny and lighthearted, but elsewhere he noted that "thoughts of the pistol, the dagger and the bowl" were never far from him.[1] When he felt up to it, he returned to medical school and ultimately passed his licensing exam at age twenty-six. Later in the same year, though, he went into a severe depression, writing in his diary, "Nature & life have unfitted me for any affectionate relations with other individuals."[2] He was in a constant state of anxiety and dreaded being alone.

James was saved by an idea from the French philosopher Charles Renouvier (1815–1903), who had characterized free will as the ability to hold on to one idea among a number of possibilities. Willing himself to hold on to the idea of health and well-being, James effectively *decided* to get well: He *willed* himself well, by concentrating all his mental energy to produce "the self-governing resistance of the ego to the world."[3] James announced, "My first act of freedom will be to believe in free will." His depression lifted like a veil, and he was at last free to follow the restless intellect he had inherited from his father. As a result of his lingering sickness and unhappiness, he developed an interest in the relationship between mind and body. Speaking of James, a friend said:

> "Active tension," uncertainty, unpredictability, extemporized adaptation, risk, change, anarchy, unpretentiousness, naturalness—these are the qualities of life which James finds most palatable, and which give him the deepest sense of well-being. They are at the same time the qualities which he deems most authentic, the accents in which the existent world speaks to him most directly.[4]

In 1872, James completed his education and took a job teaching physiology at Harvard. Within three years he was made assistant professor and remained affiliated with Harvard for nearly thirty-six years—the rest of his professional life.

In 1876, James's father announced to William, "I have met your future wife." And indeed he had. Alice Gibbens was a bright, vibrant, strikingly honest young woman. Though they fell in love, William declared himself unfit to marry her and sent her a series of self-critical, suffering letters designed to discourage any thoughts of marriage. Alice understood William well and so went to Quebec, saying she did so "to remove temptation from his path." The distance apparently diminished James's fears, however, and made Alice even more appealing. His letters became ardent efforts at courtship. Two years after his father's announcement, William and Alice were married.[5]

Though William James had found the support and care he needed to help steady his restless temperament and tendency to depression, for the rest of his life he struggled to remain healthy, using his particular good humor, aggressive intellect, and psychological insights—but he gave credit for what success he achieved to his wife for saving him.

The Philosopher as Hero

James's interest in medicine and physiology developed into curiosity about psychology, and in 1878 the Henry Holt Company signed him to write a psychology textbook. It took him twelve years to finish *Principles of Psychology* (1890), but the wait was worth it, and the book's wide appeal established James as an important figure in the early history of modern psychology.

The late nineteenth century teetered between pessimistic despair and optimistic faith in scientific progress. Thomas Eakins's painting *The Agnew Clinic* depicts the kind of medical theater William James might have attended as a medical student.

About this time, his focus began to shift once more. He became increasingly interested in philosophy, but because of his broad interests, his bouts with depression, and his experience in science, medicine, and psychology, he saw philosophy in a different light than did most professional philosophers of his time. James regarded philosophy as a matter of personal involvement, as a function of the will, and as a means to overcome despair and futility. He developed the kind of philosophy *he needed to cope* with his life and presented it in an appealing and powerful series of lectures that made it accessible to others.

Much of James's work is couched in heroic, often masculine terms, which were more fashionable and common then than they are now. But we would be doing ourselves and James a serious disservice if we rejected his philosophy for that reason. Pragmatism is not a *male* philosophy but, rather, a philosophy that includes an element of heroic struggle, a philosophy of courage and action, a philosophy of vitality. A product of his times, James expressed these values in typically masculine terms. He was trying to resist inertia, to resist giving in to self-pity and self-defeat—and he used a vocabulary of heroic action to do so. James called on us to become consciously responsible for our lives by strenuous exertion of will. In our contemporary era, which seems so often to reduce us to the helpless products of environment and heredity, a philosophy like James's is a refreshing vote of confidence in the individual human spirit.

James himself did not actually live the kind of life he described as ideal. But he wanted to. He recognized the dangers and limits of too much sentimentality,

If … man's nature … makes him do what he does, how does his action differ from that of a stone or a tree? Have we not parted with any ground for responsibility? … Holding men to responsibility may make a decided difference in their future behavior; holding a stone or tree to responsibility is a meaningless performance.

— John Dewey

too much "tender-mindedness," and offered what he saw as a healthier, more useful alternative. He understood—from his own weaknesses—the frustration of being unable to stick to anything, the frustration of not knowing what we want, the frustration of trying to make up our minds and choose one important thing. James's own experiences convinced him that life was too important, too complex, too rich to reduce to any of the philosophical systems that had gone before. And so he refused to offer a system; instead, he offered a *method* for marshaling the will. But his method was grounded in philosophy, because only philosophy "has the patience and courage to work continually at a problem when common sense and even science have long since set it aside or given it up."[6]

The Philosopher as Advocate

> *If we take the whole history of philosophy, the systems reduce themselves to a few main types which, under all the technical verbiage in which the ingenious intellect of man envelops them, are just so many visions, modes of feeling the whole push, and seeing the whole drift of life, forced on one by one's total character and experience, and on the whole preferred—there is no other truthful word—as one's best working attitude.*
>
> *— William James*

William James published his first philosophy book, *The Will to Believe and Other Essays in Popular Philosophy*, in 1896. In 1898, he was invited to give the Gifford Lectures in Edinburgh, Scotland, a rare honor for an American. These lectures were published in 1902 as *The Varieties of Religious Experience*. A classic of contemporary philosophy, this superb book still sells widely, its popularity extending far beyond academic circles.

After returning to Harvard, James delivered a series of lectures on pragmatism and repeated these lectures at Columbia University to an audience of more than one thousand people. They were published as *Pragmatism* in 1907. *Pragmatism* also sold well and attracted the interest of both scholars and the general public. James was cheered up by its reception, to the point of announcing to his brother:

> I shouldn't be surprised if ten years hence it should be rated as "epoch-making," for of the definitive triumph of that general way of thinking I can entertain no doubt whatever—I believe it to be something quite like the protestant reformation.[7]

James's work became so influential that he effectively altered the shape of what came to be known as American philosophy. He taught, among others, Supreme Court Justice Oliver Wendell Holmes, Teddy Roosevelt, writer Gertrude Stein, and philosopher George Santayana. (Of all his students, he particularly disliked Roosevelt and Santayana.)

In 1907, the same year *Pragmatism* appeared, James retired from Harvard at the age of sixty-five. Responding at last to the criticism that he had failed to present a sustained, systematic explanation of his ideas, James resolved to craft a fuller expression of pragmatism in his remaining years. To his brother he wrote, "I live in apprehension lest the Avenger should cut me off before I get my message out. I hesitate to leave the volumes I have already published without their logical complement."[8]

James compiled a volume of essays, *The Meaning of Truth*, and one of lectures, *A Pluralistic Universe*. He hoped these books would be considered more scholarly and systematic than his others, but they were not the "logical complement" he sought. Alas, the Avenger did cut off the old rebel, the anti-intellectual champion of living philosophy, and these final books were published in 1911, one year after his death. Ironically, perhaps, William James remained truer to his philosophy than if he had written a more scholarly, systematic version of it, for then he would have been required to present an appeal to the abstract and logical niceties he had spent his whole life denouncing.

The very last words of James's very last essay reflect the spirit of pragmatism better than any scholarly system: "There is no conclusion. What has been concluded that we might conclude regarding it? There are no fortunes to be told and there is no advice to be given. Farewell."[9]

Charles Sanders Peirce

The first expression of pragmatism actually appears in the work of **Charles Sanders Peirce** (1839–1914). The son of a Harvard mathematics professor, Peirce studied philosophy, science, and mathematics, and he received a master's degree in mathematics and chemistry from Harvard. After working at the Harvard astronomical observatory for three years, he went to work for the United States Coastal and Geodetic Survey, where he remained for thirty years. He also lectured briefly at Johns Hopkins University. A brilliant but eccentric man, Peirce was never able to secure a full-time university position. As a result, he had a difficult time publishing his work. The last years of his life were clouded by physical infirmity, poverty, and social isolation and rejection. Through it all, William James remained his friend, supporting him and presenting his ideas to a wide audience. After Peirce's death, his writings were collected and published. Although massive and difficult, his work has achieved a measure of success and is garnering renewed interest among philosophers.

Charles Sanders Peirce

© Cengage Learning®

Peirce's "Pragmaticism"

Peirce first presented what he referred to as "pragmatism" in an 1878 article titled "How to Make Our Ideas Clear," written for a popular magazine. This essay was ignored by philosophers until James devoted a series of lectures to it. James had intended only to present Peirce's ideas to a wider audience, but Peirce so strenuously objected to James's version of pragmatism that he "gave" him the term and coined yet another one for himself, *pragmaticism:*

> [The] word "pragmatism" has gained general recognition in a generalized sense that seems to argue power of growth and vitality. The famed psychologist, James, first took it up.... So then, the writer, finding his bantling "pragmatism" so promoted, feels that it is time to kiss his child good-by and relinquish it to a higher destiny; while to serve the precise purpose of expressing the original definition, he begs to announce the birth of the word "pragmaticism," which is ugly enough to be safe from kidnappers.[10]

Peirce was not just being cranky in insisting on clear and precise use of his term. His philosophy rested on a new theory of meaning. He coined the term *pragmaticism* from the Greek word *pragma*, which means "an act" or "a consequence." He wanted to show that the meanings of words depend on some kind of action. Peirce argued that ideas are meaningful only when they translate into actions and predict experiences associated with actions.

Pragmatic Theory of Meaning

Peirce argued that the *only differences between the meanings of words are how they test out in experience*. He thus equated meaning with the effects related to words, saying, "Our idea of anything *is* our idea of its sensible effects." Meaningful statements refer to predictable, observable, practical effects (consequences). "Consequently, the sum of experimental phenomena that a proposition implies makes up its entire bearing upon human conduct."[11] If a word cannot be tied to any observable practical results, it is thereby meaningless, for its meaning is the sum total of its practical consequences.

Peirce's scientific background and interests influenced his strong dislike for the kind of vague, abstract rationalism found in Descartes and other "impractical" system spinners. Descartes had separated the mind and thinking from any necessary connection with experience. Peirce pointed out, however, that all thinking and all meaning are *context dependent*. Context includes material, social, and emotional components, as well as an intellectual one.

Agreeing with the empiricists, Peirce argued that meaning is based on experience and determined by experiment. He did not mean just formal, scientific experiment but also the kind of informal testing we do every day, as when, say, we test a recently varnished tabletop to see whether it is hard yet. We "test" to see whether it is appropriate to apply the word *hard* to this surface; we "experiment" by looking to see whether it looks damp, by touching it lightly, and so on. Things are not hard in some abstract, ideal, constant sense but in the real world of causal and material relationships:

> Let us illustrate this rule by examples; and, to begin with the simplest one possible, let us ask what we mean by calling a thing *hard*. Evidently that it will not be scratched by many other substances. The whole conception of this quality, as of every other, lies in its conceived effects. There is absolutely no difference between a hard thing and a soft thing so long as they are not brought to the test.[12]

If there is no way of testing the effects of words (and ideas), no way of verifying their public consequences, they are meaningless. *Meaningful ideas always make a practical difference.*

Pragmatism

Like Peirce, James yearned for a philosophy free of "meaningless abstractions," a philosophy that stretched far beyond the merely technical and rationally coherent to embrace the whole of life. Building on Peirce's foundation, James advocated a new vision of a philosophical approach that he claimed others had recognized before, but only in parts. In the process, James went beyond Peirce's intentions and used pragmatism to present a moral theory and to make a case for religious belief. We might even say he made pragmatism into a kind of philosophical religion. That is, James attempted to present a philosophy that could provide values and ideals worth striving for and that could satisfy our need to believe without appealing to metaphysical abstractions.

Pragmatic Method and Philosophy

James reflected a growing trend among philosophers to resist the abstract, to demand relevance and immediacy, and to deal with the "living issues" that face us. As he put it, "The whole function of philosophy ought to be to find out what definite difference it will make to you and me, at definite instants of our life, if this world-formula or that world-formula be the true one." There is a strong moral tone implicit in this position: It is not enough for philosophers to tackle questions of consistency or spin out grand theories. People are struggling through their lives, suffering, rejoicing, searching, and dying. We have a right—indeed, an obligation—to ask, "What difference does the theory of forms make to me, *now*? How is my life *different* if a tree falling in the forest does or does not make a sound? What *practical difference* does it make to me if the mind and body are two different substances?"

James often talked about feeling "at home" in the universe. Pragmatism was meant to be a *method* for solving those problems that interfere with feeling at home. James looked for what he called the *cash value* of statements, the practical payoff, and he rejected any philosophy that lacked it. This includes virtually all metaphysics:

> The pragmatic method is primarily a method of settling metaphysical disputes that otherwise might be interminable. Is the world one or many?—fated or free?—material or spiritual?—here are notions either of which may or may not hold good of the world; and disputes over such notions are unending. The pragmatic method in such cases is to try to interpret each notion by tracing its respective practical consequences. What difference would it practically make to anyone if this notion rather than that notion were true? If no practical difference whatever can be traced, then the alternatives mean practically the same thing, and all dispute is idle. Whenever a dispute is serious, we ought to be able to show some practical difference that must follow from one side or the other's being right....
>
> A pragmatist turns his back resolutely and once and for all upon a lot of inveterate habits dear to professional philosophers. He turns away from abstraction and insufficiency, from verbal solutions, from bad *a priori* reasons, from fixed principles, closed systems, and pretended absolutes and origins. He turns toward concreteness and adequacy, toward facts, toward action and toward power.[13]

James referred to theories as "only man-made language, a conceptual shorthand...in which we write our reports of nature" and he added that "languages, as is well known, tolerate much choice of expression and many dialects."[14]

If any theory with a practical payoff is true, does it not follow that one theory is as good as another to those who believe it? It would if James were advocating sophistic relativism, but for the most part, he did not see pragmatism that way. He saw it as a *method* rather than a collection of beliefs. Thus, he saw a use for various theories of verification and meaning as long as they are ultimately used to determine the "cash value" of beliefs. We might benefit from using both empirical and rational criteria, for instance:

> Pragmatism...asks its usual question, "Grant an idea or belief to be true," it says, "what concrete difference will its being true make in any one's actual life? How will the truth be realized? What experiences will be different from those which would

> *But if materialism without idealism is blind, idealism without materialism is void.*
> — Charles Sanders Peirce

> *The philosophy which is so important in each of us is not a technical matter, it is our more or less dumb sense of what life honestly and deeply means.*
> — William James

> *Many of you are students of philosophy, and have already felt in your own persons the scepticism and unreality that too much grubbing in the abstract roots of things will breed. This is, indeed, one of the regular fruits of the overstudious career.*
> — William James

> *All our scientific and philosophic ideals are altars to unknown gods.*
> — William James

obtain if the belief were false? What, in short, is the truth's cash-value in experiential terms?"

The moment pragmatism asks this question, it sees the answer: *True ideas are those that we can assimilate, validate, corroborate and verify. False ideas are those that we cannot.* That is the practical difference it makes to us to have true ideas; that, therefore, is the meaning of truth, for it is all that truth is known as....

Our account of truth is an account of truths in the plural, of processes....Truth for us is simply a collective name for verification-processes.[15]

From a strictly logical perspective, James's position seems to contradict itself, much as strict relativism contradicts itself: He asserts the truth of his theory, which in turn seems to deny the possibility of "a truth." If a theory is merely a "man-made language," then why should we speak James's language?

A possible answer is to view James as an *advocate*, whose chief purpose isn't to present a strict *argument* but, rather, to make a broad enough case to convert and convince a wide audience. If we accept at face value James's insistence that he was offering us a *method* to live by, then we have to approach him differently from the way we would if he were offering a philosophy as such. Indeed, James himself sometimes refers to pragmatism as a *creed*. A philosophical creed is a body of beliefs we can devote our lives to, whereas a philosophical *argument* is an attempt to make a rational case; the former appeals primarily to our hearts, the latter to our minds.

Pragmatism has been called "philosophically crude" because of its apparent indifference to theoretical precision and consistency. Yet it can be argued that precision and consistency *pay* in some areas—science and medicine, for instance—but *cost* in others—for example, when we demand rigor and precision that are inappropriate for the issue before us.

James believed our lives are shaped by our beliefs. And we *need to believe more than we can ever "prove" by overly strict, objective, neutral standards*, which he calls "agnostic rules for truth-seeking." He says, "If one should assume that pure reason is what settles our opinions, he would fly in the teeth of the facts." What does settle our opinions, then? James answers, the *will to believe*. And what we believe is a function of whether we are tough or tender-minded.

The Temper of Belief

In addition to being a philosopher, James was an innovative, groundbreaking psychologist; as such, he refused to confine philosophy to the intellectual or merely academic realm. For him, the function of philosophy shifted from revealing "the truth" to learning how to live in the world. In psychological terms, pragmatic philosophy is meant to provide a way of becoming better adjusted to the world. This helps account for the kind of inconsistency that troubles more traditional philosophers: Living "at home in the universe" does *not*, at least according to James, depend on knowing and believing what is true but on believing things that suit *us*. We can classify people, James thought, into two temperamental types:

> Now the particular difference of temperament that I have in mind in making these remarks is one that has counted in literature, art, government, and manners as well as in philosophy. In manners we find formalists and free-and-easy persons.

In government, authoritarians and anarchists. In literature, purists or academi-cals, and realists. In art, classics and romantics. You recognize these contrasts as familiar; well, in philosophy we have a very similar contrast expressed in the pair of terms "rationalist" and "empiricist," "empiricist" meaning your lover of facts in all their crude variety, "rationalist" meaning your devotee to abstract and eternal principles....

I will write these traits down in two columns. I think you will practically recog-nize the two types of mental make-up that I mean if I head the columns by the titles "tender-minded" and "tough-minded" respectively.

THE TENDER-MINDED	THE TOUGH-MINDED
Rationalistic (going by "principles"),	Empiricist (going by "facts"),
Intellectualistic,	Sensationalistic,
Idealistic,	Materialistic,
Optimistic,	Pessimistic,
Religious,	Irreligious,
Free-willist,	Fatalistic,
Monistic,	Pluralistic,
Dogmatical.	Sceptical.

Each of you probably knows some well-marked example of each type, and you know what each example thinks of the example on the other side of the line. They have a low opinion of each other. Their antagonism, whenever as individuals their temperaments have been intense, has formed in all ages a part of the philosophic atmosphere of the time. It forms a part of the philosophic atmosphere today. The tough think of the tender as sentimentalists and soft-heads. The tender feel the tough to be unrefined, callous, or brutal. Their mutual reaction is very much like that that takes place when Bostonian tourists mingle with a population like that of Cripple Creek.... [But] few of us are tender-footed Bostonians pure and simple, and few are typical Rocky Mountain toughs, in philosophy. Most of us have a hankering for the good things on both sides of the line.[16]

This life is worth living, we can say, since it is what we make it, from the moral point of view; and we are determined to make it from that point of view so far as we have anything to do with it, a success.
— William James

PHILOSOPHICAL QUERY

As an experiment, analyze today's two dominant political parties according to James's tough–tender typology. Consider, especially, the seemingly intractable low opinion Democrat and Republican partisans have for their opposites. If, as James said, "most of us have a hankering for the good things on both sides of the line," why do you suppose it is so difficult to understand "them"—those folks we see as profoundly, fundamentally wrong, not wrong on an issue here or a fact there, but wrong in their vision of life, wrong to the core?

MindTap
Discussing Philosophy

James thought philosophy had been dominated historically by extremists, so that most philosophies are unbalanced in either the tough or tender direction. The same might be said of contemporary philosophy. Today's tough-minded philoso-phies view scientific knowledge as the only secure kind; they include the strictest forms of behavioristic psychology and analytically oriented philosophies, and they apply such rigid standards of meaning that most basic, meaning-of-life questions are dismissed as meaningless. The extremes of tender-minded philosophy include anti-intellectual theology, pop psychologies, and "metaphysics." Such extremism has rendered philosophy inappropriate for the vast majority of us, who are a mixture of tough and tender. But because we are easily persuaded, we end up trying to follow fashion or what James called the "most impressive philosopher in the neighborhood"—or the most impressive theologian, politician, or psychologist.

James believed that when we succumb to the "most impressive philosopher in the neighborhood," we do psychic violence to our unexpressed, preconscious sense of the world. We deny important parts of ourselves and exaggerate others. When we try to live according to beliefs that do not suit us, we become dissatisfied and unhappy. The issue, then, for James is how to find a *cause*, how to find beliefs worth living for, worth fighting and dying for—how to find a philosophical religion.

For Deeper Consideration

James says that living "at home in the universe" depends on believing things that suit us temperamentally, and he divides the human temperament into two types: the tender-minded and the tough-minded. Contrast these two types by categorizing political parties, churches, academic subjects, and tastes in art or music as tender-minded or tough-minded. Is it easy, or possible, to find pure examples of each type? Do nations and historical eras fall into these categories? What did James think happens to us if we can't find beliefs that resonate with our temperamental type? Do you agree, or do you think that we can and should mold our temperaments to fit the facts—"the truth"?

> *Individual action is a means and not our end. Individual pleasure is not our end; we are all putting our shoulders to the wheel for an end that none of us can catch more than a glimpse at—that which the generations are working out.*
> — Charles Sanders Peirce

The Will to Believe

According to James, we live according to beliefs that are products of our own temperaments and experience; our beliefs are not the products of abstract reasoning. Rather, we manage to find reasons to believe what we want and need to believe. And we have the right to do that, according to James, who once said he would have been better off titling his famous lecture *The Right to Believe* rather than *The Will to Believe*.

Because life *demands* a response, *demands* action, we have no choice but to believe *something*. Life presents us with what James calls *forced options*. We must make decisions whether we want to or not (even "not deciding" is a decision). We *cannot* remain detached and disinterested; life simply does not allow it. We are compelled to decide and to act, and reason is not a sufficient force for action. We do not act on what we understand but on what we believe. The rationalist's and skeptic's demands for certainty cannot be met, yet we continue to live and act—without intellectual certainty:

I, therefore, for one cannot see my way to accept the agnostic rules for truth-seeking, or willfully agree to keep my willing nature out of the game. I cannot do so for the plain reason that *a rule of thinking which would absolutely prevent me from acknowledging certain kinds of truth if those kinds of truth were really there, would be an irrational rule....* If we had an infallible intellect with its objective certitudes, we might feel ourselves disloyal to such a perfect organ of knowledge in not trusting to it exclusively. But if we are empiricists, if we believe that no bell in us tolls to let us know for certain when truth is in our grasp, then it seems a piece of idle fantasticality to preach so solemnly our duty of waiting for the bell. Indeed we *may* wait if we will—I hope you do not think I am denying that—(we ought, on the contrary, delicately and profoundly to respect one another's mental freedom) but if we do wait, we do so at our own peril as much as if we believed.[17]

The intellect does not discover the truths in which we believe; the will creates truth.

Truth Happens to an Idea

The rationalists' model of truth was taken from logic and mathematics. Rationalists said truth is universal, which amounts to saying it is *contextless*. The sum "2 + 2 = 4" is true at all times, in all languages, for all creeds, for all ages, ethnicities, and genders of people, in all conditions of health or sickness. Indeed, because it is true for all "rational entities," it is true throughout the universe. (See Chapters 5 and 9.)

James rejected this simplistic, universalist notion of truth. He said experience makes it clear that ideas *become* true. Elsewhere, he said "truth *happens* to an idea." We *decide* whether or not an idea is true by "testing" it, as Peirce pointed out. James extended Peirce's pragmaticist theory of truth:

Any idea upon which we can ride, so to speak; any idea that will carry us prosperously from any one part of our experience to any other part, linking things satisfactorily, working securely, simplifying, saving labor, is true for just so much, true in so far forth, true instrumentally.[18]

If James is correct, we accept ideas as true only after we test them against our past experiences. Even if we have a tendency to reject new ideas, the public, community-wide aspect of truth-seeking (which Peirce emphasized) forces us—or most of us—to test and reevaluate ideas, keeping some and discarding others as we and the world change.

We have all witnessed this process. It is especially clear in the areas of moral and religious belief (areas James thought vital to human happiness). For example, looking back over history, we see that ideas about vice have changed. Few contemporary Americans believe that it is wrong for women to appear in public with bare ankles, but many people used to believe that it was. Churches regularly convene councils to modify basic articles of faith, and entirely new religions emerge when old ones no longer *pay*.

Individuals and groups may simply refuse to accept changes, but on the whole, our beliefs do change, and thus our notion of what is true about the world changes—though, as James observed, we try to hang on to as many of our old ideas as possible until

Man is not to blame for what he is. He didn't make himself. He has no control over himself. All the control is vested in his temperament—which he did not create—and in the circumstances which hedge him round from the cradle to the grave and which he did not devise....He is as purely a piece of automatic mechanism as is a watch....He is a subject for pity, and not blame.

— Mark Twain

The individual...meets a new experience that puts them to a strain. Somebody contradicts them; or in a reflective moment he discovers that they contradict each other; or he hears of facts with which they are incompatible; or desires arise in him which they cease to satisfy. The result is an inward trouble to which his mind till then had been a stranger, and from which he seeks to escape by modifying his previous mass of opinions...until at last some new idea comes up which he can graft upon the ancient stock....

This new idea is then adopted as the true one. It preserves the older stock of truths with a minimum of modification, stretching them enough to make them admit the novelty, but conceiving them in ways as familiar as the case leaves possible. [A radical] explanation, violating all our preconceptions, would never pass as a true account....We would scratch around industriously till we found something less eccentric. The most violent revolutions in an individual's beliefs leave most of his old order standing.[19]

Ideas are tested and accepted or rejected based on how well they work for us. Sometimes we see the virtue in a new idea; other times, we can no longer live with the stress and energy it takes to hold on to an old one. So there is no such thing as disinterested truth. *Pragmatic truth is human truth.* "Purely objective truth," James asserts, "plays no role whatsoever, is nowhere to be found." He adds that the most

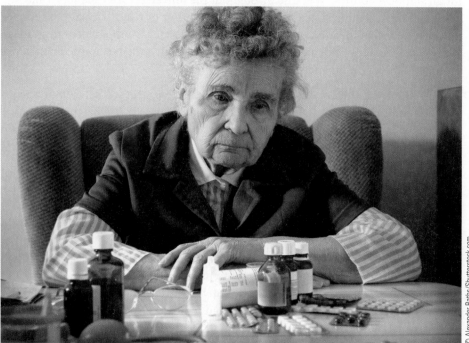

William James believed that as conditions change "truth happens to an idea." Changes in health care and medical technology have led to longer lives for more people, yet not everyone wants to stay alive at any cost. So we find ourselves wrestling with ancient philosophical questions about the meaning of life, the virtues of suffering, and the right to die. Truth is happening here.

absolute-seeming truths "also once were plastic": "They were called true for human reasons. They also mediate between still earlier truths and what in those days were novel observations."[20]

Useful, human truth is alive; rationalistic, abstract, dogmatic truth is "the dead heart of the living tree." Truth grows.

PHILOSOPHICAL QUERY

Can you think of recent examples supporting the claim that "truth happens to an idea"? Some Protestant churches, for example, have revised their once absolute policies regarding birth control, abortion, and gay marriage because older beliefs lack "cash value" for many of today's churchgoers. These churches usually experience a period of soul-searching turmoil, wrestling with the dilemma of holding on to old beliefs or losing touch with their congregations. Can you cite one or two recent examples of truth happening to an idea from current events or from your own situation?

The Dilemma of Determinism

James agreed with most moral philosophers that free will is a necessary condition for moral responsibility. He offered a unique and intriguing argument for believing in free will in a famous essay titled "The Dilemma of Determinism." James begins with a novel admission: "I disclaim openly on the threshold all pretension to prove to you that freedom of the will is true. The most I hope is to induce some of you to follow my own example in assuming it true, and acting as if it were true." Having warned us not to expect an airtight argument, James goes on to present a compelling case nonetheless.

Determinism is the belief that everything that happens must happen exactly the way it does. Some materialistic philosophers and scientists say determinism is inevitable since all matter is governed by cause and effect and follows laws of nature. Possibilities are identical to actualities; the future is already contained in the present. We cannot influence the future; it lacks ambiguity, having been sealed in the distant past. James asks:

> What does determinism profess? It professes that those parts of the universe already laid down absolutely appoint and decree what the other parts shall be.... Indeterminism, on the contrary, says that the parts have a certain amount of loose play on one another, so that the laying down of one of them does not necessarily determine what the others shall be. It admits that possibilities may be in excess of actualities, and that things not yet revealed to our knowledge may really in themselves be ambiguous.[21]

Does determinism square with our actual feelings? James suggests that we answer this question by considering a newspaper article about the brutal murder of a woman by her husband. Ignoring his wife's screams for mercy, the husband chopped her to pieces. James asks whether any sane person can read such an account

determinism
The belief that everything that happens must happen exactly the way it does because all matter is governed by cause and effect and follows laws of nature.

"The Problem Is Not a Real One"

It must be observed that those learned professors of philosophy or psychology who deny the existence of free will do so only in their professional moments and in their studies and lecture rooms. For when it comes to doing anything practical, even of the most trivial kind, they invariably behave as if they and others were free. They inquire from you at dinner whether you will choose this or that dish. They will ask a child why he told a lie, and will punish him for not having chosen the way of truthfulness. All of which is consistent with a belief in free will. This should cause us to suspect that the problem is not a real one; and this I believe is the case. The dispute is merely verbal, and is due to nothing but a confusion about the meanings of words.

W. T. Stace, *Religion and the Modern Mind* (New York: Lippincott, 1952), p. 279.

> *None of us can help the things life has done to us. They're done before you realize it, and once they're done they make you do other things until at last everything comes between you and what you'd like to be.*
> — Eugene O'Neill

and not feel deep regret. But if the determinists are right, what is the point of regret? Determinists have no reasonable grounds for regretting anything:

> The judgment of regret calls the murder bad. Calling a thing bad means, if it means anything at all, that the thing ought not to be, that something else ought to be in its stead. Determinism, in denying that anything else can be in its stead, virtually defines the universe as a place in which what ought to be is impossible—in other words, as an organism whose constitution is afflicted with an incurable taint, an irremediable flaw....
>
> It is absurd to regret the murder alone. It could not be different.... But how then about the judgments of regret themselves? If they are wrong, other judgments, judgments of approval, ought to be in their place. But as they are necessitated, nothing else could be in their place; and [for the determinist] the universe is just what it was before—namely, a place in which what ought to be appears impossible.[22]

Isn't it virtually impossible to think that such a murder "ought" to have occurred, given past conditions? Isn't it virtually impossible to be indifferent that it occurred? If James is correct, no sane person can help feeling some degree of sadness and regret when confronted by such horrors. Yet, if the determinists are correct, such feelings are utterly pointless. *There is no rational ground for moral feelings, because "ought" can have no meaning.* If the determinists are correct, we are caused to have senseless, absurd, utterly false feelings and ideas.

James acknowledged that there is no scientific and objective way to refute such a possibility. But he insisted that our deep, unshakable moral sense of right and wrong, combined with our feelings of regret, make a *compelling* case for our *need* and *right* to believe in free will. We have to believe at least in the possibility, however remote, that some children will not be abused because some adults choose to help them; we have to believe that some bad will be avoided and some good done by our actions.

The Inner Sense of Freedom

James believed that change, surprise, and chance are regular parts of our experience. "There are novelties, struggles, losses, gains...some things at least are decided here and now…the passing moment may contain some novelty, be an original starting-point of events, and not merely a push from elsewhere."[23]

James appealed directly to our *inner sense of freedom* to verify his claim, a sense shared by most people. (The possible exceptions are philosophical and psychological extremists). He was convinced that most of us have a deep "spiritual need" to believe that we are active agents who exert control over significant aspects of our lives, that we affect events, that we make a difference. We *need* this belief for our spiritual and mental well-being—and we have a *right* to believe what we need to believe.

James thought the prestige and influence of science make people try to believe in determinism, but he did not believe that the evidence supporting determinism is conclusive. Echoing Hume, he claimed that we need to believe in a "more rational shape" for nature than our individual experience reveals. Consequently, we *believe* in the uniformity of laws of nature. But this uniformity of nature cannot be conclusively proved true, as Hume showed (Chapter 10). Belief in free will cannot be conclusively proved to be correct either, James noted, but this does not make it inferior to belief in determinism. The basic unprovable status of both beliefs is similar:

> All the magnificent achievements of mathematical and physical science—our doctrines of evolution, of uniformity to law, and the rest—proceed from our indomitable desire to cast the world into a more rational shape in our minds than the shape into which it is thrown there by the crude order of our experience.…I, for one, feel as free to try conceptions of moral as of mechanical or logical rationality. If a certain formula for expressing the nature of the world violates my moral demand, I shall feel as free to throw it overboard, or at least doubt it, as if it disappointed my demand for uniformity of sequence, for example; the one demand being, so far as I can see, quite as subjective and emotional as the other is. The principle of causality, for example—what is it but a postulate, an empty name covering simply a demand that the sequence of events shall one day manifest a deeper kind of belonging of one thing with another than the mere arbitrary juxtaposition which now phenomenally appears? It is as much an altar to an unknown god as the one Saint Paul found at Athens. All our scientific and philosophic ideals are altars to unknown gods. Uniformity is as much so as is free will.[24]

In the absence of conclusive proof, we are free to *decide* which belief better suits our needs. Believing as he did in the primacy of morality, James asserted that belief in free will better serves our need for "moral rationality." And since neither belief can be conclusively rejected, he argued that we have the right to test belief in free will against our regular experiences. If it "pays" more than believing that we have no control over our lives, then clearly it is the superior belief.

Perhaps the strongest argument against determinism is the fact that almost no one really believes that absolutely everything he or she thinks, hopes, and does was determined from the first moments of the existence of the universe. Life presents us with inescapable moments of choice. How we respond is what matters most:

> Each man must act as he thinks best; and, if he is wrong, so much the worse for him. We stand on a mountain pass in the midst of whirling snow and blinding mist, through which we get glimpses now and then of paths which may be deceptive. If we stand still we shall be frozen to death. If we take the wrong road we shall be

dashed to pieces. We do not certainly know whether there is any right one. What must we do? "Be strong and of a good courage." Act for the best, hope for the best, and take what comes.[25]

How can we know what is best? James says that we must discover the essence of the good.

Discussing Philosophy

Morality and the Good

James rejected metaphysical attempts to define the good. He argued that the only way to understand the good life is to study what people actually want and strive for. He surveyed and rejected strictly Aristotelian, hedonistic, Christian, Kantian, and utilitarian ethics (Chapters 6, 7, 8, 11, and 12), though he borrowed from each:

> Various essences of good have thus been … proposed as bases of the ethical system. …
>
> No one of the measures that have actually been proposed has, however, given general satisfaction. … The best, on the whole, of these marks and measures of goodness seems to be the capacity to bring happiness. But in order not to break down fatally, this test must be taken to cover innumerable acts and impulses that never *aim* at happiness; so that, after all, in seeking for a universal principle we inevitably are carried onward to the *most* universal principle—that *the essence of good is simply to satisfy demand.* The demand may be for anything under the sun. There is really no more ground for supposing that all our demands can be accounted for by one universal underlying kind of motive than there is ground for supposing that all physical phenomena are cases of a single law.[26]

We have a basic obligation to "maximize satisfactions" and minimize frustrations, not just for ourselves but for others as well, according to James. Such a course is most likely to lead to happiness and increase the world's stock of goodness. Yet maximizing satisfaction must remain a fundamental, general obligation. The sheer number of people, coupled with the sheer number of demands we each have, makes being more specific impossible. All we can do is try our best to increase the general level of satisfaction and goodness while remaining aware of our fallibility.

James did not offer an ethical *theory* as such, though he suggested moral guidelines. He proposed a form of altruistic utilitarianism based on an optimistic vision of social progress. He believed that modern civilization is better than past eras were—he cited examples of slavery and torture—because the constant give-and-take, the "push and pull," of history results in continual refinement of satisfactions. The radical's forward drive is compensated for by the conservative's inertia; the dreamer's whimsy balances and is balanced by the scientist's objective eye, and so on.

It is important not to lose sight of the fact that James was also a psychologist and scientist. He gave more credence to observation and experience than to systematic argument. Further, he did not believe in universal moral principles or in the possibility of any finite, closed expression of morality. Thus, from his perspective, the kind of argument and system that would satisfy most philosophers would also falsify the reality of moral experience.

> *There can be no final truth in ethics any more than in physics until the last man has had his experience and said his say.*
> — William James

The Heroic Life

William James believed that life without heroic struggle is dull, mediocre, and empty. He was thinking of two approaches to life. In one, we choose (will) safety, security, and compliance. We try to avoid risks, try to avoid stress, try to avoid hassles. The other kind of life deliberately courts danger, courage, risk; it is based on a will to excitement and passion.

James was not advising us to take up hang gliding and shooting the rapids. He was talking about a "real fight" for something important, about the struggle between good and evil. He said evil is "out there" to be resisted and fought. We might find it in the form of discrimination or toxic dumping. When we do, we can ignore it, make a token effort at resisting it by voicing our objections, or actually do something. If we confront it, we could lose our jobs, money, time, or solid A grade-point average. We might fail. We might even be wrong: What we perceived as evil might not be evil. But at least we fought for or against something:

Larry Downing/Reuters/Landov

> For my own part, I do not know what the sweat and blood of this life mean, if they mean anything short of this. If this life be not a real fight, in which something is eternally gained for the universe by success, it is no better than a game of private theatricals from which we may withdraw at will. But it *feels* like a real fight—as if there were something really wild in the universe which we, with all our idealities and faithfulnesses, are needed to redeem: and first of all to redeem our own hearts from atheisms and fears. For such is a half-wild, half-saved universe adapted. The deepest thing in our nature is...this dumb region of the heart in which we dwell alone with our willingness and unwillingness, our faiths and fears.[27]

According to James, struggle and effort are vital elements of the good life. He believed that the "strenuous mood" is superior to sitting back and drifting along. Thus, he did not think much of the Epicurean ideal of the retreat to the Garden or of Stoic detachment when either meant reduced

"It is simply our total character and personal genius that are on trial," James says. "From this unsparing practical ordeal no professor's lectures and no array of books can save us." When we're tempted by the "easy-going mood," to evade our trials and ordeals, it helps to be reminded of how much more is possible. Consider Tammy Duckworth, pictured here. In 2004, as a helicopter pilot in Iraq, Duckworth lost both legs and partial use of an arm. Rather than accept medical retirement, she chose to remain in the National Guard. In 2009, Duckworth was appointed to the U.S. Department of Veterans Affairs as Assistant Secretary for Public and Intergovernmental Affairs where she actively works to ensure first-rate care for other veterans.

"Choosing a Philosophy Is a Test of Character"

It is simply our total character and personal genius that are on trial; and if we invoke any so-called philosophy, our choice and use of that also are but revelations of our personal aptitude or incapacity for moral life. From this unsparing practical ordeal no professor's lectures and no array of books can save us. The solving word, for the learned and the unlearned man alike, lies in the last resort in the dumb willingnesses and unwillingnesses of their interior characters, and nowhere else. It is not in heaven, neither is it beyond the sea; but the word is very nigh unto thee, in thy mouth and in thy heart, that thou mayst do it.

William James, "The Moral Philosopher and Moral Life," in *The Will to Believe and Other Essays in Popular Philosophy* (1897; reprinted in *Human Immortality*, New York: Dover, 1956), pp. 214–215.

involvement in life and diminished passions, though he did admire the Stoic emphasis on strength of will (Chapter 7).

James thought he had identified a natural fact of life: An active, strenuous approach is healthier and more satisfying than a passive, easygoing one:

> The deepest difference, practically, in the moral life of man is the difference between the easy-going and the strenuous mood. When in the easy-going mood, the shrinking from present ill is our ruling consideration. The strenuous mood, on the contrary, makes us quite indifferent to present ill, if only the great ideal is to be attained. The capacity for the strenuous mood probably lies slumbering in every man, but it has more difficulty in some than in others in waking up. It needs wilder passions to arouse it, the big fears, loves, and indignations; or else the deeply penetrating appeal of some of the higher fidelities, like justice, truth, or freedom. Strong belief is a necessity of its vision; and a world where all the mountains are brought down and all the valleys are exalted is no congenial place for its habitation.[28]

Discussing Philosophy

PHILOSOPHICAL QUERY

Discuss your formal and informal education in terms of the preceding passage. Have you been encouraged to adopt a strenuous mood or an easygoing one? Have customized study aids and "extra credit" options hindered or encouraged your development as a sturdy individual? Or are such things beside the point when it comes to personal development? Give some specific examples. Do you think James is on the right track? Why or why not?

Pragmatic Religion

James had deep respect for a religion that enriches our lives, that has "cash value." He noted that people in all cultures turn to a god (or gods) who *gets things done*, an active god, a god of the "strenuous mood," not a passive, ineffective god. This led

James to offer an intriguing suggestion: If people do not believe in God, it might be because God is not *doing anything* in their lives. In *The Varieties of Religious Experience*, James attempted to discover how God *works* in people's lives. Combining an empirical, psychological study of a number of cases with a keen philosophical analysis, *Varieties* is one of James's most influential, popular, and still widely read works.

James asserted that we judge the truth of religious ideas by what he calls their "immediate luminousness," adding, "in short, *philosophical reasonableness and moral helpfulness* are the only available criteria." He concluded that religious faith is important and meaningful on pragmatic grounds: Its presence or absence makes a clearly observable, practical, and concrete difference in our lives:

> The practical needs and experiences of religion seem to me sufficiently met by the belief that beyond man and in a fashion continuous with him there exists a larger power which is friendly to him and his ideals. All that the facts require is that the power shall be other and larger than our conscious selves.
>
> God is the natural appellation, for us Christians at least, for the supreme reality, so I will call this higher part of the universe by the name of God. We and God have business with each other; and in opening ourselves to his influence our deepest destiny is fulfilled.[29]

James thought that a religious orientation is more effective than a nonreligious one because it encompasses more. It derives from and addresses a wider range of experiences, including a wider, more expansive consciousness than a purely secular point of view. Besides the obvious psychological benefits of having God as a support and comfort, religious conversion can open us up and make us more responsive to all of life, according to James.

A Religious Dilemma

In his study of religious experience, James distinguished between two basic personalities: the "healthy-minded" and the "morbid-minded." Healthy-minded people "look on all things and see that they are good." Such people are vital, enthusiastic, and exuberant. In contrast, the attitude of the morbid-minded person is "based on the persuasion that the evil aspects of our life are its very essence, and that the world's meaning most comes home to us when we lay them most to heart."[30] In other words, morbid souls are negativistic and pessimistic.

Interestingly, James the optimist says morbid-minded persons have a clearer, more realistic perspective than healthy-minded ones because they recognize a wider range of experience:

> The method of averting one's attention from evil, and living simply in the light of good is splendid as long as it will work. It will work with many persons; it will work far more generally than most of us are ready to suppose; and within the sphere of its successful operation there is nothing to be said against it as a religious solution. But it breaks down impotently as soon as melancholy comes....

"What sort of thing," James asks, "would life really be, with your qualities ready for a tussle with it, if it only brought fair weather and gave those higher faculties of yours no scope?"

The normal process of life contains moments as bad as any of those which insane melancholy is filled with, moments in which radical evil gets its innings and takes its solid turn. The lunatic's visions of horror are all drawn from the material of daily fact. Our civilization is founded on the shambles, and every individual existence goes out in a lonely spasm of helpless agony. If you protest, my friend, wait till you arrive there yourself! . . . The completest religions would therefore seem to be those in which the pessimistic elements are best developed.[31]

> *The healthy-minded . . . need to be born only once. . . . sick souls . . . must be born twice—born in order to be happy. The result is two different conceptions of the universe of our experience.*
>
> — William James

To better grasp this point, think of what it means to be *always* joyful and enthusiastic in a world such as ours. This lopsided kind of "healthy-mindedness" might result from a lack of true empathy with the condition of other people. A shallow enough view of things can result in a childish (not childlike) view of life in which nothing is really bad. Or, if it is bad, it is not *that* bad. Or, if it is *that* bad, then it is somehow deserved.

In his analysis of healthy and morbid-mindedness, James is interested in identifying the most practical spiritual balance. A soul that is blocked off from a major portion of experience (which, for want of a better word, we may refer to as evil) will be less effective, less "alive," than a soul that is not blocked off.

PHILOSOPHICAL QUERY

What do you think of James's claim that morbid-minded people have a fuller, more realistic view of things than healthy-minded ones? How would you classify yourself? Discuss some of the strengths and weaknesses of both orientations.

Truth Is Always Personal

By the end of his life, James increasingly equated "true" with "useful." In "Is Life Worth Living?" he uses an analogy of a trapped mountain climber to illustrate his claim that sometimes psychological survival rests on the *will to believe whatever is necessary*:

> Suppose, for instance, that you are climbing a mountain, and have worked yourself into a position from which the only escape is by a terrible leap. Have faith that you can successfully make it, and your feet are nerved to its accomplishment. But mistrust yourself, and think of all the sweet things you have heard the scientists say of *maybes*, and you will hesitate so long that, at last, all unstrung and trembling, and launching yourself in a moment of despair, you roll into the abyss.
>
> In such a case (and it belongs to an enormous class), the part of wisdom as well as of courage is to *believe in the line of your needs*, for only by such belief is the need fulfilled.[32]

Thus, we see in James, as in Kierkegaard (Chapter 14), a turning of the tables as it were, so that subjectivity takes precedence over objectivity. Truth is always personal. In the end, then, is James merely another Sophist advocating radical relativism born of his inability or unwillingness to understand and accept objective reality and the universal truths that flow from it? Is James manifesting "weakness" in his unwillingness to accept the world as it really is, in his refusal to face the hard fact that the world does not conform to our wishes?

James's ultimate position is that beliefs are "adaptations." As such, they can only be justified if they help us navigate our way through life. He did not think that encouraging wholehearted faith in *necessary* beliefs is the same thing as asserting that any belief that one holds is necessary *simply because one holds it.*

James's basic goal was to free us from enslavement to the notion that we *must believe* whatever science asserts—regardless of the consequences to our spiritual health and general well-being. Specifically, James argued that science should be evaluated in terms of the extent to which scientific beliefs are conducive to human happiness. Accordingly, if belief in scientific determinism and materialistic reductionism are inimical to human happiness, then disbelief is necessary for psychic survival and vitality.

For example, in testimony before the Massachusetts legislature, James spoke against a bill that would have prohibited Christian Scientists from practicing what were called "mind cures." "You are not to ask yourselves," James told the legislators, "whether these mind-curers really achieve the successes that are claimed. It is enough for you as legislators to ascertain that a large number of your citizens…are persuaded that a valuable new department of medical experience is by them opening up."[33]

As we have learned, for James, "the truth" is not the chief value. Usefulness is—but usefulness in the moral sense of producing healthy results. We can turn to James's personal life for an example of the kind of "necessary belief" that James considered preferable to the truth. James considered Charles Sanders Peirce his friend and mentor, despite Peirce's rejection of James's pragmatism. Unlike James, Peirce was unable to support himself as a philosopher, and James wanted to help his friend. Knowing that Peirce would not welcome charity, James supported and protected Peirce with money that James told him came from Peirce's many anonymous admirers. In fact, the money came from James. In this kind of case, James practiced his own principle: Better a *necessary lie* than a destructive—and unnecessary—truth.

Danger Signs

Viewed from a modern or Enlightenment perspective, William James, like Kierkegaard and Nietzsche (Chapters 14 and 16), is seen as an advocate of a potentially explosive, "anti-intellectual," "unscientific," subjectivistic philosophical doctrine. James believed that there are no neutral observers of the human condition. Everything is a "point of view." According to James, moral absolutes are impossible, and attempts to impose them are especially bad. At best, we can have moral rules of thumb, flexible guidelines. James says:

> There is hardly a good which we can imagine except as competing for the possession of the same bit of space and time with some other imagined good. … Shall a man drink and smoke, or keep his nerves in condition?—he cannot do both. Shall he follow his fancy for Amelia or for Henrietta?—both cannot be the choice of his heart. Shall he have the dear old Republican party, or a spirit of unsophistication

> *Yet it is essential to realize that our way of perceiving the world in everyday life is not radically affected by scientific conceptions. For all of us—even for the astronomer, when he goes home at night—the sun rises and sets, and the earth is immobile.*
>
> — Pierre Hadot

in public affairs?—he cannot have both, etc. So that the ethical [or materialistic] philosopher's demand for the right scale of subordination in ideals is the fruit of an altogether practical need. Some part of the ideal must be butchered, and he needs to know which part. It is a tragic situation, and no mere speculative conundrum, with which he has to deal.[34]

Ultimately, James came to the "inconclusive conclusion that since nothing can be proved one way or the other, each of us is entitled to believe whatever he wants to believe."[35] "We all," he said, "scientists, and non-scientists, live on some inclined plane of credulity. The plane tips one way in one [person], another way in another; and may [the person] whose plane tips in no way be the first to cast a stone."[36] And since belief in scientific method is merely *one belief* competing among many possible beliefs, belief in scientific method is no more sacrosanct than any other belief. Science, like various philosophies and religions, must compete for our allegiance against other visions and belief systems.

According to James, faith in science can be as powerful and effective as faith in religion or philosophy. He is not advocating that we commit ourselves to whatever whim or fancy strikes us. The vision that best suits our individual natures will win out. James's position is that we are entitled to commit ourselves to whatever beliefs best express our deepest selves, the fundamental quality of our "passional life." He was less worried about being "duped" by a false belief than he was about being unhappy:

> He who says, "Better go without belief forever than believe a lie!" merely shows his own preponderant private horror of becoming a dupe. He may be critical of many of his desires and fears, but this fear he slavishly obeys. He cannot imagine any one questioning its binding force. For my own part, I have also a horror of being duped; but I can believe that worse things than being duped may happen to a [person] of this world.[37]

Aplia

We might say that for James, it is better to truly believe a personally useful lie than to pretend to believe a personally incompatible truth. James's plane tips away from theoretical completeness and purity toward the concrete, existing individual.

Commentary

William James's vigorous pragmatism straddled two philosophical worlds, the modern and the postmodern. He is said to have anticipated many contemporary philosophical questions. Whatever we make of his philosophy, James reminds us, will *not* be based on "pure," objective criteria. It will—and can only—be based on what we passionately and deeply need to believe.

Like Kierkegaard before him (Chapter 14) and Nietzsche, his great German contemporary (Chapter 16), James was a foe of the passionless life, the "uncommitted" life. Like Kierkegaard and Nietzsche, James challenged science's claim to ultimate, objective, universal, and absolute authority. For James, it is far better to believe passionately in a "lie" than it is to halfheartedly accept a "truth." He did not see the neatly ordered universe of the optimistic Enlightenment philosophers. The Jamesian universe is pluralistic, expansive, incomplete, and unpredict-able. It is *wide open*. To survive and thrive in such a universe, James thought, we need resourcefulness, good humor, stamina, and the willingness to risk living according to convictions that cannot be objectively, universally, and scientifically established beyond doubt.

The most significant weakness in James's pragmatism is so much a part of what he saw as his mission that we must con-sider it from two perspectives. By tying truth to "what works" *for us*, James cuts himself off from any possibility of objective verification. Yet many philosophers still hold that the truth must refer to something beyond and not entirely determined by the individual. James seems to blur the distinction between truth and how we discover it. Although we do test ideas by act-ing on them and by comparing them with our more established beliefs, their *truth* is independent of this process. Penicillin remains an effective antibiotic whether or not I believe that it is, for example.

Among the great philosophers, James stands out for the wonderfully engaging way he had of capturing our attention and expressing the rooted, grounded nature of our hunger for personal truth. Here's an amusing, yet touching, example: "Probably a crab would be filled with a sense of personal outrage if it could hear us classify it without ado or apology as a crustacean, and thus dispose of it. 'I am no such thing,' it would say: 'I am MYSELF, MYSELF alone.'"

There are two different issues here. If we are looking at fac-tual matters, this criticism of pragmatism is persuasive. But if we consider beliefs about moral and spiritual concerns, as well as some social and psychological beliefs, pragmatism has something important to say. We distort James's position if we lump both general categories of belief statements together.

Consider, on James's behalf, the pattern that social scientists refer to as a **self–fulfilling prophecy**. This is a belief that affects events in such a way that it causes itself to come true. For example, a man who believes his date will not like him might project a mood of surly defensiveness and hostility or passive, defeatist self-pity. Either mood could alienate his companion, who otherwise would have found him quite pleasant. If so, his prophecy of "She won't like me" has fulfilled itself. Similarly, students who expect to do poorly in a given course might not learn because they are frightened or depressed by their expectations of failure; they might unconsciously devote less energy to their studies than they would have if they had believed more in themselves. Conversely, students who expect to do well might be more open and pleasant in class, which can inspire the professor to be a better teacher; they might ask more questions and pay more attention, thereby fulfilling their own beliefs.

Ironically, in recent years, certain work emerging from the *scientific* study of belief has been interpreted as supporting James's sense that the "best" beliefs are not always the "truest" ones.[38] Lyn Abramson, of the University of Wisconsin, and Lauren Alloy, of Temple University, report that "normal, healthy" people are subject to a variety of "cognitive illusions." Among these are mild, factually unwarranted optimism and insensitivity to failure. Combined, these two "illusions" result in ten-dencies to make "straightforwardly false" judgments. Ironically, because they often do not suffer from such illusions, clinically depressed individuals are "Sadder But Wiser," to use the subtitle from one of Abramson and Alloy's better-known papers. In other research, social psychologist Shelley Taylor has found that victims of trauma and illness who are "unjustifiably optimistic" tend to be better adjusted and hap-pier than more "realistic" victims of similar circumstances. Finally, Daniel Goleman

self–fulfilling prophecy
A belief that affects events in such a way that it causes itself to come true; an example is a student doing poorly on an exam because she expects to fail it.

is one of a number of neo-Freudians who argue that forgetting unpleasant events (repression) is an important component of mental health.[39]

This raises the basic **pragmatic paradox**: *Pragmatism works only if we believe our ideas are true according to nonpragmatic criteria.* For instance, can I really just say to myself, "Well, belief in God makes people feel secure and gives their lives meaning. I would like to feel secure and find a purpose for my life. Therefore, I shall believe in God"? Does not such belief work only when I sincerely believe it to be true—objectively and factually true, not just true because I believe it is true? Paradoxically, it seems as if only by believing in a nonpragmatic view of truth can pragmatism work.

William James spoke eloquently for the person of "moderate" convictions and temperament and for the virtues of the active, vigorous struggle for good. He offered a persuasive and unique defense of our right to believe. He showed that faith in a higher power cannot be dismissed as a form of psychological infantilism and that its grounding in personal conviction is as solid as faith in science. Further, he showed that religious faith has restorative and unifying powers often missing from faith in science. James defended the common sense of the average person without pandering to it and called on us to test the higher life of the "strenuous mood." All in all, these are impressive accomplishments.

Summary of Main Points

- William James's pragmatism is based on Charles Sanders Peirce's pragmatic theory of meaning: Ideas are meaningful only when they translate into actions and predict experiences associated with actions. James argued that philosophy should make a "definite difference" in people's lives, and he attempted to construct a philosophical religion that could provide beliefs worth living and dying for. Pragmatism was meant to be a method for helping us feel "at home" in the universe.

- Pragmatism rejects any philosophy that lacks "cash value." James believed that virtually no metaphysical theory has any practical payoff (cash value). "True ideas," he said, "are those that we can assimilate, validate, corroborate and verify. False ideas are those we cannot." Pragmatic truth is human truth. James expanded the realm of philosophy beyond "revealing the truth" to providing a way to become better adjusted to the world.

- James divided people into tough-minded or tender-minded types, claiming that, historically, philosophy has been dominated by extremists of one type or the other and thus has remained unbalanced. He advocated what he saw as a more useful combination of

these two extremes. Because life demands an active response, we have no choice but to believe something. We face "forced options." The intellect does not discover the truths in which we believe; the will to believe creates truths.

- The pragmatic life rejects determinism as incompatible with our immediate sense of freedom. According to James, determinism—the idea that everything must happen exactly the way it does—is incompatible with our spiritual need for freedom. Determinism has less cash value than belief in freedom, and since neither belief can be proved conclusively, the pragmatic thing to do is believe in what we need to be happy—freedom. Feelings of regret reflect our deep belief in free will.

- Since we cannot escape choice, James advocated what he called the "heroic life," rejecting life without struggle as dull, mediocre, and empty. The heroic life is characterized by a "real fight" for something important; it is about the struggle between good and evil. James distinguished between two basic personalities: The healthy-minded personality looks at all things as good; healthy-minded people are exuberant, vital, and enthusiastic. The morbid-minded personality sees the very essence of life as evil, untrustworthy, and troublesome; morbid-minded people are negativistic and pessimistic.

- Religious faith is important on pragmatic grounds: Its presence or absence makes an observable, practical difference in people's lives. James believed a religious orientation is more effective than a non-religious one because it encompasses more. Profound religious (rebirth) experience makes it possible to be both morally decent (without descending into the pessimism of morbid-mindedness) and happy (without resorting to the limited perspective of healthy-mindedness).

Post-Reading Reflections

Now that you've had a chance to learn about the Pragmatist, use your new knowledge to answer these questions.

1. How did James's personal life influence some of his major pragmatic beliefs?

2. What prompted Charles Sanders Peirce to change the name of his philosophy to "pragmaticism"?

3. Illustrate the pragmatic theory of meaning with your own example.

4. What is the core question at the heart of the pragmatic method? Why did James believe that asking that question is so important? What does the answer to the question reveal to us?

5. Discuss James's notion of the "will to believe." In what sense do "reasons serve the will," according to James? Do you agree with him? Why or why not?

6. How does James deal with the dilemma of determinism? What do you think of his strategy? Does it square with your sense of the world and of yourself? Is his "answer" to the dilemma really an answer? If not, is there a better answer, or any answer?

7. Why was James dissatisfied with metaphysical efforts to define the good? What did he propose in their place?

8. Explain what James meant by the "heroic life." In his opinion, what aspects of life call for a heroic response? Why? What factors make it difficult for some people to live such a life?

9. What was James driving at when he claimed that a religious orientation is more effective than a nonreligious one? What reasons did he have for this belief? Do you share his opinion? Why or why not?

10. Why was James critical of optimism? What does he offer as a better—healthier—alternative?

 MindTap

Experience MindTap through the activities highlighted in this chapter. Further explore this online, personalized learning tool to deepen your comprehension and improve your grades.

16

The Anti-Philosopher
Friedrich Nietzsche

Who is most influential.–When a human being resists his whole age and stops it at the gate to demand an accounting, this must have influence. Whether that is what he desires is immaterial; that he can do it is what matters.

— *Friedrich Nietzsche*

Learning Objectives

After you complete this chapter, you should be able to:

- Describe modernity.
- Describe philosophical pessimism.
- Differentiate between Arthur Schopenhauer's will to live and Friedrich Nietzsche's will to power.
- Describe an anti-philosopher.
- Critique Nietzsche's claim that modern science and morality are mendacious.
- Give an example of a reaction formation.
- Critique Nietzsche's rejection of utilitarian ethics.
- Critique Nietzsche's claim that God is dead.
- Contrast slave morality with master morality.
- Describe *ressentiment*.
- Summarize Nietzsche's attitude toward modern, mass education.

PERHAPS NO OTHER PHILOSOPHER of modern times has provoked as much controversy as **Friedrich Nietzsche** (1844–1900). Of small physical stature, so nearsighted he was nearly blind, plagued by headaches, nausea, loneliness, and depression, Nietzsche voiced an explosive philosophy that attracts and offends people more than a century after his death. One of a handful of philosophers who can be called "best-selling" authors, Nietzsche's work has a poetic, confrontational style that is both exhilarating and disturbing.

Although he died in 1900, Nietzsche thought of himself as a cultural prophet of the next two centuries. In *The Will to Power* he says:

> What I relate is the history of the next two centuries. I describe what is coming, what can no longer come differently.... This future speaks even now in a hundred signs, this destiny announces itself everywhere; for this music of the future all ears are cocked even now. For some time now, our whole European culture has been moving as toward a catastrophe, with a tortured tension that is growing from decade to decade: restlessly, violently, headlong, like a river that wants to reach the end, that no longer reflects, that is afraid to reflect.[1]

Nietzsche saw himself as the first to recognize the symptoms of a profound sickness at the core of *modernity*. **Modernity** refers to the historical period of nineteenth- and twentieth-century nation-states and to a corresponding set of cultural conditions and beliefs dominated by Enlightenment ideals. Modernity includes faith in science, objective truth, and rationality; expectations of inevitable progress; capitalism, urbanization, and large-scale industrial enterprise; mass literacy, media, and culture; political democracy; anti-traditionalism; individualism; and secularization.

Nietzsche's most famous (or infamous) pronouncement that "God is dead" is part of a generalized assessment of modernity that consists of integrated negative and positive stages. The negative stage may be the most recognized because of Nietzsche's uniquely engaging and confrontational style of writing. Perhaps less well known—at least by the general public—is Nietzsche's life-affirming call to those who recognize the *great opportunity* for self-creation present in the death of God and all that flows from it.

Although Nietzsche is popularly credited with being the first truly postmodern philosopher, with Nietzsche nothing is that simple; or perhaps, as many philosophers insist, with Nietzsche nothing is clear. Depending on one's perspective, Nietzsche's work is either enriched or weakened by the use of cryptic utterances, biting irony, hyperbole, deliberate contradiction, and phrases and assertions that are carefully crafted to provoke the reader. Contemporary philosophers and critics disagree about whether Nietzsche was a philosopher of sustained brilliance, sporadic insight, raving irrationality—or even a philosopher at all. What is beyond dispute, however, is his enormous influence on and significance for twentieth-century and contemporary thought. Love him or hate him, Nietzsche remains an aesthetic, literary, psychological, and philosophical force to be reckoned with. He is, at the very least, a worthy adversary.

Friedrich Nietzsche, the iconoclastic son of a preacher, was a deeply spiritual atheist who lived and died in lonely obscurity. He stands outside of the common categories of philosophy. He is *sui generis*—of his own kind. I have tried to express

modernity
The historical period of nineteenth- and twentieth-century nation-states and a corresponding set of cultural conditions and beliefs dominated by Enlightenment ideals, including faith in science, objective truth, and rationality; expectations of inevitable progress; political democracy; capitalism; urbanization; mass literacy; mass media; mass culture; anti-traditionalism; large-scale industrial enterprise; individualism; and secularization.

something of this uniqueness by treating him as an *anti-philosopher*. He became that over the course of his life, but he was always an outsider.

The Outsider

Friedrich Nietzsche

Nietzsche was born in the Prussian village of Röcken. When he was four years old, his father, a Lutheran minister, died, leaving the pious little boy to the care of his mother, grandmother, two aunts, and sister. As the only male in the household, young "Fritz" became the center of attention, coddled and protected. Nietzsche's studious demeanor and religious piety earned him the nickname "the little pastor."

Nietzsche originally planned to follow in his father's footsteps and become a Lutheran minister, but in his late teens, something changed. The "good boy" lost interest in his studies. He questioned the existence of God and even sneaked away and got drunk—on a Sunday.

At twenty, Nietzsche enrolled in the University of Bonn. Freed from the pampering and domination of five women, faced with uncertainties about his faith and childhood plans for the future, Nietzsche, like Kierkegaard, went through a period of rebellious high living.

Nietzsche tried his best to fit into the raucous life of late-nineteenth-century German students: drinking, boisterous singing, romantic pursuits, duels. Nietzsche joined a student club, caroused, and even fought a halfhearted duel. Yet, for all his efforts, Nietzsche was not "one of the guys". He was personally disgusted with drunken excess, smoky beer halls, and the "coarse, Philistine spirit" of his fellows. The little pastor found that kind of student life intolerable and ultimately suffered a nervous collapse.

Nietzsche left Bonn and enrolled in the University of Leipzig. There he had the good fortune to meet Professor Friedrich Ritschl, who kindled in him a passion for philology, the study of classical philosophy and literature. Ritschl recognized that Nietzsche was a brilliant scholar and encouraged and stimulated his genius.

Despite his academic brilliance, however, Nietzsche was already a lonely man, truly an outsider. When he first moved to Leipzig, he was still shaken by his disillusionment with Bonn and by the emptiness he felt at having lost his religious faith. He went through the motions of being actively interested in his life but found himself torn by doubts. Hedonistic pursuits left him disgusted and depressed, yet the way of the church remained closed off to him.

While in this state, Nietzsche came across the work of **Arthur Schopenhauer** (1788–1860). Schopenhauer's philosophy is known as **pessimism**, the belief that life is disappointing and that for every satisfied desire, ten new unsatisfied ones emerge; our only hope is detachment and withdrawal. In his book *The World as Will and Idea*, Schopenhauer argued that life is nothing more than a constant will to survive. We are pawns of a life force, and our best hope is to detach our individual will from the cycle of wanting-getting-wanting more. Life, in Schopenhauer's vision, is an irrational, purposeless striving for a pointless existence. According to Schopenhauer, what little salvation there is comes only from resisting the blind will to *live at all costs* and curtailing our desires.

> *I have chosen for myself the word immoralist as a mark of distinction and badge of honour.*
> — Friedrich Nietzsche

pessimism
Schopenhauer's theory that life is disappointing and that for every satisfied desire, new desires emerge; our only hope is detachment and withdrawal.

Given his mental turmoil and deep dissatisfaction, Nietzsche responded enthusiastically to Schopenhauer. He craved some kind of meaning but was unable to find it in either pleasure or religion. At a precarious time in his life, Schopenhauer gave him something to hold on to:

> It seemed as if Schopenhauer were addressing me personally. I felt his enthusiasm, and seemed to see him before me. Every line cried aloud for renunciation, denial, resignation. Here I saw a mirror in which the world, life, my own mind were reflected in fearful grandeur. Here the wholly disinterested and heavenly eye of art looked at me; here I saw illness and salvation, banishment and refuge, hell and heaven.[2]

From Schopenhauer, Nietzsche concluded that life makes no objective, absolute sense. Life is not the result of a divine plan, nor is nature orderly in any way that we can discern. Rather, life is the expression of *will*. Schopenhauer characterized the ultimate will as the will to live; Nietzsche disagreed. He insisted that life is governed by the **will to power**, a universal desire to control others and impose our values on them.

> *Life is bitter and fatal, yet men cherish it and beget children to suffer the same fate.*
> — Heraclitus

will to power
Nietzsche's term for what he thought is a universal desire to control others and impose our values on them.

Beyond the Academy

Schopenhauer's pessimism, paradoxically, invigorated Nietzsche, and in 1868 Ritschl recommended him for a chair in classical philology. Ritschl was especially

Michael Tullberg/Getty Images

Nietzsche said, "Another century of readers—and the mind itself will stink. That everyone can learn to read will ruin not only writing, but thinking too." What do you suppose he might make of our culture's fondness for snarky memoirs, romance novels, self-help manuals, fantasy series, and political diatribes? In this photo, a crowd of fans waits for a book-signing appearance by Chelsea Handler, author of *Are You There, Vodka? It's Me, Chelsea*. Is universal literacy an unqualified virtue? What's the real issue here?

> *Life is no argument.*
> *The conditions of life*
> *might include error.*
> — Friedrich
>   Nietzsche

conservative, not given to excessive praise or hasty conclusions regarding the area of study to which he had devoted his life, so the recommendation he wrote for Nietzsche is all the more significant:

> However many young talents I have seen develop under my eyes for thirty-nine years...Nietzsche...is the first from whom I have ever accepted any contribution [to the philological journal *Museum*] at all while he was still a student....He is the idol, and without wishing it, the leader of the whole younger generation of philologists here in Leipzig who—and they are rather numerous—cannot wait to hear him as a lecturer. You will say, I describe a phenomenon. Well, that is just what he is—and at the same time pleasant and modest....
>
> ...He will simply be able to do anything he wants to do.[3]

Though Nietzsche lacked his doctorate, his brilliance and Ritschl's strong advocacy combined to secure the position for him. "In *Germany*," Ritschl wrote, "that sort of thing happens absolutely never."

Nietzsche was only twenty-four when he was appointed professor. The university hurriedly conferred the doctorate on him—without requiring an examination—and Nietzsche plunged into a heavy academic routine. But his heart and mind could not be confined to the limits of philology—or any other academic area as then defined.

In spite of noble intentions, Nietzsche was not a particularly effective professor. His lectures were often complex and difficult to follow, and fewer and fewer students attended them. He did not socialize well and found his colleagues difficult. Academic routine drained him. His sole comforts came from his own writing and a few close friends.

Tragic Optimism

In 1870, the Franco-Prussian War broke out. Nietzsche volunteered as a medic and served for a short time before returning to Leipzig in poor health. Germany humbled both Austria and France in the war. Under the powerful vision of Otto von Bismarck (1815–1898), small German principalities were unified into a single, powerful state dominated by Prussia. Nietzsche saw Bismarck as an example of a "higher morality" based on strength, power, and the will to dominate. He was impressed that Bismarck ruled by "blood and iron."

About this time, Nietzsche became intrigued with Darwinism. Combining Bismarck's will to power and domination with Darwin's idea of evolution, Nietzsche transformed Schopenhauer's pessimism into his own utterly unique doctrine of *overcoming*. Schopenhauer was right, Nietzsche thought, in recognizing that life consists of continual struggle and hardship. But Schopenhauer's reaction—retreat and renunciation—struck Nietzsche as weak-willed and decadent. He concluded that Schopenhauer's pessimism was unhealthy and life-denying.

tragic optimism
According to Nietzsche, the sense of joy and vitality that accompanies a superior individual's clear-sighted imposition of his or her own freely chosen values on a meaningless world.

Nietzsche's solution was **tragic optimism**, the sense of joy and vitality that accompanies a superior individual's clear-sighted imposition of his or her own freely chosen values on a meaningless world. A superior person is a person who neither shrinks from struggle nor struggles blindly, controlled by a pessimistic instinct to survive at any cost. A superior person *wills* to live deliberately and consciously.

A superior person *overcomes* pessimism without retreating into lies about ultimate meaning or purpose. In Nietzsche's view, Schopenhauer failed to recognize that the struggle to survive aims at the dominance of the strongest and the fittest. The tragic optimist imposes meaning on a meaningless universe and overcomes his or her own innate fears and weaknesses.

> One does not kill by anger but by laughter. Come, let us kill the Spirit of Gravity!
> — Friedrich Nietzsche

Zarathustra Speaks

Citing ill health, Nietzsche resigned from the university in 1879, when he was thirty-four. He was granted a pension. Nietzsche knew he needed to break free from the confines of academic scholarship and carve out his own path. He came to see himself as the prophet of a higher, healthier morality, a morality so far beyond conventional values that it required the revaluation of all values. He took to referring to himself as an *immoralist* and an *iconoclast*. He spoke of "doing philosophy with a hammer"—tapping on the statues of great idols to see which are hollow and then smashing them to bits.

Freed from the demands of the university, Nietzsche polished and refined both his thinking and his writing. His greatest work was accomplished in the ten-year period following his retirement from teaching. For a time, he lost some of his ferocity—mellowed, perhaps, by the physical and cultural climates of Switzerland and Italy, where he spent most of his time.

His most "cheerful" books, *The Dawn of Day* (1881) and *The Gay Science* (1882), were written while he was friends with Lou Salome, a witty, appealing young Jewish intellectual. Nietzsche was quite taken with her. In their walks and talks together he found a special kind of companionship. He seems to have found in her both a disciple and a lover. We do not know whether he ever proposed to her, as she later claimed. In any case, Lou Salome ultimately left Nietzsche for another man. (Years later, when Nietzsche was famous, Lou Salome capitalized on her relationship with him.)

> It is better to be envied than pitied.
> — Herodotus

Devastated by her abandonment, Nietzsche retreated to the Swiss Alps. In this agonizingly lonely, hurt, and bitter mood, he produced his most famous work, *Thus Spake Zarathustra* (1885). The title comes from the Sanskrit phrase *Iti vuttakam*, meaning "Thus spoke the Holy One."[4] Nietzsche used the name of the ancient Persian prophet Zoroaster but created his own Zarathustra. *Zarathustra* was a call to rise above decadence and mediocrity. Nietzsche later described *Zarathustra* as a revelation:

> One hears—one does not seek; one takes—one does not ask who gives; a thought suddenly flashes up like lightning, it comes with necessity, unhesitatingly—I have never had any choice in the matter.[5]

Nietzsche's Zarathustra is at once a great destroyer of false values and in the same instant a creator of new, higher, healthier values. Nietzsche said that Zarathustra "as a type...*overtook* me."[6] Zarathustra the destroyer-creator announces the arrival of the next evolutionary type, the *Übermensch*, or the overman.

Nietzsche followed *Zarathustra* with what many consider the two most coherent statements of his philosophy, *Beyond Good and Evil* (1886) and *Toward a Genealogy of Morals* (1887). Consisting mostly of aphorisms and short essays, both books are essentially commentaries on the gospel of the overman espoused in *Zarathustra*.

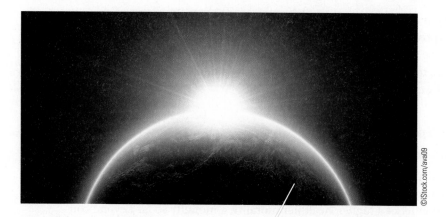

"This Is *My* Morning!"

Imagine, if you will, the solitary figure of Zarathustra as he steps from his cave at that moment just before dawn when the earth itself seems to tremble in anticipation of a new day. Better yet, listen to the famous opening chords of Richard Strauss's 1896 tone poem *Also Sprach Zarathustra* as you picture the rough-hewn prophet as he addresses the rising sun itself:

> WHEN Zarathustra was thirty years old, he left his home and the lake of his home, and went into the mountains. There he enjoyed his spirit and his solitude, and for ten years did not weary of it. But at last his heart changed,—and rising one morning with the rosy dawn, he went before the sun, and spake thus unto it:
>
> Thou great star! What would be thy happiness if thou hadst not those for whom thou shinest!
>
> For ten years hast thou climbed hither unto my cave: thou wouldst have wearied of thy light and of the journey, had it not been for me, mine eagle, and my serpent.
>
> But we awaited thee every morning, took from thee thine overflow, and blessed thee for it.

> Bless me, then, thou tranquil eye, that canst behold even the greatest happiness without envy!
>
> Bless the cup that is about to overflow, that the water may flow golden out of it, and carry everywhere the reflection of thy bliss!
>
> Thus began Zarathustra's down-going.

Now, listen to the wistful, fading end of Strauss's music and imagine Zarathustra as he leaves the world of men, returning once more to the solitude of his mountaintop. Again, the prophet addresses the sun:

> My suffering and my pity—what matter about them! Do I then strive after HAPPINESS? I strive after my WORK!
>
> Well! The lion hath come, my children are nigh, Zarathustra hath grown ripe, mine hour hath come:
>
> This is MY morning, MY day beginneth: arise now, ARISE, THOU GREAT NOONTIDE!"—
>
> Thus spake Zarathustra and left his cave, glowing and strong, like a morning sun coming out of gloomy mountains.

Modified from **Thus Spake Zarathustra**, trans. Thomas Common (Edinburgh and London: T.N. Foulis, 1892, 1909).

Nietzsche's purpose is clear: to destroy conventional morality and replace it with a higher "immoral" ideal.

The Last Philosopher

During this period of his life, Nietzsche lived modestly in rooming houses, refusing to succumb to pessimism. Overwhelmed by disappointment and loneliness,

"A Special Kind of Courage"

Writer Stefan Zweig's touching description of Nietzsche reminds us that there are many kinds of courage, many ways to be strong:

> Carefully the myopic man sits down to a table; carefully, the man with the sensitive stomach considers every item on the menu: whether the tea is not too strong, the food not spiced too much, for every mistake in his diet upsets his sensitive digestion, and every transgression in his nourishment wreaks havoc with his quivering nerves for days. No glass of wine, no beer, no alcohol, no coffee at his place, no cigar and no cigarette after his meal, nothing that stimulates, refreshes, or rests him; only the short, meager meal and a little urbane, unprofound conversation in a soft voice with an occasional neighbor (as a man speaks who for years has been unused to talking and is afraid of being asked too much).
>
> And upon entering again into the small, narrow, modest, coldly furnished *chambre garnie*, where innumerable notes, pages, writings, and proofs are piled up on the table, but no flower, no decoration, scarcely a book and rarely a letter. Back in a corner, a heavy and graceless wooden trunk, his only possession, with the two shirts and the other worn suit. Otherwise only...manuscripts, and on a tray innumerable bottles and jars and potions; against the migraines, which often render him all but senseless for hours, against his stomach cramps, against spasmodic vomiting, against the slothful intestines, and above all the dreadful sedatives against his insomnia, chloral hydrate and Veronal. A frightful arsenal of poisons and drugs, yet the only helpers in the empty silence of this strange room in which he never rests except in brief artificially conquered sleep. Wrapped in his overcoat and a woolen scarf (for the wretched stove smokes and does not give warmth), his fingers freezing, his double glasses pressed close to the paper, his hurried hand writes for hours—words the dim eyes can hardly decipher. For hours he sits like this and writes until his eyes burn.

Stefan Zweig, quoted in **The Portable Nietzsche**, trans. Walter Kaufmann (New York: Penguin, 1968), p. 104.

disturbed by what he saw as rampant mediocrity and hypocrisy, Nietzsche struggled on with his writing. Less than three years before his final collapse, he wrote:

> What found expression [in even my earliest work] was...a *strange* voice...one who concealed himself for the time being under the scholar's hood....Here was a spirit with strange, nameless needs....What spoke here was a mystical, almost maenadic [frenzied] soul that stammered with difficulty, a feat of the will, as in a strange tongue, almost undecided whether it should communicate or conceal itself. It should have *sung*, this "new soul"—and not spoken![7]

The last years of Nietzsche's life were tragic. His health deteriorated even further, and he became increasingly, bitterly isolated and lonely:

> I call myself the last philosopher because I am the last man. Nobody talks to me but myself, and my voice comes to me like that of a dying person....Though I try to conceal my loneliness from myself—the terrible loneliness of the last philosopher!—and make my way into the multitude and into love by lies, for my heart cannot bear the terror of the loneliest loneliness and compels me to talk as if I were two.[8]

As his disappointments mounted, Nietzsche quarreled with practically everyone, his human contact reduced to innkeepers, shop clerks, and others with whom

Goethe Schiller Archive

To a friend Nietzsche wrote, "If I could give you an idea of my feeling of loneliness! I have nobody among the living or among the dead, to whom I feel related. This is indescribably horrible!" To himself he wrote, "I think of myself as the scrawl which an unknown power scribbles across a sheet of paper, to try out a new pen." (This photograph was taken at Villa Silberblick in Weimar, shortly before Nietzsche's death.)

> [Nietzsche] had more penetrating knowledge of himself than any other man who ever lived or ever was likely to live.
>
> — Sigmund Freud

he had only superficial interactions. To a friend he wrote, "For the lonely one, even noise is a consolation. If I could give you an idea of my feeling of loneliness! I have nobody among the living or among the dead, to whom I feel related. This is indescribably horrible!"[9] For a soul with so much to *sing*, this must have been among the worst rebuffs of all.

In January 1889 in Turin, Italy, Nietzsche had another breakdown. His mother brought him home to Germany, and his life ended much as it had begun, in the care of his mother and sister. After their mother's death, Nietzsche's sister moved him to Weimar, where the prophet of struggle and overcoming spent the rest of his life half-paralyzed, slipping in and out of sanity. The "loneliest philosopher" died about midday August 25, 1900.

Discussing Philosophy

PHILOSOPHICAL QUERY

Some postmodern philosophers claim that all philosophy is a form of autobiography. By that they mean that all philosophy—and indeed all thinking and perceiving—expresses and reflects uniquely personal qualities of the philosopher. In your opinion, do the life circumstances of philosophers help us evaluate their philosophical writings? Do you think autobiographical considerations are significant? Insignificant?

Truth Is a Matter of Perspective

When Nietzsche says, "I call myself the last philosopher because I am the last man," he may be referring to his doctrine of the more-than-human overman. (See the preceding section.) If so, then by referring to himself as the last philosopher, Nietzsche is signaling that he is the last "merely human" philosopher. This may have been what he had in mind, since he thought that the next stage of cultural and merely human evolution would necessitate the destruction of all present value systems, including modern philosophical ones based on the possibility of objectivity.

According to Nietzsche, aesthetic vision (art or taste) is the basis of meaning—not science, not religion, not morality, not rationality. And for Nietzsche, as for his Irish contemporary Oscar Wilde (1854–1900), art is a matter of *semblance*, a *pose,* "technically" a matter of *masks* and *lies.* Nietzsche wrote:

> I never failed to sense a *hostility to life*—a furious, vengeful antipathy to life itself [behind faith in absolutes]: for all of life is based on semblance, art, deception, points of view, and the necessity of perspectives and error.[10]

Nietzsche's controversial status as a philosopher is due, at least in part, to assertions of a form of relativism known as *perspectivism.* **Nietzschean perspectivism** is the contention that every view is only one among many possible interpretations, including, especially, Nietzschean perspectivism, which itself is just one interpretation among many interpretations. But, as the critic Alexander Nehamas reminds us:

> If every view is only an interpretation, and if, as perspectivism holds, there are no independent facts against which various interpretations can be compared, what is the object at which the many interpretations that we consider interpretations *of* Nietzsche are directed? . . . If perspectivism is correct, and, as it seems to claim, every interpretation creates its own facts, then it may seem impossible to decide whether any interpretation is or is not correct. And if there is nothing of which all these are interpretations, then the very idea of interpretation, which seems to require at least that there be something there to be interpreted, begins to appear suspect itself.[11]

We have already encountered this issue of the apparent self-contradiction at the heart of radically relativistic doctrines. (See the Introduction and Chapters 3 and 4, for example.) There is, however, a characteristically postmodern quality to Nietzsche's perspectivist assertions: By repeatedly calling attention to his own aesthetic perspectivism, Nietzsche models what he asserts in a flagrantly self-referential way. He exuberantly adopts *points of view,* which he also refers to as *experiments,* thereby preventing his readers from forgetting that they, too, have points of view—from forgetting that they, too, conduct moral, philosophical, and spiritual *experiments.*

Thus, whatever positive position Nietzsche takes is also a negative position—experimentally, from one point of view. In "Attempt at a Self-Criticism," Nietzsche refers to what he labels a deep *antimoral propensity* in his writing. As we will see later, this does not mean that Nietzsche himself has no moral code whatsoever; it

Nietzschean perspectivism The contention that every view is only one among many possible interpretations, including, especially, Nietzschean perspectivism, which itself is just one interpretation among many interpretations.

means that Nietzsche's value system is anti-moral *from the perspective* of conventional (Christian) morality. Similarly, from the standpoint of most modern philosophy, Nietzsche can be considered an *anti-philosopher*.

An **anti-philosopher** is a radical critic of certain techniques and foundational doctrines of modern science and philosophy who disputes the possibility of objectivity and universality and who rejects the absolute authority of reason. In other words, the anti-philosopher rejects the possibility of a *neutral stance* or *perspectiveless perspective:*

> Most of the conscious thinking of a philosopher is secretly guided by his instincts and forced along certain lines....
>
> What tempts us to look at all philosophers half suspiciously and half mockingly is not so much that we recognize again and again how innocent they are, how often and how easily they make mistakes and lose their way, in short their childishness and childlike-ness—but rather that they are not sufficiently candid, though they make a great virtuous noisy to-do as soon as the problem of truthfulness is even remotely touched upon.... whereas, at bottom, a pre-conceived dogma, a notion, an "institution," or mostly a heart's desire, made abstract and refined, is defended by them with arguments sought after the fact. They are all of them lawyers (though wanting to be called anything but that)....
>
> Gradually I have come to realize what every great philosophy up to now has been: the personal confession of its originator, a type of involuntary and unaware memoir.[12]

anti-philosopher
A radical critic of the techniques and doctrines of modern science and philosophy. The anti-philosopher disputes the possibility of objectivity and universality and rejects the absolute authority of reason; anti-philosophers also reject the possibility of a *neutral stance* or *perspectiveless perspective.*

PHILOSOPHICAL QUERY

Do you think that the presence of a perspective makes a neutral stance impossible? What do you think neutral means in this kind of case? Does it mean *perspectiveless?* If it means something else, what else? Are perspectives the same things as biases?

Attack on Objectivity

What criteria for truth can Nietzsche, as an anti-philosopher, offer in place of objectivity and universality, and what standard of interpretation can he offer *in lieu* of rationality? Instead of offering recognizable philosophical *arguments*, Nietzsche offers a twofold *appeal*. The first component of this appeal, directed at our aesthetic sensibilities (taste), calls on us to "justify life as an aesthetic phenomenon." The second component of Nietzsche's anti-philosophical appeal rests on what he calls the *will to power*. Neither component *depends* on reason or scientific inquiry for justification.

In "On Truth and Lie in an Extra-Moral Sense," Nietzsche says that knowledge itself is an invention, and he goes so far as to doubt even our capacity for self-knowledge:

> What, indeed, does man know of himself! Can he even perceive himself completely...? Does not nature keep much the most from him, even about his body, to

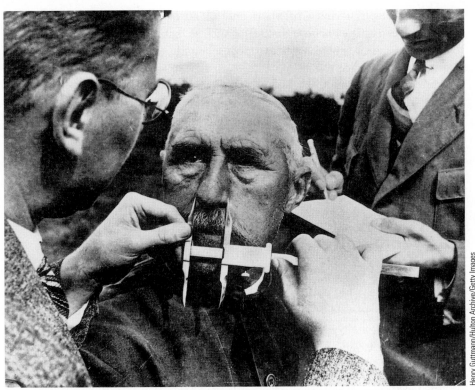

This picture depicts a Nazi-supported "scientific" system of race determination applied to a German man. Considering some of the horrific uses of "rationality" and "technology" during the past century, is optimism justified? Is the notion of "progress" intelligible on any broad scale? What better alternative is there to scientific rationality? (Is this issue framed fairly?)

spellbind and confine him in a proud, deceptive consciousness, far from the coils of his intestines, the quick current of his bloodstream? . . .

In view of this, whence the urge for truth?[13]

The clear implication is that if nature keeps "much the most" from us concerning our very own selves, we have no chance of *discovering* the objective truth about anything. We can only *invent truths* according to our individual needs. Truths are aesthetic creations that serve the will to power. Truth is seen as a function of the *physiology* and *pathology* of the individual, not some absolute, unchanging—objective—fact of nature or proposition derived from reason.

In Chapter 14, we saw how Enlightenment faith in reason and science produced Kierkegaard's sharp existential counterreaction. Among the nineteenth-century criticisms raised against faith in "scientific" rationality and objectivity (**scientism**), Nietzsche's cultural critique stands out for its intensity and scope. (See Chapter 15 for the pragmatic reaction to modern philosophy.)

Nietzsche's assault on objectivity includes rejecting the Cartesian notion of a unitary, fixed, rational self. Adopting a view similar to Hume's, Nietzsche insisted that the idea of a self that persists throughout a person's lifetime is a *fiction* or *metaphor*,

scientism
The belief that the methods of the natural sciences apply to all areas of knowledge, and that only they can overcome the vagaries of prescientific superstition, religion, and metaphysics.

not a fact. Metaphysicians, Christians, and scientists, Nietzsche said, are all prone to the same error: They believe that terms such as "substance," "God," and "gravity" refer to things as they objectively exist; consequently, they fail to grasp their metaphorical or fictive nature.

Moreover, according to Nietzsche, a *single hidden agenda* lurks behind science, philosophy, and religion: Scientists, philosophers, and "true believers" of all types seek power over the world, over other people, even over themselves. This natural impulse to dominate and control is often disguised as *influencing, controlling, managing, understanding,* or *improving* life, nature, the environment, society, and human behavior. Whatever we call them, Nietzsche insists, these desires are manifestations of the *will to power*.

The Will to Power

Call it what we wish—objectivity, truth, or wisdom—Nietzsche says the single goal of science, religion, and philosophy is the exertion of power. Thus, it is *mendacious* for scientists (or priests or philosophers) to think of themselves as disinterested, detached, rational spectators capable of neutral, objective judgment. Nietzsche equates the will to *truth* with the will to *power* and asserts that power is the basis of the distinction between good and evil:

> What urges you on and arouses your ardour, you wisest of men, do you call it "will to truth"?...
>
> [I]t is a will to power; and that is so even when you talk of good and evil and of the assessment of values....
>
> Where I found a living creature, there I found will to power; and even in the will of the servant I found the will to be master....
>
> And life itself told me this secret: "Behold," it said, "I am that *which must overcome itself again and again.*"[14]

The positive force of Nietzsche's concept is captured in contemporary philosopher Philip Novack's characterization of the will to power:

> What, then, is the will to power? It is life's intrinsic and inexorable ache for *more*. Living processes incessantly seek the enjoyment of their own sensorium, the unblocked expression of their vitality, the radiance of their health, the overcoming of resistances, and the amplification of their self-feeling. Life in each and every one of its infinite manifestations carries within it a will to fulfillment, a will to expansion, a will to deeper, fuller being.... The will to power, Nietzsche tells us, includes but exceeds the will to self-preservation. For it seeks not only the continuance of life, but *more* life, an *intensification* of life.[15]

From a Nietzschean point of view, modernity—with its mass movements, reliance on technology, science, educated *reasonableness*, and Christianized emphasis on altruism—devolves away from the *intensification* of life toward the mere extension and preservation of it.

> [W]hat one formerly did "for the sake of God" one now does for the sake of money, that is to say of that which now gives the highest feeling of power and good conscience.
> — Friedrich Nietzsche

The Diseases of Modernity

In contrast to the seemingly intelligible, manageable, tamable world of the scientist and modern philosopher, and in contrast to the God-centered, created world of the theistic believer, Nietzsche offers another perspective:

> And do you know what "the world" is to me? Shall I show it to you in my mirror? This world: a monster of energy, without beginning, without end; a firm, iron magnitude of force that does not grow bigger or smaller, that does not expend itself but only transforms itself; as a whole, of unalterable size, a household without expenses or losses, but likewise without increase or income; enclosed by "nothingness" as by a boundary; not something blurry or wasted, not something endlessly extended, but set in a definite space as a definite force, and not a space that might be "empty" here or there, but rather as force throughout....
>
> [This is] my ... world of the eternally self-creating, the eternally self-destroying, this mystery world of the twofold voluptuous delight, my "beyond good and evil," without goal, unless the joy of the circle is itself a goal; without will, unless a ring feels good-will toward itself—do you want a *name* for this world? A *solution* for all its riddles? ... *This world is the will to power—and nothing besides!* And you yourselves are also this will to power—and nothing besides![16]

Nietzsche claimed that late-nineteenth-century European culture was dominated by a superficially optimistic belief that scientific progress and Christian morality could subdue the will to power and thereby make life safe and meaningful for the masses. But just under the surface, Nietzsche said, lay a fatal, festering cultural sickness: modernity.

The cultural sickness that Nietzsche describes rests on unabashed, unwarranted faith: in science, in philosophy, and in Christianity. Each of these "decaying" belief systems is, Nietzsche asserts, hostile to the will to power, the will to exalt ourselves, the will to *live*. Science, for instance, reduces us to inevitable helpless effects, limited by the myth of objective reality, to whatever causal accounts of our world, our origins, and our selves science deigns to pronounce. Prolonged dominance of scientism results in self-contempt.

> [E]verything that elevates an individual above the herd and intimidates the neighbor is henceforth called evil; and the fair, modest, submissive, conforming mentality, the mediocrity of desires attains moral designations and honors.
>
> — Friedrich Nietzsche

The Problem of Morality

In Nietzsche's view, the same desires that attract us to science's false promise of control and objectivity attract us to such products of modern philosophy as utilitarian and Kantian ethics. (See Chapters 12 and 11, respectively.) Like science, these modernist ethical schemes reduce the great passions of *living* to thin utilitarian calculations or pinched Kantian formulae. And just as the scientist is mendacious for failing to reveal her own will to power, so too is the modern moral philosopher mendacious for being blinded to the brute fact that his philosophizing is always philosophizing from a perspective, for a *purpose:*

> With a stiff seriousness that inspires laughter, all our philosophers demanded something ... exalted, presumptuous, and solemn from themselves as soon as they approached the study of morality: they wanted to supply a *rational foundation* for

morality—and every philosopher so far has believed that he has provided such a foundation. Morality itself, however, was accepted as "given." How remote from their clumsy pride was that task which they considered insignificant and left in dust and must—the task of description—although the subtlest fingers and senses can scarcely be subtle enough for it.

Just because our moral philosophers knew the facts of morality only very approximately in arbitrary extracts or in accidental epitomes—for example, as the morality of *their* environment, *their* class, *their* church, the spirit of *their* time, *their* climate and part of the world—just because they were poorly informed and not even very curious about different peoples, times, and past ages—they never laid eyes on the real problems of morality; for these emerge only when we compare *many* moralities. In all "science of morals" so far one thing was *lacking*, strange as it may sound: the problem of morality itself; what was lacking was any suspicion that there was something problematic here. What the philosophers called "a rational foundation for morality" and tried to supply was, seen in the right light, merely a scholarly variation of the common *faith* in the prevalent morality; a new means of *expression* for this faith; and thus just another fact within a particular morality; indeed, in the last analysis a kind of denial that this morality might ever be considered problematic—certainly the very opposite of an examination, analysis, questioning, and vivisection of this very faith.[17]

Of every morality, Nietzsche says, "one can still always ask: what does such a claim tell us about the man who makes it? . . . In short, moralities are also merely a *sign language of the affects*."[18] Far from expressing objective or universal truths, or even scientific facts, moral codes reflect the desires and perspectives of those who create them.

Nietzsche accuses modern Western culture of being *moralistic*. To be **moralistic** is to express commonplace moral sentiments that conflict with one's behavior and to equate moral sentimentality with virtuous living. Being moralistic is a form of hypocrisy that resembles what Freudian psychologists refer to as a *reaction formation*. **Reaction formation** is the name of the ego defense mechanism that attempts to prevent "dangerous" desires from being exposed and expressed by endorsing opposite attitudes and types of behavior as "barriers" against them. In the following passage, Nietzsche goes so far as to say that *the most distinctive feature of modern souls and modern books is moralistic mendaciousness:*

> For if a psychologist today has *good taste* (others might say, integrity) it consists in resistance to the shamefully *moralized* way of speaking which has gradually made all modern judgments of men and things slimy. One should not deceive oneself in this manner: the most distinctive feature of modern souls and modern books is not lying but their inveterate *innocence* in moralistic mendaciousness. To have to rediscover this "innocence" everywhere—this constitutes perhaps the most disgusting job among all the precarious tasks a psychologist has to tackle today.[19]

From the perspective of modern Christian morality—and for Nietzsche, all modern morality has a Christian basis—Nietzsche is an anti-moralist, or to use his more provocative term, he is "the first immoralist."[20]

In Nietzsche's view, modernity is anti-life and anti-nature, and modern, Christianized moralities are symptoms of this *décadence*, this decay. In the following

---

Insofar as we believe in morality we pass sentence on existence.
— Friedrich Nietzsche

moralistic
Expressing commonplace moral sentiments that conflict with one's behavior and equating moral sentimentality with virtuous living; a form of hypocrisy that resembles a reaction formation.

reaction formation
A Freudian ego defense mechanism that attempts to prevent "dangerous" desires from being exposed and expressed by endorsing opposite attitudes and types of behavior as "barriers" against them.

passage, Nietzsche ascribes the "error of modernity" to all of humankind (with an oblique reference to Kantianism):

> It is *not* error as error which horrifies me . . . it is the lack of nature, it is the utterly ghastly fact that *antinature* itself has received the highest honours as morality, and has hung over mankind as law, as categorical imperative! . . . To blunder to this extent, *not* as an individual, *not* as a people, but as mankind![21]

The Problem of Generalized Accounts

At first glance, utilitarian ethics would seem to avoid the Nietzschean charge of being *anti-life*. After all, as we learned in Chapter 12, utilitarians accept an egoistic basis for their philosophy; Jeremy Bentham even hangs the principle of utility on an *egoistic hook*. But according to Nietzsche, the great Mill notwithstanding, the utilitarians sublimate the individual to the *group* (which Nietzsche sometimes refers to as the *herd*). They also manifest unwarranted faith in reason and, in Mill's case, preach altruism.

Further, according to Nietzsche, the mendacious belief that bad actions stem from curable ignorance—not evil—is as old as Socrates. In *Beyond Good and Evil*, Nietzsche links this optimistic faith in the capacity of reason to produce good behavior with utilitarian faith in science as the vehicle of social reform. He is particularly harsh toward the modern notion that through proper education and the application of scientific empiricism, society can be reformed. In the following passage, Nietzsche's contempt for this perspective is clear:

> "Nobody wants to do harm to himself, therefore all that is bad is done involuntarily. For the bad do harm to themselves: this they would not do if they knew that the bad is bad. Hence the bad are bad only because of an error; if one removes the error, one necessarily makes them—good."
>
> This type of inference smells of the *rabble* that sees nothing in bad actions but the unpleasant consequences and really judges, "it is *stupid* to do what is bad," while "good" is taken without further ado to be identical with "useful and agreeable." In the case of every moral utilitarianism one may immediately infer the same origin and follow one's nose: one will rarely go astray.[22]

If we have our own why of life, we shall get along with almost any how.
— Friedrich Nietzsche

For Nietzsche, the equation of "bad" with "stupid" and "ignorant" is both a result of and a contributor toward the modern decline of culture, the reduction of the threatening—but vital—passions to mere "errors." And, of course, errors are correctable. But, Nietzsche says, what modern society sees as progress—gained by adopting a "scientific" or "objective" attitude toward badness—is in fact a loss of grandeur. The ideal modern citizen is tame, democratic, sheeplike, and compassionate. This view, however, is merely one *fashion in morality*:

> *Fashions in morality.*—How the overall moral judgements have shifted! The great men of antique morality, Epictetus for instance, knew nothing of the now normal glorification of thinking of others, of living for others; in the light of our moral fashion they would have to be called downright immoral, for they strove with all their might *for* their *ego* and *against* feeling with others (that is to say, with the sufferings and moral frailties of others). Perhaps they would reply to us: "If you are so boring or ugly an object to yourself, by all means think of others more than yourself! It is right you should!"[23]

According to Nietzsche, our fear of being "unfair" ultimately makes us impotent in the face of danger. "There is," he says, "a point in the history of society when it becomes so pathologically soft and tender that among other things it sides even with those who harm it, criminals, and does this quite seriously and honestly. Punishing somehow seems unfair.... 'Is it not enough to render him undangerous? Why still punish? Punishing itself is terrible.' With this question, herd morality, the morality of timidity, draws its ultimate consequence."

Nietzsche's critique of culture centers on his deep and abiding suspicion of all attempts to generalize or universalize a code for living. Nietzsche insisted that science, modern philosophy, and all transcendental schemes turn away from life itself, from vitality, joy, depth, and moral health to the degree that they speak of and to *all*. They sow cultural and spiritual disease *because they generalize where one must not generalize:*

> All these moralities that address themselves to the individual, for the sake of his "happiness," as one says—what are they but counsels for behavior in relation to the degree of *dangerousness* in which the individual lives with himself; recipes against his passions, his good and bad inclinations insofar as they have the will to power and want to play the master ... they generalize where one must not generalize. All of them speak unconditionally, take themselves for unconditional, all of them flavored with more than one grain of salt.... All of it is, measured intellectually, worth very little and not by a long shot "science" much less "wisdom," but rather, to say it once more, three times more, prudence, prudence, prudence, mixed with stupidity, stupidity, stupidity.... "Morality as Timidity."[24]

So intense is modernity's assault on individual expressions of the will to power that Western society produces individuals who "side with" those who harm them. (We "forgive," we "understand," we "tolerate" and "empathize with" our abusers and enemies.)

There is a point in the history of society when it becomes so pathologically soft and tender that among other things it sides even with those who harm it, criminals, and does this quite seriously and honestly. Punishing somehow seems unfair to it, and it is certain that imagining "punishment" and "being supposed to punish" hurts it, arouses fear in it. "Is it not enough to render him *undangerous*? Why still punish? Punishing itself is terrible." With this question, herd morality, the morality of timidity, draws its ultimate consequence. Supposing that one could altogether abolish danger, the reason for fear, this morality would be abolished, too, *eo ipso:* it would no longer be needed, it would no longer *consider itself* necessary.

Whoever examines the conscience of the [citizen] today will have to pull the same imperative out of a thousand moral folds and hideouts—the imperative of herd timidity: "we want that some day there should be *nothing any more to be afraid of!*" Some day…is now called "progress."[25]

In Nietzsche's view, all of modernity's efforts to make scientific and moral *progress* are pointing toward a great cultural shift that heralds the next level of evolution, the end of human history and the beginning of the age of the overman. Like it or not, Nietzsche says, science and philosophy do not provide us with meaning; we create it. And like it or not, religion does not provide us with salvation: God is dead.

God Is Dead

Nietzsche claimed he was the first to have "discovered" the death of God. In part, he meant that the *idea of God* has lost its full creative force, its full power. The full extent of the dethronement of God is not yet felt by the great masses, who still *believe that they believe in God*. Yet if we dig deep into our own psyches, Nietzsche prophesied, we will discover that we no longer have ultimate faith in God: Our true faith is in scientific and technological progress.

Moreover, Nietzsche thought there is no turning back; authentic, fearlessly honest faith in God is not possible in the modern world. God is dead, and we have killed him, with mediocre notions of "progress," with "optimism," with faith in this world. Yet so deeply ingrained is the language of God, the idea of God, that we are unaware of the great spiritual shift. The news of God's death has not reached us— that is, it has not penetrated to our very bones. We worship, but falsely. Our faith is empty at bottom. And even though some of us may sense that the old religions are dead and dying, we remain unable to face the consequences of life without God.

And terrible those consequences can be. If there is no God, Nietzsche said, then all values must be revalued. In one of the most famous passages in Western philosophy, Nietzsche, the prophet of the death of God, delivered his message in the form of a parable:

> *The Madman.*—Have you ever heard of the madman who on a bright morning lighted a lantern and ran to the market-place calling out unceasingly: "I seek God! I seek God!"—As there were many people standing about who did not believe in God, he caused a great deal of amusement. Why! is he lost? said one. Has he strayed away like a child? said another. Or does he keep himself hidden? Is he afraid of us? Has he taken a sea-voyage? Has he emigrated?—the people cried out laughingly,

Almost two thousand years, and no new god!
— Friedrich Nietzsche

all in a hubbub. The insane man jumped into their midst and transfixed them with his glances. "Where is God gone?" he called out. "I mean to tell you! *We have killed him*—you and I! We are all his murderers! But how have we done it? How were we able to drink up the sea? Who gave us the sponge to wipe away the whole horizon? What did we do when we loosened this earth from its sun? Whither does it now move? Whither do we move? Away from all suns? Do we not dash on unceasingly? Backwards, sideways, forewards, in all directions? Is there still an above and below? Do we not stray, as through infinite nothingness? Does not empty space breathe upon us? Has it not become colder? Does not night come on continually, darker and darker? Shall we not have to light lanterns in the morning? Do we not hear the noise of the grave-diggers who are burying God? Do we not smell the divine putrefaction?—for even Gods putrefy! God is dead! God remains dead! And we have killed him!"[26]

This parable is best understood in light of Nietzsche's overall cultural critique, in which he predicted the decline of Christianity. That is, he saw the world as no longer innocent. Copernicus and Galileo had forever changed our sense of scale: The earth is a tiny, virtually invisible speck in a massive, purposeless universe. "What were we doing when we unchained the earth from its sun?" This new universe has no fixed center: "Is there still any up or down? Are we not straying as through an infinite nothing?" Darwin had forever altered our sense of ourselves as God's special creation. The new image of *merely human* beings is ignoble: We are but one species among millions struggling to survive, descendants of some primordial ooze.

What the masses think of as progress has come at a great price: the price of a way of life, the price of our vision of ourselves. It is difficult to comprehend the enormous scale of this change, this death of a worldview, Nietzsche insisted. Indeed, some of us may lack the intelligence, the courage, and the will to comprehend it:

"How shall we console ourselves, the most murderous of all murderers? The holiest and the mightiest that the world has hitherto possessed, has bled to death under our knife,—who will wipe the blood from us? With what water could we cleanse ourselves? What lustrums, what sacred games shall we have to devise? Is not the magnitude of this deed too great for us? Shall we not ourselves have to become Gods, merely to seem worthy of it? There never was a greater event,—and on account of it, all who are born after us belong to a higher history than any history hitherto!"

Here the madman was silent and looked again at his hearers; they also were silent and looked at him in surprise. At last he threw his lantern on the ground, so that it broke in pieces and was extinguished. "I come too early," he then said,

"I am not yet at the right time. This prodigious event is still on its way, and is travelling,—it has not yet reached men's ears. Lightning and thunder need time, the light of the stars needs time, deeds need time, even after they are done, to be seen and heard. This deed is as yet further from them than the furthest star—*and yet they have done it!*"

It is further stated that the madman made his way into different churches on the same day, and there intoned his *Requiem aeternam deo.* When led out and called to account, he always gave the reply: "What are these churches now, if they are not the tombs and monuments of God?"[27]

Those who claim to be hurt by words must be led to expect nothing as compensation. Otherwise, once they learn they can get something by claiming to be hurt, they will go into the business of being offended.
— Jonathan Rauch

According to Nietzsche, the death of God leads to nihilism. From the Latin word for "nothing," nihilism refers to the belief that the universe lacks objective meaning and purpose. Consequently, moral, social, and political values are *creative interpretations;* they reflect their subjective origins. Without God, there can be no objective base for values.

Nietzsche predicted that nihilism would be the wave of the future (our present). He predicted that as more and more people perceive religious values to be empty and science as having no meaning or purpose to offer us, a sense of emptiness would initially prevail: It all amounts to nothing. Life is a cosmic accident. There is no supernatural order, no divinely or rationally ordained goal. Without God, without *the* goal, what is left? Only many goals; only *this* momentary goal. Without God, we can turn only to ourselves.

In a nihilistic universe, what determines what counts? What determines which physique is beautiful? What determines whether it is better to be meek or arrogant? According to Nietzsche, the answers are always found in the particular, subjective interests of individuals and groups. We *choose* value systems and philosophies based on our sense of power: Which interpretation gives me and my kind advantage over others?

nihilism
From Latin for "nothing"; belief that the universe lacks meaning and purpose.

Overman

The death of God and the increasing democratization of Western culture signal both a great calamity and a great opportunity—depending on the individual's perspective. It is a calamity to those inferior types who cannot bear to stand on their own and who crave the security of the democratic herd. It is a glorious opportunity for the fearless individual, the overman.

The **overman** is not a product of evolution, nor is he some sort of master who will "lord" it over the masses. The overman is a "windfall" who will master his (or her) weaknesses and talents. The overman is a new "higher type" that will emerge out of the weakness and hypocrisies of the common herd. He is more than a *merely human* being. Zarathustra says the overman cannot emerge except through struggle and by abolishing the false idols of conventional morality and decadent religion:

> But my fervent will to create impels me ever again toward man; thus is the hammer impelled toward the stone, O men, in the stone there sleeps an image, the image of my images. Alas, that it must sleep in the hardest, the ugliest stone! Now my hammer rages cruelly against its prison. Pieces of rock rain from the stone; what is that to me? I want to perfect it; for a shadow came to me—the stillest and lightest of all things once came to me. The beauty of the overman came to me as a shadow. O my brothers, what are the gods to me now?
>
> Thus spoke Zarathustra.[28]

overman
Nietzsche's "higher type," a more-than-human being that will emerge only by overcoming the false idols of conventional morality and religion; announced in *Thus Spake Zarathustra.*

Without God to limit us, to define us, to smother us, we can finally grow "beyond man." In Nietzsche's philosophy, "man," meaning the *merely human* being, is defined in terms of God. We are created in "the image of God" and remain perpetual "children of God." When God dies, we are left without identity or purpose, in a vast universe that "just is." The same science that has given us so much has robbed us

If society consisted of highly valuable individuals, it would be worthwhile to adapt to it, but generally it is dominated by weak and stupid people and thus suffocates all higher individual values.

— Marie-Louise von Franz

of purpose. The deeper science looks, the less it finds: molecules, atoms, electrons, quarks, energy...the abyss.

Nietzsche, the prophet of the next stage in human evolution, predicts that conditions are ripe for the emergence, here and there, of what is virtually a new species in terms of its psychological and spiritual differences from mere man. The overman is Nietzsche's answer to the pessimism and nihilism that follow in the wake of God's death and the effects of modernity:

> The greatest recent event—that "God is dead," that the belief in the Christian god has become unbelievable—is already beginning to cast its first shadows....The event itself is far too great, too distant, too remote for the multitude's capacity for comprehension even for the tidings of it to be thought of as having *arrived* as yet. Much less may one suppose that many people know as yet *what* this event really means—and how much must collapse now that [the possibility of] faith has been undermined because it was built upon this faith [in God's existence], propped up by it, grown into it; for example, the whole of our...morality.[29]

Nietzsche never fully developed a picture of the overman. Of course, given that the overman is farther from mere man than we are from an ape, no *merely human* being can comprehend the overman. Nietzsche readily admitted that he is only the prophet of the higher type, adding, "But from time to time I may be granted a glance—only one glance—at something perfect, something that has attained its end, something happy, powerful, triumphant."[30]

For Deeper Consideration

What did Nietzsche mean when he said that God is dead, and we have killed him? What does the death of God have to do with the overman? With nihilism? If, as Nietzsche insists, God is dead, why does belief in God thrive in today's world? Indeed, poll after poll reports that America is among the most "religious" countries, with upwards of 80 percent of Americans attesting to belief in God. Controversies surrounding abortion, evolution, euthanasia, gay marriage, and attacks on Western culture by fundamentalist Muslims seem to indicate a persistently deep-seated, transnational belief in God. How would Nietzsche assess these conditions? Does widespread belief in God invalidate Nietzsche's pronouncement?

herd man
In Nietzschean philosophy, the type of person who cannot face being alone in a godless universe, an inferior individual seeking safety and identity in a group or from another; characterized by resentment and hypocrisy.

Slave Morality

Though we may never fully grasp exactly what or who the overman is, we can perhaps glimpse its shadow indirectly by taking a look at the actions and beliefs of what amounts to its opposite: the slave or herd man.

Herd man is one of the terms Nietzsche uses for the "merely human" type of person who cannot face being alone in a godless universe, a person who refuses to be an individual, a person who does not exist as an individual, a person who turns to the group or herd (Kierkegaard's "the crowd") for power, identity, and purpose. The inferior individual's awareness of his on her own inferiority produces envy and resentment of all "higher types" and elitist value systems.

In an effort to control their superiors, members of the herd create **slave morality**, a value system based on guilt, fear, and a distortion of the will to power in which the characteristics of the inferior type—humility, passivity, dependency—are praised as virtues, while the characteristics of the superior type—love of domination, delight in one's own talents, fearlessness—are condemned as arrogance and coldheartedness. Slave morality creates inhibitions, false ideals of equality, restrictive duties "owed" to our inferiors, and weakening of strong instincts by "bad conscience." The herd is always hostile to the individual.

In other words, slave morality tries to convince the powerful that they should protect the weak. According to Nietzsche, slave morality arose when rules conquered instincts in ancient Greece. Today, rationalistic Greek and Christian ethics are the two chief sources of slave morality in modern Western culture. Fairness, equality, moderation, "stepping aside," refusing to claim the full rights accompanying superior ability and talent, and resentment are all characteristics of slave morality. So are easy pity, lust for leisure, longing to fit in, and, ironically, a hunger to stand out from the crowd whose attention we need in order to stand out.

History up to the present is a record of the withering away of a noble *master morality*, as century by century the virtues of the herd weakened Western culture. Today we even resist talking about higher types. We claim that all people are fundamentally equal. Zarathustra speaks:

> You higher men learn this from me: in the market place nobody believes in higher men. And if you want to speak there, very well! But the mob blinks: "We are all equal."
>
> "You higher men"—thus blinks the mob—"there are no higher men, we are all equal, man is man; before God we are all equal."
>
> Before God! But now this God has died. And before the mob we do not want to be equal. You higher men, go away from the market place![31]

slave morality
In Nietzschean philosophy, a distortion of the will to power in which the characteristics of the inferior merely human type are praised as virtues, and the characteristics of the superior type (overman) are condemned as arrogance and coldheartedness; a morality of inhibitions, equality, restrictive duties, and "bad conscience."

PHILOSOPHICAL QUERY

Do you think todays "marketplace" mentality discourages excellence in individuals? Using specific examples, discuss why or why not.

MindTap
Discussing Philosophy

Ressentiment

Slave morality originates from a deep form of psychically polluting resentment that Nietzsche always referred to with the French word *ressentiment*. In the following passage from *Toward a Genealogy of Morals*, Nietzsche distinguishes between the slave morality of the herd man and the master morality of the overman:

> The slaves' revolt in morals begins with this, that *ressentiment* itself becomes creative and gives birth to values: the *ressentiment* of those who are denied the real reaction, that of the deed, and who compensate with an imaginary revenge. Whereas all noble morality begins out of a triumphant affirmation of

ressentiment
French for "resentment"; term used in Nietzschean philosophy for a deep form of psychically polluting resentment that generates slave morality; the dominant emotion of the herd.

"An Iconoclast Looks at Education"

There is nothing of which our culture suffers more than of the superabundance of pretentious jobbers and fragments of humanity; our universities are, *against* their will, the real hothouses for this kind of withering of the instincts of the spirit.

...No one is any longer free to give his children a noble education: our "higher schools" are all set up for the most ambiguous mediocrity, with their teachers, curricula, and teaching aims. And everywhere an indecent haste prevails, as if something would be lost if the young man of twenty-three were not yet "finished," or if he did not yet know the answer to the "main question": *which* calling? A higher kind of human being, if I may say so, does not like "callings," precisely because he knows himself to be called. He has time, he takes time, he does not even think of "finishing": at thirty one is, in the sense of high culture, a beginner, a child. Our overcrowded secondary schools, our overworked, stupefied secondary-school teachers, are a scandal: for one to defend such conditions...there may perhaps be causes—reasons there are none.

Friedrich Nietzsche, *Twilight of the Idols,* in *The Portable Nietzsche*, trans. Walter Kaufmann (New York: Penguin, 1968), pp. 502, 510–511.

"You higher men learn this from me," says Zarathustra; "in the market place nobody believes in higher men.... But the mob blinks: 'We are all equal.'" Do you agree with Nietzsche/Zarathustra's insistence that the common ideal of "blind justice" is based on the pretense that we all are equals? Is justice blind? Do we want it to be?

oneself, slave morality immediately says No to what comes from outside, to what is different, to what is not oneself: and *this* No is its creative deed. This reversal of the value-positing glance—this *necessary* direction outward instead of back to oneself—is of the nature of *ressentiment:* to come into being, slave morality requires an outside world, a counterworld; physiologically speaking, it requires external stimuli in order to react at all: its action is always at bottom a reaction.[32]

In other words, slave morality is alien to any individual—as an individual. Slave morality is so opposed to the authentic individual that his or her own self-creating urges and impulses are stifled in favor of "external stimuli" that function as guidelines from others and from the herd. Slave morality is inauthentic (phony and uncreative) because it is "always a reaction", never an originating impulse. (See Chapter 14 for more on authenticity.) Slave morality settles for the "imaginary revenge" of the afterlife: "God will punish the bad people since we are too weak to do so." Or it settles for the earthly revenge of mediocrity.

The herd man fears "the other", whether in the form of the authentic individual or in the merely different. Thus, slave morality encourages conformity; national, ethnic, gender, and religious bigotry; and unthinking patriotism: "Slave morality immediately says No to what comes from outside, to what is different, to what is not oneself." Healthy impulses are converted into repression, into sheepishly crafting ourselves to fit an external, culturally derived image. We become a type of person.

From a healthy aesthetic perspective, the merely human person is repulsive, characterized by weakness, evasion, hypocrisy, and grudge. Slave morality is a morality of resignation, deferment, withdrawal from the full range of life, and prohibition. In reality, the merely human members of the herd do not reject the lusty, fateful, self-affirming, creative aspects of the human psyche because they are bad, but because they are too weak, sick, and corrupt to live up to them—and out of *ressentiment* wants to prevent others from living up to them as well.

PHILOSOPHICAL QUERY

As you might expect, Nietzsche's characterization of slave morality was and remains controversial. Do you think it is dangerous? Is it unfair to expect most people not to have some *ressentiment*? Is today's tendency to see many people as "victims" a reflection of slave morality? Or is it a sign of moral and cultural progress?

Discussing Philosophy

Master Morality

If there are two fundamentally different types of people (merely human and overman), then there must be two radically different types of morality. One universal standard cannot apply equally to the common herd and to the superior, perfected overman.

Although both types possess the *will to power*, they differ significantly in their approaches to power. For the overman, the will to power is expressed openly, honestly, and nobly through exuberant, life-affirming self-creation and self-imposition. That is, the overman creates—experiments with—a "new law tablet," a code of values that is the opposite of the weak herd man's slave morality. Because the slave to others lacks courage and nobility, he or she must resort to appeals to a "father God," to neurotic guilt, to external guarantees of "fairness" and equality, and to demands for pity (dressed up as an "obligation" to show compassion). In the herd, the will to individual power is perverted through manipulation, *ressentiment*, and indirection shaped by unwholesome feelings of gross inadequacy—it is not expressed honestly and openly.

Master morality, in contrast to slave morality, is an *aesthetic-heroic* code of honor. That is, the overman looks only to himself or herself for value. And value is defined in aesthetic terms: noble–ignoble (shameful), glorious–degrading, honorable–dishonorable, refined–vulgar, and so on. In simple terms, for the overman, "good" equals "noble" and "evil" equals "vulgar."

According to Nietzsche:

> To be unable to take one's own enemies, accidents, and misdeeds seriously for long—that is the sign of strong and rich natures.... Such a man simply shakes off with one shrug much vermin that would have buried itself deep in others; here alone is it also possible—assuming that is possible at all on earth—that there be real "*love* of one's enemies." How much respect has a noble person for his enemies!... Conversely, imagine "the enemy" as conceived by a man of

To dream here perhaps of equal rights, equal training, equal claims and obligations: that is a typical sign of shallow-mindedness.
— Friedrich Nietzsche

master morality
In Nietzschean philosophy, the aesthetic honor code of the overman; morality that looks only to the authentic individual (overman) for values that transcend the slave's good–evil dichotomy with glorious–degrading, honorable–dishonorable, refined–vulgar, and so on; "good" equals "noble" and "evil" equals "vulgar."

ressentiment—and here precisely is his deed, his creation: he has conceived "the evil enemy," "*the evil one*"—and indeed as the fundamental concept from which he then derives, as an after-image and counterinstance, a "good one"—himself.[33]

Whereas the overman's morality begins with his affirmation of his own beloved self, herd morality begins with the invention of the "evil other" the *evil one*. For the overman, "bad" is the afterimage. For the herd man, "good" is the afterimage. Thus, master morality is positive in its orientation; slave morality is negative.

If Nietzsche is correct, we live in the twilight of a culture. The "horizon is free" because no new value system and vision have replaced the old dying one. Those who live through the twilight of the old beliefs will experience confusion, fear, a strong desire to hold on to idols; but they will also experience unlimited opportunities for growth. In the twilight of our idols, we are handed the opportunity to fashion our own way. It is up to us to define—to actually create—our very selves.

Zarathustra says:

> "I *teach you the overman*. Man is something that shall be overcome. What have you done to overcome him?
>
> "All beings so far have created something beyond themselves; and do you want to be the ebb of this great flood and even go back to the beasts rather than overcome man? What is the ape to man? A laughingstock or a painful embarrassment. And man shall be just that for the overman: a laughingstock or a painful embarrassment. You have made your way from worm to man, and much in you is still worm. Once you were apes, and even now, too, man is more ape than any ape....
>
> "Man is a rope, tied between beast and overman—a rope over an abyss. A dangerous across, a dangerous on-the-way, a dangerous looking-back, a dangerous shuddering and stopping....
>
> "I love all those who are as heavy drops, falling one by one out of the dark cloud that hangs over men; they herald the advent of lightning, and, as heralds, they perish.
>
> "Behold, I am the herald of the lightning and a heavy drop from the cloud; but this lightning is called *overman*." [34]

The very same conditions of nihilism and annihilation of values that despirit, discourage, and frighten the common, mediocre, merely human man or woman exhilarate and inspire the overman. Having overcome merely human resentment and self-loathing, the overman *looks forward to being precisely what and who he (or she) is*.

Amor Fati

In the absence of God, Nietzsche says, we must redeem ourselves with the *sacred Yes to life* expressed through **amor fati**, the love of our specific fate expressed as joyous affirmation and delight that everything is exactly as and what it is. Nihilism teaches us that there is no divine purpose or design that gives meaning and quality to our lives. Science shows us that matter follows inexorable laws. God is dead. What is left?

I mistrust all systematizers and I avoid them. The will to a system is a lack of integrity.
— Friedrich Nietzsche

amor fati
Nietzsche's term meaning "the love of fate"; expressed as joyous affirmation and delight that everything is exactly as and what it is.

What alone can *our* teaching be?—That no one *gives* a human being his qualities: not God, not society, not his parents or ancestors, not *he himself*....*No one* is accountable for existing at all, or for being constituted as he is, or for living in the circumstances and surroundings in which he lives. The fatality of nature cannot be disentangled from the fatality of all that which has been and will be. He is *not* the result of special design, a will, a purpose...it is absurd to want to *hand over* his nature to some purpose or other. *We* invented the concept of "purpose": in reality purpose is *lacking*....One is necessary, one is a piece of fate...there exists nothing which could judge, measure, compare, condemn the whole....*nothing exists apart from the whole*....We deny God; in denying God, we deny accountability: only by doing *that* do we redeem the world.[35]

Amor fati blesses everything exactly as it is. Through *amor fati*, we realize that we exist as parts of a complex whole that can be only precisely what it is and cannot be otherwise. *Amor fati* overcomes the corruption imposed by modernity and slave morality; it restores us to innocence by redeeming us from the ancient concepts of sin and guilt before the braying herd and before God. Nietzsche says:

My formula for greatness in a human being is *amor fati*: that one wants nothing to be other than it is, not in the future, not in the past, not in all eternity. Not merely to endure that which happens of necessity, still less to dissemble it...but to *love* it.[36]

> *[I]f you ever wanted one moment twice, if ever you said: "You please me, happiness, instant, moment!" then you wanted everything to return!*
> — Friedrich Nietzsche

> *He who is afraid to look back, alas, has already done so in his own heart.*
> — George Linville

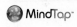 MindTap

Aplia

Commentary

Nietzsche was nothing if not authentic. And as disturbing as much of his philosophy can be, there is no escaping its power to provoke a response—often a passionate response. His assertive denial of objective meaning has influenced a whole generation of scholars and literary critics (called *new critics* and *deconstructionists*). Nietzsche's influence on postmodern scholarship cannot be overestimated. Nietzschean influences on current critical theories are found in the rejection of the possibility of unbiased (objective) interpretation, the view that all scholarship is autobiography, and unapologetic self-reference on the part of academic authors.

In the postmodern world, a world without objective value, without God, without "the truth," all that is left seems to be "my truth"—or more precisely, "my truths." Ironically, however, when nihilistic self-promotion becomes the trend and when "being an individual" becomes a consciously contrived goal, Nietzschean originality and authenticity disappear. Being "a Nietzschean" is no more possible than following someone else's orders to be free! After all, it was Nietzsche himself who insisted that "Those who understand me, understand that I can have no disciples." There is bitter (but not unexpected) irony in the notion of being "a Nietzschean."

Nietzsche's critique of contemporary culture is more subtle and profound than it may appear. On the whole, our culture does seem to have lost faith in the very idea of a single true religion and a common, shared value system that asserts more than sweeping platitudes and generalities. Education seems to have lost any central focus and seems increasingly reduced to training without purpose or to efforts by various groups (herds?) to enforce their individual points of view (today we call them agendas). Even the seemingly endless national debate over school curricula has Nietzschean roots: If there is no objective meaning, then everything is a "point of view," an expression of "diversity." If everything is a point of view, why should I have to accept your point of view or you mine? If everything is a point of view, there is no true history, no true interpretation of literature, no clear hierarchy of values.

Though it is not currently *politically correct* to suggest that we are not all equal, that some of us are entitled to more than the rest, we do not appear to believe the doctrine of equality that we preach: Each new wave of immigrants ("the evil other") generates hostility, fear, and resentment (ethnic resentment, gender resentment, class resentment, religious resentment). We certainly seem to be a culture searching for something, some clear, unifying set of values. And, for Nietzsche, that is the problem: We are looking outward for validation instead of creating ourselves according to our own, individual aesthetic codes.

So it is, that for us Nietzschean questions remain: Is God dead? If so, what next? If not, whence our widespread resentments, confusions, and fears? Are we all equal in any significant sense? If not, what then? Can we bear to ask these questions? Dare we not ask them?

I leave the last word to Nietzsche, a hopeful word, expressed in 1882 as a comment titled "For the New Year" but that speaks to the psychological possibility of renewal and affirmation of life at any moment:

> Today everyone is permitted to express his desire and dearest thoughts: so I too would like to say what I have desired of myself today and what thought was the first to cross my heart this year—what thought shall be the basis and guarantee and sweetness of all my future life! I want to learn more and more to see what is necessary in things as the beautiful in them—thus I shall become one of those who make things beautiful. *Amor fati:* may that be my love from now on! I want to wage no war against the ugly. I do not want to accuse, I do not want even to accuse the accusers. May *looking away* be my only form of negation! And, all in all: I want to be at all times hereafter only an affirmer.[37]

> *No victor believes in chance.*
> — Friedrich Nietzsche

Summary of Main Points

- Nietzsche saw himself as the first to recognize a profound sickness at the core of modernity. Modernity refers to the historical period of the nineteenth and twentieth centuries and a corresponding set of cultural conditions and beliefs dominated by Enlightenment ideals, including faith in science, objective truth, and rationality.

- Influenced by Schopenhauer's pessimism, Nietzsche concluded that life itself is an irrational, purposeless striving for a pointless existence. Nietzsche insisted that life is governed by the will to power, a universal desire to control others and impose our values on them. The will to power is also the basis of the distinction between good and evil.

- Nietzschean perspectivism, the contention that every view is only one among many possible interpretations, rejects the possibility of a neutral stance or perspectiveless perspective. According to Nietzsche, art or aesthetic vision (taste) is the basis of meaning, not science, not religion, not morality, not rationality.

- Nietzsche accuses modern Western culture of being moralistic, a form of hypocrisy that resembles what Freudian psychologists refer to as a reaction formation, the name of the ego defense mechanism that attempts to prevent dangerous desires from being exposed and expressed by endorsing opposite attitudes and types of behavior as barriers against them.

- Nietzsche claimed that he discovered the death of God: The idea of God has lost its full creative force, its full power, because science and technology have usurped God's place in people's lives. The death of God leads to nihilism, the belief that the universe lacks meaning and purpose, and that moral, social, and political values are creative interpretations because without God, there is no objective base for values.

- Slave morality is a distortion of the will to power in which the characteristics of the inferior type are praised as virtues, and the characteristics of the superior type are condemned as arrogance and cold-heartedness. Slave morality creates inhibitions, false ideals of equality, and "bad conscience."

- Master morality is an aesthetic-heroic code of honor. The overman looks only to himself or herself for value defined in aesthetic terms: noble–ignoble (shameful), glorious–degrading, honorable–dishonorable, refined–vulgar, and so on; "good" equals "noble" and "evil" equals "vulgar."

- Through *amor fati* (the love of fate), the overman approaches his life with delight that everything is and eternally will be exactly as and what it is.

Post-Reading Reflections

Now that you've had a chance to learn about the Anti-Philosopher, use your new knowledge to answer these questions.

1. How did pessimism influence Nietzsche's philosophy?

2. What role does the will to power play in Nietzsche's philosophy?

3. What is tragic about tragic optimism? What is optimistic? Why did Nietzsche reject ordinary optimism?

4. How did Nietzsche's personal experiences affect his philosophy of overcoming? What is to be overcome? Overcome by what?

5. How does Nietzsche's perspectivism free him as a thinker? Why does it result in a kind of anti-philosophy?

6. What are the diseases of modernity, and what is their cumulative effect on the herd? On the overman? How is it that the same conditions can nurture two such distinct types?

7. Explain what is meant by characterizing master morality as an aesthetic-heroic honor code. Why did Nietzsche prefer an "aesthetic" code to a moral code?

8. Why does Nietzsche associate *ressentiment* with slave morality? How does *ressentiment* lead to the development of slave morality?

9. What is the chief quality of the overman? In what sense is this quality a result of being beyond good and evil? What can we do to become overmen? Explain.

10. What does *amor fati* mean—literally, and to Nietzsche?

 MindTap

Experience MindTap through the activities highlighted in this chapter. Further explore this online, personalized learning tool to deepen your comprehension and improve your grades.

AFP/Getty Images

17

The Twentieth Century

Ludwig Wittgenstein and Martin Heidegger

When we do philosophy we are like savages, primitive people, who hear the expressions of civilized men, put a false interpretation on them, and then draw the queerest conclusions from it.

— *Ludwig Wittgenstein*

Perhaps the distinction of this age consists in the fact that the dimension of grace has been closed. Perhaps this is its unique dis-grace.

— *Martin Heidegger*

Learning Objectives

 MindTap

After you complete this chapter, you should be able to:

- Define the concept of *philosophical deconstruction*.
- Discuss the notion of philosophical realism.
- Explain what, in philosophy, is meant by the linguistic turn.
- Describe the task of the philosopher, according to the *Tractatus*.
- Define the concept of *phenomenology*.
- Define the term *ontology*.
- Explain what Martin Heidegger means when he asserts that we forget Being.
- Explain the role of idle talk for the *they*.
- Critique Heidegger's description of authentic human existence.
- Explain what happens when human beings treat themselves as *standing-reserve*.
- Describe what Heidegger sees as the supreme danger of our time.

FROM THE EIGHTEENTH CENTURY ONWARD, philosophy has grown increasingly specialized, in part due to the influence of the university system; in part due to modern philosophers' emphasis on and development of a technical philosophical vocabulary; in part due to attempts to make philosophy systematic and precise; in part due to renewed interest in the history of philosophical arguments concerning being, reality, knowledge, truth, value, and reason.[1] By the twentieth century, diverse philosophers were struggling against or furthering what has been described as the "post-Nietzschean deconstruction of metaphysics."

As a proper noun, Deconstruction*ism* refers to the writings of Jacques Derrida (1930–2004) and to an approach to literary criticism that is not confined to philosophy. As a common noun, *deconstruction* refers to the treatment of philosophical problems as conceptual and linguistic confusions that reveal their ulterior purposes when complex claims and statements are reduced to their smallest meaningful components. That is the sense we are interested in here.

Generally understood, then, philosophical **deconstruction** includes any close textual analysis that focuses on uncovering and overcoming hitherto concealed "privileges" hidden in philosophical arguments, theories, and claims. Depending on the deconstructor, philosophical assertions that cannot be clarified are set aside or rejected as empty, meaningless, nonsensical, mystical, poetic, or inauthentic.

Philosophical "deconstructors" approach philosophy historically, not as historians per se but as scrutinizers of the specific development and uses of particular philosophical notions and arguments as they pertain to actual, concrete, particular existence, to living in a specific here and now. Consequently, deconstructors challenge the notion that any text can have any definite meaning. Careful linguistic analysis is a common hallmark of otherwise divergent, even hostile, approaches to philosophical deconstruction.

In the loose sense of deconstruction, we can say that Hume deconstructed the self, causality, and ethics; Kant deconstructed Cartesian rationalism, dualism, and Humean skepticism; Bentham and Mill deconstructed the good; Marx deconstructed capitalism, philosophy, theology, and science; Kierkegaard deconstructed the crowd, objectivity, faith, truth, and existence.

Philosophical deconstruction has its most direct and influential expression in Nietzsche's critique of Western philosophy as just one more historically rooted expression of the will to power. "We are historians from top to bottom," Nietzsche said in *Human, All Too Human*, drawing a sharp line between anti-philosophers who deconstruct traditional philosophy and metaphysics and philosophers who "all to a man think unhistorically, as is the age-old custom with philosophers." To think unhistorically is to think objectively, universally, generally, and formally rather than existentially and concretely:

> "Disinterested contemplation"...is a rank absurdity....Let us, from now on, be on our guard against the hallowed philosophers' myth of a "pure, will-less, painless, timeless knower"; let us beware of the tentacles of such contradictory notions as "pure reason," "absolute knowledge," "absolute intelligence." All these concepts presuppose an eye such as no living creature can imagine, an eye required to have no direction, to abrogate its active and interpretative powers—precisely those powers that alone make seeing, *seeing something*. All seeing is essentially perspective, and so is all knowing.[2]

MindTap
Philosophy Timelines

deconstruction (philosophical)
A kind of close textual analysis focused on uncovering and overcoming "privileges" hidden in philosophical arguments and theories by taking a text apart—by deconstructing it; questions whether any text can have any definite meaning.

Against a vibrant but unstable backdrop of two world wars, fast-paced scientific advances, and changing social mores, twentieth-century philosophers questioned the very possibility of philosophy itself, asking a series of increasingly narrow and specialized questions about the future of metaphysics and the possibility of universal truth that prompted the pragmatist John Dewey (1859–1952) to declare that "despair of any integrated outlook and attitude is the chief intellectual characteristic of the twentieth century." The philosopher and novelist Iris Murdoch (1919–1999) said of twentieth-century philosophy that "There may be no deep structure," that is, no objective, independent, universal metaphysical reality "out there." Alasdair MacIntyre quipped, "Epitaph-writing has been added to the list of accredited philosophical activities."[3]

Twentieth-century philosophy was by far too diverse, too complex, too specialized, and too recent to know which—if any—among its many impressive philosophers will emerge as archetypal philosophers. As you might suspect, such divisive figures cannot be summarized without more risk than less controversial and complex philosophers can. We can minimize the risk of serious distortion, however, if our goals are modest, and they are. So here, to get a sense—and only a sense—of two influential trends in twentieth-century philosophy, are sketches of two (so far) major twentieth-century philosophers' struggles to find a unique role for philosophy in a complex, contentious, and invigorating cultural milieu. I hope they entice you to dig further—not just into their philosophies but also into your own.

Two Approaches to Philosophy

Analytic philosophy emerged in England around 1912, when Ludwig Wittgenstein began to study philosophy with Bertrand Russell at Cambridge University. As generally understood, analytic philosophy refers to a nonliterary approach to philosophy that stresses logic, testability, precision, and clarity. Analytic philosophers do not belong to a single school of philosophy but to a philosophical tradition that goes back to Locke and Hume.

Common to the analytic tradition is the notion that the universe consists of independent (atomic) entities, although individual philosophers disagree about whether these entities are material particles, sense data, impressions, "facts," or something else. Philosophy is restricted to analyzing complex statements and claims in order to reduce them to elemental, unanalyzable components. Logical and linguistic analyses are thought to be the only proper methods for sorting out philosophical confusions. The goal is to "do philosophy," not drift into theology, sociology, or history dressed up as philosophy.[4]

Philosophers often contrast analytic philosophy with what is broadly referred to as **continental philosophy**. Of course, a quick bit of linguistic analysis reveals a certain conceptual lack of symmetry: "Analytic" refers to a method, whereas "continental" refers to a locale. Be that as it may, there is, nonetheless, a useful contrast to be made. As it is currently used, the phrase "continental philosophy" came into vogue after World War II to acknowledge a growing divide between the English-speaking philosophical world and that of continental Europe, although continental philosophy as such began just before the death of Kant and includes Hegel, Schopenhauer, Kierkegaard, Marx, Nietzsche, and Martin Heidegger.[5]

analytic philosophy
An influential nonliterary approach to philosophy that stresses logic, testability, precision, and clarity with antecedents in an anglophile tradition that includes John Locke, David Hume, Bertrand Russell, and Ludwig Wittgenstein; contends that close logical and linguistic analyses are the only proper methods for sorting out philosophical confusions; commonly contrasted with continental philosophy.

continental philosophy
A broad term referring to philosophies associated with European philosophers such as Kant, Hegel, Kierkegaard, Marx, Nietzsche, Husserl, and Heidegger; not a school of philosophy as such or single way of doing philosophy; includes phenomenology, existentialism, deconstructionism; commonly contrasted with analytic philosophy.

Continental philosophers tend to explain things not by reducing them to simple entities but by understanding them in a broader, holistic context. Like analytic philosophy, twentieth-century continental philosophy is not a school of philosophy as such or a single way of doing philosophy but a diverse, often interdisciplinary approach to philosophy. Formalism, idealism, phenomenology, and existentialism are examples of continental approaches to philosophy.

Ludwig Wittgenstein

Ludwig Wittgenstein (1889–1951) has been described as a philosopher's philosopher and as a genius whose work and thinking are audacious, complicated, austere, obscure, and unsystematic. His admirers see him as a—if not the—major figure in twentieth-century philosophy. His detractors see him as a marginal, overrated character, a perplexing footnote in the history of analytic philosophy, which, these detractors insist, will itself turn out to be just a blip in the history of philosophy. Consequently, there is as yet no consensus concerning Wittgenstein's place in the history of philosophy.

Ludwig Wittgenstein

And yet, in an era in which philosophers are largely unknown among the general public, Wittgenstein is famous *as a great philosopher* because, it has been suggested, he fits the general public's notions of a philosopher: eccentric, otherworldly, cryptic, and arrogant.[6]

The youngest of eight children, Ludwig Josef Wittgenstein was born on April 26, 1889, in Vienna to one of Europe's most cultured and influential families. The Wittgensteins were wealthy, artistic, brilliant, and talented.

Wittgenstein's gifts and interests were broad. As an adult, he taught himself to play the clarinet, whistled entire musical scores from memory, dabbled in architecture, taught grade school, considered becoming a monk, devoured pulp fiction, and spent hours in the front rows of the cinema watching the same movies again and again. As a child he is supposed to have made a working model of a sewing machine.

After being home-schooled in the arts, Wittgenstein was sent to a technical college in Berlin-Charlottenburg. Unhappy, he left without completing his studies and went to England. In 1908, he began studying aeronautical engineering at Manchester University but spent most of the two years he was officially registered there living on the continent. While working on a design for a propeller with jet nozzles on the tips, Wittgenstein became intrigued by the mathematics of his design. This led to a general interest in mathematics, which, in turn, led to an interest in the philosophy of pure mathematics.

When he returned to England, Wittgenstein met the logician and mathematician Gottlob Frege (1848–1925) and read Bertrand Russell's (1872–1970) *Principles of Mathematics*. Intrigued by their new work in logic and philosophy, he took Frege's advice and in 1912 registered at Cambridge University in order to study with Russell.

From 1911 to 1913, Wittgenstein discussed the foundations of logic and philosophy with Russell and with important figures such as the philosopher G. E. Moore (1873–1958), the economist John Maynard Keynes (1883–1946), and the mathematician and philosopher Frank Ramsey (1903–1930). Retreating to Norway for months at a time, he would wrestle with philosophical and logical problems and work on solutions to them by himself.

> *"The essence is hidden from us"; this is the form our problem now assumes. We ask: "What is language?"*
> — Ludwig Wittgenstein

Imagno/Hulton Archive/Getty Images

In 1925, Wittgenstein's sister Margaret hired an architect to design a town house. Wittgenstein became enthralled by the project and designed the windows, doors, radiators, door knobs, and other aspects of what has come to be known as Haus Wittgenstein. When everything was nearly complete, Wittgenstein insisted that one of the ceilings be raised just over an inch to meet his exacting standards. After its completion, his sister Hermine said that, at first, it felt as if the "house embodied logic" and seemed "much more a dwelling for the gods than for a small mortal like me."

In 1913, Wittgenstein returned to Austria. In 1914, at the start of World War I (1914–1918), he joined the Austrian army, which essentially put an end to his close relationship with Russell, who was a pacifist. In 1917, he was captured and spent the rest of the war in an Italian prison camp, where he wrote the notes and drafts of what was to become the influential *Tractatus Logico-Philosophicus*, his first book.

Although they were no longer close, Russell thought Wittgenstein's work buttressed his own and so he helped Wittgenstein get the *Tractatus* published, first in German in 1921 and then in English in 1922. Wittgenstein accepted Russell's help, even though he was convinced that Russell did not understand what he was trying to express in the *Tractatus*, noting as early as 1919 that neither Russell nor Frege understood him.

In 1920, Wittgenstein temporarily gave up philosophy, convinced that in the *Tractatus* he had, once and for all, solved all philosophical problems. He also gave away his share of the family fortune and worked variously as a gardener in a monastery, a grade school teacher, and an architect in and around Vienna. He also contemplated becoming a monk.

By 1929, Wittgenstein was back in Cambridge, where he used the *Tractatus* to secure a Ph.D., supposedly prompting G. E. Moore, one of his examiners, to write in his report, "The *Tractatus* is a work of genius, but it otherwise satisfies the requirements for a Ph.D."[7] With a five-year fellowship to Cambridge, Wittgenstein was free to study and write, which he did with energy and intensity. His notions of philosophy and philosophical problems changed radically during this so-called middle-period, as he rejected all dogmatic philosophy, including his own *Tractatus*.

During the 1930s and 1940s, Wittgenstein conducted a series of lectures and seminars and became known as much for his odd behavior and apparent animosity toward his students as for his philosophy. During his seminars, Wittgenstein would struggle aloud with philosophical problems, occasionally bursting out, "I'm stupid today!" and other times sitting for long periods, silently sunk in thought. In this halting way, he worked out many of the ideas that were eventually published as his *Philosophical Investigations*, his second groundbreaking book—his second book, period.

The *Philosophical Investigations*, which includes sections on psychology and mathematics, reflects a deep, pervasive skepticism about philosophy's "pretensions." It signals a turn away from formal logic toward an analysis of ordinary language. By this time, the later Wittgenstein considered most philosophical problems to be nonsense (more about this below) and once jokingly and unfavorably compared

Wittgenstein retreated to a mountain cabin when he wanted to get away from Cambridge.

the intellectual—and moral—quality of a prestigious philosophy journal to detective magazines.[8]

Wittgenstein almost published his *Philosophical Investigations* in 1945 but changed his mind, preferring instead that it be published posthumously. In addition to *Investigations*, other posthumously published writings include, in the order Wittgenstein wrote them, *Notebooks 1914–16* (1961), *The Blue and Brown Books* (1958), *Zettel* (1967, revised 1981), *Remarks on the Philosophy of Psychology* (1980), and *On Certainty* (1969).

In 1939, Wittgenstein was made a professor of philosophy at Cambridge, but World War II interfered, and he worked as a hospital porter until 1944. After the war, he lectured at Cambridge but found the task distasteful. Wittgenstein resigned and moved to Ireland. In 1949, he briefly visited America and then returned to England, where he stayed with various friends in Oxford and Cambridge until his death.

Upon his return to Cambridge from America, Wittgenstein was diagnosed with prostate cancer. He spent his last days at the home of Dr. Edward Bevan and his wife, Joan. On April 28, 1951, Wittgenstein fell ill just after he and Mrs. Bevan returned from their nightly stroll. Before losing consciousness, he said to Mrs. Bevan, "Tell them I've had a wonderful life." Ludwig Wittgenstein died the next day without regaining consciousness.[9]

A few days before he died, the man who took language so seriously wrote, "God may say to me: 'I am judging you out of

Although Wittgenstein once said, "It is very hard not to be understood by a single soul," the troubled philosopher's last words were "Tell them I've had a wonderful life."

your own mouth. Your own actions have made you shudder with disgust when you have seen other people do them.'"[10]

What Are You Talking About?

As the sciences appropriated more and more questions that had once belonged chiefly to philosophers, philosophers felt challenged to "put up or shut up." That is, they needed to demonstrate that philosophy is, indeed, a specific, identifiable discipline, not just a loose set of issues historically categorized as "philosophical" until science comes up with measurable, practical ways to address and—more importantly—settle them.

The analytic tradition in philosophy began with a recognition that philosophers need to be sure they know what they are saying before they can philosophize with any confidence. Just as the epistemological turn began when Descartes recognized that the thinking thing had been taken for granted, the linguistic turn began when philosophers such as Locke began to wonder about the effects of linguistic confusions on philosophy:

> Vague and insignificant forms of speech, and abuse of language, have…long passed for mysteries of science; and hard or misapplied words, with little or no meaning, have [been] mistaken for deep learning.… They are but covers of ignorance, [and] hindrance of true knowledge.[11]

From the first, analytically oriented philosophers concentrated on clarifying our experience of experience by clarifying what we say about it—and what we can say about anything. "Saying," in this context, is different from "uttering." We utter all sorts of things that, upon reflection, do not mean much of anything. So an important, primary task of philosophy is to clear up language confusions so that we, philosophers and nonphilosophers alike, do not waste ourselves haggling over empty noises and, worse, worshiping nonsensical expressions and fighting one another over what they "really mean."

As analytic philosophy developed, it became increasingly technical—more professional than traditional philosophy; some would say, less "sloppy," less existential and personal, focusing on logic and language rather than on life. Now, of course, this is a broad characterization, and individual analytic philosophers such as Bertrand Russell took a great interest in social issues—but not technically, not professionally, not *as philosophers*.

Finally, analytic philosophers rejected traditional, idealistic metaphysics in favor of what they took to be a hard-headed, down-to-earth **realism**, the belief that there exists an independent, objective world of things, facts, and states of affairs that are accessible to us. From this perspective, the proper task of philosophy is to identify and then to toss aside mistaken claims about reality and replace them, when possible, with sensible—meaningful, testable—assertions identified through rigorous analysis. Things are what they are, and all we have to do is to clear up our understanding of them by learning how to talk about them in ways that do not allow language to "bewitch" our intelligence.

realism

In philosophy, the belief that there exists an independent, objective world of things, facts, and states of affairs that are accessible to us.

Discussing Philosophy

> **PHILOSOPHICAL QUERY**
>
> Has language ever "bewitched" your intelligence? Think carefully before you say no. Consider, as just three bewitching possibilities, "he changed his mind," "she is not being her true self," "God is everywhere."

The *Tractatus*

Wittgenstein's *Tractatus Logico-Philosophicus* is widely seen as one of the first major examples of the linguistic-analytic turn in twentieth-century philosophy. It begins with a clarion call for clarity:

> The book deals with the problems of philosophy and shows, I believe, that the reason why these problems are posed is that the logic of our language is misunderstood. The whole sense of the book might be summed up in the following words: what can be said at all can be said clearly, and what we cannot talk about must be passed over in silence.
>
> Thus the aim of the book is to set a limit to thought, or rather, not to thought but to the expression of thoughts: for in order to be able to set a limit to thought, we should have to find both sides of the limit thinkable (i.e., we should have to be able to think what cannot be thought).
>
> It will therefore only be in language that the limit can be set, and what lies on the other side of the limit will simply be nonsense.[12]

Although Wittgenstein himself ultimately moved beyond the *Tractatus*, it remains an important, influential, difficult work. Philosophers continue to argue about what Wittgenstein was getting at and whether or not he succeeded. Nonphilosophers also are fascinated by the little book— partly, no doubt, because of its cryptic, aphoristic style and partly, perhaps, by its odd, numerical arrangement.

The *Tractatus* consists of seven main numbered propositions and comments on those seven, arranged numerically. So, for instance,

1	is a distinct proposition
1.1	is a comment on proposition 1
1.11	is a comment on 1.1, which is itself a comment

Following common practice, extracts from the *Tractatus* will be referenced with these numbers rather than via endnotes with page citations.

In the *Tractatus*, Wittgenstein confidently rejects earlier philosophers' attempts to grapple directly with problems of existence, knowledge, truth, and value because, he says, those so-called problems are illusory, linguistic, results of misunderstanding what language is and how it works. These bogus "philosophical problems" will—not might—disappear once their true nature is recognized:

> The truth of the thoughts that are here set forth seems to me to be unassailable and definitive. I therefore believe myself to have found, on all essential points, the final solutions of the problems.[13]

> *It is the peculiar business of philosophy to ascertain and make clear the meaning of statements and questions. The chaotic state in which philosophy found itself during the greater part of its history is due to the unfortunate fact that, in the first place, it took certain questions to be real questions before carefully ascertaining whether they really made any sense.*
>
> — Moritz Schlick

Accordingly, the *Tractatus* is Wittgenstein's attempt to *show*—not explain or prove—the underlying structure of language. What can be *said* is what can be said meaningfully. What can be said is the same as what can be *thought*—grasped, understood. What cannot be said cannot be thought, and trying to say the unsayable—as philosophers have heretofore done—amounts to trying to think the unthinkable:[14]

1	The world is all that is the case.
1.1	The world is the totality of facts, not things.
1.11	The world is determined by the facts, and by their being *all* the facts.
1.12	For the totality of facts determines what is the case, and also whatever is not the case.

Wittgenstein believed that he had set the stage to show, among other things, that complex propositions, including all the propositions we assert in ordinary, everyday language, are *meaningful* only if they are analyzable into simpler and simpler, ultimately elemental, propositions that consist only of names (not descriptions or relationships). Analysis must end in simple, unanalyzable names that refer to objects.

Sentences that cannot be reduced to simple symbols—primitive names—are meaningless. Objects themselves cannot be analyzed, only pictured. That there are objects, that they exist, cannot be proved, only shown. So where does all of this leave philosophy?

4.003	Most of the propositions and questions to be found in philosophical works are not false but nonsensical. Consequently we cannot give any answer to questions of this kind, but can only establish that they are nonsensical. Most of the propositions and questions of philosophers arise from our failure to understand the logic of our language.

Consider, for instance, the so-called problem of skepticism about knowledge of the external world generated by Locke's egocentric predicament and the sort of withering arguments Hume made about what we can and cannot know. (See Chapter 10.) These seemingly difficult philosophical problems cannot be refuted in the conventional way because the conventional way rests on linguistic misunderstandings. The way out is to see that Humean skepticism is not the powerful expression of an irrefutable philosophical problem at all but a garbled way of speaking. It is *nonsensical:*

6.51	Skepticism is not irrefutable, but obviously nonsensical, when it tries to raise doubts where no question can be asked.

For doubt can exist only where a question exists, a question only where an answer exists, and an answer only where something can be said.

Does this mean that aesthetics, ethics, religion, the "problems of life," are themselves nonsensical? No, they themselves are not nonsensical, but trying to *say anything* about them is.

Then what is left for philosophers to do? Believe it or not, if philosophers do their jobs properly, they will see that all meaningful propositions fall into the bailiwick of the natural sciences and, hence, will allow science to deal with them. So much for Plato, Aristotle, Augustine, Hume, and Kant; so much for the history of traditional philosophy; so much even for Wittgenstein and the *Tractatus*, for even its propositions are senseless, meant to be discarded after they have shown the way out of traditional philosophical nonsense:

> 6.53   The correct method in philosophy would really be the following: to say nothing except what can be said, i.e., propositions of natural science—i.e., something that has nothing to do with philosophy—and then, whenever someone else wanted to say something metaphysical, to demonstrate to him that he had failed to give a meaning to certain signs in his propositions. Although it would not be satisfying to the other person—he would not have the feeling that we were teaching him philosophy—*this* method would be the only strictly correct one.

You are not alone if you sense something going on here besides philosophical analysis. Wittgenstein realized that for all its successes, science will never touch the really important problems of life. Wittgenstein, it turns out, is, like so many of his philosophical predecessors, concerned with the meaning of life. His deconstruction of traditional philosophy is not intended to leave us with nothing of value. It is, rather, an ethical and therapeutic enterprise, a way out of cloudy, empty babble, an encouragement to shut up and look. If we do, we might see the world not just aright but afresh:

> 7.   What we cannot speak about we must pass over in silence.

If a person tells me he has been to the worst places I have no right to judge him, but if he tells me it was his superior wisdom that enabled him to go there, then I know he is a fraud.
— Ludwig Wittgenstein

PHILOSOPHICAL QUERY

Do you believe that there is anything whereof we cannot—not *should* not but *cannot*—speak? Explain. (Is an explanation—a linguistic response of any sort—a refutation of this assertion? That is, if there are things of which we *cannot* speak, are they also things of which we *cannot* think?)

MindTap
Discussing Philosophy

Wittgenstein's Turn

Following his own advice, Wittgenstein did not return to Cambridge after the war and the completion of the *Tractatus*. Instead, as we have seen, he tried to abandon philosophy but was eventually drawn back after nearly a decade of trying other things. The more he reflected on language uses, the more Wittgenstein became convinced that rather than solve the problems of philosophy, the *Tractatus* had succumbed to the problem it set out to combat: The claim that the only meaningful language was one in which sentences stated facts in ways that reflected the logical

Some philosophers (or whatever you call them) suffer from what may be called "loss of problems." Then everything seems quite simple to them, no deep problems seem to exist anymore, the world becomes broad and flat and loses all depth, and what they write becomes immeasurably shallow and trivial. Russell and H. G. Wells suffer from this.

— Ludwig
    Wittgenstein

structure of the world was itself a metaphysical assumption, a misunderstanding of the uses—the logic—of language.

In the *Tractatus*, Wittgenstein had said that the structure of the real world determines the structure of language. In the *Investigations*, he begins to think of words as tools and sentences as instruments. In this and his later work, he makes a turnabout and says that the structure of our language determines the structure of thought and, so, the structure of our experience. Fact-stating is only one language use (tool); there are countless others and, hence, countless other ways of experiencing the world.[15]

In the *Investigations* and other writings, Wittgenstein talks about language as we use it in ordinary life, using such expressions as "forms of life," "language games," and "family resemblances," not as once-and-for-all, fixed, logically exact relationships but rather as certain kinds of *natural human practices*. In this light, Wittgenstein once described his own work as "one of the heirs of the subject that used to be called philosophy."[16]

"We may not advance any kind of theory," Wittgenstein says in the *Investigations*, frustrating traditional and even some analytic philosophers. In *Culture and Value*, he indicates that his unease with theorizing in philosophy is part of a broader unease, an ethical, nearly religious discomfort:

> Our civilization is characterized by the word "progress." ... Typically it constructs. It is occupied with building an ever more complicated structure and even clarity is sought only as a means to this end, not as an end in itself. For me on the contrary clarity, perspicuity are valuable in themselves.[17]

Rather than replace mistaken philosophical theories with his own new, correct, "progressive" philosophical theory, Wittgenstein suggests that, when it succeeds, philosophy allows us to give philosophical questions—and ourselves—a rest:

> The real discovery is the one that makes me capable of stopping doing philosophy when I want to.—The one that gives philosophy peace, so that it is no longer tormented by questions which bring *itself in* question.—Instead, we now demonstrate a method by examples, and the series of examples can be broken off.—Problems are solved (difficulties eliminated), not a *single* problem.
> There is not a philosophical method, though there are indeed methods, like different therapies.[18]

Our task as philosophers consists not in solving grand—super—problems but in "assembling reminders for a particular purpose," the purpose of seeing how language really works:

> We must do away with all *explanation*, and description alone must take its place. And this description gets its light, that is to say its purpose—from the philosophical problems. These are, of course, not empirical problems; they are solved, rather, by looking into the workings of our language, and that in such a way as to make us realize these workings: *in despite of an* urge to misunderstand them. The problems are solved not by giving new information but by arranging what we have always known. Philosophy is a battle against the bewitchment of our intelligence by means of language.[19]

PHILOSOPHICAL QUERY

What do you think? Are philosophical problems really problems of language? Is philosophy a funny way of talking that appears to be more substantive than it, in fact, is? If so, why does it persist? If not, what is philosophy really about and for?

Martin Heidegger

Depending on whom you ask, **Martin Heidegger** (1889–1976) is "one of the most significant and influential philosophers of the twentieth century" and "in all likelihood the most influential existentialist figure after Kierkegaard and Nietzsche"—or he is an untrustworthy incoherent, lifelong Nazi sympathizer.

The impartial observer cannot help but wonder what accounts for such extreme reactions. Part of the explanation, no doubt, has to do with the divisiveness of twentieth-century philosophy, reflected, for example, in the distrust, even contempt, some analytic and continental philosophers feel for "the other way" of doing philosophy. But that sort of philosophical wrangling cannot be the whole story. Part of the explanation no doubt has to do with Heidegger's notoriously difficult language, so difficult that he has been described as a purveyor of audacious "nonsense" and "humbug and mystification," a "dismal windbag whose influence has been completely disastrous."[20]

Still, something more than philosophical disagreements seems to be going on when some analytic philosophers refuse to read any continental philosophy on the grounds that whatever "it" is, it is not philosophy, and some continental philosophers respond by dismissing analytic philosophy as mere word games and sterile logic-chopping. Gauging from these most extreme reactions, it would appear that something more important than a philosophical disagreement about this argument or that theory is thought to be at stake in these extreme positions. What? For some contemporary philosophers, the future of philosophy itself is at stake. For others, human existence is at stake— not just in a physical sense but in an existential sense. Heidegger falls into both camps.

Martin Heidegger

> *You do not get to philosophy by reading many and multifarious philosophical books, nor by torturing yourself with solving the riddles of the universe…philosophy remains latent in every human existence and need not be first added to it from somewhere else.*
> — Martin Heidegger

Roots and Ground

Martin Heidegger, the eldest of three children born to Friedrich Heidegger, the sexton of the Catholic Church of St. Martin, and Johanna Kemp, the daughter of a farmer from a nearby village, was born into a lower-middle-class Catholic family on September 26, 1889, in the village of Messkirch in Baden, South Germany.

As a child, Heidegger spent a great deal of time with his mother's family on a farm that had belonged to them for hundreds of years. Except for a five-year period spent teaching at Marburg University, Heidegger lived and worked in Messkirch, Freiburg, and in a mountain cottage he built for himself in Todtnauberg in the Black Forest. When he was fourteen, a local priest noted that Heidegger was unusually intelligent and arranged for him to attend a Jesuit grammar school in Kostanz on a church scholarship. Three years later, Heidegger attended a Jesuit high school in Freiburg, where he developed an interest in Aristotle and philosophy after reading Franz

Brentano's (1838–1917) *On the Manifold Meaning of Being According to Aristotle.* Brentano's book triggered Heidegger's lifelong quest for "the meaning of Being."

In 1909, with the priesthood in mind, Heidegger entered a Jesuit novitiate in Austria but was dismissed in only two weeks for health reasons. He returned to Freiburg and studied at both a Jesuit seminary and the University of Freiburg. In about 1911, Heidegger had a nervous breakdown that forced him to abandon his studies briefly. During his recuperation, he gave up the idea of the priesthood and concentrated on the study of mathematics, natural science, and philosophy. In 1913, he completed his doctorate in philosophy.

In 1914, at the outbreak of World War I, Heidegger enlisted in the German army but was almost immediately discharged due to poor health. In 1915, he was recruited as a censor with the Central Board of the Post Office at Freiburg. During this period, hoping to secure an appointment as the chair of Catholic Philosophy at the University of Freiburg, Heidegger began to write a habilitation dissertation on the Catholic philosopher Duns Scotus. Habilitation dissertations were scholarly works that, if adequate, qualified would-be professors to teach at the university. Meanwhile, Heidegger lectured on ancient and scholastic philosophy, Immanuel Kant, and Aristotle as a *privatdozent*, an unpaid lecturer. In 1916, **Edmund Husserl** (1859–1938), whose phenomenology was to play a big role in Heidegger's philosophy, began to teach at Freiburg.

In 1917, Heidegger married Thea Elfride Petri, a Lutheran economics student who had been attending his courses since 1915, with whom he had two sons, Jorge and Hermann. In 1918, Heidegger was recalled for active military duty and sent to Verdun, where he served as a meteorologist for the last few months of the war.

At the end of the war, Husserl convinced the university to hire Heidegger as his assistant. Soon thereafter, Heidegger's lectures and seminars began to attract a following. About this time, Heidegger announced that he was "breaking with" Catholicism, personally and philosophically: "I [quickly] gave up my theological studies and dedicated myself entirely to philosophy."[21]

As he worked with Husserl, Heidegger also broke, though less dramatically, from Husserl's way of doing phenomenology. Pursuing a new line of inquiry, Heidegger was determined to apply the phenomenological method to what he saw as a momentous spiritual crisis rooted in modernity's "forgetting" of Being.

Thinking Has Come to Life Again

After he was rejected for the chair in Catholic Philosophy at Freiburg, Heidegger secured a position as a junior professor at Marburg University in 1927. At Marburg, Heidegger knew Karl Jaspers (1883–1969), Max Scheler (1874–1928), Paul Tillich (1886–1965), and Hans-Georg Gadamer (1900–2002) and held regular discussions in theology with Rudolf Bultmann (1884–1976). Gadamer said that Heidegger's reputation as a teacher was so strong that he was able to fill classes beginning at seven o'clock in the morning. Referring to the transformative effect of Heidegger's "orality" and "word-genius," the critic George Steiner said that

> Witnesses...are of one voice saying that those who did not hear Martin Heidegger lecture or conduct his seminars can have only an imperfect, even distorted notion of his purpose. It is the lectures, the seminars already prior to *Sein und Zeit*, which,

Stephen Studd/Getty Images

Throughout his life, Heidegger sought solace and renewal in the mountains, forests, and valleys of the Black Forest.

in Marburg in the very early 1920s, came as a shock and a revelation to colleagues and students. The "secret king of thought," as [Hannah] Arendt memorably called her master, acted through the spoken word.[22]

Hannah Arendt (1906–1975) was an eighteen-year-old Jewish student with whom a thirty-five-year-old Heidegger had a romantic and academic relationship. During World War II, Arendt's relationship with Heidegger came to a halt because of Heidegger's Nazi affiliations. It resumed, in a different form, in 1950 when Arendt renewed their friendship. Subsequently, Arendt played a major role in introducing Heidegger's work to America. In the following passage, as a mature and influential philosopher in her own right, Arendt describes Heidegger's long-ago impact as a teacher:

> The rumor about Heidegger put it quite simply: Thinking has come to life again; the cultural treasures of the past, believed to be dead, are being made to speak, in the course of which it turns out that they propose things altogether different from the familiar worn-out trivialities that they had been presumed to say. There exists a teacher; one can perhaps learn to think.[23]

Heidegger's power as a teacher stemmed, in great part, from his conviction that philosophy cannot be divorced from life. Like Kierkegaard, he believed that philosophy is grounded in living, or, more precisely, grounded in concerns about concrete human existence. Thus, philosophy cannot be divorced from the existence of the

We do not know how to harmonize the contradictory tasks contemporary society imposes upon us. We can only try to reach an uncertain balance between these tasks because we have no blueprint for a conflictless and secure society.

— Leszek Kowlakowski

philosopher. Philosophy cannot be done in a detached relational way but only in an existential, involved, concerned way. This belief was not an attempt to turn philosophy into biography, however. Arendt notes, for instance, that Heidegger once summarized Aristotle's life as "Aristotle was born, worked and died."

Heidegger's point is that life itself is always at stake—the way of life of the particular philosopher, to be sure, but also the life of the university. Our thinking and existing are at stake when we philosophize. Our own *being* is always—somehow—implicated.[24]

PHILOSOPHICAL QUERY

Have you had a truly charismatic teacher? If so, was his or her influence positive or negative? How does a *charismatic* teacher differ from a merely appealing, powerful one? (You might want to double-check the meaning of *charismatic* before deciding.)

> *We cannot by philosophical analysis decide whether anything is real, but only what it means to say that it is real.*
> — Moritz Schlick

In 1927, Heidegger published an incomplete version of *Being and Time*. He planned to develop it further but never did. Even in its incomplete form, *Being and Time* secured Heidegger's reputation as a major figure, both in Germany and internationally. In 1928, Heidegger was called back to the University of Freiburg to succeed Husserl upon the latter's retirement. Almost immediately, Heidegger distanced himself from his former advocate, for philosophical reasons, to be sure, but also, it seems, because Husserl was Jewish. From about 1930 to 1936, Heidegger reassessed this original expression of philosophy in a way that led to *die Kehre*, the turning. This "turning" was not so much a radical shift away from Heidegger's early ideas as it was a new focus on them from a different direction.

In 1933, Heidegger, an ardent Nazi supporter at the time, was named rector of the university. By 1934, his relationship with the Nazis changed, and he resigned the rectorship but retained his professorship under the watchful eye of the Gestapo. In 1944, the Nazis sent Heidegger to dig trenches along the Rhine, declaring him to be the most "expendable" member of the Freiburg faculty.

In 1945, Heidegger was forbidden to teach, and in 1946 he lost his chair in philosophy due to concerns about his Nazi affiliations. In 1949, the ban against teaching was lifted, and in 1951 Heidegger was granted emeritus status by the University of Freiburg and allowed to conduct seminars and lectures into the late 1960s.

After the war, Heidegger divided his time between Freiburg, Messkirch, and his hut in the mountains of the Black Forest. He continued to write and publish such essays and lectures as "What Are Poets For?" (1946), "Letter on Humanism" (1947), "The Question Concerning Technology" (1953), "The Way to Language" (1959), "Time and Being" (1962), and "The End of Philosophy and the Task of Thinking" (1964). Much of

Although Edmund Husserl introduced Heidegger to phenomenology and helped him secure a university job, because Husserl was a Jew, Heidegger later backed away from his elderly mentor to avoid offending the Nazis.

his work focused on modernity and the history of being as he struggled to find appropriate ways to express and clarify his thinking after *die Kehre*.

During this prolific period, Heidegger was visited by Hannah Arendt, Rudolf Bultmann, and such other notable figures as the physicist Werner Heisenberg (1901–1976) and the psychologist Ludwig Binswanger (1881–1966). He died on May 26, 1976. Martin Heidegger was buried in the Messkirch churchyard, with his nephew serving as sextant.

Heidegger's Children

We can get some sense of Heidegger's impact on philosophy and other disciplines by considering some of the notable twentieth-century figures he has influenced, many of whom disagree with one another about the scope and purposes of philosophy. A partial list includes Jean-Paul Sartre and Hannah Arendt in existentialism and phenomenology; Hans-Georg Gadamer (1900–2002) in hermeneutics; Jacques Derrida (1930–2004) in Deconstructionism; Richard Rorty (1931–2007) in pragmatism; Rudolf Bultmann and Paul Tillich (1886–1965) in theology—even Charles Taylor (b. 1931) and Stanley Cavell (b. 1926) in analytic philosophy.[25]

Despite Heidegger's significant and growing influence, troublesome matters persist. One is his infamously difficult writing style, a style so complex and arcane that it prompts some philosophers—especially analytically inclined philosophers— to dismiss Heidegger's work as irretrievably ambiguous, vague, even meaningless, an inflated pseudo-philosophy tinged with messianic religious overtones that do not square with Heidegger's purported focus on existential matters. According to such critics, Heidegger's influence is not due to the quality of his thought but the opposite: The ambiguity and unintelligibility of Heidegger's language allows readers to make his dense prose mean whatever they wish it to mean.

Of course, as we have seen, Heidegger is not unique among philosophers when it comes to difficult writing. Kant (Chapter 11), for instance, immediately comes to mind, as do a number of other important philosophers. Difficult, so-called bad writing can be an impediment to understanding and accessibility, to be sure, but does not, of itself, tell us whether a philosopher's ideas are important and worthwhile any more than simplicity and clarity, of themselves, guarantee philosophical merit.

For many philosophers, the most notorious, controversial, complicating factor when it comes to Heidegger is his troubling and seemingly absolute refusal to repudiate his early affiliations with the Nazis and his utter—some say devastating— silence in regard to the Nazi death camps. This, critics note, is particularly difficult to explain away in light of Heidegger's concerns about modern technology and science—tools the Nazis used to objectify and destroy millions of people.

In 1966, Heidegger tried to justify his involvement with the Nazis in an interview titled "Only a God Can Save Us," which was not published until after his death. There, he said that, like many others, he at first had been misled and then had been pressured by the Nazis. When asked why he deleted the dedication to his mentor Husserl from the editions of *Being and Time* published under the Nazis, Heidegger suggested that it was only sensible, given that Husserl was a Jew.

Most troubling of all to many observers was Heidegger's absolute public silence regarding the Holocaust in the 1966 interview and, so far as we know, in any of

> *The case of Heidegger's Nazism has generated considerable scholarship and journalism over the years, some of it thoughtful, much of it dreadful. Most authors who have chosen to tackle the subject succumb to one of two temptations, both of which reflect a failure of moral judgment. Either they are led by indignation to dismiss Heidegger as a demonic charlatan or they arrogantly defend him without stooping to confront the serious moral concerns raised by his actions and ideas.*
>
> — Damon Linker

Many of Heidegger's critics are troubled by his refusal to repudiate his early affiliations with the Nazis and his persistent silence regarding the Nazi death camps. This silence is particularly difficult to explain away given Heidegger's concerns about modern technology and science—the very tools the Nazis used to objectify and destroy millions of people.

his later writings. These, however, are so voluminous that some philosophers advise us to wait and see, to which critics retort that Heidegger's public silence in the face of such an unprecedented assault on humanity cannot be mitigated by any comments buried in a mass of writings—if such comments even exist. In the following passage, George Steiner expresses the unease of those who find Heidegger's early support of National Socialism (Nazism) and subsequent silence difficult, if not impossible, to justify:

> It is an ill-kept secret that cloistered intellectuals…who spend their lives immersed in words, in texts, can experience with especial intensity the seductions of violent political proposals, most particularly where such violence does not touch their own person. There can be in the sensibility and outlook of the charismatic teacher, of the philosophical absolutist, more than a touch of surrogate sadism….
>
> Martin Heidegger's…notorious address in support of Hitler's break with the League of Nations, his elegy on a nationalist thug…whom the Nazis made a martyr, are nauseating documents….
>
> Once more: the disabling fact is Heidegger's silence after 1945.…the thinker of Being found nothing to say of the Holocaust and the death-camps.[26]

Does such unease help us assess Heidegger's philosophy? When all is said and done, probably not, as Richard Rorty explains:

> A bad reason for caring [about Heidegger's Nazism] is the notion that learning about a philosopher's moral character helps one evaluate his philosophy. It does not, any more than our knowledge of Einstein's character helps us evaluate his physics. You can be a great, original, and profound artist or thinker, and also a complete bastard….
>
> …[A]ttempts to simplify the thought of original thinkers by reducing them to moral or political attitudes should be avoided…[they] are of no use when dealing with authors of the complexity and originality of a Heidegger….They are merely excuses for not reading them.[27]

I appeal to the philosophers of all countries to unite and never again mention Heidegger or talk to another philosopher who defends Heidegger. This man was a devil. I mean, he behaved like a devil to his beloved teacher [Husserl], and he was a devilish influence in Germany.

— Karl Popper

For Deeper Consideration

Do you agree with Rorty that Heidegger's Nazism is irrelevant to his philosophy? Would his religious beliefs be relevant? Is the issue the same for logicians as it is for existentialists? Does it matter *philosophically* if a proponent of vegetarianism eats meat? When, if ever, are a philosopher's personal beliefs and habits *philosophically relevant*? As you reflect on this, take into account not only the matter of personal integrity—harmony with one's professed beliefs—but also the nature of those beliefs. For example, is anti-Semitism on a par with eating meat? Is dissembling about one's diet on a par with dissembling about one's support for fascism? What are the benefits and harms associated with distinguishing arguments from their advocates? Are there some areas of philosophy that cannot or should not be depersonalized?

Phenomenology: The Science of Beings

In 1919, Edmund Husserl secured a position for Heidegger as his assistant in Husserl's "phenomenological workshop," where Heidegger said he received the "step-by-step training in phenomenological 'seeing,'" that was to play a vital role in the development of his own philosophy.[28]

Phenomenology is a method of philosophical analysis first developed by Husserl that uses purely descriptive statements to provide a "descriptive analysis" of consciousness in all its forms. Phenomenology focuses on concrete "experienced facts" rather than abstractions in order to reveal the "essence" of human consciousness. Borrowing from Franz Brentano's "descriptive psychology" Husserl held that consciousness is *intentional*—that is, *consciousness of something*. It is not a representation, not a subjective reflection of some private, inner state, but an experience of something that exists in its own way and in its own right.

According to Husserl, Descartes was on the right track when he said that one thing is certain and undoubtable—our own conscious awareness—and that this is the place to start if we want a solid philosophical foundation. What Descartes failed to see, Husserl said, is that consciousness is always *consciousness of something*. Consciousness—thinking—cannot exist as a Cartesian cogito, an objectless state of mind, a "thinking thing" detached from bodily experience. In theory, we might be able to distinguish between thinking (consciousness) and thoughts (objects of consciousness), but in experience, in practice, we cannot make such a distinction.

It is at this point that Husserl thinks he has found the solution to the age-old skeptical argument that we can never be sure that objects of consciousness exist objectively—that is, independently of us. (See Chapters 9–11.) Remarkably, Husserl's solution is that *we do not need to answer* the skeptics' challenge because it is enough for human purposes that objects of consciousness exist—*as objects of consciousness*. We have no reason to get all tangled up in academic disputes about whether or not they exist in other ways, too. We can investigate objects *as they appear* to us, study them and know them, without struggling with what are, after all, *unanswerable* questions.

Husserl's project was part of his overarching concern with what he and many others, including Heidegger, saw as a European crisis associated with the spread of relativism, skepticism, and the use of science to "objectivize" psychic life, the life of the spirit, and reduce the spiritual realm—which includes judging and valuing—to matter:

> To speak of the spirit as [an] annex to bodies and having its supposedly spatiotemporal being within nature is an absurdity....
>
> There are all sorts of problems that stem from this naiveté, according to which objectivistic science holds what it calls the objective world to be the totality of what is, without paying any attention to the fact that no objective science can do justice to the subjectivity that achieves science.[29]

For Husserl, careful, phenomenological observation—attending to the objects of consciousness without "interfering"—reveals clearly and without any ambiguity the true natures of the various modes of being. Modes of being are not inferred, not deduced; they are seen—disclosed—when we learn how to look, how to attend to reality. Being is present all around us; we do not need to look for it in some super,

phenomenology
A method of philosophical analysis first developed by Husserl that uses purely descriptive statements to provide a "descriptive analysis" of consciousness in all its forms; focuses on concrete "experienced facts" rather than abstractions in order to reveal the "essence" of human consciousness.

Philosophers were hired by the comfortable classes to prove that everything is all right.

— Oliver Wendell Holmes

transcendental, Platonic level of reality. It is right here. All we have to do to see it is to look deeper and deeper into the one-and-only reality, this one. Enter Heidegger.

Being Human

Heidegger believed that Husserl's real insight was the recognition of a kind of thinking that is concealed by modern technological and scientific thought and that by treating phenomenology as a method, rather than a subject matter, he could reach back to the ancient Greeks and "revitalize thought and overcome the spiritual crisis of the twentieth century."[30] Husserl saw phenomenology as the science of beings (in the plural), but, according to Heidegger, it is more properly understood as the science of Being with a capital *B*.

Taking off from Husserl's conviction that what we see phenomenologically is what is the thing itself, Heidegger held that in our everyday experience we encounter "Being itself." This is not the Being of transcendental metaphysics, some other level of Being, but Being as it exists in the world.

In *Being and Time*, Heidegger begins his search for Being with a phenomenological study of humans, looking to see what our very nature discloses to us, or, as he puts it, what is "unconcealed." Concerned with both *human* be-ing (humanity) and with individual human beings, Heidegger develops a complex terminology to try to uncover a uniquely human way of existing that is distinct from other ways of existing as mere objects of scientific inquiry.

In that spirit, let us concentrate on getting a basic sense of Heidegger's "questioning of Being," a task he undertakes on our behalf. Anything more is beyond the scope and purposes of this survey. Given the enormity of Heidegger's writings and the complexity of the language he uses, initial forays into his philosophy run the risk of focusing so heavily on terminology that they pay short shrift to Heidegger's spirit—to the "marvel of all marvels," the fact that we exist at all, that alone among all other kinds of things that exist, human beings care about existence itself, and as such, we are the "shepherds of Being" in this world.

According to Heidegger, what makes us uniquely human is not, as so many other philosophers have suggested, detached and objective knowing. That is, we are not unique because we *think about* the world. Rather, our fundamental human condition is *concern* about our fundamental—human—condition. It is our nature to care about how we exist in the world, to care about human be-ing. Alone among all other beings, we are concerned about our fate in an alien world. Consequently, any inquiry into the nature of human nature, into the conditions of human be-ing, is, ultimately, also an inquiry into the nature of Being itself, into our ownmost existence.

Heidegger notes that we can be described from two different "levels." One is the ordinary, day-to-day level of facts (Heidegger calls this the *ontic* level). Considered from the ordinary level of facts, we are understood in quantitative and objective ways in terms of our particular bodies, temperaments, histories, and worldviews. But that is not all there is to us. Thus, we resist and resent being "treated like an object" or being "reduced to a thing." We instinctively and intuitively recognize that treating human beings this way exclusively amounts to stripping away their humanity or humanness.

> *From Plato until the present, with a few notable exceptions, reason rather than emotion has been regarded as the indispensable faculty for acquiring knowledge.*
>
> — Alison M. Jaggar

> *Yet the knowledge that is craved today tends to be very different from that sought by the cultivated elite of an earlier age. The present-day knowledgeable man may lack any cultivation, and the well-informed person may be but a cheerful robot. The increase of information may indeed have led, contrary to the belief of the Enlightenment, to a decrease in rationality.*
>
> — Lewis A. Coser

We are unique among beings because our nature and the fact that we exist at all is something we care about, something that matters to us. Indeed, our concern with the deeper meaning of our own existence is part of our very essence, part of who and what we are, a reflection of a deeper level of Being. Heidegger calls this the *ontological* level of Being; this is the level of our uniquely *human* way of existing in the world. At this level, we discover that unlike all other entities, our very existence (our Being) is an *issue* for us. We do not "just occur" as one entity among other entities.[31]

Ontology, recall, is the study of being. So when Heidegger says that our nature *is* ontological, he is telling us that our essence is to try to understand our essence. It is not enough for us humans to merely exist. We want to know what we are, not just in a day-to-day ordinary way—not, say, how tall we are or how well we can play the piano—but what makes us *human*. So we "question Being" and in doing so discover that we do not just react. Things just react. We, on the other hand, "comport ourselves." That is, we respond to things in accordance with our own idea of what makes us, us.

If some of this seems alien to you or meaningless or a waste of your valuable time, stop for a moment and ask yourself what it would mean to have absolutely no, none, zip, nada interest in, not to have even the dimmest flicker of concern with the "meaning" of your life in a fundamental, "philosophical," thoughtful, and reflective way.

Think about what you would lose if you were content to just exist as an organism, a set of urges, appetites, immediate goals, and conditioned responses. I bet you cannot—literally cannot—exist like that, certainly not for very long. If, somehow, you could shut off all philosophical (ontological) concerns, wouldn't you be more of an "entity" or automaton than a human being in the fullest, truest sense? This is not to say that being human means being "a philosopher" in a technical sense or having a specific "quantifiable" and "measurable" level of intelligence. Having ontological concerns is primarily caring about how you live in a way that goes beyond exclusively pragmatic and means-to-ends ways.

As you begin to think about these things, see, too, if you can't identify "echoes of Being" in some of your ordinary conversations and reflections about life. Consider, also, the common experience of feeling as if we're "merely existing" as opposed to really, fully *living!* Isn't this sort of feeling a way of questioning our own existence? Most of us, at times of tribulation or disappointment especially, but not only then, ask: What's it all about? Is this it? Why am I here? Without knowing it, we are ontologists "questioning Being," whether or not we ever explicitly refer to Being and even if we have never heard the word *ontology*.

Today's widespread unawareness of our ontological needs is most likely a function of the fact that we commonly use the terms *exist, existing*, and *existence* to mean "merely existing," which we contrast with "being alive!" This kind of everyday linguistic confusion contributes to minimizing the force of Heidegger's concern with the "fundamental ontology of Being" (human existence).

We would do well to remind ourselves that, although we tend to be unaware of it, we are already familiar with the "interrogation of Being" even if we have never thought about it in Heidegger's terms. We are so familiar with it, in fact, that we don't always recognize what we're doing or what we most deeply care about. This is what it means to "forget" Being. Heidegger's unusual language is grounded in his

ontology
The study of being.

We ought to ask whether the increase of these variegated types of knowledge has made us happier or wiser, whether it has enriched or impoverished the quality of our lives, whether the increased production of intellectual knowledge necessarily had to be accompanied by an even greater increase of trivialized and trashy knowledge.

— Lewis A. Coser

struggle to help us recover what we have lost and forgotten. He wants to awaken us from a kind of amnesia that constitutes what he sees as the spiritual crisis of the present age, an amnesia that induces us to squander our humanity by settling for "merely existing."

What makes us human is that we, alone among beings, engage the world and wrest meaning and significance from it; in so doing we confront and engage our very selves. We are, thus, active, creative participants in our own existence. Alone among beings, we reflect on the nature of existence itself. We alone wonder what it means to *exist*.

What Is the Meaning of Being?

At its core, Heidegger's ambitious, therapeutic task is to remind us of what we and our culture have lost by taking existence so much for granted, lost by "forgetting" Being. What we have lost is the primordial sense of wonder that there is anything at all, the amazement that *something exists!*—that *we* exist! So Heidegger "questions Being" on our behalf. *Being and Time* begins with a quotation from Plato's *The Sophist* followed by a question from Heidegger that, together, alert us to this:

> For manifestly you have long been aware of what you mean when you use the expression "being." We, however, who used to think we understood it have now become perplexed.
>
> Do we in our time have an answer to the question of what we really mean by the word "being"? Not at all. So it is fitting that we should raise anew *the question of the meaning of Being*. But are we nowadays even perplexed at our inability to understand the expression "Being"? Not at all. So first of all we must reawaken an understanding for the meaning of this question.[32]

We modern men and women "forget" Being to such an extent that we are not even perplexed by it. We get "lost" in the everyday world as we become so involved in mundane affairs that we do not even wonder that we no longer wonder. All the while, Heidegger says, Being remains in the background, always ready to disclose itself. The world is imbued with "signs" and "markers" "waiting" to "point the way" for us, waiting to remind us of what it really means to be human.

The spiritual stakes here are high, especially so because we think they are not. In our fallen state, we debunk this sort of philosophical/ontological inquiry as a waste, as frivolous, impractical. "What's the big deal?" we grouse. "Everybody knows what human beings are." Knowing "what human beings are" in the ordinary, scientific, technical, taken-for-granted everybody-knows way is one thing. Knowing and caring about what is essential and authentic about being *human* is another. Equating these distinct kinds of knowing puts us at risk of diminishing ourselves by, to borrow Kant's language, treating humanity, in our own case and in that of others, as means-only and not as ends-in-ourselves. What's lost by not seeing people (ourselves and others) as people is humanity, human nature itself.

The "question of being" then, is not about this or that being—not, say, why are there roses or stones or Doug Soccio—but why, especially, is there Being itself and,

Particular questions must receive particular answers; and if the series of crises which we have lived through since the beginning of this century can teach us anything at all, it is, I think, the simple fact that there are no general standards to determine our judgments unfailingly, no general rules under which to subsume the particular cases with any degree of certainty.
— Hannah Arendt

more importantly, what does it mean to be us, to be you and me, to be human. What a wondrous, amazing thing being human is, Heidegger thinks—and yet we do not seem to notice, so absorbed are we in our immediate tasks.

This is our tragedy, for to be truly and fully *human* is to be amazed in the presence of being human. This alone and uniquely makes us human, not mastering objects, not uninvolved, disengaged, objective knowledge. The special task of philosophy, as Heidegger conceives it, is to evoke the wonder and amazement that are necessary to reveal us to ourselves as *human* beings—as opposed to just beings. And because traditional metaphysics talked about Being as if it were an entity, a thing, our way back to authentic humanity requires that we "overcome" metaphysics:

> Due to the manner in which it thinks of beings, metaphysics almost seems to be, without knowing it, the barrier which keeps man from the original involvement of Being in human nature.
>
> What if the absence of this involvement and the oblivion of this absence determined the entire modern age.... [and] abandoned man more and more exclusively to beings, leaving him forsaken and far from any involvement of Being in his nature, while this forsakenness itself remained veiled? What if this were the case—and had been the case for a long time now? What if there were signs that this oblivion will become still more decisive in the future?[33]

For Deeper Consideration

Do we take Being for granted? Do you? If so, is that a symptom of a loss or evidence of cultural progress and stability? That is, does it matter if we take being human for granted in a world that, for all of its problems, is a better world than ever before? Or is it—really—better? Is the modern, technological, busy-busy world more, or less, human than it once was? Does ever-present technology free us or does it, ironically, constrain us by enthralling us, by making us depend on it? What kind of being—not who—communicates via tweets and emoticons? Is such a question appropriate? That is, does the manner of communicating really matter that much? Can we ever know?

The Attitude of Humanity

Scientists and philosophers have long sought, and quarreled over, the distinctly "human" part of human nature, which they have variously defined as being created in God's image, rationality, tool making, the development of agriculture, the ability to use language and create symbols, DNA. We are, from the scientific-technological point of view, human animals existing alongside nonhuman animals, one kind of organism among many other organisms, one entity among many entities.

For Heidegger, however, living authentically, being human, means living with an attitude in "a" world, as opposed to "the" world. According to Heidegger, "the" world, as most of us understand it, is merely one dualistic Cartesian (Chapter 9) world among many other possible worlds. This distinctly modern worldview dehumanizes us, de-humans us, as it were. We need only catalogue the distinctive features that make us human to see this because reflecting on what it means to be a *human* being reveals the general (fundamental) nature of humanity. When we do this, we see that we are at our most human when we are concerned with our world, not "the" world but "a" world—our world as we experience it, inhabit it, exist in it. We are at our most human when, contrary to Enlightenment notions, we are engaged rather than disinterestedly and objectively knowing. We *exist as an attitude toward a world*—not toward the single, one-and-only world but toward our particular world. We do not *exist* as the cogito (Chapter 9) or some sort of empirical perceiver (Chapter 10) or as "disinterested rational agents" (Chapter 11).

Other beings, including nonhuman animals, respond automatically to their worlds according to their various fixed natures and the fixed natures of whatever stimulates them. We alone do not have a fixed nature that endures and persists across time like an unvarying clockwork. It is our nature to choose our existence. We cannot avoid choosing: Choosing not to choose is itself a choice. Neglecting to choose is choosing to neglect to choose. We are not things, not automatic responses to stimuli, not objects that are "just there" in "the" world. We are subjects, beings with attitudes that we call "existence."

Humanity cannot be separated—abstracted, understood, analyzed—in isolation from the existing individual. We do not and cannot exist as a separate "thinking thing" or as a neutral "perceiver." When we try to adopt an uninvolved, transcendental, purely rational, or neutral mode of existence, we objectify ourselves and our world, thereby losing sight of the nature of authentic (concerned) human existence. This sort of independent existence is "merely existing," existing without interest, concern, or engaged involvement. It is nonhuman. The difference between the way we *exist* in the human world and the way things are "just there" in the world of things is that in the human world things are not neutral, they are for us or against us, ready to fulfill some purpose, to be *of* us.

In the human world, things appear "inviting" to us, useful for our purposes, or off-putting and uncongenial to our purposes. We have dealings with the things we encounter, dealings that involve more than mere perceptual or rational cognition. The things that matter are not "just there," not just things-in-themselves, but things-for-a-purpose, things-for-my-purpose, things that *matter* to *us*. Descartes, Hume, Kant, and other philosophers who have struggled to find a solution to the "problem" of things-in-themselves, the so-called problem of the external world, have forgotten what it means to *exist as a human being*. In their philosophizing—not in their living—they lost touch with humanity.

Existence, Heidegger says, is not a "property," which we sometimes have and sometimes do not have, and *without* which we could live just as well. Human existence *is* a relationship with the world. We exist because and to the extent that we are "in a relationship" with our world. The human way of existing (Being) in the world is not, as Heidegger repeatedly warns us, one of cold calculation or detachment, but one of involvement and concern.

PHILOSOPHICAL QUERY

Sociopaths are commonly characterized in terms of their extreme detachment from others, a radical detachment that leads some experts to suggest that sociopaths see other people as objects, things, entities, things "just there." Discuss the possibility that sociopaths are examples of entities most out of touch with humanity—with humanness. Do we want to go so far as to say that, in their inability to see others as human beings, sociopaths are themselves not human? Why or why not?

The "They"

When the burdens of human concern seem too great to bear, we try to absolve ourselves from having to choose among many possibilities and seek to lose ourselves in what Heidegger calls **the "they."** The "they-self" is sometimes called our social self. Unlike our authentic self, a self of open possibilities and potentiality, the inauthentic they-self is "neat and tidy," defined by the anonymous "they." The they-self conforms to a socially contrived "nature" by living as a type rather than *existing* authentically. When we live inauthentically, we lose sight of others as others. Instead of empathetically existing with others, we see ourselves as "one-another" among an averaged aggregate, a vague, amorphous, abstracted norm: the "they." The "they" is a diminished, inauthentic way of Being in which "one speaks of oneself" from the outside.

When we hide out in the amorphous "they," we busy ourselves by taking stock of where we stand and calculating how well or poorly we are conforming to social norms, checking to see how we stack up:

> The "they" has its own ways in which to be…grounded in…*averageness*, which is an existential characteristic of the "they." The "they" in its Being, essentially makes an issue of this. Thus the "they"…keeps watch over everything exceptional that thrusts itself to the fore. Every kind of priority gets noiselessly suppressed. Overnight, everything that is primordial gets glossed over as something that has been well known. Everything gained by a struggle becomes just something to be manipulated. Every secret loses its force. This care of averageness reveals in turn an essential tendency of [human beings] which we call the "leveling down" of all possibilities of being....
>
> Thus the particular [human being] in its everydayness is *disburdened* by the "they." Not only that: by this disburdening of its Being, the "they" accommodates [the particular human being] if [he or she] has any tendency to take things easily and make them easy. And because the "they" constantly accommodates…the "they" retains and enhances its stubborn dominion.[34]

Idle Talk

Among the "they," there is only **idle talk**, chatter. There can be no *dialogue*. "Dialogue" occurs when we see others as others. In dialogue, each participant is

the "they"
Heidegger's name for being-with-another; an inauthentic way of avoiding anxiety by allowing an "aggregate average" to determine how we live and think; enemy of authenticity.

idle talk
Heidegger's name for superficial "they talk"; includes chatter, gossip, and merely verbal understanding; contrasted with conversation or dialogue.

concerned with understanding the other and with being understood. In idle talk, no one is concerned with genuine understanding and caring. Idle talk never rises above verbal understanding; it seeks nothing more penetrating:

> [W]hat the talk is about is understood only approximately and superficially...following the route of *gossiping* and *passing the word along....* Things are so because one says so....
>
> The groundlessness of idle talk is no obstacle to its becoming public; instead it encourages this...Idle talk...releases one from the task of genuinely understanding.[35]

In everyday life, we evade the burden of being fully human (deeply concerned) by speaking of the "they" as "one," as "everybody," as "people," as "nobody": "Everybody knows that is wrong." "People will talk if you go through with that." "One hardly knows what to say." "Nobody believes in God anymore." "The American people are fed up."

Such chatter absolves us of the responsibility of knowing whereof we speak. Idle talk lowers expectations and exalts "public opinion." Evading the task of genuinely understanding, we feel free—nay, encouraged—to spout off without bothering to understand, free to treat information as understanding. In idle talk, we do not *experience* the full majesty and mystery of the human world. Whatever we do see is dimmed so that beauty is averaged down, terror is averaged, joy, diversity, mystery—everything is averaged, made safe, put in its place. We live up—or down—to our way

> *With Americanism nihilism reaches its zenith...since with the appearance of "happiness" for everyone, they destroy everything.*
> — Martin Heidegger

During the 2008 presidential campaign, Barack Obama declared, "We are the ones we have been waiting for." Both he and his opponent John McCain routinely referred to "the American people" and spoke of "we" to huge, enthusiastic crowds. Do the "American people" actually *exist*, or were Obama and McCain appealing to the *they* by engaging in what Heidegger called idle talk—chatter that "releases one from the task of genuinely understanding"?

of talking (and attending to what is said). Our lives lack majesty and grandeur if we rarely speak of majesty and grandeur. They lack awe when we routinely describe the most trivial things as "Awesome!" It is as if Being has no meaning for us, as if existence did not exist.

You might wonder why we allow the "they" to rob us this way. We do not *allow* it. We *encourage* it as a way of evading the hard decisions about which aspects of life to put aside and which to pursue. Instead of struggling with how and what to *be*, we focus on what to *do*. We rely on the "they" to disburden us of our humanity by telling us what we are "supposed to do," by conforming to what has been predetermined for us by the "they." The "they" absolves us from the agony of deciding. No longer need we choose: One simply does whatever is normal for "people like us." We make a virtue out of conforming to the norms and expectations of an ethnic group, profession, political party, gender, or social class—we eagerly fall in step with some they-determined set of expectations, purposes, and values.

When we succumb to the dictates of the "they," our mode of Being is inauthenticity, a kind of existence dominated by and lost in "the" world rather than being responsive to "our" world and concerned with our own Being, with our humanity. We are consumed with being with one another, absorbed by idle talk, curiosity, ambiguity. We are lost, fallen:

"Inauthenticity"...is completely fascinated by the "world" and by...the "they."[36]

Satisfied with trivial knowledge, with "information," the they-self is alternately indifferent to and actively discouraging of the kind of inquiry necessary for authenticity. Its attitude is distant, manipulative, and thereby indifferent to what it means to be a human being.

> *Man is not the lord of beings. Man is the shepherd of Being.*
> — Martin Heidegger

For Deeper Consideration

Apply the notion of disburdening idle talk to today's mass media pundits and experts. Scrutinize op-ed articles, blogs—especially blogs—and television and radio talk shows for examples of "they" talk. Be alert for different "theys": conservatives and liberals: fundamentalists and secularists: males and females: blacks, whites, and Hispanics, for example. Does it strike you as odd when television hosts ask viewers to tweet or Facebook or e-mail them comments and then refer to selected respondents, about whom they know nothing personal, in chatty, personal terms: "Jamal from Omaha tweets..." or "Here's one from Louise in Bemidji..."? Are folksiness and informality on a mass scale always inauthentic? Must all such mass talk be idle? Why or why not?

Authenticity and Death

Authentic individuals know that they are "there" in the world, without any say in the matter, and denied a comforting, metaphysical explanation. They understand and accept that they are going to die. This is an existential (and ontological) understanding of death, not the detached, objective, "averaged" understanding of death in the abstract but the subjective, concerned knowledge of death in our very own case.

Among all other entities, only we know that our specific existence will inevitably come to an end. Knowing this—and only knowing this—allows us to understand ourselves as a totality, a whole, an end-in-ourselves. Only we humans have the capacity to know ourselves explicitly—that is, only we have the capacity to articulate what we sometimes realize implicitly: Our existence has a beginning, and it will come to an end. We are inauthentic to the extent that we deny and suppress the fact that we are going to die. We lose touch with our humanness and get lost in discrete particularities, reducing ourselves to "a this" or "a that" only. The only way back from this fallen state is by living authentically in the full knowledge that we will die—that you and I *will* die—not in some vague, abstract way but really, truly, finally, inescapably *die*:

> [The particular human being] does not...have any explicit or theoretical knowledge of the fact that it has been delivered over to its death, and that death thus belongs to Being-in-the-world. Thrownness into death reveals itself...in a more primordial and impressive manner in that state-of-mind which we have called "anxiety."[37]

The objective world itself, "the" world as opposed to "our" world, is indifferent to our hopes, fears, questions, and projects. It is "out there," objectified, "just there"—alien. In Heidegger's vivid description, the world "tarries alongside" of us but is not of us, nor are we of it. So, as we have seen, we try our best to suppress even the vaguest sense that, objectively, scientifically, technologically understood we are homeless, orphaned, insignificant entities, one more thing "just there" in the world of things.

Given all the creative energy expended on not-knowing, on disappearing into the "they" and busy-ness, how do we ever come to exist as *human* beings rather than just beings? One way is by experiencing a mood that Heidegger labels "anxiety." Anxiety is directed toward nothing in particular. We experience it when we are aware of the world's indifference to us. Whereas fear alerts us to something specific—the snake in the grass, failing to pass algebra—anxiety does not focus on a specific thing. Anxiety discloses our fundamental human condition, our way of being in the world.

What threatens our sense of belonging here is not a thing or a place but the nature of the world *as such* and the nature of human beings *as such* rather than as things among other things that are "just there." Understood this way, anxiety is "friendly" toward us. Anxiety shows us how the world is for us and how we exist in the world. Anxiety prevents us from feeling at home in the world of mere things. More precisely, anxiety shows us that we cannot exist as authentic human beings if we feel at home in "the" world.

If we want to live authentically, we must constantly resist the temptation to escape from anxiety by diluting what we experience, by numbing it, as it were, into a be-happy-don't-worry lightness or by distracting ourselves with an infinite series of multi-tasks, projects, and undertakings that rob us of the richness of what it means to be human.

Philosophy will be unable to effect any immediate change in the current state of the world. This is true not only of philosophy but of all purely human reflection and endeavor. Only a god can save us.

— Martin
   Heidegger

The Age of Technology

In *The Question Concerning Technology*, Heidegger raises questions that are especially timely and interesting in this era of multi-tasking and seemingly perpetual information seeking and leveling. He begins by noting that even when we are not actively concerned with fundamental matters, Being sends us clues about ourselves that we can recognize, if we are open to them. These clues correspond to particular historical epochs or ages. They invite, but do not compel, us to recognize what it means to exist (in the fullest human sense) under the conditions of the present age. They call us to authentic existence at this particular time, the age of technology.

PHILOSOPHICAL QUERY

Compare Kierkegaard's and Nietzsche's critique of "the present age" with Heidegger's. What do these critiques have in common? How do such "existentially oriented" critiques differ from, say, Plato's critique of democracy? In regard to Kierkegaard, Nietzsche, and Heidegger, what do you think of their "shared suspicion that modernity is a disease?" Do you share it? (See Chapters 5, 14, and 16.)

MindTap

Discussing Philosophy

It is important to note that Heidegger's understanding of technology goes beyond the common notion of technology as neutral instruments, as tools and devices that we are free to use for whatever purposes we wish. It's not that we are wrong to think about technology in such a neutral means-to-ends way. On one level, technology is clearly "neutral." Prior to and during World War II, the Nazis, for instance, were master technologists who used the latest technology to efficiently "relocate," "eliminate," and "recycle" those they deemed unfit or undesirable. Almost as soon as that war ended, some of those same technologies were used for humane and peaceful purposes. Today, the same technology that allows students to produce sophisticated, computer-researched papers also allows for the clandestine buying, selling, copying, and taking credit for others' work. It seems obvious that, considered this way, technology is neutral, deserving neither praise nor blame for the way it is used.

Does this particular attitude toward technology disclose its essence, or does it, perhaps, hide the true nature of technology from us? What is concealed or revealed when we correspondingly see ourselves and, by extension, humanity as masters of a neutral, your-wish-is-my-command servant, a magical servant to whom we look to give us whatever we desire and save us from whatever we want to be saved from? Does the common conception of technology help us recognize the full extent and nature of technology's role in our day-to-day dealings and in our sense of ourselves?

Even a superficial look at the current technological age reveals that we are the benefactors of such wondrous technological marvels as smart phones and tablets more powerful than computers of only a few years past; streaming video on demand; personal GPS navigators; big, thin television screens; teeny-tiny digital cameras we can wear so as to record our every activity; online classes taken at our convenience; smart vehicles that apply their brakes on our behalf; and classroom "clickers" that allow professors to get instant feedback from students. So widespread and constant is the parade of technological superstars that it is easy to forget about less glamorous, but nonetheless equally technological, aspects of our lives, forget how deeply and pervasively our lives and consciousness are imbued with such taken-for-granted technology as dental braces; indoor plumbing; central heating and air conditioning; no-wrinkle, no-stain fabrics; eyeglasses and contact lenses; hearing aids and cochlear implants; prosthetic limbs and artificial joints; ATM cards; microwave ovens; television and radio; ballpoint pens and mechanical pencils; electricity; skateboards, mountain bikes, automobiles, and motorcycles; running shoes; vaccinations; running water; multivitamins; paperback books—all technology.

Maybe we don't "forget" that these things are technology so much as we just don't think about *what it means that they are technology*. Maybe we are so comfortable with them—so dependent on them, so involved with them—that we don't really pay close attention to how pervasively technological our present way of living is. And, so, we slip into taking technology as a whole for granted, assuming that, as a rule, we are the masters of our own contrivances. But are we? Are we in "control" when we cannot stray too far from our smart phones and when we must make sure we have plenty of batteries, chargers, cords, and other "necessities" before we can comfortably go about our business? What kind of freedom and ease are provided by *depending on* so much technology?

Are we in control when *we are afraid not to take advantage* of the latest technological improvements in athletic performance lest we be outperformed by those who do use them: HGH, steroids, blood doping, metal alloy bats, high-tech tennis rackets, customized alloy golf clubs, and space-age, speed-enhancing swimsuits? Are we in control if we are unable to study without background music and a laptop, incapable of talking on the phone without simultaneously checking our e-mail or surfing the Web? Are we in control when we cannot—not *will not* but *cannot*—write a research paper without a computer and Internet access? In other words, are we in control when we feel lost and naked without the technological umbilical cords that link us to the "they" 24/7?

Are we in control when our lives are based on an endless series of calculations, technical assessments of advantages versus disadvantages, long- and short-range projections? What is the effect on our lives and psyches of continuously scrutinizing studies, surveys, charts, statistics, longevity tables, and BMI calculators to "figure out" if it is okay to consume gluten or meat or caffeine and, if so, when and how much? What happens to the *human* experience of eating when I preface each meal with a careful study of its nutritional content, down to grams, ounces, micrograms, recommended daily percentages for "average" adults or "typical" diabetics or…?

When we take technology and technical knowledge and mastery so much for granted, we unavoidably take ourselves and our humanness for granted because this era's default approach to the world is "calculative," focused on solving problems and organizing

What are we doing to the *human* experience of eating when we subject everything we eat to a technical analysis of its nutritional content, down to grams, ounces, micrograms, when we subject ourselves to averaged recommendations based on conglomerations of "data"?

©iStock.com/RiverNorthPhotography

knowledge and accomplishing our goals scientifically, efficiently, quickly, and predictably. Without great care, we risk "doing" more and "being" less. We take existence (Being) itself for granted, overlooking what Heidegger described as "the marvel of all marvels; that what-is *is*."[38]

This taken-for-granted, crudely pragmatic, so-what attitude is a dominant feature of the present age. We modern men and women are action-oriented, "proactive" folks, prone to "getting things done" rather than dwelling on them, more interested in results than in reflecting on the nature or essence of things. To us, existence = doing, calculating, negotiating, consuming, and manipulating everything freely and as fully as possible. Even our efforts to "save the environment" are based on calculations, carbon credits, species counts.

So fully have we embraced and absorbed technology and the kind of thinking that comes along with it that we believe that we can fix technology by coming up with better technology. If technology has polluted our atmosphere, better technology will clean it up. When our streams and waterways are dirtied, we calculate ways to filter out pollutants. We'll save water with low-flush toilets, operate our increasing cache of gadgets with solar and wind power, cut our consumption of oil by driving technologically complex and sophisticated vehicles that can "think" for themselves. We'll save trees by going to the "paperless office" and downloading e-books. We'll end killing and war by creating some technologically "smart" weapons that can disable other weapons without hurting living things and by finding alternative sources of energy so there is plenty for all. We'll "cure" philosophical anxiety with medication. And we'll "figure out" how to accomplish all of these goals without pain, at no cost to the environment or to ourselves.

PHILOSOPHICAL QUERY

Take a technology inventory of your own life. Here are some obvious places to start: What role does the Internet play in your study habits, music and video consumption, social interaction, work? As a consumer, look for less-than-obvious forms of technology, from UPC scanners to the things you buy or want to buy. Look around your school and classroom for examples of technology. Then reflect on how technology affects how you think about life and what you want from it.

Human Resources

Occasionally, we may have a flickering sense that somehow something is amiss here, that something seems lacking in our lives. What could it be? A first temptation might be to think that we only need to figure out how to have more money, more gadgets, more freedom. But what if we are thinking about all of this in a flawed way, calculating and analyzing and looking for the *wrong kind of answer* in the wrong places and in the wrong way—and not seeing what could save us, could enrich our lives? What if we must stop thinking technologically before we can respond to what technology "wants" to reveal to us—the *truth of Being*.

Premodern technology used nature as a means in a kind of ongoing exchange. Consider the way a windmill shares the power of the wind to create energy. It relies

According to Heidegger, modern technology "puts to nature the unreasonable demand that it supply energy which can be extracted and stored as such" and then calculates ways to accomplish this, treating everything as a means, a tool, a source of energy to be stored as a "standing-reserve" of potential power to be "ordered," "challenged," and stored according to our whims.

on the wind and works only when there is wind. The windmill waits for the wind. Not so modern technology "which puts to nature the unreasonable demand that it supply energy which can be extracted and stored as such" and then calculates ways to accomplish this. Modern technological thinking treats everything as a means, a tool, a source of energy to be stored to await our beck and call. In Heidegger's language, modern technology sees everything as a "standing-reserve" of potential power to be "ordered" and "challenged" (arranged and manipulated) and stored:

> [A] tract of land is challenged in the hauling out of coal and ore. The earth now reveals itself as a coal mining district, the soil as a mineral deposit.... Agriculture is now the mechanized food industry. Air is now set upon to yield nitrogen, the earth to yield ore, ore to yield uranium, for example; uranium is set upon to yield atomic energy, which can be released either for destruction or for peaceful use.[39]

Today the rhythms of nature are disrupted; we no longer wait for the wind, we create it (or its equivalent) in fuel cells and turbines and generators. Corn is "challenged" to yield ethanol, which "stands in reserve" in refineries and fuel tanks until we tap into its "stored" energy. Nothing is allowed to "arrive" or to exist as an end-in-itself. Everything serves a calculated, pragmatic purpose, is seen as a potential source of something else, as a means, an instrument, something passively waiting to be "taken."

Technologically understood, you and I are human resources. Most likely, your college or business has a human resources department. You can even major in

Heidegger was [possibly] a small character, an ageing man haunted by ruse, by ambition, by certain deeply-incised "agrarian" traditions of concealment and exploitation. His acre of ground might have seen the harvest of Hell, but it was his.

— George Steiner

human resources management or work for a temporary employment agency that keeps human resources "ordered" by experience, training, and skill sets, "standing in reserve" until needed.

Danger

For Heidegger, the supreme danger of our time is the transformation of the human being into something fundamentally less than human, even nonhuman. Technology itself—essentially, by its nature—transforms how we think and, thereby, how we live more than any particular technological device or practice. Thus, technology and pragmatic calculation dominate our existence and, tragically, human beings are folded into the standing-reserve.

"The essence of technology is by no means anything technological," Heidegger notes. Rather, the essence of technology is a way of looking at the world as raw material to be used. Technology is a frame of mind, a way of thinking. But it is not a frame of mind that we have chosen. It is a frame of mind shaped by the way technology sees nature itself as an instrument. Today, unlike in other eras, we literally experience the entire world as standing-reserve, and we tarry alongside it rather than exist in it.

We do not come to this of our own accord but are thrown into a technological and scientific relationship to the world. The technological frame of mind constitutes our modern destiny. We even approach spiritual matters scientifically and technologically, conducting studies to prove or disprove the efficacy of prayer or meditation or life after death. We carbon-date pages of Scripture and bones of saints, looking for scientific answers to age-old questions. We conduct sociological and anthropological studies of religion. We conduct "placebo-controlled, double-blind" studies of spiritual practices. We scan our brains as we listen to music and poetry and as we look at paintings and sunsets to better "understand" music or poetry or art or beauty.

We measure—"order"—the cosmos itself, looking to outer space for new sources of energy to add to the ever-expanding standing-reserve. We presume to calculate the age of the universe itself and to measure and identify "the" causes of climate change across centuries. When nature as a whole is threatened by technology, we employ technology to count and record ("order") endangered species via wireless transmitters. We scientifically analyze soil and air samples, track storms via satellite, and obsessively tweak additives and supplements to enhance our food supply. We seek out new superdrugs to kill off superbugs created by older drugs crafted to kill off older bugs.

The technological frame of mind is as blind to human essence as chemical analysis of the paint applied to the Sistine Chapel is blind to the majesty of Michelangelo's frescoes.

Yet in these very attempts to control the world and to come to technically "correct" understandings of the world, "the truth will withdraw," Heidegger warns. Correct, calculative, objective understanding of particulars, though not sufficient for grasping the truth of existence, is potently useful, seductive, and distracting and induces complacency. This, says Heidegger, is "the supreme danger" of technology, a danger rooted in our overall indifference to everything that is not part of the standing-reserve. So long as we are chiefly interested in things as means, as instruments, as standing-reserve, we inevitably come to a point where we take ourselves for standing-reserve. Then, ironically and monstrously,

> ...precisely as the one so threatened, [man] exalts himself to the posture of the lord of the earth. In this way the illusion comes to prevail that everything man encounters exists only insofar as it is his construct. This illusion gives rise in turn to one final delusion: it seems as though man everywhere and always encounters only himself....*In truth, however, precisely nowhere does man today any longer encounter himself, i.e., his essence.*[40]

Demanding that we ourselves produce "on call" reduces us to mere means (a danger Kant, Kierkegaard, and Nietzsche so vehemently warned against). This way of thinking hides the truth of Being from us and prevents us from existing authentically.

The technological frame of mind is, we might say, as blind to human essence as a chemical analysis of the paint applied to the Sistine Chapel is blind to the majesty of Michelangelo's frescoes. So long as we consign ourselves to a technological frame of mind, we remain hidden from ourselves. Unaware that we are hidden from ourselves, we are blindly confident that nothing can hide from us. This is an irony of tragic, and to use Heidegger's term, monstrous proportions because we no longer encounter anything but caricatures of ourselves: Our great tragedy is to be unable to recognize our great tragedy:

> [Technological reasoning] blocks the shining-forth and holding sway of truth....What is dangerous is not technology. Technology is not demonic; but its essence is mysterious. The essence of technology...is the danger....
>
> The threat to man does not come...from the potentially lethal machines and apparatuses of technology. The actual threat has already afflicted man in its essence...with the possibility that it could be denied to him to...experience the call of a more primal truth.[41]

For Deeper Consideration

Assess Heidegger's assessment of technology. What does he mean by technology? How is that different from more common notions of technology? Most importantly, why is Heidegger interested in technology at all? That is, what role does he see technology playing in living authentically?

Wither Philosophy? (A Pun)

From its inception, philosophy has been self-conscious, self-assessing, and self-correcting. Philosophers have argued about particular issues and about "meta-issues"—that is, about questions concerning what constitutes legitimate philosophy and the *philosophical* treatment of *philosophical* issues—as opposed to, say, scientific, literary, historical, or theological treatments of nonphilosophical issues.

By the twentieth century, philosophers began to accuse other philosophers of not *being* philosophers. This was an altogether different kind of criticism than accusing one another of not being *good* philosophers. Existentialists contemned idealists; postmodernists contemned existentialists; analytic philosophers rejected continental philosophy and vice versa. Some philosophers, as we have seen, questioned even the possibility of philosophy. In a 1987 address to the American Philosophical Association, Kai Nielsen went so far as to say, "There is no defending the tradition. Systematic analytic philosophy and its Continental cousins along with their historical ancestors must be given up."[42]

In some ways, this is hardly surprising. Indeed, it would have been more troubling if twentieth-century Western philosophy had remained aloof from the divisiveness, the diversity, and the unease of the polarized world around it: on the one hand, the smashing of boundaries and shibboleths; on the other, the anxiety of nearly absolute personal freedom without the guiding hand of tradition. Sophisticated and specialized techniques work exceptionally well in their own domains, yet mere technical mastery cannot satisfy our hunger for meaningfulness. The very same scrupulous attention to language that clarifies cloudy thinking and reveals hidden assumptions simultaneously nurtures widespread suspicion that, at base, nothing *really means* anything.

Wittgenstein and Heidegger were sensitive to these themes and sensitive to the crisis twentieth-century philosophy faced. Each in his own way tried to "save" philosophy and, in the process, spoke at times in a prophetic, quasi-biblical poetic voice that reflected and reinforced their charismatic personalities and seriousness. Whether one, both, or neither stand(s) the test of time is not for us to know, but this much we can say with confidence: Wittgenstein and Heidegger deserve our thanks for trying to find or recover the archetypal voice of philosophy, the voice that speaks beyond the academic and the technical, the voice that speaks directly to the problems of life and the challenges of living authentically in an unsettled age.

If, at times, they stammer and seem, paradoxically, both over-simple and unnecessarily complex, perhaps it is because they are trying to say precisely what, in the end, can be heard but not spoken. If *that* (what I just said) seems nonsensical, then you may already be an analytic philosopher. If it seems—feels—as if it is *about something*, then you may be more of a continentalist. In either case, if you care at all about such things, then perhaps you are a philosopher.

Whatever that may be.

> *The Enlightenment's "natural light of reason" turns out to have been a myth. Reason is not a light. It is more like a transformer.*
> — Huston Smith

Aplia

Summary of Main Points

- By the twentieth century, philosophers were struggling with the "post-Nietzschean deconstruction of metaphysics." Philosophical deconstruction is a kind of close textual analysis focused on uncovering and overcoming "privileges" hidden in philosophical arguments and theories—"texts."

- Analytic philosophers stress logic, testability, precision, and clarity. Common to this way of approaching philosophy is the notion that the universe consists of independent (atomic) entities, material particles, sense data, impressions, "facts," or something else. Logical and linguistic analyses are said to be the only proper methods for sorting out philosophical confusions. Continental philosophers tend to explain things not by reducing them to simple entities but by understanding them in a broader, holistic, historical context. This approach to philosophy includes formalism, idealism, phenomenology, and existentialism.

- In the *Tractatus Logico-Philosophicus*, Ludwig Wittgenstein tried to show the underlying structure of language, asserting that what can be said is what can be said meaningfully, that what can be said is the same as what can be thought, and that what cannot be said cannot be thought. Trying to say the unsayable, as earlier philosophers did, amounts to trying to think the unthinkable. According to Wittgenstein, this applies to the *Tractatus* as well, for its propositions are senseless and meant to be discarded after they have shown the way out of traditional philosophical nonsense.

- In the *Philosophical Investigations*, Wittgenstein questions his own earlier work and says that the structure of language determines the structure of thought and, therefore, the structure of our experience, not the other way around. Rather than replace mistaken philosophical theories with his own new, correct, philosophical theory, the later Wittgenstein suggests that, when it succeeds, philosophy allows us to give philosophical questions a rest.

- Martin Heidegger's unique blend of phenomenology, ontology, and existentialism grew out of his study of Edmund Husserl's phenomenology. According

to Heidegger, Husserl saw phenomenology as the science of beings (in the plural), whereas it is more properly understood as the science of Being with a capital *B*. Toward that end, Heidegger attempted to articulate the fundamental condition of uniquely human existence.

- According to Heidegger, the fundamental human condition is concern about our unique condition, our be-ing. Thus, any inquiry into the nature of human existence, is, ultimately, an inquiry into the nature of Being. Heidegger wants to remind us of what we have lost, our primal amazement that we (humanity) exist. Unlike any other entity, we "comport" ourselves toward "the" world. We exist as human beings with an attitude toward a human world, not toward the single, detached, objective, one-and-only world.

- According to Heidegger, most philosophers have lost sight of Being because they have treated detached, calculative thinking as the defining characteristic of being human. But unless we have an attitude and a relationship toward things, we cannot understand them. We understand something only when we are involved with it and "attuned" to it.

- According to Heidegger, we exist without any explanation no matter how hard we try to make it otherwise. When the burden and anxiety of the human condition are too great to bear, we escape by losing ourselves in the "they." When we do this, our mode of being is inauthenticity, a way of being dominated by "the" world. In this condition, there can be no dialogue, only idle talk. Idle talk never rises above verbal understanding.

- In his analysis of technology, Heidegger says that calculative technological thinking sees everything as "standing-reserve," a source of energy to be stored to await our beck and call. This way of thinking transforms human beings into beings "just there," entities to be used and treated like everything else in the standing-reserve. The essence of technology is a way of looking at the world as raw material to be used. Technology is a frame of mind that we have not chosen and that characterizes and dominates our era.

Post-Reading Reflections

Now that you've had a chance to learn about Ludwig Wittgenstein and Martin Heidegger, use your new knowledge to answer these questions.

1. Why do philosophers distinguish between the "early" and "later" Wittgenstein? How do they differ?

2. How is the *Tractatus* organized? Why is it organized that way?

3. What is the significance of "saying" in the *Tractatus*?

4. How does Wittgenstein's attitude toward language as expressed in the *Tractatus* change in his later work?

5. Why are some philosophers troubled by Heidegger's attitude toward Nazism? What was his attitude? Why is this issue particularly significant given Heidegger's overriding concerns with authenticity?

6. What is the central question in Heidegger's philosophy? Why is it important?

7. What does Heidegger mean by existence? What kinds of things can exist?

8. What is the "they," and what function does it serve in dealing with the burden of being human?

9. What kind of thinking characterizes technology (the technological frame of mind), and what role does that kind of thinking play in Heidegger's critique of technology?

10. What are human resources, according to Heidegger?

11. How does idle talk differ from dialogue? Is one "better" than the other? Why?

 MindTap™

Experience MindTap through the activities highlighted in this chapter. Further explore this online, personalized learning tool to deepen your comprehension and improve your grades.

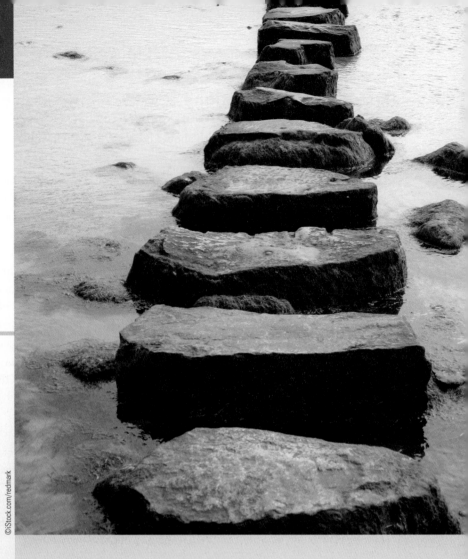
©iStock.com/redmark

18

Philosophy as a Way of Life

Let no one be slow to seek wisdom when he is young, nor weary in the search thereof when he is grown old. For no age is too early or too late for the health of the soul. And to say that the season for studying philosophy has not yet come or that it is past and gone, is like saying that the season for happiness is not yet or that it is now no more.

— *Epicurus*

Learning Objectives

 MindTap

After you complete this chapter, you should be able to:

- Define the notion of *philosophical advocacy*.
- Describe the influence that World War II had on Jean-Paul Sartre personally and philosophically.
- Analyze Sartre's assertion that existence precedes essence.
- Describe Sartrean despair.
- Describe what Carol Gilligan identifies as the different voice.
- Analyze the issue of representation in academic philosophy.
- Critique Martin Luther King, Jr.'s doctrine of creative moral tension.
- Critique the argument Peter Singer makes in *The Singer Solution to World Poverty*.
- Critique Martha C. Nussbaum's claim that philosophers ought to be lawyers for humanity.
- Justify Pierre Hadot's claim that it often happens that a poem or a biography is more philosophical than a philosophical treatise.

🅜 MindTap™

Philosophy Timelines

WHAT is the role of the philosopher in contemporary society? Do philosophers have a role to play beyond that of philosophy teachers and scholars?

Traditionally, the philosopher has been viewed as a detached observer, someone outside the mainstream of society. Beginning with the apocryphal story of Thales falling into a well, one popular stereotype of the philosopher remains the befuddled, impractical critic, the character who gives advice and asks silly riddles about God making rocks too large to lift and trees falling in empty forests—but who bakes no bread. Less benign philosophical stereotypes include that of the icy, impersonal *logic chopper*, the individual who has mastered the art of exposing contradictions and ambiguities in other people's arguments and beliefs but who has no positive, practical skills to offer. A more charitable picture of the contemporary philosopher is of the well-intentioned intellectual who asks "good questions" but who, nonetheless, fails to understand and come to grips with "practical matters."

The popular notion of the philosopher as somehow irrelevant to modern life probably owes a great deal to the importance placed on theory, argument, and, most of all, objectivity and rationality by most modern philosophers. With the notable exceptions of philosophers such as Kierkegaard, James, and Nietzsche (Chapters 14–16), most modern philosophers write in a detached, impersonal voice. Even Marx (Chapter 13) wrote in an impersonal voice when he said that the time had come for philosophers to change the world, as did Wittgenstein and Heidegger (Chapter 17) when they attempted to introduce a "therapeutic" element into philosophy.

In this last chapter, we will take a *selective look* at some contemporary philosophers I have chosen to refer to under the broad heading of *philosophical advocates*. A **philosophical advocate** is a philosopher whose work identifies, clarifies, and actively opposes a perceived injustice; philosophical advocates give philosophical credence to personal experience based on gender, ethnic background, and social status.

Although philosophical advocates are not always academically trained philosophers, they always address philosophical questions in ways that speak to present-day concerns. They raise questions about the relationships of means to ends; about the effects of technology or culture or class structure on our individual and communal well-being. Jeremy Bentham, John Stuart Mill, Karl Marx, and William James are examples of philosophical advocates who were also public philosophers (Chapters 12–13 and 15).

Public philosophers are writers or speakers whose philosophical positions are expressed in ways accessible to a broad audience. The most effective public philosophers tap into—or identify—vital philosophical issues of the day. When public philosophers also "practice what they preach," they function much like sages or prophets in their capacity to provoke individual self-assessment and collective consciousness-raising.

Philosophical advocates refuse to remain on the sidelines of the major social controversies of our time. These include, but are not limited to, issues of poverty, quality of life, cultural equality, women's rights, and gender influences. I believe that any new philosophical archetypes are likely to include some form of public philosophical advocacy. I also believe that it is unwise to predict precisely who the chief exemplars of these new archetypes will be, since that determination must be made over time. Consequently, I recommend treating this last chapter as a kind of *philosophical preview of coming attractions* indicating some (but certainly not all) fertile and important areas of contemporary philosophical activity.

Knowledge for the sake of knowledge is, say what you will, nothing but a dismal begging of the question.
— Miguel de Unamuno

philosophical advocate A philosopher whose work identifies, clarifies, and actively opposes a perceived injustice; philosophical advocates give philosophical credence to personal experience based on gender, ethnic background, or social status.

public philosophers A compelling writer or speaker whose philosophical positions are expressed in ways accessible to a broad audience; public philosophers tap into—or identify—vital philosophical issues of the day.

"It Is the Age of Socrates Again"

Philosophers and social historians have been interested in and troubled by "technology" from the Classical age to today. Socrates, for example, lamented the invention of writing and reading as impediments to memory. In this early twentieth-century extract, the historian of philosophy Will Durant makes observations that remain as timely as when he made them:

> Human conduct and belief are now undergoing transformations profounder and more disturbing than any since the appearance of wealth and philosophy put an end to the traditional religion of the Greeks. It is the age of Socrates again: our moral life is threatened, and our intellectual life is quickened and enlarged by the disintegration of ancient customs and beliefs. Everything is new and experimental in our ideas and our actions; nothing is established or certain any more. The rate, complexity, and variety of change in our time are without precedent...all forms about us are altered, from the tools that complicate our toil, to the wheels that whirl us restlessly about the earth, to the innovations in our sexual relationships, and to the hard disillusionment of our souls....
>
> Our culture is superficial today, and our knowledge dangerous, because we are rich in mechanisms and poor in purposes. The balance of mind which once came of a warm religious faith is gone; science has taken from us the supernatural bases of our morality, and all the world seems consumed in a disorderly individualism that reflects the chaotic fragmentation of our character....We move about the earth with unprecedented speed, but we do not know, and have not thought, where we are going, or whether we shall find any happiness there for our harassed souls. We are being destroyed by our knowledge, which has made us drunk with our power. And we shall not be saved without wisdom.

Will Durant, *The Mansions of Philosophy: A Survey of Human Life and Destiny* (Garden City, N.Y.: Simon and Schuster, 1929), pp. vii, viii, xff.

idiot: *originally from the Greek* idiotes, *a disparaging term for private person; one who does not participate in community affairs; one who shuns the body politic; sometimes translated as "good for nothing."*

For Deeper Consideration

Take a moment to reflect on Will Durant's characterization of ours being an "age of Socrates" (see box on this page), "rich in mechanisms and poor in purposes," an age "consumed in a disorderly individualism." Do you think our culture is, on balance, superficial? Fragmented? Are we distracted by information, too easily drawn away from substantial pursuits and fully human engagement with one another? Or are Durant's fears the usual lamentations older generations express in the face of progress? Is there a way to distinguish progress from change that amounts to more than merely liking what's new? As you reflect on Durant's diagnosis, keep in mind that he made it in 1929.

Contemporary philosophers disagree among themselves about whether or not it is proper for philosophers—as philosophers—to base philosophical views on *autobiography* (the philosopher's specific life circumstances) or *advocacy* ("taking sides" by promoting specific social and political positions based on the philosopher's gender,

The association of rationality with masculinity is being challenged by contemporary women (and men) philosophers, reaffirming some of the earliest, most compelling archetypal representations of woman as a symbol of both wisdom (Athena, right) and love (Aphrodite, left). Many of these contemporary philosophers also challenge the association of femininity with emotions, pointing out that both men and women can be wise.

ethnic, or economic circumstances). One camp argues that philosophers should strive for detached (objective) rationality—not become personally attached to their philosophical conclusions. Another camp argues that philosophers have both *rights* and *obligations* to take personal stands on timely issues—as philosophers.

In simplified terms, we can summarize the general critique of modern (Enlightenment) philosophy as follows: With rare exceptions, Western philosophers have failed to recognize that they have personal, social, gendered, and ethnic perspectives. When philosophers do this, they overlook the fact that their philosophy reflects the special interests of only a small portion of the human community.

Critics of modern philosophy assert that until relatively recently this blindness has resulted in a separation of professional philosophy from the real-life concerns of all persons not of the typical (privileged) philosophical classes: highly educated white males. The result, it is argued, is a tradition that has systematically excluded or marginalized the voices of philosophers concerned with family matters, children's interests, and other traditionally "unphilosophical" and "private" topics.

Jean-Paul Sartre: A Way of Life Is a Philosophy

Combined with his literary talent, **Jean-Paul Charles Aymard Sartre's** (1905–1980) rejection of the traditional distinction between "philosophical" concerns and everyday life made him one of the most influential public philosophers of the "existential" 1950s and 1960s. More than anything else, Sartre's philosophy was shaped by his

Jean-Paul Sartre

experiences during World War II. He was drafted into the French army in 1939 and in 1940 was captured by the Germans. Sartre spent nine months as a prisoner of war, teaching Heidegger to fellow prisoners, before being released because of poor health. He returned to Paris and soon became an influential member of the French Resistance movement. During this time he met **Albert Camus** (1913–1960), his only near-rival in contemporary existential influence, and the brilliant **Simone de Beauvoir** (1908–1986), who became Sartre's lover and lifelong friend.

The German occupation of France drove home to Sartre the fact that evil is not a mere abstraction; it is real and concrete. He concluded that civilization and order are a thin veneer: At any moment "the beast" can break loose and reveal "the absurd," which most of us try to deny through rationalizations in the form of abstractions and philosophical and religious beliefs. Failure to face the absurd is always accompanied by excessive denial, which prevents us from recognizing evil for what it is. "It was the war," Sartre stated, "which made the obsolete frames of our thought explode, the war, occupation, resistance, the years that followed."[1]

After the war, Sartre devoted his life to reading, writing, and speaking out on various topics relating to social injustice and personal responsibility. Throughout this time, he maintained a rich and rewarding friendship with Simone de Beauvoir. She challenged and stimulated him as a man and as a thinker, greatly influencing both his ideas and their written expression, as he did hers. Sartre and de Beauvoir were a unique couple whose influence extended beyond their individual works to their lives, as they became role models for postwar intellectuals.

Buoyed by the popularity of Sartre's and others' existential plays and novels, existentialism became the "in" philosophy of hipsters, beats, hippies, artists, students, and avant-garde thinkers. Sartre became a kind of philosophical godfather to radical French students and remained a well-known public figure throughout his life. He flirted with Maoism, a form of communism practiced in China. In 1968, Sartre

> *The essential predicament of man has assumed a peculiar urgency in our time, living as we do in a civilization where factories were established in order to exterminate millions of men, women, and children; where soap was made of human flesh. What have we done to make such crimes possible? What are we doing to make such crimes impossible?*
>
> — Abraham Joshua Heschel

As their writing became widely known and controversial, Jean-Paul Sartre and Simone de Beauvoir emerged as one of history's most unlikely celebrity couples.

Francois Lochon/Gamma-Rapho/Getty Images

spoke out on behalf of a student revolt and two years later edited a Maoist newspaper called *The People's Cause*. During the Vietnam War, Sartre spoke out vehemently against American "war crimes."

Yet Sartre remained an enigma. He never joined the Communist Party. Though he has been described as arrogant and snobbish, he enjoyed the company of younger thinkers. His affair with Simone de Beauvoir grew into a complex friendship in which each party remained fiercely loyal to the other, while continuing to have affairs with others. When he was awarded the Nobel Prize in Literature 1964, Sartre refused it because he did not want to be "turned into an institution."

Freedom and Forlornness

For Sartre and countless others, living with the horror and irrationality of the Nazi occupation shattered any hope for an ordered universe governed by a wise, powerful, and loving God. Science provides no certainty either; indeed, the Nazi concentration camps were "scientific" and "rationally ordered." For Sartre, even nature is only another bourgeois delusion, a mental construct designed to cover up the hideous absurdity of existence. By pretending that facts dictate choices or that certain choices are "natural," we obscure our own responsibility. Like it or not, we are free to choose "the facts" or to reject them, free to "follow nature" or not, because we are free to define the facts and to define what is natural.

Sartre concluded that to *be* an authentic self is not possible. There is no fixed "essence" lingering behind the roles we play. We are whatever we do, the totality of our actions. Thus, *an authentic self exists as and through the choices it makes for itself, uncontrolled by the values of others.* Put another way, we do not *have* a given nature; we *become* a certain kind of person. We are existentially free. There is no fixed self on which we build.

The characters in Sartre's most famous play, *No Exit*, are dead people who never lived authentically, who identified themselves according to others' opinions of them. As a result, they became caricatures, mere sketches of living, real human beings. They meet in a hell fashioned by their own superficial choices. They have no exit from the consequences of their choices. They now *are* what they once only pretended to be—merely what others think of them. There is no real person behind the social mask.

In *No Exit*, Sartre attacked the hypocrisy, inauthenticity, and cowardice of living for others ("social self") rather than for one's "authentic self." So long as we do this, we are mere "social types," not *living individuals*. In Kierkegaard's terms, we live through the crowd without actually *existing*. In a Heideggerian sense, we disappear into the "they."

Consider an example illustrating Sartre's point. A young woman might try to conform to an image of what she conceives to be a stylish, successful type—say, a having-it-all businesswoman who wears trendy-but-casual clothes and drives a "green" hybrid car. She will try to work for Apple or Google or some other "cool," "unique," "creative" company or individual and learn to talk about following her "passion" and not selling out. Consciously and unconsciously, she will emulate people who fit her idealized type. She will make a point of telling herself and everyone else how independent,

Roger Viollet/Getty Images

Sartre's philosophy was shaped by the Holocaust, which made it difficult to simply dismiss the death of God and the Nietzschean abyss (Chapter 16). Perhaps "forlornness" is too tame a term for the human condition following such atrocities. How could God let something like this happen? How could "decent, average" people let it happen?

Man is but a foundling in the cosmos, abandoned by the forces that created him. Unparented, unassisted, and undirected by omniscient or benevolent authority, he must fend for himself, and with the aid of his own limited intelligence find his way about in an indifferent universe.
— Carl Becker

Galerie Bilderwelt/Hulton Archive/Getty Images

satisfied, and honest—authentic—she is. For the most part, however, these qualities, and her relationship to them, are external to the individual. Their meaning and value are created and controlled by social groups.

To succeed, the young woman will have to sacrifice until she becomes nothing more than a type of person. Her "success" will rest on her conceptions of other people's opinions of her. She might live under the delusion that she will be herself when she gets powerful enough or rich enough or when she retires or is phenomenally famous or notorious. This delusion protects her from a terrifying truth: There is no real self waiting. She has "no exit."

> *Man is nothing else but what he makes of himself. Such is the first principle of existentialism.*
>
> — Jean-Paul Sartre

PHILOSOPHICAL QUERY

Identify some common social types from your own experience. What social type are you? Are you, perhaps, many social types? Is it possible to be both a social type and an authentic self?

Condemned to Be Free

According to Sartre, since nothing limits our choices, we are not psychologically required to be this or that person. We are not chained to the past through heredity or environmental conditioning. Science and nature cannot tell us what to do, and neither can God. God is truly dead: He does not answer us but remains silent in the face of absurdity and horror. Thus we face life alone, without God, without certainty—we experience Sartrean forlornness—with only absolute freedom and the chilling responsibility that accompanies it:

> Nowhere is it written that the Good exists, that we must be honest, that we must not lie; because the fact is we are on a plane where there are only men. Dostoievsky said, "If God didn't exist, everything would be possible." That is the very starting point of existentialism. Indeed, everything is permissible if God does not exist, and as a result man is forlorn, because neither within him nor without does he find anything to cling to. He can't start making excuses for himself.[2]

Sartre denounced secular ethics that attempt to take ethical values seriously in such a way that "nothing will be changed if God does not exist." But if God does not exist, and if science cannot provide certainty, and if "nature" is a middle-class invention, *then everything has changed radically.* (See also Chapter 16.)

Most significant, in Sartre's view, is that without God, there is no fixed human nature, no "essence" that infuses us. *We* are not governed by fixed laws: We are free, not determined. First we exist; then we choose; then we act. We fashion our essence by how we actually live our lives—without God to guide and console us:

> If existence really does precede essence, there is no explaining things away by reference to a fixed and given human nature. In other words, there is no determinism, man is free, man is freedom. On the other hand, if God does not exist, we find no values or commands to turn to which legitimise our conduct. So, in the bright realm of values, we have no excuse behind us, nor justification before us. We are alone with no excuses.[3]

forlornness
Sartre's term for his belief that we face life alone, without God, without certainty, with only absolute freedom and the responsibility that accompanies it.

PHILOSOPHICAL QUERY

Given the horrors of our age—the threat of nuclear annihilation, chemical weapons, terrorism, child abuse, rampant pollution, AIDS and cancer, homelessness, ecological disasters, and famine—which do you see as more horrible: the absence of God or the silence of God? Is God silent?

What good three thousand years of so-called civilization, of religion, philosophy, and education, when . . . men go on torturing, killing, repressing their fellowmen? In fact, was there not a retrogression here? In my own brief time we have vastly multiplied our capacity to kill and destroy.

— William L. Shirer

A strong case can be made that our age is indeed forlorn, at least psychologically. Though science continues to explain human conduct in biochemical terms and according to behavioristic models, we cannot fail to see signs of forlornness in desperate attempts to find guidelines, guarantees, certainty: We look to science to "cure" everything from warts to character defects. We seek to absolve ourselves with excuses: "I come from a disadvantaged background." "I couldn't help it." "I was drunk." "I was overcome by my emotions."

Sartre insisted that in at least one aspect we are indeed not free: *We are not free not to be free.* In his famous phrase, *we are condemned to be free.* No divine commandments, no prophecies or omens, limit or lead us; no powerful, "irresistible" feeling excuses us.

Sartre illustrated the forlornness of freedom with a story about one of his students. The young man's father had collaborated with the Nazis during the occupation of France, but his older brother had been killed fighting the Germans, and the young man wanted to avenge him. The boy and his mother lived alone, and the mother was upset by the father's betrayal of his country and dead son. Sartre's student was her sole consolation and reason for living. He faced the choice of leaving for England to fight or staying in France to support his mother. What should the student do, and how could he know?

> Who could help him choose? Christian doctrine? No. Christian doctrine says, "Be charitable, love your neighbor, take the more rugged path, etc., etc." But which is the more rugged path? Whom should he love as a brother? The fighting man or his mother? Which does the greater good, the vague act of fighting in a group or the concrete one of helping a particular human being to go on living? Who can decide *a priori?* Nobody. No book of ethics can tell him. The Kantian ethic says, "Never treat any person as a means, but as an end." Very well, if I stay with my mother, I'll treat her as an end and not as a means; but by virtue of this very fact, I'm running the risk of treating the people around me who are fighting, as means; and, conversely, if I go to join those who are fighting, I'll be treating them as an end, and, by doing that, I run the risk of treating my mother as a means.[4]

No system of ethics, no philosophy, could tell the student what choice to make, and if feelings "are formed by the act one performs," he could not seek the answer within himself. And so he turned to Sartre for advice:

> But if you seek advice from a priest, for example, you have chosen this priest; you already knew, more or less, just about what advice he was going to give you. In other words, choosing your adviser is choosing yourself. . . . Which to choose? If the young man chooses a priest who is resisting or collaborating, he has already decided on the kind of advice he's going to get. Therefore, in coming to see me he

We are left alone, without excuse. That is what I mean when I say that man is condemned to be free.

— Jean-Paul Sartre

knew the answer I was going to give: "You're free, choose, that is, invent." No general ethics can show you what is to be done; there are no omens in the world. The Catholics will reply, "But there are." Granted—but, in any case, I myself choose the meaning they have.

... Therefore, he is fully responsible for the interpretation. Forlornness implies that we ourselves choose our being.[5]

MindTap

Discussing Philosophy

PHILOSOPHICAL QUERY

If valuing depends on choosing, and not the other way around, what do you value? Assess your values with a Sartrean analysis of your actions. For instance, do you value your job more than school? To find out, see which receives most of your time, thoughts, and actions. Test other aspects of your life. What are the strengths and weaknesses of such a view of valuing and choosing?

Out of Despair, Toughness

If we adopt a rigorous Sartrean philosophy, then we must confine our planning and our efforts to what is under our immediate influence or control. We must stick to what falls under the domain of our will and ability. But this realistic, responsible approach, Sartre says, leads to *despair*. We are stripped of hoping that God, or society, or luck, or science, or the general goodwill of others will come to our aid or rescue:

As for despair, the term has a very simple meaning. It means that we shall confine ourselves to reckoning only with what depends upon our will, or on the ensemble of probabilities which make our action possible.

... Given that man is free and that there is no human nature for me to depend on, I cannot count on men whom I do not know by relying on human goodness or man's concern for the good of society.... I've got to limit myself to what I see.[6]

We must not confuse *possibilities* with *probabilities*. Many improbable things are possible. Someone might possibly walk up to you on the street and hand you a million dollars. But it would be extremely foolish and irresponsible for you to run up thousands of dollars on a credit card based on that possibility. It is possible that your philosophy final exam will be canceled, and your professor will give you an A on it anyway. But ...

Sartre says:

According to this, we can understand why our doctrine horrifies certain people. Because often the only way they can bear their wretchedness is to think, "Circumstances have been against me. What I've been and done doesn't show my true worth. To be sure, I've had no great love, no great friendship, but that's because I haven't met a man or woman who was worthy. The books I've written haven't been very good because I haven't had the proper leisure. I haven't had children to devote myself to because I didn't find a man with whom I could have spent my life. So there remains within me, unused and quite viable, a host of propensities, inclinations, possibilities, that one wouldn't guess from the mere series of things I've done."[7]

Modern man may be characterized as a being who is callous to catastrophes. A victim of enforced brutalization, his sensibility is being increasingly reduced; his sense of horror is on the wane. The distinction between right and wrong is being blurred. All that is left to us is our being horrified at the loss of our sense of horror.

— Abraham
Joshua Heschel

To those who object to Sartre's apparently harsh doctrine, he replies that his philosophy actually calls us to "optimistic toughness." Though it seeks to strip us of our dreams, hopes, and expectations, it does so for the purpose of turning our attention, and hence our lives, to the reality of here and now—not the fantasy of maybe there later:

> To be sure, this may seem a harsh thought to someone whose life hasn't been a success. But, on the other hand, it prompts people to understand that reality alone is what counts, that dreams, expectations, and hopes warrant no more than to define a man as a disappointed dream, as miscarried hopes, as vain expectations. In other words, to define him negatively and not positively....
>
> When all is said and done, what we are accused of, at bottom, is not our pessimism, but an optimistic toughness.... When the existentialist writes about a coward, he says that this coward is responsible for his cowardice. He's not like that because he has a cowardly heart or lung or brain; he's not like that on account of his physiological make-up; but he's like that because he has made himself a coward by his acts. There is no such thing as a cowardly constitution; there are nervous constitutions; there is poor blood, as the common people say, or strong constitutions. But the man whose blood is poor is not a coward on that account, for what makes cowardice is the act of renouncing or yielding. A constitution is not an act; the coward is defined on the basis of the acts he performs. People feel, in a vague sort of way, that this coward we're talking about is guilty of being a coward, and the thought frightens them. What people would like is that a coward or a hero be born that way.
>
> ... What the existentialist says is that the coward makes himself cowardly, that the hero makes himself heroic. There's always a possibility for the coward not to be cowardly any more and for the hero to stop being heroic. What counts is total involvement; some one particular action or set of circumstances is not total involvement. [8]

Ironically, excuses and explanations, though superficially comforting and compassionate, are ultimately pessimistic: They reduce us to the effects of uncontrollable forces (genes, childhood, culture). Our choices, if we believe such scientifically sophisticated explanations, are severely restricted. Our dignity is reduced to coping with the rough deal we've been dealt. "I've done pretty well, considering the way I was treated as a child." "It's not my fault I went to inferior schools. I'm doing pretty well, considering that my reading skills are weak."

Perhaps the loss of free will is a small price to pay for being able to blame luck, heredity, and my past for the present condition of my life. Perhaps the comforts provided by excuses, grudges, self-pity, wishes, dreams, and expectations are worth the price of losing sight of opportunities to act differently right now. Sartre, clearly, does not think so. For inevitably, with the loss of freedom comes the loss of human dignity.

The Reemergence of Other Voices

Whether or not philosophers must have particular experiences before they can philosophize about them is a difficult and controversial issue. Must one be a woman in order to philosophize about the oppression of women? Can philosophers of one social class or ethnic group really understand the particularities of members of some other group? And if they cannot, how can they speak for people in general when they deal with ethical issues or social philosophy—or the nature of knowledge?

Such questions are difficult to answer for many reasons. In the first place, there is the problem of who can possibly judge among competing claims of unique insight. Consider, for instance, the notion that only women are qualified to philosophize about "women's issues." Must we then also argue that women cannot speak out on "men's issues"? Are we thus committed to the principle that only those who suffer a particular form of oppression are qualified to address its identification and remedy?

If we are, then does it also follow that only African American working-class women can speak to the oppression of African American working-class women— but not to the oppression of African American middle-class women or Laotian American professional women or Haitian American working-class women? Should philosophers who have not given birth and raised children philosophize about motherhood?

These are not frivolous questions; they address important and controversial issues that extend beyond philosophy into campus politics, elections, legislation, the composition of juries. Answering these sorts of questions is fraught with peril, since any answer must appeal to some foundational principle of justification, which can— in turn—be questioned.

In this context, modern philosophy's emphases on objectivity and personal detachment have become increasingly disturbing to growing numbers of philosophers. Converging social, political, and intellectual movements are contributing to reawakened interest in *other voices* and other approaches to doing philosophy and practicing science. Susan Bordo (Chapter 9) does not see this as a complete rejection of modern philosophy but rather as a *complement*, a completion or enrichment:

> This is not to say that detachment, clarity, and precision will cease to have enormous value in the process of understanding. Rather, our culture needs to reconceive the status of what Descartes assigned to the shadows. Such revaluation has been a constant, although "recessive" strain in the history of philosophy since Descartes.... Hume's insistence that "reason is and ought to be the slave of the passions," and, perhaps most importantly, Kant's revelation that objectivity itself is the result of human structuring, opened various doors that in retrospect now appear as critical openings.
>
> Hume, for example, may now be seen as having a rightful place—along with Nietzsche...[and]...James...in the critical protest against the Cartesian notion that reason can and should be a "pure" realm free from contamination by emotion, instinct, will, sentiment, and value. Within this protest, we see the development both of a "naturalist" *anthropology* of the Cartesian ideals of precision, certainty, and neutrality (Nietzsche...and James), and a complementary *metaphysics*...in which "vagueness" as well as specificity, tentativeness, and valuation are honored as essential to thought.[9]

Now perhaps you may think it not fitting for a woman to philosophize, just as it is not fitting for her to ride horses or speak in public. But I think that some things are peculiar to a man, some to a woman, some are common to both.... I say that courage and justice and wisdom are common to both.

— Phintys of Sparta

Contemporary philosophers and social scientists pose a series of interrelated questions that challenge the exclusive status of the traditional (masculinized) model of rationality as detached, objective knowing: Is there only one way of reasoning? Is objective reasoning the only or best way of knowing? To what extent, if any, are personal detachment and objectivity possible? Perhaps most important, when—if ever—are personal detachment and objectivity undesirable?

In 1982, Harvard psychologist **Carol Gilligan** (b. 1936) published her ground-breaking book *In a Different Voice: Psychological Theory and Women's Development*, a work that prompted a necessary reassessment of moral reasoning. The following passage conveys some sense of the importance and delicacy of research into the area of gender bias—and how pervasive such bias can be:

Carol Gilligan

© Cengage Learning®

> A word, finally, about the politics and the controversy of this research. The stark fact of the all-male research sample, accepted for years as representative by psychologists studying human development, in one sense speaks for itself. That such samples were not seen long ago as problematic by women or men points to different blindnesses on the part of each sex. The fact that these samples passed the scrutiny of peer review boards, that studies of…moral development…using all-male samples were repeatedly funded and widely published in professional journals indicates that the psychological research community needs to reexamine its claims to objectivity and dispassion. If the omission of half the human population was not seen, or not seen as significant, or not spoken about as a problem (by women or men), what other omissions are not being seen? The contribution of women's thinking…is a different voice, a different way of speaking about relationships and about the experience of the self. The inclusion of this voice changes the map of the moral domain. Listening to girls and women, we have come to listen differently to boys and men. And we have come to think differently about human nature and the human condition, and in turn, about…disciplines devoted to improving human life.…
>
> The different voice I describe is characterized not by gender but by theme. Its association with women is an empirical observation, and it is primarily through women's voices that I trace its development. But this association is not absolute, and the contrasts between male and female voices…highlight a distinction between two modes of thought and…focus [on] a problem of interpretation rather than represent a generalization about either sex.[10]

When female philosophers publish feminist interpretations of Marx, Nietzsche, Kant, Aristotle, and others, they have implicitly accepted the dead White male tradition, docilely agreeing to read the works singled out by men for men to read.

— Laurie
    Calhoun

Gilligan notes that excessive reliance on "rationality" results in injustice by excluding those who do not speak in the "objective voice" from full participation in philosophy, science, law, higher education—and by denying everyone access to the full range of knowledge necessary for wise choices. When we confine our standard of reasoning to the "impersonal" modern model, we fail to recognize wisdom as it is expressed in some Asian, Native American, African, and Hispanic philosophies that are not built on the objective, rationalistic model. One result is a tendency to classify wisdom philosophies as religions or mythologies rather than as "real" philosophies.

Inclusive Philosophy

In 2007—more than a quarter of a century after Carol Gilligan called contemporary philosophers' attention to the exclusion of "other voices" from philosophy—organizers of the first meeting of the Collegium of Black Women Philosophers were able to identify only thirty full-time black women philosophy teachers in America. That's correct: thirty.[11]

Kathryn T. Gines, the black assistant professor at Vanderbilt University who founded the Collegium, points out that, "If you're a black woman, you cannot identify with the majority of the people in the profession." Jacqueline R. Scott, an associate professor of philosophy at Loyola University Chicago, expressed similar frustrations: "I spend a lot of time being the only woman and the only black person.... Every once in a while it hits me, and I wonder what I'm doing here." Although philosophy is academe's oldest discipline, the first Ph.D. was not awarded to a black woman until 1965, when Joyce Mitchell Cook earned her philosophy doctorate at Yale University.

Anna Stubblefield, chair of the philosophy department at Rutgers University's Newark campus and head of the APA's Committee on Blacks and Philosophy, estimated that about one hundred, or 1 percent, of the ten thousand academic philosophers in North America are black, and of those, perhaps twenty are female, while Gines put the number at twenty-nine.

Representation in Philosophy? Do the Math

In "Feminism is a Humanism," Laurie Calhoun, a philosopher and Research Fellow at the Independent Institute, noted that:

> Although, in theory, it may seem that the necessary conditions for the intellectual flourishing of women have already been achieved, in fact, considering the history of philosophy, even in the late twentieth century the appearance and influence of women has been rather limited. Still today, in the twenty-first century, one finds respected philosophy departments with few or no tenured women faculty....[12]

When Sally Haslanger, a philosophy professor at the Massachusetts Institute of Technology, first discovered that the American Philosophical Association (APA) did not keep records of how many of its ten thousand philosophers are women (or members of other minority groups), she and other concerned philosophers began collecting their own data from America's philosophy departments. (Thanks to the APA Committee on the Status of Women's requests, the APA has started to collect demographic data about its members.)

In 2013, the *New York Times* published "Women in Philosophy? Do the Math," the first essay in a five-part series addressing the treatment of women philosophers in academia.[13] In her *Times* article, Haslanger notes that, for many reasons, it is particularly difficult to determine the true percentages of women philosophy professors and teachers. According to Julie Van Camp, a California State University at Long Beach professor who keeps track of tenured and tenure-track women faculty at 98 U.S. doctoral programs, in 2014, of the 1,044 positions available in the top fifty-one philosophy programs, only 237 were held by women. That's a 22.22 percent median average.

Such numbers can be misleading, Haslanger cautions. For instance, according to the most current data from the *Digest of Educational Statistics*, in 2003, women

More generally, professional philosophy itself forms a higher-order ghetto within academia. People in other disciplines generally pay no attention whatsoever to what White male philosophers do and say, except in rare cases....

— Laurie
    Calhoun

accounted for 16.6 percent of thirteen thousand full-time postsecondary academic jobs in philosophy—despite the fact that women received 27.1 percent of the philosophy doctorates awarded that year. Why the gap between student achievement and professional inclusion? For women of color, the percentage was particularly disturbing: *zero*. There was not enough data about non-white women to generate a percentage.

In 2009, the U.S. Department of Education reported that black philosophers—both men and women—accounted for only 2.48 percent of the Ph.D.s awarded in philosophy. According to Haslanger, the American Philosophical Committee on the Status of Black Philosophers and the Society of Young Black Philosophers could identify only 156 black philosophers (both doctoral students and Ph.D.s). Of those, 55 were black women—only 31 of whom were tenured or in tenure-track positions. "Assuming that there are still 13,000 full-time philosophy instructors in the United States," Haslanger writes, "the representation of scholars of color is plausibly worse than in *any other field in the academy*, including not only physics, but also engineering. Inexcusable."

Does this sort of thing matter *philosophically*, as opposed to, say, sociologically or legally? Surely it does, for, as we have seen throughout our journey together, philosophy, from its origins, has been associated with a love of wisdom. From its inception, philosophers have struggled to articulate, assess, and establish moral principles and universal standards of justice, or to show that there are no such principles. What philosophers have not done, because to do so would render them unphilosophical, is to ignore unspoken, uncritiqued epistemological assumptions and prejudicial social practices and preferences once they are pointed out, whether by social scientists, theologians, poets, protestors, or other philosophers.

This is not to say that philosophers, as philosophers, are free from biases and always open to new questions and modes of inquiry. They are, obviously, not immune to human frailties. But philosophers, as philosophers, are expected to base their philosophical conclusions on arguments, evidence, and reasons—not on preferences pertaining to personalities, nationality, gender, religion, ethnicity, appearance.

As a truly critical and reflective discipline, philosophy cannot tolerate the systemic and persistent exclusion and suppression of philosophers based solely on social, gender, or other autobiographical considerations—nor can it include or make exceptions for individuals or ideas on those bases. And this is where the role of the contemporary philosophical advocate can get particularly tricky.

Whether it is done deliberately or not, systematically limiting the participation of "outsiders" and "minorities" in the ranks of professional, academic philosophy is clearly unreasonable because doing so deprives us of the contributions of individuals who may have insights and capacities that we lack. It is also unfair because it creates a caste system based not on talent, experience, or character, but on luck, custom, and ethnocentrism. Yet one common "fix" for the underrepresentation of certain groups in the ranks of professional philosophy may be exacerbating the very problem it seeks to redress by increasing rather than reducing the role of autobiography in philosophy. "There is a certain type of research done by black scholars that isn't accepted by the larger white academy," reports Carol M. Swain, a black professor of political science and law at Vanderbilt, who worries about what she describes as the "self-segregation" that can result by "Encouraging black people to marginalize themselves by pursuing a line of philosophy not accepted by the mainstream [and that] just reinforces the stereotype that blacks can't do philosophy the way other scholars can."

Laurie Calhoun concludes "Feminism Is a Humanism" in the strong, inviting, inclusive voice of the best philosophical advocates, the fully human voice that addresses our hearts as well as our minds, reminding us, as Carol Swaim reminds us, that just as we rightly resist and resent being marginalized by others, we must take care not to marginalize ourselves:

> If feminism has done much too much to facilitate the entry of women into the respected world of letters, it will only have triumphed when the word "feminism" itself holds merely historical interest. That women should be free to flourish intellectually and to make their own original contributions to philosophy is a goal toward which all waves of feminism have, in one way or another, strived. That goal will have been reached when women, no less than men, are able to achieve professional success in philosophy simply through being themselves.[14]

What, then, does it mean to philosophize *as a woman*, or *as a black woman*, or *as a Native American*, or *as an Italian American*, or *as a gay man*, or *as a lesbian*? And what, if any, is the limit to such categories? That is, is the category black-lesbian *philosophically* different from black-woman or black-gay-person? Whatever their social, political, and legal ramifications, such considerations also raise epistemological, moral, and philosophical questions.

> *Who knows? Perhaps someday in the not-too-distant future, women in philosophy will finally reach critical mass; all philosophers will live in balmy warmth; and no APA meetings will involve blizzards.*
>
> — Peggy DesAutels

PHILOSOPHICAL QUERY

Does categorizing philosophical areas of specialization along gender, ethnic, and other autobiographical lines turn "doing philosophy" into sociology or social work? Is this a philosophical question? If not, why not? If so, who is qualified to deal with it?

🅜 MindTap™

Discussing Philosophy

Martin Luther King, Jr.: Philosophic Activist

Perhaps more than any other figure in recent American history, **Martin Luther King, Jr.** (1929–1968) brought important philosophical and moral concerns into the public arena. In the process, he became a figure of reverence and contempt, idolized and ridiculed during his life, analyzed and debated in death. King had the vision, intellect, and courage to take action against injustice without demonizing his oppressors—a most rare, beautiful, and needful quality, indeed. King's powerful speaking skills, combined with his courageous actions on behalf of racial justice, make him a compelling exemplar of philosophical advocacy in action.

Just as it is impossible to separate the sage's life from his or her philosophical beliefs, it is also impossible to separate the public philosophical advocate from his or her place in history. In the case of King, that place is at the beginning of what has come to be known as the American civil rights movement.

Martin Luther King, Jr.

© Cengage Learning®

> *We must never forget that everything Hitler did in Germany was "legal."... It was "illegal" to aid and comfort a Jew in Hitler's Germany. But I am sure that if I had lived in Germany during that time I would have aided and comforted my Jewish brothers even though it was illegal.*
> — Martin Luther King, Jr.

Underwood Archives/Getty Images

Rosa Parks is shown being booked in jail after her arrest for refusing to give up her bus seat to a white passenger. Speaking of civil disobedience, Martin Luther King, Jr., said, "This is not a method for cowards; it *does* resist."

On May 17, 1954, in *Linda Brown et al. v. Board of Education of Topeka*, the U.S. Supreme Court ordered the desegregation of all public schools "with all deliberate speed." Chief Justice Earl Warren wrote the unanimous opinion that "in the field of public education the doctrine of 'separate but equal' has no place. Separate educational facilities are inherently unequal." The Court's ruling sent shock waves throughout the country, and white racist and separatist groups such as the Ku Klux Klan and White Citizens' Council initiated an escalating series of violent attacks on blacks. Shortly after the ruling, the black press in Mississippi recorded three cases of antiblack terrorism.

On December 1, 1955, Mrs. Rosa Parks, a forty-two-year-old black seamstress in Montgomery, Alabama, defied the law when she refused to yield her seat on a bus to a white man when ordered to by the bus driver. Rosa Parks was arrested, and the resulting controversy attracted national attention.[15] The reaction to the *Brown* case had divided the country. When Rosa Parks refused to give up her seat on the bus a year and a half after the *Brown* decision, the South erupted with murderous racial violence: The Reverend George W. Lee was lynched in Belzoni, Mississippi, after he tried to register to vote in Humphreys County; Lamar Smith was lynched in Brookhaven, Mississippi; fourteen-year-old Emmett Till was lynched in Money, Mississippi.[16]

Character Is Destiny

Acting as president of the Montgomery Improvement Association created to support Rosa Parks, King led a 381-day nonviolent boycott of the Montgomery public transportation system by blacks. The boycotters initially demanded that black bus drivers be hired for buses serving mostly black areas. They also protested the many insults and discourtesies blacks suffered. Ultimately, the boycotters demanded an end to segregated seating. During the boycott, four black churches were bombed, as were the homes of King and another protesting black pastor, the Reverend Ralph Abernathy. Rosa Parks lost her job, as did other blacks who participated in the boycott. Despite the lynchings, bombings, arson, and general intimidation, the push toward civil equality continued.

The Montgomery bus boycott was the first of many nonviolent black demonstrations aimed at securing for blacks those rights already enjoyed by whites. It marked a major turning point in King's life. In addition to making him an internationally recognized black leader and advocate of Christian nonviolent civil disobedience, the boycott crystallized King's vision for America. Referring to that time, he said, "After prayerful consideration, I am convinced that the psychological moment has come when a concentrated drive against injustice can bring great tangible gains."[17] In short, the bus boycott showed that King's nonviolent philosophy of civil disobedience *worked*.

> *I will believe that standing up for the truth of God is the greatest thing in the world. This is the end of life. The end of life is not to be happy. The end of life is not to achieve pleasure and avoid pain. The end of life is to do the will of God, come what may.*
> — Martin Luther King, Jr.

Francis Miller/Time & Life Pictures/Getty Images

On August 28, 1963, Martin Luther King, Jr., delivered one of the great speeches in American history to a crowd of more than 200,000 civil rights demonstrators gathered around the Lincoln Memorial. Later, King said, "I started out reading the speech, and...the audience response was wonderful that day....And all of a sudden this thing came to me that...'I have a dream.'...And at that point I just turned aside from the manuscript altogether. I didn't come back to it."

King's method of "nonviolent direct action" worked slowly and involved great struggle. It took seven years to desegregate Southern buses, for instance, and we've just noted the violence that followed Rosa Parks's refusal to give up her seat on the bus. The national fight over integrating schools took years, and remnants of that issue face us today in the form of questions regarding affirmative action, job quotas, and so forth.

Clearly, attempts to overcome racism and gain equal rights took great stamina and courage. In this context, King's efforts to *live out a philosophy* of active, direct nonviolence are especially impressive. Risking his life, and surviving scorn, ridicule, beatings, and jail, King expressed a powerful moral and social philosophy that led to cultural changes that affect all Americans. In 1964, King received the Nobel Peace Prize. On April 4, 1968, he was assassinated in Memphis, Tennessee.

King belongs to a special class of activist philosophers whose philosophies and lives are inseparable. Because his chief concerns were social progress and improvement of the human condition for *all people*, his philosophy of nonviolence is expressed in dialogical sermons and lectures aimed at stirring the soul and calling the mind and body to action—not in detailed philosophical analysis or rarefied theoretical disputations.

The Value of Moral Tension

King's active nonviolent resistance differed from passive acceptance of injustice in that nonviolent resistance *deliberately interferes* with whatever is being opposed. Refusing to move to the back of the bus, refusing to leave a segregated lunch counter, and marching to protest discriminatory voter registration laws created *moral* tension by calling attention to injustice and trying to stop it.

If you have ever seen newsreels of civil rights demonstrators being clubbed, dragged away, attacked by police dogs, or beaten back by powerful fire hoses, you know that actively fighting for civil rights required considerable physical courage. *Public* resistance of injustice affected those who participated in that resistance and those who merely witnessed it from the safety and comfort of their living rooms.

King insisted that great care be taken to ensure the means used to achieve righteous goals did not tarnish the ultimate goal of a just society. The tricky part, then, was developing a way of producing timely change without resorting to methods that violated anyone else's basic rights. King insisted that no matter how reprehensible the wrong, the ends do not justify unjust means:

> The movement is based on the philosophy that ends and means must cohere. Now, this has been one of the long struggles in history, the whole idea of means and ends. Great philosophers have grappled with it, and sometimes they have emerged with the idea, from Machiavelli on down, that the end justifies the means....
>
> ...For in the long run, we must see that the end represents the means in process and the ideal in the making. In other words, we cannot believe, or we cannot go with the idea that the end justifies the means because the end is preexistent in the means. So the idea of nonviolent resistance, the philosophy of nonviolent resistance, is the philosophy which says that means must be as pure as the end, that in the long run of history, immoral destructive means cannot bring about moral and constructive ends.[18]

To those who argued for "negotiation" rather than "confrontation," King replied that negotiation was the very essence of active, public, nonviolent resistance. With

> *You don't have to be a man to fight for freedom. All you have to do is be an intelligent human being. And automatically your intelligence makes you want freedom so badly that you'll do anything, by any means necessary, to get that freedom.*
>
> — Malcolm X

Imagno/Hulton Archive/Getty Images

Take a good look at this photo. It is representative of the climate of hatred, fear, and danger that Martin Luther King, Jr., said could never be changed by violent means. According to King, the philosophy of nonviolent resistance holds that "in the long run of history, immoral destructive means cannot bring about moral and constructive ends." Understood in the context of King's life, this was more than just a philosophical notion. It was a lived principle, a philosophical way of life, knowingly adhered to in the face of grave personal risk.

time an indefensible luxury, the only course left for decent people was nonviolent direct action. Good people had to be awakened from their moral slumbers; the ability to feel satisfied in the midst of great injustice had to be shattered. Complacency had to be set aside, conscience had to be aroused. But how?

King's answer was to create a kind of moral tension that is always associated with genuine philosophical advocacy. When a philosophical advocate "practices what he (or she) preaches," the rest of us are confronted with something more powerful than a merely rigorous scholarly argument presented as a written or spoken claim. If the issues raised by a public philosopher touch on our own fundamental beliefs and principles, then we are faced with Socratic questions: *What about you? What do you believe? Does your life reflect your highest principles? If not, which is false, your life or your principles?*

These are not easy questions to face, and when our interlocutor possesses philosophical rigor, moral courage, and overall integrity, we may experience the kind of moral "shock treatment" Socrates administered as a way of awakening his conversants to the injustices of their time. According to King, moral tension is *exposed by* non-violent resisters; it is not *created*. In the following statement, King characterizes the role of active nonviolent resisters as "midwives," without actually using that term. (See Chapter 4 for a review of Socrates' characterization of himself as a midwife.)

> Actually, we who engage in nonviolent direct action are not the creators of tension. We merely bring to the surface the hidden tension that is already alive. We bring it out in the open where it can be seen and dealt with. Like a boil that can never be cured as long as it is covered up but must be opened with all its pus-flowing ugliness to the natural medicines of air and light, injustice must likewise be exposed, with all of the tension its exposing creates, to the light of human conscience and the air of national opinion before it can be cured.[19]

Public philosophical advocates like King appeal to what may be thought of as our "higher" or "better" selves by speaking directly to our consciences, our capacity to reflect and reason, and to our moral sentiments. Even when we disagree with them, we benefit from the philosophical reflection they trigger in us.

For Deeper Consideration

Try this thought experiment: Imagine that you are a philosophical detective assigned to determine your own deepest, truest, most sacred beliefs—but you are only allowed to draw conclusions from behavior observed over an extended period of time, say the past six months or more. That is, you must base your conclusions on behavior that occurred before you knew your lived choices would be used to draw a description of your lived—as opposed to your felt or idealized—philosophy. Is it fair to use only actual behavior as the determinant of what we "really believe"? If not, why not? Do we too easily let ourselves off the hook by placing considerable weight on beliefs and intentions? What would Kant say? James? Sartre?

Peter Singer: "The Dangerous Philosopher"

Peter Singer

The Australian philosopher **Peter Singer** (b. 1946) is an important professional philosopher who believes in making people uncomfortable as a way of raising moral consciousness. For nearly forty years, Singer has advocated a rigorous brand of contemporary utilitarianism (Chapter 12). Due to the potent combination of the life-and-death topics he addresses, the clarity of his prose, and the relentless quality of reasoning, Singer has become the rare philosopher whose philosophical writings and arguments are widely discussed among academic philosophers and the non-professional mass media.

Singer emerged as an international figure with the publication of *Animal Liberation* in 1975; in 1979 he published *Practical Ethics*. *Animal Liberation* has sold half a million copies, and *Practical Ethics* more than one hundred twenty thousand copies—remarkable figures for carefully reasoned philosophy books.

By the time of his 1999 appointment as Princeton University's first professor of bioethics, Singer was already one of the most famous—and controversial—philosophers writing and speaking. His influence is a product of a relentless application of utilitarian principles to some of the most troublesome and important issues of our era: euthanasia, abortion, suicide, poverty. Even Singer's position at Princeton is controversial. The philosophy department wanted a theoretical philosopher, not a practical (or applied) ethicist. The biology department was uneasy about appointing someone who openly opposed animal experimentation. As a result, Singer's bioethics professoriate is in the Center for Human Values. Because of protests against the university and death threats against Singer, Princeton has had to take extraordinary security precautions, carefully guarding the exact location of Singer's office and varying his routine.

Singer has long argued that euthanasia and infanticide (the killing of babies) are sometimes "necessary," given the complexities of the modern world. "It is ridiculous to pretend that old ethics still make sense when plainly they do not," Singer says in his characteristically straightforward way.[20] He also argues that a human's life is not necessarily "more sacred" than a dog's. Singer suggests that it might even be more compassionate to conduct medical experiments on permanently disabled unconscious orphans than on conscious, sentient animals. Following Bentham, Singer argues that what matters most is not whether any animal (including human animals) can reason or talk but whether it can suffer: "The notion that human life is sacred just because it's human is medieval," Singer says. "It's time to stop pretending that the world is not the way we know it to be."[21]

As if such ideas are not disturbing enough to many people, Singer challenges everyone not already living in abject poverty—and that is most of the readers of this text—with forceful arguments for giving away all income over $30,000 (a 1999 figure he accepted as the baseline for adequately supporting a typical middle-class household). Today, a comparable income would be approximately $46,000. Single adults could, of course, live on much less and so give away much more. Singer himself gives one-fifth of his income (including royalties from his books) to famine-relief agencies.

The Singer Solution to World Poverty

In "The Singer Solution to World Poverty," an article published in the *New York Times* rather than in a philosophy journal, Singer considers the hypothetical case of "Bob," who would rather see an innocent child run over by a train than throw a switch that would save the child's life by diverting the train onto the track where Bob's precious Bugatti automobile is stalled. In the hypothetical scenario, Bob, who is close to retirement age, has invested most of his savings in the Bugatti. If it is destroyed, he will not have a chance to recoup his losses. So he chooses the car over the child.

Singer then presents a series of Socratic arguments designed to challenge us to think long and hard about how (or if) we are morally different from Bob. In the passage that follows, the figure of $200 is borrowed from the work of the philosopher Peter Unger, who had calculated that approximately $200 ($300 to $350 today) donated to UNICEF or Oxfam of America could provide enough aid to transform a sickly two-year-old into a healthy six-year-old. (This includes the costs of administrative fees.) As you read, note how deftly Singer anticipates some of the more

Discourse about philosophy is not the same thing as philosophy.
— Pierre Hadot

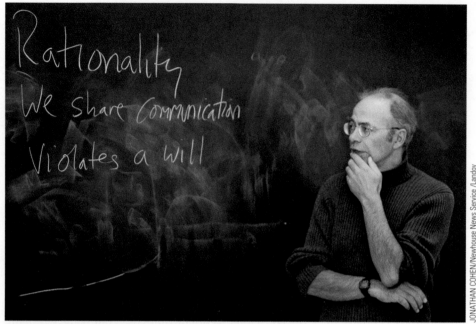

JONATHAN COHEN/Newhouse News Service /Landov

Peter Singer has devoted much of his life to questions of moral significance, including the matter of what characteristics (if any) distinguish human animals from nonhuman animals. This is dangerous stuff: "We like to distinguish ourselves from animals by saying that only humans are rational, can use language, are self-aware, or are autonomous. But...there are many humans who are not rational, self-aware, or autonomous, and who have no language—all humans under three months of age, for a start."

> *Our campuses educate our citizens. Becoming an educated citizen means learning a lot of facts and mastering techniques of reasoning. But it means something more. It means learning how to be a human being capable of love and imagination.*
>
> — Martha C. Nussbaum

common arguments we offer to explain why we do not give more to those in dire need. Singer writes:

> To show how practical philosophical argument can be, Unger even tells his readers that they can easily donate funds by using their credit card and calling one of these toll-free numbers: (800) 367-5437 for UNICEF; [(800) 77-OXFAM] for Oxfam America....
>
> Now you, too, have the information you need to save a child's life. How should you judge yourself if you don't do it? Think again about Bob and his Bugatti....
>
> If you still think that it was very wrong of Bob not to throw the switch that would have diverted the train and saved the child's life, then it is hard to see how you could deny that it is also very wrong not to send money to one of the organizations listed above. Unless, that is, there is some morally important difference between the two situations that I have overlooked.
>
> Is it the practical uncertainties about whether aid will really reach the people who need it? Nobody who knows the world of overseas aid can doubt that such uncertainties exist. But Unger's figure of $200 to save a child's life was reached after he had made conservative assumptions about the proportion of the money donated that will actually reach its target.
>
> One genuine difference between Bob and those who can afford to donate to overseas aid organizations but don't is that only Bob can save the child on the tracks, whereas there are hundreds of millions of people who can give $200 to

overseas aid organizations. The problem is that most of them aren't doing it. Does this mean that it is all right for you not to do it?…

We seem to lack a sound basis for drawing a clear moral line between Bob's situation and that of any reader of this article with $200 to spare who does not donate it to an overseas aid agency. These readers seem to be acting at least as badly as Bob was acting when he chose to let the runaway train hurtle toward the unsuspecting child. In the light of this conclusion, I trust that many readers will reach for the phone and donate that $200. Perhaps you should do it before reading further.

Now that you have distinguished yourself morally from people who put their vintage cars ahead of a child's life, how about treating yourself and your partner to dinner at your favorite restaurant? But wait. The money you will spend at the restaurant could also help save the lives of children overseas! True, you weren't planning to blow $200 tonight, but if you were to give up dining out just for one month, you would easily save that amount. And what is one month's dining out, compared to a child's life? There's the rub. Since there are a lot of desperately needy children in the world, there will always be another child whose life you could save for another $200. Are you therefore obliged to keep giving until you have nothing left? At what point can you stop?…

In the world as it is now, I can see no escape from the conclusion that each one of us with wealth surplus to his or her essential needs should be giving most of it to help people suffering from poverty so dire as to be life-threatening. That's right: I'm saying that you shouldn't buy that new car, take that cruise, redecorate the house or get that pricey new suit. After all, a $1,000 suit could save five children's lives.

So how does my philosophy break down in dollars and cents? An American household with an income of $50,000 spends around $30,000 annually on necessities, according to the Conference Board, a nonprofit economic research organization. Therefore, for a household bringing in $50,000 a year, donations to help the world's poor should be as close as possible to $20,000. The $30,000 required for necessities holds for higher incomes as well. So a household making $100,000 could cut a yearly check for $70,000. Again, the formula is simple: whatever money you're spending on luxuries, not necessities, should be given away….

When Bob first grasped the dilemma that faced him as he stood by that railway switch, he must have thought how extraordinarily unlucky he was to be placed in a situation in which he must choose between the life of an innocent child and the sacrifice of most of his savings. But he was not unlucky at all. We are all in that situation.[22]

For Deeper Consideration

Whew! Well, what do you think of Singer's reasoning? Assess Singer's views regarding our obligations toward alleviating world poverty. Is he too strict? Make your case that he is or is not. Should you save up your pizza and beer money, your latté and movie money, and send it to the poor? What principles or reasons are there—if any—for not doing so? Do you think Singer's argument would be more compelling if it addressed local—rather than world—poverty? (Has Singer succeeded in creating moral tension for you?)

Martha C. Nussbaum

Philosophy heals human diseases, diseases produced by false beliefs. Its arguments are to the soul as the doctor's remedies are to the body.

— Martha C. Nussbaum

Can one live in reason's kingdom... and still be a creature of wonder, grief, and love?

— Martha C. Nussbaum

Martha C. Nussbaum: "Lawyer for Humanity"

The philosopher **Martha C. Nussbaum** (b. 1947) speaks for many public philosophers when she notes that, too often, professional intellectuals fail to use their theories and talents to improve the human condition by fighting for equality, justice, and freedom.[23] Nussbaum's background in classics and theology enriches and informs her work. Nussbaum believes that philosophers ought to be "lawyers for humanity" (a term she borrows from Seneca):

> For any view you put forward the next question has to be, "What would the world be like if this idea were actually taken up?"... It's what happens in the long haul that really matters. You just never know where or how your ideals will be realized.[24]

Nussbaum's conviction that philosophy should make a practical difference in our lives has both theoretical and experiential roots. Trained in philosophy and classics, Nussbaum now holds a joint appointment in divinity and law at the University of Chicago. In *Cultivating Humanity: A Classical Defense of Reform in Liberal Education*, Nussbaum comments on the experience of exclusion and expresses a contemporary version of the Stoic concept of the *cosmopolis*, or universal city:

> When I arrived at Harvard in 1969, my fellow first-year graduate students and I were taken up to the roof of the Widener Library by a well-known professor of classics. He told us how many Episcopal churches could be seen from that vantage point. As a Jew (in fact a convert from Episcopalian Christianity), I knew that my husband and I would have been forbidden to marry in Harvard's church, which had just refused to accept a Jewish wedding. As a woman I could not eat in the main dining room for the faculty club, even as a member's guest. Only a few years before, a woman would not have been able to use the undergraduate library. In 1972 I became the first female to hold the Junior Fellowship that relieved certain graduate students from teaching so that they could get on with their research. At that time I received a letter of congratulation from a prestigious classicist saying that it would be difficult to know what to call a female fellow, since "fellowess" was an awkward term. Perhaps the Greek language could solve the problem: since the masculine for "fellow" in Greek was *hetairos*, I could be called a *hetaira*. *Hetaira*, however, as I knew, is the ancient Greek word not for "fellowess" but for "courtesan."
>
> In a setting in which exclusions and such "jokes" were routine, is it any wonder that the academic study of women's history, of literature written by women, of the sociology and politics of gender—that all of these perfectly normal and central topics were unavailable for serious study? They were just as unavailable as was (in most places) the serious academic study of Judaism, of African and of African-American cultures, of many other ethnic minorities, of many non-Western religions and cultures, of the variety and diversity of human sexuality. Exclusions of people and exclusions of their lives from the domain of knowledge went hand in hand. The exclusions seemed natural and apolitical; only the demand for inclusion seemed motivated by a "political agenda." From the rooftop of the Widener, there were many people and many lives that my colleague could not see.
>
> We are now trying to build an academy... in which to be a "fellowess" need not mean being called a "courtesan," an academy in which the world will be seen

to have many different types of citizen and in which we can all learn to function as citizens of that entire world.[25]

Nussbaum functions as a citizen of the world by writing about philosophical issues for the general public in *The New York Review of Books, The New Republic,* national newspapers, and other nonacademic publications. Her work generates mixed reviews, as is to be expected when any serious writer takes strong positions. The debate over the extent to which philosophy can—and should—be made accessible to a broad audience has always been contentious among American philosophers. Nussbaum sides with those philosophers who want to extend philosophy's reach. Referring to her own privileged background (her mother's family has roots going back to the *Mayflower,* and her father was a prosperous lawyer), Nussbaum says, "a lot of my impatience with [the work of elitist philosophers] grew out of my repudiation of my own aristocratic upbringing. I don't like anything that sets itself up as an in-group or an elite."[26]

Philosophy for the Sake of Humanity

With notable exceptions, as Western philosophy developed, philosophers increasingly dismissed and distrusted subjective—private—emotional responses to philosophical problems, focusing more on the dangers inherent in subjectivity than on the cost of pursuing objectivity at all costs. Yet objectivity and detachment are as susceptible to abuse as are overreliance on emotions and indiscriminate personal responses to life's predicaments. To the extent that being *fully human* is characterized as always deferring to a universal, objective, impersonal way of knowing, the responsible person is defined as one who exhibits the capacity to think in an objective, impersonal, unemotional way.

Nussbaum challenges modern philosophy's wariness of emotions and what she sees as its correspondingly limited view of philosophy (and life) in *The Therapy of Desire* and *Upheavals of Thought: The Intelligence of Emotions,* two books that have attracted the attention of readers from inside and outside of academic circles. Building on her knowledge of Hellenistic philosophy, Nussbaum presents what she describes as a "Neo-stoic" philosophy that takes the "art of life" seriously by treating philosophy as more than an intellectual or academic exercise. In the following passage, note how Nussbaum opens *The Therapy of Desire* by characterizing her role as a writer and teacher of philosophy in a broad way that excludes neither reason nor feeling. Note, too, her appeal to the practical nature of ancient philosophy:

> The idea of a practical and compassionate philosophy—a philosophy that exists for the sake of human beings, in order to address their deepest needs, confront their most urgent perplexities, and bring them from misery to some greater measure of flourishing—this idea makes the study of Hellenistic ethics riveting for a philosopher who wonders what philosophy has to do with the world. The writer and teacher of philosophy is a lucky person, fortunate, as few human beings are, to spend her life expressing her most serious thoughts and feelings about the problems that have moved and fascinated her most. But this exhilarating and wonderful life is also part of the world as a whole, a world in which hunger, illiteracy, and disease are the daily lot of a large portion of the human beings who still exist, as

The association of cognitive style with gender is in itself nothing new. We find it in ancient mythology, in archetypal psychology, in philosophical and scientific writings, and in a host of enduring popular stereotypes about men and women (for example, that women are more "intuitive," men are more "logical," etc.).

— Susan Bordo

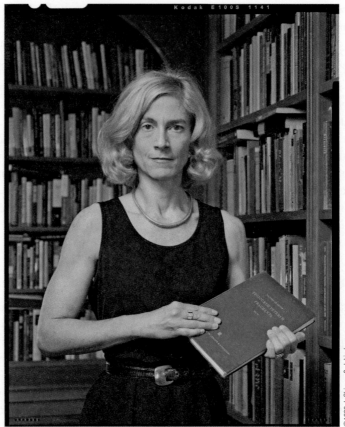

©1999 J. Shimon & J. Lindermann

When a reporter asked Martha Nussbaum if she takes philosophy "too seriously," the lawyer for humanity replied: "For any view you put forward, the next question simply has to be, 'What would the world be like if this idea were actually taken up?' It's what happens in the long haul that really matters. You just never know where or how your ideals will be realized." How might our lives change if we took our beliefs seriously enough to ask—to really ask—*What would the world be like if my beliefs were actually taken up?*

well as the causes of death of many who do not still exist. A life of leisured self-expression is, for most of the world's people, a dream so distant that it can rarely even be formed. The contrast between these two images of human life gives rise to a question: what business does anyone have living in the happy, self-expressive world, so long as the other world exists and one is a part of it?

One answer to this question may certainly be to use some portion of one's time and material resources to support relevant types of political action and social service. On the other hand, it seems possible that philosophy itself, while remaining itself, can perform social and political functions, making a difference in the world by using its own distinctive methods and skills.

[The Epicureans and Stoics]...saw the philosopher as a compassionate physician whose arts could heal many pervasive types of human suffering. They practiced philosophy not as a detached intellectual technique dedicated to the display of cleverness but as an immersed and worldly art of grappling with human misery. They focused their attention, in consequence, on issues of daily and urgent human significance—the fear of death, love and sexuality, anger and aggression—issues that are sometimes avoided as embarrassingly messy and personal by the more detached varieties of philosophy. They confronted these issues as they arose in ordinary human lives, with a keen attention to the vicissitudes of those lives, and to what would be necessary and sufficient to make them better.[27]

In the final analysis, Nussbaum reminds us that although it cannot perfect human life, philosophy has unique skills to help us tell our stories in ways that can free us from at least some unhappiness and guide us toward better lives:

> Here, I think, we must turn, with Seneca, to mercy and narrative—trying to respond to what has taken place without strict punishment, asking the watchful eyes of wisdom to look with narrative understanding into the complexities of another's motivation and one's own. The bold…attempt to purify social life of all its ills, rigorously carried through, ends by removing, as well, its finite humanity, its risk-taking loyalty, its passionate love. Abandoning the zeal for absolute perfection as inappropriate to the life of a finite being, abandoning the thirst for punishment and self-punishment that so frequently accompanies that zeal, the education I recommend looks with mercy at the ambivalent excellence and passion of a human life.[28]

For Deeper Consideration

Some philosophers argue that personal or "autobiographical" considerations are irrelevant when it comes to philosophy. Others are not so sure. What do philosophers mean by autobiographical considerations, and why is this issue significant? Is this even a philosophical issue? Why or why not?

Philosophy and Human Development

Although much of her work focuses on problems inhibiting the flourishing and development of women around the world, Nussbaum articulates a "big" vision of philosophy that I find wholesome, compelling, and congenial because it recognizes that, for all of its inevitable human limitations and periodic setbacks, the kind of philosophy that mattered to Confucius, Socrates, Diogenes, Marcus Aurelius, Augustine, Marx, Mill, Kierkegaard, James, Nietzsche, Heidegger, and so many others still matters—at least as much now as ever before.

All times are perilous. All cultures and individuals remain blind to certain of their own weaknesses and, equally often, unaware of some of their greatest strengths. Even so, collectively and individually, we persist in trying to understand our lives in particular and humanity in general, and to discern what matters most and why, and to do right by what we learn as we go. What better friend can we have

All I knew of the Tao was what a vinegar-fly stuck inside of a barrel can know of the universe. If the master had not lifted the lid, I would still be unaware of the universe in its integral grandeur.
— Chuang-tzu

in our perennial search for meaning than philosophy—richly, open-heartedly, and humanely understood? Here's Nussbaum:

> But we do not need philosophy only as a counterweight to…philosophical assumptions….We need it to help us think through our own intuitive ideas, to criticize them, and to figure out which ones we are willing to hold on to. People do not go through life without forming views about the human good and the right, about what has value and what does not, about what choice is, about what justice and mercy and aggression and grief are. They have views about these things and they use them—not least when they enter the political arena. Often these views embed pieces of highly general theory, derived from custom, or religion, or social science. When public policies are chosen, then, they are the product of many people's intuitions and theories, some of them examined, and many of them unexamined. It seems sensible to deliberate about which theories we really want to hold onto, which intuitions are really the most deeply rooted in our moral sensibility. In the absence of such public deliberation, the most influential views are likely to be those, simply, that are held by the most powerful or rhetorically adept people. This way of proceeding, defective in itself, is especially defective when we consider the interests of the powerless, who rarely get a chance to bring their own ideas about such matters to the table.
>
> Philosophy asks for public deliberation instead of the usual contest of power. It asks us to choose the view that stands the test of argument, rather than the view that has the most prestigious backers; the view that gets all the details worked out coherently and clearly, rather than the view whose proponents shout the loudest. At its best, its conceptual fussiness is profoundly practical: only if things are worked out in all their detail will we know whether we really do have the alternative that can stand up to objection better than another, and sometimes the fatal objection to a view emerges only after considerable probing. It makes sense for public deliberation to take account of these apparently fussy debates, because this is how we think through what we have to do, see what we really want to stand for.
>
> Philosophy often fails to impress people with its relevance, and sometimes this is the fault of philosophers. Philosophy can offer good guidance to practice, I believe, only if it is responsive to experience and periodically immersed in it….Philosophers…should be able to show that their work responds to the complexity of experience and has been shaped by a mature being's sense of that complexity. Feminists rightly demand that the theories dealing with women's lives show their understanding of women's experience of subordination and exclusion. Much of what philosophers of the past (in all traditions) have written about women, sex, and the family has not shown such understanding. Again, it is right to demand that philosophers writing about poverty show that they have some understanding of the complex interaction of agency and constraint in the lives of those concerning whom they make recommendations. Again, many traditions of thought have approached these problems with either naïveté or callousness. The solution to these problems, however, is not to reject philosophy, or even the tradition; it is to learn from them and move forward, with an even more passionate commitment to inclusiveness, precision, and sound argument.[29]

Philosophy as a Way of Life

It is tempting to dismiss the search for wisdom as a form of sophomoric naivete and self-indulgence—or to romanticize it as the cure-all for the ills of our confused, technological, crowded society. Both views miss the true splendor and power of one important aspect of searching for wisdom: the *therapeutic* unifying function of seriously valuing such a search. One of the best ways to achieve this therapeutic effect is to make philosophical reading and reflection a regular part of our lives—as regular as exercise, recreation, and work. Without deluding ourselves or trying to become sages ourselves, we can nonetheless join the sages by living our own examined lives.

Pierre Hadot (1922–2010), Professor Emeritus of the History of Hellenistic and Roman Thought at the College de France, took seriously the sage's goal that philosophy become a way of life. Hadot's *Philosophy as a Way of Life* is one of my favorite books. Although somewhat technical and scholarly, Hadot's text contains many accessible passages that capture the richness of lived philosophy, the therapeutic action of philosophy done out of love of wisdom. According to Hadot, the true philosopher

Pierre Hadot

> knows that the normal, natural state of [human beings] should be wisdom, for wisdom is nothing more than the vision of things as they are, the vision of the cosmos as it is in the light of reason, and wisdom is also nothing more than the mode of being and living that should correspond to this vision. But the philosopher also knows that this wisdom is an ideal state, almost inaccessible. For such a [lover of wisdom], daily life, as it is organized and lived by other [people], must necessarily appear abnormal, like a state of madness, unconsciousness, and ignorance of reality.... And it is precisely in this daily life that [lovers of wisdom] must seek to attain that way of life which is utterly foreign to the everyday world. The result is a perpetual conflict between the philosopher's effort to see things as they are from the standpoint of universal nature and the conventional vision of things underlying human society, a conflict between the life one should live and the customs and conventions of daily life. This conflict can never be totally resolved.[30]

Even though Hadot asserts that the conflict between philosophy and "the world" can never be totally resolved, he nonetheless promises what the sages have always promised: Life is better with philosophy than without it, and if wisdom is hard to define precisely, it is still worth seeking because taking wisdom seriously raises our sights and requires more of us than does abandoning the search. Whatever wisdom is or is not, we do know that technology, possessions, fame, fortune, high grades, attractive figures, and disease-free years are not enough to make life meaningful.

As attractive and pleasing as these things can be, nothing external can make us happy if being happy means more than satisfied or pleased. In one form or another, this is the teaching of Socrates, Epicurus, Epictetus, Marcus Aurelius, the Buddha, Jesus, Muhammad, Kierkegaard, our grandparents, pastors, and wiser elders. Who are we to refute the teachings of the wise? But how wise is it to accept such teachings without testing and questioning them? Hadot offers some advice:

> The trick is to maintain oneself on the level of reason, and not allow oneself to be blinded by political passions, anger, resentments, or prejudices. To be sure, there is

Receive each moment of accumulating time as though it came about by an incredible stroke of luck.
— Pierre Hadot

an equilibrium—almost impossible to achieve—between the inner peace brought about by wisdom, and the passions to which the sight of the injustices, sufferings, and misery of mankind cannot help but give rise. Wisdom, however, consists in precisely such an equilibrium, and inner peace is indispensable for efficacious action.

Such is the lesson of ancient philosophy: an invitation to each human being to transform himself. Philosophy is a conversion, a transformation of one's way of being and living, and a quest for wisdom. This is not an easy matter. As Spinoza wrote at the end of the *Ethics:*

If the way which I have pointed out as leading to this result seems exceedingly hard, it may nevertheless be discovered. It must indeed be hard, since it is so seldom found. How would it be possible, if salvation were easy to find, and could without great labour be found, that it should be neglected by almost everybody? But all excellent things are as difficult as they are rare.[31]

Hadot reminds us that part of the difficulty Baruch Spinoza recognizes is due to the very nature of the human condition:

Everything which is "technical" in the broad sense of the term, whether we are talking about the exact sciences or the humanistic sciences, is perfectly able to be communicated by teaching or conversation. But everything that touches the domain of the existential—which is what is most important for human beings—for instance, our feeling of existence, our impressions when faced by death, our perception of nature, our sensations... is not directly communicable. The phrases we use to describe them are conventional and banal; we realize this when we try to console someone over the loss of a loved one. That's why it often happens that a poem or a biography are more philosophical than a philosophical treatise, simply because they allow us to glimpse this unsayable in an indirect way.[32]

To Live Like a Philosopher

In *What Is Ancient Philosophy?* Hadot expresses his conviction that the ancient concept of philosophy as a practical way of life is still possible and that the rediscovery of philosophy as a way of life has a certain urgency in today's world:

Isn't there an urgent need to rediscover the ancient notion of the "philosopher"—the living, choosing philosopher without whom the notion of philosophy has no meaning? Why not define the philosopher not as a professor or a writer who develops a philosophical discourse but, in accordance with the concept which was constant in antiquity, as a person who leads a philosophical life? Shouldn't we reverse the habitual use of the word "philosopher" (which usually refers only to the theoretician) so that it applies to the person who practices philosophy, just as Christians can practice Christianity without being theorists or theologians? Do we ourselves have to construct a philosophical system before we can live philosophically? This does not mean, of course, that we needn't reflect upon our own experience, as well as that of philosophers both past and present.

Yet what does it mean to "live like a philosopher"? What is the practice of philosophy?...

The medicines for the soul were discovered by the ancients—but it is our job to find out how to apply them and when. Our predecessors accomplished a lot, but not everything.
— Seneca

. . . There is an abyss between fine phrases and becoming genuinely aware of oneself, truly transforming oneself. . . . Throughout the history of ancient philosophy . . . we encounter the same warnings against the danger the philosopher incurs, if he thinks his philosophical discourse can be sufficient unto itself without being linked to a philosophical life. Plato already sensed this ever-present danger when . . . he wrote: "I was afraid that I would see myself as a fine talker, incapable of resolutely undertaking an action."

Another danger, the worst of all, is to believe that one can do without philosophical reflection. . . . Without such reflection, the philosophical life risks sinking into vapid banality, "respectable" feelings, or deviance. To be sure, we cannot wait until we have read Kant's *Critique of Pure Reason* in order to live as philosophers. Nevertheless, living as a philosopher also means to reflect, to reason, to conceptualize, in a rigorous, technical way. . . . The philosophical life is a never-ending quest.

Finally, and despite all the tenacious clichés which still clog philosophy manuals, we must never forget that the ancient philosophical life was always linked to the care for others, and that this demand is inherent in the philosophical life, especially when it is lived in the contemporary world. . . . The philosopher is cruelly aware of his solitude and impotence in a world which is torn between two states of unconsciousness: that which derives from the idolatry of money, and that which results in the face of the misery and suffering of billions of human beings. In such conditions, the philosopher will surely never be able to attain the absolute serenity of the sage. . . . But ancient philosophy also teaches us not to resign ourselves, but to continue to act reasonably and try to live according to the norm constituted by the Idea of wisdom, whatever happens, and even if our action seems very limited to us. In the words of Marcus Aurelius: "Do not wait for Plato's Republic, but be happy if one little thing leads to progress, and reflect on the fact that what results from such a little thing is not, in fact, so very little."[33]

> *Soon we shall breathe our last. Meanwhile, while we live, while we are among human beings, let us cultivate humanity.*
> — Seneca

For Deeper Consideration

Imagine Socrates, Epictetus, and Diogenes wandering through a modern bookstore. Imagine them watching hours of TED talks, listening to podcasts, watching YouTube videos of "life coaches," and perusing blogs devoted to happiness, peace of mind, self-therapy, and their ilk. Describe a detailed scenario—including philosophical conversations and comments—in which these sages confront today's claimants to wisdom. Would they be impressed? Angry? Amused? Saddened? Generate a rational, respectful discussion of specific books, guru figures, "philosophical" belief systems. This is dangerous stuff—but it's also invigorating and important stuff. To what extent can/does technology affect philosophical insight and growth? Can you imagine, for example, Socrates holding forth on the Internet or Diogenes writing a daily blog? Are such questions fair? Or do they confuse the mechanisms of communication with the substance?

The Heart of Philosophy

Perhaps more than any other academic professionals, Western philosophers quarrel among themselves over who is a legitimate member of the profession. Sociologists and physicists and pathologists, more often than not, quarrel over the quality of one another's arguments or research; less often do they quarrel over who is "really a sociologist" or "really a physicist" or "really a pathologist." That's not to say that such fundamental issues never arise in other disciplines but to remind ourselves that philosophy, much to its credit, stands out as a self-critical discipline.

If we allow just about any form of critical analysis to count as philosophy, we risk expanding the practice of philosophy to meaninglessness. If any kind of thinking and commenting about love, say, equals a philosophy of love, or assessing demographic data about philosophers constitutes, on its own, a social philosophy, then we will be hard pressed to distinguish philosophy from literature or social science or statistics. If we limit philosophy to a set of "historically identified" philosophical issues and sub-disciplines, we reduce philosophy to a history of philosophy and to an unchanging set of traditional topics, thereby overlooking its origins as an interrogator of conventional beliefs and critic of popular assumptions and questioner of codified methods for assessing truth and error. If we equate philosophy with logical analysis and highly specialized critical thinking, we risk dehumanizing what began as, and what for many remains, a search for wisdom and meaningfulness broadly understood.

If we value philosophy as a way of life, our task, as tricky as it is important, will be to preserve philosophy's rigor without abandoning its living heart and mind and without losing sight of philosophy's capacity to keep up with us. Broadly understood, the give-and-take between let-it-all-in openness and highly specialized narrowness is as old as philosophy. Indeed, it is, I believe, the heart of philosophy.

From their earliest incarnations to today's practitioners, philosophers have refused to accept others'—even and especially other philosophers'—definitions of philosophy and what is off-limits for philosophical scrutiny. Consider, for example, Plato's contributions to politics, art, and law, in addition to his seminal work in epistemology, metaphysics, ontology, and ethics. Consider Aristotle's contributions to physics, biology, botany, politics, law, theology, and drama.

Note, too, Descartes's work in optics as well as philosophy, Kierkegaard's influence on psychologists and theologians. Marx's and Mill's philosophies involve sociological, economic, political, legal, and psychological aspects, as do elements of the work of John Rawls, Alison Jaggar, Susan Moller Okin, Susan Bordo, Sarah Conly, Sally Haslanger, Laurie Calhoun, Carol Swain, Kathryn Gines, Carol Gilligan, Martin Luther King, Jr., Martha Nussbaum, and Peter Singer. And then consider the Stoic foundation of Viktor Frankl's logotherapy, William James's broad-ranging influence on everything from education to Alcoholics Anonymous, and Friedrich Nietzsche's many appearances in works of criticism, theology, social theory, classical music, and popular media. The list is, like philosophy, a living, growing, evolving thing.

A Vision for You

It is too soon to tell whether or not philosophical advocacy will produce new philosophical archetypes. But we can reasonably expect that some of the topics touched on in this chapter will continue to attract serious philosophical attention. Complex questions concerning the effects of gender, ethnicity, and social climate on philosophizing are not easily answered. Indeed, some of these issues hearken back to those raised by Socrates in his encounters with Sophists. That is why I have written *Archetypes of Wisdom* not just to convey philosophical facts and arguments but also to evoke philosophical yearnings that most of us experience—but don't always recognize as being philosophical. I can think of no better way to say "Fare thee well" than to encourage you not to diminish, forget, or forsake the love of wisdom. Think of this last section as a personal invitation to keep company with the sages.

I hope that in addition to any intellectual satisfaction you have found in philosophy, you have also *experienced* something special: a sense of the majesty of the human condition that is simultaneously poignant, profound, encouraging, humbling, and comforting. The special experience I am referring to evokes a longing to be a better, wiser person—not in any specific way but in a fundamental way. This longing is the *love of wisdom*, and it triggers a "felt need" for an honest vision of the human condition and of our particular place in it.

Once felt, the need to see the human condition and our particular place in it "as a whole" never leaves us. The need to find meaning in a capricious, dangerous world never leaves us. Life assaults us with questions of choice, value, meaning— *philosophical* questions: issues of fairness; choices among evils; existential conditions that demand action; forced choices that, once made, obliterate all other possibilities. Highly specialized professional philosophers properly see themselves as scholars rather than as sages. Scholars and other experts abound, but sages are rare.

Today, with the exception of a limited number of public philosophers, the public function of the *sophos*, or sage, has been taken over by the priest, the scientist, the psychologist, and the all-too-eager celebrity guru. Every year seems to produce another celebrity guru, another blockbuster book about the soul, wisdom, metaphysics, ancient secrets, past lives, angels, wise entities, simple secrets of happiness.

Without wisdom, intelligence has no guide. When Empedocles told Xenophanes that it was impossible to find a wise man, Xenophanes is said to have replied: "Naturally, for it takes a wise man to recognize a wise man."

Passages from many philosophical masterpieces are included throughout *Archetypes of Wisdom*. Others are listed in the Bibliography of Philosophical Delights. I find myself returning again and again to a select few for consolation, encouragement, and wisdom. Of all of my favorites, I have probably read the small collection of teachings of Epictetus's known as the *Handbook* or *Enchiridion* more than any other book. I think so highly of it that I have handed out hundreds of copies to students, friends, and family members. You will recall that the little at-hand book was originally compiled for Roman soldiers to carry on long, difficult military campaigns. We might also think of it as a handbook to carry and consult in our daily campaign against the confusions, deceptions, and distractions of modern life. So it is especially fitting that I say, "Fare thee well, philosopher," with a message from Epictetus:

Douglas J. Soccio

How long do you put off thinking yourself worthy of the best things, and [worthy of] never going against the definitive capacity of reason? You have received the philosophical propositions that you ought to agree to and you have agreed to them. Then what sort of teacher are you still waiting for, that you put off improving yourself until he comes? You are not a [child] anymore, but

Remember that it is no chance matter that we are discussing but how one should live.
— Socrates

already…full grown.…If you now neglect things and are lazy and are always making delay after delay and set one day after another as the day for paying attention to yourself, then without realizing it you will make no progress but will end up a non-philosopher all through life and death. So decide now that you are worthy of living as a full-grown [human being] who is making progress, and make everything that seems best be a law you cannot go against. And if you meet with any hardship or anything pleasant or reputable or disreputable, then remember that the contest is now and the Olympic games are now and you cannot put things off any more and that your progress is made or destroyed by a single day and a single action. Socrates became fully perfect in this way.… You, even if you are not yet Socrates, ought to live as one wanting to be [like] Socrates.[34]

Aplia

Summary of Main Points

- A philosophical advocate is a philosopher whose work identifies, clarifies, and actively opposes a perceived injustice. Philosophical advocates give philosophical credence to personal experience based on gender, ethnic background, or social status.

- Jean-Paul Sartre's experiences during World War II convinced him that actions create values and that our choices create our selves. Thus, rather than a philosophy producing a way of life, a way of life produces a philosophy. We create our essence by how we live. Freedom makes us anxious and God's silence makes us forlorn.

- Critics of modern philosophy associate the dominance of the detached philosophical specialist with modern philosophy's emphasis on philosophical arguments presented in a detached—masculinized, objective—voice that deliberately minimizes the philosopher's personal qualities (social status, gender, ethnicity). Consequently, some modern and contemporary philosophers remain indifferent to the fact that their philosophy reflects the interests of only a small portion of the human community.

- Carol Gilligan's research into moral development has led her to distinguish between a traditional, masculine-oriented "voice" and a feminine-oriented "different voice" that is not confined to objective argument (or scientific evidence) but that expresses other "ways of knowing." Gilligan argues that excessive reliance on "rationality" results in injustice by excluding those who do not speak in the "objective voice" from full participation in philosophy, science, law, and higher education.

- Public philosophers are writers or speakers whose philosophical positions are expressed in ways accessible to a broad audience. The most effective public philosophers tap into—or identify—vital philosophical issues of the day. When public philosophers also "practice what they preach," they function much like sages or prophets in their capacity to provoke individual self-assessment and collective consciousness-raising.

- Martin Luther King, Jr., is an example of a public philosopher and activist. King practiced a form of nonviolent direct action characterized as "active nonviolent resistance." King belongs to a special class of activist philosophers whose philosophies and lives are inseparable. King hoped to awaken good people from their moral slumbers.

- Peter Singer is a controversial public philosopher who believes in making people uncomfortable as a way of raising moral consciousness. Singer applies utilitarian principles to such current issues as animal rights, infanticide, euthanasia, and world poverty. Singer challenges everyone not already living in abject poverty to give away all income over $30,000. Single adults could, of course, give away much more. Singer himself gives one-fifth of his income (including royalties from his books) to famine-relief agencies.

- Martha C. Nussbaum describes public philosophers as "lawyers for humanity." Nussbaum suggests that too many professional intellectuals fail to use their theories and talents to improve the human condition by fighting for equality, justice, and freedom.

- Pierre Hadot's *Philosophy as a Way of Life* presents a distillation of his accumulated knowledge and experience as a professional scholar and lover of wisdom. Hadot takes seriously the sage's goal that philosophy become a way of life. Although Hadot asserts that the conflict between wisdom and "the world" can never be totally resolved, he believes that life is better with philosophy than without it, because taking wisdom seriously raises our sights and requires more of us than does abandoning the search.

Post-Reading Reflections

Now that you've had a chance to learn about Philosophy as a Way of Life, use your new knowledge to answer these questions.

1. What philosophical issues are associated with the problem of advocacy?
2. What does "essence precedes existence" mean? Why is the issue important?
3. What is Sartrean forlornness, and what causes it?
4. What is meant by the claim that we are condemned to be free?
5. What is the "problem of representation" in academic philosophy, and why is it so difficult to determine its true extent?
6. Briefly contrast the two "voices" alluded to in this chapter.
7. What is "active nonviolent resistance"?
8. What was Martin Luther King, Jr.'s, position regarding means and ends? Why was the issue so important to him?
9. What is Singer's solution to world poverty?
10. Why is Singer such a controversial philosopher?
11. Discuss the insult Martha C. Nussbaum experienced in a letter of congratulation, paying special attention to the context in which this occurred.
12. Why does Nussbaum think that we need philosophy today?
13. What is the tension Hadot sees between wisdom and "the world"?
14. What does Pierre Hadot mean when he says that our lives are better with philosophy than without it and that even wisdom is hard to define precisely?
15. What, according to Hadot, is the lesson of ancient philosophy?
16. Compare Nussbaum's and Hadot's arguments on behalf of philosophy as a way of life.

 MindTap

Experience MindTap through the activities highlighted in this chapter. Further explore this online, personalized learning tool to deepen your comprehension and improve your grades.

Notes

Introduction   Philosophy and the Search for Wisdom

1. Mary Ellen Waithe, *Introduction to the Series, A History of Women Philosophers*, vol. 1, 600 B.C.–500 A.D., ed. Mary Ellen Waithe (Dordrecht: Martinus Nijhoff, 1987), pp. IX–X.

2. James Q. Wilson, *The Moral Sense* (New York: Free Press, 1993), pp. 8–9.

Chapter 1   The Asian Sages: Lao-tzu, Confucius, and Buddha

1. Wing-Tsit Chan, *A Source Book in Chinese Philosophy* (Princeton, N.J.: Princeton University Press, 1963), p. 98.

2. See Michael C. Brannigan, *The Pulse of Wisdom*, 2nd ed. (Belmont, Calif.: Wadsworth, 2000), pp. 23–27; and Warren Matthews, *World Religions*, 3rd ed. (Belmont, Calif.: Wadsworth, 1999), p. 209.

3. Chad Hansen, "Classical Chinese Ethics," in *A Companion to Ethics*, ed. Peter Singer (Oxford: Blackwell, 1993), p. 69.

4. A. C. Graham, *Disputers of the Tao* (La Salle, Ill.: Open Court, 1989), pp. 1–4.

5. Brannigan, p. 24.

6. Graham, pp. 216–217.

7. Holmes Welch, *Taoism: The Parting of the Way* (Boston: Beacon Press, 1965), p. 2.

8. Lao-tzu, *Tao Te Ching*, in Chan, p. 136.

9. Lao-tzu, *The Wisdom of Laotse*, trans. and ed. Lin Yutang (New York: Modern Library, 1976), p. 41. Reprinted by permission of Random House, Inc.

10. Lao-tzu, *Te-Tao Ching: A New Translation Based on the Recently Discovered Mawang-tui Texts*, trans. with introduction and commentary by Robert G. Henricks (New York: Ballantine, 1989), p. 53.

11. Graham, p. 219.

12. Ibid., p. 220.

13. Ibid., p. 221.

14. Ibid., p. 221.

15. Ibid., p. 223.

16. Lao-tzu, in Chan, p. 140.

17. After Graham, pp. 223f.

18. Graham, p. 232.

19. Ibid., p. 235.

20. Lao-tzu, in Chan, pp. 162–163.

21. *Tao te Ching*, #57, Graham, p. 233.

22. Lin Yutang, *The Wisdom of Confucius* (New York: Modern Library, 1938), p. 6.

23. Ibid., pp. 26–27.

24. Ibid., p. 29.

25. Chan, p. 17.

26. Yutang, p. 52.

27. Ibid., p. 98.

28. Chan, p. 15.

29. Confucius, *Analects*, 7:21, in Graham, p. 15.

30. Graham, p. 15.

31. Confucius, *Analects*, 6:22, in Graham, pp. 15f.

32. Graham, p. 10.

33. Confucius, *Analects*, 7:1, in Graham, p. 10.

34. Ibid., 15:31, in Graham, p. 11.

35. *The Doctrine of the Mean*, Chu Hsi arrangement, trans. Wing-Tsit Chan, in Chan, pp. 98–99. Copyright © 1963 by Princeton University Press. Reprinted by permission.

36. Ibid., pp. 98–101.

37. Graham, p. 13.

38. Ibid.

39. Ibid.

40. Confucius's disciple Yu-tzu, quoted in Graham, p. 12.

41. Chan, pp. 15f.

42. Graham, p. 19.

43. Confucius, *Analects*, 12:1, in Graham, p. 22.

44. Yutang, p. 24.

45. Ibid., pp. 19–20.

46. Confucius, *Analects*, 6:28, in Chan, p. 31.

47. *The Doctrine of the Mean*, in Chan, p. 105.

48. Confucius, *Analects*, 4:6, in Chan, p. 26.

49. The brief sketch that follows is based on Nancy Wilson Ross, *Buddhism: A Way of Life and Thought* (New York: Vintage, 1981); see also Edward Conze, *Buddhism: Its Essence and Development* (New York: Harper Torchbooks, 1965); *Stories of the Buddha: Being Selections from the Jakata*, trans. and ed. Caroline A. F. Rhys Davids (New York: Dover, 1989); Richard H. Robinson and Willard L. Johnson, *The Buddhist Religion* (Encino, Calif.: Dickenson, 1977); and Donald S. Lopez, Jr., *The Story of Buddhism* (San Francisco: Harper San Francisco, 2001).

50. Ross, p. 6.

51. Ibid., p. 10.

52. Ibid., p. 18.

53. Ibid.

54. Ibid., p. 33.

55. The Buddha, "The Discourse on Universal Love," in Ross, p. 32.

56. Padmasiri de Silva, "Buddhist Ethics," in *A Companion to Ethics*, ed. Peter Singer, p. 58.

57. Ibid., pp. 59–60.

58. Ibid., p. 61; and Rev. Master P.T.N.H. Jiyu-Kennett, M.O.B.C. "Basic Original Doctrines Essential to Zen," in Jiyu-Kennett, *Zen Is Eternal Life* (Mt. Shasta, Calif.: Shasta Abbey, 1987), p. 9.

59. Ross, pp. 23ff.

60. Modified from Ross, p. 24.

61. See Ross, pp. 24ff.

62. Ibid., p. 26.

63. Ibid., p. 27.

64. Ibid., pp. 26f.

65. Ibid., p. 37.

66. A. Burtt, ed., *The Teachings of the Compassionate Buddha* (New York: Mentor, 1982), pp. 202ff.

67. Ibid., pp. 34ff, 36.

68. Ibid., p. 204.

Chapter 2 The Presocratic Sophos

1. Pierre Hadot, *Philosophy As a Way of Life*, trans. Arnold I. Davidson (Oxford: Blackwell, 1995), pp. 56–61.

2. *Ibid.*

3. Christopher Janaway, "Ancient Greek Philosophy I: The Pre-Socratics and Plato," in *Philosophy: A Guide Through the Subject*, ed. A. C. Grayling (Oxford: Oxford University Press, 1995), p. 338.

4. Plato, *Theatetus*, 174A, trans. F. M. Cornford in *The Collected Dialogues of Plato: Including the Letters* (New York: Pantheon, 1961), p. 879.

5. Aristotle, *Metaphysics*. M'Mahon translation, i, 3.

6. J. Barnes, *The Presocratic Philosophers: Arguments of the Philosophers* (London, 1989), p. 72.

7. *Ibid.*, p. 74.

8. Will Durant, *The Story of Civilization, vol. 2: The Life of Greece* (New York: Simon & Schuster, 1966), pp. 138–139.

9. Janaway, p. 342.

10. Charles H. Kahn, *The Art and Thought of Heraclitus* (Cambridge: Cambridge University Press, 1979), pp. 1–3.

11. Giovanni Reale, *A History of Ancient Philosophy, vol. 1, From the Origins to Socrates*, trans. John R. Catan (Albany: State University of New York Press, 1987), p. 53.

12. Janaway, p. 343.

13. Reale, p. 53.

14. Heraclitus, Fragment 23, *Herakleitos and Diogenes*, trans. Guy Davenport (San Francisco: Grey Fox, 1979), p. 15.

15. W. T. Jones, *The Classical Mind: A History of Western Philosophy*, 2nd ed. (New York: Harcourt Brace Jovanovich, 1970), p. 16.

16. Heraclitus, Fragment 116, Davenport, p. 31.

17. Heraclitus, Fragment 117, Davenport, p. 31.

18. Plato, *Parmenides*, 127A, in Cornford, *The Collected Dialogues of Plato*, p. 921.

19. Parmenides, Fragment 3, trans. Freeman, in Reale, p. 84.

20. John Dillon, "The Question of Being," in *Greek Thought: A Guide to Classical Knowledge,* trans. under the direction of Catherine Porter, eds. Jacques Brunschwig and Geoffrey E. R. Lloyd, with the collaboration of Pierre Pellegrin (Cambridge, Mass.: Belknap Press, 2000), p. 51.

21. Reale, p. 87.

22. Jones, pp. 21–22.

23. G. S. Kirk and J. E. Raven, *The Presocratic Philosophers* (Cambridge: Cambridge University Press, 1957), p. 345.

24. Jones, p. 27.

25. Anaxagoras, Fragment 10, Kirk and Raven, p. 378.

26. Jones, p. 29; Peter Angeles, *Dictionary of Philosophy* (New York: Barnes & Noble Books, 1981), p. 191.

27. Reale, p. 114.

28. Anaxagoras, Fragment 11; in J. Burnet, *Early Greek Philosophy*, 4th ed. (London, 1930), p. 259.

29. Anaxagoras, Fragment 21, in Jones, p. 29.

30. Amaury de Riencourt, *Sex and Power in History* (New York: David McKay, 1974), pp. 97 ff.

31. *Ibid.*, p. 99.

Chapter 3 The Sophist: Protagoras

1. Plato, *The Republic*, trans. H. D. P. Lee (London: Penguin, 1955), bk. 7, sec. 6.

2. See W. K. C. Guthrie, *The Sophists* (Cambridge: Cambridge University Press, 1971); Giovanni Reale, *A History of Ancient Philosophy*, vol. 1, *From the Origins to Socrates*, trans. John R. Catan (Albany: State University of New York Press, 1987), p. 84; Will Durant, *The Story of Civilization*, vol. 2, *The Life of Greece* (New York: Simon & Schuster, 1939); Frederick Copleston, S. J., *A History of Philosophy*, vol. 1, *Greece and Rome* (New York: Image, 1985).

3. Will Durant, *The Story of Philosophy* (New York: Simon & Schuster, 1953), p. 358.

4. Guthrie, p. 35.

5. Plato, *The Sophist*, 231D–E, in Reale, p. 149.

6. Xenophon, *Memorabilia*, trans. E. C. Marchant, in *Xenophon, Memorabilia and Oeconomics* (London: Loeb Classical Library, 1959), bk. 1, sec. 6, line 13.

7. Plato, *Theaetetus*, trans. F. M. Cornford, 151E–152A, in Reale, p. 157.

8. Ibid., p. 166D, in Reale, pp. 160ff.

9. Plato, *Gorgias*, trans. W. C. Helmbold (Indianapolis: Bobbs-Merrill, 1952), pp. 482–486.

10. Ibid., p. 457B.

Chapter 4 The Wise Man: Socrates

1. W. K. C. Guthrie, *Socrates* (Cambridge: Cambridge University Press, 1971), p. 6.

2. Plato, *Phaedo*, 60C–D, trans. Benjamin Jowett, in *The Dialogues of Plato*, 3rd ed. (Oxford: Clarendon, 1892).

3. Guthrie, p. 4.

4. Ibid.

5. Xenophon, *Symposium*, trans. E. C. Marchant (London: Loeb Classical Library, 1959), ch. 2, line 18.

6. Plato, *Gorgias*, 470E, in Giovanni Reale, *A History of Ancient Philosophy*, vol. 1, *From the Origins to Socrates*, trans. John R. Catan (Albany: State University of New York Press, 1987), p. 219.

7. Xenophon, *Symposium*, ch. 5, in Guthrie, pp. 67–68.

8. Xenophon, *Memorabilia*, bk. 1, sec. 6, line 10, in Reale, p. 216.

9. Ibid, sec. 2, lines 29–30. See also Mary Renault's novel *The Last of the Wine* (New York: New English Library, 1968), pp. 120ff.

10. Xenophon, *Memorabilia*, bk. 4, sec. 5, lines 9ff., in Reale, p. 218.

11. Plato, *Apology*, 34D, trans. Benjamin Jowett, in *The Dialogues of Plato: Phaedo*, 60A.

12. Will Durant, *The Story of Civilization*, vol. 2, *The Life of Greece* (New York: Simon & Schuster, 1939), p. 367.

13. Karl Jaspers, *Socrates, Buddha, Confucius, Jesus: The Paradigmatic Individuals*, trans. Ralph Manheim, ed. Hannah Arendt (New York: Harcourt Brace Jovanovich, 1962), p. 87.

14. Pierre Hadot, *Philosophy as a Way of Life*, trans. Arnold I. Davidson (Oxford: Blackwell, 1995), p. 147.

15. Plato, *Apology*, 17A.

16. Plato, *Republic*, 336, trans. Benjamin Jowett, in *The Dialogues of Plato*, 3rd ed., vol. III, (Oxford University Press: London, 1892), pp. 12–16, edited and elided.

17. Reale, p. 202.

18. Plato, *Apology*, 21B–E.

19. Ibid., 20C.

20. Ibid., 22D, 23A.

21. Ibid., 29–30.

22. Plato, *Gorgias*, trans. W. C. Helmbold (Indianapolis: Bobbs-Merrill, 1952), pp. 468b–468c.

23. Plato, *Protagoras*, 345e, trans. Benjamin Jowett, rev. ed., Martin Ostwald (Indianapolis: Bobbs-Merrill, 1956), p. 49.

24. Meno, 77b–78b, trans. Benjamin Jowett in *Plato's Meno: Text and Criticism*, eds. Alexander Sesonske and Noel Fleming (Belmont, Calif.: Wadsworth, 1965), pp. 12–13.

25. Ibid., 87–89, pp. 23–25.

26. Plato, *Apology*, 40A.

27. Plato, *Phaedo*, 115Dff.

28. Ibid., 117Bff.

Chapter 5 The Philosopher-King: Plato

1. Diogenes Läertius, *Life of Plato*, trans. R. H. Hicks, in *Lives of Eminent Philosophers* (Cambridge, Mass.: Harvard University Press, 1925).

2. Plato, *Letter: VII*, 324E, trans. L. A. Post, in *Plato: The Collected Dialogues* (New York: Pantheon, 1961), p. 1575.

3. See A. W. Levi, "Ancient Philosophy: The Age of the Aristocrat," ch. 2 in *Philosophy as Social Expression* (Chicago: University of Chicago Press, 1974), for a full discussion of the influence of social class on Plato.

4. Ibid, p. 66.

5. Plato, *Letter: VII*, 325D–326B, p. 1576.

6. A. E. Taylor, *Plato: The Man and His Works* (London: Methuen, 1966), pp. 6ff.

7. Luc Brisson, "Platonism," trans. Rita Guerlac and Anne Slack, in *Greek Thought: A Guide to Classical Knowledge*, trans. under the direction of Catherine Porter, eds. Jacques Brunschwig and Geoffrey E. R. Lloyd, with the collaboration of Pierre Pellegrin (Cambridge, Mass.: Belknap Press, 2000), p. 893.

8. Christopher Janaway, "Ancient Greek Philosophy I: The Pre-Socratics and Plato," in *Philosophy: A Guide Through the Subject*, ed. A. C. Grayling (Oxford: Oxford University Press, 1995), pp. 378, 380. In the *Parmenides*, Plato revisits some of the difficult questions generated by the theory of forms.

9. Janaway, p. 378.

10. Peter A. Angeles, *Dictionary of Philosophy* (New York: Barnes & Noble, 1981), p. 124.

11. Plato, *Timaeus*, 27D–28A, trans. Benjamin Jowett, in *The Dialogues of Plato*, 3rd ed. (Oxford: Clarendon, 1892).

12. Plato, *Republic*, 506, pp. 269–270.

13. Ibid., 510–511, pp. 276–277.

14. Ibid., 508–509, pp. 272–273.

15. Ibid., 511, p. 278.

16. Plato, *Republic*, 514–516, trans. Jowett, in *The Dialogues of Plato*, 3rd ed., vol. III, (Oxford University Press: London, 1892), pp. 214–216, edited and elided.

17. Ibid., 517, p. 217, edited and elided.

18. Plato, *Republic*, bk. 1, Prelude, Lee, pp. 327–328.

19. H. D. P. Lee, Introduction to Plato, *Republic* (London: Penguin, 1955), p. 87.

20. B. A. G. Fuller, *History of Greek Philosophy*, vol. 2 (New York: Henry Holt, 1931), p. 214.

21. Plato, *Republic*, bk. 2, 363, pp. 94ff.

22. Taylor, *Plato: The Man and His Works*, p. 270.

23. Plato, *Republic*, bk. 4, 442E–443A, p. 194.

24. Ibid., bk. 8, sec. 6, p. 326.

25. Ibid., 555C, p. 327.

26. Ibid., 557, pp. 329ff.

27. Ibid., p. 330.

28. Ibid., p. 351.

29. Ibid., 561, p. 334.

30. Ibid., 563, pp. 336–337.

31. Ibid., bk. 9, 573–574, pp. 346ff.

Chapter 6   The Naturalist: Aristotle

1. In the 1970s, psychologists Daniel Levinson and G. E. Vailant identified something called a "mid-life crisis," which, they claimed, prompted major disruptions in men's lives. Since then, other psychologists, like Carol Gilligan, have pointed out that in mid-life both men and women try to establish better balance in their lives. Earlier, Erik Erikson had proposed a theory of personal development based on psychosocial stages. He coined the term *identity crisis* to characterize typical changes during adolescence. See Philip G. Zimbardo, *Psychology and Life*, 12th ed. (Glenview, Ill.: Scott, Foresman, 1988), pp. 98–99.

2. Will Durant, *The Story of Civilization*, vol. 2, *The Life of Greece* (New York: Simon & Schuster, 1966), p. 526.

3. Diogenes Läertius, *Life of Plato*, trans. R. H. Hicks, in *Lives of Eminent Philosophers* (Cambridge, Mass.: Harvard University Press, 1925), sec. 25.

4. Samuel Enoch Stumpf, *Philosophy: History and Problems*, 4th ed. (New York: McGraw-Hill, 1989), bk. 1, p. 83.

5. Durant, *Life of Greece*, p. 525.

6. W. T. Jones, *The Classical Mind*, 2nd ed. (New York: Harcourt Brace Jovanovich, 1970), p. 219.

7. Aristotle, *Metaphysics*, bk. 7, ch. 1, 1028A10, in *The Philosophy of Aristotle*, ed. Renford Bambrough (New York: New American Library, 1963).

8. Aristotle, *Physics*, bk. 2, ch. 7, 198A20, trans. Phillip Wheelwright, in *Aristotle* (New York: Odyssey, 1951).

9. Ibid., bk. 2, ch. l, 93A10.

10. Ibid., bk. 2, ch. 1, 193A36–193B6.

11. Ibid., bk. 2, ch. 7, 198A, 33–35.

12. Ibid., bk. 2, ch. 8, sec. 199b.

13. Sir David Ross, *Aristotle* (London: Methuen, 1966), p. 129.

14. Pierre Pellegrin, "Aristotle," trans. Rita Guerlac and Anne Slack, in *Greek Thought: A Guide to Classical Knowledge*, trans. under the direction of Catherine Porter, eds. Jacques Brunschwig and Geoffrey E. R. Lloyd, with the collaboration of Pierre Pellegrin (Cambridge, Mass.: Belknap Press, 2000), p. 572.

15. Aristotle, *Nicomachean Ethics*, bk. 1, 1094A, trans. J. C. Welldon, in *Philosophers Speak for Themselves*, ed. T. V. Smith (Chicago: University of Chicago Press, 1934).

16. Ibid., 1094B.

17. Ibid., 1095A.

18. Ibid., 1095B.

19. Ibid., 1096A.

20. Ibid., 1095B.

21. This treatment of *eudaimonia* is based in part on material found in Burton F. Porter, *Reasons for Living: A Basic Ethics* (New York: Macmillan, 1988), pp. 204–207.

22. Aristotle, *Nicomachean Ethics*, trans. Wheelwright, bk. 1, 1095Bff.

23. Aristotle, *Nicomachean Ethics*, 1103B30, trans. Martin Ostwald (Indianapolis: Library of Liberal Arts, 1962).

24. Ibid., 1104A13–25.

25. Ibid., 1104Aff.

26. Aristotle, *Nicomachean Ethics*, 1103A17ff., trans. W. D. Ross, in *Basic Works of Aristotle*, p. 952.

27. Ibid., 1144A6.

28. Aristotle, *Nicomachean Ethics*, trans. Ostwald, 1143B22.

29. Ibid., 1106B15.

Chapter 7   The Stoics: Epictetus and Marcus Aurelius

1. Epicurus, Fragment 221, in Giovanni Reale, *A History of Ancient Philosophy*, vol. 3, *The Systems of the Hellenistic Age*, ed. and trans. John R. Catan (Albany: State University of New York Press, 1985), p. 111.

2. Will Durant, *The Story of Civilization*, vol. 2, *The Life of Greece* (New York: Simon & Schuster, 1939), p. 645.

3. Epicurus, *Letter to Menoeceus*, trans. George D. Strodach, quoted in *Hellenistic Philosophy*, eds. Herman Shapiro and Edwin M. Curley (New York: Modern Library, 1965), p. 6.

4. Ibid., pp. 7ff.

5. Ibid., p. 8.

6. Epictetus, *Discourses*, trans. P. E. Matheson (Oxford: Clarendon, 1916), in William Sahakian and Mabel Lewis Sahakian, *Realms of Philosophy* (Cambridge, Mass.: Schenkman, 1965), p. 133.

7. Epictetus, *Discourses as Reported by Arrian, The Manual, and Fragments*, vol. 2, trans. W. A. Oldfather (Cambridge, Mass.: Harvard University Press, 1928), bk. xxii, pp. 139–149.

8. Ibid., p. 159.

9. Epictetus, *Handbook of Epictetus*, trans. Nicholas P. White (Indianapolis: Hackett, 1983), p. 13.

10. This sketch of Epictetus's life is based on Philip Hallie's entry on Epictetus in *The Encyclopedia of Philosophy*, vol. 3, eds. Paul Edwards et al. (New York: Macmillan and the Free Press, 1967), p. 1.

11. Marcus Aurelius, *Meditations*, bk. 7, sec. 54, trans. George Long, in *Plato, Epictetus, Marcus Aurelius* (Harvard Classics edition) (New York: Collier, 1937).

12. Ibid., bk. 6, sec. 2.

13. Ibid., bk. 7, sec. 58, 59.

14. From Maxwell Staniforth's entry in *Encyclopedia of Philosophy*, vol. 5, p. 156.

15. Seneca, "On Tranquility," in *The Stoic Philosophy of Seneca*, trans. Moses Hadas (New York: Norton, 1958), p. 93.

16. Epictetus, *Enchiridion*, sec. 27, trans. George Long, in *The Discourses of Epictetus with the Enchiridion and Fragments* (New York: A. L. Burt, 1929).

17. Seneca, Letter 41, in *The Stoic Philosophy of Seneca*, p. 188.

18. Ibid.

19. Marcus Aurelius, *Meditations*, bk. 7, sec. 22, 23, 25, trans. Maxwell Staniforth (Middlesex: Penguin, 1970).

20. Ibid.

21. Seneca, "On Self-Control," trans. Gunmere, in *Philosophers Speak for Themselves: Guides and Readings for Greek, Roman, and Early Christian Philosophy*, by T. V. Smith (Chicago: University of Chicago Press, 1934), pp. 623ff.

22. Epictetus, *Enchiridion*, sec. 1.

23. Ibid., sec. 4.

24. Ibid., sec. 1.

25. Ibid.

26. Ibid., sec. 30.

27. Ibid., sec. 25.

28. Seneca, "On Providence," in *The Stoic Philosophy of Seneca*, p. 37.

29. Ibid., pp. 38–39.

30. From "The World of Epictetus," by James B. Stockdale, *Atlantic Monthly*, April 1978. Used by permission of the author.

31. James Bond Stockdale, "Epictetus' Enchiridion," in *Text and Teaching: The Search for Human Excellence*, eds. Michael J. Collins and Frances J. Ambosio (Washington, D.C.: Georgetown University Press, 1991), pp. 39–42.

Chapter 8 The Scholar: Thomas Aquinas

1. Augustine, *Confessions*, trans. R. S. Pine-Coffin (Harmondsworth, England: Penguin, 1961), 2.3.

2. Paul, Epistle to the Romans, 13:13, The Revised English Bible (Oxford: Oxford University Press, and Cambridge: Cambridge University Press, 1989).

3. Ibid., 2.2.

4. Ibid., 8.5.

5. Augustine, *Letters*, New Advent (electronic version copyright © 1997 by New Advent, Inc.), 118.21.

6. Paul, Acts of the Apostles, 17:18–34, The Revised English Bible.

7. Vernon J. Bourke, in *Aquinas' Search for Wisdom* (Milwaukee: Bruce, 1965), identifies discrepancies in many biographical sketches of Thomas Aquinas, since most are based on William of Tocco. Bourke points out that all we know for sure is that Thomas was born between 1220 and 1227. The commonly cited date of 1225 originated with Tocco and cannot be verified.

8. A. W. Levi, *Philosophy as Social Expression* (Chicago: University of Chicago Press, 1974), p. 106.

9. William of Tocco in Bourke, *Aquinas' Search for Wisdom*, p. 37.

10. Based on Peter A. Angeles, *Dictionary of Philosophy* (New York: Barnes & Noble, 1981), p. 250.

11. Levi, *Philosophy as Social Expression*, pp. 122ff.

12. Ibid., p. 124.

13. From Thomas Aquinas's commentary on Aristotle's *Metaphysics*, quoted in Levi, *Philosophy as Social Expression*, p. 102.

14. The Five Ways are found in *Summa Theologica*, trans. the Dominican Fathers, *Basic Writings of Saint Thomas Aquinas*, ed. A. C. Pegis (New York: Random House, 1945), part 1, ques. 2, art. 3.

15. Ibid.

16. Ibid.

17. Ibid.

18. Ibid.

19. W. T. Jones, *A History of Western Philosophy: The Medieval Mind*, 2nd ed. (New York: Harcourt Brace Jovanovich, 1969), pp. 220ff.

20. Augustine, *City of God*, trans. M. Dods (Edinburgh: T. & T. Clark, 1872), xi, 26.

21. Thomas Aquinas, *Summa contra Gentiles*, trans. English Dominican Fathers (London: Bunns Oates, 1924), part 3, ques. 25.

Overview of Modern Themes

1. Quoted in William K. Hartmann, *Astronomy: The Cosmic Journey* (Belmont, Calif.: Wadsworth, 1991), p. 64.

Chapter 9 The Rationalist: René Descartes

1. René Descartes, *Discourse on Method*, trans. Elizabeth Haldane and G. R. T. Ross, in *The Philosophical Works of Descartes*, vol. 1 (Cambridge: Cambridge University Press, 1931; reprint, New York: Dover), p. 83. Reprinted by permission.

2. Ibid., p. 87.

3. Quoted in Levi, *Philosophy as Social Expression* (Chicago: University of Chicago Press, 1974), p. 185.

4. Descartes, *Rules for the Direction of the Mind*, in *Philosophical Works*, vol. 1, p. 6.

5. Ibid., pp. 9, 14.

6. Descartes, *Discourse on Method*, p. 88.

7. Ibid., pp. 81ff.

8. Descartes, *Meditation I*, in *Philosophical Works*, vol. 1, pp. 144–145.

9. Ibid., pp. 145–146.

10. Ibid., p. 148.

11. Descartes, *Meditation II*, in *Philosophical Works*, vol. 1, p. 150.

12. Ibid., pp. 151–153.

13. Descartes, *Meditation III*, in *Philosophical Works*, vol. 1, p. 159.

14. Ibid., p. 157.

15. Ibid., p. 165.

16. Ibid., p. 166.

17. Ibid., p. 163.

18. Ibid., p. 169.

19. Ibid., p. 170.

20. Ibid., pp. 170–171.

21. Descartes, *Meditation V*, in *Philosophical Works*, vol. 1, pp. 181–182.

22. Descartes, *Meditation VI*, in *Philosophical Works*, vol. 1, p. 185.

23. Ibid., p. 191.

24. Ibid., p. 195.

25. Gilbert Ryle, *The Concept of Mind* (New York: Harper & Row, 1941), p. 11.

26. Descartes, *Meditation VI*, in *Philosophical Works*, vol. 1, p. 192.

27. Amaury de Riencourt, *Sex and Power in History* (New York: David McKay, 1974), pp. 97ff.

28. Ibid., p. 99.

29. Susan Bordo, "The Cartesian Masculinization of Thought," in *From Modernism to Postmodernism: An Anthology*, ed. Lawrence Cahoone (Cambridge, Mass.: Blackwell, 1996), p. 638.

30. Ibid., pp. 638.

31. Ibid.

32. Ibid., p. 643.

33. Ibid., p. 645.

34. Ibid., p. 656.

35. See "Introduction: Feminism, Western Culture, and the Body," in Susan Bordo, *Unbearable Weight: Feminism, Western Culture, and the Body*, Tenth Anniversary Edition (Oakland, Ca.: University of California Press, 2004), pp. 13–14.

Chapter 10 The Skeptic: David Hume

1. H. R. Fox Bourne, *The Life of John Locke*, vol. 1 (New York: Harper, 1876), pp. 200–201.

2. John Locke, "Epistle to the Reader" in *An Essay Concerning Human Understanding*, ed. A. C. Fraser (Oxford: Clarendon, 1894), p. 9.

3. John Locke, "The Art of Medicine" (a paper written in 1669), quoted in Fox Bourne, vol. I, p. 224, and John Locke, *An Essay Concerning Human Understanding*, bk. 4, ch. 7, sec. 11.

4. Ibid., bk. 1, ch. 3, secs. 24–25.

5. Ibid., bk. 2, ch. 11, sec. 17.

6. Ibid., bk. 2, ch. 1, sec. 2.

7. Ibid., bk. 2, ch. 23, sec. 1.

8. Ibid., sec. 2.

9. Ibid., sec. 3.

10. Ibid., sec. 5.

11. Ibid., sec. 29.

12. George Berkeley, *Three Dialogues Between Hylas and Philonous*, in *Selections*, ed. Mary W. Calkins (New York: Scribner's, 1957), pp. 268–269.

13. Ibid., pp. 238–239.

14. George Berkeley, *A Treatise Concerning the Principles of Human Knowledge*, in *The Works of George Berkeley*, vol. 1, ed. A. C. Fraser (Oxford: Clarendon, 1901), pt. 1, sec. 3.

15. Ernest C. Mossner, *Life of David Hume* (1954; reprint, Oxford: Clarendon, 1970), p. 51.

16. Thomas H. Huxley, *Hume* (New York, 1901), p. 3.

17. Mossner, p. 94.

18. Richard Watson, *The Philosopher's Diet: How to Lose Weight and Change the World* (Boston: Atlantic Monthly Press, 1985), p. 97.

19. Mossner, p. 111.

20. Ibid., p. 213.

21. Ibid., pp. 223, 318.

22. David Hume, "My Own Life," in *Dialogues Concerning Natural Religion*, ed. Henry D. Aiken (New York: Hafner, 1948), p. 239.

23. Mossner, p. 568.

24. Hume, "My Own Life," p. 239.

25. Ibid., p. 244.

26. Mossner, pp. 598–600.

27. David Hume, *An Enquiry Concerning Human Understanding*, ed. L. A. Selby-Bigge (Oxford: Clarendon, 1894), sec. 1.

28. Ibid., sec. 2.

29. Ibid.

30. David Hume, *A Treatise of Human Nature*, ed. L A. Selby-Bigge (Oxford: Clarendon, 1896), bk. 1, pt. 4, sec. 6.

31. Ibid.

32. Ibid.

33. Hume, *Enquiry Concerning Human Understanding*, bk. 12, pt. 1.

34. Hume, *Treatise*, bk. 1, pt. 4, sec. 2.

35. Ibid.

36. Hume, *Enquiry Concerning Human Understanding*, sec. 7, pts. 1, 2.

37. Hume, *Dialogues Concerning Human Religion*, ed. Norman Kemp-Smith (Edinburgh: Nelson, 1947), pts. 2, 11. Used by permission of Thomas Nelson & Sons Limited.

38. Ibid., pts. 10, 11.

39. Ibid.

40. Ibid., bk. II, sec. III.

41. David Hume, *An Enquiry Concerning the Principles of Morals*, ed. L. A. Selby-Bigge (Oxford: Clarendon, 1894), Appendix I.

42. Ibid., sec. I.

43. Hume, *Treatise*, bk. 2, pt. 3, sec. 3.

44. Ibid., bk. 3, pt. 1, sec. 1.

45. Hume, *An Enquiry Concerning the Principles of Morals*, sec. I.

46. Hume, *Treatise*, bk. 3, pt. 1, sec. 2.

47. Hume, *An Enquiry Concerning the Principles of Morals*, Appendix II.

48. Ibid.

49. Ibid.

50. See Alison Jaggar, "Love and Knowledge: Emotion in Feminist Epistemology," in *Gender/Body/Knowledge: Feminist Reconstructions of Being and Knowing*, eds. Alison Jaggar and Susan Bordo (Rutgers, N.J.: University Press, 1989), pp. 145–146.

51. Ibid., p. 155.

52. Hume, *Dialogues*, pt. 10, 11.

53. Hume, *Treatise*, bk. 1, pt. 4, sec. 7.

54. Hume, *Enquiry Concerning Human Understanding*, pt. 1.

Chapter 11 The Universalist: Immanuel Kant

1. In A. D. Lindsay, *Kant* (London: Oxford University Press, 1934), p. 2.

2. Henry Thomas and Dana Lee Thomas, *Living Biographies of Great Philosophers* (Garden City, N.Y.: Blue Ribbon, 1941), p. 191.

3. Josiah Royce, *The Spirit of Modern Philosophy* (Boston: Houghton Mifflin, 1892), p. 108.

4. Norman Kemp Smith, *Commentary to Kant's "Critique of Pure Reason"* (London: Macmillan, 1923), p. xix.

5. Immanuel Kant, preface, *Critique of Pure Reason*, 1st ed., trans. Norman Kemp Smith (London: Macmillan, 1929), p. 13.

6. Thomas and Thomas, *Living Biographies*, p. 196.

7. Friedrich Schiller, *Poems in Works* (London, 1901).

8. Immanuel Kant, *Prolegomena to Any Future Metaphysics*, trans. Lewis White Beck (Indianapolis: Liberal Arts, 1950), intro., pp. 5–6.

9. W. T. Jones, *A History of Western Philosophy: Kant and the Nineteenth Century*, rev. 2nd ed. (New York: Harcourt Brace Jovanovich, 1975), pp. 19ff.

10. Immanuel Kant, *Critique of Pure Reason*, 2nd ed., unabridged ed., trans. Norman Kemp Smith (New York: St. Martin's, 1929), pp. 41–42.

11. Ibid., p. 532.

12. Ibid., pp. 557ff.

13. Ibid., pp. 558ff.

14. Ibid., p. 559.

15. Roger Scruton, "The Rationalists and Kant," in *Philosophy: A Guide Through the Subject*, ed. A. C. Grayling (Oxford: Oxford University Press, 1995), p. 475.

16. Ibid., pp. 475–476.

17. See Immanuel Kant, *Critique of Practical Reason and Other Essays*, trans. Lewis White Beck (Chicago: University of Chicago Press, 1949), p. 8, B, ix.

18. S. Körner, *Kant* (Baltimore: Penguin, 1955), pp. 129ff.

19. Immanuel Kant, *Fundamental Principles of the Metaphysics of Morals*, trans. T. K. Abbott (London: Longmans, Green, 1927), sec. 1, p. 10.

20. Ibid., p. 16.

21. Ibid., p. 17.

22. Ibid., sec. 2, p. 36.

23. Ibid., sec. 1, p. 18.

24. Kant, *Metaphysics of Morals*, sec. 2, pp. 46–47.

25. Immanuel Kant, *Groundwork of the Metaphysics of Morals*, in H. J. Paton, trans., *Kant's Groundwork of the Metaphysics of Morals*, 3rd ed. (New York: Harper & Row Torchbook, 1964), p. 96.

26. John Rawls, *A Theory of Justice* (Cambridge, Mass.: Harvard University Press, 1971), p. 12.

27. Ibid., pp. 60–61.

28. Ibid., p. 13.

29. Susan Moller Okin, *Justice, Gender, and the Family* (New York: Basic, 1989), p. 8.

30. Ibid., p. 91.

31. Rawls, p. 12.

32. Okin, p. 91.

Chapter 12 The Utilitarian: John Stuart Mill

1. W. T. Jones, *Kant and the Nineteenth Century: A History of Western Philosophy*, rev. 2nd ed. (New York: Harcourt Brace Jovanovich, 1975), p. 162.

2. Thomas Malthus, *An Essay on the Principle of Population as It Affects the Future Improvement of Society* (J. Johnson, in St. Paul's Church-Yard London, 1798), p. 4.

3. Jeremy Bentham, *An Introduction to Principles of Morals and Legislation* (Oxford: Oxford University Press, 1823 ed.), ch. 1, sec. 1.

4. Richard Watson, *Cogito, Ergo Sum: The Life of René Descartes* (Boston: David R. Godine, 2002), p. 11.

5. Benedict de Spinoza, *The Ethics*, trans. R. H. M. Elwes (New York: Dover, 1955), proposition 37, note 1.

6. Immanuel Kant, "Duties towards Animals and Spirits," in *Lectures on Ethics*, trans. L. Infeld (New York: Harper & Row, 1963), pp. 239–240.

7. Jeremy Bentham, *An Introduction to Principles of Morals and Legislation* (New York: Hafner, 1948), p. 311n.

8. A. Bain, *John Stuart Mill* (1882; reprint, New York: Augustus M. Kelley, 1966), pp. 334f, and B. Mazlish, *James and John Stuart Mill* (New York: Basic Books, 1975), p. 66.

9. John Stuart Mill, *Autobiography*, ed. J. D. Stillinger (London: Oxford University Press, 1971), pp. 6, 9.

10. John Stuart Mill, *Autobiography* (New York: Columbia University Press, 1924), pp. 21–22.

11. Mill, *Autobiography*, ed. J. D. Stillinger, p. 20.

12. Ibid., p. 33, note 3.

13. Mazlish, pp. 201–202, and M. St. John Packe, *The Life of John Stuart Mill* (London: Stecker & Warburg, 1954), pp. 66–68.

14. Mill, *Autobiography*, ed. J. D. Stillinger, pp. 32, 33, note 3.

15. Mill, *Autobiography* (Columbia), pp. 97–98.

16. Mill, *Autobiography*, ed. J. D. Stillinger, pp. 83–84.

17. Mill, *Autobiography* (Columbia), p. 122.

18. Lewis S. Feuer, "John Stuart Mill as a Sociologist: The Unwritten Ethology," in John Stuart Mill, *On Socialism* (1879; reprint, Buffalo, N.Y.: Prometheus, 1987), p. 10.

19. Jeremy Bentham, *The Rationale of Reward*, in *The Works of Jeremy Bentham* (Edinburgh: Tait, 1838–1843), part 2, sec. 1, p. 253.

20. John Stuart Mill, *Utilitarianism*, ch. 2, "What Utilitarianism Is," in *The Utilitarians* (Garden City, N.Y.: Dolphin, 1961), p. 407.

21. Ibid., pp. 408–409.

22. Ibid., p. 409.

23. Ibid., pp. 410–411.

24. Ibid., p. 418.

25. Ibid., p. 415.

26. Ibid., pp. 412–413.

27. Ibid., pp. 414–415.

28. Ibid., pp. 415ff.

29. Ibid., p. 416.

30. Ibid., ch. 3, p. 437.

31. Sarah Conly, *Against Autonomy: Justifying Coercive Paternalism* (Cambridge, U.K. University Press, 2012), p. 9.

32. Ibid., p. 2.

33. Ibid.

34. Ibid., p. 39.

35. Ibid., pp. 2–3.

36. Mill, *Autobiography* (Columbia), p. 100.

Chapter 13   The Materialist: Karl Marx

1. Quoted in Isaiah Berlin, *Karl Marx* (New York: Oxford University Press, 1939), p. 73.

2. Condensed from "Karl Marx's Funeral," in Robert Payne, *Marx* (New York: Simon & Schuster, 1968), pp. 500–502.

3. Karl Marx, *Critique of Political Economy*, trans. N. I. Stone, in *Marx and Engels: Selected Works*, vol. 1 (Moscow: Foreign Languages Publishing, 1955), pp. 362–364.

4. In Sidney Hook, *Towards the Understanding of Karl Marx* (New York: John Day, 1932), pp. 80–81, and "Theses on Feuerbach, III," in *Karl Marx and Friedrich Engels on Religion*, ed. Reinhold Niebuhr (New York: Schocken, 1964), p. 70.

5. Karl Marx, *Economic and Philosophic Manuscripts*, trans. T. B. Bottomore, in Erich Fromm, *Marx's Concept of Man* (New York: Ungar, 1961), p. 181.

6. Karl Marx, *Critique of Political Economy*, trans. N. I. Stone (Chicago: C. H. Kerr, 1911), p. 11.

7. Karl Marx and Friedrich Engels, *Manifesto of the Communist Party*, 1888 ed., reprinted in *Introductory Readings in Philosophy*, eds. Avrum Stroll and Richard H. Popkin (New York: Holt, Rinehart & Winston, 1972), p. 412.

8. Ibid., p. 413.

9. Ibid., p. 415.

10. Ibid.

11. Ibid., p. 416.

12. Ibid., pp. 416–417.

13. Ibid., p. 418.

14. Karl Marx, *Economic and Philosophic Manuscripts* (1844), in *Writings of the Young Marx on Philosophy and Society*, eds. and trans. Loyd D. Easton and Kurt H. Guddat (Garden City, N.Y.: Anchor Doubleday, 1967), p. 290. Used by permission of Loyd D. Easton and Mrs. Kurt H. Guddat.

15. Ibid., p. 292.

16. Ibid., p. 294.

Chapter 14   The Existentialist: Søren Kierkegaard

1. Samuel Enoch Stumpf, *Philosophy: History and Problems*, 4th ed. (New York: McGraw-Hill, 1989), bk. 1, p. 475.

2. Søren Kierkegaard, *The Journals of Søren Kierkegaard*, trans. Alexander Dru (New York: Oxford University Press, 1938), p. 94.

3. Morten Høi, *A Keeper of Love's Flame: Regine Olsen and Søren Kierkegaard*, Los Angeles Review of Books, April 9, 2014; see also Joakim Garff's *Regines gåde: Historien om Kierkegaards forlovede og Schlegels hustru (Regine's Mystery: The Story of Kierkegaard's Fiancée and Schlegel's Wife)* (Copenhagen: Gads Forlag, 2013).

4. Kierkegaard, *Journals*, p. 4.

5. Kierkegaard, *Concluding Unscientific Postscript*, 1846 ed., trans. D. F. Swenson, L. M. Swenson, and W. K. Lowrie, in *A Kierkegaard Anthology*, p. 276, and *The Journals of Kierkegaard*, trans. and ed. Alexander Dru (London: Collins, 1958), p. 46.

6. Søren Kierkegaard, *Either/Or*, vol. 1: *Diapsalmata*, trans. D. F. Swenson, L. M. Swenson, and W. K. Lowrie, in *A Kierkegaard Anthology*, p. 33.

7. William Barrett, *Irrational Man: A Study in Existential Philosophy* (Garden City, N.Y.: Doubleday Anchor, 1958), p. 173.

8. Søren Kierkegaard, in *The Present Age*, trans. Alexander Dru, "The Individual and the Public," in *A Kierkegaard Anthology*, pp. 260–261.

9. Ibid., p. 263.

10. Søren Kierkegaard, "Conclusion of" *The Point of View for My Work as an Author*, trans. Walter K. Lowrie (abridged), in *A Kierkegaard Anthology*, ed. Robert Bretall (New York: Modern Library, 1946), pp. 330, 332. Used by permission of Princeton University Library.

11. Kierkegaard, *Concluding Unscientific Postscript*, in Bretall, p. 198.

12. Søren Kierkegaard, *Kierkegaard's Concluding Unscientific Postscript*, trans. D. F. Swenson, with notes and introduction by W. Lowrie (Princeton, N.J.: Princeton University Press, 1941), p. 276.

13. David R. Law, *Kierkegaard as Negative Theologian* (Oxford: Clarendon Press, 1993), p. 115.

14. *Journals*, in Bretall, p. 11.

15. Ibid., p. 7.

16. Søren Kierkegaard, *The Point of View for My Work as an Author*, trans. W. Lowrie, ed. B. Nelson (New York: Harper & Row, 1962), p. 18.

17. *Journals*, in Bretall, p. 8.

18. Søren Kierkegaard, *Christian Discourses*, trans. Howard V. Hong and Edna H. Hong (Princeton, N.J.: Princeton University Press, 1978–2000), *Kierkegaard's Writings*, vol. 17, p. 317.

19. Søren Kierkegaard, *Philosophical Fragments*, trans. Howard V. Hong and Edna H. Hong (Princeton, N.J.: Princeton University Press, 1978–2000), *Kierkegaard's Writings*, vol. 7, pp. 190–191.

20. *Kierkegaard's Concluding Unscientific Postscript*, pp. 25–30.

21. David E. Cooper, "Kierkegaard," *The Blackwell Guide to Continental Philosophy*, eds. Robert C. Solomon and David Sherman (Malden, Mass.: Blackwell, 2003), p. 54.

22. Søren Kierkegaard, *Sickness Unto Death*, trans. Walter Lowrie, in Bretall, p. 338.

23. For a discussion regarding the implication that the crowd level is also a stage on life's way, see A. Rudd, *Kierkegaard and the Limits of the Ethical* (Oxford: Blackwell, 1997), p. 24.

24. Søren Kierkegaard, *Purity of Heart (is to will one thing)*, trans. D. Steered (London: Fontana, 1961), p. 54.

25. Søren Kierkegaard, *Either/Or: A Fragment of Life*, trans. David F. Swenson, Lillian Marvin Swenson, and Walter K. Lowrie, in Bretall, pp. 22–24.

26. Ibid., p. 34.

27. Søren Kierkegaard, *Either/Or*, vol. II, trans. W. Lowrie (Princeton, N.J.: Princeton University Press, 1971), p. 229.

28. Ibid., p. 164.

29. *Either/Or*, in Bretall, pp. 106–108.

30. Kierkegaard, *Journals*, pp. 181–182.

31. *Kierkegaard's Concluding Unscientific Postscript*, p. 276.

32. Søren Kierkegaard, *Fear and Trembling*, trans. Walter Lowrie, in Bretall, pp. 132–134.

33. *Kierkegaard's Concluding Unscientific Postscript*, pp. 31–32.

34. *Fear and Trembling*, in Bretall, p. 129.

35. Ibid., p. 130.

36. Søren Kierkegaard, quoted in Bruce H. Krimmse, *Encounters with Kierkegaard: A Life as Seen by His Contemporaries* (Princeton, N.J.: Princeton University Press, 1996), p. 464.

37. Ibid., pp. 471ff.

38. Ibid., p. 462.

39. *Either/Or*, in Bretall, p. 81.

Chapter 15 The Pragmatist: William James

1. G. W. Allen, *William James: A Biography* (New York: Viking, 1967), p. 134.

2. Ibid., p. 163.

3. Ibid., pp. 168–169.

4. Ralph Barton Perry, *The Thought and Character of William James* (Cambridge, Mass.: Harvard University Press, 1948), p. 386.

5. Allen, pp. 214–220.

6. Guy W. Stroh, *American Philosophy from Edwards to Dewey: An Introduction* (Princeton, N.J.: Van Nostrand, 1968), p. 123.

7. Perry, p. 300.

8. Ibid.

9. Quoted in Robert F. Davidson, *Philosophies Men Live By* (Fort Worth: Holt, Rinehart & Winston, 1971), p. 296.

10. Charles Sanders Peirce, *Collected Papers of Charles Sanders Peirce*, vol. 5, eds. Charles Hartshorne and Paul Weiss (Cambridge, Mass.: Harvard University Press, 1931–1935), pp. 276ff.

11. Ibid., pp. 284ff.

12. Ibid., pp. 272–273, 259–262.

13. William James, *The Will to Believe and Other Essays in Popular Philosophy* (1897; reprinted in *Human Immortality: Two Supposed Objections to the Doctrine*, New York: Dover, 1956), pp. 146–147.

14. Ibid., p. 177.

15. William James, *Pragmatism*, 1907 text, in *William James: Writings 1902–1910* (New York: Library of America, 1987), pp. 573ff.

16. Ibid., pp. 489, 490, 491.

17. James, *The Will to Believe*, pp. 28, 30.

18. William James, *Pragmatism* (New York: Longmans, Green, 1907), p. 58.

19. Ibid., pp. 59–64.

20. Ibid., p. 64.

21. William James, "The Dilemma of Determinism," in *The Will to Believe*, p. 150.

22. Ibid., pp. 161–163.

23. William James, "Some Problems in Philosophy," in *The Moral Equivalent of War and Other Essays*, ed. John K. Roth (New York: Harper & Row, 1971), p. 164.

24. William James, "The Dilemma of Determinism," in *The Will to Believe*, pp. 146–147.

25. James, *The Will to Believe*, p. 31.

26. Ibid., pp. 200–201.

27. William James, "Is Life Worth Living?", an address to the Harvard Young Men's Christian Association, published in *International Journal of Ethics*, October 1895, and in *The Search for Meaning in Life: Readings in Philosophy*, ed. Robert F. Davidson (New York: Holt, Rinehart & Winston, 1962), p. 61.

28. William James, "The Moral Philosopher and Moral Life," in *The Will to Believe*, pp. 211ff.

29. William James, *The Varieties of Religious Experience* (New York: Longmans, Green, 1902), pp. 525, 516–517.

30. James, *The Varieties of Religious Experience*, in *William James: Writings 1902–1910*, p. 124.

31. Ibid., p. 152.

32. William James, "Is Life Worth Living?" cited in Dmitri Tymoczko, "The Nitrous Oxide Philosopher," *Atlantic Monthly*, May 1996, pp. 98–99.

33. Quoted in Tymoczko, p. 100.

34. James, *The Will to Believe*, pp. 202ff.

35. W. T. Jones, *Kant and the Nineteenth Century: A History of Western Philosophy*, rev. 2nd ed. (New York: Harcourt Brace Jovanovich, 1975), p. 323.

36. James, *The Will to Believe*, p. 320.

37. Ibid., pp. 18–19.

38. Tymoczko, pp. 99–100.

39. Ibid.

Chapter 16   The Anti-Philosopher: Friedrich Nietzsche

1. Friedrich Nietzsche, *The Will to Power*, ed. Walter Kaufmann, trans. Walter Kaufmann and R. J. Hollingdale (New York: Vintage, 1967), p. 3.

2. Friedrich Nietzsche, *The Birth of Tragedy*, trans. W. A. Haussmann (New York: Russell & Russell, 1964), p. xvii.

3. Letter from Friedrich Ritschl in *The Portable Nietzsche*, trans. Walter Kaufmann (New York: Penguin, 1968), pp. 8–9.

4. R. J. Hollingdale, introduction to his translation of *Thus Spake Zarathustra* (Baltimore, Md.: Penguin, 1967), p. 26.

5. Friedrich Nietzsche, *Ecce Homo*, quoted in *Thus Spake Zarathustra*, trans. Thomas Cotton (New York: Modern Library, 1967), pp. 18–19.

6. Friedrich Nietzsche, *Ecce Homo*, in *The Portable Nietzsche*, p. 298.

7. Friedrich Nietzsche, "Attempt at a Self-Criticism," in *The Birth of Tragedy*, trans. Walter Kaufmann (New York: Vintage, 1967), sec. 3, pp. 19–20.

8. Quoted in Karl Jaspers, *Nietzsche: An Introduction to the Understanding of His Philosophical Activity* (Tucson: University of Arizona Press, 1965), p. 56.

9. Nietzsche, letter to Franz Overbeck, quoted in Jaspers, p. 87.

10. Nietzsche, "Attempt at a Self-Criticism," sec. 5, p. 23.

11. Alexander Nehamas, *Nietzsche: Life as Literature* (Cambridge, Mass.: Harvard University Press, 1985), p. 2.

12. Friedrich Nietzsche, *Beyond Good and Evil*, trans. M. Cowan (Chicago: Henry Regnery, 1955), pp. 3–6.

13. Friedrich Nietzsche, "On Truth and Lie in an Extra-Moral Sense," in *The Portable Nietzsche*, pp. 42, 44.

14. Nietzsche, "Of Self-Overcoming," *Thus Spake Zarathustra*, pp. 136, 137, 138.

15. Philip Novak, *The Vision of Nietzsche* (Rockport, Mass.: Element, 1996), pp. 8–9.

16. Nietzsche, *The Will to Power*, sec. 1067, pp. 549–550.

17. Friedrich Nietzsche, "The Natural History of Morals," Part Five of *Beyond Good and Evil*, trans. Walter Kaufmann and R. J. Hollingdale, sec. 186, in *From Modernism to Postmodernism: An Anthology*, ed. Lawrence Cahoone (Cambridge, Mass.: Blackwell, 1966), pp. 104–105.

18. Ibid.

19. Nietzsche, *On the Genealogy of Morals*, in *On the Genealogy of Morals and Ecce Homo*, ed. Walter Kaufmann, trans. Walter Kaufmann and R. J. Hollingdale (New York: Vintage, 1969), Third Essay, sec. 19, pp. 136–137.

20. Friedrich Nietzsche, "Why I Am a Destiny," *Ecce Homo*, sec. 6, in *On the Genealogy of Morals and Ecce Homo*, p. 331.

21. Ibid., sec. 7, p. 332.

22. Nietzsche, *Beyond Good and Evil*, sec. 190, in Cahoone, p. 108.

23. Nietzsche, *Daybreak*, in Novak, sec. 131, p. 78.

24. Nietzsche, *Beyond Good and Evil*, sec. 198, in Cahoone, p. 113.

25. Ibid., sec. 201, p. 117.

26. Friedrich Nietzsche, *The Joyful Wisdom*, trans. Thomas Common, in *The Complete Works of Friedrich Nieztsche*, vol. 10, ed. Oscar Levy, (New York: Macmillan: 1924), bk. 3, sec. 125, pp. 167–168.

27. Ibid., pp. 168–169.

28. Nietzsche, *Thus Spoke Zarathustra*, in *The Portable Nietzsche*, pp. 199–200.

29. Nietzsche, *The Gay Science*, sec. 343, p. 279.

30. Quoted in Jaspers, p. 162.

31. Nietzsche, *Thus Spoke Zarathustra*, in *The Portable Nietzsche*, p. 398.

32. Nietzsche, *Toward a Genealogy of Morals*, trans. Walter Kaufmann, "Good and Evil Versus Good and Bad," sec. 10, in *The Portable Nietzsche*, pp. 451–452.

33. Ibid.

34. Nietzsche, *Thus Spoke Zarathustra*, in *The Portable Nietzsche*, pp. 124–128.

35. Friedrich Nietzsche, "Four Great Errors," sec. 8, in *Twilight of the Idols and The Anti-Christ*, trans. R. J. Hollingdale (Middlesex: Penguin, 1968), p. 54.

36. Nietzsche, "Why I Am So Clever," *Ecce Homo*, sec. 10, p. 258.

37. Nietzsche, *The Gay Science*, sec. 276, Novak, p. 160.

Chapter 17 The Twentieth Century: Ludwig Wittgenstein and Martin Heidegger

1. See Albert William Levi, *Philosophy as Social Expression* (Chicago: University of Chicago Press, 1974), pp. 239–241.

2. Friedrich Nietzsche, *The Genealogy of Morals*, trans. F. Golffing (Garden City, N.Y.: 1956), p. 255.

3. Alasdair MacLntyre, "Philosophy: Past Conflict and Future Direction," address delivered to the Pacific Division of the American Philosophical Association, March 1987, quoted in Huston Smith, *Beyond the Postmodern Mind*, updated and revised (Wheaton, Ill.: Quest Books, 1982, 1989, 2003), p. 119.

4. See W. T. Jones, *The Twentieth Century to Wittgenstein and Sartre: A History of Philosophy*, vol. 5 (San Diego: Harcourt Brace Jovanovich, 1975), pp. 88–93.

5. Robert C. Solomon, "Introduction," *The Blackwell Guide to Continental Philosophy*, eds. Robert C. Solomon and David Sherman (Malden, Mass.: Blackwell, 2003), p. 3.

6. See A. C. Grayling, *Wittgenstein: A Very Short Introduction* (Oxford: Oxford University Press, 1996), p. 134.

7. Ibid., p. 11.

8. Jaakko Hintikka, *On Wittgenstein* (Belmont, Calif.: Wadsworth, 2000), p. i.

9. Ray Monk, *Wittgenstein: The Duty of Genius* (New York: Penguin, 1990), p. 579.

10. Ibid., p. 580.

11. John Locke, "Epistle to the Reader," in *An Essay Concerning Human Understanding*, ed. A. C. Fraser (Oxford: Clarendon Press, 1894).

12. Ludwig Wittgenstein, *Tractatus Logico-Philosophicus*, trans. D. F. Pears and B. F. McGuinness (London: Routledge and Kegan Paul, 1961), p. 3.

13. Ibid.

14. Grayling, p. 18.

15. See Hans Sluga, "Introduction," *The Cambridge Companion to Wittgenstein*, pp. 16–17, and Bryan Magee's interview with John Searle in *The Great Philosophers: An Introduction to Western Philosophy* (Oxford: Oxford University Press, 1988), pp. 326–327.

16. Ludwig Wittgenstein, *The Blue and Brown Books* (Oxford: Blackwell, 1960), p. 28.

17. Ludwig Wittgenstein, *Culture and Value*, ed. G. G. von Wright, trans. P. Winch (Oxford: Blackwell, 1980), pp. 6–10 and 79.

18. *Philosophical Investigations*, par. 133.

19. Ibid., par. 109.

20. Jeff Malpas, "Martin Heidegger," *The Blackwell Guide to Modern Philosophy*, eds. Robert C. Solomon and David Sherman (Malden, Mass.: Blackwell, 2003), p. 143; Richard Gill and Ernest Sherman, *The Fabric of Existentialism: Philosophical and Literary Sources*, eds. Richard Gill and Ernest Sherman (Englewood Cliffs, N.J.: Prentice-Hall, 1973), pp. 415–416; Simon Blackburn, "Enquivering," *The New Republic* (Oct. 30, 2000), p. 43; A. J. Ayer, cited in *L'Espresso* (Rome), May 25, 1980, p. 199; Paul Edwards, *Heidegger on Death: A Critical Evaluation* (La Salle, Ill.: Hegeler, 1979), p. v.

21. Martin Heidegger, "My Way to Phenomenology," in *On Being and Time*, trans. J. Stambaugh (New York: Harper & Row, 1972), p. 75.

22. George Steiner, "Introduction—Heidegger: In 1991," in *Martin Heidegger* (Chicago: University of Chicago Press, 1989), p. xv.

23. Hannah Arendt, "Martin Heidegger at Eighty," trans. A. Hofstadter, in *Heidegger and Modern Philosophy*, ed. M. Murray (New Haven, Conn.: Yale University Press, 1971), p. 295.

24. Malpas, pp. 146–147.

25. Malpas, pp. 143–161; and Gill and Sherman, pp. 415–416.

26. Steiner, pp. xxvi–xxviii.

27. Richard Rorty, "Heidegger et la Nazisme," in *The New Republic*, April 11, 1988, pp. 32–33.

28. Heidegger, "My Way to Phenomenology," p. 78.

29. Edmund Husserl, "Philosophy and the Crisis of European Man," trans. Q. Lauer, in *Phenomenology and the Crisis of Philosophy* (New York: Harper & Row, 1965), p. 184f.

30. Patricia Altenbernd Johnson, *On Heidegger* (Belmont, Calif.: Wadsworth, 2000), p. 5.

31. Martin Heidegger, *Being and Time*, trans. J. Macquarrie and E. Robinson (New York: Harper & Row, 1962), p. 32.

32. Ibid., p. 19.

33. Martin Heidegger, "The Way Back into the Ground of Metaphysics," in *Existentialism from Dostoevsky to Sartre*, trans. Walter Kaufmann (New York: Meridian, 1957), pp. 209ff.

34. Heidegger, *Being and Time*, pp. 163–165.

35. Ibid., pp. 212–213.

36. Ibid., pp. 219–220.

37. Ibid., pp. 294–295.

38. Martin Heidegger, "Postscript to *What Is Metaphysics?*" in *Existence and Being*, ed. Werner Brock (Chicago: Henry Regnery, 1949), p. 355.

39. Martin Heidegger, *The Question Concerning Technology*, trans. William Lovitt, in *Basic Writings*, ed. David Farrell Krell (New York: Harper & Row, 1977), p. 296.

40. Ibid., p. 308.

41. Ibid., p. 309.

42. Kai Nielsen, "Philosophy: Past Conflict and Future Direction," an address delivered to the Pacific Division of the American Philosophical Association, March 1987.

Chapter 18 Philosophy as a Way of Life

1. Jean-Paul Sartre, *Critique of Dialectical Reason*, trans. H. E. Barnes (New York: Vintage, 1960), p. 24.

2. Jean-Paul Sartre, *Existentialism Is a Humanism*, trans. Bernard Frechtman, in *The Fabric of Existentialism: Philosophical and Literary Sources*, eds. Richard Gill and Ernest Sherman (Englewood Cliffs, N.J.: Prentice-Hall, 1973), p. 523.

3. Ibid., pp. 523–524.

4. Ibid., pp. 524–525.

5. Ibid., p. 525.

6. Ibid., pp. 525–526.

7. Ibid., pp. 526–527.

8. Ibid.

9. Susan Bordo, "The Cartesian Masculinization of Thought," in *From Modernism to Postmodernism: An Anthology*, ed. Lawrence Cahoone (Cambridge, Mass.: Blackwell, 1966), pp. 656–657.

10. Carol Gilligan, *Mapping the Moral Domain: A Contribution of Women's Thinking to Psychological Theory and Education*, eds. Carol Gilligan, Janie Victoria Ward, and Jill McLean Taylor, with Betty Baridge (Cambridge, Mass.: Center for the Study of Gender Education and Human Development, distributed by Harvard University Press, 1988), p. v; Carol Gilligan, *In a Different Voice: Psychological Theory and Women's Development* (Cambridge, Mass.: Harvard University Press, 1982), pp. 1–2.

11. This material is based on Robin Wilson's article "Black Women Seek a Role in Philosophy," *The Chronicle of Higher Education* (September 28, 2007), vol. 54, issue 5, p. B4.

12. Laurie Calhoun, "Feminism Is a Humanism," *APA Newsletter on Feminism and Philosophy* (2005), vol. 05, issue 1, p. 10.

13. Sally Haslanger, "Women in Philosophy? Do the Math," *New York Times*, September 2, 2013.

14. Calhoun, p. 13.

15. James M. Washington, ed., *A Testament of Hope: The Essential Writings of Martin Luther King, Jr.* (San Francisco: Harper & Row, 1986), pp. xviii–xix.

16. Ibid., p. xix.

17. Quoted in Sydney E. Ahlstrom, "The Radical Turn in Theology and Ethics: Why It Occurred in the 1960s," *Annals of the American Academy of Political and Social Science 387* (January 1970), p. 10.

18. Martin Luther King, Jr., "Love, Law and Civil Disobedience," address before the Fellowship of the Concerned, November 16, 1961, in Washington, *A Testament of Hope*, p. 45.

19. Martin Luther King, Jr., "Letter from Birmingham Jail," in Washington, *Testament of Hope*, pp. 295–296.

20. Michael Specter, "The Dangerous Philosopher," *New Yorker*, September 6, 1999, p. 46.

21. Ibid.

22. Peter Singer, "The Singer Solution to World Poverty," *New York Times*, September 5, 1999.

23. This sketch is based on Robert Boynton's article, "Who Needs Philosophy?" *New York Times Magazine*, November 12, 1999.

24. Ibid.

25. Martha C. Nussbaum, *Cultivating Humanity: A Classical Defense of Reform in Liberal Education* (Cambridge, Mass.: Harvard University Press, 1997), pp. 6–7.

26. Quoted by Boynton.

27. Martha C. Nussbaum, *The Therapy of Desire: Theory and Practice in Hellenistic Ethics* (Princeton, N.J.: Princeton University Press, 1994), pp. 3–4.

28. Ibid., p. 510.

29. Martha C. Nussbaum, *Women and Human Development: The Capabilities Approach* (New York: Cambridge University Press, 2000), pp. 299–301.

30. Pierre Hadot, *Philosophy as a Way of Life*, trans. Arnold I. Davidson (Oxford: Blackwell, 1995), p. 58.

31. Ibid., p. 274.

32. Ibid., p. 285.

33. Pierre Hadot, *What Is Ancient Philosophy?* trans. Michael Chase (Cambridge, Mass.: Harvard University Press, 2002), pp. 275–281.

34. Epictetus, *Handbook of Epictetus*, trans. Nicholas P. White (Indianapolis: Hackett, 1983), pp. 28ff.

Glossary

This Glossary contains all of the terms defined in the margins of the text. It also includes a few additional terms that are not defined in the margins. Chapter and page number notations for margin definitions are indicated in parentheses. Consult the index for terms and concepts not listed here.

absolute Hegelian idealism, see *idealism (absolute or Hegelian)*

ad hominem (fallacy of) From the Latin for "at the man"; logical fallacy of arguing against the person making the argument rather than the argument itself. (Overview of Classical Themes, p. 20)

aesthetics A branch of philosophy that studies all forms of art.

alienated life Unconscious, unspontaneous, and unfulfilled life; deprived of fundamental conditions necessary for self-actualization. (Ch. 13, p. 384)

alienation According to Marx, the condition of workers separated from the products of their labor; primarily an objective state but can also refer to not feeling "at one" with the product of labor. (Ch. 13, p. 382)

altruism From Latin for "other"; the capacity to promote the welfare of others; opposed to egoism. (Ch. 12, p. 354)

amor fati Nietzsche's term meaning "the love of fate"; expressed as joyous affirmation and delight that everything is exactly as and what it is. (Ch. 16, p. 470)

amoral, see *nonmoral*

analytic philosophy An influential nonliterary approach to philosophy that stresses logic, testability, precision, and clarity with antecedents in an anglophile tradition that includes John Locke, David Hume, Bertrand Russell, and Ludwig Wittgenstein; contends that close logical and linguistic analyses are thought to be the only proper methods for sorting out philosophical confusions; commonly contrasted with continental philosophy. (Ch. 17, p. 476)

anti-philosopher A radical critic of the techniques and doctrines of modern science and philosophy. The anti-philosopher disputes the possibility of objectivity and universality and rejects the absolute authority of reason; anti-philosophers also reject the possibility of a *neutral stance* or *perspectiveless perspective*. (Ch. 16, p. 456)

apeiron According to Anaximander, the first principle from which all existing things develop, a vast "Indefinite–Infinite"; the *apeiron* is an infinite mass of forces with no specific qualities. (Ch. 2, p. 62)

***a posteriori* knowledge** Empirical knowledge derived from sense experience and not regarded as universal because the conditions under which it is acquired change, perceivers vary, and factual relationships change. (Ch. 9, p. 257)

***a priori* ideas,** see *innate ideas*

***a priori* knowledge** Knowledge derived from reason without reference to sense experience. Examples include "All triangles contain 180°" and "Every event has a cause." (Ch. 9, p. 257)

archetypal (paradigmatic) individual A special class of teachers, philosophers, and religious figures whose nature becomes a standard by which a culture judges the "ideal" human being; a rare human being whose very nature represents something elemental about the human condition. (Ch. 4, p. 100)

archetype A basic image that represents our conception of the essence of a certain type of person; according to

559

psychologist C. G. Jung, some of the images have been shared by the whole human race from the earliest times. (Introduction, p. 5)

archetype (philosophical) A philosopher who represents an original or influential point of view in a way that significantly affects philosophers and nonphilosophers: cynic, saint, pessimist, optimist, atheist, rationalist, idealist, and so on. (Introduction, p. 5)

argument from design, see *teleological argument*

argument from gradation An argument for the existence of God based on the idea that being progresses from inanimate objects to increasingly complex animated creatures, culminating in a qualitatively unique God; Aristotelian argument that forms the basis for the fourth of Aquinas's Five Ways. (Ch. 8, p. 230)

argument from motion An attempt to prove the existence of God based on the reasoning that to avoid an infinite regress, there must be an Unmoved Mover capable of imparting motion to all other things; Aristotelian argument that forms the basis for the first of Thomas Aquinas's Five Ways. (Ch. 8, p. 226)

argument from necessity An argument for the existence of God based on the idea that if nothing had ever existed, nothing would always exist; therefore, there is something whose existence is necessary (an eternal something); Aristotelian argument that forms the basis for the third of Aquinas's Five Ways. (Ch. 8, p. 229)

ascetic An individual who turns away from pleasure and severely limits all sensual appetites in order to achieve salvation or peace of mind. (Ch. 1, p. 43)

atomism An early Greek philosophy developed by Leucippus and Democritus and later refined by Epicurus and Lucretius; materialistic view that the universe consists entirely of empty space and ultimately simple entities that combine to form objects. (Ch. 2, p. 71)

atoms From the Greek *atomos*, meaning "indivisible," "having no parts," or "uncuttable"; minute material particles; the ultimate material constituents of all things. Atoms have such properties as size, shape, position, arrangement (combination), and motion, but lack qualities like color, taste, temperature, or smell. (Ch. 2, p. 72)

authenticity A subjective condition of an individual living honestly and courageously in the moment, refusing to make excuses, and not relying on groups or institutions for meaning and purpose; for Heidegger, living in and with the "understanding" of our death. (Ch. 14, p. 396)

axiology A branch of philosophy that studies values in general.

barbarian From a rude "bar-bar" noise used to mock dialects considered crude by the ancient Athenians; originally referred

to other cultures considered "less than human" or uncivilized. (Ch. 3, p. 78)

belief Conviction or trust that a claim is true; an individual's subjective mental state; distinct from knowledge. (Introduction, p. 13)

belief (mere) A conviction that something is true for which the only evidence is the sincerity of the believer. (Introduction, p. 13)

bodhisattva An enlightened being who voluntarily postpones his own nirvana in order to help all other conscious life-forms find "supreme release"; not a savior. (Ch. 1, p. 45)

bourgeoisie All those who do not produce anything yet own and control the means of production. (Ch. 13, p. 372)

bundle theory of the self Humean theory that there is no fixed self but that the self is merely a "bundle of perceptions"; a self is merely a habitual means for discussing certain perceptions. (Ch. 10, p. 293)

capitalism An economic system in which the means of production and distribution are all (or mostly) privately owned and operated for profit under fully competitive conditions; tends to be accompanied by concentration of wealth and growth of great corporations. (Ch. 13, p. 377)

categorical imperative According to Kant, a command that is universally binding on all rational creatures; the ultimate foundation of all moral law: "Act as if the maxim of thy action were to become a universal law of nature." (Ch. 11, p. 328)

character From the Greek *charakter*, a word derived from *charassein,* "to make sharp" or "to engrave," the sum total of a person's traits, including behavior, habits, likes and dislikes, capacities, potentials, and so on; a key element of Aristotelian ethics and psychology, meaning the overall (generally fixed) nature or tone of a person's habits. (Ch. 6, p. 179)

chun-tzu Literally, "the lord's son"; originally the sovereign himself or a "cultivated gentleman"; Confucian morally superior man; a great or noble soul. (Ch. 1, p. 39)

chung-yung Literally, "centrality and universality," the Golden Mean of Confucius, consisting of moderation and normality; universal moral law; also equilibrium or harmony. (Ch. 1, p. 36)

Cogito, ergo sum Latin for "I think, therefore I am." (Ch. 9, p. 261)

coherence theory of truth A truth test in which new or unclear ideas are evaluated in terms of rational or logical consistency and in relation to already established truths. (Ch. 9, p. 251)

continental philosophy A broad term referring to philosophies associated with European philosophers such as Kant, Hegel, Kierkegaard, Marx, Nietzsche, Husserl, and

Heidegger; not a school of philosophy as such or single way of doing philosophy; includes phenomenology, existentialism, deconstructionism; commonly contrasted with analytic philosophy. (Ch. 17, p. 476)

co-opted In Marxian social analysis, co-option occurs when workers identify with the economic system that oppresses them by confusing the remote possibility of accumulating wealth with their actual living and working conditions; being co-opted also refers to anyone who is somehow convinced to further interests that are to her or his ultimate disadvantage. (Ch. 13, p. 380)

correspondence (copy or representation) theory of truth A truth test which holds that an idea (or belief or thought) is true if whatever it refers to actually exists (corresponds to a fact). (Ch. 10, p. 280)

cosmological argument From the Greek word *kosmos*, meaning "world," "universe," or "orderly structure"; argument for the existence of God that because it is impossible for any natural thing to be the complete and sufficient source of its own existence, there must be an Uncaused Cause capable of imparting existence to all other things; Aristotelian argument that forms the basis for the second of Aquinas's Five Ways. (Ch. 8, p. 228)

cosmology From the Greek word *kosmos*, meaning "world," "universe," or "orderly structure," the study of the universe as an ordered system or cosmos. (Ch. 2, p. 66)

cosmos Greek term for "ordered whole"; first used by the Pythagoreans to characterize the universe as an ordered whole consisting of harmonies of contrasting elements. (Ch. 2, p. 64)

critical philosophy Kant's term for his effort to assess the nature and limits of "pure reason," unadulterated by experience, in order to identify the actual relationship of the mind to knowledge. (Ch. 11, p. 318)

Cynic An individual who lives an austere, unconventional life based on Cynic doctrine. (Ch. 7, p. 192)

Cynicism A philosophy based on the belief that the very essence of civilization is corrupt and that civilization destroys individuals by making them soft and subject to the whims of fortune. (Ch. 7, p. 191)

Cyrenaic hedonism, see *hedonism (Cyrenaic)*

Dao, see *Tao*

deconstruction (philosophical) A kind of close textual analysis focused on uncovering and overcoming "privileges" hidden in philosophic arguments and theories by taking a text apart—by deconstructing it; questions whether any text can have any definite meaning. (Ch. 17, p. 475)

despair Sartre's term for refusing to base our choices and actions on possibilities; the condition of confining ourselves to what directly falls under our present influence and control.

determinism The belief that everything that happens must happen exactly the way it does because all matter is governed by cause and effect and follows laws of nature. (Ch. 15, p. 433)

dialectic (Hegelian) According to Hegel, a three-step pattern in which an original idea, known as a thesis, struggles with a contrary idea, known as an antithesis, to produce a new synthesis that combines elements of both. (Ch. 13, p. 367)

dialectic (Socratic), see *Socratic method*

dialectical process (Hegelian) An internally governed evolutionary cycle in which progress occurs as the result of a struggle between two opposing conditions. (Ch. 13, p. 372)

dualism Any philosophical position that divides existence into two completely distinct, independent, unique substances. (Ch. 9, p. 268)

dualism (epistemological) The view that knowing consists of two distinct aspects: the knower and the known. (Ch. 10, p. 283)

economic As used by Marx, the complete array of social relationships and arrangements that constitutes a particular social order. (Ch. 13, p. 375)

Efficient Cause The triggering cause that initiates activity; the substance by which a change is brought about; close to the contemporary meaning of cause; the third of Aristotle's Four Causes. (Ch. 6, p. 169)

egocentric predicament A problem generated by epistemological dualism: If all knowledge comes in the form of my own ideas, how can I verify the existence of anything external to them? (Ch. 10, p. 283)

egoism The belief that self-interest is or ought to be the basis of all deliberate action; psychological egoists deny that altruism is even possible.

Eightfold Path Buddha's prescription for rooting out suffering: (1) right understanding; (2) right purpose; (3) right speech; (4) right conduct; (5) right livelihood; (6) right effort; (7) right mindfulness; (8) right meditation. (Ch. 1, p. 50)

empirical criterion of meaning Meaningful ideas are those that can be traced back to sense experience (impressions); beliefs that cannot be reduced to sense experience are not "ideas" at all but meaningless utterances. (Ch. 10, p. 292)

empiricism The belief that all knowledge is ultimately derived from the senses (experience) and that all ideas can be traced to sense data. (Ch. 10, p. 278)

entelechy From the Greek for "having its end within itself"; according to Aristotle, an inner urge that drives all things to blossom into their own unique selves; inner order or design that governs all natural processes. (Ch. 6, p. 170)

epistemological dualism see *dualism (epistemological)*

epistemology A branch of philosophy that studies the nature and possibility of knowledge. (Ch. 10, p. 278)

Esse est percipi Latin for Berkeley's belief that "to be is to be perceived." (Ch. 10, p. 286)

ethical hedonism, see *hedonism (ethical)*

ethics A branch of philosophy concerned with the good life and with moral value and moral reasoning.

ethnocentrism From Greek roots meaning "the race is the center"; belief that the customs and beliefs of one's own culture are inherently superior to all others. (Ch. 3, p. 78)

eudaimonia Often translated as "happiness"; term Aristotle used to refer to fully realized existence; state of being fully aware, vital, alert. (Ch. 6, p. 175; see also Ch. 13, p. 383)

existentialism A term used to refer to philosophy that emphasizes fundamental questions of meaning and choice as they affect existing individuals; existential themes include choice, freedom, identity, alienation, inauthenticity, despair, and awareness of our own mortality. (Ch. 14, p. 390)

fallacy of anachronism Error in reasoning that results from uncritically and rigidly applying contemporary values to past practices and ideas. (Overview of Classical Themes, p. 20)

Final Cause That for which an activity or process takes place; a thing's very reason for being (*raison d'être*); the fourth of Aristotle's Four Causes. (Ch. 6, p. 169)

forces of production In philosophical Marxism, factories, equipment, technology, knowledge, and skill; a part of the substructure of society. (Ch. 13, p. 375)

forlornness Sartre's term for his belief that we face life alone, without God, without certainty, with only absolute freedom and the responsibility that accompanies it. (Ch. 17, p. 517)

form (Aristotle) From the Greek word for essence (*ousia*), that which is in matter and makes a thing what it is; can be abstracted from matter but cannot exist independently of matter. (Ch. 6, p. 165)

Formal Cause The shape, or form, into which matter is changed; the second of Aristotle's Four Causes. (Ch. 6, p. 168)

forms, see *Platonic Forms*

Four Noble Truths The foundation of Buddha's teachings: (1) to exist is to suffer; (2) self-centeredness is the chief cause of human suffering; (3) the cause of suffering can be understood and rooted out; (4) suffering can be alleviated by following the Eightfold Path. (Ch. 1, p. 49)

functionalist theory of morality A moral position that right and wrong can be understood only in terms of their effect on anything's natural function; each kind of thing has a natural purpose (function). (Ch. 5, p. 148)

hedonism From the Greek root for "pleasure"; general term for any philosophy that asserts that pleasure = good and pain = evil (bad). (Ch. 7, p. 187)

hedonism (Cyrenaic) A philosophy that advocates the unreflective pursuit of intense, immediate pleasure; makes no qualitative distinctions among pleasures. (Ch. 7, p. 188)

hedonism (ethical) The belief that although it is possible to deliberately avoid pleasure or choose pain, it is morally wrong to do so. (Ch. 12, p. 342)

hedonism (psychological) The belief that all decisions are based on considerations of pleasure and pain because it is psychologically impossible for human beings to do otherwise. (Ch. 12, p. 342)

herd man In Nietzschean philosophy, the type of person who cannot face being alone in a godless universe, an inferior individual seeking safety and identity in a group or from another; characterized by resentment and hypocrisy. (Ch. 16, p. 466)

hsiao-jen Small or vulgar man; in Confucian philosophy, the opposite of the *chun-tzu;* a petty and base individual. (Ch. 1, p. 39)

humanism The name given to any philosophy that emphasizes human welfare and dignity; the belief that human intelligence and effort are capable of improving conditions in the here and now. (Ch. 1, p. 36)

hypothetical imperatives Propositions that tell us what to do under specific, variable conditions. (Ch. 11, p. 327)

idealism (absolute or Hegelian) Term used to identify Hegel's particular form of German idealism; a monistic philosophy that is based on an all-encompassing Absolute Spirit that is self-actualizing into perfection; Reality (Absolute Mind or Absolute Spirit) is independent of any individual's mind; not to be confused with Berkeleian idealism (immaterialism), in which objective reality is said to exist in the individual's mind. (Ch. 13, p. 367)

idealism (immaterialism) The belief that only ideas (mental states) exist; the material world is a fiction—it does not exist. (Ch. 10, p. 285)

idealism (Kantian) Kant's theory that knowledge is the result of the interaction between the mind and sensation and is structured by regulative ideas called categories; also known as *Kantian formalism* and *transcendental idealism.* (Ch. 11, p. 316)

idiot From the Greek *idiotes,* a disparaging term for a private person; one who does not participate in community affairs; one who shuns the body politic; sometimes translated as "good for nothing."

idle talk Heidegger's name for superficial "they talk"; includes chatter, gossip, and merely verbal understanding; contrasted with conversation or dialogue. (Ch. 17, p. 497)

immoral Morally wrong, bad, or not right; a moral value judgment or prescriptive claim. (Ch. 11, p. 310)

inauthenticity A condition that results when the nature and needs of an individual are ignored, denied, and obscured or sacrificed for institutions, abstractions, or groups. (Ch. 14, p. 396)

inductive reasoning A reasoning pattern that proceeds from the particular to the general or from "some" to "all" and results in generalized rules or principles established with degrees of probability. (Ch. 10, p. 296)

innate ideas (*a priori* ideas) Truths that are not derived from observation or experiment; characterized as being certain, deductive, universally true, and independent of all experience. (Ch. 9, p. 251; see also Ch. 10, p. 280)

instrumental theory of morality A moral position that right and wrong must be determined by the consequences of acts; right and wrong viewed as means (instruments) for getting something else. (Ch. 5, p. 147)

intellectualism A term used to refer to the claim that behavior is always controlled by beliefs about what is good and the means to that good. (Ch. 4, p. 117)

irony Communication on at least two levels, a literal or obvious level and a hidden or real level; favored by Socrates as a technique for keeping his listeners alert and involved. (Ch. 4, p. 104)

jen General human virtue; translated as human, humane, humanitarian, humanity, and benevolence; can mean both humankind and kindness; also a man or woman who is truly himself or herself; a "real person." (Ch. 1, p. 40)

justice (platonic) Excellence of function for the whole; in a just society each individual performs his or her natural function according to class; in a just individual, reason rules the spirit and the appetites. (Ch. 5, p. 150)

Kantian formalism, see *idealism (Kantian)*

Kantian idealism, see *idealism (Kantian)*

karma From the Pali *kamma;* according to Buddhist tradition, the law of moral causation (moral cause and effect); it includes past and present actions and is not to be confused with fate or predestination; good or bad karma results from our own actions. (Ch. 1, p. 48)

knowledge True belief. (Introduction, p. 12)

knowledge (practical) The skills needed to do things like play the piano, use a band saw, remove a tumor, or bake a cake. (Introduction, p. 13).

knowledge (theoretical) The accurate compilation and assessment of factual and systematic relationships. (Introduction, p. 12)

knowledge, see a posteriori *knowledge*

knowledge, see a priori *knowledge*

law of contradiction A rule of inference which says that no statement can be both true and false at the same time and under the same conditions; sometimes known as the law of noncontradiction. (Ch. 8, p. 219)

law of noncontradiction, see *law of contradiction*

li Literally, "ceremony"; encompasses rites, customs, and conventions ranging from ritual sacrifices honoring one's ancestors to everyday etiquette and good manners. (Ch. 1, p. 38)

logic A branch of philosophy that studies the rules of correct reasoning.

logos One of the richest and most complex terms in ancient philosophy; associated meanings include: "intelligence," "speech," "discourse," "thought," "reason," "word," "meaning"; the root of "log" (record), "logo," "logic," and the "ology" suffix found in terms like *sociology* and *physiology*. According to Heraclitus, the rule according to which all things are accomplished and the law found in all things. (Ch. 2, p. 63)

Logos (Stoic) According to Stoic doctrine, World Reason, also referred to as Cosmic Mind, God, Zeus, Nature, Providence, Cosmic Meaning, and Fate; force that governs the universe; also see Chapter 2. (Ch. 7, p. 199)

master morality In Nietzschean philosophy, the *aesthetic* honor code of the overman; morality that looks only to the authentic individual (overman) for values that transcend the slave's good–evil dichotomy with glorious–degrading, honorable–dishonorable, refined–vulgar, and so on; "good" equals "noble" and "evil" equals "vulgar." (Ch. 16, p. 469)

Material Cause The material (substance) from which a thing comes and in which change occurs; the first of Aristotle's Four Causes. (Ch. 6, p. 168)

materialism (or behaviorism, mechanism, reductionism) The belief that everything is composed of matter (and energy) and can be explained by physical laws, that all human activity can be understood as the natural behavior of matter according to mechanical laws, and that thinking is merely a complex form of behaving: The body is a fleshy machine. (Ch. 9, p. 267)

materialism (Marxian) A form of social determinism based on a reciprocal relationship between individuals and their environment; distinguished from strict materialism and hard determinism. (Ch. 13, p. 374)

matter (Aristotle) From the Greek *hyle*, the common material stuff found in a variety of things; it has no distinct characteristics until some form is imparted to it or until the form inherent in a thing becomes actualized. (Ch. 6, p. 165)

564 GLOSSARY

mean From the Latin *medius*, the midpoint between two other points; for Aristotle, moral virtue was characterized as a mean between too little (deficiency) and too much (excess). (Ch. 6, p. 180)

means of production In philosophical Marxism, natural resources such as water, coal, land, and so forth; a part of the substructure of society. (Ch. 13, p. 375)

mere belief, see *belief (mere)*

metaphysics A branch of philosophy that addresses the problem of what is real.

methodic doubt A Cartesian strategy of deliberately doubting everything it is possible to doubt in the least degree so that what remains will be known with absolute certainty. (Ch. 9, p. 256)

modernity The historical period of nineteenth- and twentieth-century nation-states and a corresponding set of cultural conditions and beliefs dominated by Enlightenment ideals, including faith in science, objective truth, and rationality; expectations of inevitable progress; political democracy; capitalism; urbanization; mass literacy; mass media; mass culture; anti-traditionalism; large-scale industrial enterprise; individualism; and secularization. (Ch. 16, p. 447)

monism The general name for the belief that everything consists of only one, ultimate, unique substance such as matter or spirit. (Ch. 2, p. 61; Ch. 9, p. 268)

moral From the Latin *moralis*, meaning "custom," "manner," or "conduct"; refers to what people consider good or bad, right or wrong; used descriptively as a contrast to *amoral* or *nonmoral* and prescriptively as a contrast to *immoral*. (Ch. 11, p. 310)

moral realism A pragmatic social philosophy unfettered by moral considerations; expressed in the formula "might makes right." (Ch. 3, p. 87)

moralistic Expressing commonplace moral sentiments that conflict with one's behavior and equating moral sentimentality with virtuous living; a form of hypocrisy that resembles a reaction formation. (Ch. 16, p. 460)

mystification Use of cloudy abstractions to create elaborate metaphysical systems that distract us from concrete material reality. (Ch. 13, p. 374)

naturalism The belief that reality consists of the natural world; denial of the existence of a separate supernatural order of reality; belief that nature follows orderly, discoverable laws. (Ch. 6, p. 162)

Nietzschean perspectivism The contention that every view is only one among many possible interpretations, including, especially, Nietzschean perspectivism, which itself is just one interpretation among many interpretations. (Ch. 16, p. 455)

nihilism From Latin for "nothing"; belief that the universe lacks meaning and purpose. (Ch. 16, p. 465)

nirvana Annihilation of the ego; a state of emptiness or "no-thing-ness"; a state of bliss; "pure consciousness" that leads to release from suffering while remaining conscious. (Ch. 1, p. 45)

nonmoral (amoral) Not pertaining to moral; a value-neutral descriptive claim or classification. (Ch. 11, p. 310)

noumenal reality Kant's term for reality as it is, independent of our perceptions; what is commonly called "objective reality." (Ch. 11, p. 318)

Nous From the Greek for "mind"; according to Anaxagoras, "the all-pervading Mind which imposes (brings about) an intelligible pattern in an otherwise unintelligible universe"; a material being that affects all things without being in them. (Ch. 2, p. 69)

ontological argument An attempt to prove the existence of God either by referring to the meaning of the word *God* when it is understood a certain way or by referring to the purportedly unique quality of the concept of God. (Ch. 9, p. 265)

ontology The study of being. (Ch. 2, p. 66; Ch. 17, p. 493)

original position John Rawls's imaginary setting in which we can identify the fundamental principles of justice from an objective, impartial perspective, as rational agents rather than as "interested parties"; similar to the "state of nature" in the social contract theories of Thomas Hobbes, Jean-Jacques Rousseau, and John Locke. (Ch. 11, p. 331)

overman Nietzsche's "higher type," a more-than-human being that will emerge only by overcoming the false idols of conventional morality and religion; announced in *Thus Spake Zarathustra*. (Ch. 16, p. 465)

paradigmatic individual, see *archetypal individual*

perspectivism, see *Nietzschean perspectivism*

pessimism Schopenhauer's theory that life is disappointing and that for every satisfied desire, new desires emerge; our only hope is detachment and withdrawal. (Ch. 16, p. 448)

phenomenal reality Kant's term for the world as we experience it. (Ch. 11, p. 318)

phenomenology A method of philosophical analysis first developed by Husserl that uses purely descriptive statements to provide a "descriptive analysis" of consciousness in all its forms; focuses on concrete "experienced facts" rather than abstractions in order to reveal the "essence" of human consciousness. (Ch. 17, p. 491)

philophaster A pretender or dabbler in philosophy. (FYI)

philosophical advocate A philosopher whose work identifies, clarifies, and actively opposes a perceived injustice; philosophical advocates give philosophical credence to personal experience based on gender, ethnic background, or social status. (Ch. 18, p. 511)

philosophical archetype, see *archetype (philosophical)*

philosophy From Greek roots meaning "the love of wisdom." (Introduction, p. 2)

philosophy (political) A branch of philosophy concerned with the state and issues of sovereignty.

philosophy (social) A branch of philosophy concerned with social institutions and relations.

Platonic Forms Independently existing, nonspatial, nontemporal "somethings" ("kinds," "types," or "sorts") known only through thought and that cannot be known through the senses; independently existing objects of thought; that which makes a particular thing uniquely and essentially what it is. (Ch. 5, p. 133)

Platonic virtue, see *virtue (Platonic)*

plenitude, see *principle of plenitude*

pluralism The belief that there exist many realities or substances. (Ch. 2, p. 69; Ch. 9, p. 268)

pneuma According to Anaximenes, the ultimate, pervasive spirit that holds the world together; all things are produced by either "rarefaction" of the *pneuma*, which creates fire, or condensation of the *pneuma*, which creates (in order of density) wind, cloud, water, earth, and stone. (Ch. 2, p. 63)

practical imperative (or principle of dignity) Kant's formulation of the categorical imperative based on the concept of dignity: "Act in such a way that you always treat humanity, whether in your own person or in the person of another, never simply as a means but always at the same time as an end." (Ch. 11, p. 330)

practical knowledge, see *knowledge (practical)*

practical reason, see *reason (practical)*

pragmatic paradox The paradox that pragmatism works only if we believe that our ideas are true according to nonpragmatic criteria. (Ch. 15, p. 444)

pragmatism From the Greek for "deed"; belief that ideas have meaning or truth value to the extent that they produce practical results and effectively further our aims; empirically based philosophy that defines knowledge and truth in terms of practical consequences. (Ch. 3, p. 84; see also Ch. 15, p. 420)

primary qualities According to Locke, objective sensible qualities that exist independently of any perceiver; shape, size, location, and motion are examples of primary qualities. (Ch. 10, p. 282)

principle of dignity, see *practical imperative*

principle of plenitude The name given by American historian of ideas Arthur O. Lovejoy (1873–1962) to the metaphysical principle that, given infinity, any real possibility must occur (at least once). (Ch. 8, p. 229)

principle of sufficient reason The principle that nothing happens without a reason; consequently, no adequate theory or explanation can contain any brute, crude, unexplained facts. First specifically encountered in the work of the medieval philosopher Peter Abelard (1079–1142), it is usually associated with the rationalist philosopher Gottfried Wilhelm Leibniz (1646–1716), who used it in his famous "best of all possible worlds" argument. (Ch. 2, p. 62; Ch. 8, p. 229)

principle of utility, see *utility (principle of)*

principles of reason (or rules of inference) Principles (such as the law of contradiction) that define the limits of rationality by their very structure and that cannot be rationally refuted since we rely on them in order to reason. (Ch. 8, p. 219)

problem of evil If God can prevent the suffering of the innocent yet chooses not to, He is not good. If God chooses to prevent the suffering but cannot, He is not omnipotent. If God cannot recognize the suffering of the innocent, He is not wise. (Ch. 8, p. 235)

proletariat All those whose labor produces goods and provides essential services yet who do not own the means of production. (Ch. 13, p. 372)

psyche Greek for "soul"; in today's terms, a combination of mind and soul, including the capacity for reflective thinking. (Ch. 2, p. 63; see also Ch. 4, p. 110)

psychological hedonism, see *hedonism (psychological)*

public philosopher A compelling writer or speaker whose philosophical positions are expressed in ways accessible to a broad audience; public philosophers tap into—or identify—vital philosophical issues of the day. (Ch. 18, p. 511)

qualities, see *primary qualities* and *secondary qualities*

rational discourse The interplay of carefully argued ideas; the use of reason to order, clarify, and identify reality and truth according to agreed upon standards of verification. (Ch. 2, p. 62)

rationalism An epistemological position in which reason is said to be the primary source of all knowledge, superior to sense evidence. Rationalists argue that only reason can distinguish reality from illusion and give meaning to experience. (Ch. 9, p. 250)

reaction formation A Freudian ego defense mechanism that attempts to prevent "dangerous" desires from being exposed and expressed by endorsing opposite attitudes and types of behavior as "barriers" against them. (Ch. 16, p. 460)

realism In philosophy, the belief that there exists an independent, objective world of things, facts, and states of affairs that are accessible to us. (Ch. 17, p. 480)

reality (noumenal), see *noumenal reality*

reality (phenomenal), see *phenomenal reality*

reason (practical) According to Kant, a moral function of reason that produces religious feelings and intuitions based on knowledge of moral conduct. (Ch. 11, p. 322)

reason (theoretical) According to Kant, a function of reason confined to the empirical, phenomenal world. (Ch. 11, p. 322)

reductio ad absurdum From the Latin for "reduce to absurdity"; form of argument that refutes an opponent's position by showing that accepting it leads to absurd, unacceptable, or contradictory conclusions because (1) accepting it leads to a logical contradiction, or (2) it leads to a logical conclusion that is somehow obviously ridiculous because it offends either our reason or common sense. (Ch. 2, p. 66)

regulative ideas (transcendental ideas) In Kantian philosophy, a special class of transcendental ideas that bridges the gap between the phenomenal and noumenal worlds: the ideas of self, cosmos (totality), and God. (Ch. 11, p. 316)

relationships of production In philosophical Marxism, who does what, who owns what, and how this affects members of both groups; a part of the substructure of society. (Ch. 13, p. 375)

relativism The belief that knowledge is determined by specific qualities of the observer, including age, ethnicity, gender, and cultural conditioning. (Introduction, p. 10; see also Ch. 3, p. 82)

ressentiment French for "resentment"; term used in Nietzschean philosophy for a deep form of psychically polluting resentment that generates slave morality; the dominant emotion of the herd. (Ch. 16, p. 467)

rules of inference, see *principles of reason*

sage An archetypal figure who combines religious inspiration and extraordinary insight into the human condition; the English word *sage* is derived from the Latin *sapiens*, meaning "wise." (Ch. 1, p. 23)

Scholasticism A Christian philosophy dominating medieval Europe from about 1000 to 1300 that stressed logical and linguistic analysis of texts and arguments in order to produce a systematic statement and defense of Christian beliefs. (Ch. 8, p. 224)

scientism The belief that the methods of the natural sciences apply to all areas of knowledge, and that only they can overcome the vagaries of prescientific superstition, religion, and metaphysics. (Ch. 16, p. 457)

secondary qualities According to Locke, subjective qualities whose existence depends on a perceiver; color, sound, taste, and texture are examples of secondary qualities. (Ch. 10, p. 282)

self-fulfilling prophecy A belief that affects events in such a way that it causes itself to come true; an example is a student doing poorly on an exam because she expects to fail it. (Ch. 15, p. 443)

skeptic From the Greek *skeptesthai,* "to consider or examine"; a person who demands clear, observable, undoubtable evidence before accepting any knowledge claim as true. (Ch. 10, p. 277)

slave morality In Nietzschean philosophy, a distortion of the will to power in which the characteristics of the inferior merely human type are praised as virtues, and the characteristics of the superior type (overman) are condemned as arrogance and coldheartedness; a morality of inhibitions, equality, restrictive duties, and "bad conscience." (Ch. 16, p. 467)

Socratic dialectic, Socratic method A question-and-answer technique Socrates used to draw truth out of his pupils, often by means of achieving a clearer, more precise definition of a key term or concept. (Ch. 4, p. 104)

sophistry The teachings and practices of the original Sophists; modern usage refers to subtle, plausible, but fallacious reasoning used to persuade rather than discover truth. (Ch. 3, p. 81)

Sophists In fifth century B.C.E., teachers of rhetoric (who were paid); relativists who taught that might makes right, truth is a matter of appearance and convention, and power is the ultimate value. (Ch. 3, p. 79)

sophos Sage or wise man; term applied to the first philosophers; from the Greek word for "wise." (Ch. 2, p. 59)

sophrosyne Wisdom as moderation; hitting the mark; quality of finding the mean between excess and deficiency. (Ch. 6, p. 178)

species-life Fully human life lived productively and consciously; not alienated. (Ch. 13, p. 384)

Stoic An individual who attempts to live according to Stoic doctrine. (Ch. 7, p. 186)

Stoicism A philosophy that counsels self-control, detachment, and acceptance of one's fate as identified by the objective use of reason. (Ch. 7, p. 186)

substructure of society In philosophical Marxism, the material substructure or base of society that determines the nature of all social relationships, as well as religions, art, philosophies, literature, science, and government. (Ch. 13, p. 375)

sufficient reason, see *principle of sufficient reason*

superstructure of society According to philosophical Marxism, the ideas and institutions (religious beliefs, educational systems, philosophies, the arts, and such) compatible with and produced by the material substructure of the society. (Ch. 13, p. 376)

surplus value The term Marx used to refer to the capital accumulated by owners; the result of keeping prices higher than the costs of production at the expense of workers. (Ch. 13, p. 377)

tabula rasa Latin expression for a "clean slate," used by John Locke to challenge the possibility of innate ideas by characterizing the mind at birth as a blank tablet or clean slate. (Ch. 10, p. 281)

Tao Literally "way" or "path," Tao (or Dao) is variously translated as the source of all existence, the principle of all things, the way or path of the universe or the moral law; key concept in Confucian and Taoist philosophy. (Ch. 1, p. 23)

te Traditionally, moral neutral virtue; potency, the power to affect others without using physical force; expanded by Confucius to mean the capacity to act according to Tao and to bring others to Tao. (Ch. 1, p. 37)

techne From the Greek for "art," "skill," "craft," "technique," "trade," "system," or "method of doing some thing"; root of English words such as technique, technical, and technology; term Socrates used when he asserted that virtue (*arete*) is knowledge or wisdom (*techne*). (Ch. 4, p. 116)

teleological argument Also called the argument from design, a widely known argument for the existence of God which claims that the universe manifests order and purpose that can only be the result of a conscious intelligence (God); Aristotelian argument that forms the basis for the fifth of Aquinas's Five Ways. (Ch. 8, p. 231)

teleological thinking A way of explaining things in terms of their ultimate goals; understanding things functionally in terms of the relationship of the parts to the whole. (Ch. 6, p. 174)

the "they" Heidegger's name for Being-with-another; an inauthentic way of avoiding anxiety by allowing an "aggregate average" to determine how we live and think; enemy of authenticity. (Ch. 17, p. 497)

theology From the Greek *theos* (God) and *logos* (study of); "talking about God" or "the study or science of God." (Ch. 8, p. 217)

theoretical reason, see *reason (theoretical)*

thought experiment A way of using our imaginations to test a hypothesis; we think rather than field-test a hypothesis, using reasoned imagination to provide the necessary conditions for the experiment, and carefully reasoning out the most likely consequences according to our hypothesis. (Ch. 11, p. 331)

tragic optimism According to Nietzsche, the sense of joy and vitality that accompanies a superior individual's clear-sighted imposition of his or her own freely chosen values on a meaningless world. (Ch. 16, p. 450)

transcendental idealism, see *idealism (Kantian)*

transcendental ideas, see *regulative ideas*

tyranny A form of government in which all power rests in a single individual, known as the tyrant. (Ch. 5, p. 154)

utility (principle of) A principle which says to always act to promote the greatest happiness for the greatest number. (Ch. 12, p. 343)

utopia Term for a perfect or ideal society derived from Sir Thomas More's 1516 novel of the same name; the word was created from the Greek root meaning "nowhere." (Ch. 5, p. 151)

veil of ignorance John Rawls's mechanism for imaginatively entering into the original position by avoiding all personal considerations in the process of determining principles of justice; the veil of ignorance is a problem-solving device that prevents us from knowing our social status, what property we own, what we like and don't like, how intelligent we are, what our talents and strengths are, and so on. (Ch. 11, p. 331)

virtue From the Greek *arete*, meaning "that at which something excels," or "excellence of function." (Ch. 4, p. 116)

virtue (Platonic) Excellence of function. (Ch. 5, p. 148)

void (the) Democritus's term for no-thing (no-bodies); empty space in Atomist theory. (Ch. 2, p. 72)

will to power Nietzsche's term for what he thought is a universal desire to control others and impose our values on them. (Ch. 16, p. 449)

willed ignorance An attitude of indifference to the possibility of error or enlightenment that holds on to beliefs regardless of the facts. (Introduction, p. 14)

wisdom A fundamental understanding of reality as it relates to living a good life; reasonable and practical, focusing on the true circumstances and character of each individual; good judgment about complex situations involving reflection, insight, and a plausible conception of the human condition. (Introduction, p. 12)

wu wei Literally, "not to act"; in the *Tao te Ching*, a warning against unnatural or demanding action. (Ch. 1, p. 32)

yang In Ancient Chinese metaphysics, strong, positive, light, and constructive natural force or principle; linked with yin. (Ch. 1, p. 23)

yin In Ancient Chinese metaphysics, weak, negative, dark, and destructive natural force or principle; linked with yang. (Ch. 1, p. 23)

Bibliography of Philosophical Delights

Here is a small sampling of some especially well-written, interesting, and engaging books that complement the material covered in Archetypes of Wisdom, *9th edition. They are some of my favorite philosophical and philosophy books. What is the difference? "Philosophical books" do not have to be written by philosophers, nor do they have to present technical, scholarly philosophical arguments. Rather, philosophical books, as I see them, express, nurture, and encourage philosophical themes. They flow from and touch upon our "meaning needs" our innate curiosities about what matters and why. Not only can they be valuable in a philosophically technical way, they are also practically—that is, humanly—valuable. As such, most of them are "good reads."*

With only a few exceptions, this list does not duplicate the main philosophical sources cited in the text since these are fully annotated in the Notes section.

General Sources

Blackburn, Simon. *The Oxford Dictionary of Philosophy*, 2nd rev. ed. Oxford: Oxford University Press, 2008. This witty and authoritative philosophical dictionary includes excellent cross-references.

Craig, Edward. *The Shorter Routledge Encyclopedia of Philosophy*. New York: Routledge, 2005. Here's a handy one-volume desk reference culled from the ten-volume *Routledge Encyclopedia of Philosophy*.

Critchley, Simon. *The Book of Dead Philosophers*. New York: Vintage Books, 2008. Now here's a truly delightful book! Critchley's little sketches of the deaths of philosophers from Thales to Simon Critchley (yes, *that* Simon Critchley) is a refreshing blend of humor and seriousness that amounts to a précis of the history of philosophy. Substance in disguise.

Edwards, Paul, ed. in chief. *The Encyclopedia of Philosophy*. New York: Macmillan & the Free Press, 1967. Two versions of this indispensable source are available: the regular edition of eight separate volumes and a four-volume "student edition" that contains exactly the same material.

Honderich, Ted, ed. *The Oxford Companion to Philosophy*, 2nd ed. Oxford: Oxford University Press, 2005. Checking in at a massive 1,076 pages, Honderich's text is one of the most thorough single-volume reference books available—nearly an encyclopedia.

Introduction Philosophy and the Search for Wisdom

Gaarder, Jostein. *Sophie's World*. New York: Farrar, Straus and Giroux, 1994. Paulette Møller's excellent translation of Gaarder's clever story of an eighteen-year-old girl's intriguing introduction to philosophy is highly recommended.

Needleman, Jacob. *The Heart of Philosophy*. New York: Jeremy P. Tarcher/Penguin, 2003. Needleman's adventures teaching philosophy through dialogue to high school students and their parents produced intriguing ideas about education, society, and the need for philosophy.

Rand, Ayn. *Philosophy: Who Needs It?* Ayn Rand Library, vol. 1. New York: Signet, 1982. Rand ranks as one of the few best-selling philosophical writers of the twentieth century. In this collection of essays, she argues for her own objectivist philosophy. Even when her argument is weak, her confrontational style raises questions about the value of philosophy rarely asked in popular literature.

Overview of Classical Themes

Cook, Elizabeth. *Achilles*. New York: Macmillan, 2003. I can't resist recommending this tiny, short (107 pages) retelling of Homer's *Iliad* in poetic, contemporary English. It is a haunting, moving evocation of mythic themes and human longing—superb!

Hadot, Pierre. *What Is Ancient Philosophy?* Translated by Michael Chase. Cambridge, Mass.: Harvard University Press, 2002. Don't be misled by the title; this is a magnificent book—technically informative, evocatively written, and generous in its view of philosophy and the human condition.

Homer. *Iliad and Odyssey*. I'm partial to the Robert Fagels translations of these compelling epics, but almost any of the many inexpensive, widely available versions is well worth reading. If you've never read Homer, don't deprive yourself of "conversing" with one of the most profound voices in Western history.

Chapter 1 The Asian Sages: Lao-tzu, Confucius, and Buddha

Bankei. *The Unborn*. Translated by Norman Waddell. San Francisco: North Point Press, 1984. Delightful collection of talks and sermons by a seventeenth-century Japanese sage. Bankei's wisdom is funny, profound, and relevant. An excellent introduction to Buddhism without technical language.

Benares, Camden. *Zen Without Zen Masters*. Berkeley, Calif.: And/Or Press, 1977. Bizarre collection of Buddhist-like tales, most with punch lines. A kind of stand-up comedy approach to philosophy.

Confucius. *The Wisdom of Confucius*. Translated and edited by Lin Yutang. New York: Modern Library, 1994. An elegant and especially readable treatment of Confucius's *Analects* along with engaging stories and Lin Yutang's helpful commentaries.

Emerson, Ralph Waldo, and Lao-tzu. *The Tao of Emerson: The Wisdom of the Tao te Ching as Found in the Words of Ralph Waldo Emerson*. Edited by Richard Grossman. New York: Modern Library, 2007. This is a creative, engaging pairing of two popular philosophical writers whose words, although separated by 2,500 years and two radically distinct cultures, often echo each other. Goodman positions passages from Lao-tzu and Emerson on facing pages as a way of testing Emerson's assertion that "all philosophy, East and West, has the same centerpiece." What do you think? Or should I ask, how does your psyche answer?

Lao-tzu. *The Wisdom of Laotse*. Translated and edited by Lin Yutang. New York: Modern Library, 1948. This is one of my favorite books. It's a modestly priced little hardback containing excellent translations of both Lao-tzu and Chuang-tzu. Wise and witty.

Maugham, W. Somerset. *The Razor's Edge*. New York: Penguin, 1979. A classic of spiritual discovery.

Pirsig, Robert. *Zen and the Art of Motorcycle Maintenance: An Inquiry into Values*. New York: Morrow, 1974. A remarkably moving book that works on many levels. It's about motorcycles, parenthood, traveling, mental breakdowns, values, Plato, Buddhism, courage, loneliness, and wisdom.

Chapter 2 The Presocratic Sophos

Davenport, Guy. *Herakleitos & Diogenes*. San Francisco: Grey Fox Press, 1979. Davenport's little book is a real treat. His poetic, contemporary translations of these fragments bring roaring to life the sting, wisdom, and wit of these compelling figures from our archaic past. A true little treasure.

Greenblatt, Stephen. *The Swerve: How the World Became Modern*. New York: W.W. Norton & Co., 2011. On the surface this is the story of the rediscovery of Lucretius's great poem *De Rerum Natura* ("On the Nature of Things") and a story of books as physical artifacts. At its heart, it is an inviting inquiry into Lucretius's philosophical poem and its influence on philosophers, artists, and scientists.

Kirk, G. S., J. E. Raven, and M. Schofield. *The Presocratic Philosophers*. Cambridge: Cambridge University Press, 1983. One of the best single-volume commentaries and a great collection of original sources covering this era of philosophy.

Chapter 3 The Sophist: Protagoras

Davenport, Guy. *7 Greeks*. New York: New Directions, 1995. The late Guy Davenport is one of my favorite translators of ancient Greek poetry. This colorful and sophisticated collection includes five poets and two philosophers. These lusty and poignant fragments reveal a complex, beautiful, and disturbing culture.

Grant, Michael. *The Classical Greeks*. New York: Scribner's, 1989. This nicely written history of classical Greece often reads like a novel. Good index, useful for selective research.

Guthrie, W. K. C. *The Sophists*. Cambridge: Cambridge University Press, 1971. Thorough, major source of general information. Best read in conjunction with a general history of the period.

Henry, Jules. *Culture Against Man*. New York: Vintage, 1963. The section on advertising as a philosophical system, though dated in its examples, is a stinging indictment of modern sophistry.

Chapter 4 The Wise Man: Socrates

Guthrie, W. K. C. *Socrates*. Cambridge: Cambridge University Press, 1971. Comprehensive survey of Socrates' life and philosophy. Sophisticated reading level, but valuable source for research papers.

Jaspers, Karl. *Socrates, Buddha, Confucius, Jesus: The Paradigmatic Individuals*. Edited by Hannah Arendt. Translated by Ralph Manheim. New York: Harcourt Brace Jovanovich, 1962. This excerpt from Jaspers's history of philosophy presents his fascinating notion of the paradigmatic individual. Worth tracking down for those interested in wise people.

Stone, I. F. *The Trial of Socrates*. Toronto: Little, Brown, 1988. Valuable as an alternative view of Socrates and as an example of a first-rate mind driven by wonder. Working outside the academic establishment, Stone, like Joseph Campbell, reminds us of the virtues of curiosity and independence.

Chapter 5 The Philosopher-King: Plato

Levi, A. W. *Philosophy as Social Expression*. Chicago: University of Chicago Press, 1974. See Chapter 2, "Ancient Philosophy: The Age of the Aristocrat," for a full discussion of the influence of social class on Plato.

Taylor, A. E. *Plato: The Man and His Work*. London: Methuen, 1966. Scholarly and sometimes difficult, but useful for research papers.

Chapter 6 The Naturalist: Aristotle

Andrews, Lewis M. *To Thine Own Self Be True: The Rebirth of Values in the New Ethical Therapy*. New York: Doubleday/

Anchor, 1987. Intriguing blend of philosophy and psychology. Andrews's ethical therapy is based on universal moral principles derived from Plato and Aristotle.

MacIntyre, Alasdair. *After Virtue*, 3rd ed. Notre Dame, Ind.: University of Notre Dame Press, 2007. MacIntyre argues that virtues are necessary for society and human development. An impressive assessment of excellence and community.

Merton, Thomas. *New Seeds of Contemplation*. New York: New Directions, 1961. This is one of Merton's best, a rare combination of literature, philosophy, psychology, and Catholic theology. A gem.

Chapter 7 The Stoics: Epictetus and Marcus Aurelius

Epictetus. *Handbook of Epictetus*. Translated by Nicholas P. White. Indianapolis: Hackett, 1983. First-rate translation, inexpensive edition.

Frankl, Viktor E. *Man's Search for Meaning: An Introduction to Logotherapy*. New York: Beacon Press, 2006. A modern classic. Frankl's account of his concentration camp experiences is harrowing, and the conversion of those experiences into a form of philosophical therapy is inspiring. If I had my way, this would be required reading for just about everyone.

Hadot, Pierre. *The Inner Citadel: The Meditations of Marcus Aurelius*. Translated by Michael Chase. Cambridge, Mass.: Harvard University Press, 1998. Hadot is one of my very favorite contemporary philosophical writers, and this extended meditation on Marcus's *Meditations* is simply magnificent. It is scholarly, to be sure, but is also deep, rich, and profoundly affecting.

Lin Yutang. *The Importance of Living*. New York: Morrow, 1937, 1965. A genuinely delightful book that raises questions about what's important and what's not. Some dated passages, but much of this is elegant, pleasant—everything a hedonist looks for. William Morrow's 1996 hardcover edition of this gem is itself appropriately elegant. An excellent edition.

Lippmann, Walter. *A Preface to Morals*. 1929. Reprint. New Brunswick, N.J.: Transaction, 2009. Though dated, the opening and closing chapters present a stirring Stoic analysis of American culture.

Marcus Aurelius. *The Essential Marcus Aurelius*. Translated by Jacob Needleman and John Piazza. New York: Tarcher/Penguin, 2008. This compact, truncated new translation of the heart of the *Meditations* boasts Needleman's magnificent introduction, a rare attempt to articulate precisely why and how Marcus's notes to himself act on our souls.

Marcus Aurelius. *Meditations*. Translated by Gregory Hays. New York: Modern Library, 2002. Stoicism seems to be enjoying a mini-revival, and Hays's new translation of the *Meditations* includes a first-rate introduction; this attractive edition makes a great gift. A number of inexpensive editions of George Long's elegant Victorian translation are widely available as well. Truly timeless.

Seneca. *The Stoic Philosophy of Seneca*. Translated by Moses Hadas. New York: Norton, 1958. This excellent translation is still available as a paperback reprint. Seneca's letters remain edifying.

Stockdale, Jim. *Thoughts of a Philosophical Fighter Pilot*. Stanford, Calif.: Hoover Institution Press, 1995. An inspiring and accessible collection of essays, articles, lectures, and speeches focusing on the human capacity for meeting adversity with courage, dignity, and wisdom; Stockdale was the Epictetus of our time.

Chapter 8 The Scholar: Thomas Aquinas

Armstrong, Karen. *A History of God: The 4,000-Year Quest of Judaism, Christianity, and Islam*. New York: Ballantine, 1993. Written by a former Roman Catholic nun, this comparative history of Western monotheism is also a profoundly moving search for a sense of God that "works for us in the empirical age."

Augustine. *Confessions*. Translated by R. S. Pine-Coffin. Middlesex, England: Penguin, 1961. The first "autobiography" as such. You'll be surprised how contemporary Augustine sounds in this honest, introspective blend of philosophy and journal writing.

Dawkins, Richard. *The God Delusion*. New York: Houghton Mifflin, 2008. Dawkins's entry into the "religious wars" of the early twenty-first century derides Aquinas's proofs for God's existence as "fatuous" and religion itself as "nonsense." Contrast this tone—independent of any arguments—with that of Thomas Merton and C. S. Lewis to see how much religion and philosophy still matter.

Hitchens, Christopher. *God Is Not Great: How Religion Poisons Everything*. New York: Twelve Books/Hachette, 2007. This pungent indictment of religion—Hitchens describes religious education as "child abuse"—is deliberately provocative and disturbing. It's also biased. But it raises a foundational question: If religion is as foolish and harmful as Hitchens claims, what accounts for its persistence?

Kaufmann, Walter. *The Faith of a Heretic*. New York: New American Library, 1978. A wholly different kind of critique of theology from those of Dawkins and Hitchens. Intense, to be sure, yet reasonable rather than mostly polemical.

Lewis, C. S. *Mere Christianity*. New York: Macmillan, 1976. One of the most popular examples of contemporary apologetics. Lewis attempts to construct a rational argument for Christianity. Quite interesting and persuasive to many.

Russell, Bertrand. *Why I Am Not a Christian, and Other Essays on Religion and Related Subjects*. New York: Simon & Schuster, 1957. Russell's tightly argued but clear account of his objections to Christianity. Intelligent atheism at its best. (For an interesting take on cultural changes, compare Russell to Dawkins and Hitchens.)

Chapter 9 The Rationalist: René Descartes

Descartes, René. *Objections and Replies to Descartes' Meditations*, in *The Philosophical Works of Descartes*, vol. 2. Translated by Elizabeth S. Haldane and G. R. T. Ross. Cambridge: Cambridge University Press, 1968. This witty exchange of letters between Descartes and Hobbes (and others) is philosophically important and has the added virtue of showing us philosophy in action.

Goldstein, Rebecca. *Betraying Spinoza: The Renegade Jew Who Gave Us Modernity*. New York: Nextbook/Schoken, 2006. If space were no object, I would have devoted a chapter of this book to the great rationalist Baruch Spinoza, a radical thinker whose integrity branded him a heretic, led to his excommunication, and puts him in a league with Socrates. I like this short (287 pages) book for its humanity and the way Goldstein's Spinoza makes me think about religion, rationality, and what courage it sometimes takes to be a philosopher.

Jaggar, Alison M., and Susan R. Bordo, eds. *Gender/Body/ Knowledge: Feminist Reconstructions of Being and Knowing*. New Brunswick, N.J.: Rutgers University Press, 1989. Sophisticated anthology of feminist analyses of epistemological and metaphysical issues.

Ryle, Gilbert. *The Concept of Mind*. New York: Barnes & Noble, 1949. Important work in the analytic tradition. Quite readable introduction to early analytic method.

Watson, Richard. *Cogito Ergo Sum: The Life of René Descartes*. Boston: Godine, 2002. Hold on to your hats! Watson's written a quirky (in a good sense), witty biography that manages to be both scholarly and entertaining.

Chapter 10 The Skeptic: David Hume

Annas, Julia, and Jonathan Barnes. *The Modes of Scepticism: Ancient Texts and Modern Interpretations*. Cambridge: Cambridge University Press, 1985. First-rate contemporary look at skepticism.

Hallie, Phillip P. "Classical Scepticism—A Polemical Introduction," in *Sextus Empiricus, Selections from the Major Writings on Scepticism, Man, & God*. Edited by Phillip P. Hallie. Translated by Sanford G. Etheridge. Indianapolis: Hackett, 1985. Lucid commentary on classical skepticism.

Russell, Bertrand. *Our Knowledge of the External World*. Chicago: Open Court, 1915. First-rate assessment of some fundamental epistemological problems.

Santayana, George. *Scepticism and Animal Faith*. 1923. Reprint. New York: Dover, 1955. Santayana's challenge to skepticism is an excellent example of precise thinking presented in nontechnical terms. Very well written.

Watson, Richard. *The Philosopher's Diet: How to Lose Weight and Change the World*. Boston: Atlantic Monthly Press, 1985. Watson talks about diets, exercise, philosophy, and David Hume in a powerful, witty, surprisingly effective manner. This is a delightful book you'll want to reread. A refreshing change of pace.

Chapter 11 The Universalist: Immanuel Kant

Campbell, Jeremy. *The Liar's T... : History of Falsehood*. New York: Norton, 2002. An intriguing look at the possibility that not only is deception unavoidable but also downright valuable and necessary for human well-being; chock-full of examples.

Okin, Susan Moller. *Justice, Gender, and the Family*. New York: Basic, 1989. Disturbing (in a valuable way) challenge to John Rawls's influential theory of justice and the possibility of gender-free rationality. Excellent discussion of "original position" reasoning.

Stout, Martha. *The Sociopath Next Door*. New York: Broadway, 2005. What would life be like with absolutely no conscience, no moral sense, no empathy whatsoever? Would it be glorious and successful, as some of the most radical Sophists suggested? Stout, a clinical psychologist, thinks not, going so far as to say that conscience makes us fully human. A chilling and worthwhile survey of what social scientists have been saying about morality.

Chapter 12 The Utilitarian: John Stuart Mill

Capaldi, Nicholas. *John Stuart Mill: A Biography*. Cambridge: Cambridge University Press, 2004. "The two most important factors about the life of John Stuart Mill were that he was the son of James Mill and that he fell in love with Harriet Taylor." To the dismay of some philosophers, Capaldi's intellectual biography of Mill is more sympathetic to Mrs. Taylor than other assessments of Mill's life are. It is also rich in engaging anecdotes and analysis of Mill's place in Victorian culture and the evolution of his thought. The result is thought-provoking and moving.

Sarah Conly. *Against Autonomy: Justifying Coercive Paternalism*. Cambridge: Cambridge University Press, 2012. Whether you find this little book a delight or provocation, it's almost guaranteed to make you think. Conly confronts one of the persistent tensions for free societies: the tension between maximizing individual liberty and maximizing the good of the many.

Mill, John Stuart. *Autobiography*. New York: Columbia University Press, 1924. A classic autobiography, readable, and, I think, commendable for its brevity and modesty—which, considering Mill's gifts and accomplishments, is particularly enlightening in this era of the pervasive, bloated memoir.

Reeves, Richard. *John Stuart Mill: Victorian Firebrand*. New York: Overlook, 2008. Reeves's new biography of Mill puts the philosopher's ideas and life together in an engaging way that diminishes neither the personal nor the philosophical.

Chapter 13 The Materialist: Karl Marx

Berlin, Isaiah. *Karl Marx*. Edited by Henry Hardy with a foreword by Alan Ryan. Princeton, NJ: Princeton University Press, 2013. A superb biography. Berlin's characterizations of Marx's ideas are clear, and his portrait of the man is sympathetic without going overboard. Here's an example of fair and balanced treatment of a philosopher with whom one (in this case Berlin) disagrees. That in itself is a lesson for these hyper-partisan times.

Fromm, Erich. *The Art of Loving*. 1956. Reprint. New York: Perennial Library, 1974. Another good book with a potentially misleading title. This is not a self-help book; it's much more. The chapter on the disintegration of love is a fine humanistic analysis of modern capitalism that raises worthwhile questions more than half a century after it was written.

Marcuse, Herbert. *One-Dimensional Man: Studies in the Ideology of Advanced Industrial Society*, 2nd ed. Introduction by Douglas

Kellner. Boston: Beacon, 2013. Critique of modern capitalism's "flattening effect" on our psyches.

Wheen, Francis. *Karl Marx: A Life*. New York: Norton, 2001. More personal (biographical) than philosophical, this is an "odd" biography of an "odd" man. Nonetheless, and perhaps because of this, it is unsettling but entertaining. Good as a change of pace, but not so good if you're looking to dig deeper in to Marx's ideas.

Chapter 14 The Existentialist: Søren Kierkegaard

Barrett, William. *Irrational Man: A Study in Existential Philosophy*. Garden City, N.Y.: Doubleday/Anchor, 1962. This impressive analysis of the 1960s intellectual and social scene is still widely read and discussed.

Camus, Albert. *The Stranger*. Translated by Matthew Ward. New York: Vintage, 1989. "Maman died today. Or maybe yesterday. I don't know. I got a telegram from the home: 'Mother deceased. Funeral tomorrow. Faithfully yours.' That doesn't mean anything. Maybe it was yesterday." Thus begins one of the most intriguing, disturbing "existential novels" of the twentieth century. The book is small; its wallop is not.

Garff, Joakim. *Søren Kierkegaard: A Biography*. Translated by Bruce H. Kimmse. Princeton, N.J.: Princeton University Press, 2005. I think Kierkegaard would have gotten a kick out of Garff's beautifully written search for the self-created individual hiding behind Kierkegaard's fictional personae, particularly since this is not a philosophical analysis as such. It is a life story—or is that "a life's" stories, one of many?

Chapter 15 The Pragmatist: William James

James, William. *William James: Writings 1902–1910*. New York: Literary Classics of the United States, Library of America—vol. 38, 1987. Excellent edition, though both Collier and Dover have inexpensive paperback editions available of *The Will to Believe* and *Varieties of Religious Experience*.

Richardson, Robert D. *Emerson: The Mind on Fire*. Berkeley: University of California Press, 1995. Although not a philosopher in the academic, technical sense, the "sage of Concord" expressed spiritual, literary, social, and philosophical interests in such compelling ways that he became one of the most influential and—gasp—popular intellectuals of his era. He's still widely read today, and this biography provides an exciting and moving background to James's life and work.

Richardson, Robert D. *William James: In the Maelstrom of American Modernism*. New York: Mariner/Houghton Mifflin, 2007. This big-hearted biography of what Richardson calls James's "matchless incandescent spirit" is chock-full of quotations and anecdotes, such as the time a friend tried to praise James by comparing him to St. Paul and Isaiah to which James retorted, "Why drag in Saint Paul and Isaiah?"

Chapter 16 The Anti-Philosopher: Friedrich Nietzsche

Hollingdale, R. J. *Nietzsche: The Man and His Philosophy*. Revised. Cambridge: Cambridge University Press, 1999. More than a biography, this updated edition of one of the most humane and accessible treatments of Nietzsche includes excellent translations of key passages, illuminating notes, and a fascinating new Appendix that discusses some of the more recent Nietzsche scholarship.

Kaufmann, Walter. *Without Guilt and Justice: From Decidophobia to Autonomy*. New York: Delta, 1973. Kaufmann's attempt to construct a Nietzschean ethic is easy to read and guaranteed to get you thinking about contemporary values. His assessment of the various strategies of "decidophobia" (fear of making decisions) is especially effective.

Leopardi, Giacomo. *Zibaldone*. Edited by Michael Caesar and Franco D'Intino. Translated by Kathleen Baldwin, et al. New York: Farrar, Straus and Giroux, 2013. Leopardi's remarkable, monumental collection of observations, quoted passages, and cross-referenced entries comes in at 2,502 pages. Don't be intimidated by the physical size of this book—a *zibaldone* is a hodge-podge. You can dip into this one at your leisure. Acknowledged by Nietzsche as a master of prose, Leopardi comes across as engaging, provoking, and real—like Nietzsche and Kierkegaard. He deserves a wider audience.

MacIntyre, Ben. *Forgotten Fatherland: The Search for Elisabeth Nietzsche*. New York: Farrar, Straus and Giroux, 1992. This fascinating account of efforts to establish a "New Germany" in South America raises disturbing questions about ways that Nietzsche's sister distorted her brother's reputation.

Nietzsche, Friedrich. *The Portable Nietzsche*. Edited and translated by Walter Kaufmann. New York: Penguin, 1968. A "best buy," this handy collection includes Kaufmann's helpful comments.

Ratner-Rosenhagen, Jennifer. *American Nietzsche: A History of an Icon and His Ideas*. Chicago: The University of Chicago Press, 2012. This insightful scholarly blend of intellectual and social history identifies forgotten and overlooked swirls and eddies in the many currents of Nietzsche's influence on American culture, from early twentieth-century celebrities, radical reformers, artists, and isolated admirers. I found much of it eye-opening, touching, and thought-provoking.

Safranski, Rüdiger. *Nietzsche: A Philosophical Biography*. New York: Norton, 2002. In the words of one reviewer, "a graceful and elegant book"; Safranski delivers on his subtitle by commingling Nietzsche's life and philosophy in a way that illuminates both.

Solomon, Robert, and Kathleen M. Higgins. *What Nietzsche Really Said*. New York: Schocken, 2000. I suspect that Nietzsche would have been simpatico with this exuberant, nose-tweaking, error-busting romp through his life and ideas, perhaps all the more so because Solomon and Higgins are respected philosophers who deflate thirty common misconceptions about the bogeyman along the way.

Yalom, Irvin D. *When Nietzsche Wept: A Novel of Obsession*. New York: Perennial Classics, 2003. Friedrich Nietzsche walks into a psychoanalyst's office.... What seems at first glance like a joke is in fact the premise of Yalom's touching novel. An existentially oriented psychiatrist himself, Yalom uses a fictional encounter between Freud's student Josef Breuer and the troubled philosopher to explore the roots of classical psychotherapy and the inspiration for *Thus Spoke Zarathustra*.

One of those special books that combine fiction and historical narrative to the benefit of both.

Chapter 17   The Twentieth Century: Ludwig Wittgenstein and Martin Heidegger

Barison, David, and Daniel Ross. *The Ister*. Brooklyn, N.Y.: First Run/Icarus Films, 2004. This intriguing film uses a journey from the mouth of the Danube upstream to its source in the Black Forest as a background for a conversation among three philosophers (Philippe Lacoue-Labarthe, Jean-Luc Nancy, Bernard Stiegler) and a filmmaker (Hans-Jürgen Syberberg) about Heidegger's life, work, and historical place. The title comes from a course Heidegger gave on Hölderin's poem "The Ister."

Edmonds, David, and John Eidinow. *Wittgenstein's Poker: The Story of a Ten-Minute Argument Between Two Great Philosophers*. New York: HarperCollins, 2001. This look at a legendary, disputed argument between Ludwig Wittgenstein and Karl Popper makes for a fascinating blend of philosophy and story telling. Bracing, informed, and entertaining. Works on many levels.

Magee, Bryan. *Confessions of a Philosopher: A Personal Journey Through Western Philosophy; From Plato to Popper*. New York: Modern Library, 1999. Magee chronicles his development as a philosopher as he discovers and reacts to the Presocratics, Schopenhauer, Nietzsche, Russell, and Wittgenstein. A contemporary philosophical memoir that is as personally interesting as it is intellectually engaging.

McGinn, Colin. *The Making of a Philosopher: My Journey Through Twentieth-Century Philosophy*. New York: HarperCollins, 2002. Well-written, funny, intelligent memoir that truly does describe the making of a twentieth-century philosopher. McGinn's descriptions of fellow philosophers and their thinking are crisp and elegant. His stories about famous and not-so-famous thinkers are engaging, warm, and philosophically interesting.

Monk, Ray. *Ludwig Wittgenstein: The Duty of Genius*. New York: Penguin, 1991. Philosophically interesting and personally moving account of one of the most fascinating figures in recent philosophy. Engrossing.

Smith, Huston. *Beyond the Postmodern Mind: The Place of Meaning in a Global Civilization*. Wheaton, Ill.: Quest, 2003. Smith's reflections on what he sees as a "crisis" of meaning that affects philosophy, religion, and science. Smith raises important questions and provides captivating, if somewhat skewed, overviews of postmodern philosophy. Thought-provoking take on modernity from a philosopher of religion.

Solomon, Robert C., and David Sherman, eds. *The Blackwell Guide to Continental Philosophy*. Malden, Mass.: Blackwell, 2003. Excellent introductory essays on continental philosophers from Hegel to Derrida and related trends in contemporary philosophy. Good starting point for serious readers.

Wolin, Richard. *Heidegger's Children: Hannah Arendt, Karl Löwith, Hans Jonas, and Herbert Marcuse*. Princeton, N.J.: Princeton University Press, 2003. Wolin uses four of Heidegger's most famous students as a springboard for an examination of the relationship between philosophy and history. Itself a controversial book about an ongoing, contentious issue that extends beyond academic philosophy.

Wolin, Richard. *The Seduction of Unreason: The Intellectual Romance with Fascism from Nietzsche to Postmodernism*. Princeton, N.J.: Princeton University Press, 2004. Difficult, tough-minded critique of postmodernism that asks why—and how—it is that philosophers can be seduced by tyranny and fascism. Disturbing yet important questions here.

Chapter 18   Philosophy as a Way of Life

Davies, Robertson. *The Cunning Man*. New York: Penguin, 1994. A truly magnificent novel, Davies's last book presents a fine account of the journey from intelligence to wisdom; the fictional Jonathan Hullah is warm, wise, and kind. The sort of book you can't wait to finish but don't want to end.

Hadot, Pierre. *Philosophy as a Way of Life*. Translated by Arnold I. Davidson. Oxford: Blackwell, 1995. Hadot's book deserves wider attention than it has received. This valedictory statement by one of our era's premier intellectuals combines the scholarly authority of a lifetime with passion, spiritual depth, and superlative philosophical taste. I recommend it without qualification. A "must read" for anyone even remotely interested in the *sophos*.

Hadot, Pierre. *The Veil of Isis: An Essay on the History of the Idea of Nature*. Translated by Michael Chase. Cambridge, Mass.: Harvard University Press, 2006. This elegant, sophisticated, and moving inquiry is the result of Hadot's twenty-five-year meditation on Heraclitus's statement "Nature loves to hide." Rather than choose between the extreme positions of technologically "stripping" nature or mystically idolizing it by demonizing technology, Hadot invites us to treat nature as art and art as nature.

King, Martin Luther, Jr. *A Testament of Hope: The Essential Writings of Martin Luther King, Jr.* Edited by James M. Washington. New York: Harper & Row, 1986. All of King's important speeches, essays, and books are included. An impressive collection.

Marinoff, Lou. *Therapy for the Sane: How Philosophy Can Change Your Life*. New York: Bloomsbury, 2003. Here's an unusual collection of case studies from Marinoff's "philosophical counseling" practice, which Marinoff describes as the application of useful philosophical ideas to the concrete problems of living or "advanced common sense." This accessible book is a good place to start if you are intrigued by—or uneasy with—the notion that philosophers can and should practice therapy.

Nussbaum, Martha C. *Frontiers of Justice: Disability, Nationality, Species Membership*. Cambridge, Mass.: Harvard University Press, 2006. This extension of Nussbaum's "capabilities approach" to social justice focuses on three unsolved problems, with attention to Kant, Marx, Rawls, and Singer among others: doing justice to people with physical and mental disabilities; extending justice to people throughout the world; facing up to matters of justice for nonhuman animals.

Nussbaum, Martha C. *The Therapy of Desire*. Princeton, N.J.: Princeton University Press, 1994. I like this book for many reasons, but most of all because of the way it makes a contemporary case for the Hellenistic philosophers—and for their unshakable faith in philosophy's therapeutic virtues.

Singer, Peter. *The Life You Can Save: How to Do Your Part to End World Poverty*. New York: Random House, 2010. Singer writes that the point of this book is "to bring about change in how we live." I'm not sure how successful any single book can be in that regard, but Singer does a masterful job of making me uncomfortable about some of my priorities. I count that as a philosophical success. You might find it rewarding to test your present way of life against Singer's inquiry.

Singer, Peter. *Writings on an Ethical Life*. New York: HarperCollins, 2000. Here's a handy one-volume introduction to one of today's most controversial and influential public philosophers; it contains excerpts from some of Singer's best work.

X, Malcolm. *Autobiography*. New York: Grove Press, 1965. Stunning story of a civil rights activist who challenged both blacks and whites.

Index of Margin Quotes

© KUCO/Shutterstock.com

INDEX

FIGURES		EVENTS AND PUBLICATIONS	
Ludwig Feuerbach	1804–1872	Age of Reform	c. 1800–1900
John Stuart Mill	1806–1873		
Charles Darwin	1809–1882	*The Phenomenology of Mind (or Spirit)* (Hegel)	1807
Søren Kierkegaard	1813–1855		
Karl Marx	1818–1883		
Friedrich Engels	1820–1895		
Leo Tolstoy	1828–1910	Industrial Revolution ends	c. 1835
William Dilthey	1833–1911		
Franz Brentano	1838–1917		
Charles Sanders Peirce	1839–1914		
William James	1842–1910	*Either/Or: A Fragment of a Life; Fear and Trembling; and Repetition: An Essay in Experimental Psychology* (Kierkegaard)	1843
Friedrich Nietzsche	1844–1900	*The Present Age* (Kierkegaard)	1846
Gottlob Frege	1848–1925	*Communist Manifesto* (Marx and Engels)	1848
John Dewey	1859–1952	Thoreau expresses doctrine of civil disobedience	1848
		The Sickness Unto Death (Kierkegaard)	1849
		Training in Christianity (Kierkegaard)	1850
		Attack Upon "Christendom" (Kierkegaard)	1854
Sigmund Freud	1856–1939		
Edmund Husserl	1859–1938	*Utilitarianism* (Mill)	1863
		Volume One of *Das Kapital* (Marx)	1867
Bertrand Russell	1872–1970		
G. E. Moore	1873–1958		
Max Scheler	1874–1928		
C. G. Jung	1875–1961	Pragmaticism appears in "How to Make Our Ideas Clear" (Peirce)	1878
Karl Jaspers	1883–1969		
Rudolf Bultmann	1884–1976	The Gay Science (Nietzsche)	1882
Paul Tillich	1886–1965	"God is dead!"—*Thus Spake Zarathustra* (Nietzsche)	1883–1892
Ludwig Wittgenstein	1889–1951		
Martin Heidegger	1889–1976	*Beyond Good and Evil* (Nietzsche)	1886
		Principles of Psychology (James)	1890
Lin Yutang	1895–1976	*The Will to Believe and Other Essays* (James)	1896
Herbert Marcuse	1898–1979		
Hans-Georg Gadamer	1900–2002	*The Varieties of Religious Experience* (James)	1902
Gilbert Ryle	1900–1976		
Frank Ramsey	1903–1930		
Jean-Paul Sartre	1905–1980	*Pragmatism* (James)	1907
Hannah Arendt	1906–1975		
Simone de Beauvoir	1908–1986	World War I and advent of modern nihilism	1914–1917
Albert Camus	1913–1960	Age of Anxiety	1919–1939
Iris Murdoch	1919–1999	Russian (Communist) Revolution	1917–1920